Handwritten notes:

1. Deutsch
2. Dye + Ziegler
3. Roche
4. Smith
5. Flist #51

Flism:
1) Riker, The Origins. / Flism
2) Leach, Flism + Theory

Interest Groups
— all —

Pol. Parties:
Keefer, Broder arts.

Alan Shank

☆☆☆☆☆☆☆☆☆☆☆☆☆☆☆☆☆☆☆☆☆☆☆☆☆☆☆☆☆☆☆☆☆☆☆☆☆

American Politics, Policies, and Priorities

THIRD EDITION

ALLYN AND BACON, INC. / Boston, London, Sydney, Toronto

Library of Congress Cataloging in Publication Data

Shank, Alan, 1936–   comp.
    American politics, policies, and priorities.

    Includes bibliographical references and index.
    1.   United States—Politics and government—Addresses,
essays, lectures. I. Title.
JK21.S4 1981   320.973   80–17235
ISBN 0–205–07165–1

Production editor: Jane de Groot

Printed in the United States of America

10 9 8 7 6 5 4 3 2 1   85 84 83 82 81 80

Contents

Preface

The third edition of *American Politics, Policies, and Priorities* explores
and analyzes the principal components of the American political system.
A sound basis is established for understanding the foundations of
American government, the ways of influencing government through
political participation, the institutional processes of the presidency,
Congress and the courts, and various aspects of public policy problems
and issues relevant to the contemporary setting.

The forty-three selected readings in eleven chapters provide a
comprehensive overview of American government. This book encourages students and instructors to discuss and debate the controversies in
our polity. The various selections include theory and concepts of
American politics as well as examples of actual practices and performances of the system. This is facilitated by chapter introductions which
place the readings into a context. Additionally, there are introductory
paragraphs before each selection which summarize major points and
raise key questions. The introductory paragraphs also tie together
preceding and subsequent titles by showing their interrelationships.

The Appendix contains the texts of the Declaration of Independence
and the Constitution which can be used as reference materials for
Chapters Two, Three, and Ten on the Constitution, the Bill of Rights
and the Supreme Court.

New features of the third edition include twenty-five articles that were not contained in the second edition. Chapter Three, "The Bill of Rights," has been added to introduce key concepts of civil liberties and civil rights, including freedom of speech, freedom of religion, equal protection of the laws in school desegregation, school busing, and equal opportunity in employment, and due process of law affecting the rights of the accused in criminal proceedings. Other major changes for this edition include five new articles for Chapter Eight, The Presidency and the Bureaucracy; four different selections for Chapter Nine, Congress; and three new public policy articles in Chapter Eleven dealing with Proposition 13 (the taxpayers' revolt in California), race and housing discrimination, and excerpts from the commission report to President Carter on the nuclear power plant accident at Three Mile Island.

The materials for the third edition were compiled, edited, and revised during the summer and fall months of 1979, a time of increasing dissatisfaction toward government, focusing particularly on inflation in the economy and lack of solutions for the energy problem. President Carter faced strong challenges from Republicans and within his own party from Senator Edward Kennedy.

I wish to acknowledge the support of several people who assisted in developing, organizing, and completing this edition. Al Levitt, the political science editor of Allyn and Bacon, encouraged the project and provided excellent faculty reviews suggesting additions, changes, and deletions. Ken Deutsch, my colleague and friend at Geneseo, provided suggestions, materials, and wrote the chapter and article introductions for the Bill of Rights section. Also, Ken's article on ideological perspectives was revised for inclusion in Chapter One. Loretta Chrzan Brown provided outstanding editorial, typing, and clerical assistance. Her efforts in obtaining the permissions for the various selections were exceptional. My wife Bernice and Thelma Dua provided many hours of typing assistance. Sam Bickel from Columbia University helped with library research and assembling of the articles.

I hope the third edition of this book will inspire students of American politics to comprehend the sources of our nation's strengths as well as to identify new approaches to the domestic and foreign policy problems that directly affect our lives. The major objective of this edition is to encourage active participation in the political life of the community, state, and nation. Students need to develop a basis for positive action in dealing with the complex and often frustrating problems we now face.

☆☆☆☆☆☆☆☆☆☆☆☆☆☆☆☆☆☆☆☆☆☆☆☆☆☆☆☆☆☆☆☆☆☆☆☆

American Politics, Policies, and Priorities

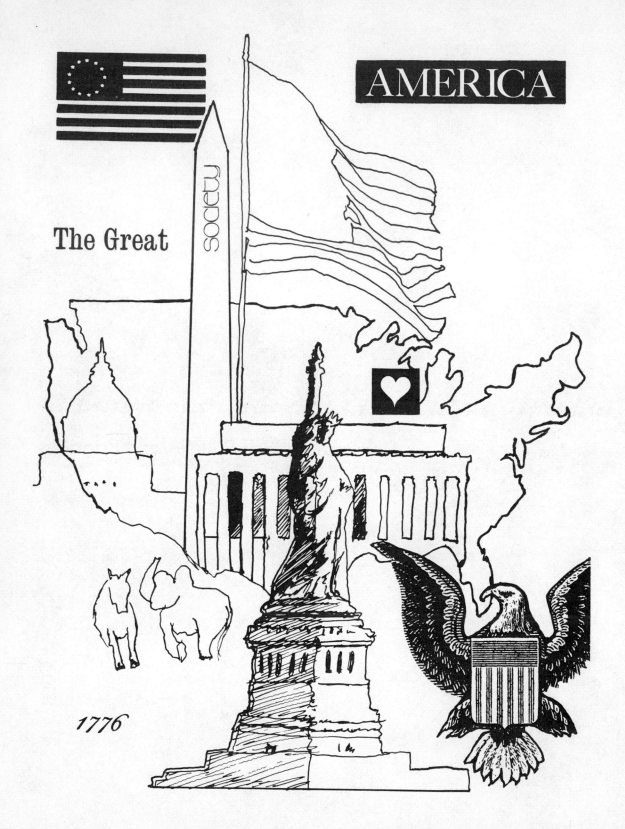

America

The Great

society

1776

PART ONE

✯✯

THE FOUNDATIONS
OF AMERICAN GOVERNMENT

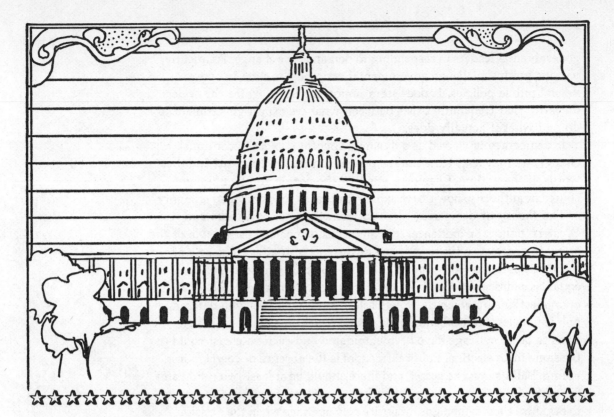

★★

Democracy and the American Political System

1

What are the fundamental principles of American government? Most Americans believe that the United States is governed by democratic processes, although we often disagree about how these principles should be applied to specific situations.

During the last decade, American national government and its policies have experienced many controversies. The 1960s produced serious questions concerning the credibility and accountability of our political leaders in such areas as civil rights, urban decay, and the Vietnam War. Such questioning persisted in the 1970s. Conflicts ensued over managing the economy, protecting the environment, the expansion of presidential war-making authority, growth of the bureaucracy, and energy shortages.

American democracy requires a constant testing between the traditional values that underlie our system and the actual performance of our governmental leaders in responding to demands for change. Frequently, various groups challenge governmental action or inaction in controversial public policies. It does seem important to recognize the wide disparity that frequently exists between what we expect government to do and what it actually does.

If democracy is viewed as a dynamic concept subject to continual change, we may ask: How can the people control government? In other words, if the notion of democracy is that the people are the ultimate source of authority, how do we explain the bases for popular sovereignty?

The *theory* of democracy, derived from the ancient Greeks and Western political experiences, distinguishes democracy as the *rule of the many* in contrast to the *rule of one* or the *rule of the few*. The rule of the many is achieved by popular control of policymakers, political equality, political freedoms, and majority rule. Popular control is based upon elections in which the voters select representatives who determine public policies. Political equality is voting equality in which all restrictions to adult suffrage have been eliminated and each vote cast counts the same in an election. Political freedom is the absence of coercion in voting. Ballots must be secret, and there should be at least two candidates for each office. Candidates must be free to express their views as well as to organize their campaigns. Majority rule operates when the decision of the majority prevails in any divided decisions made by the elected representatives. Also, the minority has the right to criticize and oppose majority decisions, although the minority also agrees to accept majority decisions. Thus, rule by democracy has been defined as "one in which public policies are made, on a majority basis, by representatives subject to effective popular control at periodic elections which are conducted on the principles of political equality and under conditions of political freedom."

Kenneth Deutsch provides an overview of American politics by reviewing the major *ideological* components or value systems associated with our governmental system. In Article 1, Deutsch claims that "liberal pluralism" has been the major bias throughout our political development. Various critics, however, have attacked liberal pluralism either because of distrust in the masses, fear of governmental interference with personal freedom, the imbalances and inequities of economic resources, or the oppression of bureaucratic structures. By carefully assessing the major claims of each competing political vision, Deutsch provides a useful summary which can promote better understanding of the intellectual roots of American politics.

Another approach to comparing democratic theory with governmental performance is to identify the sources of political power. The democratic elitist approach contends that small and unrepresentative groups gain dominance by monopolizing the sources of power and authority. Dye and Zeigler (Article 2) argue that "elites, not masses, govern America." Democratic elitism challenges the principles of popular sovereignty by observing that American political life is controlled by an "establishment" or "power structure" of relatively few actors and groups which make the key decisions in government.

Democratic elitism includes interpretations of both closed or open responsiveness to mass influences. In contrast to the conspiratorial or self-interest motivations of elite power, Dye and Zeigler take the position that elites must reflect the wishes of the people. The irony of democracy, they observe, is that "elites must govern wisely if government 'by the people' is to survive." Thus, elites are not opposed to popular sovereignty; in fact, they may act in the public interest and actively seek to improve the welfare of the masses. But elites clearly differ from the masses in the amount of power and resources at their disposal. Elites maintain governmental stability They have the power to act when the masses are ill-informed, passive, and apathetic, and elites generally agree on the "rules of the game" by which to conduct government.

1

Competing Visions of American Politics

Kenneth L. Deutsch

What is the ideological basis of American politics? Kenneth Deutsch considers the normative or value judgments associated with power and participation in American politics. He shows that political ideology affects the forms of acceptable political action in any society. In America, the dominant ideology has been "liberal pluralism." What are the major components of this ideology? What accounts for the consistency of liberal pluralism since the founding of the nation? Challengers from the left and the right of the political spectrum have attacked various deficiencies of liberal pluralism. What is the major problem according to the con-

servatives? How do the "collectivist" conservatives differ from the "libertarians"? What do the libertarians mean by "negative freedom"? How is this applied to policy questions? What are the differences in strategy between the gradualist and revolutionary socialists? How does existentialism define the "authentic individual"? How does this relate to problems of bureaucracy? At the conclusion of his essay, Deutsch raises several interesting questions regarding the practices, impacts, and prescriptions for public policy. He also compares and contrasts the different ideological approaches in a chart.

The Chinese have a curse: "May you live in interesting times." Assassinations, overt deceptions, an unpopular war in Vietnam, electoral corruption, the perversion of our political institutions, oil crises, and inflation have all contributed to our "interesting" times during the past decade. During such crisis periods, a nation becomes more critically conscious of those rhetorical and operative values which tend to bind the political process and serve to maintain the rules of our political game. Every political culture has a "political mind" or ideology which provides its inhabitants with a particular normative picture of political reality. This picture of political reality covertly and overtly lays out those forms of political action that are considered "acceptable" or

"functional" and those political forms considered to be deviant and worthy of rejection. Over the past two hundred years the American political and social system has developed a political perspective which many political scientists refer to as "liberal pluralism." Although the American culture experiences considerable intellectual diversity, liberal pluralism has provided Americans with explicit ideological claims and supports that have been crucial in defending our federal system, party system, interest group activities, and state intervention in the economy:

(a) The claim that there is open access to the political arena. There are no barriers to a group getting a hearing. Participation is open.
(b) The support for a constitutional democracy which operates within clearly defined rules and restraints. The rules are considered generally fair.
(c) The claim that there is a sufficiently large number of groups ("plural" or diverse) that no one group can dominate the political power structure. Power is tamed, balanced, and "civilized."

This essay was written especially for this book. Kenneth L. Deutsch is associate professor of political science at SUNY at Geneseo. He is co-author of two books on political theory and civil liberties. His most recent publication is *Constitutional Rights and Student Life* (West Publishing Co., 1979).

It is my particular purpose to discuss the liberal pluralist perspective. The focus includes problems of *access* to the political system; the fairness of the political *process*; and the equitable *impact* this process and its decisions have in dealing with a variety of groups in our society. I shall also examine groups whose perspectives—conservative, libertarian, socialist and existentialist—have attempted to challenge the dominance of liberal pluralism.

Every political system that seriously considers itself "democratic" must grapple with two serious issues: the danger of *domination* by a minority—ethnic, religious, regional or economic—and the *responsiveness*, or lack thereof, to needs among its citizens. The issues of *power* and *participation* provide a comparative basis of analysis of how various ideological perspectives view the American political order as well as suggest future directions. A study of a "democratic" political system is not only concerned with describing precisely who has power and who participates in the political process; it is also concerned with who should be involved in the future of that political system.

THE DOMINANCE OF LIBERAL PLURALISM

Liberal pluralism has a long lineage in American political history. I can only begin to indicate here some of its more salient features. It was James Madison, the "father" of the Constitution and the principal author of the *Federalist Papers*, who encouraged within our political system an already deep seated pluralism (or group diversity). Madison stressed that, "Whilst all authority . . . will be derived from and dependent on the society, the society itself will be broken into so many parts, interests and classes of citizens, that the rights of individuals or of the minority, will be in little danger from interested combinations of the majority. In a free government, the security for civil rights must be the same as for religious rights. It consists in the one case in the multiplicity of interests, and in the other, in the multiplicity of sects." For Madison majority tyranny could be a major threat to property rights, the most precarious of natural rights. Pluralism of interest and the precise fragmentation of political power (checks and balances) could serve to protect those natural rights.

It was Alexis de Toqueville, the great nineteenth-century foreign analyst of American civil society, who made it quite clear that our society is basically a nation of joiners when he stated: "Americans of all ages, all conditions, and all dispositions constantly form associations. . . . Whenever at the head of some new undertaking you see the government in France, or a man or rank in England, in the United States you will be sure to find an association." This nation of joiners, the pluralists claim, is the foundation for our political genius —a genius based upon openness, moderation, compromise and political consensus.

Robert Dahl, a contemporary political scientist, provides the liberal pluralists with the most convincing and explicit rationale for a moderate and restrained view of politics.

For Dahl, "the fundamental axiom" of American politics is found in the following: "Instead of a single center of sovereign power there must be multiple centers of power, none of which is or can be wholly sovereign. Although the only legitimate sovereign is the people in the perspective of American pluralism even the people ought never to be an absolute sovereign; consequently, no part of the people, such as a majority, ought to be absolutely sovereign." For Dahl this fundamental axiom contains an inherent practical vision of American politics. He claims that "the theory and practice of American pluralism tend to assume . . . that the existence of multiple centers of power, none of which is wholly sovereign, will help (may indeed be necessary) to tame power, to secure the consent of all, and to settle conflicts peacefully. Power is tamed by being divided. Policy is moderate because of the existence of "veto groups" which are necessary for coalitions. Peaceful resolution of conflicts of interests and values is assured through the need of all groups and power centers to compromise in order to obtain *at least* part of their desired objectives."

The liberal pluralist vision of American politics, then, includes the following analytical and prescriptive standards by which liberals evaluate the needs and realities of American politics.

Procedual Consensus

There is a need to sustain a "culture" of constitutional democracy. One must operate within the rules and defeats must be accepted because of the strong value support attached to the manner of resolving conflicts (i.e. elections).

Open Access to the Public Policy-Making Arena

There are no barriers to a socioeconomic or political group getting a hearing. Dissatisfied groups must be encouraged to translate their hostilities into political demands, find coalition partners among other established political groups, and create reforms where possible which can remedy the unsatisfactory conditions. The political system offers multiple points of access (the Administration, Congress, and the Supreme Court) at which to pursue one's demands.

Countervailing Power is the Key

Political parties will eventually woo those disaffected groups that have developed some de-

gree of organization, either to broaden their electoral support or frustrate their opposition. Existing pressure or interest groups with similar interests will be motivated to facilitate the organization of such dissatisfied groups—perceiving them as potential allies. Plural points of access to the public policy-making arena will encourage participation by providing a number of potential points of influence. This political condition will encourage a value commitment on the part of all competitors to an open access. Pluralism civilizes and moderates our political system.

Balance of Power

In our political system, with its sufficiently large number of groups, no one group can prevail over the others at all times. Coalitions are flexible and impermanent. These coalitions are created more or less anew for each social, economic, or political issue. As Dahl writes, "because one center of power is set against another (in terms of groups and political institutions) power itself will be tamed, civilized, controlled, and limited to decent human purposes, while coercion, the most evil form of power, will be reduced to a minimum."

The liberal pluralist vision never assumes perfection in the political realm. The United States, they claim, has avoided "extreme polarization." As Dahl puts it, "Extreme polarization is rare in American politics, and it never persists over long periods. Most of the time political life displays the characteristics of moderate conflict." The liberal pluralists consider it fair to say that "few groups . . . who are determined to influence the government—certainly few if any groups of citizens who are organized, active and persistent—lack the capacity and opportunity to influence some officials somewhere in the political system in order to obtain at least some of its goals." The American political system is *reasonably* responsive to the needs of most of its citizens most of the time. Power is dispersed and participation is open and encouraged. What more can one expect from political life? As will be shown, critics of liberal pluralism, including the socialists and the existentialists, expect far more while the conservatives and the libertarians expect far less.

THE COUNTER-IDEOLOGICAL ATTACK ON LIBERAL PLURALISM

Since liberal pluralism has been the dominant ideology throughout American history, its critics claim that this has kept the spectrum of political issues narrow and circumscribed to include only those issues which are in the *interest* of the well financed and well organized at various pressure points in the political system. Right wing critics claim that the flexibility of the liberal pluralists has eroded standards of the public interest and individual excellence. Left wing critics have argued that the liberal pluralist system weighs more heavily on some groups than on others, and that the function of public decisions should be to correct the gross inequities of the society. Within each of these factions are a variety of fascinating variations which we shall examine in turn.

THE CONSERVATIVE AGONY: YEARNING FOR THE ENLIGHTENED ELITE

Conservatives in American politics are generally those individuals who clearly stand in opposition to the political coalitions that favor regulation of private property, social welfare legislation, and popular control over the reins of political power. As we shall see, American conservatives break into two distinct ideological groups—*collectivist conservatives* who emphasize the importance of preserving the social order and a common social ethic and *individualist conservatives* or "libertarians" who emphasize the primacy of individual rights and personal autonomy. Let us first examine the collectivists who are politically referred to as conservatives and then the individualists who presently wish to be referred to as libertarians.

Ideologically, conservatism accepts and defends most of the institutions and values of the Western traditions which they consider to include deference to enlightened elites, traditions of civility, the awareness of rights and responsibilities, and the concern for slow change grounded in the ethical bond that maintains the political order. American conservatives consider the great English philosopher, Edmund Burke, to be their intellectual father. His concern was to control the passions of individuals who can potentially overwhelm the economic and spiritual resources of a society. Government and the political process exist for a very specific purpose. Let Burke speak for himself:

Government is a contrivance of human wisdom to provide for human wants. Men have a right that these wants should be provided for by this wisdom. Among these wants is to be reckoned the want, out of civil society, of a sufficient restraint upon their passions. Society requires not only that the passions of individuals should be subjected, but then even in the mass and body, as well as in the individuals, the inclinations of men should frequently be thwarted, their will controlled, and their passions brought into subjection. This can only be done by *a power outside of* themselves. . . . In this sense the restraints on men, as well as their liberties, are reckoned among their rights.

The Burkean conservatives are reluctant to count on even the best of men to behave with *complete* rationality: "History consists, for the greater part, of the miseries brought upon the world by pride, ambition, avarice, revenge, lust, sedition, hypocrisy, ungoverned zeal, and all the train of disorderly appetites. . . ."

If we are to minimize these tendencies of man we must cling to traditions which have worked to maintain stability. We must look upon civil society as an organic and ordered partnership between "those who are living, those who are dead, and those who are to be born." This kind of order is best maintained if there is a well defined class structure which minimizes the participation of the masses in the political process. The passions of the people must be restrained for their own good. Men are entitled to fair and equal treatment under the law, "but not to equal things." Social or property distinctions should not be leveled to the *lowest* common denominator. The conservative emphasis on property is quite important. It is one of the great bastions of "ordered liberty" since property provides a suitable base for the security required by a wise, talented, and enlightened elite. Two American conservatives that express a Burkean criticism of liberal pluralism are the scholar-journalist, Walter Lippmann, and the influential political scientist, Edward Banfield.

Conservatives criticize liberal pluralism for its undermining of respect for authority by turning it into a mere contrivance of temporarily dominant coalitions of groups and thus robbing it of its continuity and clearly defined moral standards. The conservatives look upon the liberal pluralists as far too pragmatic, flexible and willing to alter public policies at the whim of newly formed majority coalitions. Under liberal pluralism passions (interests) rule rather than the needs of the *entire* community.

Walter Lippmann sums up the conservative concern for a self-limiting view of politics in his famous work, *The Public Philosophy*, in the following words:

The public philosophy is addressed to the government of our appetites and passions by the reason for a second, civilized, and, therefore, *acquired* nature. Therefore, the public policy cannot be popular. For it aims to resist and to *regulate* those very desires and opinions which are most popular. The warrant of the public philosophy is that while the regime it imposes is hard, the results of rational

and disciplined government will be good. And so, while the right but hard decisions are not likely to be popular when they are taken, the wrong and *soft* decisions will, if they are frequent and big enough, bring on a disorder in which freedom and democracy are destroyed.

The contemporary conservative political analyst, Edward Banfield, in his book, *The Unheavenly City*, has argued that liberal pluralists have allowed a new majority coalition to throw money at urban problems that represent unrealistic needs rather than setting up those public policies which deal with the inherent inequality of the "lower classes." The only policy which would deal with the unrestrained passions of the "lower class" (i.e. blacks) is to provide the "lower class" with what Lippmann called a "second, civilized . . . , acquired nature." Parents in a "lower class" culture could be encouraged to give or sell their children to parents outside that culture or permit the state to place them in "boarding schools" or "day nurseries." This would give the "lower class" children an "American" character which would teach self-restraint and the work ethic. As Banfield puts it:

If lower class ways constitute a culture (strictly speaking, a sub-culture) that is learned in childhood, it would seem that the only way to eliminate it is to prevent children from being brought up in it. This means taking the child from his "lower class" parents at an early age and either giving him to adoptive parents who are not "lower class" or putting him in an orphanage.

Conservatives consider themselves to be "realists" in the public policy-making process. The power of a majority coalition does not make right policy—it does not solve the problems of disorder and the lack of productivity in a community. In sum, the best we can hope for is an enlightened elite that can guide us out of the morass of social decay and the attacks on political freedoms. Peter Viereck has expressed the conservative "irony of democracy" in the following terms:

The American masses are overwhelmingly more hostile to civil liberties than their supposed exploiters and corrupters, the powers-that-be. What saves civil liberties from the intolerant majority is not universal suffrage, not equality, not universal rational Rights of Man, but an educated, self-restrained elite, the Constitution, the Supreme Court, and an organic, historical community of the unwritten, concrete habits of free men ("prescriptive rights").

If these traditions of civility and restraint are destroyed, we will be facing the passions of a tyrannical majority.

THE LIBERTARIAN ALTERNATIVE: IN PRAISE OF THE AUTONOMOUS INDIVIDUAL

The "libertarians" in contemporary American politics have much in common with the "classical liberal" tradition of the nineteenth century which focused its political attention on "negative freedom" and "laissez-faire" ("let-alone" in the economic and social realms). The libertarians offer to the American political debate, the notion of "negative" freedom—the freedom *from* governmental interference in our economic and personal lives. This emphasis on the moral autonomy and sovereignty of the individual and the moral justification of capitalism as the basis for individual initiative and survival has been popularly argued by the novelist Ayn Rand and by such economic and philosophical supporters as Murray Rothbard and Tibor Machan. This position had wide currency in the Nixon-Ford Administrations by the statements and economic policy objectives of William Simon, Secretary of the Treasury, and Alan Greenspan, Chairman of the Council of Economic Advisors. Recently, the libertarian movement has attracted a relatively large number of people from the left and the right who have been seeking an overarching justification for individual freedom and choice

in all realms of social life. Politically, they have been particularly active in supporting a new constitutional convention which would establish an amendment for a balanced budget that enshrines the principle of extremely limited government.

Ayn Rand must be considered the "mother" of the recent libertarian movement, although many of her progeny have taken their own roads. In her widely read series of essays, *The Virtue of Selfishness*, Rand laid out the basic values and precepts which undergird most of its advocates. For Rand, what makes us human (or rational) is the *act* of individuals making their own *decisions* based on their own *interests*—this maximizes the prospect for personal survival and creativity (the virtue of selfishness). Power prevents an individual from making his or her own personal choices. Therefore to *initiate* a power relationship is immoral. Evil stems from the unbridled exercise of governmental power in the name of some collectivity ("the people," the "nation," the "majority") which submerges the individual in the morass of bureaucracy, coercion, and control. Governmental power can only be justified to protect the individual's right to "life, liberty, and property" when those rights are jeopardized by the initiation of coercion on the part of some other person or group. The government should only be a "nightwatchman" protecting the rights of individuals to pursue their interests in a uncoercive social environment. Those who show initiative and utilize their resources (the productive) will (and should) prevail. A pure capitalist system with a limited "night-watchman" state can provide the structural foundations for the maximum utilization of all human and material resources.

Murray Rothbard, a professor of economics and editor of *Libertarian Forum*, has provided the movement with very specific defenses of "laissez-faire" capitalism as the foundation of personal freedom, particularly as the libertarians differentiate themselves from the liberal pluralists. Rothbard argues that:

If we are to keep the term "capitalism" at all . . . we must distinguish between free-market capitalism [which the libertarians support] on the one hand, and "state capitalism" [which the liberal pluralists support] on the other. The two are as different as day and night in their nature and consequences. Free-market capitalism is a network of free and voluntary exchanges in which producers work, produce and exchange their products for the products of others through prices voluntarily arrived at. State capitalism consists of one or more groupings making use of the coercive apparatus of the government—the state to accumulate capital for themselves by expropriating the production of others by force and violence. As free-market capitalism has been replaced by state capitalism, more and more of our economy has begun to decay and our liberties to erode.

Rothbard cites a number of public policy areas where governmental monopoly and action have not been successful, such as: crime in the streets, the welfare system, the postal service, the military-industrial complex, railroads, highways, the schools, wire-tapping, and inflation. As Rothbard indicates, "Examine the problem areas, and everywhere, like a red thread, there lies the overweening stain of government." Rothbard's libertarian critique of liberal pluralism focuses in on what he terms, "Liberalism's solution to every domestic problem is to tax and inflate more and to allocate more federal funds; its solution for foreign crises is to send the Marines (accompanied, of course, by politico-economic planners to alleviate the destruction that the Marines cause). Surely we cannot continue to accept the proffered solutions of a liberalism [the liberal pluralist approach] that has failed."

The libertarian critique of our contemporary public policy making process should now be quite clear. The political process is coercive; it is controlled by coalitions which work to "steal" from productive individuals; and its impact has been inefficient and manipulative.

The prescription for dealing with our political malady is support for individual self-interest and the total absence of government interference in the free market.

The libertarian "ideal" has been expressed by the philosopher, Tibor Machan, in these terms: "The right of every man to be free from coercion by others and groups of others, including governments, is based on the fact that it is *wrong* to incapacitate a person in his ability to exercise choice and to aspire, possibly, to moral goodness. This is a *human* right that everyone possesses by virtue of his being human and thus having the capacity for choice and the capacity for making himself a good man."

The Left in the United States, as we shall see, has taken issue with this libertarian individualist "ideal" in our society as well as with the liberal pluralist "ideal" of consensus and compromise. We next examine the vision of the American Left in its attempt to resolve what they consider the basic unfairness of the American political process and the radical remedies needed to establish political justice.

THE SOCIALIST VISION: DEMOCRATIZATION OF THE POLITICAL AND ECONOMIC REALMS

The Left has never lived comfortably in the political world of coalition-building, "moderation," and respect for the rules of the political game as they are laid out by the liberal pluralists. A constant theme runs through the Leftist attack on liberal pluralism. That theme has been articulated by E. E. Schattschneider when he stated, "The flaw in the pluralist heaven is that the heavenly chorus sings with a strong upper-class accent. Probably about 90% of the people cannot get into the pressure system." The socialist places great emphasis on the inequality of economic resources and the inadequacy of democratic control as the major problems of the political system which require a radical (from the roots up) transformation. The existentialists place their emphasis on the modern development of bureaucratic structures that resist democratic control and responsiveness and require radical decentralization and individual action. We shall examine the socialists first and then the existentialists.

American socialists have been expressing their criticisms and alternatives for over eight decades. They perceive our socio-political system in the following terms:

(1) a system dominated by a small elite who own or control the most important areas of private property (the productive capacity which provides goods and services).
(2) a military-industrial complex that is outside of popular control and unaccountable and unresponsive to the society at large.

Political scientist Michael Parenti states:

In looking to the political system as a means of rectifying the abuses and inequities of the socio-economic system we are confronted with the inescapable fact that any political system, including one that observes democratic forms, is a system of power. As such, it best serves those who have the wherewithal to make it serviceable to their *interests*—those who own and control the resources of money, property, organization, jobs, social prestige, legitimacy, time and expertise, and who thereby command the attentive responses of political decision-makers. Indeed, our political system works well for those large producer and corporate interests that control the various loci of power in the state and federal legislatures and bureaucracies. One can find no end to the instances in which public agencies have become the captives of private business interests. Economic power is to political power as fuel is to fire, but in this instance the 'fire' actually feeds back and adds to the fuel; for political power when properly harnessed becomes a valuable resource in expanding the prerogatives of those economic interests that control it. To think of government as nothing more than a broker or referee (as the liberal pluralists view it) amid a vast array of competing groups . . . is to forget that

government best serves those who can best serve themselves.

In effect, the socialists claim that *access* to the political system is inherently unequal and that the *process* of policy making is neither neutral nor in the interest of the masses. The only way the masses can be in control of their own destiny is to obtain the "fuel" of economic resources or power in order to control the political instruments of society. Socialism, then, requires mass (or social) control of the means of production. This implies a radical reconstruction of the socio-economic foundations of society. Reform of the political structures alone is insufficient to democratize our society or to reorient our social priorities. Radical socialist transformation requires that no inherited wealth exist, the organization of social and political structures so that all persons may develop their respective talents while participating in a fair share of the labor and responsibilities, the provision for each person of the necessities of life, and the development of comprehensive planning of public policy for the communal interest. An example of this would be national ownership of the oil companies, which could provide such planning in the interest of the community.

Socialists are not optimistic at all about the prospect of changing our political mind or actions. They assume that the "guardians of the public trust" will not stop behaving like creatures of the dominant private interests. They see no reason to assume that these political actors can respond to such *social* problems as fuel scarcities, ecology, urban blight, mass transportation or national health insurance. Socialists continue to lament the inability of the dominant politico-economic elites to meet the demands for structural changes while continuing to support their own interests. As Michael Parenti put it, socialists must make the masses aware of the bias of the liberal pluralist system in favor of the monied and organized interests and the fact that ". . . the essence of politics itself (is) an appreciation of the inescapability of *interest and power* in determining what solutions will be deemed suitable, what allocations will be thought supportable, and indeed, what variables (or social "facts") will be considered as interrelating and salient." "Power to the People" for socialists means nothing short of controlling economic resources and well-being as the foundation for political freedom and democracy. The socialist vision of politics requires far more than compromise and consensus; it requires mass control of their destiny.

THE EXISTENTIALIST EXPANSION OF PUBLIC SPACE: AN UNCONVENTIONAL PERSPECTIVE

The existentialist posture is an unconventional one. It has emerged as an important political position as a result of the complex problems of modern life (such as human manipulation and degradation) that have particularly faced us during the past three decades. Existentialism is a response to the "unauthentic" (irresponsible) arguments of those who practiced or accepted brutality with the following kind of claims: "I was only following orders." "Politics is always some form of deception." "One person cannot make a difference." "The leadership must protect national security."

Existentialism is an outlook concerned with the submergence of the individual to the overwhelming political, military and ideological *structures*, which serve to reduce the individual to a manipulated object rather than an *authentic* person capable of exercising freedom of choice. The existentialists claim that human beings can freely choose not to obey inhumane orders; we can refuse to submerge ourselves within the social group; we can choose to disobey an unjust law; we can choose to fight an unfair bureaucratic decision. Authentic

existence, then, is accepting one's freedom to choose and recognizing the limitations and restrictive attempts of other political positions which attempt to define "human nature" according to predefined terms (whether it is the norm of "consensus" of liberal pluralists, the norm of elite rule of the conservatives, the norm of "productive" individuals of the libertarians or the norm of "mass" liberation of the socialists). The existentialists claim that we are capable of transcending the confining and unauthentic thought systems that reduce human beings to the definition of humanity proffered by rigid ideologies.

Although a major dimension of the existentialist political perspective is critical, they have offered what they consider to be a positive political ethic. Contemporary existentialists in this nation have suggested reforms of American "liberal democracy" on four levels: the attack on the "pyramidal prism" in which underdeveloped or unauthentic individuals have become "colonists" in an overdeveloped (centralized and bureaucratized) nation; the need for an open political process which will replace authoritarianism with new areas of political participation; a redefined socio-political ethic which emphasizes the complex responsibilities of socio-political life; and an educational and political socialization process which will resist training automatons and begin educating individuals willing and able to accept the "tensions" of human freedom. The existentialists claim that only by solving these basic problems of *existence* within our own political system can our so-called "liberal" democracy begin to realize the rhetorical values of freedom and participation we have so long espoused as a nation. As Marcus Raskin, one of the most important of American existentialists, has put it, the task of a philosophy of reconstruction of American democracy requires us "to break the bounds of absurdity—an absurdity created by institutions, expressed in official ideologies and reflected in the anxieties of man's inner life." But what specifically have been offered as concrete reforms which can open the political process and extend those areas of individual action in determining their own lives?

Marcus Raskin, co-director of the Washington Institute for Policy Studies, has provided a comprehensive existentialist analysis of the American "pyramidal State" (hierarchical, elitist, bureaucratic and irresponsible) and of the "colonized reality" that it produces. In his book, *Being and Doing*, Raskin finds that the American socio-political order is dominated by a "colonized reality," where an approach to citizenship has emerged which *shapes* the individual to accept exploitation and manipulation. The United States, according to Raskin, is in the thrall of colonialism (individual subordination to hierarchical elites), the American Revolution notwithstanding. Specifically, there are four internal colonies that frequently overlap. There is the *Violence Colony* which uses its citizens as hostages in wars in which hardly anyone believes. Commerce and industry compose the *Plantation Colony*, in which jobs are parceled out by huge corporations beyond the reach of democratic access or control and where the workers are locked into a rhythm of working at alienating jobs. Raskin views our schools as a *Channeling Colony* in which youngsters are graded and conditioned for the shifting needs of the organization life. What is learned in schools is the specialization which buttresses the pyramidal structure. Finally, there exists the *Dream Colony*, which provides the masses with an opiate of fantasies confected by the mass media for the purpose of cultivating the popular taste for the *Plantation* and *Violence Colonies*.

These "colonies" constitute a total pyramidal structure which reinforce each other. Each colony arises as a result of our over-centralized and over-bureaucratized society, and each can create people who are merely agents of its support. In effect, *access* to the political process is limited by the "colonized reality," the *process* itself is elitist and hierarchical, and the *impact* of policy is found in support of entrenched members of the pyramidal state which represents their "needs" rather than the common good.

For existentialists such as Raskin, the reconstruction of our pyramidal state can only occur when individuals feel free. They must learn to accept their instinctive feeling for freedom or they cannot act independently of their pyramidal role. Raskin uses the concept of the "colony" not only as a descriptive concept useful in examining exploitation, but it also provides existentialists with an identification of the kind of power that is behind various types of active agents of political control in our society. The existentialists claim that we must go beyond the formal institutions of political power in America (such as Congress, the presidency, etc.) and examine other institutions as well (such as the education and communication centers, etc.) that deeply affect American citizen expectations and aspirations.

What kind of reforms will provide arenas of political action and authenticity for individuals and "open" the system? We can only hint at the comprehensive reforms that Raskin suggests. In addition to *absolute* support for First Amendment freedoms of expression, Raskin claims that "consciousness seeking" projects (like the People's Park project in Berkeley), communities that operate by contract (the "communal" movement), and social units that are not coordinated by central policies can aid the person in rejecting the colonized "outer layer," can help the person resist being "characterized" and resist playing the "role" that the pyramidal state either seduces, coerces, or implores us to play.

Raskin's radical reforms also find a role for certain modes of political power that can foster authenticity. These recommendations include "neighborhood sovereignty" and worker assemblies within unions to indicate the importance of "being and doing," of thinking independently and having an opportunity to interact with others who affect your existential (or actual) political condition. Raskin and the existentialists clearly wish to expand the arena of what is considered public or political and put this arena or space under the control of all individuals who must act out their lives within it.

For the existentialists, politics and public policy must be more than the province of elites or periodic elections, rather public space must be expanded to find new arenas of political action where more people can act out their choices in interaction with others. Only when more individuals act publicly can we break out of our "pyramidal" and "colonized" existence.

THE INEVITABILITY OF IDEOLOGICAL DEBATE

Ideologies are frequently described as a set of coherent ideas or levers for political action, that is, ideas that describe and delimit what is to be viewed as "political," such as who shall have power and who shall participate. Every political system has developed, over time, a dominant ideology that supports particular rules of the political game and challengers who wish to reorient power and participation in the society. We have examined the dominant ideology of liberal pluralism with its emphasis on process and accommodation and the challengers who advocate either "enlightened" elites (conservatives), "selfish" individuals (libertarians), "mass" ownership of the means of production (socialists), or "authentic" public actors (existentialists). There has never been an "end of ideology" in this nation and there is every likelihood that ideological debate will be more enlivened in the future as we face such problems as national health insurance, multinational corporations, revival of the central

cities and governmental reorganization. As we shall see throughout this book, such problems cannot be dealt with on technical grounds alone. They also require basic choices in *values* and *ideology* which are the essence of political life.

The chart on page 17 summarizes the richness of political positions that are part of the American public dialogue.

As you read about particular features of the American political system, keep in mind the various perspectives that have been introduced. Consider which of them (one or more) satisfactorily answers the following questions about American politics:

(a) Which of the perspectives best describes the *actual* practice of who governs and who participates?
(b) Which of the perspectives most satisfactorily deals with the social, economic, and political impact of policy as it affects a wide variety of groups in this society?
(c) Which of the perspectives provides the most effective set of prescriptions for dealing with the *substantive* problems of American society?
(d) Do you view any of the ideological challengers as possible successors to or modifiers of liberal pluralism?

The culture, language and process of liberal pluralism is so strong in America that many political scientists such as H. Mark Roelofs contend that "Americans are trapped inside their historically given political mind, that they cannot escape from it, and that they are bound to go on repeating patterns of political behavior which are essentially unproductive if not worse." As we move into the third century of the American "experiment," we shall all have the opportunity to make basic political choices which will either refute or support Roelofs' contention. Fate will not determine the outcome. Ours is a burden of choice—a burden

The dominant ideology and its challengers

	Access to the Political Process	Who Actually Controls the Political Process?	Who Should Rule?	Impact of Contemporary Policy	The Good Political Order	The Prospects for Change
(1) Liberal Pluralists (Dahl and most political figures and political scientists)	It is open to those who are organized or are willing to organize.	representative elites of organized groups who accept the rules of the political game	a majority coalition that forms on any given issue	flexible policy that meets the needs of shifting coalitions and needs	a process which allows for accommodation and consensus	We have a flexible system that has worked
(2) Conservatives (Banfield and many cultural elitists)	It is far too open and responsive to human passions.	intellectuals and welfare-oriented politicians who seek to uplift the "lower classes"	a talented and educated "enlightened elite" that seeks the public interest	policy that deals with the "real" problems of inequality of talent and culture	a proper relationship between elites and masses where each knows its place	We can only change when the passions of groups can be restrained by reasoned leadership
(3) Libertarians (Rand and some very influential economic advisors)	It is a reflection of groups that are able to crush individual initiative.	bureaucrats who seek to level the society to lowest common denominator and tax the productive in the process	individuals should direct their own talents and resources in all areas	policies that protect the individual's right to life, liberty, and property	a society of free individuals where each can freely exchange with the other and the state is only an umpire	We can only change when more individuals realize that their society steals from them and destroys them
(4) Socialists (Harrington, Parenti and a growing number of radical social activists)	It is dominated by economic elites and their interests.	a military-industrial complex or elite that reenforce each other in their domination of all aspects of social life	the masses should control the means of production and the political system	policy controlled by the masses that meets their needs rather than special economic interests	a community of individuals where all control the productivity of the society and all basic needs are satisfied	We can only change when we break the dominance of the corporate elite on the political structure
(5) Existentialists (Raskin, Kariel and a number of sympathizers)	It is dominated by centralized elites and the subordinate masses.	a centralized and hierarchial elite which sets up a "colonized reality"	authentic individuals develop new areas of public space in order to act out with others their needs	policy that breaks the colonized reality and allows the person to maximize authenticity	a public order where the individuals have direct impact on policy and people are made responsible for their acts	We can only change when individuals are willing to "rebel" against the colonized reality

that must be accepted in light of concrete knowledge of the political process and its substantive problems, not mere feeling or opinion.

SELECTED BIBLIOGRAPHY

Below are some of the major primary and secondary sources that were consulted in developing this essay. They should be of value to all readers who wish to examine in more depth some of the major ethical problems of American politics.

PRIMARY SOURCES

Liberal Pluralism:

Dahl, Robert. *Pluralist Democracy in the United States: Conflict and Consensus*. Chicago: Rand McNally, 1967.

———. *Preface to Democratic Theory*. Chicago: University of Chicago Press, 1963.

Schlesinger, Arthur M., Jr. *The Crisis of Confidence: Ideas, Power and Violence in America*. Boston: Houghton Mifflin, 1969.

Conservatism:

Kirk, Russell. *A Program for Conservatives*. Chicago: Regency, 1954.

Lippmann, Walter. *The Public Philosophy*. Boston: Little, Brown, 1955.

Viereck, Peter. *Conservatism Revisited and the New Conservatives: What Went Wrong*. New York: Free Press, 1965.

Libertarianism

Friedman, Milton. *Capitalism and Freedom*. Chicago: University of Chicago Press, 1962.

Rand, Ayn. *The Virtue of Selfishness*. New York: New American Library, 1966.

———. *Capitalism: The Unknown Ideal*. New York: Signet Books, 1966.

Rothbard, Murray. *For a New Liberty*. New York: Harper & Row, 1975.

Socialism

Galbraith, John Kenneth. *Economics and the Public Purpose*. Boston: Houghton Mifflin, 1973.

Harrington, Michael. *Socialism*. New York: Saturday Review Press, 1972.

Lynd, Staughton and Gar Alperovitz. *Strategy and Program: Two Essays Toward a New American Socialism*. Boston: Beacon Press, 1973.

Wolfe, Alan. *The Seamy Side of Democracy*. New York: David McKay Co., 1973.

Existentialism

Kariel, Henry S. *The Promise of Politics*. New Jersey: Prentice-Hall, 1966.

———. *Open Systems: Arenas for Political Action*. Itasca, Ill.: F. E. Peacock, 1969.

Raskin, Marcus. *Being and Doing*. Boston: Beacon Press, 1973.

SECONDARY SOURCES

General Discussions of American Political Ideologies:

Dolbeare, Kenneth and Patricia Dolbeare. *American Ideologies: The Competing Beliefs of the 1970's* (3rd edition). Chicago: Rand McNally, 1976.

Etzkowitz, Henry and Peter Schwab (eds.). *Is America Necessary? Conservative Liberal and Socialist Perspectives of United States Political Institutions*. St. Paul: West Publishing Co., 1976.

James, Dorothy Buckton (ed.). *Outside, Looking In: Critiques of American Policies and Institutions, Left and Right*. New York: Harper and Row, 1972.

Roelofs, H. Mark. *Ideology and Myth in American Politics: A Critique of a Political Mind*. Boston: Little, Brown, & Co., 1976.

Critical Analyses of Particular Ideologies:

Liberal Pluralism

Connolly, William (ed.). *The Bias of Liberalism*. New York: Atherton Press, 1969.

Conservatism

Rossiter, Clinton. *Conservatism in America*. New York: Knopf, 1965.

Libertarianism

Tucille, Jerome. *Radical Libertarianism*. Indianapolis: Bobbs-Merrill, 1970.

Socialism

Clecak, Peter. *Radical Paradoxes: Dilemmas of the American Left, 1945–1970*. New York: Harper and Row, 1973.

Existentialism

Pranger, Robert, Jr. *Action, Symbolism and Order: The Existential Dimensions of Politics in Modern Citizenship*. Nashville: Vanderbilt University Press, 1968.

2

The Irony of Democracy

Thomas R. Dye and L. Harmon Zeigler

Dye and Zeigler suggest that elites are necessary to maintain American democracy. Elites comprise the educationally, socially, and economically advantaged groups in society. They are the leadership corps responsible for preserving government by the people. In contrast, the masses have a relatively weak commitment to democratic values. Self-government and popular participation do not occur spontaneously but require motivation by elites. Most people are not interested in public life, vote infrequently, and are not concerned with policy issues. The authors also define "pluralism" as "a system of multiple, competing elites who determine public policy," by bargaining, negotiation, and accommodation of competing objectives. They also consider mass and elite threats to democracy. The masses may tend toward "left" or "right" extremist movements led by demagogues who promote communism or fascism. Extremists reject democratic values in seeking to correct serious economic or political problems. They argue that "the ends justify the means." The overthrow of existing political regimes considered oppressive may lead to equally repressive dictatorships which deny political liberties. Elite threats to democracy may also reduce liberty and freedom by imposing police or military forces as instruments of "law and order" or "national security" in the face of mass threats. Many questions are left unanswered by this essay: Are self-restraints by elites a sufficient protection to maintain democratic values? Can we always depend on elites to recognize the existence of public problems that they will respond to? Or, do elites cause as many problems as they solve?

Elites, not masses, govern America. In an industrial, scientific, and nuclear age, life in a democracy, just as in totalitarian society, is shaped by a handful of men. In spite of differences in their approach to the study of power in America, scholars—political scientists and sociologists alike—agree that "the key political, economic, and social decisions are made by 'tiny minorities.'"[1]

An *elite* is the few who have power; the *masses* are the many who do not. Power is deciding who gets what, when, and how; it is participation in the decisions that allocate values for a society. Elites are the few who participate in the decisions that shape our lives; the masses are the many whose lives are shaped by institutions, events, and leaders over which they have little direct control. Harold Lasswell writes, "the division of society into elite and mass is universal," and even in a democracy "a few exercise a relatively great weight of power, and the many exercise comparatively little."[2]

Elites are not necessarily conspiracies to oppress or exploit the masses. On the contrary, elites may be very "public-regarding" and deeply concerned with the welfare of the masses. Membership in an elite may be relatively open to ambitious and talented individuals from the masses, or it may be closed to all except top corporate, financial, military, civic, and governmental leaders. Elites may be competitive or consensual; they may agree or disagree over the direction of foreign and domestic policy. Elites may form a pyramid, with a top group exercising power in many sectors of the society; or plural elites may divide power, with separate groups making key decisions in different issue areas. Elites may be responsive to the demands of the masses and influenced by the outcome of elections, or they may be unresponsive to mass movements and unaffected by elections. But whether elites are public-minded or self-seeking, open or closed, competitive or consensual, pyramidal or pluralistic, responsive or unresponsive, it is elites and not the masses who govern the modern nation.

Democracy is government "by the people," but the responsibility for the survival of democracy rests on the shoulders of elites. This is the irony of democracy: Elites must govern wisely if government "by the people" is to survive. If the survival of the American system depended upon an active, informed, and enlightened citizenry, then democracy in America would have disappeared long ago; for the masses of America are apathetic and ill-informed about politics and public policy, and they have a surprisingly weak commitment to democratic values—individual dignity, equality of opportunity, the right to dissent, freedom of speech and press, religious toleration, due process of law. But fortunately for these values and for American democracy, the American masses do not lead, they follow. They respond to the attitudes, proposals, and behavior of elites. V. O. Key wrote:

The critical element for the health of the democratic order consists of the beliefs, standards, and competence of those who constitute the influentials, the political activists, in the order. That group, as has been made plain, refuses to define itself with great clarity in the American system: yet analysis after analysis points to its existence. If democracy tends toward indecision, decay, and disaster, the responsibility rests here, not with the mass of people.[3]

Although the symbols of American politics are drawn from democratic political thought, the reality of American politics can often be better understood from the viewpoint of *elite theory*. The questions posed by elite theory are the vital questions of politics: Who governs America? What are the roles of elites and masses in American politics? How do people acquire power? What is the relationship between economic and political power? How open and accessible are American elites? How do American elites change over time? How widely is power shared in America? How much real competition takes place among elites? What is the basis of elite consensus? How do elites and masses differ? How responsive are elites to mass sentiments? How much influence do masses have over policies decided by elites? How do elites accommodate themselves to mass movements?

This book, *The Irony of Democracy*, is an attempt to explain American political life on the basis of elite theory. It attempts systematically to organize the evidence of American history and contemporary social science in order to come to grips with the central questions posed by elite theory. But before we turn to this examination of American political life, it is important that we understand the meaning of *elitism*, *democracy*, and *pluralism*.

THE MEANING OF ELITISM

The central proposition of elitism is that all societies are divided into two classes—the few who govern and the many who are governed. The Italian political scientist Gaetano Mosca expressed this basic concept as follows:

In all societies—from societies that are very under-developed and have largely attained the dawnings of civilization, down to the most advanced and powerful societies—two classes of people appear—a class that rules and a class that is ruled. The first class, always the less numerous, performs all of the political functions, monopolizes power, and enjoys the advantages that power brings, whereas the second, the more numerous class, is directed and controlled by the first, in a manner that is now more or less legal, now more or less arbitrary and violent.[4]

For Mosca it was inevitable that elites and not masses would govern all societies, because elites possess organization and unity of purpose.

An organized minority, obeying a single impulse, is irresistible against an unorganized majority in which each individual stands alone before the totality of the organized minority. A hundred men acting uniformly in concert, with a common understanding, will triumph over a thousand men who are not in accord and can be dealt with one by one.[5]

Contemporary writers generally attribute elitism to the impact of urbanization, industrialization, technological development, and the growth of the social, economic, and political organizations in modern societies. Robert Dahl writes, "The key political, economic, and social decisions . . . are made by tiny minorities. . . . It is difficult—nay impossible—to see how it could be otherwise in large political systems."[6] Sociologist Suzanne Keller writes, "The democratic ethos notwithstanding, men must become accustomed to bigger, more extensive and more specialized elites in their midst as long as industrial societies keep growing and becoming more specialized."[7] And according to Harold Lasswell, "The discovery that in all large-scale societies the decisions at any given time are typically in the hands of a small number of people" confirms a basic fact: "Government is always government by the few, whether in the name of the few, the one, or the many."[8]

Elitism also asserts that the few who govern are not typical of the masses who are governed. Elites possess more control over resources—power, wealth, education, prestige, status, skills of leadership, information, knowledge of political processes, ability to communicate, and organization—and elites (in America)

are drawn disproportionately from among wealthy, educated, prestigiously employed, socially prominent, white, Anglo-Saxon, and Protestant groups in society. In short, elites are drawn from a society's upper classes, which are made up of those persons in a society who own or control a disproportionate share of the societal institutions—industry, commerce, finance, education, the military, communications, civic affairs, and law.

On the other hand, elite theory admits of some social mobility that enables non-elites to become elites; elitism does not necessarily mean that individuals from the lower classes cannot rise to the top. In fact, a certain amount of "circulation of elites" (upward mobility) is essential for the stability of the elite system. Openness in the elite system siphons off potentially revolutionary leadership from the lower classes, and an elite system is strengthened when talented and ambitious individuals from the masses are permitted to enter governing circles. However, it is important that the movement of individuals from non-elite positions be a slow and continuous assimilation rather than a rapid or revolutionary change. Moreover, only those non-elites who have demonstrated their commitment to the elite system itself and to the system's political and economic values can be admitted to the ruling class.

Elites share in a *consensus* about fundamental norms underlying the social system. They agree on the basic "rules of the game," as well as on the continuation of the social system itself. The stability of the system, and even its survival, depends upon this consensus. According to David Truman, "Being more influential, they (the elites) are privileged; and being privileged, they have, with few exceptions, a special stake in the continuation of the system in which their privileges rest."[9] Elite consensus does not mean that elite members never disagree or never compete with each other for preeminence; it is unlikely that there ever was a society in which there was no competition among elites. But elitism implies that competition takes place within a very narrow range of issues and that elites agree on more matters than they disagree on. Disagreement usually occurs over *means*, rather than *ends*.

In America, the bases of elite consensus are the sanctity of private property, limited government, and individual liberty. Richard Hofstadter writes about American elite struggles:

The fierceness of political struggles has often been misleading; for the range of vision embodied by the primary contestants in the major parties has always been bounded by the horizons of property and enterprise. However much at odds on specific issues, the major political traditions have shared a belief in the rights of property, the philosophy of economic individualism, the value of competition; they have accepted the economic virtues of capitalist culture as necessary qualities of man.[10]

Hofstadter's analysis of consensus among leaders in American history echoes a central principle of elitism.

Elitism implies that public policy does not reflect demands of "the people" so much as it reflects the interests and values of elites. Changes and innovations in public policy come about as a result of redefinitions by elites of their own values. However, the general conservatism of elites—that is, their interest in preserving the system—means that changes in public policy will be incremental rather than revolutionary. Public policies are frequently modified but seldom replaced.

Basic changes in the nature of the political system occur when events threaten the system. Elites, acting on the basis of enlightened self-interest, institute reforms to preserve the system and their place in it. Their motives are not necessarily self-serving; the values of elites may be very "public-regarding," and the welfare of the masses may be an important element in elite decision making. Elitism does not mean that public policy will ignore or be against the welfare of the masses but only that the responsibility for the mass welfare rests upon the shoulders of elites, not upon the masses.

Finally, elitism assumes that the masses are largely passive, apathetic, and ill-informed. Mass sentiments are manipulated by elites more often than elite values are influenced by the sentiments of the masses. For the most part, communication between elites and masses flows downward. Policy questions of government are seldom decided by the masses through elections or through the presentation of policy alternatives by political parties. For the most part, these "democratic" institutions —elections and parties—are important only for their symbolic value. They help tie the masses to the political system by giving them a role to play on election day and a political party with which they can identify. Elitism contends that the masses have at best only an indirect influence over the decision-making behavior of elites.

Naturally, elitism is frequently misunderstood in America, because the prevailing myths and symbols of the American system are drawn from democratic theory rather than elite theory. Therefore, it is important here to emphasize what elitism is *not*, as well as to briefly restate what it *is*.

Elitism does not mean that those who have power are continually locked in conflict with the masses or that powerholders always achieve their goals at the expense of the public interest. Elitism is not a conspiracy to oppress the masses. Elitism does not imply that powerholders constitute a single impenetrable monolithic body or that powerholders in society always agree on public issues. Elitism does not pretend that power in society does not shift over time or that new elites cannot emerge to compete with old elites. Elites may be more or less monolithic and cohesive or more or less pluralistic and competitive. Power need not rest exclusively on the control of economic resources but may rest instead upon other leadership resources—organization, communication, or information. Elitism does not imply that the masses *never* have any impact on the attitudes of elites but only that elites influence masses more than masses influence elites.

Elitism can be summarized as follows:

1. Society is divided into the few who have power and the many who do not. Only a small number of persons allocate values for society; the masses do not decide public policy.
2. The few who govern are not typical of the masses who are governed. Elites are drawn disproportionately from the upper socioeconomic strata of society.
3. The movement of non-elites to elite positions must be slow and continuous to maintain stability and avoid revolution. Only non-elites who have accepted the basic elite consensus can be admitted to governing circles.
4. Elites share a consensus on the basic values of the social system and the preservation of the system. Disagreement is confined to a narrow range of issues.
5. Public policy does not reflect demands of masses but rather the prevailing values of the elite. Changes in public policy will be incremental rather than revolutionary.
6. Active elites are subject to relatively little direct influence from apathetic masses. Elites influence masses more than masses influence elites.

THE MEANING OF DEMOCRACY

Ideally, democracy means individual participation in the decisions that affect one's life. John Dewey wrote, "The keynote of democracy as a way of life may be expressed as the necessity for the participation of every mature human being in formation of the values that regulate the living of men together."[11] In other words, democracy means popular participation in the allocation of values in a society.

In traditional democratic theory, popular participation has been valued as an opportunity for individual self-development: Responsibility for the governing of one's own conduct develops one's character, self-reliance, intelligence, and moral judgment—in short, one's dignity. Even if a benevolent despot could govern in the public interest, he would be rejected by the classic democrat. The English political philosopher J. S. Mill asks, "What sort of human beings can be formed under such a regime? What development can either their thinking or active faculties attain under it?" The argument for citizen participation in public affairs is based not upon the policy outcomes it would produce but on the belief that such involvement is essential to the full development of human capacities. Mill argues that man can know truth only by discovering it for himself.[12]

Procedurally, popular participation was to be achieved through majority rule and respect for the rights of minorities. Self-development means self-government, and self-government can be accomplished only by encouraging each individual to contribute to the development of public policy and by resolving conflicts over public policy through majority rule. Minorities who have had the opportunity to influence policy but whose views have not succeeded in winning majority support would accept the decisions of majorities. In return, majorities would permit minorities to openly attempt to win majority support for their views. Freedom of speech and press, freedom to dissent, and freedom to form opposition parties and organizations are essential to insure meaningful individual participation. This freedom of expression is also necessary for ascertaining what the majority views really are.

The procedural requirements and the underlying ethics of democracy are linked. Carl Becker writes about democracy:

Its fundamental assumption is the worth and dignity and creative capacity of the individual, so that the chief aim of government is the maximum of individual self-direction, the chief means to that end, the minimum of compulsion by the state. . . .

Means and ends are conjoined in the concept of freedom; freedom of thought so that the truth may prevail; freedom of occupation, so that careers may be open to talent; freedom of self-government, so that none may be compelled against his will.[13]

The underlying value of democracy is, as we have noted, individual dignity. Man, by virtue of his existence, is entitled to life, liberty, and property. A "natural law," or moral tenet, guarantees to every man both liberty and the right to property; and this natural law is morally superior to man-made law. John Locke, the English political philosopher whose writings most influenced America's founding elites, argues that even in a "state of nature"—that is, a world in which there were no governments—an individual possesses inalienable rights to life, liberty, and property. Locke meant that these rights were antecedent to government, that these rights are not given to the individual by governments, and that no governments may legitimately take them away.[14]

Locke believed that the very purpose of government was to protect individual liberty. Men form a "social contract" with each other in establishing a government to help protect their rights; they tacitly agree to accept governmental activity in order to better protect life, liberty, and property. Implicit in the social contract and the democratic notion of freedom is the belief that governmental activity and social control over the individual be kept to a minimum. This involves the removal of as many external restrictions, controls, and regulations on the individual as is consistent with the freedom of his fellow citizens.

Moreover, since government is formed by the consent of the governed to protect individual liberty, it logically follows that government cannot violate the rights it was established to protect. Its authority is limited. Locke's ultimate weapon to protect individual dignity against abuse by government was the right of revolution. According to Locke, whenever governments violate the natural rights of the governed, they forfeit the authority placed in them under the social contract.

Another vital aspect of classic democracy is a belief in the equality of all men. The Declaration of Independence expresses the conviction that "all men are created equal." Even the Founding Fathers believed in equality for all men *before the law*, notwithstanding the circumstances of the accused. A man was not to be judged by social position, economic class, creed, or race. Many early democrats also believed in *political equality*—equal access of individuals to political influence, that is, equal opportunity to influence public policy. Political equality is expressed in the concept of "one man, one vote."

Over time, the notion of equality has also come to include *equality of opportunity* in all aspects of American life—social, educational, and economic, as well as political. Roland Pennock writes:

The objective of equality is not merely the recognition of a certain dignity of the human being as such, but it is also to provide him with the opportunity—equal to that guaranteed to others—for protecting and advancing his interests and developing his powers and personality.[15]

Thus, the notion of equality of opportunity has been extended beyond political life to encompass equality of opportunity in education, employment, housing, recreation, and public accommodations. Each person has an equal opportunity to develop his individual capacities to their natural limits.

It is important to remember, however, that the traditional democratic creed has always stressed *equality of opportunity* to education, wealth, and status and not *absolute equality*. Thomas Jefferson recognized a "natural aristocracy" of talent, ambition, and industry, and liberal democrats since Jefferson have always accepted inequalities that are a product of individual merit and hard work. Absolute equality, or "leveling," is not a part of liberal democratic theory.

In summary, democratic thinking involves the following ideas:

1. popular participation in the decisions that shape the lives of individuals in a society;
2. government by majority rule, with recognition of the rights of minorities to try to become majorities. These rights include the freedom of speech, press, assembly, and petition and the freedom to dissent, to form opposition parties, and to run for public office;
3. a commitment to individual dignity and the preservation of the liberal values of life, liberty, and property;
4. a commitment to equal opportunity for all men to develop their individual capacities.

THE MEANING OF PLURALISM

Despite political rhetoric in America concerning citizen participation in decision making, majority rule, our protection of minorities, individual rights, and equality of opportunity, no scholar or commentator, however optimistic about life in this country, would contend that these conditions have been fully realized in the American political system. No one contends that citizens participate in *all* the decisions which shape their lives, or that majority preferences *always* prevail. Nor do they argue that the rights of minorities are *always* protected, or that the values of life, liberty, and property are *never* sacrificed, or that *every* American has an equal opportunity to influence public policy.

However, modern *pluralism* seeks to reaffirm the democratic character of American society by asserting that:

1. Although citizens do not directly participate in decision making, their many leaders do make decisions through a process of bargaining, accommodation, and compromise.
2. There is competition among leadership groups which helps to protect the interests of individuals. Countervailing centers of power—for example, competition between business leaders,

labor leaders, and governmental leaders—can check each other and keep each interest from abusing its power and oppressing the individual.
3. Individuals can influence public policy by choosing between competing elites in elections. Elections and parties allow individuals to hold leaders accountable for their action.
4. While individuals do not participate directly in decision making, they can join organized groups and make their influence felt through their participation in these organizations.
5. Leadership groups are not closed; new groups can be formed and gain access to the political system.
6. Although political influence in society is unequal, power is widely dispersed. Frequently, access to decision making is based on the level of interest people have in a particular decision, and because leadership is fluid and mobile, power depends upon one's interest in public affairs, skills in leadership, information about issues, knowledge of democratic processes, and skill in organization and public relations.
7. There are multiple leadership groups within society. Those who exercise power in one kind of decision do not necessarily exercise power in others. No single elite dominates decision making in all issue areas.
8. Public policy is not necessarily majority preference, but it is an equilibrium of interest interaction. Such equilibrium is the approximate balance of competing interest group influences and is therefore a reasonable approximation of society's preferences.

Pluralism, then, is the belief that democratic values can be preserved in a system of multiple, competing elites who determine public policy through a process of bargaining and compromise, in which voters exercise meaningful choices in elections and new elites can gain access to power.

But pluralism, even if it accurately describes American society, is *not* the equivalent of democracy. Let us explain why. First of all, the pluralist notion of decision making by elite interaction is not the same as the democratic ideal of direct *individual* participation in decision making. Pluralists recognize that mass participation in decision making is not possible in a complex, urban, industrial society and that decision making must be accomplished through elite interaction, rather than individual participation. But a central value of classical democratic politics is *individual* participation in decision making. In modern pluralism, however, individual participation has given way to interaction—bargaining, accommodation, and compromise—between leaders of institutions and organizations in society. Individuals are represented in the political system only insofar as they are members of institutions or organizations whose leaders participate in policy making. Government is held responsible not by individual citizens but by leaders of institutions, organized interest groups, and political parties. The principal actors are leaders of corporations and financial institutions, elected and appointed government officials, the top ranks of military and governmental bureaucracies, and leaders of large organizations in labor, agriculture, and the professions.

Yet, decision making by elite interaction, whether it succeeds in protecting the individual or not, fails to contribute to individual growth and development. In this regard, modern pluralism diverges sharply from classic democracy, which emphasizes as a primary value the personal development that would result from the individual's actively participating in decisions that affect his life.

Pluralism stresses the fragmentation of power in society and the influence of public opinion and elections on the behavior of elites. But this fragmentation of power is not identical with the democratic ideal of political equality. Who rules, in the pluralist view of America? According to political scientist Aaron Wildavsky, "different small groups of interested and active citizens in different issue areas with some overlap, if any, by public officials, and occasional intervention by a large number of people at the polls."[16] This is not government by the people. While citizen influence can be felt through leaders who anticipate the reaction of citizens, decision making is still in the hands of the leaders—the elites. According to the pluralists, multiple elites decide public policy in America, each in their own area of interest.

Traditional democratic theory envisions public policy as a rational choice of individuals with equal influence, who evaluate their needs and reach a decision with due regard for the rights of others. This traditional theory does not view public policy as a product of elite interaction or interest group pressures. In fact, interest groups and even political parties were viewed by classical democratic theorists as intruders into an individualistic brand of citizenship and politics.

There are several other problems in accepting pluralism as the legitimate heir to classical democratic theory. First of all, can pluralism assure that membership in organization and institutions is really an effective form of individual participation in policy making? Robert Presthus argues that the organizations and institutions on which pluralists rely "become oligarchic and restrictive insofar as they monopolize access to government power and limit individual participation."[17] Henry Kariel writes, "The voluntary organization or associations which the early theorists of pluralism relied upon to sustain the individual against a unified omnipotent government, have themselves become oligarchically governed hierarchies."[18] The individual may provide the numerical base for organizations, but what influence does he have upon the leadership? Rarely do corporations, unions, armies, churches, government bureaucracies, or professional associations have any *internal* mechanisms of democracy. They are usually run by a small elite of officers and activists. Leaders of corporations, bank, labor unions, churches, universities, medical associations, and bar associations remain in control year after year. Only a small number of people attend meetings, vote in organizational elections, or make their influence felt within their organization. The pluralists offer no evidence that the giant organizations and institutions in American life really represent the views or interests of their individual members.

Also, can pluralism really assume that the dignity of the individual is being protected by elite competition? Since pluralism contends that different groups of leaders make decisions in *different* issue areas, why should we assume that these leaders compete with each other? It seems more likely that each group of leaders would consent to allow other groups of leaders to govern their own spheres of influence without interference. Accommodation, rather than competition, may be the prevailing style of elite interaction.

Pluralism answers with the hope that the power of diverse institutions and organizations in society will roughly balance out and that the emergence of power monopoly is unlikely. Pluralism (like its distant cousin, the economics of Adam Smith) assures us that no interests can ever emerge the complete victor in political competition. Yet inequality of power among institutions and organizations is commonplace. Examples of narrow, organized interests achieving their goals at the expense of the broader but unorganized public are quite common. Furthermore, it is usually producer interests, bound together by economic ties, which turn out to dominate less organized consumer groups and groups based upon non-economic interests. The pluralists offer no evidence that political competition can prevent monopoly or oligopoly in political power, any more than economic competition could prevent monopoly or oligopoly in economic power.

Finally, pluralism must contend with the problem of how private non-governmental elites can be held accountable to the people. Even if the people can hold governmental elites accountable through elections, how can corporation elites, union leaders, and other kinds of private leadership be held accountable? Pluralism usually dodges this important question by focusing primary attention on *public* decision making involving governmental elites and by largely ignoring *private* decision making involving non-governmental elites. Pluralists focus on rules and orders which are enforced by *governments*, but certainly men's lives are vitally affected by decisions made by private institutions and organizations—corporations, banks, universities, medical associations, newspapers, and so on. In an ideal democracy, individuals would participate in *all* decisions which significantly affect their lives; but pluralism largely excludes individuals from participation in many vital decisions by claiming that these decisions are "private" in nature and not subject to public accountability.

In summary, the pluralism diverges from classical democratic theory in the following respects:

1. Decisions are made by elite interaction—bargaining, accommodation, compromise—rather than by direct individual participation.
2. Key political actors are leaders of institutions and organizations rather than individual citizens.
3. Power is fragmented, but inequality of political influence among powerholders is common.
4. Power is distributed among governmental and non-governmental institutions and organizations, but these institutions and organizations are generally governed by oligarchies, rather than by their members in democratic fashion.
5. Institutions and organizations divide power and presumably compete among themselves, but there is no certainty that this competition guarantees political equality or protects individual dignity.
6. *Governmental* elites are presumed to be accountable to the masses through elections, but many important decisions affecting the lives of individuals are made by *private* elites, who are not directly accountable to the masses.

Frequently confusion arises in distinguishing *pluralism* from *elitism*. Pluralists *say* that the system they describe is a reaffirmation of democratic theory in a modern, urban, industrial society. They offer pluralism as "a practical solution" to the problem of achieving democratic ideals in a large complex social system where direct individual participation and decision making are simply not possible. But many critics of pluralism assert that it is a covert form of elitism—that pluralists are closer to the elitist position than to the democratic tradition they revere. Thus Peter Bachrach describes pluralism as "democratic elitism":

Until quite recently democratic and elite theories were regarded as distinct and conflicting. While in their pure form they are still regarded as contradictory, there is, I believe, a strong if not dominant trend in contemporary political thought incorporating major elitist principles within democratic theory. As a result there is a new theory which I have called democratic elitism.[19]

MASS THREATS TO DEMOCRACY

Democratic theory assumes that liberal values —individual dignity, equality of opportunity, the right of dissent, freedom of speech and press, religious toleration, and due process of law—are best protected by the expansion and growth of mass political participation. Historically, the masses and not elites were considered the guardians of liberty. For example, in the eighteenth and nineteenth centuries, the threat of tyranny arose from corrupt monarchies and decadent churches. But in the twentieth century, it has been the masses who have been most susceptible to the appeals of totalitarianism.

It is the irony of democracy in America that elites, not masses are most committed to democratic values. Despite a superficial commitment to the symbols of democracy, the American people have a surprisingly weak commitment to individual liberty, toleration of diversity, or freedom of expression for those who would challenge the existing order. Social science research reveals that the common man is not attached to the causes of liberty, fraternity, or equality. On the contrary, support for free

speech and press, for freedom of dissent, and for equality of opportunity for all is associated with high educational levels, prestigious occupations, and high social status. Authoritarianism is stronger among the working classes in America than among the middle and upper classes. Democracy would not survive if it depended upon support for democratic values among the masses in America.

Democratic values have survived because elites, not masses, govern. Elites in America— leaders in government, industry, education, and civic affairs; the well-educated, prestigiously employed, and politically active—give greater support to basic democratic values and "rules of the game" than do the masses. And it is because masses in America respond to the ideas and actions of democratically minded elites that liberal values are preserved. In summarizing the findings of social science research regarding mass behavior in American democracy, political scientist Peter Bachrach writes:

A widespread public commitment to the fundamental norms underlying the democratic process was regarded by classical democratic theorists as essential to the survival of democracy . . . today social scientists tend to reject this position. They do so not only because of their limited confidence in the commitment of non-elites to freedom, but also because of the growing awareness that non-elites are, in large part, politically activated by elites. The empirical finding that mass behavior is generally in response to the attitudes, proposals and modes of action of political elites gives added support to the position that responsibility for maintaining "the rules of the game" rests not on the shoulders of the people but on those of the elites.[20]

In short, it is the common man, not the elite, who is most likely to be swayed by antidemocratic ideology; and it is the elite, not the common man, who is the chief guardian of democratic values.

Elites must be insulated from the antidemocratic tendencies of the masses if they are to fulfill their role as guardians of liberty and property. Too much mass influence over elites threatens democratic values. Mass behavior is highly unstable. Usually, established elites can depend upon mass apathy; but, occasionally, mass activism will replace apathy, and this activism will be extremist, unstable, and unpredictable. Mass activism is usually an expression of resentment against the established order, and it usually occurs in times of crisis, when a counter-elite, or demagogue, emerges from the masses to mobilize them against the elites.

Democracies, where elites are dangerously accessible to mass influence, can survive only if the masses are absorbed in the problems of everyday life and are involved in primary and secondary groups which distract their attention from mass politics. In other words, the masses are stable when they are absorbed in their work, family, neighborhood, trade union, hobby, church, recreational group, and so on. It is when they become alienated from their home, work, and community—when existing ties to social organizations and institutions become weakened—that mass behavior becomes unstable and dangerous. It is then that the atttention and activity of the masses can be captured and directed by the demagogue, or counter-elite. The demagogue can easily mobilize for revolution those elements of the masses who have few ties to the existing social and political order.

These ties to the existing order tend to be weakest during crisis periods, when major social changes are taking place. According to social psychologist William Kornhauser:

. . . communism and fascism have gained strength in social systems undergoing sudden and extensive changes in the structure of authority and community. Sharp tears in the social fabric caused by widespread unemployment or by major military defeat are highly favorable to mass politics.[21]

Counter-elites are mass-oriented leaders who express hostility toward the established order and appeal to mass sentiments—extremism, in-tolerance, racial identity, anti-intellectualism, equalitarianism, and violence. Counter-elites can easily be distinguished from elites: *Elites*, whether liberal or conservative, support the fundamental values of the system—individual liberty, majority rule, due process of law, limited government, and private property; *counter-elites*, whether "left" or "right," are anti-democratic, extremist, impatient with due process, contemptuous of law and authority, and violence-prone. The only significant difference between "left" and "right" counter-elites is their attitude toward change: "right" counter-elites express mass reaction against change—political, social, economic, technological—while "left" counter-elites demand radical and revolutionary change.

All counter-elites claim to speak for "the people." Both "left" and "right" counter-elites assert *the supremacy of "the people"* over laws, institutions, procedures, or individual rights. Right-wing counter-elites, including fascists, justify their policies as "the will of the people," while left-wing radicals cry "all power to the people" and praise the virtues of "people's democracies." In describing this populism, sociologist Edward Shils writes:

the will of the people as such is supreme over every other standard, over the standards of traditional institutions, over the autonomy of institutions, and over the will of other strata. Population identifies the will of the people with justice and morality.[22]

Extremism is another characteristic of mass politics—the view that compromise and coalition-building are immoral. Indeed "politics" and "politicians" are viewed with hostility, because they imply the possibility of compromising mass demands.[23] Occasionally counter-elites will make cynical use of politics, but only as a short-term tactical means to other goals. A commentator on radical student activists observes that they are

indistinguishable from the far right. . . . They share a contempt for rational political discussion and constitutional legal solutions. Both want to be pure. They know nothing about the virtue of compromise. They know nothing about the horror of sainthood or the wickedness of saints.[24]

Counter-elites frequently charge that a *conspiracy* exists among established elites to deliberately perpetuate evil upon the people. The "left" counter-elite charges that the established order knowingly exploits and oppresses the people for its own benefit and amusement; the "right" counter-elite charges that the established order is falling prey to an international communist conspiracy whose goal is to deprive the people of their liberty and property and to enslave them. Richard Hofstadter refers to this phenomena as "the paranoid style of politics."[25] A related weapon in the arsenal of the counter-elite is *scapegoatism*—the designation of particular minority groups in society as responsible for the evils suffered by the people. Throughout American history various scapegoats have been designated—Catholics, immigrants, Jews, blacks, communists, intellectuals, "Wall Street Bankers," munitions manufacturers, etc.

The masses define politics in *simplistic* terms. The masses want simple answers to all of society's problems, regardless of how complex these problems may be. Thus, black counter-elites charge that "white racism" is responsible for the complex problems of under-education, poverty, unemployment, crime, delinquency, ill-health, and poor housing of ghetto dwellers. In a similar fashion the white counter-elites dismiss ghetto disturbances as a product of "communist agitation." These simplistic answers are designed to relieve both black and white masses of any difficult thinking about social issues and to place their problems in simple, emotion-laden terms. Anti-intellectualism and antirationalism are an important part of mass politics.

Counter-elites often reflect mass *propensities toward violence*. Rap Brown inspired black masses in Cambridge, Maryland, in 1967 with:

Don't be trying to love that honky to death. Shoot him to death. Shoot him to death, brother, cause that's what he's out to do to you. Like I said in the beginning, if this town don't come around, this town should be burned down, it should be burned down, brother.[26]

Early in his political career, George C. Wallace's references to violence were only slightly more subtle:

Of course, if I did what I'd like to do I'd pick up something and smash one of these federal judges in the head and then burn the courthouse down. But I'm too genteel. What we need in this country is some Governors that used to work up here at Birmingham in the steel mills with about a tenth-grade education. A Governor like that wouldn't be so genteel. He'd put out his orders and he'd say, "The first man who throws a brick is a dead man. The first man who loots something what doesn't belong to him is a dead man. My orders are to shoot to kill."[27]

The similarity between the appeals of black and white counter-elites is obvious.

In summary, elite theory views the critical division in American politics as the division between elites and masses. "Left" and "right" counter-elites are similar. Both appeal to mass sentiments; assert the supremacy of "the people" over laws, institutions, and individual rights; reject compromise in favor of extremism; charge that established elites are a conspiracy; designate scapegoat groups; define social problems in simple emotional terms and reject rational thinking; express equalitarian sentiments and hostility toward men who have achieved success within the system; and express approval of mass violence.

ELITE THREATS TO DEMOCRACY

While elites are relatively more committed to democratic values than masses, elites themselves frequently abandon these values in crisis periods and become repressive. Anti-democratic mass activism has its counterpart in elite repression. Both endanger democratic values.

Mass activism and elite repression frequently interact to create multiple threats to democracy. Mass activism—riots, demonstrations, extremism, violence—generate fear and insecurity among elites, who respond by curtailing freedom and strengthening "security." Dissent is no longer tolerated, the news media are censored, free speech curtailed, potential counter-elites jailed, and police and security forces strengthened—usually in the name of "national security" or "law and order." Elites convince themselves that these steps are necessary to preserve liberal democratic values. The irony is, of course, that the elites make society less democratic in trying to preserve democracy.

In short, neither elites nor masses in America are totally and irrevocably committed to democratic values. Elites are generally more committed to democratic procedures than the masses. This is true for several reasons. In the first place, persons who are successful at the game of democratic politics are more amenable to abiding by the rules of the games than those who are not. Moreover, many elite members have internalized democratic values learned in childhood. Finally, the achievement of high position may bring a sense of responsibility for, and an awareness of, societal values. However, elites can and do become repressive when they perceive threats to the political system and their position in it.

NOTES

[1] Robert A. Dahl, "Power, Pluralism, and Democracy: A Modest Proposal," paper delivered at 1964 annual meeting of the American Political Science Association, p. 3. See also Peter Bachrach, *The Theory of Democratic Elitism* (Boston: Little, Brown and Co., 1967).

[2] Harold Lasswell and Abraham Kaplan, *Power and Society* (New Haven, Conn.: Yale University Press, 1950), p. 219.

[3] V. O. Key, Jr., *Public Opinion and American Democracy* (New York: Alfred A. Knopf, 1961), p. 558.

[4] Gaetano Mosca, *The Ruling Class* (New York: McGraw-Hill Book Co., 1939), p. 50.

[5] Mosca, p. 51.

[6] Dahl, "Power, Pluralism and Democracy," p. 3.

[7] Suzanne Keller, *Beyond the Ruling Class* (New York: Random House, 1963), p. 71.

[8] Harold Lasswell and Daniel Lerner, *The Comparative Study of Elites* (Stanford, Calif.: Stanford University Press, 1952), p. 7.

[9] David Truman, "The American System in Crisis," *Political Science Quarterly* (December 1959), 489.

[10] Richard Hofstadter, *The American Political Tradition* (New York: Alfred A. Knopf, 1948), p. viii.

[11] John Dewey, "Democracy and Educational Administration," *School and Society* (April 3, 1937).

[12] John Stuart Mill, *Representative Government* (New York: E. P. Dutton, Everyman's Library), p. 203.

[13] Carl Becker, *Modern Democracy* (New Haven, Conn.: Yale University Press, 1941), pp. 26–27.

[14] For a discussion of John Locke and the political philosophy underlying democracy, see George Sabine, *A History of Political Theory* (New York: Holt, Rinehart and Winston, 1950), pp. 517–541.

[15] Roland Pennock, "Democracy and Leadership," in William Chambers and Robert Salisbury (eds.), *Democracy Today* (New York: Dodd, Mead & Co., 1962), pp. 126–127.

[16] Aaron Wildavsky, *Leadership in a Small Town* (Totawa, N.J.: Bedminster Press, 1964), p. 20.

[17] Robert Presthus, *Men at the Top* (New York: Oxford University Press, 1964), p. 20.

[18] Henry Kariel, *The Decline of American Pluralism* (Stanford, Calif.: Stanford University Press, 1961), p. 74.

[19] Peter Bachrach. *The Theory of Democratic Elitism* (Boston: Little, Brown and Co., 1967), p. xi.

[20] Bachrach, pp. 47–48.

[21] William Kornhauser, *The Politics of Mass Society* (New York: Free Press, 1959), p. 99.

[22] Edward A. Shils, *The Torment of Secrecy* (New York: Free Press, 1956), p. 98.

[23] See John H. Bunzel, *Anti-Politics in America* (New York: Knopf, 1967).

[24] Quotation from Nan Robertson, "The Student Scene: Angry Militants," *New York Times*, November 20, 1967, p. 30.

[25] Richard Hofstadter, *The Paranoid Style of American Politics* (New York: Knopf, 1965).

[26] U.S. Congress, Senate, Committee on the Judiciary, Hearings on H.R. 421, "Anti-riot Bill," 90th Congress, 1st Session, 2 August 1967, p. 32.

[27] Quoted in Seymour Martin Lipset and Earl Raab, *The Politics of Unreason* (New York: Harper and Row, 1970), p. 356.

✩✩✩✩✩✩✩✩✩✩✩✩✩✩✩✩✩✩✩✩✩✩✩✩✩✩✩✩✩✩✩✩✩✩✩✩✩

The Constitution

2

The political heritage of Western democracy is strongly rooted in constitutionalism and the rule of law. We noted in Chapter 1 that a fundamental premise of democratic theory is that government receives its authority from the consent of the governed. What are the legal and constitutional relationships between government and the people? The American colonists considered this basic question when they sought to sever their ties to Britain in the eighteenth century. To fully appreciate the philosophic foundations of the colonists' rationale in the Declaration of Independence (see the Appendix), we turn first to John Locke, whose writings had great influence on Thomas Jefferson, the principal author of the Declaration.

Locke, the noted British philosopher of the seventeenth century, was concerned with the essential reason why men establish political societies (governments). In his *Second Treatise, Of Civil Government*, he focused upon the legal obligations between people and government that are established in a "social contract." Upon forming government, individuals move from a state of nature where their security is uncertain and where justice is a personal matter, to an organized society which is required to arbitrate and decide disputes impartially. The role of government is to enforce the law fairly and without personal bias or prejudice. At the same time, the members of society retain certain basic natural rights (the Declaration's "inalienable rights") which government may not take away. These include the rights to life, liberty, and property. Government may not deprive the people of their natural rights, nor may it act contrary to the expectations of the citizenry. Thus, the rulers of society are limited—they derive their authority from the consent of the governed, and they may be deposed if their actions are no longer considered legitimate.

Locke's ideas on the social contact, the natural rights of the people, and the reserved authority to alter the people's contractual obligations with government were incorporated directly into the Declaration of Independence. The Declaration provided the moral and legal basis for American separation from Britain in 1776. This was (and still is) a truly revolutionary statement of principles. Not only does the Declaration assert such "self-evident truths" as political equality and the rights to "life, liberty, and the pursuit of happiness," but it also states that "whenever any form of government becomes destructive of these ends, it is the right of the people to alter or to abolish it. . . ." Moreover, since changes in government are serious matters, the statement is qualified by warning: "Prudence, indeed, will dictate, that governments long established should not be changed for light and transient causes."

Following the Revolutionary War and preceding the Constitutional Convention of 1787, the United States was governed by the Articles of Confederation, a document that provided for a very weak central government that was dependent upon the thirteen states for nearly all of its powers. The national legislature lacked the power to tax and to regulate interstate commerce. It could not act in any matters relating to war, foreign relations, money, or requisitions without the approval of at least nine of the thirteen states; and Congress could not enforce sanctions against the states for any of the decisions it made. The executive and judicial branches were even weaker than the legislature. There were no provisions for a chief executive (a president) nor was there any system of federal courts, except those that settled disputes on the high seas. Finally, the Articles were nearly impossible to change or amend since unanimous consent of the states was required. This was an obstacle that permitted any one state to exercise veto power over changes that the others might desire.

Obviously, the confederation of states lacked unity and a strong national purpose. Serious commercial and trading disputes occurred between the states under the Articles. The fifty-five men who went to Philadelphia in 1787 were determined to overcome the political and institutional defects of the national government by framing a new constitution. What were the intentions, purposes, and objectives of the Founding Fathers? John P. Roche (Article 3) indicates that the Constitutional Convention was confronted with many serious problems that required a whole series of compromise solutions. Foremost among the issues facing the delegates were those dealing with representation in Congress, the conflicting interests of the larger and smaller states, and the regional disputes between North and South, particularly over slavery. In resolving these conflicts, Roche argues that the framers were, above all else, consummate practical politicians who engaged in bargaining, negotiation, and accommodation to produce the American Constitution, which has withstood the test of time with relatively few changes (see text of the Constitution in the Appendix).

In Article 4, David G. Smith further examines the motivations of the Founding Fathers. He considers the representativeness of the framers in relation to the major social and economic forces in American society in 1787: Was the Constitution primarily an economic document reflecting the biases of a small ruling elite or was it a democratic charter expressing the majority will of the nation? This debate has raged ever since Charles A. Beard wrote his famous book, *An Economic Interpretation of the Constitution* (1913). Beard and others claimed that the framers were an unrepresentative elite who wrote the Constitution to protect and enhance their private property interests. Property was restricted to a powerful few in post-colonial society and voting privileges depended upon one's property holdings. The masses did not participate in drafting the Constitution. In fact, the calling of the Convention was an "act of usurpation" not authorized by the Articles of Confederation or by a majority of the voters. Finally, the Constitution was "antidemocratic" in design and substance because the propertied elite wanted to improve commercial relationships between the states disrupted under the Articles.

Smith answers these charges by showing that private property was more widely distributed in post-colonial America. A majority owned some land and most believed in the natural right of property ownership. The major problem was not between an unrepresentative elite and a powerless mass, but the tensions and conflicts of a disharmonious society. The new nation was divided by region, section, and the lack of national unity. The Constitution was an important step toward uniting the disparate parts of the nation.

From the Roche and Smith discussions, we can conclude that the foundation of American government is *constitutional* democracy. As originally established in 1789, the national government was limited in exercising power. Powers were separated between the executive, legislative, and judicial branches; the three branches checked and balanced each other. Powers not exercised by the national government were reserved for the states. Certain basic civil liberties were retained by the people.

The *Federalist Papers*, written by Alexander Hamilton, John Jay, and James Madison, are exceptionally useful sources for understanding the goals, purposes, and objectives of the Constitution. These essays were intended to convince the New York State convention to ratify the Constitution. In *Federalist*, no. 51, we find the basic arguments for limiting concentrated political power. Do these arguments still apply? Has the national government become too powerful? What are the options for controlling such influences?

3

The Founding Fathers: A Reform Caucus in Action

John P. Roche

The U.S. Constitution is a remarkable document; since it was drafted in 1787 it has withstood the test of time with relatively few changes (although various interpretations by the Supreme Court have changed its meaning in many important ways). What were the intents and purposes of the Founding Fathers at the Constitutional Convention? What political strategies did they employ to achieve their objectives? John P. Roche shows that the framers engaged in considerable bargaining, negotiation, and accommodation. This is quite similar to the notion of "pluralism" as previously discussed by Deutsch in Article 1 and Dye and Zeigler in Article 2. The political in-fighting of the Convention is especially interesting in regard to the battles over representation. What were the differing objectives of the Virginia and New Jersey plans? How did the Connecticut Compromise resolve these differences? Why was the struggle over representation so crucial to the success of the Convention? Do you agree that the framers were less interested in abstract political theories and more interested in developing workable forms of government?

Over the last century and a half, the work of the Constitutional convention and the motives of the Founding Fathers have been analyzed under a number of different ideological auspices. To one generation of historians, the hand of God was moving in the assembly; under a later dispensation, the dialectic (at various levels of philosophical sophistication) replaced the Deity: "relationships of production" moved into the niche previously reserved for Love of Country. Thus in counterpoint to the Zeitgeist, the Framers have undergone miraculous metamorphoses: at one time acclaimed as liberals and bold social engineers, today they appear in the guise of sound Burkean conservatives, men who in our time would subscribe to *Fortune*, look to Walter Lippman for political theory, and chuckle patronizingly at the antics of Barry Goldwater. The implicit assumption is that if James Madison were among us, he would be President of the Ford Foundation, while Alexander Hamilton would chair the Committee for Economic Development.

The "Fathers" have thus been admitted to our best circles; the revolutionary ferocity which confiscated all Tory property in reach and populated New Brunswick with outlaws has been converted by the "Miltown School" of American historians into a benign dedication to "consensus" and "prescriptive rights." The Daughters of the American Revolution have, through the ministrations of Professors Boorstin, Hartz, and Rossiter, at last found ancestors worthy of their descendants. It is not my purpose here to argue that the "Fathers" were, in fact, radical revolutionaries; that proposition has been brilliantly demonstrated by Robert R. Palmer in his *Age of the Democratic Revolution*. My concern is with the further position that not only were they revolu-

Reprinted from John P. Roche, "The Founding Fathers: A Reform Caucus In Action," *American Political Science Review* 55, no. 4 (December 1961): 799–816. Reprinted by permission of the American Political Science Association and John P. Roche.

tionaries, but also they were democrats. Indeed, in my view, there is one fundamental truth about the Founding Fathers that *every* generation of Zeitgeisters has done its best to obscure: They were first and foremost superb democratic politicians. I suspect that in a contemporary setting, James Madison would be Speaker of the House of Representatives and Hamilton would be the *eminence grise* dominating (*pace* Theodore Sorenson or Sherman Adams) the Executive Office of the President. They were, with their colleagues, *political men* —not metaphysicians, disembodied conservatives or Agents of History—and as recent research into the nature of American politics in the 1780s confirms, they were committed (perhaps willy-nilly) to working within the democratic framework, within a universe of public approval. Charles Beard *and* the filiopietists to the contrary notwithstanding, the Philadelphia Convention was not a College of Cardinals or a council of Platonic guardians working within a manipulative, pre-democratic framework; it was a *nationalist* reform caucus which had to operate with great delicacy and skill in a political cosmos full of enemies to achieve the one definitive goal—popular approbation.

Perhaps the time has come, to borrow Walton Hamilton's fine phrase, to raise the Framers from immortality to mortality, to give them credit for their magnificent demonstration of the art of democratic politics. The point must be reemphasized; they *made* history and did it within the limits of consensus. There was nothing inevitable about the future in 1787; the *Zeitgeist*, that fine Hegelian technique of begging casual questions, could only be discerned in retrospect. What they did was to hammer out a pragmatic compromise which would both bolster the "National interest" and be acceptable to the people. What inspiration they got came from their collective experience as professional politicians in a democratic society. As John Dickinson put it to his fellow delegates on

August 13, "Experience must be our guide. Reason may mislead us."

In this context, let us examine the problems they confronted and the solutions they evolved. The Convention has been described picturesquely as a counter-revolutionary junta and the Constitution as a *coup d'etat*, but this has been accomplished by withdrawing the whole history of the movement for constitutional reform from its true context. No doubt the goals of the constitutional elite were "subversive" to the existing political order, but it is overlooked that their subversion could only have succeeded if the people of the United States endorsed it by regularized procedures. Indubitably they were "plotting" to establish a much stronger central government than existed under the Articles, but only in the sense in which one could argue equally well that John F. Kennedy was, from 1956 to 1960, "plotting" to become President. In short, on the fundamental *procedural* level, the Constitutionalists had to work according to the prevailing rules of the game. Whether they liked it or not is a topic for spiritualists—and is irrelevant: one may be quite certain that had Washington agreed to play the De Gaulle (as the Cincinnati once urged), Hamilton would willingly have held his horse, but such fertile speculation in no way alters the actual context in which events took place.

I

When the Constitutionalists went forth to subvert the Confederation, they utilized the mechanisms of political legitimacy. And the roadblocks which confronted them were formidable. At the same time, they were endowed with certain potent political assets. The history of the United States from 1786 to 1790 was largely one of a masterful employment of political expertise by the Constitutionalists as against bumbling, erratic behavior by the opponents of reform. Effectively, the Constitutionalists had to induce the states, by democratic techniques of coercion, to emasculate themselves. To be specific, if New York had refused to join the new Union, the project was doomed; yet before New York was safely in, the reluctant state legislature had *sua sponte* to take the following steps: 1) agree to send delegates to the Philadelphia Convention; 2) provide maintenance for these delegates (these were distinct stages: New Hampshire was early in naming delegates, but did not provide for their maintenance until July); 3) set up the special *ad hoc* convention to decide on ratification; and 4) concede to the decision of the *ad hoc* convention that New York should participate. New York admittedly was a tricky state, with a strong interest in a *status quo* which permitted her to exploit New Jersey and Connecticut, but the same legal hurdles existed in every state. And at the risk of becoming boring, it must be reiterated that the *only* weapon in the Constitutional arsenal was an effective mobilization of public opinion.

The group which undertook this struggle was an interesting amalgam of a few dedicated nationalists with the self-interested spokesmen of various parochial bailiwicks. The Georgians, for example, wanted a strong central authority to provide military protection for their huge, underpopulated state against the Creek Confederacy; Jerseymen and Connecticuters wanted to escape from economic bondage to New York; the Virginians hoped to establish a system which would give that great state its rightful place in the councils of the republic. The dominant figures in the politics of these states therefore cooperated in the call for the Convention. In other states, the thrust towards national reform was taken up by opposition groups who added the "national interest" to their weapons system; in Pennsylvania, for instance, the group fighting to revise the Consti-

tution of 1776 came out four-square behind the Constitutionalists, and in New York, Hamilton and the Schuyler *ambiance* took the same tack against George Clinton. There was, of course, a large element of personality in the affair: there is reason to suspect that Patrick Henry's opposition to the Convention and the Constitution was founded on his conviction that Jefferson was behind both, and a close study of local politics elsewhere would surely reveal that others supported the Constitution for the simple (and politically quite sufficient) reason that the "wrong" people were against it.

To say this is not to suggest that the Constitution rested on a foundation of impure or base motives. It is rather to argue that in politics there are no immaculate conceptions, and that in the drive for a stronger general government, motives of all sorts played a part. Few men in the history of mankind have espoused a view of the "common good" or "public interest" that militated against their private status; even Plato with all his reverence for disembodied reason managed to put philosophers on top of the pile. Thus it is not surprising that a number of diversified private interests joined to push the nationalist public interest; what would have been surprising was the absence of such a pragmatic united front. And the fact remains that, however motivated, these men did demonstrate a willingness to compromise their parochial interests in behalf of an ideal which took shape before their eyes and under their ministrations.

As Stanley Elkins and Eric McKitrick have suggested in a perceptive essay, what distinguished the leaders of the Constitutionalist caucus from their enemies was a "Continental" approach to political, economic and military issues. To the extent that they shared an institutional base of operations, it was the Continental Congress (thirty-nine of the delegates to the Federal Convention had served in Congress), and this was hardly a locale which inspired respect for the state governments. Robert de Jouvenal observed French politics half a century ago and noted that a revolutionary Deputy had more in common with a non-revolutionary Deputy than he had with a revolutionary non-Deputy; similarly one can surmise that membership in the Congress under the Articles of Confederation worked to establish a continental frame of reference, that a Congressman from Pennsylvania and one from South Carolina would share a universe of discourse which provided them with a conceptual common denominator *vis à vis* their respective state legislatures. This was particularly true with respect to external affairs: the average state legislator was probably about as concerned with foreign policy then as he is today, but Congressmen were constantly forced to take the broad view of American prestige, were compelled to listen to the reports of Secretary John Jay and to the dispatches and pleas from their frustrated envoys in Britain, France and Spain. From considerations such as these, a "Continental" ideology developed which seems to have demanded a revision of our domestic institutions primarily on the ground that only by invigorating our general government could we assume our rightful place in the international arena. Indeed, an argument with great force—particularly since Washington was its incarnation—urged that our very survival in the Hobbesian jungle of world politics depended upon a reordering and strengthening of our national sovereignty.

Note that I am not endorsing the "Critical Period" thesis; on the contrary, Merrill Jensen seems to me quite sound in his view that for most Americans, engaged as they were in self-sustaining agriculture, the "Critical Period" was not particularly critical. In fact, the great achievement of the Constitutionalists was their ultimate success in convincing the elected representatives of a majority of the white male population that change was imperative. A small group of political leaders with a Continental vision and essentially a consciousness of the United States' *international* impotence provided the matrix of the movement. To their standard other leaders rallied with their own parallel ambitions. Their great assets were 1) the presence in their caucus of the one authentic American "father figure," George Washington, whose prestige was enormous; 2) the energy and talent of their leadership (in which one must include the towering intellectuals of the time, John Adams and Thomas Jefferson, despite their absence abroad), and their communications "network," which was far superior to anything on the opposition side; 3) the preemptive skill which made "their" issue The Issue and kept the locally oriented opposition permanently on the defensive; and 4) the subjective consideration that these men were spokesmen of a new and compelling credo: *American* nationalism, that ill-defined but nonetheless potent sense of collective purpose that emerged from the American Revolution.

Despite great institutional handicaps, the Constitutionalists managed in the mid-1780s to mount an offensive which gained momentum as years went by. Their greatest problem was lethargy, and paradoxically, the number of barriers in their path may have proved an advantage in the long run. Beginning with the initial battle to get the Constitutional Convention called and delegates appointed, they could never relax, never let up the pressure. In practical terms, this meant that the local "organizations" created by the Constitutionalists were perpetually in movement building up their cadres for the next fight. (The word *organization* has to be used with great caution: a political organization in the United States—as in contemporary England—generally consisted of a magnate and his following, or a coalition of magnates. This did not necessarily mean that it was "undemocratic" or "aristocratic," in the Aristotelian sense of the word: while a few magnates such as the Livingstons could draft their followings, most exercised their leadership without coercion on the basis of popular endorsement. The absence of organized opposition did not imply the impossibility of competition any more than low public participation in elections necessarily indicated an undemocratic suffrage.)

The Constitutionalists got the jump on the "opposition" (a collective noun: oppositions would be more correct) at the outset with the demand for a Convention. Their opponents were caught in an old political trap: they were not being asked to approve any specific program of reform, but only to endorse a meeting to discuss and recommend needed reforms. If they took a hard line at the first stage, they were put in the position of glorifying the *status quo* and of denying the need for *any* changes. Moreover, the Constitutionalists could go to the people with a persuasive argument for "fair play"—"How can you condemn reform before you know precisely what is involved?" Since the state legislatures obviously would have the final say on any proposals that might emerge from the Convention, the Constitutionalists were merely reasonable men asking for a chance. Besides, since they did not make any concrete proposals at that stage, they were in a position to capitalize on every sort of generalized discontent with the Confederation. . . .

II

With delegations safely named, the focus shifted to Philadelphia. While waiting for a quorum to assemble, James Madison got busy and drafted the so-called Randolph or Virginia Plan with the aid of the Virginia delegation. This was a political master-stroke. Its consequence was that once business got underway, the framework of discussion was established on Madison's terms. There was no interminable argument over agenda; instead the delegates took the Virginia Resolutions—"just for purposes of discussion"—as their point of de-

parture. And along with Madison's proposals, many of which were buried in the course of the summer, went his major premise: a new start on a Constitution rather than piece-meal amendment. This was not necessarily revolutionary—a little exegesis could demonstrate that a new Constitution might be formulated as "amendments" to the Articles of Confederation—but Madison's proposal that this "lump sum" amendment go into effect after approval by nine states (the Articles required unanimous state approval for any amendment) was thoroughly subversive.

Standard treatments of the Convention divide the delegates into "nationalists" and "states'-righters" with various improvised shadings ("moderate nationalists," etc.), but these are *a posteriori* categories which obfuscate more than they clarify. What is striking to one who analyzes the Convention as a case-study in democratic politics is the lack of clear-cut ideological divisions in the Convention. Indeed, I submit that the evidence—Madison's *Notes*, the correspondence of the delegates, and debates on ratification—indicates that this was a remarkably homogeneous body on the ideological level. Yates and Lansing, Clinton's two chaperones for Hamilton, left in disgust on July 10. (Is there anything more tedious than sitting through endless disputes on matters one deems fundamentally misconceived? It takes an iron will to spend a hot summer as an ideological *agent provocateur*.) Luther Martin, Maryland's bibulous narcissist, left on September 4 in a huff when he discovered that others did not share his self-esteem; others went home for personal reasons. But the hard core of delegates accepted a grinding regimen throughout the attrition of a Philadelphia summer precisely because they shared the Constitutionalist goal.

Basic differences of opinion emerged, of course, but these were not ideological; they were *structural*. If the so-called "states'-rights" group had not accepted the fundamental purposes of the Convention, they could simply have pulled out and by doing so have aborted the whole enterprise. Instead of bolting, they returned day after day to argue and to compromise. An interesting symbol of this basic homogeneity was the initial agreement on secrecy: these professional politicians did not want to become prisoners of publicity; they wanted to retain that freedom of maneuver which is only possible when men are not forced to take public stands in the preliminary stages of negotiation. There was no legal means of binding the tongues of the delegates: at any stage in the game a delegate with basic principled objections to the emerging project could have taken the stump (as Luther Martin did after his exit) and denounced the convention to the skies. Yet Madison did not even inform Thomas Jefferson in Paris of the course of the deliberations and available correspondence indicates that the delegates generally observed the injunction. Secrecy is certainly uncharacteristic of any assembly marked by strong ideological polarization. This was noted at the time: the *New York Daily Advertiser*, August 14, 1787, commented that the ". . . profound secrecy hitherto observed by the Convention [we consider] a happy omen, as it demonstrates that the spirit of party on any great and essential point cannot have arisen to any height."

Commentators on the Constitution who have read *The Federalist* in lieu of reading the actual debates have credited the Fathers with the invention of a sublime concept called "Federalism." Unfortunately *The Federalist* is probative evidence for only one proposition: that Hamilton and Madison were inspired propagandists with a genius for retrospective symmetry. Federalism, as the theory is generally defined, was an improvisation which was later promoted into a political theory. Experts on "federalism" should take to heart the advice of David Hume, who warned in his *Of the Rise and Progress of the Arts and Sciences*

that ". . . there is no subject in which we must proceed with more caution than in [history], lest we assign causes which never existed and reduce what is merely contingent to stable and universal principles." In any event, the final balance in the Constitution between the states and the nation must have come as a great disappointment to Madison, while Hamilton's unitary views are too well known to need elucidation.

It is indeed astonishing how those who have glibly designated James Madison the "father" of Federalism have overlooked the solid body of fact which indicates that he shared Hamilton's quest for a unitary central government. To be specific, they have avoided examining the clear import of the Madison-Virginia Plan, and have disregarded Madison's dogged inch-by-inch retreat from the bastions of centralization. The Virginia Plan envisioned a unitary national government effectively freed from and dominant over the states. The lower house of the national legislature was to be elected directly by the people of the states with membership proportional to population. The upper house was to be selected by the lower and the two chambers would elect the executive and choose the judges. The national government would be thus cut completely loose from the states.

The structure of the general government was freed from state control in a truly radical fashion, but the scope of the authority of the national sovereign as Madison initially formulated it was breathtaking—it was a formulation worthy of the Sage of Malmesbury himself. The national legislature was to be empowered to disallow the acts of state legislatures, and the central government was vested, in addition to the powers of the nation under the Articles of Confederation, with plenary authority wherever ". . . the separate States are incompetent or in which the harmony of the United States may be interrupted by the exercise of individual legislation." Finally, just to lock the door against state intrusion, the national Congress was to be given the power to use military force on recalcitrant states. This was Madison's "model" of an ideal national government, though it later received little publicity in *The Federalist*.

The interesting thing was the reaction of the Convention to this militant program for a strong autonomous central government. Some delegates were startled, some obviously leery of so comprehensive a project of reform, but nobody set off any fireworks and nobody walked out. Moreover, in the two weeks that followed, the Virginia Plan received substantial endorsement *en principe*; the initial temper of the gathering can be deduced from the approval "without debate or dissent," on May 31, of the Sixth Resolution which granted Congress the authority to disallow state legislation ". . . contravening *in its opinion* the Articles of Union." Indeed, an amendment was included to bar states from contravening national treaties.

The Virginia Plan may therefore be considered, in ideological terms, as the delegates' Utopia, but as the discussions continued and became more specific, many of those present began to have second thoughts. After all, they were not residents of Utopia or guardians in Plato's Republic who could simply impose a philosophical ideal on subordinate strata of the population. They were practical politicians in a democratic society, and no matter what their private dreams might be, they had to take home an acceptable package and defend it—and their own political futures—against predictable attack. On June 14 the breaking point between dream and reality took place. Apparently realizing that under the Virginia Plan, Massachusetts, Virginia and Pennsylvania could virtually dominate the national government—and probably appreciating that to sell this program to "the folks back home" would be impossible—the delegates from the small states dug in their heels and demanded time for a consideration of alternatives. One gets a graphic sense of the inner politics from John Dickinson's reproach to Madison: "You see the consequences of pushing things too far. Some of the members from the small States wish for two branches in the General Legislature and are friends to a good National Government; but we would sooner submit to a foreign power than . . . be deprived of an equality in suffrage in both branches of the Legislature, and thereby be thrown under the domination of the large States."

III

According to the standard script, at this point the "states'-rights" group intervened in force behind the New Jersey Plan, which has been characteristically portrayed as a reversion to the *status quo* under the Articles of Confederation with but minor modifications. A careful examination of the evidence indicates that only in a marginal sense is this an accurate description. It is true that the New Jersey Plan put the states back into the institutional picture, but one could argue that to do so was a recognition of political reality rather than an affirmation of states'-rights. A serious case can be made that the advocates of the New Jersey Plan, far from being ideological addicts of states'-rights, intended to substitute for the Virginia Plan a system which would both retain strong national power and have a chance of adoption in the states. The leading spokesman for the project asserted quite clearly that his views were based more on counsels of expediency than on principle; said Paterson on June 16: "I came here not to speak my own sentiments, but the sentiments of those who sent me. Our object is not such a Governmt. as may be best in itself, but such a one as our Constituents have authorized us to prepare, and as they will approve." This is Madison's version; in Yates' transcription, there is a crucial sentence following the remarks above: "I believe that a little practical virtue is to be preferred to the finest theoretical principles, which cannot be carried into effect." In his preliminary speech on June 9, Paterson had stated ". . . to the public mind we must accommodate ourselves," and in his notes for this and his later effort as well, the emphasis is the same. The *structure* of government under the Articles should be retained:

2. Because it accords with the Sentiments of the People
   [Proof:]
   1. Coms. [Commissions from state legislatures defining the jurisdiction of the delegates]
   2. News-papers—Political Barometer. Jersey never would have sent Delegates under the first [Virginia] Plan—
   Not here to sport Opinions of my own. Wt. [What] can be done. A little practicable Virtue preferable to Theory.

This was a defense of political acumen, not of states'-rights. In fact, Paterson's notes of his speech can easily be construed as an argument for attaining the substantive objectives of the Virginia Plan by a sound political route, *i.e.*, pouring the new wine in the old bottles. With a shrewd eye, Paterson queried:

Will the Operation and Force of the [central] Govt. depend upon the mode of Representn.—No —it will depend upon the Quantum of Power lodged in the leg. ex. and judy. Departments— Give [the existing] Congress the same Powers that you intend to give the two Branches, [under the Virginia Plan] and I apprehend they will act with as much Propriety and more Energy . . .

In other words, the advocates of the New Jersey Plan concentrated their fire on what they held to be the *political liabilities* of the Virginia Plan—which were matters of institutional structure—rather than on the proposed scope of national authority. Indeed, the Supremacy Clause of the Constitution first saw the light of day in Paterson's Sixth Resolution;

the New Jersey Plan contemplated the use of military force to secure compliance with national law; and finally Paterson made clear his view that under either the Virginia or the New Jersey systems, the general government would ". . . act on individuals and not on states." From the states'-rights viewpoint, this was heresy: the fundament of that doctrine was the proposition that any central government had as its constituents the states, not the people, and could only reach the people through the agency of the state government.

Paterson then reopened the agenda of the Convention, but he did so within a distinctly nationalist framework. Paterson's position was one of favoring a strong central government in principle, but opposing one which in fact *put the big states in the saddle*. (The Virginia Plan, for all its abstract merits, did very well by Virginia.) As evidence for this speculation, there is a curious and intriguing proposal among Paterson's preliminary drafts of the New Jersey Plan:

Whereas it is necessary in Order to form the People of the U.S. of America in to a Nation, that the States should be consolidated, by which means all the Citizens thereof will become equally entitled to and will equally participate in the same Privileges and Rights . . . it is therefore resolved, that all the Lands contained within the Limits of each state individually, and of the U.S. generally be considered as constituting one Body or Mass, and be divided into thirteen or more integral parts.
    Resolved, That such Divisions or integral Parts shall be styled Districts.

This makes it sound as though Paterson was prepared to accept a strong unified central government along the lines of the Virginia Plan if the existing states were eliminated. He may have gotten the idea from his New Jersey colleague Judge David Brearley, who on June 9 had commented that the only remedy to the dilemma over representation was ". . . that a map of the U.S. be spread out, that all the existing boundaries be erased, and that a new partition of the whole be made into 13 equal parts." According to Yates, Brearley added at this point, ". . . then a government on the present [Virginia Plan] system will be just."

This proposition was never pushed—it was patently unrealistic—but one can appreciate its purpose: it would have separated the men from the boys in the large-state delegations. How attached would the Virginians have been to their reform principles if Virginia were to disappear as a component geographical unit (the largest) for representational purposes? Up to this point, the Virginians had been in the happy position of supporting high ideals with that inner confidence born of knowledge that the "public interest" they endorsed would nourish their private interest. Worse, they had shown little willingness to compromise. Now the delegates from the small states announced that they were unprepared to be offered up as sacrificial victims to a "national interest" which reflected Virginia's parochial ambition. Caustic Charles Pinckney was not far off when he remarked sardonically that ". . . the whole [conflict] comes to this": "Give N. Jersey an equal vote, and she will dismiss her scruples, and concur in the Natil. system." What he rather unfairly did not add was that the Jersey delegates were not free agents who could adhere to their private convictions; they had to take back, sponsor and risk their reputations on the reforms approved by the Convention—and in New Jersey, not in Virginia.

Paterson spoke on Saturday, and one can surmise that over the weekend there was a good deal of consultation, argument, and caucusing among the delegates. One member at least prepared a full length address: on Monday Alexander Hamilton, previously mute, rose and delivered a six-hour oration. It was a remarkably apolitical speech: the gist of his position was that *both* the Virginia and New Jersey Plans were inadequately centralist, and he detailed a reform program which was reminiscent of the Protectorate under the Crom-

wellian *Instrument of Government* of 1653. It has been suggested that Hamilton did this in the best political tradition to emphasize the moderate character of the Virginia Plan, to give the cautious delegates something *really* to worry about; but this interpretation seems somehow too clever. Particularly since the sentiments Hamilton expressed happened to be completely consistent with those he privately—and sometimes publicly—expressed throughout his life. He wanted, to take a striking phrase from a letter to George Washington, a "strong well mounted government"; in essence, the Hamilton Plan contemplated an elected life monarch, virtually free of public control, on the Hobbesian ground that only in this fashion could strength and stability be achieved. The other alternatives, he argued, would put policy-making at the mercy of the passions of the mob; only if the sovereign was beyond the reach of selfish influence would it be possible to have government in the interests of the whole community.

From all accounts, this was a masterful and compelling speech, but (aside from furnishing John Lansing and Luther Martin with ammunition for later use against the Constitution) it made little impact. Hamilton was simply transmitting on a different wave-length from the rest of the delegates; the latter adjourned after his great effort, admired his rhetoric, and then returned to business. It was rather as if they had taken a day off to attend the opera. Hamilton, never a particularly patient man or much of a negotiator, stayed for another ten days and then left, in considerable disgust, for New York. Although he came back to Philadelphia sporadically and attended the last two weeks of the Convention, Hamilton played no part in the laborious task of hammering out the Constitution. His day came later when he led the New York Constitutionalists into the savage imbroglio over ratification—an arena in which his unmatched talent for dirty political infighting may well have won the day. . . .

IV

On Tuesday morning, June 19, the vacation was over. James Madison led off with a long, carefully reasoned speech analyzing the New Jersey Plan which, while intellectually vigorous in its criticisms, was quite conciliatory in mood. "The great difficulty," he observed, "lies in the affair of Representation; and if this could be adjusted, all others would be surmountable." (As events were to demonstrate, this diagnosis was correct.) When he finished, a vote was taken on whether to continue with the Virginia Plan as the nucleus for a new constitution: seven states voted "Yes"; New York, New Jersey, and Delaware voted "No"; and Maryland, whose position often depended on which delegates happened to be on the floor, divided. Paterson, it seems, lost decisively; yet in a fundamental sense he and his allies had achieved their purpose: from that day onward, it could never be forgotten that the state governments loomed ominously in the background and that no verbal incantations could exorcise their power. Moreover, nobody bolted the convention: Paterson and his colleagues took their defeat in stride and set to work to modify the Virginia Plan, particularly with respect to its provisions on representation in the national legislature. Indeed, they won an immediate rhetorical bonus; when Oliver Ellsworth of Connecticut rose to move that the word "national" be expunged from the Third Virginia Resolution ("Resolved that a *national* Government ought to be established consisting of a *supreme* Legislative, Executive and Judiciary"), Randolph agreed and the motion passed unanimously. The process of compromise had begun.

For the next two weeks, the delegates circled around the problem of legislative representation. The Connecticut delegation appears to have evolved a possible compromise quite early in the debates, but the Virginians and particularly Madison (unaware that he would later be acclaimed as the prophet of "federalism") fought obdurately against providing for equal representation of states in the second chamber. . . .

It would be tedious to continue a blow-by-blow analysis of the work of the delegates; the critical fight was over representation of the states and once the Connecticut Compromise was adopted on July 17, the Convention was over the hump. Madison, James Wilson, and Gouverneur Morris of New York (who was there representing Pennsylvania!) fought the compromise all the way in a last-ditch effort to get a unitary state with parliamentary supremacy. But their allies deserted them and they demonstrated after their defeat the essentially opportunist character of their objections—using "opportunist" here in a non-pejorative sense, to indicate a willingness to swallow their objections and get on with the business. Moreover, once the compromise had carried (by five states to four with one state divided), its advocates threw themselves vigorously into the job of strengthening the general government's substantive powers—as might have been predicted, indeed, from Paterson's early statements. It nourishes an increased respect for Madison's devotion to the art of politics, to realize that this dogged fighter could sit down six months later and prepare essays for *The Federalist* in contradiction to his basic convictions about the true course the Convention should have taken.

V

Two tricky issues will serve to illustrate the later process of accommodation. The first was the institutional position of the Executive. Madison argued for an executive chosen by the National Legislature and on May 29 this had been adopted with a provision that after his seven-year term was concluded, the chief magistrate should not be eligible for reelection. In late July this was reopened and for a week the matter was argued from several different points of view. A good deal of desultory speech-making ensued, but the gist of the problem was the opposition from two sources to election by the legislature. One group felt that the states should have a hand in the process; another small but influential circle urged direct election by the people. There were a number of proposals: election by the people, election by state governors, by electors chosen by state legislatures, by the National Legislature (James Wilson, perhaps ironically, proposed at one point that an Electoral College be chosen by lot from the National Legislature!), and there was some resemblance to three-dimensional chess in the dispute because of the presence of two other variables, length of tenure and reeligibility. Finally, after opening, re-opening, and re-opening the debate, the thorny problem was consigned to a committee for resolution.

The Brearley Committee on Postponed Matters was a superb aggregation of talent and its compromise on the Executive was a masterpiece of political improvisation. (The Electoral College, its creation, however, had little in its favor as an *institution*—as the delegates well appreciated.) The point of departure for all discussion about the presidency in the Convention was that in immediate terms, the problem was non-existent; in other words, everybody present knew that under any system devised, George Washington would be President. Thus they were dealing in the future tense and to a body of working politicians the merits of the Brearley proposal were obvious: everybody got a piece of cake. (Or to put it more academically, each viewpoint could leave the Convention and argue to its constituents that it had *really* won the day.) First, the state legislatures had the right to determine the mode of selection of the electors; second, the small states received a bonus in the Electoral College in the form of a guaranteed minimum of three votes while the big states got acceptance of the

principle of proportional power; third, if the state legislatures agreed (as six did in the first presidential election), the people could be involved directly in the choice of electors; and finally, if no candidate received a majority in the College, the right of decision passed to the National Legislature with each state exercising equal strength. (In the Brearley recommendation, the election went to the Senate, but a motion from the floor substituted the House; this was accepted on the ground that the Senate already had enough authority over the executive in its treaty and appointment powers.)

This compromise was almost too good to be true, and the Framers snapped it up with little debate or controversy. No one seemed to think well of the College as an *institution*; indeed, what evidence there is suggests that there was an assumption that once Washington had finished his tenure as President, the electors would cease to produce majorities and the chief executive would usually be chosen in the House. George Mason observed casually that the selection would be made in the House nineteen times in twenty and no one seriously disputed this point. The vital aspect of the Electoral College was that it got the Convention over the hurdle and protected everybody's interests. The future was left to cope with the problem of what to do with this Rube Goldberg mechanism.

In short, the Framers did not in their wisdom endow the United States with a College of Cardinals—the Electoral College was neither an exercise in applied Platonism nor an experiment in indirect government based on elitist distrust of the masses. It was merely a jerry-rigged improvisation which has subsequently been endowed with a high theoretical content. When an elector from Oklahoma in 1960 refused to cast his vote for Nixon (naming Byrd and Goldwater instead) on the ground that the Founding Fathers intended him to exercise his great independent wisdom, he was indulging in historical fantasy. If one were to indulge in counter-fantasy, he would be tempted to suggest that the Fathers would be startled to find the College still in operation—and perhaps even dismayed at their descendants' lack of judgment or inventiveness.

The second issue on which some substantial practical bargaining took place was slavery. The morality of slavery was, by design, not at issue; but in its other concrete aspects, slavery colored the arguments over taxation, commerce, and representation. The "Three-Fifths Compromise," that three-fifths of the slaves would be counted both for representation and for purposes of direct taxation (which was drawn from the past—it was a formula of Madison's utilized by Congress in 1783 to establish the basis of state contributions to the Confederation treasury) had allayed some Northern fears about Southern over-representation (no one then foresaw the trivial role that direct taxation would play in later Federal financial policy), but doubts still remained. The Southerners, on the other hand, were afraid that Congressional control over commerce would lead to the exclusion of slaves or to their excessive taxation as imports. Moreover, the Southerners were disturbed over "navigation acts," *i.e.*, tariffs, or special legislation providing, for example, that exports be carried only in American ships; as a section depending upon exports, they wanted protection from the potential voracity of their commercial brethren of the Eastern states. To achieve this end, Mason and others urged that the Constitution include a proviso that navigation and commercial laws should require a two-thirds vote in Congress.

These problems came to a head in late August and, as usual, were handed to a committee in the hope that, in Gouverneur Morris' words, ". . . these things may form a bargain among the Northern and Southern states." The Committee reported its measures of reconciliation on August 25, and on August 29 the package was wrapped up and delivered. What

occurred can best be described in George Mason's dour version (he anticipated Calhoun in his conviction that permitting navigation acts to pass by majority vote would put the South in economic bondage to the North—it was mainly on this ground that he refused to sign the Constitution):

The Constitution as agreed to till a fortnight before the Convention rose was such a one as he would have set his hand and heart to. . . . [Until that time] The 3 New England States were constantly with us in all questions . . . so that it was these three States with the 5 Southern ones against Pennsylvania, Jersey and Delaware. With respect to the importation of slaves, [decision-making] was left to Congress. This disturbed the two Southernmost States who knew that Congress would immediately suppress the importation of slaves. Those two States therefore struck up a bargain with the three New England States. If they would join to admit slaves for some years, the two Southern-most States would join in changing the clause which required the ⅔ of the Legislature in any vote [on navigation acts]. It was done.

On the floor of the Convention there was a virtual love-feast on this happy occasion. Charles Pinckney of South Carolina attempted to overturn the committee's decision, when the compromise was reported to the Convention, by insisting that the South needed protection from the imperialism of the Northern states. But his Southern colleagues were not prepared to rock the boat and General C. C. Pinckney arose to spread oil on the suddenly ruffled waters; he admitted that:

It was in the true interest of the S[outhern] States to have no regulation of commerce; but considering the loss brought on the commerce in the Eastern States by the Revolution, their liberal conduct towards the views of South Carolina [on the regulation of the slave trade] and the interests the weak Southn. States had in being united with the strong Eastern states, he thought it proper that no fetters should be imposed on the power of making commercial regulations; *and that his constituents, though prejudiced against the Eastern States, would be reconciled to this liberality.* He had himself prejudices agst the Eastern States before he came here, but would acknowledge that he had found them as liberal and candid as any men whatever. (Italics added)

Pierce Butler took the same tack, essentially arguing that he was not too happy about the possible consequences, but that a deal was a deal. Many Southern leaders were later—in the wake of the "Tariff of Abominations"—to rue this day of reconciliation; Calhoun's *Disquisition on Government* was little more than an extension of the argument in the Convention against permitting a congressional majority to enact navigation acts.

VI

Drawing on their vast collective political experience, utilizing every weapon in the politician's arsenal, looking constantly over their shoulders at their constituents, the delegates put together a Constitution. It was a makeshift affair; some sticky issues (for example, the qualification of voters) they ducked entirely; others they mastered with that ancient instrument of political sagacity, studied ambiguity (for example, citizenship), and some they just overlooked. In this last category, I suspect, fell the matter of the power of the federal courts to determine the constitutionality of acts of Congress. When the judicial article was formulated (Article III of the Constitution), deliberations were still in the stage where the legislature was endowed with broad power under the Randolph formulation, authority which by its own terms was scarcely amenable to judicial review. In essence, courts could hardly determine when ". . . the separate States are incompetent or . . . the harmony of the United States may be interrupted"; the National Legislature, as critics pointed out, was free to define its own jurisdiction. Later the definition of legislative authority was changed into the form

we know, a series of stipulated powers, *but the delegates never seriously reexamined the jurisdiction of the judiciary under this new limited formulation.* All arguments on the intention of the Framers in this matter are thus deductive and *a posteriori*, though some obviously make more sense than others.

The Framers were busy and distinguished men, anxious to get back to their families, their positions, and their constituents, not members of the French Academy devoting a lifetime to a dictionary. They were trying to do an important job, and do it in such a fashion that their handiwork would be acceptable to very diverse constituencies. No one was rhapsodic about the final document, but it was a beginning, a move in the right direction, and one they had reason to believe the people would endorse. In addition, since they had modified the impossible amendment provisions of the Articles (the requirement of unanimity which could always be frustrated by "Rogues Island") to one demanding approval by only three-quarters of the states, they seemed confident that gaps in the fabric which experience would reveal could be rewoven without undue difficulty.

So with a neat phrase introduced by Benjamin Franklin (but devised by Gouverneur Morris) which made their decision sound unanimous, and an inspired benediction by the Old Doctor urging doubters to doubt their own infallibility, the Constitution was accepted and signed. Curiously, Edmund Randolph, who had played so vital a role throughout, refused to sign, as did his fellow Virginian George Mason and Elbridge Gerry of Massachusetts. Randolph's behavior was eccentric, to say the least—his excuses for refusing his signature have a factitious ring even at this late date; the best explanation seems to be that he was afraid that the Constitution would prove to be a liability in Virginia politics, where Patrick Henry was burning up the countryside with impassioned denunciations. Presumably, Randolph wanted to check the temper of the populace before he risked his reputation, and perhaps his job, in a fight with both Henry and Richard Henry Lee. Events lend some justification to this speculation: after much temporizing and use of the conditional subjunctive tense, Randolph endorsed ratification in Virginia and ended up getting the best of both worlds.

Madison, despite his reservations about the Constitution, was the campaign manager in ratification. His first task was to get the Congress in New York to light its own funeral pyre by approving the "amendments" to the Articles and sending them on to the state legislatures. Above all, momentum had to be maintained. The anti-Constitutionalists, now thoroughly alarmed and no novices in politics, realized that their best tactic was attrition rather than direct opposition. Thus they settled on a position expressing qualified approval but calling for a second Convention to remedy various defects (the one with the most demagogic appeal was the lack of a Bill of Rights). Madison knew that to accede to this demand would be equivalent to losing the battle, nor would he agree to conditional approval (despite wavering even by Hamilton). This was an all-or-nothing proposition: national salvation or national impotence with no intermediate positions possible. Unable to get congressional approval, he settled for second best: a unanimous resolution of Congress transmitting the Constitution to the states for whatever action they saw fit to take. The opponents then moved from New York and the Congress, where they had attempted to attach amendments and conditions, to the states for the final battle.

At first the campaign for ratification went beautifully: within eight months after the delegates set their names to the document, eight states had ratified. Only in Massachusetts had the result been close (187-168). Theoretically, a ratification by one more state convention would set the new government in motion, but

in fact until Virginia and New York acceded to the new Union, the latter was a fiction. New Hampshire was the next to ratify; Rhode Island was involved in its characteristic political convulsions (the Legislature there sent the Constitution out to the towns for decision by popular vote and it got lost among a series of local issues); North Carolina's convention did not meet until July and then postponed a final decision. This is hardly the place for an extensive analysis of the conventions of New York and Virginia. Suffice it to say that the Constitutionalists clearly outmaneuvered their opponents, forced them into impossible political positions, and won both states narrowly. The Virginia Convention could serve as a classic study in effective floor management. Patrick Henry had to be contained, and a reading of the debates discloses a standard two-stage technique. Henry would give a four- or five-hour speech denouncing some section of the Constitution on every conceivable ground (the federal district, he averred at one point, would become a haven for convicts escaping from state authority!); when Henry subsided, "Mr. Lee of Westmoreland" would rise and literally pole-axe him with sardonic invective (when Henry complained about the militia power, "Lighthorse Harry" really punched below the belt; observing that while the former Governor had been sitting in Richmond during the Revolution, *he* had been out in the trenches with the troops and thus felt better qualified to discuss military affairs). Then the gentlemanly Constitutionalists (Madison, Pendleton and Marshall) would pick up the matters at issue and examine them in the light of reason.

Indeed, modern Americans who tend to think of James Madison as a rather dessicated character should spend some time with this transcript. Probably Madison put on his most spectacular demonstration of nimble rhetoric in what might be called "The Battle of the Absent Authorities." Patrick Henry in the course of one of his harangues alleged that

Jefferson was known to be opposed to Virginia's approving the Constitution. This was clever: Henry hated Jefferson, but was prepared to use any weapon that came to hand. Madison's riposte was superb: First, he said that with all due respect to the great reputation of Jefferson, he was not in the country and therefore could not formulate an adequate judgment; second, no one should utilize the reputation of an outsider—the Virginia Convention was there to think for itself; third, if there were to be recourse to outsiders, the opinions of George Washington should certainly be taken into consideration; and finally, he knew from privileged personal communications from Jefferson that in fact the latter *strongly favored* the Constitution. To devise an assault route into this rhetorical fortress was literally impossible.

VII

The fight was over; all that remained now was to establish the new frame of government in the spirit of its framers. And who were better qualified for this task than the Framers themselves? Thus victory for the Constitution meant simultaneous victory for the Constitutionalists; the anti-Constitutionalists either capitulated or vanished into limbo—soon Patrick Henry would be offered a seat on the Supreme Court and Luther Martin would be known as the Federalist "bull-dog." And irony of ironies. Alexander Hamilton and James Madison would shortly accumulate a reputation as the formulators of what is often alleged to be our political theory, the concept of "federalism." Also, on the other side of the ledger, the arguments would soon appear over what the Framers "really meant"; while these disputes have assumed the proportions of a big scholarly business in the last century, they began almost before the ink on the Constitution was dry. One of the best early ones featured Hamilton

versus Madison on the scope of presidential power, and other Framers characteristically assumed positions in this and other disputes on the basis of their political convictions.

Probably our greatest difficulty is that we know so much more about what the Framers *should have meant* than they themselves did. We are intimately acquainted with the problems that their Constitution should have been designed to master; in short, we have read the mystery story backwards. If we are to get the right "feel" for their time and their circumstances, we must in Maitland's phrase, ". . . think ourselves back into a twilight." Obviously, no one can pretend completely to escape from the solipsistic web of his own environment, but if the effort is made, it is possible to appreciate the past roughly on its own terms. The first step in this process is to abandon the academic premise that because we can ask a question, there must be an answer.

Thus we can ask what the Framers meant when they gave Congress the power to regulate interstate and foreign commerce, and we emerge, reluctantly perhaps, with the reply that (Professor Crosskey to the contrary notwithstanding) they may not have known what they meant, that there may not have been any semantic consensus. The Convention was not a seminar in analytic philosophy or linguistic analysis. Commerce was *commerce*—and if different interpretations of the word arose, later generations could worry about the problem of definition. The delegates were in a hurry to get a new government established; when definitional arguments arose, they characteristically took refuge in ambiguity. If different men voted for the same propositon for varying reasons, that was politics (and still is); if later generations were unsettled by this lack of precision that would be their problem.

There was a good deal of definitional pluralism with respect to the problems the delegates did discuss, but when we move to the question of extrapolated intentions, we enter the realm of spiritualism. When men in our time, for instance, launch into elaborate talmudic exegesis to demonstrate that federal aid to parochial schools is (or is not) in accord with the intentions of the men who established the Republic and endorsed the Bill of Rights, they are engaging in historical Extra-Sensory Perception. . . .

The Constitution, then, was not an apotheosis of "constitutionalism," a triumph of architectonic genius; it was a patch-work sewn together under the pressure of both time and events by a group of extremely talented democratic politicians. They refused to attempt the establishment of a strong, centralized sovereignty on the principle of legislative supremacy for the excellent reason that the people would not accept it. They risked their political fortunes by opposing the established doctrines of state sovereignty because they were convinced that the existing system was leading to national impotence and probably foreign domination. For two years, they worked to get a convention established. For over three months, in what must have seemed to the faithful participants an endless process of give-and-take, they reasoned, cajoled, threatened, and bargained amongst themselves. The result was a Constitution which the people, in fact, by democratic processes, did accept, and a new and far better national government was established.

Beginning with the inspired propaganda of Hamilton, Madison and Jay, the ideological build-up got under way. *The Federalist* had little impact on the ratification of the Constitution, except perhaps in New York, but this volume had enormous influence on the image of the Constitution in the minds of future generations, particularly on historians and political scientists who have an innate fondness for theoretical symmetry. Yet, while the shades of Locke and Montesquieu *may* have been hovering in the background, and the delegates *may* have been unconscious instruments of a transcendent *telos*, the careful observer of the day-to-day work of the Convention finds no overarching principles. The "separation of powers" to him seems to be a by-product of suspicion, and "federalism" he views as a *pis aller*, as the farthest point the delegates felt they could go in the destruction of state power without themselves inviting repudiation.

To conclude, the Constitution was neither a victory for abstract theory nor a great practical success. Well over half a million men had to die on the battlefields of the Civil War before certain constitutional principles could be defined—a baleful consideration which is somehow overlooked in our customary tributes to the farsighted genius of the Framers and to the supposed American talent for "constitutionalism." The Constitution was, however, a vivid demonstration of effective democratic political action, and of the forging of a national elite which literally persuaded its countrymen to hoist themselves by their own boot straps. American pro-consuls would be wise not to translate the Constitution into Japanese, or Swahili, or treat it as a work of semi-Divine origin; but when students of comparative politics examine the process of nation-building in countries newly freed from colonial rule, they may find the American experience instructive as a classic example of the potentialities of a democratic elite.

4

The Framers' Intentions

David G. Smith

What were the primary motives of the constitutional framers? Did the Constitution serve to protect men of property rather than the rest of society? Were the Founding Fathers fundamentally opposed to democratic principles? David Smith offers a useful summary of the principal accusations and defense of the framers' intentions. He reviews the major charges in Charles A. Beard's (and others) indictment: that the convention was an act of usurpation, that the framers sought to protect private property, and that the Constitution was antidemocratic in design and substance. While admitting the partial validity of these charges, Smith responds by defending the framers in the context of their efforts to develop effective political institutions to overcome the fragmentation of a "disharmonious" society. In Smith's view, the Constitution was a political rather than an economic document. This essay is interesting in raising questions about: (1) the responsiveness of political elites to serious societal problems (discussed earlier in Article 1); (2) the factionalism which may disrupt a nation united only by weak bonds, a theme discussed in the classic Federalist, No. 10 by James Madison; and (3) the construction of our system of separation of powers and checks and balances in the national government to limit the tendencies toward disharmony and disunity, also discussed by James Madison in Federalist, No. 51 (See Article 5).

This chapter has two objects. One is an inquiry into the intentions of the Founding Fathers, necessary because of the enormous controversy over their original purpose. But the same inquiry also establishes the historical and theoretical perspectives needed to understand the original constitution itself.

THE CONTROVERSY OVER MOTIVES

Early controversies over the Constitution, especially those engaged in by antebellum political leaders, appear to have been over what the Constitution ought to say or mean. When Madison and Jefferson drafted the Virginia

Reprinted by permission of the publisher from David G. Smith, *The Convention and The Constitution: The Political Ideas of the Founding Fathers* (New York: St. Martin's Press, 1965). Copyright © 1965 St. Martin's Press, Inc.

and Kentucky Resolutions (1799) to protest broad interpretations of national power, or when John C. Calhoun wrote his *Exposition of 1828* to defend state sovereignty, they looked to basic constitutional theory rather than to an alleged intention or motivation of the Founding Fathers. The quarrel over motives first arose after the Civil War. The generation that followed the Compromise of 1877[1] faced many new social and economic problems attendant upon rapid industrial development and population movements, and it searched anew for the fundamentals of American politics. Out of this era came a spirit of "constitution worship" and an interpretation of the Federal Convention

[1] The Compromise followed the disputed Hayes-Tilden presidential election and resulted in an end to Reconstruction policies and a number of agreements between economic interests of the North and the South.

termed by one historian the "chaos and patriots to the rescue" theme.[2]

John Fiske, a historian widely influential at the turn of the century, was one of the leading worshippers. The title of Fiske's book—*The Critical Period in American History, 1783-1789*—suggests his point of view.[3] For him, the period under the Articles of Confederation was a time of economic chaos, depression, and group and local struggles that were rapidly moving the thirteen states toward anarchy and dissolution, if not civil war. The convention delegates were patriots distressed at the fate of their country, seeking to ward off either anarchy or dictatorship. The Constitution they made necessarily curbed liberty and confined democracy, but they established a sturdy republican frame of government—conservative though it may have been—that proved itself immune to the worst diseases of popular government. Is not the lesson clear? At least by implication? The Constitution is the salvation of the country. Learn its principles and abide by them, no matter how attractive mass democracy or sharing-the-wealth may for the moment seem to be.

Constitution-worship profaned early in the twentieth century by a generation led by the historians Charles Beard and J. Allen Smith.[4]

According to Beard, who wrote the most controversial interpretation of the Convention, the Constitution was not the fruition of Anglo-Saxon liberty; still less was it an impartial judicial instrument protecting the good of all. Behind "justice" and "the Constitution," Beard saw groups of men and economic interest, even a hint of conspiracy. The Constitution, he said, was not the creation of disinterested patriots, nor did it represent the will of the whole people. The men who drafted the Constitution had personal pecuniary interests. The adoption of the Constitution also was originated and accomplished principally by "four groups of personalty interests which had been adversely affected under the Articles of Confederation: money, public securities, manufactures, trading and shipping."[5] J. Allen Smith had earlier drawn a conclusion that Beard might well have endorsed: "In the United States at the present time we are trying to make an undemocratic Constitution the vehicle of democratic rule."[6]

Whether right or wrong, Beard's interpretation of the Convention has been enormously influential. It shocked some and comforted others of the Wilsonian era, and was almost received doctrine during the New Deal.[7] Historians and political scientists have continued to this day to reinterpret the Convention and to quarrel with Beard and his spiritual kinsmen.[8]

[2] Merrill Jensen, *The New Nation—A History of the United States During the Confederation—1781–1789* (New York: Alfred A. Knopf, 1950), p. xiii.

[3] New York: Houghton Mifflin Co., 1888.

[4] Of course other influential works on the Convention appeared during this period. Some were important in shaping later views: for example, Max Farrand, *The Framing of the Constitution of the United States* (New Haven: Yale University Press, 1913); and Andrew C. McLaughlin, *The Confederation and the Constitution* (New York and London: Harper and Brothers Publishers, 1905). Farrand described the Constitution as a "bundle of compromises" achieved by practical men with practical and immediate aims. McLaughlin argued that the Constitution was the natural culmination of colonial experience. The views of these men were influential, but did not disturb anyone. The theses of Beard and Smith, however, have upset a good many people since the early 1900's. They also produced one of the "great issues" of American historiography that

has continued to this day. For this reason, the ensuing discussion deals principally with their arguments.

[5] Charles A. Beard, *An Economic Interpretation of the Constitution* (New York: Macmillan, 1913), "Conclusion," especially pp. 324–325.

[6] J. Allen Smith, *The Spirit of American Government* (New York: Macmillan, 1907), p. 31.

[7] One author states that 37 of 42 new college texts adopted Beard's interpretation in 1937. Robert E. Brown, *Charles Beard and the American Constitution* (Princeton: Princeton University Press, 1956), p. 9.

[8] See, for example: Lee Benson, *Turner and Beard—American Historical Writing Reconsidered* (Glencoe, Ill.: The Free Press, 1960); Forrest McDonald, *We the People—The Economic Origins of the Constitution*

The alleged economic motivations or antidemocratic intent of the Founding Fathers, even if the allegations are true, do not rob the Constitution of legitimacy nor destroy the importance of the political theory underlying it. For whatever the intent, the result stands independently. The dispute over original intentions has, however, directed attention away from the larger principles of the Constitution to an inconclusive debate over the interests, motives, and group loyalties of the Founding Fathers. For this reason, alternate interpretations of the delegates' motives, or different ways of looking at the same facts are important to an understanding of the Constitution itself.

Beard argued that the motivation of the Founding Fathers and of the supporters of the Constitution was principally economic. Yet the men who made the Constitution, and many who were active—either for or against ratification—had also serious political motivations. Without denying that economics may have been important, the political motives of the delegates must be included to establish the context within which they acted. In some instances the latter motives were, properly, separable from the economic, and in some instances they were directed toward larger and more inclusive objectives than the economic ones.

Smith, Parrington, and others have stressed the antidemocratic intent of the delegates and compared the Convention and the adoption to a counter-revolution. But they paid little attention to the society for which the Constitution was made. In fact, the political objectives of the delegates were sensible ones, given the society in which they lived.[9]

According to the interpretation suggested in this chapter, the delegates were attempting *in the main* to create a political system and not to protect property. They were also attempting *principally* not to defeat democracy but to devise strong constitutional and political supports for a federal republic. They had a large and generous vision of the future. They also understood the limitations of their constitutional and political resources. They sought to connect their ambitious vision of the future with their present political world.

THE FOUNDING FATHERS: ACCUSED AND DEFENDED

The indictment by Beard, Smith, and Parrington includes three counts. One is that making and adopting the Constitution was an act of usurpation. Another is that the Constitution was designed largely to protect property interests, especially personalty or property other than land. The last count is that the Constitution was antidemocratic both in design and in substance. We shall deal with each of these charges, but first, an elaboration of the indictment as a whole.

A bill of particulars can be made, with no great difficulty, that the delegates acted without authorization, that they usurped power, and that they acted on their own account. Following the Annapolis Convention of 1786,[10] Congress had passed a cautiously worded resolution calling upon the states to send delegates for the "sole and express purpose of revising the Articles . . . ," and providing that any amendments required the approval of Congress and of all the state legislatures.[11]

(Chicago: Chicago University Press, 1958); John P. Roche, "The Founding Fathers: A Reform Caucus in Action," *The American Political Science Review*, Vol. 55 (1961), pp. 799–816.

[9] The argument to be made with respect to this point depends upon Chapter II.

[10] Convened to consider commerce along the Potomac. The resolution appears to have been the work primarily of Hamilton, and was the most important act of the Convention.

[11] A proviso that would seem reasonable given the authority under which the Convention was to meet and the explicit provisions of the Articles.

Under these instructions, delegates from twelve states convened in Philadelphia. No one would dispute that they went beyond their mandate; and indeed, most of them apparently intended to do so even before they met as an assembled convention. In Convention, with organization and procedure settled and a secrecy rule adopted, they passed the first of the Randolph Resolutions: "That a National Government ought to be established consisting of a supreme Legislature, Executive, and Judiciary."[12] With no more ado, the Articles were discarded, so far at least as the activities of the Convention were concerned. The Convention also violated the provisions of the Articles by stipulating that the Constitution be ratified by approval of conventions in nine of the states. We can argue, as did the delegates, that a "higher trust" bade them strike boldly and carry the Constitution to the "people."[13] Yet there was a taint of usurpation in their action.

The delegates constituted a small, cohesive elite, perhaps one of the most powerful and tightly knit groups of men that have acted upon the American national scene. They were financially and professionally successful: merchants, planters, bankers and lawyers. They were knit together by ties of family and acquaintance, and by years of service in national activities—in the army, the Congress, and the diplomacy and administration of the peacetime years. They were also men of great political influence: former and present governors, leaders in national administration, and representatives in Congress. The company has often been cited for its talent and intellectual ornaments. It is equally noteworthy for the collective influence it could and did wield. If we say that the Convention usurped power, we ought to add that from the nature of the company and

their political relations they were in a good position to make a constitution inimical to the real interests or desires of the people.

The delegates did not subscribe to that complex of values today associated with liberal democracy. They openly declared their hostility to democracy as a method of government, to popular state legislatures, and to the democratic provisions of the Articles. They were concerned particularly to withdraw the power of decison from the "grass roots" and to strengthen the less directly representative branches of government. They attempted as well to *fragment* the public will by such devices as separation of powers, the independence of the judiciary, diverse representation and "filtration,"[14] and separating the states into politically "isolated compartments." By the interpretation of many of their own radical contemporaries, they were undoing the Revolution and preparing the ground for a future aristocracy.[15]

Finally, a principal object of the Constitution was, simply and plainly, to restrain the states in order to protect property. The Constitution, Beard pointed out, can be largely described as a creation of central authority to protect and advance property interests through the four great powers of taxation, war, commercial control, and the disposition of western lands, and as an instrument designed to withhold from the states a power to menace property: the ban on paper money and the protection of contract.[16] Furthermore, personalty was given a distinct preference, despite the overwhelmingly rural and agrarian character of the country.

The Founding Fathers were not, by the

---

[12] Warren, *op. cit.*, p. 146; *Records*, Vol. I, p. 30. Notice the use of the word "National." It does not appear in the final draft.

[13] Warren, *op. cit.*, p. 346; *Records*, Vol. I, pp. 122, 123.

[14] "Refinement" of political opinion by indirect election.

[15] See Jackson Turner Main, *The Antifederalists—Critics of the Constitution, 1781–1788* (Chapel Hill: University of North Carolina Press, 1961).

[16] Charles A. Beard, *op. cit.*, pp. 176–178; Forrest McDonald, *op. cit.*, p. 9.

standards of their time, democrats. They acted to protect property and to restrain the states. They used their influence to make a constitution "over the heads" of the local assemblies, the states, and the Congress of the Articles. From this recital alone, Beard's principal contention of an overriding economc motivation is persuasive. So, too, is the charge of Smith and Parrington that the delegates undemocratically made an undemocratic constitution.

Defense: An Alternate Interpretation

The bill of particulars given above is, so far as it goes, true. The main issue with Beard, Smith, Parrington and other idol-smashers, however, is the interpretation of the acts of the delegates. Interpretation depends upon context; and an alternate interpretation depends upon enlarging the context within which the delegates acted. That enlarged context is the "disharmonious society" for which the Constitution was made. That context does not destroy the anti-Convention indictment. It simply demonstrates that the indictment can be subsumed as incidental to a bigger purpose: to erect a large political edifice upon weak constitutional foundations.

We return briefly to the eighteenth-century society described in the preceding chapter. The society was disharmonious because it tended toward group and sectional particularism, and because the political attitudes needed to support common republican government were not firmly set nor strongly entrenched. There were few of the moderating influences that we associate with democracy in modern, urban, and industrialized societies: intersectional ties, a national economy, and a wide sharing and communication of common political attitudes. Eighteenth century society, furthermore, lacked many of the institutional resources with which to create a "reasonable" or "moderate" politics, to borrow the language of that time.

Parties were loose factional assemblages; and political communication was poorly organized. Under all these circumstances, and despite all that worked in favor of republican government, the danger of expanding or "cumulative" political conflict was a very real, if not always present, threat.

The language of the delegates in Convention supports a view that they were primarily concerned with creating a constitution for a "disharmonious society" lacking adequate supports for a moderate federal republic. Their speeches and their language do not support an interpretation that they wanted primarily to defeat democracy or erect an antipopular oligarchy. In the florid oratory of the opening days of the Convention the delegates denounced the democratic provisions of the Articles and of the state constitutions, the rage for paper money, and the unreasonableness of the people. But for the most part, they spoke of different fears: of cabal and faction; of dissolution or consolidation; of monarchy or popular upheaval. They were fearful mainly not of democracy or attacks upon property, but of continuing, unchecked tendencies to an extreme, and of political expressions that would undermine republican government itself.

The constitution the delegates constructed indicates also that, whatever may have been their other concerns, they were fundamentally engaged in an attempt to strengthen the American polity so that the future republican government could function effectively. Their strategy—logical under the circumstances—included three principal methods or aims. One was to withdraw especially fruitful sources of contention from the most quarrelsome and heated centers of political dispute and thereby limit a tendency toward cumulative political conflict. Another technique of the delegates was to strengthen both the political and nonpolitical bonds of unity. And lastly, also in keeping with rational strategy under prevalent political conditions, they sought to create an artificial frame of government to limit and to sublimate the natural tendencies of politics in their "disharmonious society."

The delegates withdrew power from the states; especially they withdrew some principal objects of political contention from the reach of local democracy. The Constitution prohibited interference with contracts or with commerce among the states. It also enjoined each state to grant "full faith and credit" to the public acts, records, and judicial proceedings of other states and to recognize for the citizens of each state the "privileges and immunities" of citizens in the several states.

By one account, in these provisions the delegates acted to limit democracy and to protect property. By another, they attempted to remove sources of contention from the power of the states, to provide for a national citizenship and for a new government with power to act as representative and trustee of citizens possessed of a dual citizenship.

Actually, the delegates in Convention seemed to be relatively indifferent to the *internal* politics of the states. They did not consistently take the side of debtors or creditors, democrats or oligarchs. Nor did they appear to fear local democracy as such. They did not care, either, how many heads were broken on the local level. But they were intensely and continuously concerned with political conflict that weakened the union, undermined a growing nationhood, or threatened the stability of a republican government.

Aside from the provisions cited and those designed to secure national control of foreign relations, the states were left substantially in charge of their own affairs. They retained their traditional police power almost in its entirety, along with control over property, crime, civil injuries, and social arrangements. The delegates removed from the states very little. Indeed, to have done so would have, in their view, both threatened to create a monarchy, centralized discontent, and made the common government itself too much subject to con-

tention. Instead, they sought to create an additional tier of government and a new constituency principally to defend and represent what citizens enjoyed in common as Americans.

Those objects of political controversy that the delegates sought to protect from the states were critical in amending the major defects of their disharmonious society. A national commerce and protection of common rights would contribute both to a national citizenship and to removing causes of dissension among the states. Their protection would encourage both political and economic growth. And by putting them out of the reach of the states and local governments, some of the heat would be removed from a politics that tended dangerously toward cumulative and uncontrollable conflict.

Aside from an attempt to withdraw certain subjects of contention from state action, the delegates were also especially concerned to strengthen the bonds of union. The contract and commerce clauses, indeed all of those clauses of the Constitution that deal with property, need to be read in this context. The delegates set up protections for property, for commerce, and for sound money. They particularly sought to protect the foundations upon which personalty and economic endeavor rested. To follow the delegates in Convention is revealing. They discuss property, the commerce clause, and conflicts of debtors and creditors. But they talked directly about these matters very little. They are discussed almost wholly in conjunction with *other* objects: navigation acts, the slave trade, the burden of taxation, etc.

Property found its place among many other interests, and especially as an adjunct to *political* objectives such as military strength and corporate unity, or *social* objectives such as access to unappropriated resources and equality of status. Usually, the delegates seemed primarily interested in settling upon one or another social or political objective. The battles in the Convention about these interests or ends were often fierce. When agreement was reached, economic arrangements appeared to follow pretty much as a matter of course and even of indifference. Often they were simply taken over from some clause in the Articles, or from a practice made familiar by their colonial experience. One may say, then, that economic and property arrangements were subordinate to the interests of federal union, political stability, and the future economic and social development within the United States. The delegates adopted those property arrangements they felt would conduce the long-term interests of the nation they saw growing from their efforts.

Property was protected: and a measure of control over property and especially personalty was withdrawn from the states. The delegates may have incidentally benefited the interests of creditors or merchants or speculators. In fact, they did not seem specifically to want to protect them. In any case, they had other ends. One was withdrawing a source of controversy from direct political action by the states. The delegates were also filling out and giving specific character to a conception of national citizenship and of future national development. And they were, finally, artificially strengthening the polity by associating union and common republican government with economic advantage and development.

The delegates' treatment of democracy, or popular government, probably appears by contemporary standards the most suspect of all their deeds. Notice again, however, that an interpretation of their actions depends upon the context in which they are read. Their actions could have been aimed at weakening democracy. They could also have been intended to strengthen artificially a republican government under circumstances, requiring precisely that approach to secure a popular government on a national scale. The delegates sought to erect a national government. They sought to establish a dual citizenship under which people would be at once members of a locale and of a state, but would share in a joint venture of federal and republican government. They created scope for an additional layer or level of government, an independent government with its own machinery of courts, its own taxing powers, and a capacity to develop loyalties. They knew the tendencies of the politics of their time. Consequently, they sought equally to guard against the most dangerous tendencies of the government they were creating.

The Founding Fathers called themselves supporters of republican government, by which they meant representative government, derived from the great bulk of the people, but so arranged as to secure stability and government of the wise and virtuous. They meant by "wise and virtuous" primarily wise in the ways of politics and filled with republican virtue. The delegates understood from their own experience that the government, to work at all, required political leaders at the national level with considerable disinterested devotion to the republic. Remember their experience: their enormous efforts and great difficulty in getting the project started and their many frustrations. They had seen how readily jealousies could set individuals and sections against each other. From their experience—under colonial governments, during the Revolution, under the Articles—they knew that a stratum of patriots was not only a necessary support to government, but a needed security against factionalism, cabal, or disruptive parochialism.

A prime objective of the Convention was, therefore, to provide for moderate and independent leadership for the nation in spite of the masses or popular majorities, especially those within the states. The delegates feared also a plebiscitary chief on the national scene or a widespread populistic democracy. Against these dangers, they devised a set of "republican remedies" to apply to the federal government itself. Their "republican remedies" had another purpose: to complete and perfect the representative republic itself.

The representative devices in the Constitution serve both to temper political will and to supplement and complete it by providing representation for interests that might otherwise remain unheard. Representation in the Constitution was the subject of sectional and factional compromise. These compromises had also (and were understood to have) a broad tendency to supplement and expand political representation. In sum, the representative arrangements in the Constitution, whatever other purposes they had, were also designed to offset the defects of political representation that arose from an inadequately organized politics.

Today, we are apt to think of checks and balances, separation of powers, and indirect representation as devices to restrain the "tyranny of the majority," and to thwart popular government. In part they have that effect. But in the eighteenth century, they were good republican and democratic devices and, in fact, applied consistently and rigorously by radical republicans in the states. When commending such devices in the Convention, the delegates sometimes spoke of the danger of majorities or omnipotent legislatures. A more central concern was cabal and faction: the threats of silent and sinister accumulations of power and of the disruption of the polity by minority interests. The delegates were trying to generate a national will, not defeat it. A central danger, as they saw it, was that such a will would not be representative, that it would be a will proclaiming itself the representative of the whole but masking designs for power, pelf, and preferment. Separation of powers, checks and balances, and representative formulae would work to counteract the natural tendencies of politics built on a primitive economic and social base. Such devices were also vital for nourishing the government itself: to secure confidence in it; to win the support of disinterested patriots; and to afford a security against fecund evils.

A democrat might say that the delegates took too low a view of politics. Perhaps they did. But that judgment misses one of the unique and original contributions of the Founding Fathers. They contrived an alternate and supplementary system of institutions to remedy the deficiencies of their own political society. The delegates' constitutional methods of fragmentation, of withdrawal and delegation, and of nourishing a patriot elite are directed to this object. They wished to stimulate loyalty to the principles of republican government. They wanted also to generate power in the whole system. They sought to achieve both these ends by limiting politics— that is, politics in the ordinary sense of the word. But in constraining and narrowing the method of politics, they supplemented the Constitution, providing for alternate methods, other modes for the resolution of conflict, and for stimulating patriotic energies.

Eighteenth-century philosophers often spoke of a social contract and of a political contract or contract of government. These terms are useful in the present context. The task for the delegates was to build a nationwide political contract upon an untried and possibly inadequate foundation. For this purpose, they required more than a simple principal-agent model of government. Neither the existing society nor contemporary political institutions could sustain a republican government based upon a direct connection between political will and government response. Supporting the political contract required artful measures. Consequently, the delegates contrived methods to strengthen particular political institutions by formal constitutional provisions and to sublimate intense political passions by utilizing the forces of social and economic evolution. American politics was "judicialized." Many issues that involved property, citizenship, and the development of the nation were reserved from the direct or speedy expression of popular will. Even ordinary political decision was closely associated with the politics of federalism and an intricate constitutional system of representation and separation of powers. According to one view of democracy, the delegates dethroned the people and set up an antidemocratic scheme of government. But "politics" in the narrow usage of that term is a small part of the whole of the life of man, and even a small part of what most understand democracy to be. Whether the delegates' conception of the right relation between citizens, the society, and the state, between the social contract and the contract of government, was an ungenerous one or even an antipopular one, remains to be discussed in later chapters. Certainly we can say, however, that their conception was statesmanlike.

Conclusion

The intention of the delegates probably cannot be finally known. But if we establish a purpose that included a wider intention and motive than that imputed by Beard or Smith, we lay a foundation for the ensuing discussion. Without alleging proof, it would be useful to state what seems the most plausible interpretation of the delegates' intentions.

In the context of their society and their experience with the colonial and revolutionary governments, the delegates' activities in behalf of the new government seem to have been directed primarily at a simple, coherent set of *political* objectives. They seem to have been aiming at (1) withdrawing particular objects of contention from local majorities; (2) attempting to secure a common interest; (3) securing the support for the "representative republic" of a stratum of "wise and virtuous" leaders who would put republican principles above personal and factional interest; and (4) devising a scheme of representation and checks and balances that would complete that government and prevent it in turn from developing cumulative tendencies toward an extreme.

The delegates, in Convention and out of it, appear to have been doing what people have generally thought they were. They protected property, but especially in order to remove sources of discord, foster economic growth,

and develop interest in the government. They destroyed the dependence of the government upon the states, but more in the interests of a national citizenship than fear of democracy. Similarly, they added to central government the "salutary checks" of republican government as much to complete a representative will as to restrain it. In Convention and out of it they did not act as if they were trying to execute a *coup* for their faction, defend property, or silence democrats in the states. They were men engaged in a task intellectually and practically of enormous difficulty: to conceive a successful constitution and launch a nation: That task required great initiative and sound principles of strategy and philosophy.

The difficulty of the task answers at least partly the charge of usurpation. Without any doubt the delegates violated their mandate. They also appealed from the Congress and the states to the ratifying conventions. While their deeds lacked constituted political legitimacy, that same defect also puts a different face upon their actions. The Convention was not a government. The delegates could at most hope to persuade the active electorate, assuming that elections to the conventions would be held. Against their cause they had two of the most powerful of political influences: inertia and fear of the unknown. Under the circumstances, the charge of usurpation does not seem a grave one.

Beard and Smith remind us that the Founding Fathers lived long ago and that they made a Constitution to serve, initially, a society of a few million farmers. There is no security that their philosophy will continue to serve us, especially at times when new popular creeds are struggling for recognition. To their credit, however, the Founding Fathers did not finally settle the issue between republican government and responsiveness to popular creeds or democratic majorities. Instead, they initiated a dialogue between the people as ultimate sovereign and the people as *populus*, as trustee for the nation.

5

The Federalist, Number Fifty-One

Alexander Hamilton or James Madison

Factions and uncontrolled political power are the major problems addressed in Federalist, *No. 51. Too much governmental power causes abuses which endanger personal liberty and security. This is a problem in relationships within the national government and between government and the people. For example, if the president gains excessive power at the expense of congress, our constitutional system may be threatened by abusive exercise of executive authority. This is highly relevant to our recent experiences with Vietnam and Watergate. The federal system is a second check on possible excesses of concentrated political power. Since we have two governmental systems functioning on the same geographic territory, individuals are protected because the national govern-*

ment and the states can counterbalance each other. This argument is related to the centralization-decentralization discussions in Chapter 4 as well as the strengths and weaknesses of political parties reviewed in Chapter 6. A major question from this Federalist *essay concerns the exercise of negative as opposed to positive political power: If separation of powers and checks and balances prevent abuses of authority, how can the government deal effectively with serious crises and policy priorities? Clearly, our governmental structure is not organized to facilitate hasty decisions. At the same time, we may be frustrated by the lack of governmental response to pressing social and economic problems.*

To the People of the State of New York:

To what expedient, then, shall we finally resort, for maintaining in practice the necessary partition of power among the several departments, as laid down in the Constitution? The only answer that can be given is, that as all these exterior provisions are found to be inadequate, the defect must be supplied, by so contriving the interior structure of the government as that its several constituent parts may, by their mutual relations, be the means of keeping each other in their proper places. Without presuming to undertake a full development of this important idea, I will hazard a few general observations, which may perhaps place it in a clearer light, and enable us to form a more correct judgment of the principles and structure of the government planned by the convention.

From the *New York Packet*, Friday, February 8, 1788.

In order to lay a due foundation for that separate and distinct exercise of the different powers of government, which to a certain extent is admitted on all hands to be essential to the preservation of liberty, it is evident that each department should have a will of its own; and consequently should be so constituted that the members of each should have as little agency as possible in the appointment of the members of the others. Were this principle rigorously adhered to, it would require that all the appointments for the supreme executive, legislative, and judiciary magistrates should be drawn from the same fountain of authority, the people, through channels having no communication whatever with one another. Perhaps such a plan of constructing the several departments would be less difficult in practice than it may in contemplation appear. Some difficulties, however, and some additional expense would attend the execution of it. Some deviations, therefore, from the principle must be admitted. In the constitution of the judiciary department in particular, it might be inexpedient to insist rigorously on the principle: first, because peculiar qualifications being essential in the members, the primary consideration ought to be to select that mode of choice which best secures these qualifications; secondly, because the permanent tenure by which the appointments are held in that department, must soon destroy all sense of dependence on the authority conferring them.

It is equally evident, that the members of each department should be as little dependent as possible on those of the others, for the emoluments annexed to their offices. Were the executive magistrate, or the judges, not independent of the legislature in this particular, their independence in every other would be merely nominal.

But the great security against a gradual concentration of the several powers in the same department, consists in giving to those who administer each department the necessary constitutional means and personal motives to resist encroachments of the others. The provision for defence must in this, as in all other cases, be made commensurate to the danger of attack. Ambition must be made to counteract ambition. The interest of the man must be connected with the constitutional rights of the place. It may be a reflection on human nature, that such devices should be necessary to control the abuses of government. But what is government itself, but the greatest of all reflections on human nature? If men were angels, no government would be necessary. If angels were to govern men, neither external nor internal controls on government would be necessary. In framing a government which is to be administered by men over men, the great difficulty lies in this: you must first enable the government to control the governed; and in the next place oblige it to control itself. A dependence on the people is, no doubt, the primary control on the government; but experience has taught mankind the necessity of auxiliary precautions.

This policy of supplying, by opposite and rival interests, the defect of better motives, might be traced through the whole system of human affairs, private as well as public. We see it particularly displayed in all the subordinate distributions of power, where the constant aim is to divide and arrange the several offices in such a manner as that each may be a check on the other—that the private interest of every individual may be a sentinel over the public rights. These inventions of prudence cannot be less requisite in the distribution of the supreme powers of the State.

But it is not possible to give to each department an equal power of self-defence. In republican government, the legislative authority necessarily predominates. The remedy for this inconveniency is to divide the legislature into different branches; and to render them, by different modes of election and different principles of action, as little connected with each other as the nature of their common functions and their common dependence on the society will admit. It may even be necessary to guard against dangerous encroachments by still further precautions. As the weight of the legislative authority requires that it should be thus divided, the weakness of the executive may require, on the other hand, that it should be fortified. An absolute negative on the legislature appears, at first view, to be the natural defence with which the executive magistrate should be armed. But perhaps it would be neither altogether safe nor alone sufficient. On ordinary occasions it might not be exerted with the requisite firmness, and on extraordinary occasions it might be perfidiously abused. May not this defect of an absolute negative be supplied by some qualified connection between this weaker department and the weaker branch of the stronger department, by which the latter may be led to support the constitutional rights of the former, without being too much detached from the rights of his own department?

If the principles on which these observations are founded to be just, as I persuade myself they are, and they be applied as a criterion to the several State constitutions, and to the federal Constitution, it will be found that if the latter does not perfectly correspond with them, the former are infinitely less able to bear such a test.

There are, moreover, two considerations particularly applicable to the federal system of America, which place that system in a very interesting point of view.

First In a single republic, all the power surrendered by the people is submitted to the administration of a single government; and the usurpations are guarded against by a division of the government into distinct and separate departments. In the compound republic of America, the power surrendered by the people is first divided between two distinct governments, and then the portion allotted to each subdivided among distinct and separate departments. Hence a double security arises to the rights of the people. The different governments will control each other, at the same time that each will be controlled by itself.

Second It is of great importance in a republic not only to guard the society against the oppression of its rulers, but to guard one part of the society against the injustice of the other part. Different interests necessarily exist in different classes of citizens. If a majority be united by a common interest, the rights of the minority will be insecure. There are but two methods of providing against this evil: the one by creating a will in the community independent of the majority—that is, of the society itself; the other, by comprehending in the society so many separate descriptions of citizens as will render an unjust combination of a majority of the whole very improbable, if not impracticable. The first method prevails in all governments possessing an hereditary or self-appointed authority. This, at best, is but a precarious security; because a power independent of the society may as well espouse the unjust views of the major, as the rightful interests of the minor party, and may possibly be turned against both parties. The second method will be exemplified in the federal republic of the United States. Whilst all authority in it will be derived from and dependent on the society, the society itself will be broken into so many parts, interests and classes of citizens, that the rights of individuals, or of the minority, will be in little danger from interested combinations of the majority. In a free government the security for civil rights must be the same as that for religious rights. It consists in the one case in the multiplicity of interests, and in the other in the multiplicity of sects. The degree of security in both cases will depend on the number of interests and sects; and this may be presumed to depend on the extent of country and number of people comprehended under the same government. This view of the subject must particularly recommend a proper federal system to all the sincere and considerate friends of republican government, since it shows that in exact proportion as the territory of the Union may be formed into more circumscribed Confederacies, or States, oppressive combinations of a majority will be facilitated; the best security, under the republican forms, for the rights of every class of citizens, will be diminished; and consequently the stability and independence of some member of the government, the only other security, must be proportionately increased. Justice is the end of government. It is the end of civil society. It ever has been and ever will be pursued until it be obtained, or until liberty be lost in the pursuit. In a society under the forms of which the stronger faction can readily unite and oppress the weaker, anarchy may as truly be said to reign as in a state of nature, where the weaker individual is not secured against the violence of the stronger; and as, in the latter state, even the stronger individuals are prompted, by the uncertainty of their condition, to submit to a government which may protect the weak as well as themselves; so, in the former state, will the more powerful factions or parties be gradually induced, by a like motive, to wish for a government which will protect all parties, the weaker as well as the more powerful. It can be little doubted that if the State of Rhode Island was separated from the Confederacy and left to itself, the insecurity of rights under the popular form of government within such narrow limits would be displayed by such reiterated oppressions of factious majorities that some power altogether independent of the people would soon be called for by the voice of the very factions whose misrule had proved the necessity of it. In the extended republic of the United States, and among the great variety of interests, parties, and sects which it embraces, a coalition of a majority of the whole society could seldom take place on any other principles than those of justice and the general good; whilst there being thus less danger to a minor from the will of a major party, there must be less pretext, also, to provide for the security of the former, by introducing into the government a will not dependent on the latter, or, in other words, a will independent of the society itself. It is no less certain than it is important, notwithstanding the contrary opinions which have been entertained, that the larger the society, provided it lie within a practical sphere, the more duly capable it will be of self-government. And happily for the *republican cause*, the practicable sphere may be carried to a very great extent, by a judicious modification and mixture of the *federal principle*.

Publius

The Bill of Rights

3

The original Constitution contained a number of provisions regarding
individual rights such as protections against the writ of habeas corpus,
which prohibits government officials from jailing a person without
specific charges, or the passage of any bills of attainder, a statute which
declares a person or a group guilty of a crime and establishes punishment
without a fair trial. Many anti-Federalists considered these protections to
be inadequate. They demanded a bill of rights and were prepared to use
this as an issue in the original fight for ratification of the Constitution.
The Federalists (the strong supporters of the Constitution) finally agreed
to set up a new convention to be held for the express purpose of
passing a comprehensive Bill of Rights.

The ten amendments to the Constitution were finally ratified in 1791.

Kenneth L. Deutsch prepared the introduction and assembled the case materials
for Articles 6, 7, 10 and 11 in this chapter.

Such explicit protections as the First Amendment freedom of speech, press, assembly and religious belief were included as well as rights against unreasonable searches and seizure (the Fourth Amendment); the protection against double jeopardy and forceful testimony against oneself (the Fifth Amendment); the right of due process of law that protects citizens against arbitrary procedures; the right to a speedy and public trial (the Sixth Amendment); and the protection against excessive bail and cruel and unusual punishment (the Eighth Amendment). This basic core of rights provides the foundation for the idea of limited government as it deals with the individual citizen.

Additional amendments have been added to the Constitution since 1791 that have applied these basic rights to the various states. Important examples are the Fourteenth Amendment, due process of law, and equal protection of the laws clauses that have greatly enhanced procedural protections for those accused of a crime and the provision of equality of opportunity for blacks and other minorities.

FREEDOM OF EXPRESSION

The cornerstone of free expression rests on the right of freedom of speech. A vital debate on public issues was considered to be of particular importance to the architects of the Bill of Rights. Although the First Amendment spells out in clear terms that Congress may make "no law . . . abridging freedom of speech," the Supreme Court has never claimed that this right to free speech is guaranteed in all circumstances and situations. The great jurist Oliver Wendell Holmes was quick to state that the First Amendment does not give a person the right to shout "Fire" in a crowded theater. How much freedom should Americans possess in contributing to an open public debate on public policy issues? Can we distinguish between the expression of ideas, which is guaranteed under the First Amendment, and the expression of political action, which may not always be protected under the First Amendment? The Supreme Court has grappled with these difficult questions in the important case of *Brandenburg* v. *Ohio* (Article 6) decided in 1969. The case deals with the right of a Ku Klux Klan member to express his hatred of blacks, Jews, and Catholics.

The First Amendment also directly guarantees the "free exercise" of religious belief. For many years the Supreme Court has encountered a variety of cases dealing with unconventional forms of religious worship and beliefs. These include, for example, state laws against members of the Mormon faith, who in the nineteenth century practiced polygamy. Should individuals who adhere to a particular set of religious beliefs be exempt from prosecution under a criminal statute that prohibits polygamy? To what extent should society limit certain kinds of religious worship? Can a proper distinction be made by the Supreme Court between the expression of religious belief and practices of religious ritual? The Supreme Court addressed these important questions in the case of *Wisconsin* v. *Yoder (1972)* which involved the refusal of the Old Order Amish parents to abide by Wisconsin's compulsory school attendance law (see Article 7).

EQUAL PROTECTION OF THE LAWS

Racial discrimination against blacks has been an American dilemma since 1619 when slavery was introduced in the colony of Virginia. Efforts to deal with the inherently unequal conditions that blacks have experienced culminated in the Civil War amendments which sought to provide them "Equal protection of the laws" (the Fourteenth Amendment). "Jim Crow" laws, however, implemented throughout the South after the Civil War established the systematic legal segregation of the races, in schools, trains, prisons, even restaurants and water fountains. In 1896, the Supreme Court delivered a decisive blow to advocates of racial equality. In the case of *Plessy* v. *Ferguson*, the Court upheld the conviction of Homer Plessy, a man of "one-eighth African blood," for violation of the segregation rules of the Louisiana Railroad Accommodation Law. The Court in an 8 to 1 decision claimed that Louisiana could *separate* the races if it provided "equal" facilities.

During the period from the 1930's to the 1950's, the Supreme Court began to erode the odious mantle of inferiority placed on blacks by the *Plessy* decision. These discussions set the stage for the 1954 landmark *Brown* v. *Board of Education of Topeka* decision. The *Brown* decision was a unanimous opinion in which the Court spoke in clarion terms: "We conclude that in the field of public education the doctrine of 'separate but equal' has no place" (see Article 8).

Although the *Brown* decision declared segregation in the public schools unconstitutional, the Court merely specified that the desegregation process must be "with all deliberate speed." The Court has subsequently been criticized for not being firmer, for little progress toward desegregation was made by the eleven Southern states practicing segregation during the succeeding decade. By the 1960's and the 1970's the

Supreme Court became concerned with the slow pattern of desegregation. The important case of *Swann* v. *Charlotte-Mecklenburg Board of Education* (1971) represents the Court's support for a wide variety of remedies to eradicate school segregation, including the highly controversial remedy of school busing to eliminate racial imbalance (see Article 9).

The notion that all people are created equal has never meant that all people possess the same talents or interests. When we try to put the principle of equality into practice in American society, we face the problem of determining which differences between people are relevant to differential treatment and which are not. Should the government ever establish public policies which in some significant way discriminate on the basis of race, religion, sex, or national origin? More specifically, should the government establish programs to aid minority groups in competition for jobs and higher education? Are these special treatment programs valid forms of "compensatory treatment" for past racial discrimination or do they establish an unfair policy of "reverse discrimination" against whites? The Supreme Court recently dealt with these troubling questions in context of special minority admissions programs in medical school (*Bakke* v. *Regents of the State of California, 1978*) and in the context of special minority programs in employment (*United Steelworkers of America* v. *Weber, 1979*) (see Article 10).

Beliefs in the inferior (or unequal) status of women are at least as old as written history. Women have experienced laws in this nation which claimed that because of their "timidity" and "delicacy" they are unfit for many occupations of civil life. Although many recent Supreme Court decisions have struck down some particularly odious forms of sexual discrimination, many women's rights advocates are concerned that an Equal Rights Amendment (ERA) is still needed to provide the legal status whereby "equality of rights under the law shall not be denied or abridged by the United States or by any state on account of sex." Although three states are needed to ratify this Amendment by 1982, proponents of the ERA remain hopeful that eventual ratification will be a victory in granting new and equal dignity to women under the law.

DUE PROCESS OF LAW: THE RIGHTS OF THE ACCUSED

The Anglo-American legal tradition has been concerned with the fair treatment of those accused of a crime. One of the great controversies of American politics in the last decade or so has been to determine how much "fairness" is due to the criminally accused. For some, fairness means procedural justice, that is, investigative and judicial proceedings conducted according to clearly established and predictable rules. For others, this scrupulous attention to established rules only "coddles" criminals. They believe that the law should provide for a quick retribution against criminals so security can be established. Still others in our society contend that "due process of law" principles found in the Fifth and Fourteenth Amendments must mean a great equalizing of legal resources in the criminal justice system, giving every person, rich or poor, the same opportunity to establish an effective defense when accused of a crime.

The Supreme Court of Chief Justice Earl Warren was particularly concerned with the issue of due process of law and criminal justice. In the 1966 case of *Miranda* v. *Arizona,* the Supreme Court made it clear that procedural safeguards must be expanded in dealing with the accused. This extremely controversial case is presented in Article 11.

The recent Supreme Court of Chief Justice Warren Burger has been quite reticent about expanding the procedural safeguards established in *Miranda.* Instead, this Court has chosen to focus on protection of the public against the criminal forces of society.

In reviewing these landmark decisions of the Supreme Court, it is clear that the Bill of Rights is the focus of resolving controversial issues. Today, the Bill of Rights remains a cornerstone of our legal and political systems, particularly when the elected branches are unable or unwilling to settle conflicts over basic rights and freedoms.

6

Brandenburg v. Ohio

U.S. Supreme Court

In 1966, Clarence Brandenburg invited a Cincinnati newscaster to attend a Ku Klux Klan meeting in Hamilton County, Ohio. One of the films taken by the newscaster's crew showed Brandenburg in the full dress of a Klansman stating that the Klan might have to seek "revenge" against the government for its desegregation policies. Brandenburg stated: "Personally, I believe the nigger should be returned to Africa and the Jew returned to Israel."

Based upon the content of these films, Brandenburg was arrested, tried and convicted under a 1919 Ohio criminal syndicalism statute which prohibited "advocating . . . the duty, necessity or pro-

priety of crime, sabotage, violence or unlawful methods of terrorism. . ."

Brandenburg appealed his conviction to the U.S. Supreme Court, claiming his right to free speech was abridged by the Ohio law. The Supreme Court agreed and overturned Brandenburg's conviction as well as declaring the state law unconstitutional.

In this opinion, the Court presented what is perhaps the clearest position to date concerning the limits to which government may abridge the individual's freedom of speech. Do you agree that Brandenburg should have been permitted to say what he did, or were his words so inflammatory that the state had a right to stop him?

. . . The Ohio Criminal Syndicalism Statute was enacted in 1919. From 1917 to 1920, identical or quite similar laws were adopted by 20 States and two territories. In 1927, this Court sustained the constitutionality of California's Criminal Syndicalism Act, the text of which is quite similar to that of the laws of Ohio. *Whitney* v. *California*, 274 U.S. 357 (1927). The Court upheld the statute on the ground that, without mere "advocating" violent means to effect political and economic change involves such danger to the security of the State that the State may outlaw it. But *Whitney* has been thoroughly discredited by later decisions. See *Dennis* v. *United States*, (1951). These later decisions have fashioned the principle that the constitutional guarantees of free speech and free press do not permit a State to forbid or proscribe advocacy of the use of force or of law violation except where such advocacy

is directed to inciting or producing imminent lawless action and is likely to incite or produce such action. As we said in *Noto* v. *United States*, (1961), "the mere abstract teaching . . . of the moral propriety or even moral necessity for a resort to force and violence, is not the same as preparing a group for violent action and steeling it to such action." A statute which fails to draw this distinction impermissibly intrudes upon the freedoms guaranteed by the First and Fourteenth Amendments. It sweeps within its condemnation speech which our Constitution has immunized from governmental control.

Measured by this test, Ohio's Criminal Syndicalism Act cannot be sustained. . . . Neither the indictment nor the trial judge's instructions to the jury in any way refined the statute's bald definition of the crime in terms of mere advocacy not distinguished from incitement to imminent lawless action.

Accordingly, we are here confronted with a

395 U.S. 444, 89 S.Ct. 1827, 23 L.Ed.2d 430 (1969)

statute which, by its own words and as applied, purports to punish mere advocacy and to forbid, on pain of criminal punishment, assembly with others merely to advocate the described type of action. Such a statute falls within the condemnation of the First and Fourteenth Amendments. The contrary teaching of *Whitney* v. *California*, cannot be supported, and that decision is therefore overruled.

Reversed.

Mr. Justice Black, concurring.

I agree with the views expressed by Mr. Justice Douglas in his concurring opinion in this case that the "clear and present danger" doctrine should have no place in the interpretation of the First Amendment. I join the Court's opinion, which, as I understand it, simply cites *Dennis* v. *United States*, (1951), but does not indicate any agreement on the Court's part with the "clear and present danger" doctrine on which *Dennis* purported to rely.

Mr. Justice Douglas, concurring.

While I join the opinion of the Court, I desire to enter a *caveat*.

The "clear and present danger" test was adumbrated by Mr. Justice Holmes in a case arising during World War I—a war "declared" by the Congress, not by the Chief Executive. The case was *Schenck* v. *United States*, where the defendant was charged with attempts to cause insubordination in the military and obstruction of enlistment. The pamphlets that were distributed urged resistance to the draft, denounced conscription, and impugned the motives of those backing the war effort. The First Amendment was tendered as a defense. Mr. Justice Holmes in rejecting that defense said:

"The question in every case is whether the words are used in such circumstances and are of such a nature as to create a clear and present danger that

they will bring about the substantive evils that Congress has a right to prevent. It is a question of proximity and degree. . . ."

(Justice Douglas reviews the World War I "clear and present danger" cases.)

Those, then, were the World War I cases that put the gloss of "clear and present danger" on the First Amendment. Whether the war power—the greatest leveler of them all—is adequate to sustain that doctrine is debatable. The dissents . . . show how easily "clear and present danger" is manipulated to crush what Brandeis called "[t]he fundamental right of free men to strive for better conditions through new legislation and new institutions" by argument and discourse even in time of war. Though I doubt if the "clear and present danger" test is congenial to the First Amendment in time of a declared war, I am certain it is not reconcilable with the First Amendment in days of peace.

The Court quite properly overrules *Whitney* v. *California*, which involved advocacy of ideas which the majority of the Court deemed unsound and dangerous.

Mr. Justice Holmes, though never formally abandoning the "clear and present danger" test, moved closer to the First Amendment ideal when he said in dissent in *Gitlow* v. *New York*:

"Every idea is an incitement. It offers itself for belief and if believed it is acted on unless some other belief outweighs it or some failure of energy stifles the movement at its birth. The only difference between the expression of an opinion and an incitement in the narrower sense is the speaker's enthusiasm for the result. Eloquence may set fire to reason. But whatever may be thought of the redundant discourse before us it had no chance of starting a present conflagration. If in the long run the beliefs expressed in proletarian dictatorship are destined to be accepted by the dominant forces of the community, the only meaning of free speech is that they should be given their chance and have their way."

We have never been faithful to the philosophy of that dissent. . . .

Out of the "clear and present danger" test came other offspring. Advocacy and teaching of forcible overthrow of government as an abstract principle is immune from prosecution. *Yates* v. *United States*. But an "active" member, who has a guilty knowledge and intent of the aim to overthrow the Government by violence, *Noto* v. *United States*, may be prosecuted. *Scales* v. *United States*. And the power to investigate, backed by the powerful sanction of contempt, includes the power to determine which of the two categories fits the particular witness. *Barenblatt* v. *United States*. And so the investigator roams at will through all of the beliefs of the witness, ransacking his conscience and his innermost thoughts.

Judge Learned Hand, who wrote for the Court of Appeals in affirming the judgment in *Dennis*, coined the "not improbable" test, which this Court adopted and which Judge Hand preferred over the "clear and present danger" test. Indeed, in his book, *The Bill of Rights* 59 (1958), in referring to Holmes' creation of the "clear and present danger" test, he said, "I cannot help thinking that for once Homer nodded."

My own view is quite different. I see no place in the regime of the First Amendment for any "clear and present danger" test, whether strict and tight as some would make it, or free-wheeling as the Court in *Dennis* rephrased it.

When one reads the opinions closely and sees when and how the "clear and present danger" test has been applied, great misgivings are aroused. First, the threats were often loud but always puny and made serious only by judges so wedded to the *status quo* that critical analysis made them nervous. Second, the test was so twisted and perverted in *Dennis* as to make the trial of those teachers of Marxism an all-out political trial which was part and parcel

of the cold war that has eroded substantial parts of the First Amendment.

Action is often a method of expression and within the protection of the First Amendment.

Suppose one tears up his own copy of the Constitution in eloquent protest to a decision of this Court. May he be indicted?

Suppose one rips his own Bible to shreds to celebrate his departure from one "faith" and his embrace of atheism. May he be indicted?

. . . The act of praying often involves body posture and movement as well as utterances. It is nonetheless protected by the Free Exercise Clause. Picketing, as we have said on numerous occasions, is "free speech plus." That means that it can be regulated when it comes to the "plus" or "action" side of the protest. It can be regulated as to the number of pickets and the place and hours, because traffic and other community problems would otherwise suffer.

. . . One's beliefs have long been thought to be sanctuaries which government could not invade. *Barenblatt* is one example of the case with which that sanctuary can be violated. The lines drawn by the Court between the criminal act of being an "active" Communist and the innocent act of being a nominal or inactive Communist mark the difference only between deep and abiding belief and casual or uncertain belief. But I think that all matters of belief are beyond the reach of subpoenas or the probings of investigators. That is why the invasions of privacy made by investigating committees were notoriously unconstitutional. That is the deep-seated fault in the infamous loyalty-security hearings which, since 1947 when President Truman launched them, have processed 20,000,000 men and women. Those hearings were primarily concerned with one's thoughts, ideas, beliefs, and convictions. They were the most blatant violations of the First Amendment we have ever known.

The line between what is permissible and

not subject to control and what may be made impermissible and subject to regulation is the line between ideas and overt acts.

The example usually given by those who would punish speech is the case of one who falsely shouts fire in a crowded theatre.

This is, however, a classic case where speech is brigaded with action. They are indeed inseparable and a prosecution can be launched for the overt acts actually caused. Apart from rare instances of that kind, speech is, I think, immune from prosecution. Certainly there is no constitutional line between advocacy of abstract ideas as in *Yates* and advocacy of political action as in *Scales*. The quality of advocacy turns on the depth of the conviction; and government has no power to invade that sanctuary of belief and conscience.

7

Wisconsin v. Yoder

U.S. Supreme Court

This case deals with the Amish Church's refusal to comply with the Wisconsin State Education Law, which compelled children to attend school through age 16. The Amish contended that public education beyond age 14 was not proper because it exposed their children to worldly values and interfered with parental influence on the children's character. The Amish thereby asserted that state compulsion of requiring their offspring to attend high school interfered with the free exercise of the parents' religion. Such state laws violated the First Amendment protection of freedom of religion. The U.S. Supreme Court agreed with the Amish, stating that the Amish community was successful, peaceful and orderly for its members. The State failed to show how the extra two years of required schooling was of greater benefit to the children than the vocational education they would receive on their family farms. Do you agree with the Court's reasoning?

Mr. Chief Justice Burger delivered the opinion of the Court.

. . . Respondents Jonas Yoder and Wallace Miller are members of the Old Order Amish religion, and respondent Adin Yutzy is a member of the Conservative Amish Mennonite Church. They and their families are residents of Green County, Wisconsin. Wisconsin's compulsory school-attendance law required them to cause their children to attend public or private school until reaching age 16 but the respondents declined to send their children, ages 14 and 15, to public school after they complete the eighth grade. The children were not enrolled in any private school, or within any recognized exception to the compulsory-attendance law, and they are conceded to be subject to the Wisconsin statute.

On complaint of the school district administrator for the public schools, respondents were charged, tried, and convicted of violating the compulsory-attendance law in Green County Court and were fined the sum of $5 each. Respondents defended on the ground

406 U.S. 205, 92 S.Ct. 1526, 32 L.Ed.2d 15 (1972)

that the application of the compulsory-attendance law violated their rights under the First and Fourteenth Amendments. The trial testimony showed that respondents believed, in accordance with the tenets of Old Order Amish communities generally, that their children's attendance at high school, public or private, was contrary to the Amish religion and way of life. They believed that by sending their children to high school, they would not only expose themselves to the danger of the censure of the church community, but as found by the county court, also endanger their own salvation and that of their children. . . .

Formal high school education beyond the eighth grade is contrary to Amish beliefs, not only because it places Amish children in an environment hostile to Amish beliefs with increasing emphasis on competition in class work and sports and with pressure to conform to the styles, manners, and ways of the peer group, but also because it takes them away from their community, physically and emotionally, during the crucial and formative adolescent period of life. During this period, the children must acquire Amish attitudes favoring manual work and self-reliance and the specific skills needed to perform the adult role of an Amish farmer or housewife. They must learn to enjoy physical labor. Once a child has learned basic reading, writing, and elementary mathematics, these traits, skills, and attitudes admittedly fall within the category of those best learned through example and "doing" rather than in a classroom. And, at this time in life, the Amish child must also grow in his faith and his relationship to the Amish community if he is to be prepared to accept the heavy obligations imposed by adult baptism. In short, high school attendance with teachers who are not of the Amish faith— and may even be hostile to it—interposes a serious barrier to the integration of the Amish child into the Amish religious community. . . .

The Amish do not object to elementary education through the first eight grades as a general proposition because they agree that their children must have basic skills in the "three R's" in order to read the Bible, to be good farmers and citizens, and to be able to deal with non-Amish people when necessary in the course of daily affairs. They view such a basic education as acceptable because it does not significantly expose their children to worldly values or interfere with their development in the Amish community during the crucial adolescent period. . . .

The Wisconsin Circuit Court affirmed the convictions. The Wisconsin Supreme Court, however, sustained respondents' claim under the Free Exercise Clause of the First Amendment and reversed the convictions. A majority of the court was of the opinion that the State had failed to make an adequate showing that its interest in "establishing and maintaining an educational system overrides the defendants' right to the free exercise of their religion."

There is no doubt as to the power of a State, having a high responsibility for education of its citizens, to impose reasonable regulations for the control and duration of basic education. Providing public schools ranks at the very apex of the function of a State. Yet even this paramount responsibility was, in *Pierce*, made to yield to the right of parents to provide an equivalent education in a privately operated system. . . . Thus, a State's interest in universal education, however highly we rank it, is not totally free from a balancing process when it impinges on fundamental rights and interests, such as those specifically protected by the Free Exercise Clause of the First Amendment, and the traditional interest of parents with respect to the religious upbringing of their children so long as they, in the words of *Pierce*, "prepare [them] for additional obligations."

. . . A way of life, however virtuous and admirable, may not be interposed as a barrier to reasonable state regulation of education if it is based on purely secular considerations; to have the protection of the Religion Clauses, the claims must be rooted in religious belief. Although a determination of what is a "religious" belief or practice entitled to constitutional protection may present a most delicate question, the very concept of ordered liberty precludes allowing every person to make his own standards on matters of conduct in which society as a whole has important interests. Thus, if the Amish asserted their claims because of their subjective evaluation and rejection of the contemporary secular values accepted by the majority, much as Thoreau rejected the social values of his time and isolated himself at Walden Pond, their claims would not rest on a religious basis. Thoreau's choice was philosophical and personal rather than religious, and such belief does not rise to the demands of the Religion Clauses.

Giving no weight to such secular considerations, however, we see that the record in this case abundantly supports the claim that the traditional way of life of the Amish is not merely a matter of personal preference, but one of deep religious conviction, shared by an organized group, and intimately related to daily living. That the Old Order Amish daily life and religious practice stem from their faith is shown by the fact that it is in response to their literal interpretation of the Biblical injunction from the Epistle of Paul to the Romans, "be not conformed to this world. . . ." This command is fundamental to the Amish faith. Moreover, for the Old Order Amish, religion is not simply a matter of theocratic belief. As the expert witnesses explained, the Old Order Amish religion pervades and determines virtually their entire way of life, regulating it with the detail of the Talmudic diet through the strictly enforced rules of the church community.

The record shows that the respondents' religious beliefs and attitude toward life, family, and home have remained constant— perhaps some would say static—in a period of unparalleled progress in human knowledge generally and great changes in education. The respondents freely concede, and indeed assert as an article of faith, that their religious beliefs and what we would today call "life style" have not altered in fundamentals for centuries. Their way of life in a church-oriented community, separated from the outside world and "worldly" influences, their attachment to nature and the soil, is a way inherently simple and uncomplicated, albeit difficult to preserve against the pressure to conform. Their rejection of telephones, automobiles, radios, and television, their mode of dress, of speech, their habits of manual work do indeed set them apart from much of contemporary society; these customs are both symbolic and practical.

As the society around the Amish has become more populous, urban, industrialized, and complex, particularly in this century, government regulation of human affairs has correspondingly become more detailed and pervasive. The Amish mode of life has thus come into conflict increasingly with requirements of contemporary society exerting a hydraulic in-

sistence on conformity to majoritarian standards. So long as compulsory education laws were confined to eight grades of elementary basic education imparted in a nearby rural schoolhouse, with a large proportion of students of the Amish faith, the Old Order Amish had little basis to fear that school attendance would expose their children to the worldly influence they reject. But modern compulsory secondary education in rural areas is now largely carried on in a consolidated school, often remote from the student's home and alien to his daily home life. As the record so strongly shows, the values and progress of the modern secondary school are in sharp conflict with the fundamental mode of life mandated by the Amish religion; modern laws requiring compulsary secondary education have accordingly engendered great concern and conflict. The conclusion is inescapable that secondary schooling, by exposing Amish children to worldly influences in terms of attitudes, goals, and values contrary to beliefs, and by substantially interfering with the religious development of the Amish child and his integration into the way of life of the Amish faith community at the crucial adolescent stage of development, contravenes the basic religious tenets and practice of the Amish faith, both as to the parent and the child.

The impact of the compulsory-attendance law on respondents' practice of the Amish religion is not only severe, but inescapable, for the Wisconsin law affirmatively compels them, under threat of criminal sanction, to perform acts undeniably at odds with fundamental tenets of their religious beliefs. . . . As the record shows, compulsory school attendance to age 16 for Amish children carries with it a very real threat of undermining the Amish community and religious practice as they exist today; they must either abandon belief and be assimilated into society at large, or be forced to migrate to some other and more tolerant region. . . .

Wisconsin concedes that under the Religion Clauses religious beliefs are absolutely free from the State's control, but it argues that "actions," even though religiously grounded, are outside the protection of the First Amendment. . . . It is true that activities of individuals, even when religiously based, are often subject to regulation by the States in the exercise of their undoubted power to promote the health, safety, and general welfare, or the Federal Government in the exercise of its delegated powers. But to agree that religiously grounded conduct must often be subject to the broad police power of the State is not to deny that there are areas of conduct protected by the Free Exercise Clause of the First Amendment and thus beyond the power of the State to control, even under regulations of general applicability. This case, therefore, does not become easier because respondents were convicted for their "actions" in refusing to send their children to the public high school; in this context belief and action cannot be neatly confined in logic-tight compartments.

. . . The State advances two primary arguments in support of its system of compulsory education. It notes, as Thomas Jefferson pointed out early in our history, that some degree of education is necessary to prepare citizens to participate effectively and intelligently in our open political system if we are to preserve freedom and independence. Further, education prepares individuals to be self-reliant and self-sufficient participants in society. We accept these propositions.

However, the evidence adduced by the Amish in this case is persuasively to the effect that an additional one or two years of formal high school for Amish children in place of their long-established program of informal vocational education would do little to serve those interests. Respondents' experts testified at trial, without challenge, that the value of all education must be assessed in terms of its capacity to prepare the child for life. It is one thing to say that compulsory education for a year or two beyond the eighth grade may be necessary when its goal is the preparation of the child for life in modern society as the majority live, but it is quite another if the goal of education be viewed as the preparation of the child for life in the separated agrarian community that is the keystone of the Amish faith.

The State attacks respondents' position as one fostering "ignorance" from which the child must be protected by the State. No one can question the State's duty to protect children from ignorance but this argument does not square with the facts disclosed in the record. Whatever their idiosyncrasies as seen by the majority, this record strongly shows that the Amish community has been a highly successful social unit within our society, even if apart from the conventional "mainstream." Its members are productive and very law-abiding members of society; they reject public welfare in any of its usual modern forms. The Congress itself recognized their self-sufficiency by authorizing exemption of such groups as the Amish from the obligation to pay social security taxes. . . .

The State, however, supports its interest in providing an additional one or two years of compulsory high school education to Amish children because of the possibility that some such children will choose to leave the Amish community, and that if this occurs they will be ill-equipped for life. The State argues that if Amish children leave their church they should not be in the position of making their way in the world without the education available in the one or two additional years the State requires. However, on this record, that argument is highly speculative. There is no specific evidence of the loss of Amish adherents by attrition, nor is there any showing that upon leaving the Amish community Amish children, with their practical agricultural training and habits of industry and self-reliance, would become burdens on society because of educational shortcomings. . . .

There is nothing in this record to suggest that the Amish qualities of reliability, self-reliance, and dedication to work would fail to find ready markets in today's society. . . .

The requirement for compulsory education beyond the eighth grade is a relatively recent development in our history. Less than 60 years ago, the educational requirements of almost all of the States were satisfied by completion of the elementary grades, at least where the child was regularly and lawfully employed. . . .

. . . The origins of the requirement for school attendance to age 16, an age falling after the completion of elementary school but before completion of high school, are not entirely clear. But to some extent such laws reflected the movement to prohibit most child labor under age 16 that culminated in the provisions of the Federal Fair Labor Standards Act of 1938. . . .

The requirement of compulsory schooling to age 16 must therefore be viewed as aimed not merely at providing educational opportunities for children, but as an alternative to the equally undesirable consequence of unhealthful child labor displacing adult workers, or, on the other hand, forced idleness. The two kinds of statutes—compulsory school attendance and child labor laws—tend to keep children of certain ages off the labor market and in school; this regimen in turn provides opportunity to prepare for a livelihood of a higher order than that which children could pursue without education and protects their health in adolescence.

In these terms, Wisconsin's interest in compelling the school attendance of Amish children to age 16 emerges as somewhat less substantial than requiring such attendance for children generally. . . .

. . . Contrary to the suggestion of the dissenting opinion of Mr. Justice Douglas, our holding today in no degree depends on the assertion of the religious interest of the child as contrasted with that of the parents. It is the parents who are subject to prosecution here for failing to cause their children to attend school, and it is their right of free exercise, not that of their children, that must determine Wisconsin's power to impose criminal penalties on the parent. The dissent argues that a child who expresses a desire to attend public high school in conflict with the wishes of his parents should not be prevented from doing so. There is no reason for the Court to consider that point since it is not an issue in the case. The children are not parties to this litigation. The State has at no point tried this case on the theory that respondents were preventing their children from attending school against their expressed desires, and indeed the record is to the contrary. . . .

. . . For the reasons stated we hold, with the Supreme Court of Wisconsin, that the First and Fourteenth Amendments prevent the State from compelling respondents to cause their children to attend formal high school to age 16. Our disposition of this case, however, in no way alters our recognition of the obvious fact that courts are not school boards or legislatures, and are ill-equipped to determine the "necessity" of discrete aspects of a State's program of compulsory education. This should suggest that courts must move with great circumspection in performing the sensitive and delicate task of weighing a State's legitimate social concern when faced with religious claims for exemption from generally applicable educational requirements. It cannot be overemphasized that we are not dealing with a way of life and mode of education by a group claiming to have recently discovered some "progressive" or more enlightened process for rearing children for modern life.

Aided by a history of three centuries as an identifiable religious sect and a long history as a successful and self-sufficient segment of American society, the Amish in this case have convincingly demonstrated the sincerity of their religious beliefs, the interrelationship of belief with their mode of life, the vital role that belief and daily conduct play in the continued survival of Old Order Amish communities and their religious organization, and the hazards presented by the State's enforcement of a statute generally valid as to others. . . . In light of this convincing showing, one that probably few other religious groups or sects could make, and weighing the minimal difference between what the State would require and what the Amish already accept, it was incumbent on the State to show with more particularity how its admittedly strong interest in compulsory education would be adversely affected by granting an exemption to the Amish.

Nothing we hold is intended to undermine the general applicability of the State's compulsory school-attendance statutes or to limit the power of the State to promulgate reasonable standards that, while not impairing the free exercise of religion, provide for continuing agricultural vocational education under parental and church guidance by the Old Order Amish or others similarly situated. The States have had a long history of amicable and effective relationships with church-sponsored schools, and there is no basis for assuming that, in this related context, reasonable standards cannot be established concerning the content of the continuing vocational education of Amish children under parental guidance, provided always that state regulations are not inconsistent with what we have said in this opinion.

Affirmed.

☆ EQUAL PROTECTION OF THE LAWS: SCHOOL DESEGREGATION ☆

8

Brown v. Board of Education of Topeka

U.S. Supreme Court

One of the most dramatic decisions of the U.S. Supreme Court took place in May 1954 when Chief Justice Warren, speaking for a unanimous court, declared that racial segregation for the public schools was unconstitutional. Brown v. Board of Education arose from challenges by the National Association for the Advancement of Colored People (NAACP) against racially "separate but equal" school facilities in Kansas, South Carolina, Virginia, Delaware, and the District of Columbia. Southern school segregation was a bulwark of white supremacy over blacks, since most white schools were far superior in regard to buildings, curriculum, and qualifications and salaries of teachers. In 1896, the Supreme Court had upheld the "separate but equal" doctrine for railway passenger coaches in Louisiana. However, the Court was now impressed with the overwhelming evidence indicating the relationship between segregated schools and the "sense of inferiority" affecting the motivation of black children to learn. Racial segregation produced unequal education and therefore violated the provisions of the Fourteenth Amendment. The Court's decision opened an era of political controversy between the South and the Supreme Court. The court brought some of the problems to itself by the vaguely worded "with all deliberate speed" implementation of desegregation. It took nearly two decades to end southern resistance. By then the problem of school busing to eliminate racial imbalance was in full force, a difficulty that spread beyond the South to the major urban centers of the nation.

Mr. Chief Justice Warren, delivering the opinion of the Court . . . said in part:

These cases come to us from the States of Kansas, South Carolina, Virginia, and Delaware. They are premised on different facts and different local conditions, but a common legal question justifies their consideration together in this consolidated opinion.

In each of the cases, minors of the Negro race, through their legal representatives, seek the aid of the courts in obtaining admission to the public schools of their community on a non-segregated basis. In each instance, they had been denied admission to schools attended by white children under laws requiring or permitting segregation according to race. This segregation was alleged to deprive the plaintiffs of the equal protection of the laws under the Fourteenth Amendment. . . .

The plaintiffs contend that segregated public schools are not "equal" and cannot be made "equal" and that hence they are deprived of the equal protection of the laws. Because of the obvious importance of the question presented, the Court took jurisdiction. Argument was heard in the 1952 Term, and reargument was heard this Term on certain questions propounded by the Court.

Reargument was largely devoted to the circumstances surrounding the adoption of the Fourteenth Amendment in 1868. It covered exhaustively consideration of the Amendment in Congress, ratification by the states, then existing practices in racial segregation, and the views of proponents and opponents of the Amendment. This discussion and our own in-

347 U.S. 483; 74 S. Ct. 686; 98 L. Ed. 873 (1954)

vestigation convince us that, although these sources cast some light, it is not enough to resolve the problem with which we are faced. At best, they are inconclusive. The most avid proponents of the post-War Amendments undoubtedly intended them to remove all legal distinctions among "all persons born or naturalized in the United States." Their opponents, just as certainly, were antagonistic to both the letter and the spirit of the Amendments and wished them to have the most limited effect. What others in Congress and the state legislatures had in mind cannot be determined with any degree of certainty.

An additional reason for the inconclusive nature of the Amendment's history, with respect to segregated schools, is the status of public education at that time. In the South, the movement toward free common schools, supported by general taxation, had not yet taken hold. Education of white children was largely in the hands of private groups. Education of Negroes was almost nonexistent, and practically all of the race were illiterate. In fact, any education of Negroes was forbidden by law in some states. Today, in contrast, many Negroes have achieved outstanding success in the arts and sciences as well as in the business and professional world. It is true that public school education at the time of the Amendment had advanced further in the North, but the effect of the Amendment on Northern States was generally ignored in the congressional debates. Even in the North, the conditions of public education did not approximate those existing today. The curriculum was usually rudimentary; ungraded schools were common in rural areas; the school term was but three months a year in many states; and compulsory school attendance was virtually unknown. As a consequence, it is not surprising that there should be so little in the history of the Fourteenth Amendment relating to its intended effect on public education.

In the first cases in this Court construing the Fourteenth Amendment, decided shortly after its adoption, the Court interpreted it as proscribing all state-imposed discriminations against the Negro race. The doctrine of "separate but equal" did not make its appearance in this Court until 1896 in the case of Plessy v. Ferguson involving not education but transportation. American courts have since labored with the doctrine for over half a century. In this Court, there have been six cases involving the "separate but equal" doctrine in the field of public education. In Cumming v. Board of Education of Richmond County [1899] and Gong Lum v. Rice [1927] the validity of the doctrine itself was not challenged. In more recent cases, all on the graduate school level, inequality was found in that specific benefits enjoyed by white students were denied to Negro students of the same educational qualifications. State of Missouri ex rel. Gaines v. Canada [1938], Sipuel v. Board of Regents of University of Oklahoma [1948], Sweatt v. Painter [1950], McLaurin v. Oklahoma State Regents [1950]. In none of these cases was it necessary to reexamine the doctrine to grant relief to the Negro plaintiff. And in Sweatt v. Painter the Court expressly reserved decision on the question whether Plessy v. Ferguson should be held inapplicable to public education.

In the instant cases, that question is directly presented. Here, unlike Sweatt v. Painter, there are findings below that the Negro and white schools involved have been equalized, or are being equalized, with respect to buildings, curricula, qualifications and salaries of teachers, and other "tangible" factors. Our decision, therefore, cannot turn on merely a comparison of these tangible factors in the Negro and white schools involved in each of the cases. We must look instead to the effect of segregation itself on public education.

In approaching this problem, we cannot turn the clock back to 1868 when the Amendment was adopted, or even to 1896 when *Plessy* v. *Ferguson* was written. We must consider public education in the light of its full development and its present place in American life throughout the Nation. Only in this way can it be determined if segregation in public schools deprives these plaintiffs of the equal protection of the laws.

Today, education is perhaps the most important function of state and local governments. Compulsory school attendance laws and the great expenditures for education both demonstrate our recognition of the importance of education to our democratic society. It is required in the performance of our most basic public responsibilities, even service in the armed forces. It is the very foundation of good citizenship. Today it is a principal instrument in awakening the child to cultural values, in preparing him for later professional training, and in helping him to adjust normally to his environment. In these days, it is doubtful that any child may reasonably be expected to succeed in life if he is denied the opportunity of an education. Such an opportunity, where the state has undertaken to provide it, is a right which must be made available to all on equal terms.

We come then to the question presented: Does segregation of children in public schools solely on the basis of race, even though the physical facilities and other "tangible" factors may be equal, deprive the children of the minority group of equal education opportunities? We believe that it does.

In *Sweatt* v. *Painter*, in finding that a segregated law school for Negroes could not provide them equal educational opportunities, this Court relied in large part on "those qualities which are incapable of objective measurement but which make for greatness in a law school." In *McLaurin* v. *Oklahoma State Regents*, the Court, in requiring that a Negro admitted to a white graduate school be treated like all other students, again resorted to intangible consider-

ations: ". . . his ability to study, to engage in discussions and exchange views with other students, and, in general, to learn his profession." Such considerations apply with added force to children in grade and high schools. To separate them from others of similar age and qualifications solely because of their race generates a feeling of inferiority as to their status in the community that may affect their hearts and minds in a way unlikely ever to be undone. The effect of this separation on their educational opportunities was well stated by finding in the Kansas case by a court which nevertheless felt compelled to rule against the Negro plaintiffs:

"Segregation of white and colored children in public schools has a detrimental effect upon the colored children. The impact is greater when it has the sanction of the law; for the policy of separating the races is usually interpreted as denoting the inferiority of the Negro group. A sense of inferiority affects the motivation of a child to learn. Segregation with the sanction of law, therefore, has a tendency to [retard] the educational and mental development of Negro children and to deprive them of some of the benefits they would receive in a racial[ly] integrated school system." Whatever may have been the extent of psychological knowledge at the time of *Plessy* v. *Ferguson*, this finding is amply supported by modern authority.* Any language in *Plessy* v. *Ferguson* contrary to this finding is rejected.

* K. B. Clark, Effect of Prejudice and Discrimination on Personality Development (Midcentury White House Conference on Children and Youth, 1950); Witmer and Kotinsky, Personality in the Making (1952), ch VI; Deutscher and Chein, The Psychological Effects of Enforced Segregation: A Survey of Social Science Opinion, 26 J Psychol 259 (1948); Chein, What Are the Psychological Effects of Segregation Under Conditions of Equal Facilities?, 3 Int J Opinion and Attitude Res 229 (1949); Brameld, Educational Costs, in Discrimination and National Welfare (MacIver, ed. 1949), 44–48; Frazier, The Negro in the United States (1949), 674–681. And see generally Myrdal, An American Dilemma (1944).

We conclude that in the field of public education the doctrine of "separate but equal" has no place. Separate educational facilities are inherently unequal. Therefore, we hold that the plaintiffs and others similarly situated for whom the actions have been brought are, by reason of the segregation complained of, deprived of the equal protection of the laws guaranteed by the Fourteenth Amendment. This disposition makes unnecessary any discussion whether such segregation also violates the Due Process Clause of the Fourteenth Amendment.

Because these are class actions, because of the wide applicability of this decision, and because of the great variety of local conditions, the formulation of decrees in these cases presents problems of considerable complexity. On reargument, the consideration of appropriate relief was necessarily subordinated to the primary question—the constitutionality of segregation in public education. We have now announced that such segregation is a denial of the equal protection of the laws. In order that we may have the full assistance of the parties in formulating decrees, the cases will be restored to the docket, and the parties are requested to present further argument on Questions 4 and 5 previously propounded by the Court for the reargument this Term.† The Attorney General of the United States is again invited to participate. The Attorneys General of the states requiring or permitting segregation in public education will also be permitted to appear as amici curiae upon request to do so by September 15, 1954, and submission of briefs by October 1, 1954.

It is so ordered.

---

† "4. Assuming it is decided that segregation in public schools violates the Fourteenth Amendment

"(a) would a decree necessarily follow providing that, within the limits set by normal geographic school districting, Negro children should forthwith be admitted to schools of their choice, or

"(b) may this Court, in the exercise of its equity powers, permit an effective gradual adjustment to be brought about from existing segregated systems to a system not based on color distinctions?

"5. On the assumption on which questions 4(a) and (b) are based, and assuming further that this Court will exercise its equity powers to the end described in question 4(b)."

9

Swann v. Board of Education

U.S. Supreme Court

After the Brown *decision, the Supreme Court was faced with the constitutionality of busing as a remedy for desegregating the public schools. The* Swann *case developed over disputes between the federal district court and school officials to develop a plan to desegregate the Charlotte-Mecklenburg, North Carolina school system. The key questions in this case were whether the school board had acted to maintain racial segregation and whether the district court could validly order the school board to develop a busing plan to carry out*

desegregation. The U.S. Supreme Court was asked to determine the appropriateness of the busing remedy. In its decision, the Court upheld busing as a tool of school desegregation unless "the time or distance is so great as to risk either the health of the children or significantly impinge on the educational process." Many more school busing cases have come to the Court in recent years. The busing issue remains a perplexing problem for the courts at all levels.

Mr. Chief Justice Burger delivered the opinion of the Court, saying in part:

We granted certiorari in this case to review important issues as to the duties of school authorities and the scope of powers of federal courts under this Court's mandates to eliminate racially separate public schools established and maintained by state action. *Brown* v. *Board of Education* (1954) (*Brown I*).

This case and those argued with it arose in States having a long history of maintaining two sets of schools in a single school system deliberately operated to carry out a governmental policy to separate pupils in schools solely on the basis of race. That was what *Brown* v. *Board of Education* was all about. These cases present us with the problem of defining in more precise terms than heretofore the scope of the duty of school authorities and district courts in implementing *Brown I* and the mandate to eliminate dual systems and es-

tablish unitary systems at once. Meanwhile district courts and courts of appeals have struggled in hundreds of cases with a multitude and variety of problems under this Court's general directive. Understandably, in an area of evolving remedies, those courts had to improvise and experiment without detailed or specific guidelines. This Court, in *Brown I*, appropriately dealt with the large constitutional principles; other federal courts had to grapple with the flinty, intractable realities of day-to-day implementation of those constitutional commands. Their efforts, of necessity, embraced a process of "trial and error," and our effort to formulate guidelines must take into account their experience.

I

The Charlotte-Mecklenburg school system, the 43d largest in the Nation, encompasses the city of Charlotte and surrounding Mecklenburg County, North Carolina. The area is large—550 square miles—spanning roughly 22

Reprinted from *United States Supreme Court Reports, Swann, et al.* v. *Charlotte-Mecklenburg Board of Education, et al.*, 402 U.S. 1 (1971). Washington, D.C.: U.S. Government Printing Office, 1972.

miles east-west and 36 miles north-south. During the 1968-1969 school year the system served more than 84,000 pupils in 107 schools. Approximately 71% of the pupils were found to be white and 29% Negro. As of June 1969 there were approximately 24,000 Negro students in the system, of whom 21,000 attended schools within the city of Charlotte. Two-thirds of those 21,000—approximately 14,000 Negro students—attended 21 schools which were either totally Negro or more than 99% Negro.

This situation came about under a desegregation plan approved by the District Court at the commencement of the present litigation in 1965, based upon geographic zoning with a free-transfer provision. The present proceedings were initiated in September 1968 by petitioner Swann's motion for further relief based on *Green* v. *County School Board* (1968), and its companion cases. All parties now agree that in 1969 the system fell short of achieving the unitary school system that those cases require.

The District Court held numerous hearings and received voluminous evidence. In addition to finding certain actions of the school board to be discriminatory, the court also found that residential patterns in the city and county resulted in part from federal, state, and local government action other than school board decisions. School board action based on these patterns, for example, by locating schools in Negro residential areas and fixing the size of the schools to accommodate the needs of immediate neighborhoods, resulted in segregated education. These findings were subsequently accepted by the Court of Appeals.

II

Nearly 17 years ago this Court held, in explicit terms, that state-imposed segregation by race in public schools denies equal protection of the laws. At no time has the Court deviated in the slightest degree from that holding or its constitutional underpinnings. None of the parties before us challenges the Court's decision of May 17, 1954, that

in the field of public education the doctrine of 'separate but equal' has no place. Separate educational facilities are inherently unequal. Therefore, we hold that the plaintiffs and others similarly situated . . . are, by reason of the segregation complained of, deprived of the equal protection of the laws guaranteed by the Fourteenth Amendment. . . .

Because these are class actions, because of the wide applicability of this decision, and because of the great variety of local conditions, the formulation of decrees in these cases presents problems of considerable complexity. (*Brown* v. *Board of Education*).

None of the parties before us questions the Court's 1955 holding in *Brown II* . . .

Over the 16 years since *Brown II*, many difficulties were encountered in implementation of the basic constitutional requirement that the State not discriminate between public school children on the basis of their race. Nothing in our national experience prior to 1955 prepared anyone for dealing with changes and adjustments of the magnitude and complexity encountered since then. Deliberate resistance of some to the Court's mandates has impeded the good-faith efforts of others to bring school systems into compliance. The detail and nature of these dilatory tactics have been noted frequently by this Court and other courts.

By the time the Court considered *Green* v. *County School Board* in 1968, very little progress had been made in many areas where dual school systems had historically been maintained by operation of state laws. In *Green*, the Court was confronted with a record of a freedom-of-choice program that the District Court had found to operate in fact to preserve a dual system more than a decade after *Brown II*. While acknowledging that a freedom-of-choice concept could be a valid remedial measure in some circumstances, its failure to be effective in *Green* required that:

The burden on a school board today is to come forward with a plan that promises realistically to work . . . *now* . . . until it is clear that state-imposed segregation has been completely removed.

This was plain language, yet the 1969 Term of Court brought fresh evidence of the dilatory tactics of many school authorities. . . .

The problems encountered by the district courts and courts of appeals make plain that we should now try to amplify guidelines, however incomplete and imperfect, for the assistance of school authorities and courts. The failure of local authorities to meet their constitutional obligations aggravated the massive problem of converting from the state-enforced discrimination of racially separate school systems. This process has been rendered more difficult by changes since 1954 in the structure and patterns of communities, the growth of student population, movement of families, and other changes, some of which had marked impact on school planning, sometimes neutralizing or negating remedial action before it was fully implemented. Rural areas accustomed for half a century to the consolidated school systems implemented by bus transportation could make adjustments more readily than metropolitan areas with dense and shifting population, numerous schools, congested and complex traffic patterns. . . .

V

The central issue in this case is that of student assignment, and there are essentially four problem areas:

1. to what extent racial balance or racial quotas may be used as an implement in a remedial order to correct a previously segregated system;

2. whether every all-Negro and all-white school must be eliminated as an indispensable part of a remedial process of desegregation;
3. what the limits are, if any, on the rearrangement of school districts and attendance zones, as a remedial measure; and
4. what the limits are, if any, on the use of transportation facilities to correct state-enforced racial school segregation.

1. Racial balances or racial quotas.   The constant theme and thrust of every holding from *Brown I* to date is that state-enforced separation of races in public schools is discrimination that violates the Equal Protection Clause. The remedy commanded was to dismantle dual school systems.

We are concerned in these cases with the elimination of the discrimination inherent in the dual school systems, not with myriad factors of human existence, which can cause discrimination in a multitude of ways on racial, religious, or ethnic grounds. The target of the cases from *Brown I* to the present was the dual school system. . . .

Our objective in dealing with the issues presented by these cases is to see that school authorities exclude no pupil of a racial minority from any school, directly or indirectly, on account of race; it does not and cannot embrace all the problems of racial prejudice, even when those problems contribute to disproportionate racial concentrations in some schools.

In this case it is urged that the District Court has imposed a racial balance requirement of 71%-29% on individual schools. The fact that no such objective was actually achieved—and would appear to be impossible —tends to blunt that claim, yet in the opinion and order of the District Court of December 1, 1969, we find that court directing

that efforts should be made to reach a 71–29 ratio in the various schools so that there will be no basis for contending that one school is racially different from the others . . ., [t]hat no school [should] be operated with an all-black or predominantly black student body, [and] [t]hat pupils of all grades [should] be assigned in such a way that as nearly as practicable the various schools at various grade levels have about the same proportion of black and white students.

The District Judge went on to acknowledge that variation "from that norm may be unavoidable." This contains intimations that the "norm" is a fixed mathematical racial balance reflecting the pupil constituency of the system. If we were to read the holding of the District Court to require, as a matter of substantive constitutional right, any particular degree of racial balance or mixing, that approach would be disapproved and we would be obliged to reverse. The constitutional command to desegregate schools does not mean that every school in every community must always reflect the racial composition of the school systems as a whole.

As the voluminous record in this case shows, the predicate for the District Court's use of the 71%-29% ratio was twofold: first, its express finding, approved by the Court of Appeals and not challenged here, that a dual school system had been maintained by the school authorities at least until 1969; second, its finding, also approved by the Court of Appeals, that the school board had totally defaulted in its acknowledged duty to come forward with an acceptable plan of its own, notwithstanding the patient efforts of the District Judge who, on at least three occasions, urged the board to submit plans. As the statement of facts shows, these findings are abundantly supported by the record. It was because of this total failure of the school board that the District Court was obliged to turn to other qualified sources, and Dr. Finger was designated to assist the District Court to do what the board should have done.

We see therefore that the use made of mathematical ratios was no more than a starting point in the process of shaping a remedy, rather than an inflexible requirement. From that starting point the District Court proceeded to frame a decree that was within its discretionary powers, as an equitable remedy for the particular circumstances. . . .

2. One-race schools. The record in this case reveals the familiar phenomenon that in metropolitan areas minority groups are often found concentrated in one part of the city. In some circumstances certain schools may remain all or largely of one race until new schools can be provided or neighborhood patterns change. Schools all or predominantly of one race in a district of mixed population will require close scrutiny to determine that school assignments are not part of state-enforced segregation.

In light of the above, it should be clear that the existence of some small number of one-race, or virtually one-race, schools within a district is not in and of itself the mark of a system that still practices segregation by law. The district judge or school authorities should make every effort to achieve the greatest possible degree of actual desegregation and will thus necessarily be concerned with the elimination of one-race schools. No *per se* rule can adequately embrace all the difficulties of reconciling the competing interests involved; but in a system with a history of segregation the need for remedial criteria of sufficient specificity to assure a school authority's compliance with its constitutional duty warrants a presumption against schools that are substantially disproportionate in their racial composition. Where the school authority's proposed plan for conversion from a dual to a unitary system contemplates the continued existence of some schools that are all or predominately of one race, they have the burden of showing that such school assignments are genuinely nondiscriminatory. The court should scrutinize such schools, and the burden upon the school authorities will be to satisfy the court that their racial composition is not the result of present or past discriminatory action on their part.

An optional majority-to-minority transfer provision has long been recognized as a useful part of every desegregation plan. Provision for optional transfer of those in the majority racial group of a particular school to other schools where they will be in the minority is an indispensable remedy for those students willing to transfer to other schools in order to lessen the impact on them of the state-imposed stigma of segregation. In order to be effective, such a transfer arrangement must grant the transferring student free transportation and space must be made available in the school to which he desires to move. . . . The court orders in this and the companion *Davis* case now provide such an option.

3. Remedial altering of attendance zones. The maps submitted in these cases graphically demonstrate that one of the principal tools employed by school planners and by courts to break up the dual school system has been a frank—and sometimes drastic—gerrymandering of school districts and attendance zones. An additional step was pairing, "clustering," or "grouping" of schools with attendance assignments made deliberately to accomplish the transfer of Negro students out of formerly segregated Negro schools and transfer of white students to formerly all-Negro schools. More often than not, these zones are neither compact nor contiguous; indeed they may be on opposite ends of the city. As an interim corrective measure, this cannot be said to be beyond the broad remedial powers of a court. . . .

No fixed or even substantially fixed guidelines can be established as to how far a court can go, but it must be recognized that there are limits. The objective is to dismantle the dual school system. "Racially neutral" assignment plans proposed by school authorities to a district court may be inadequate; such plans may fail to counteract the continuing effects of past school segregation resulting from discrimina-

tory location of school sites or distortion of school size in order to achieve or maintain an artificial racial separation. When school authorities present a district court with a "loaded game board," affirmative action in the form of remedial altering of attendance zones is proper to achieve truly nondiscriminatory assignments. In short, an assignment plan is not acceptable simply because it appears to be neutral. . . .

We hold that the pairing and grouping of noncontiguous school zones is a permissible tool and such action is to be considered in light of the objectives sought. . . .

4. Transportation of students. The scope of permissible transportation of students as an implement of a remedial decree has never been defined by this Court and by the very nature of the problem it cannot be defined with precision. No rigid guidelines as to student transportation can be given for application to the infinite variety of problems presented in thousands of situations. Bus transportation has been an integral part of the public education system for years, and was perhaps the single most important factor in the transition from the one-room schoolhouse to the consolidated school. Eighteen million of the Nation's public school children, approximately 39%, were transported to their schools by bus in 1969-1970 in all parts of the country.

The importance of bus transportation as a normal and accepted tool of educational policy is readily discernible in this and the companion case. The Charlotte school authorities did not purport to assign students on the basis of geographically drawn zones until 1965 and then they allowed almost unlimited transfer privileges. The District Court's conclusion that assignment of children to the school nearest their home serving their grade would not produce an effective dismantling of the dual system is supported by the record.

Thus the remedial techniques used in the

District Court's order were within that court's power to provide equitable relief; implementation of the decree is well within the capacity of the school authority.

The decree provided that the buses used to implement the plan would operate on direct routes. Students would be picked up at schools near their homes and transported to the schools they were to attend. The trips for elementary school pupils average about seven miles and the District Court found that they would take "not over 35 minutes at the most." This system compares favorably with the transportation plan previously operated in Charlotte under which each day 23,600 students on all grade levels were transported an average of 15 miles one way for an average trip requiring over an hour. In these circumstances, we find no basis for holding that the local school authorities may not be required to employ bus transportation as one tool of school desegregation. Desegregation plans cannot be limited to the walk-in school.

An objection to transportation of students may have validity when the time or distance of travel is so great as to either risk the health of the children or significantly impinge on the educational process. . . .

VI

The Court of Appeals, searching for a term to define the equitable remedial power of the district courts, used the term "reasonableness." In *Green, supra,* this Court used the term "feasible" and by implication, "workable," "effective," and "realistic" in the mandate to develop "a plan that promises realistically to work, and . . . to work *now.*" On the facts of this case, we are unable to conclude that the order of the District Court is not reasonable, feasible and workable. However, in seeking to define the scope of remedial power or the limits on remedial power of courts in an area as sensitive as we deal with here, words are poor instruments to convey the sense of basic fairness inherent in equity. Substance, not semantics, must govern, and we have sought to suggest the nature of limitations without frustrating the appropriate scope of equity.

At some point, these school authorities and others like them should have achieved full compliance with this Court's decision in *Brown I.* The systems would then be "unitary" in the sense required by our decisions in *Green* and *Alexander.*

It does not follow that the communities served by such systems will remain demographically stable, for in a growing, mobile society, few will do so. Neither school authorities nor district courts are constitutionally required to make year-by-year adjustments of the racial composition of student bodies once the affirmative duty to desegregate has been accomplished and racial discrimination through official action is eliminated from the system. This does not mean that federal courts are without power to deal with future problems; but in the absence of a showing that either the school authorities or some other agency of the State has deliberately attempted to fix or alter demographic patterns to affect the racial composition of the schools, further intervention by a district court should not be necessary.

For the reasons herein set forth, the judgment of the Court of Appeals is affirmed as to those parts in which it affirmed the judgment of the District Court. The order of the District Court, dated August 7, 1970, is also affirmed.

It is so ordered.

10

United Steelworkers of America v. Weber

U.S. Supreme Court

In 1978, in the Bakke case, the Supreme Court invalidated a quota system for minorities in educational institutions not having an historical pattern of discrimination. The Bakke decision invalidated an affirmative action-minority admission program at the University of California-Davis medical school. However, the Court indicated that special admissions programs for minorities could use race as a consideration for selecting applicants. It also hinted that quotas may be acceptable if such university programs showed evidence of an historic pattern of discrimination.

Brian Weber, an employee of Kaiser Aluminum's Gramercy, Louisiana plant, filed suit in 1974, charging that the company's affirmative action-minority jobs programs, as included in a negotiated union contract, violated Title VII of the 1964 Civil Rights Act, because such provisions reserved special job opportunities for blacks. Both the district court and the Fifth Circuit Court of Appeals upheld Weber's claim. Both courts noted that the company had never been found guilty of discriminating against black employees. Under these conditions, no person could be discriminated against under Title VII, including whites. In 1979, the U.S. Supreme Court overruled the lower courts. In a 5–2 decision, the Court ruled that voluntary affirmative action programs, even those with numerical quotas, do not automatically violate Title VII of the 1964 Civil Rights Act that bars discrimination on the basis of race. The Court now claimed that race-conscious affirmative action quotas are not inconsistent with the purpose of the Civil Rights law, which was established to improve the economic conditions of blacks. Both the Bakke and Weber cases raise the conflicting interests of improving economic conditions for blacks and the concern for the performance merits of white workers. Which interest has the better argument?

Mr. Justice Brennan delivered the opinion of the Court, saying in part:

We emphasize at the outset the narrowness of our inquiry. Since the Kaiser-USWA plan does not involve state action, this case does not present an alleged violation of the Equal Protection Clause of the Constitution. Further, since the Kaiser-USWA plan was adopted voluntarily, we are not concerned with what Title VII requires or with what a court might order to remedy a past proven violation of the act. The only question before us is the narrow statutory issue of whether Title VII forbids private

The U.S. Supreme Court decision was issued on June 27, 1979.

employers and unions from voluntarily agreeing upon bona fide affirmative action plans that accord racial preferences in the manner and for the purpose provided in the Kaiser-USWA plan. That question was expressly left open in McDonald v. Santa Fe Trail Trans. Co., which held, in a case not involving affirmative action, that Title VII protects whites as well as blacks from certain forms of racial discrimination.

Respondent argues that Congress intended in Title VII to prohibit all race-conscious affirmative action plans. Respondent's argument rests upon a literal interpretation of Sec. 703 (a) and (d) of the Act. Those sections make it unlawful to "discriminate . . . Because of . . . race" in hiring and in the selection of apprentices for training programs. Since, the argument runs, McDonald v. Santa Fe Trans. Co., supra, settled that Title VII forbids discrimination against whites as well as blacks, and since the Kaiser-USWA affirmative action plan operates to discriminate against white employees solely because they are white, it follows that the Kaiser-USWA plan violates Title VII.

AFFIRMATIVE ACTION PLAN

Respondent's argument is not without force. But it overlooks the significance of the fact that the Kaiser-USWA plan is an affirmative action plan voluntarily adopted by private parties to eliminate traditional patterns of racial segregation. In this context respondent's reliance upon a literal construction of Sec. 703 (a) and (d) and upon McDonald is misplaced. The prohibition against racial discrimination in Sec. 703 (a) and (d) of Title VII must therefore be read against the background of the legislative history of Title VII and the historical context from which the Act arose. Examination of those sources makes clear that an interpretation of the sections that forbade all race-conscious affirmative action would "bring about an end completely at variance with the purpose of the statute" and must be rejected.

Congress' primary concern in enacting the prohibition against racial discrimination in Title VII of the Civil Rights Act of 1964 was with "the plight of the Negro in our economy." (remarks of Sen. Humphrey). Before 1964, blacks were largely relegated to "unskilled and semiskilled jobs." Because of automation the number of such jobs was rapidly decreasing. As a consequence "the relative position of the Negro worker (was) steadily worsening. In 1947 the nonwhite unemployment rate was only 64 percent higher than the white rate; in 1962 it was 124 percent higher." Congress considered this a serious social problem.

Congress feared that the goals of the Civil Rights Act—the integration of blacks into the mainstream of American society—could not be achieved unless this trend were reversed. And Congress recognized that that would not be possible unless blacks were able to secure jobs "which have a future."

TITLE VII PROHIBITION

Accordingly, it was clear to Congress that "the crux of the problem (was) to open employment opportunities for Negroes in occupations which have been traditionally closed to them," and it was to this problem that Title VII's prohibition against racial discrimination in employment was primarily addressed.

It plainly appears from the House Report accompanying the Civil Rights Act that Congress did not intend wholly to prohibit private and voluntary affirmative action efforts as one method of solving this problem.

Given this legislative history, we cannot agree with respondent that Congress intended to prohibit the private sector from taking effective steps to accomplish the goal that Congress designed Title VII to achieve. The very statutory words intended as a spur or catalyst to cause "employers and unions to self-examine and to self-evaluate their employment practices and to endeavor to eliminate, so far as possible, the last vestiges of an unfortunate and ignominious page in this country's history," Albemarle v. Moody, cannot be interpreted as an absolute prohibition against all private, voluntary, race-conscious affirmative action efforts to hasten the elimination of such vestiges. It would be ironic indeed if a law triggered by a Nation's concern over centuries of racial injustice and intended to improve the lot of those who had "been excluded from the American dream for so long," constituted the first legislative prohibition of all voluntary, private, race-conscious efforts to abolish traditional patterns of racial segregation and hierarchy.

HISTORY OF SECTION 703

Our conclusion is further reinforced by examination of the language and legislative history of Section 703 (j) of Title VII. Opponents of Title VII raised two related arguments against the bill. First, they argued that the Act would be interpreted to require employers with racially imbalanced work forces to grant preferential treatment to racial minorities in order to integrate. Second, they argued that employers with racially imbalanced work forces would grant preferential treatment to racial minorities, even if not required to do so by the Act. Had Congress meant to prohibit all race-conscious affirmative action, as respondent urges, it easily could have answered both objections by providing that Title VII would not require or permit racially preferential integration efforts. But Congress did not choose such a course. Rather Congress added Section 703 (j) which addresses only the first objection. The section provides that nothing contained in Title VII "shall be interpreted to require any employer . . . to grant preferential treatment . . . to any group because of the race . . . of such . . . group on account of" a de facto racial imbalance in the employer's work force. The section does not state that "nothing in Title VII shall be interpreted to permit" voluntary affirmative efforts to correct racial imbalances. The natural inference is that Congress chose not to forbid all voluntary race-conscious affirmative action.

The reasons for this choice are evident from the legislative record. Title VII could not have been enacted into law without substantial support from legislators in both Houses who traditionally resisted Federal regulation of private business. Those legislators demanded as a price for their support that "management prerogatives and union freedoms . . . be left undisturbed to the greatest extent possible." Section 703 (j) was proposed by Senator Dirksen to allay any fears that the Act might be interpreted in such a way as to upset this compromise. In view of this legislative history and in view of Congress' desire to avoid undue Federal regulation to private businesses, use of the word "require" rather than the phrase "require or permit" in Section 703 (j) fortifies the conclusion that Congress did not intend to limit traditional business freedom to such a degree as to prohibit all voluntary, race-conscious affirmative action.

LIMITS OF PROHIBITION

We therefore hold that Title VII's prohibition in Sec. 703 (a) and (d) against racial discrimination does not condemn all private, voluntary, race-conscious affirmative action plans.

We need not today define in detail the line of demarcation between permissible and impermissible affirmative action plans. It suffices to hold that the challenged Kaiser-USWA affirmative action plan falls on the permissible side of the line. The purposes of the plan mirror those of the statute. Both were designed to break down old patterns of racial segregation and hierarchy. Both were structured to "open employment opportunities for Negroes in occupations which have been traditionally closed to them."

At the same time the plan does not unnecessarily trammel the interests of the white employees. The plan does not require the discharge of white workers and their replacement with new black hires. Nor does the plan create an absolute bar to the advancement of white employees; half of those trained in the program will be white. Moreover, the plan is a temporary measure; it is not intended to maintain racial balance, but simply to eliminate a manifest racial imbalance. Preferential selection of craft trainess at the Gramercy plant will end as soon as the percentage of black skilled craft workers in the Gramercy plant approximates the percentage of blacks in the local labor force.

We conclude, therefore, that the adoption of the Kaiser-USWA plan for the Gramercy plant falls within the area of discretion left by Title VII to the private sector voluntarily to adopt affirmative action plans designed to eliminate conspicuous racial imbalance in traditionally segregated job categories. Accordingly, the judgment of the Court of Appeals for the Fifth Circuit is reversed.

Mr. Justice Powell and Mr. Justice Stevens took no part in the consideration or decision of this case.

Mr. Justice Blackmun, concurring, said in part:

Respondents' reading of Title VII, endorsed by the Court of Appeals, places voluntary compliance with Title VII in profound jeopardy. The only way for the employer and the union to keep their footing on the "tightrope" it creates would be to eschew all forms of voluntary affirmative action. Even a whisper of emphasis on minority recruiting would be forbidden. Because Congress intended to encourage private efforts to come into compliance with Title VII, Judge Wisdom concluded that employers and unions who had committed "arguable violations" of Title VII should be free to take reasonable responses without fear of liability to whites.

The "arguable violation" theory has a number of advantages. It responds to a practical problem in the administration of Title VII not anticipated by Congress. It draws predictability from the outline of present law, and closely effectuates the purpose of the Act. Because I agree that it is the soundest way to approach this case, my preference would be to resolve this litigation by applying it and holding that Kaiser's craft training program meets the requirement that voluntary affirmative action be a reasonable response to an "arguable violation" of Title VII.

The Court, however, declines to consider the narrow "arguable violation" approach and adheres instead to an interpretation of Title VII that permits affirmative action by an employer whenever the job category in question is "traditionally segregated."

"Traditionally segregated job categories," where they exist, sweep far more broadly than the class of "arguable violations" of Title VII. The Court's expansive approach is somewhat disturbing for me because, as Mr. Justice Rehnquist points out, the Congress that passed Title VII probably thought it was adopting a principle of nondiscrimination that would apply to blacks and whites alike.

A closer look at the problem, however, reveals that in each of the principal ways in which the Court's "traditionally segregated job categories" approach expands on the "arguable violation" theory, still other considerations point in favor of the broad standard adopted by the Court, and make it possible for me to conclude that the Court's reading of the statute is an acceptable one.

Mr. Chief Justice Burger, dissenting, said in part:

The Court reaches a result I would be inclined to vote for were I a Member of Congress considering a proposed amendment of Title VII. I cannot join the Court's judgment, however, because it is contrary to the explicit language of the statute and arrived at by means wholly incompatible with long-established principles of separation of powers. Under the guise of statutory "construction," the Court effectively rewrites Title VII to achieve what it regards as a desirable result.

Often we have difficulty interpreting statutes either because of imprecise drafting or because legislative compromises have produced genuine ambiguities. But here there is no lack of clarity, no ambiguity. The quota embodied in the collective-bargaining agreement between Kaiser and the Steelworkers unquestionably discriminates on the basis of race against individual employees seeking admission to on-the-job training programs. And, under the plain language of Section 703 (d), that is "an unlawful employment practice."

Oddly, the Court seizes upon the very clarity of the statute almost as a justification for evading the unavoidable impact of its language. The Court blandly tells us that Congress could not really have meant what it said, for a "literal construction" would defeat the "purpose" of the statute—at least the Congressional "purpose" as five Justices divine it today.

Arguably, Congress may not have gone far enough in correcting the effects of past discrimination when it enacted Title VII. But that statute was conceived and enacted to make discrimination against any individual illegal, and I fail to see how "voluntary compliance" with the no-discrimination principle that is the heart and soul of Title VII as currently written will be achieved by permitting employers to discriminate against some individuals to give preferential treatment to others.

It is often observed that hard cases make bad law. I suspect there is some truth to that adage, for the "hard" cases always tempt judges to exceed the limits of their authority, as the Court does today by totally rewriting a crucial part of Title VII to reach a desirable result.

Mr. Justice Rehnquist, with whom the Chief Justice joins, dissenting, said in part:

We have never waivered in our understanding that Title VII "prohibits all racial discrimination in employment, without exception for any particular employees."

Today, however, the Court behaves as if it had been handed a note indicating that Title VII would lead to a result unacceptable to the Court if interpreted here as it was in our prior decisions. Accordingly, without even a break in syntax, the Court rejects "a literal construction of Sec. 703 (a)" in favor of newly discovered "legislative history," which leads it to a conclusion directly contrary to that compelled by the "uncontradicted legislative history" unearthed in McDonald and our other prior decisions.

Thus, by a tour de force reminiscent not of jurists such as Hale, Holmes, and Hughes, but of escape artists such as Houdini, the Court eludes clear statutory language, "uncontradicted" legislative history, and uniform precedent in concluding that employers are, after all, permitted to consider race in making employment decisions.

Were Congress to act today specifically to prohibit the type of racial discrimination suffered by Weber, it would be hard pressed to draft language better tailored to the task than that found in Sec. 703 (d) of Title VII:

"It shall be an unlawful employment practice for any employers, labor organization, or joint labor-management committee controlling apprenticeship or other training or retraining, including on-the-job training programs to discriminate against any individual because of his race, color, religion, sex, or national origin in admission to, or employment in, any program established to provide apprenticeship or other training." 43 U.S.C. Sec. 2000e-2 (d). Equally suited to the task would be Sec. 703 (a) (2), which makes it unlawful for an employer to classify his employees "in any way which would deprive or tend to deprive any individual of employment opportunities or otherwise adversely affect his status as an employee, because of such individual's race, color, religion, sex, or national origin."

Entirely consistent with these two express prohibitions is the language of Sec. 703 (j) of Title VII, which provides that the Act is not to be interpreted "to require any employer . . . to grant preferential treatment to any individual or to any group because of the race . . . of such individual or group" to correct a racial imbalance in the employer's work force. Seizing on the word "require," the Court infers that Congress must have intended to "permit" this type of racial discrimination. Not only is this read-

ing of Sec. 703 (j) outlandish in the light of the flat prohibitions of Sec. 703 (a) and (d), but, it is totally belied by the Act's legislative history.

Quite simply, Kaiser's racially discriminatory admission quota is flatly prohibited by the plain language of Title VII.

11

Miranda v. Arizona

U.S. Supreme Court

On March 13, 1963, Ernesto Miranda was arrested by the Phoenix police, brought to a local police station, and placed in a lineup for identification by a woman who had recently been robbed. The woman selected Miranda. An 18-year-old girl who had been recently raped also identified Miranda as her assailant. Miranda was then taken to a room for questioning. His interrogators did not state that he had a right to an attorney. There was some uncertainty as to whether Miranda was told that any of his statements would be used against him in court. Miranda eventually confessed to both crimes. At the rape trial, Miranda's lawyer objected to the prosecutor's introduction of Miranda's confession as valid evidence, stating that the accused was entitled to a lawyer at the time of his arrest. The trial judge, however, ad-mitted the confession into evidence over the lawyer's objections. The jury found Miranda guilty of both the robbery and the rape charges at separate trials. Miranda was sentenced to prison for 40–45 years for both convictions. The appellate courts of Arizona sustained the convictions. The U.S. Supreme Court reversed Miranda's convictions by a narrow 5–4 majority. The Court's decision also provided concrete guidelines for law enforcement agencies, police, and courts to follow, which are presented in Chief Justice Warren's majority opinion. These so-called Miranda rules became a source of major controversy in criminal justice policy. Justice Harlan's dissent, also excerpted below, indicated the deep concerns for effective police investigations as against protections for the individuals accused of crimes.

Mr. Chief Justice Warren delivered the opinion of the Court.

The cases before us raise questions which go to the roots of our concepts of American criminal jurisprudence: the restraints society must observe consistent with the Federal Constitution in prosecuting individuals for crime. More specifically, we deal with the admissibility of statements obtained from an individual who is subjected to custodial police interrogation and the necessity for procedures which assure that the individual is accorded his privilege under the Fifth Amendment to the Constitution not to be compelled to incriminate himself.

. . . We start here, as we did in *Escobedo*, with the premise that our holding is not an in-novation in our jurisprudence, but is an application of principles long recognized and applied in other settings. We have undertaken a thorough re-examination of the *Escobedo* decision and the principles it announced, and we reaffirm it. That case was but an explication of basic rights that are enshrined in our Constitution—that "No person . . . shall be compelled in any criminal case to be a witness against himself," and that "the accused shall . . . have the Assistance of Counsel"—rights which were put in jeopardy in that case through official overbearing. These precious rights were fixed in our Constitution only after centuries of persecution and struggle. And in the words of Chief Justice Marshall, they were secured "for ages to come, and . . . designed to approach immortality as nearly as human institutions can approach it."

384 U.S. 436, 86 S.Ct. 1602, 16 L.Ed.2d 694 (1966)

I.

. . . The constitutional issue we decide in each of these cases is the admissibility of statements obtained from a defendant questioned while in custody or otherwise deprived of his freedom of action in any significant way. In each, the defendant was questioned by police officers, detectives, or a prosecuting attorney in a room in which he was cut off from the outside world. In none of these cases was the defendant given a full and effective warning of his rights at the outset of the interrogation process. In all the cases, the questioning elicited oral admissions, and in three of them, signed statements as well which were admitted at their trials. They all thus share salient features—incommunicado interrogation of individuals in a police-dominated atmosphere, resulting in self-incriminating statements without full warnings of constitutional rights.

An understanding of the nature and setting of this in-custody interrogation is essential to our decisions today. The difficulty in depicting what transpires at such interrogations stems from the fact that in this country they have largely taken place incommunicado. From extensive factual studies undertaken in the early 1930's including the famous Wickersham Report to Congress by a Presidential Commission, it is clear that police violence and the "third degree" flourished at that time. In a series of cases decided by this Court long after these studies, the police resorted to physical brutality—beating, hanging, whipping—and to sustained and protracted questioning incommunicado in order to extort confessions. The Commission on Civil Rights in 1961 found much evidence to indicate that "some policemen still resort to physical force to obtain confessions." The use of physical brutality and violence is not, unfortunately, relegated to the past or to any part of the country. . . .

. . . the modern practice of in-custody interrogation is psychologically rather than physi-

cally oriented. . . . Interrogation still takes place in privacy. Privacy results in secrecy and this in turn results in a gap in our knowledge as to what in fact goes on in the interrogation rooms. A valuable source of information about present police practices, however, may be found in various police manuals and texts which document procedures employed with success in the past, and which recommend various other effective tactics.

[A review of manuals and texts follows.]

. . . From these representative samples of interrogation techniques, the setting prescribed by the manuals and observed in practice becomes, clear. In essence, it is this: To be alone with the subject is essential to prevent distraction and to deprive him of any outside support. The aura of confidence in his guilt undermines his will to resist. He merely confirms the preconceived story the police seek to have him describe. Patience and persistence, at times relentless questioning, are employed. To obtain a confession, the interrogator must "patiently maneuver himself or his quarry into a position from which the desired objective may be attained." When normal procedures fail to produce the needed result, the police may resort to deceptive stratagems such as giving false legal advice. It is important to keep the subject off balance, for example, by trading on his insecurity about himself or his surroundings. The police then persuade, trick, or cajole him out of exercising his constitutional rights.

Even without employing brutality, the "third degree" or the specific stratagems described above, the very fact of custodial interrogation exacts a heavy toll on individual liberty and trades on the weakness of individuals. . . .

In these cases, we might not find the defendants' statements to have been involuntary in traditional terms. Our concern for adequate safeguards to protect precious Fifth Amendment rights is, of course, not lessened in the slightest. In each of the cases, the defendant was thrust into an unfamiliar atmosphere and run through menacing police interrogation procedures. The potentiality for compulsion is forcefully apparent, for example, in *Miranda*, where the indigent Mexican defendant was a seriously disturbed individual with pronounced sexual fantasies, and in *Stewart*, in which the defendant was an indigent Los Angeles Negro who had dropped out of school in the sixth grade. To be sure, the records do not evince overt physical coercion or patent psychological ploys. The fact remains that in none of these cases did the officers undertake to afford appropriate safeguards at the outset of the interrogation to insure that the statements were truly the product of free choice.

It is obvious that such an interrogation environment is created for no purpose other than to subjugate the individual to the will of his examiner. This atmosphere carries its own badge of intimidation. To be sure, this is not physical intimidation, but it is equally destructive of human dignity. The current practice of incommunicado interrogation is at odds with one of our Nation's most cherished principles —that the individual may not be compelled to incriminate himself. Unless adequate protective devices are employed to dispel the compulsion inherent in custodial surroundings, no statement obtained from the defendant can truly be the product of his free choice....

III.

Today, . . . there can be no doubt that the Fifth Amendment privilege is available outside of criminal court proceedings and serves to protect persons in all settings in which their freedom of action is curtailed in any significant way from being compelled to incriminate themselves. We have concluded that without proper safeguards the process of in-custody interrogation of persons suspected or accused of crime contains inherently compelling pressures which work to undermine the individual's will to resist and to compel him to speak where he would not otherwise do so freely. In order to combat these pressures and to permit a full opportunity to exercise the privilege against self-incrimination, the accused must be adequately and effectively apprised of his rights and the exercise of those rights must be fully honored.

. . . At the outset, if a person in custody is to be subjected to interrogation, he must first be informed in clear and unequivocal terms that he has the right to remain silent. For those unaware of the privilege, the warning is needed simply to make them aware of it—the threshold requirement for an intelligent decision as to its exercise. More important, such a warning is an absolute prerequisite in overcoming the inherent pressures of the interrogation atmosphere. It is not just the subnormal or woefully ignorant who succumb to an interrogator's imprecations, whether implied or expressly stated, that the interrogation will continue until a confession is obtained or that silence in the face of accusation is itself damning and will bode ill when presented to a jury. Further, the warning will show the individual that his interrogators are prepared to recognize his privilege should he choose to exercise it.

. . . The warning of the right to remain silent must be accompanied by the explanation that anything said can and will be used against the individual in court. This warning is needed in order to make him aware not only of the privilege, but also of the consequences of forgoing it. It is only through an awareness of these consequences that there can be any assurance of real understanding and intelligent exercise of the privilege. Moreover, this warning may serve to make the individual more acutely aware that he is faced with a phase of the adversary system—that he is not in the presence of persons acting solely in his interest....

. . . we hold that an individual held for interrogation must be clearly informed that he has the right to consult with a lawyer and to have the lawyer with him during interrogation under the system for protecting the privilege we delineate today. As with the warnings of the right to remain silent and that anything stated can be used in evidence against him, this warning is an absolute prerequisite to interrogation. No amount of circumstantial evidence that the person may have been aware of this right will suffice to stand in its stead. Only through such a warning is there ascertainable assurance that the accused was aware of this right.

If an individual indicates that he wishes the assistance of counsel before any interrogation occurs, the authorities cannot rationally ignore or deny his request on the basis that the individual does not have or cannot afford a retained attorney. The financial ability of the individual has no relationship to the scope of the rights involved here. The privilege against self-incrimination secured by the Constitution applies to all individuals. The need for counsel in order to protect the privilege exists for the indigent as well as the affluent. In fact, were we to limit these constitutional rights to those who can retain an attorney, our decisions today would be of little significance. The cases before us as well as the vast majority of confession cases with which we have dealt in the past involve those unable to retain counsel. While authorities are not required to relieve the accused of his poverty, they have the obligation not to take advantage of indigence in the administration of justice. . . .

In order fully to apprise a person interrogated of the extent of his rights under this system then, it is necessary to warn him not only that he has the right to consult with an attorney, but also that if he is indigent a lawyer will be appointed to represent him. Without this additional warning, the admonition of the right to consult with counsel would often be understood as meaning only that he can consult with a lawyer if he has one or has the funds to obtain one. The warning of a right to counsel would be hollow if not couched in terms that would convey to the indigent—the person most often subjected to interrogation—the knowledge that he too has a right to have counsel present. As with the warnings of the right to remain silent and of the general right to counsel, only by effective and express explanation to the indigent of this right can there be assurance that he was truly in a position to exercise it.

Once warnings have been given, the subsequent procedure is clear. If the individual indicates in any manner, at any time prior to or during questioning, that he wishes to remain silent, the interrogation must cease. At this point he has shown that he intends to exercise his Fifth Amendment privilege; any statement taken after the person invokes his privilege cannot be other than the product of compulsion, subtle or otherwise. Without the right to cut off questioning, the setting of in-custody interrogation operates on the individual to overcome free choice in producing a statement after the privilege has been once invoked. If the individual states that he wants an attorney, the interrogation must cease until an attorney is present. At that time, the individual must have an opportunity to confer with the attorney and to have him present during any subsequent questioning. If the individual cannot obtain an attorney and he indicates that he wants one before speaking to police, they must respect his decision to remain silent. . . .

Our decision is not intended to hamper the traditional function of police officers in investigating crime. When an individual is in custody on probable cause, the police may, of course, seek out evidence in the field to be used at trial against him. Such investigation may include inquiry of persons not under restraint. General on-the-scene questioning as to facts surrounding a crime or other general questioning of citizens in the fact-finding process is not affected by our holding. It is an act of responsible citizenship for individuals to give whatever information they may have to aid in law enforcement. In such situations the compelling atmosphere inherent in the process of in-custody interrogation is not necessarily present.

In dealing with statements obtained through interrogation, we do not purport to find all confessions inadmissible. Confessions remain a proper element in law enforcement. Any statement given freely and voluntarily without any compelling influences is, of course, admissible in evidence. The fundamental import of the privilege while an individual is in custody is not whether he is allowed to talk to the police without the benefit of warnings and counsel, but whether he can be interrogated. There is no requirement that police stop a person who enters a police station and states that he wishes to confess to a crime, or a person who calls the police to offer a confession or any other statement he desires to make. Volunteered statements of any kind are not barred by the Fifth Amendment and their admissibility is not affected by our holding today.

To summarize, we hold that when an individual is taken into custody or otherwise deprived of his freedom by the authorities in any significant way and is subjected to questioning, the privilege against self-incrimination is jeopardized. Procedural safeguards must be employed to protect the privilege, and unless other fully effective means are adopted to notify the person of his right of silence and to assure that the exercise of the right will be scrupulously honored, the following measures are required. He must be warned prior to any questioning that he has the right to remain silent, that anything he says can be used against him in a court of law, that he has the right to the presence of an attorney, and that if he cannot afford an attorney one will be appointed for him prior to any questioning if he so desires. Opportunity to exercise these rights must be afforded to him throughout the in-

terrogation after such warnings have been given, and such opportunity afforded him, the individual may knowingly and intelligently waive these rights and agree to answer questions or make a statement. But unless and until such warnings and waiver are demonstrated by the prosecution at trial, no evidence obtained as a result of interrogation can be used against him.

IV.

. . . In announcing these principles, we are not unmindful of the burdens which law enforcement officials must bear, often under trying circumstances. We also fully recognize the obligation of all citizens to aid in enforcing the criminal laws. This Court, while protecting individual rights, has always given ample latitude to law enforcement agencies in the legitimate exercise of their duties. The limits we have placed on the interrogation process should not constitute an undue interference with a proper system of law enforcement. As we have noted, our decision does not in any way preclude police from carrying out their traditional investigatory functions. Although confessions may play an important role in some convictions, the cases before us present graphic examples of the overstatement of the "need" for confessions. In each case authorities conducted interrogations ranging up to five days in duration despite the presence, through standard investigating practices, of considerable evidence against each defendant. . . .

Mr. Justice Clark, dissenting and concurring. . . .

Mr. Justice Harlan, whom Mr. Justice Stewart and Mr. Justice White join, dissenting.

. . . The new rules are not designed to guard against police brutality or other unmistakably banned forms of coercion. Those who use third-degree tactics and deny them in court are equally able and destined to lie as skillfully about warnings and waivers. Rather, the thrust of the new rules is to negate all pressures, to reinforce the nervous or ignorant suspect, and ultimately to discourage any confession at all. . . .

To incorporate this notion into the Constitution requires a strained reading of history and precedent and a disregard of the very pragmatic concerns that alone may on occasion justify such strains. I believe that reasoned examination will show that the Due Process Clauses provide an adequate tool for coping with confessions and that, even if the Fifth Amendment privilege against self-incrimination be invoked, its precedents taken as a whole do not sustain the present rules. Viewed as a choice based on pure policy, these new rules prove to be a highly debatable, if not one-sided, appraisal of the competing interests, imposed over widespread objection, at the very time when judicial restraint is most called for by the circumstances. . . .

There are several relevant lessons to be drawn from . . . constitutional history. The first is that with over 25 years of precedent the Court has developed an elaborate, sophisticated, and sensitive approach to admissibility of confessions. It is "judicial" in its treatment of one case at a time, . . . flexible in its ability to respond to the endless mutations of fact presented, and ever more familiar to the lower courts. Of course, strict certainty is not obtained in this developing process, but this is often so with constitutional principles, and disagreement is usually confined to that borderland of close cases where it matters least.

The second point is that in practice and from time to time in principle, the Court has given ample recognition to society's interest in suspect questioning as an instrument of law enforcement. . . .

. . . The Court's opening contention, that the Fifth Amendment governs police station confessions, is perhaps not an impermissible extension of the law but it has little to commend itself in the present circumstances. Histori-

cally, the privilege against self-incrimination did not bear at all on the use of extra-legal confessions, for which distinct standards evolved: . . . Even those who would readily enlarge the privilege must concede some linguistic difficulties since the Fifth Amendment in terms proscribes only compelling any person "in any criminal case to be a witness against himself." . . . It then emerges from a discussion of *Escobedo* that the Fifth Amendment requires for an admissible confession that it be given by one distinctly aware of his right not to speak and shielded from "the compelling atmosphere" of interrogation. From these key premises, the Court finally develops the safeguards of warning, counsel, and so forth. I do not believe these premises are sustained by precedents under the Fifth Amendment. . . .

A closing word must be said about the Assistance of Counsel Clause of the Sixth Amendment, which is never expressly relied on by the Court but whose judicial precedents turn out to be linchpins of the confession rules announced today. . . . While the Court finds no pertinent difference between judicial proceedings and police interrogation, I believe the differences are so vast as to disqualify wholly the Sixth Amendment precedents as suitable analogies in the present cases. . . .

Examined as an expression of public policy, the Court's new regime proves so dubious that there can be no due compensation for its weakness in constitutional law.

Without at all subscribing to the generally black picture of police conduct painted by the Court, I think it must be frankly recognized at the outset that police questioning allowable under due process precedents may inherently entail some pressure on the suspect and may seek advantage in his ignorance or weaknesses. The atmosphere and questioning techniques, proper and fair though they be, can in themselves exert a tug on the suspect to confess, and in this light "[t]o speak of any confessions of crime made after arrest as being 'voluntary' or 'uncoerced' is somewhat inaccurate, although traditional. A confession is wholly and incontestably voluntary only if a guilty person gives himself up to the law and becomes his own accuser." Until today, the role of the Constitution has been only to sift out *undue* pressure, not to assure spontaneous confessions. . . .

What the Court largely ignores is that its rules impair, if they will not eventually serve wholly to frustrate, an instrument of law enforcement that has long and quite reasonably been thought worth the price paid for it. There can be little doubt that the Court's new code would markedly decrease the number of confessions. To warn the suspect that he may remain silent and remind him that his confession may be used in court are minor obstructions. To require also an express waiver by the suspect and an end to questioning whenever he demurs must heavily handicap questioning. And to suggest or provide counsel for the suspect simply invites the end of the interrogation.

How much harm this decision will inflict on law enforcement cannot fairly be predicted with accuracy. Evidence on the role of confessions is notoriously incomplete. . . . We do know that some crimes cannot be solved without confessions, that ample expert testimony attests to their importance in crime control, and that the Court is taking a real risk with society's welfare in imposing its new regime on the country. The social costs of crime are too great to call the new rules anything but a hazardous experimentaton. . . .

. . . it may make the analysis more graphic to consider the actual facts of one of the four cases reversed by the Court. *Miranda* v. *Arizona* serves best, being neither the hardest nor easiest of the four under the Court's standards.

On March 3, 1963, an 18-year-old girl was kidnapped and forcibly raped near Phoenix, Arizona. Ten days later, on the morning of March 13, petitioner Miranda was arrested and taken to the police station. At this time Miranda was 23 years old, indigent, and educated to the extent of completing half the ninth grade. He had "an emotional illness" of the schizophrenic type, according to the doctor who eventually examined him; the doctor's report also stated that Miranda was "alert and oriented as to time, place, and person," intelligent within normal limits, competent to stand trial, and sane within the legal definition. At the police station, the victim picked Miranda out of a lineup, and two officers then took him into a separate room to interrogate him, starting about 11:30 a. m. Though at first denying his guilt, within a short time Miranda gave a detailed oral confession and then wrote out in his own hand and signed a brief statement admitting and describing the crime. All this was accomplished in two hours or less without any force, threats or promises and—I will assume this though the record is uncertain,—without any effective warnings at all.

Miranda's oral and written confessions are now held inadmissible under the Court's new rules. One is entitled to feel astonished that the Constitution can be read to produce this result. These confessions were obtained during brief, day-time questioning conducted by two officers and unmarked by any of the traditional indicia of coercion. They assured a conviction for a brutal and unsettling crime, for which the police had and quite possibly could obtain little evidence other than the victim's identifications, evidence which is frequently unreliable. There was, in sum, a legitimate purpose, no perceptible unfairness, and certainly little risk of injustice in the interrogation. Yet the resulting confessions, and the responsible course of police practice they represent, are to be sacrificed to the Court's own finespun conception of fairness which I seriously doubt is shared by many thinking citizens in this country. . . .

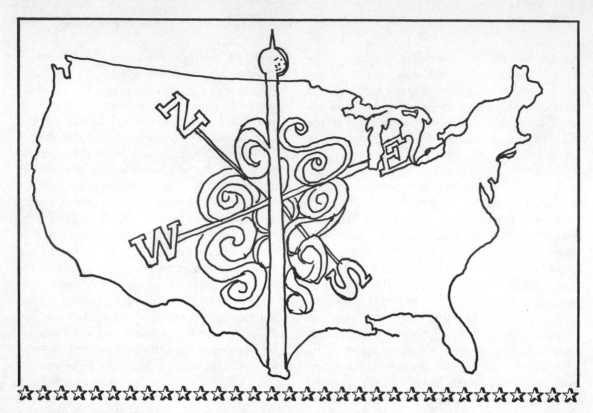

Federalism

4

American government can only be partially understood by focusing attention on the institutions, functions, and processes of the national government. The Constitution recognizes that the United States is a *federal system*, that is, a governmental framework characterized by the division and sharing of powers between the nation and the states. Federalism differs from *unitary systems*, such as in Britain or France, where one central government has authority over the entire nation. Federalism is also distinguished from *confederation*, where several member states have coequal status. Confederacies, such as the United Nations, consist of weak central authorities that lack power to enforce decisions without agreement of the participating members.

Thus, federal-state relations must be considered in any serious study of American government. What were some of the basic reasons for establishing our federal system? When the Founding Fathers debated the new Constitution in 1787, they were concerned with the weakness of the national government. Not only did the state predominate under the Articles of Confederation, but the new nation lacked unified military capability to protect itself from foreign attacks. General George Washington had encountered this problem during the Revolutionary War when many of the colonies were reluctant to supply him with arms and troops. The United States was weak militarily and diplomatically in 1787. Consequently, according to William Riker in Article 12, there were two essential foundations of the federal bargain: an *expansion* condition and a *military* condition. The framers created centralized federalism by expanding territorial control to meet an external threat. Such expansion could not be achieved by conquest, so concessions were made to the constituent units. In addition, the federal bargain was accepted by the constituent units because of external military-diplomatic threats or opportunities. The federal arrangement provided more protection to member states than if they acted alone.

The Constitution reflects the federal bargain by defining the basic *legal* boundaries of national and state authority. The national government has "delegated" responsibilities over such matters as taxation, interstate commerce, money, war, the military, and federal courts. These grants of power are subject to specific prohibitions. More precisely, the first eight amendments to the Constitution prevent interference with individual liberties by the national government. In contrast, the states have "reserved" powers that are relatively unrestricted, as indicated in the Tenth Amendment.

What is the relationship between the formal constitutional provisions dealing with national and state powers and the realities of intergovernmental cooperation and conflict? Obviously, the Founding Fathers could not anticipate future nation-state problems and the political processes by which these controversies would be resolved. The Supreme Court assumed the role of umpire in the federal system. Under the leadership of Chief Justice John Marshall, the Supreme Court became involved in deciding nation-state disputes. When the State of Maryland challenged the authority of Congress to charter a national bank, Marshall wrote a landmark decision which greatly expanded the powers of Congress. In the case of *McCulloch* v. *Maryland* (1819), the Chief Justice declared that the so-called "elastic clause" of Article 1, Section 8 of the Constitution, which refers to congressional authority "to make all laws which shall be necessary and proper," requires a very broad interpretation and implementation because:

... This provision is made in a constitution intended to endure for ages to come, and, consequently, to be adapted to the various crises of human affairs. ...

Thus, even though the delegated powers of Congress include no provisions to charter a national bank, such power is implied from the "necessary and proper" clause. Such implied powers are quite broad and subject only to the following conditions:

... Let the end be legitimate, let it be within the scope of the Constitution, and all means which are appropriate, which are plainly adapted to that end, which are not prohibited, but consist with the letter and spirit of the Constitution. ...

Chief Justice Marshall's decision in *McCulloch* v. *Maryland* not only expanded the powers of Congress by broadening the interpretation of the elastic clause, but it also established the principle of national supremacy in disputes with the states. When national and state authority clashed over controversial issues, the Supreme Court decided in favor of Congress, particularly when such legislative authority was constitutionally permissible. Throughout his tenure as Chief Justice, Marshall consistently strengthened national power. As America expanded its territory during the early decades of the nineteenth century, many of his decisions affirmed national authority.

Marshall's "nation-centered" interpretation is not the only view of American federalism. As Richard Leach indicates in Article 13, there have been other theories dealing with states' rights, dual federalism, intergovernmental cooperation, creative federalism, and new federalism. However, Leach is less concerned with examining theories about the federal system than he is with understanding the practical nature of nation-state relations. He argues that intergovernmental cooperation is the key to analyzing how the national, state, and local governments work with each other. Thus, federalism is a *"process . . . a way of doing things,* rather than . . . a set of abstract principles." If there is no set pattern of intergovernmental relations, then theorizing about federalism may be irrelevant. Most importantly, Leach observes, our federal system should be viewed pragmatically. "Workable federalism is marked by diversity, trial and error, and experimentation on the one hand, and it is problem-oriented on the other."

Cooperation is the keynote of modern federal-state relations. Our federal system is characterized by the sharing of government functions and responsibilities. Rather than a "layer cake" of legal separation, the nation works together to overcome the formal fragmentation of many units of government. Centralization and decentralization are not competing concepts. Rather, "government close to the people" depends upon the nature of cooperative policies which best serve national, state, and local needs. In fact, our governmental and political structure in Congress, the bureaucracy, pressure groups, and political parties illustrate the accommodation required to achieve common policy objectives.

The president may encounter problems by attempting to impose "decentralization by order" in federal-state programs. By trying to return federally sponsored programs to the states and localities, the president may be interposing his preferences against various constituencies that perceive benefits from continued national involvement. President Eisenhower was unable to overcome such objections in the 1950s but President Nixon attempted to do the same with his policies of welfare reform and revenue sharing in the 1970s. His New Federalism agenda attempted to reduce the power of federal bureaucracies by providing an *income strategy* for needy groups and "no strings attached" federal funds to states and localities.

Revenue sharing, discussed by Michael Reagan in Article 14, attempted to reduce federal requirements associated with a wide variety of grant-in-aid programs. Revenue sharing developed within the context of long-standing federal commitments to grants-in-aid programs for state and localities. Before enactment, revenue sharing was a test of power between President Nixon and the Democratic-controlled Congress. At its early stages, revenue sharing was proposed in two different forms: the "add on" or supplemental no-strings-attached plan of economic adviser Walter Heller and the "substitute" or replacement of grants-in-aid proposal of Republican Congressman Melvin Laird. After his 1968 election, President Nixon sent a special message to Congress on revenue sharing. After encountering stiff resistance from House Ways and Means Chairman Wilbur Mills, Nixon reformulated revenue sharing in 1971 to consist of "no-strings-attached" general revenue sharing and six block grants of special revenue sharing. After minor changes by the senate and conference committee agreements, revenue sharing was enacted as the 1972 State and Local Fiscal Assistance Act. The act was administered by the Office of Revenue Sharing, a rather small agency of the Treasury Department. This was a rather unusual example of not establishing complex bureaucratic machinery to implement a new federal policy. Reagan's discussion deals with the administration of revenue sharing, its impact on state and local governments, and suggestions for improving the policy.

Revenue sharing was renewed for another five years in 1977. During the Carter Administration, intergovernmental cooperation was threatened by emerging regional rivalries. As discussed in Article 15, population shifts and the drain of business and industry from the Northeastern and Midwestern states resulted in a competition for federal aid with the more prosperous Southern and Southwestern states. Consequently, the so-called Snowbelt states formed a lobbying coalition in Washington. Their objective was to gain more access to federal programs during a time of economic stagnation and severe inflation.

In summary, federalism is a dynamic concept of the American governmental system. The key to strengthening the intergovernmental partnership is not more centralized administrative direction from Washington, but encouragement of resource redistribution in such a way that regional rivalries do not become politically destructive.

12

The Origin and Purposes of Federalism

William H. Riker

If the U.S. Constitution was based upon political objectives within a pluralistic system of bargaining and tradeoffs (as argued by Roche and Smith in Articles 3 and 4) rather than reflecting the economic motives of an unrepresentative elite (see Article 2 by Dye and Ziegler and Smith's discussion of Charles A. Beard in Article 4), William Riker offers yet another interpretation of the framers' intentions: a military or diplomatic view of the Constitution. He claims that the creation of "centralized federalism" was the major objective of the Founding Fathers. The federal bargain was based upon an expansion condition and a military condition. British and Spanish threats could not be met by a very weak nation governed under the decentralized system of the Articles of Confederation. Similarly, the Virginia Plan, which offered a unitary governmental system, was unacceptable to many of the state delegations. Riker argues that the battle over representation was tied to the modification made in achieving a federal system. How was the Virginia Plan adjusted to establish federalism? How does Riker justify the framers' concerns for military and diplomatic threats in designing the federal system? Was the new federal system more effective in meeting such threats than the decentralized arrangements under the Articles of Confederation?

I CONDITIONS OF THE FEDERAL BARGAIN

As bargains, the acts of making federal constitutions should display the main feature of bargains generally, which is that all parties are willing to make them. Assuming that they do display this feature, one may ask what it is that predisposes the parties to favor this kind of bargain. From the theory set forth in the previous chapter, I infer the existence of at least two circumstances encouraging a willingness to strike the bargain of federalism:

1. The politicians who offer the bargain desire to expand their territorial control, usually either to meet an external military or diplomatic threat or to prepare for military or diplomatic aggression and aggrandizement. But, though they

Reprinted by permission of the author from William H. Riker, *Federalism: Origin, Operation, Significance* (Boston: Little, Brown and Company, 1964).

desire to expand, they are not able to do so by conquest, because of either military incapacity or ideological distaste. Hence, if they are to satisfy the desire to expand, they must offer concessions to the rulers of constituent units, which is the essence of the federal bargain. The predisposition for those who offer the bargain is, then, that federalism is the only feasible means to accomplish a desired expansion without the use of force.

2. The politicians who accept the bargain, giving up some independence for the sake of union, are willing to do so because of some external military–diplomatic threat or opportunity. Either they desire protection from an external threat or they desire to participate in the potential aggression of the federation. And furthermore the desire for either protection or participation outweighs any desire they may have for independence. The predisposition is the cognizance of the pressing need for the military strength or diplomatic maneuverability that comes with a larger and presumably stronger government. (It is not, of course, necessary that their assessment of the military-diplomatic circumstances be objectively correct.)

For convenience of abbreviation I shall refer to these two predispositions as (1) the expansion condition and (2) the military condition.

The hypothesis of this chapter is that these two predispositions are *always* present in the federal bargain and that each one is a necessary condition for the creation of a federalism. I am tempted, on the basis of my immersion in this subject, to assert that these two conditions are together sufficient. But, since I cannot possibly collect enough information to prove sufficiency, I am constrained to assert only the more modest hypothesis of necessity. . . .

II THE INVENTION OF CENTRALIZED FEDERALISM

American historians have long disputed about the reason for the replacement of the peripheralized federalism of the Articles of Confederation by the centralized federalism of the Constitution. The traditional and long-prevailing explanation, which reached its most complete formulation in the writings of John Fiske (ca. 1890), was the teleological assertion that a more centralized union than the Articles could provide was needed for the United States to fulfill its destiny. This notion, however flattering to American readers, was, of course, chronological nonsense since the politicians of the 1780's could have at best a dim view of the "destiny" of the United States of 1890 or 1960.

As against this mystical explanation, Charles Beard in 1913 offered a wholly naturalistic explanation that, however, so denigrated heroes and assumed so naive a theory of social causation that it continued to be a center of controversy for nearly 50 years. Beard called his explanation an *economic* interpretation, by which he meant that the motive of those who wrote and supported the Constitution as against the Articles was simply the desire to

get rich or stay rich. Assuming that the central feature of politics was the struggle between the haves and the have-nots, Beard argued that the have-nots preferred the peripheralized federalism of the Articles to the centralized Constitution proposed by the haves. In some places, he even goes so far as to argue that the evil rich succeeded in imposing their Constitution on the meek poor only by chicanery. Naturally, this oversimplified attribution of motives and morals is easy to challenge and in the last decade the so-called revisionist historians have in fact shown, *inter alia*, that in some states it was the rich who opposed and the poor who favored the Constitution.[1]

Mere revision of Beard's historical errors is not likely, however, to improve our understanding of the constitutional change. What is needed is a broader conception of the nature of politics than Beard's narrow progressivism. In the following paragraphs, therefore, I have outlined what I call the "Military Interpretation of the Constitution of the United States" and have demonstrated that it accounts for the total local, national, and international features of the process of constitution-writing.

The Military Interpretation of the Constitution. From the end of the War of 1812 until the manufacture of an atomic bomb by the Soviet Union, most Americans felt safe from European invasion. During that long period (in the latter part of which Beard wrote), it was difficult to conceive of the international situation of the American states in the 1780's, when European aggression seemed both imminent and inevitable. (Probably this continental security that permitted exclusive preoccupation with domestic affairs was a precondition of Beard's misinterpretation of history.) But in

[1] Charles Beard, *An Economic Interpretation of the Constitution of the United States* (New York: Macmillan, 1913); Robert E. Brown, *Charles Beard and the Constitution* (Princeton: Princeton University Press, 1956).

the 1950's and 1960's it is again easy to sympathize with the fears and calculations of politicians of the era of the Articles. Consider the objective international situation they found themselves in. The thirteen states concluded in 1783 a very uneasy peace with the imperial power, uneasy because significant politicians in Britain regretted the outcome and hoped to reopen the war, and uneasy because it appeared likely that some of the states would give them occasion to do so. The British occupied forts in the Northwest Territory, forts which they were obligated to surrender under the terms of the Treaty of Paris but which they refused to surrender until the states paid the arrears in the treaty-obligated indemnity for Tory property seized during the war. The English threat in the Northwest was matched by the Spanish threat in the Southwest, where New Orleans was a base for potential expansion into the Ohio and Tennessee valleys. The States had neither fleet to forestall invasion nor army to repel it. In such circumstances wise politicians could seldom be free of the fear of war and in fact they were not. The chief criticisms they made of the peripheralized federalism of the Articles was that the system as a whole, central and constituent governments together, was inadequate for war and the prospect of war. I cite three instances: (1) Washington in his semi-annual political surveys to Lafayette throughout 1785 to 1787 emphasized the military weakness of government under the Articles. He seemed especially disturbed by the possibility that Kentucky might even voluntarily go with Spain. The military emphasis of these summaries, which presumably give Washington's considered judgment of the total political situation, probably explains why he attended the Philadelphia convention and by his sanction gave it a chance of success; (2) Madison, who is often called the father of the Constitution in the sense that he came to Philadelphia with a considered plan of reform and succeeded, of course, with

Washington's approval, in writing the substance of it into the Constitution, circulated in 1786 a manuscript criticism of the Articles. The first, the longest, and the most passionately argued items in the list of weaknesses of the Articles all refer to the military or diplomatic inadequacies of Congress. Indeed, five items out of eleven are on this subject. Because Madison subsequently wrote the tenth *Federalist* paper, with its interpretation of domestic conflict in economic terms, Beard and his followers have supposed that Madison, like them, saw the great issue of the times as a domestic conflict among a variety of economic interests. But Madison's own writings on the Articles say otherwise and, as I shall show in item (3), only a wilful misinterpretation of *The Federalist* can align Madison with Beard.[2] (3) *The Federalist* papers, the main propaganda document issued in support of the ratification of the Constitution, emphasizes the military-diplomatic advantages of centralized federalism. *The Federalist* has, I recognize, been used to prove many and contradictory propositions about the Constitution. Nevertheless I point out that the first five papers— and presumably the first papers were regarded by its authors as of primary importance—are concerned with military and foreign affairs and were written by John Jay, who was then regarded as the great specialist on diplomacy. The structure of *The Federalist* and the content of its first papers thus suggests the primacy of military considerations in the process of centralization, at least in the understanding of the authors of that work.

These three instances, chosen from the main writers and writings responsible for the Con-

---

[2] See for example J. Fitzpatrick, *Writings of George Washington* (Washington, D.C.: Government Printing Office) Vol. 29, pp. 260–261 (15 Aug. 1787, to Lafayette); G. Hunt, *Writings of James Madison* (New York: G. P. Putnam and Sons, 9 vols., 1900–1910) Vol. 2, pp. 361–369, "Vices of the Political System of the United States."

stitution, do strongly suggest the primacy of the military motive in the adoption of centralized federalism. The suggestion is in fact so strong that one wonders how Beard and his followers could ever have believed that the main issues at Philadelphia were domestic matters of the distribution of income. The conflict between the military and economic interpretations is over what was the "main" issue. Naturally, the fathers of the Constitution were interested in both international and domestic affairs and when they talked about a better army sometimes they referred to the international scene and sometimes to the maintenance of order at home (especially to the policing of revolts by poor farmers, such as Shay's rebellion). Unquestionably the Beardians were right when they said that some economic concerns were felt, but they were perversely wrong when they magnified the domestic concerns and ignored the foreign concerns almost entirely. Probably they did so because in their day foreign concerns were not very important anyway; but as I have shown, the preconceptions of their era were such that they could not easily sympathize with politicians who daily expected to be involved in European wars on the American continent. This is why they have distorted the message and the structure of *The Federalist*, why they have written incessantly of Shays' rebellion (which did indeed disturb Washington), but totally ignored Washington's much greater fear that the Kentuckians might join Spain, why they have emphasized the writings and views of provincial and insignificant leaders like Luther Martin, George Mason, *et al.*, and largely ignored the writings of a really national and significant leader like Washington. It is almost as if some future historians of India were to interpret the history of constitution-making in that country with the words of Ambedekar and Narayan without discussing the words of Gandhi and Nehru.

The Bargain at Philadelphia. Taking it as proved that the fathers of the Constitution were primarily concerned with rendering their federalism better able to meet military and diplomatic threats, we may ask now how they proposed to improve its capabilities. This question leads us directly into the nature both of centralized federalism and of the bargain invented at Philadelphia in 1787.

The Virginia delegation at Philadelphia came prepared with a plan for a new constitution (presumably written by Madison and endorsed by Washington) which was essentially unitary in character. It provided that the people at large would elect the lower house of the national legislature and that this body in turn would choose all the remaining parts of a national government: an upper house, an executive, and a judiciary. Furthermore, it proposed to give an essentially unlimited grant of power to the national legislature

to legislate in all cases to which the separate States are incompetent, or in which the harmony of the United States may be interrupted by the exercise of individual Legislation; to negative all laws passed by the several States, contravening in the opinion of the National Legislature the articles of Union; and to call forth the force of the Union agst any member of the Union failing to fulfill its duty under the articles thereof.[3]

This arrangement seems to be an adaptation of the unitary English constitution to fit a society lacking a formal aristocracy and royalty. Had the Virginia Plan been adopted and successfully imposed, federalism in North America would have ceased to exist. But the Virginia Plan was far too extreme a change to win acceptance in the Convention and so it was repeatedly modified. The invention of centralized federalism was thus a byproduct of modifications made to render the plan acceptable to ruling factions in the states. One cannot say that the framers tried to invent what they did—rather they tried to construct, by

[3] M. Farrand, *Records of the Federal Convention of 1787* (New Haven: Yale Univ. Press, rev. ed., 4 vols., 1937) Vol. 1, 21.

means of *ad hoc* arrangements, a government that would work in their own peculiar circumstances. By happenstance it embodied a principle that could also work in numerous other circumstances.[4]

The general theme of the modifications in the Virginia Plan was, as I have just indicated, to deviate from the unitary form just enough to render the plan acceptable to ruling factions in the states. In practice, this meant guaranteeing that the governments of the states have something to say about the formation of the central government and that they also have important areas of governing left to themselves. The main deviations from the Virginia Plan were in the selection and structure of the upper house of the legislature, the selection of the executive, and the grant of legislative authority to the national government. In each instance, the framers went just as far from the unitary form as they thought necessary to obtain adherence of state-centered politicians and then backed sharply away from going further.

The great debate, as every American school child knows, was over the representation of states in the national government. The essential modification that the proponents of the Virginia Plan were forced to accept was the equal representation of state governments in one house of the national legislature. The issue arose out of the fear of the nine small states that they would be swamped by the preponderant weight of the four large states. This was probably an unreasonable fear since the subsequent politics of the federation has seldom, if ever, seen the small states pitted directly against the large ones. Whether reasonable or not, however, the fear was real

(possibly because the small states had generally been lax in their payments to the Congress whereas the large ones had not) and it led the small states to insist on some kind of equal representation. The large states acceded in order to keep the Convention in session and this modification rendered the states a formal part of the central government and ensured the retention of some of the federalism of the Articles.

Once the proponents of unitary government had made this one great concession, however, they were extremely loath to make additional ones. And it was this systematic resistance on their part that produced a federalism of an essentially different kind from the peripheralized federalism of the Articles.

Consider, for example, the way the framers handled the election of the executive, which was a problem with at least two dimensions. Given the traditions in the states, it was natural for the framers to suggest that the legislature elect the executive; but, since most of the framers were mild conservatives fearing too much authority in popularly elected legislatures, this natural method was undesirable. Given the existence of the federation of the Articles, the next most obvious method was election by some agency of the states; but, since the framers mostly wanted something, approaching unitary government, state-controlled elections were also undesirable. Faced with this two-dimensional set of considerations, the framers had a terrible time. Twelve different methods of election were proposed, two of which were actually adopted in a preliminary way, before the electoral college was finally devised. Though this expedient was a poor one (for it had to be revised in the Twelfth Amendment and is still subject to constant criticism today), it satisfied them on both dimensions. From the point of view of the federal-unitary dimension, it is important to note that, however great the difficulty of decision, the proponents of unitary government managed to avoid giving the states a part in the

---

[4] For a demonstration of the *ad hoc* character of this federalism, see William H. Riker, "Dutch and American Federalism," *Journal of the History of Ideas*, Vol. 18 (1956), pp. 495–526, where it is shown that the framers' invention owed nothing, either positively or negatively, to the most well-known federalism then in existence.

process of election. Thus, having capitulated on the election of the upper house of the legislature, the proponents of centralism refused to capitulate further, even though the way out of their difficulty was hard to discover.[5]

Or consider, as a further illustration of the resistance of centralizers to peripheralization, the development during the course of the convention of the grant of legislative power to the national government. It started out in the Virginia Plan as the (previously quoted) unlimited grant. It reappeared just after the large states' capitulation on equal representation as substantially the list of the powers delegated to Congress by the Articles. Having capitulated on one thing, it appeared that the large states were capitulating on everything. But then revisions began to appear in debates and committee reports. For example, the first list gave the Congress simply the power to call the militia into its service. Then it was proposed to give Congress full authority to regulate and discipline the militia, which was then the only military force in existence and therefore of central importance to men who wanted a stronger central government for military reasons. This proposal failed quite probably because, as one delegate remarked, "If it be agreed to by the Convention, this plan will have as black a mark as was set on Cain." What resulted, however, was a compromise that allowed the Congress not only to call out the militia but also to "provide for organizing, arming, and disciplining" it and to govern "such Part of them as may be employed in the Service of the United States." This compromise, which seems quite weak to us today, was probably as far as the proponents of centralized government dared go, for, as it turned out, the militia provisions came under extremely heavy criticism in the ratifying conventions and the Second Amendment was

tacked onto the Constitution to ensure that the militia would never be fully transferred to the central authority.[6] For another example, the first list of delegated powers did go much beyond the Articles in that it enabled the Congress to "lay and collect" taxes. But in subsequent revisions this power was expanded almost into a general grant of power of the sort originally intended in the Virginia Plan by the addition of the phrase "to pay the Debts and provide for the common Defense and general Welfare of the United States." The meaning of this statement has always been ambiguous, for it is not clear whether the grant of power to provide for the general welfare is a grant for taxing or for all legislative purposes. The tradition of constitutional jurisprudence has been to assume the former, but the plain English of the sentence and the probable intent of the framers suggests that one ought to assume the latter. Under either interpretation, however, there occurred a considerable expansion of the power of the central government.

In short, the proponents of a centralized government made the concessions to federalism that they were obliged to make in order to keep the Convention in session and to offer a Constitution with a reasonable expectation of ratification. Beyond that they would not go and so resulted the centralized federalism of the new Constitution.

The foregoing description of the development of centralized federalism at the Philadelphia Convention of 1787 has demonstrated, I believe, the validity with respect to the United States of the hypothesis set forth at the beginning of this chapter. The military interpretation of the Constitution has demonstrated the existence of the military condition, whereas the determination of the centralizing framers to grant to the decentralizers only so much as was necessary to keep the convention in ses-

---

[5] William H. Riker, *Democracy in the United States* (New York: Macmillan, 1953) pp. 146–49.

[6] William H. Riker, *Soldiers of the States* (Washington, D.C.: Public Affairs Press, 1957) pp. 14ff.

sion and to produce an agreed-upon document demonstrates the expansion condition. In connection with the latter condition, I suppose it should be shown also that imperial expansion was impossible. It is conceivable that Virginia, Pennsylvania, and Massachusetts could have conquered some of their immediate neighbors; but no one thought of doing so probably because the cost would have been thoroughly prohibitive. Hence there was but one means to centralize, namely to bargain rather than to conquer, and that is what the centralizers did.

13

Federalism and Theory

Richard H. Leach

How has American federalism developed over time? Richard Leach shows that federal-state relations reflect a variety of approaches, each of which represents an adjustment to different political circumstances. Denying that federalism is a fixed "theory," Leach argues there have been a variety of pragmatic responses to nation-state relations. For example, Chief Justice John Marshall was a leading advocate of "nation-centered" federalism. He tried to strengthen the authority of the national government against challenges made by the states, (McCulloch v. Maryland, 1819). *Other competitive and cooperative varieties of federalism have characterized American political experiences. Since Leach's views were written in 1970, how has federalism developed? What is the most effective balance between the goals of centralization and decentralization? How does revenue sharing fit into the pattern of intergovernmental relations? Michael Reagan (Article 14) provides further discussion of this policy issue.*

Federalism has been a subject of controversy in American government and politics since the beginning of the Republic. It continues so today. For it is at the center of American governmental action. It is, as the late Morton Grodzins wrote, "a device for dividing decisions and functions of government . . . It is a means, not an end."[1] It ordinarily involves two major levels of government, each, at least in democratic societies, assumed to derive its powers directly from the people and therefore to be supreme in the areas of power assigned to it. Each level of government in a federal system insists upon its right to act directly upon the people. Each is protected constitutionally from undue encroachment or destruction by the other. To this end, federalism entails a point of final reference, usually a judiciary. The people in federal systems are held to possess what amounts to dual citizenship. Sovereignty, in the classic sense, has no meaning; divided as power is, the element of absoluteness which is essential to the concept of sovereignty is not present. Federalism is concerned with process and by its very nature is a dynamic, not a static, concept. In operation, it requires a willingness both to cooperate across governmental lines and to exercise restraint and forebearance in the interests of the entire nation. . . .

But precisely what "federalism" means is not now and never has been clear. We can only be sure that the framers of the Constitution regarded it as one of several ways to limit the power of government in the United States. Thus any attempt to argue for a particular relation between the national government and the states—in particular for a precise division of powers between them—must fall flat for lack of constitutional corroboration. Nor are clear directions given with regard to other aspects of federalism. Instead of a rigid set of

Selection is reprinted from *American Federalism* by Richard H. Leach, with the permission of W. W. Norton & Company, Inc. Copyright © 1970 by W. W. Norton & Company, Inc.

[1] Morton Grodzins, "The Federal System," Ch. 12 in *Goals for Americans. The Report of the President's Commission on National Goals* (Englewood Cliffs, N.J., Prentice-Hall, 1965), p. 265.

principles, what the framers gave us was a flexible instrument concerned with function and the practice of government. Federalism is thus something which is able to resound to changing needs and circumstances and is not bound by the tenets of a particular political theory.

But that there is in effect no basic theory of American federalism has not prevented both plain and eminent men from arguing vehemently that such a theory exists. So many and so vociferous have proponents of various conceptions of federalism been over the years that the literature is voluminous. The leading theoretical contentions are summarized under two main categories in the paragraphs that follow.

COMPETITIVE THEORIES

Nation-centered Federalism

The concept of nation-centered federalism was the first to be advanced. Alexander Hamilton laid the basis for nation-centered federalism in his numbers of *The Federalist*, in his state papers, and by his actions as Secretary of the Treasury under George Washington. Later, John Marshall, as Chief Justice of the United States, constantly emphasized national power and indeed visualized judicial review "as a means of keeping the states within bounds."[2] The nation-centered theory of federalism posits the idea that the Constitution is a document emanating from and ratified by the American people as a whole. It follows that the government which the whole people created is the focal point of political power in the United States and that it has the principal responsibility for meeting the needs of the American people. Between them, Hamilton and Marshall

expounded the idea that, in Marshall's words in *McCulloch* v. *Maryland*, the national government "is the government of all; its powers are delegated by all; it represents all, and acts for all . . . The nation, on those subjects on which it can act, must necessarily bind its component parts. But this question is not left to mere reason; the people have, in express terms, decided it by saying, 'this constitution, and the laws of the United States, which shall be made in pursuance thereof, . . . shall be the supreme law of the land' . . ." Nor is it merely its popular base which gives the nation primacy. As Abraham Lincoln pointed out in his first Inaugural Address, "The Union is much older than the Constitution. It was formed, in fact, by the Articles of Association in 1774. It was matured and continued by the Declaration of Independence in 1776. It was further matured, and the faith of all the then thirteen States expressly plighted and engaged that it be perpetual, by the Articles of Confederation. . . . And finally, in 1787, one of the declared objects for ordaining and establishing the Constitution was 'to form a more perfect Union.' " What else needs to be pointed out to demonstrate the centrality of the Union at the outset? And the intervening years did nothing to alter the original emphasis on the national government.

Nor is there anything incompatible in emphasizing the national government and at the same time defending the existence and utility of states and state governments. As Chief Justice Roger Taney put it in 1869 in *Texas* v. *White*[3] (the case which tested whether the government of Texas was responsible for the bonds issued by the state's Confederate government during the Civil War),

. . . the perpetuity and indissolubility of the Union, by no means implies the loss of distinct and individual existence, or of the right of self-government by the States. Under the Articles of Confed-

---

[2] The phrase of Benjamin F. Wright, *The Growth of American Constitutional Law* (Boston: Houghton Mifflin, 1942), p. 38.

[3] 7 Wallace 700 (1869).

eration each State retained its sovereignty, freedom, and independence, and every power, jurisdiction, and right not expressly delegated to the United States. Under the Constitution, though the powers of the States were much restricted, still, all powers not delegated to the United States, nor prohibited to the States, are reserved to the States respectively, or to the people. And we have already had occasion to remark at this term, that "the people of each State compose a State, having its own government, and endowed with all the functions essential to separate and independent existence," and that "without the States in union, there could be no such political body as the United States." Not only, therefore, can there be no loss of separate and independent autonomy to the States, through their union under the Constitution, but it may be not unreasonably said that the preservation of the States, and the maintenance of their governments, are as much within the design and care of the Constitution as the preservation of the Union and the maintenance of the National government. The Constitution, in all its provisions, looks to an indestructible Union, composed of indestructible States.

Thus the national government has a dual responsibility to the people under the Constitution, a responsibility for the preservation and defense of both the Union as a whole and each and every individual state, which adds but a further reason for its primacy.

State-centered Federalism

State-centered federalism developed in resistance to the nationalism of Hamilton and Marshall and was first articulated in the Virginia and Kentucky Resolutions in 1798. Later on, the full-blown theory of state-centered federalism was polished and perfected, particularly by southerners, as its usefulness in rationalizing the differences between that section of the country and the rest of the nation became more apparent. Thomas Jefferson and John C. Calhoun were the chief (but far from the only developers of this variation on the theme.[4]

[4] See Alpheus T. Mason, *The States' Rights Debate.* A Spectrum Paperback (New York, 1964).

The theory of state-centered federalism holds that the Constitution resulted from state action. It was, after all, the states which sent delegates to Philadelphia, and state ratifying conventions which confirmed the completed document. Moreover, to protect the states, the framers set absolute limits to the power of the national government in Article I, section 8, and specifically guaranteed state power in the Tenth Amendment. James Madison spoke to the point in *Federalist 45:*

. . . is it not preposterous, to urge as an objection to a government, without which the objects of the Union cannot be attained, that such a government may derogate from the importance of the governments of the individual states? . . . The powers delegated by the proposed Constitution to the federal government are few and defined. Those which are to remain in the State governments are numerous and indefinite. The former will be exercised principally on external objects. . . . The powers reserved to the several States will extend to all the objects which, in the ordinary course of affairs, concern the lives, liberties, and properties of the people, and the internal order, improvement, and prosperity of the States.

The chief focus of citizen and governmental attention, believers in this theory are convinced, should be to guard against any enlargement of national power. For basic to the theory of state-centered federalism is the conviction that there is only a limited amount of power available to government in the United States and that the constitutional delegation of power, as narrowly construed as possible, is all that safely can be exercised by the national government. Any expansion beyond those narrow limits amounts to usurpation of power which rightfully belongs to the states.

Dual Federalism

In one sense, the Civil War was fought between the proponents of nation-centered and state-centered federalism. With the victory of the North, it might be assumed that the nationalist concept became the dominant and unchallenged interpretation of federalism in the United States. In fact, this was not the case. Even before the war, the Taney Court had begun to develop the concept of dual federalism, which the Supreme Court after the war embellished and utilized well into the twentieth century; and it gained adherents outside the bar and the judiciary as the corporation, which sought freedom from the restraints of both national and state government, came fully into its own. Proponents of dual federalism profess to believe that the Constitution created a governmental system with "collateral political spheres," to use John Taylor of Carolina's phrase. The national and state governments form two separate centers of power, from each of which the other is barred and between which is something like a jurisdictional no-man's land, into which both are barred from entering. Each government in its own sphere is sovereign, and there is an essential equality between them. As Taylor put it in his *Construction Construed and Constitutions Vindicated*, published in 1820, "the federal constitution, so far from intending to make its political spheres morally unequal in powers, or to invest the greatest with any species of sovereignty over the least, intended the very reverse"—the distribution of equal power between the states and the national government. "The reason," Taylor continued, "why great spheres derive no authority from magnitude to transgress upon small spheres, is, that both are donations from the same source [i.e., the people]; and that the donor did not intend that one donation should pilfer another, because it was smaller." The donation is inviolable, and it is the clear duty of the several branches of the national government, as well as of state governments, to maintain it so, not so much to protect the governments involved, but to assure the freedom of the people. For "the strength of the government lies in the people," Taylor concluded.

They are the protectors and supervisors of the collateral political spheres, which they have created. If one of these spheres should acquire sufficient power to controul the others, it would, like an officer of a monarch, who can controul all the other officers of the government, obtain a supremacy over the monarch himself. . . .

COOPERATIVE THEORIES

Cooperative Federalism

Despite the triumph of dual federalism in the years following the Civil War, neither the nation-centered nor the state-centered varieties were abandoned, in part probably because the heat of the Civil War was so long in dying down, both sides continuing to fight the battle long after the war was over. Perhaps because the arena of argument seemed to be full, the concept of cooperative federalism was slow in jelling and was not given explicit expression much before Morton Grodzins described it in the 1950's. The flavor of the cooperative theory is best caught in the title of a book by Grodzin's student, Daniel Elazar, *The American Partnership*.[5] Elazar illustrates how from the very beginning all levels of government in the United States have collaborated in performing governmental functions. Far from comprising separate and independent layers of government as suggested by proponents of the competitive theories, the American form of government is cooperative, a blending of governments, resembling a "rainbow or marble cake, characterized by an inseparable mingling of differently colored ingredients, the colors appearing in vertical and diagonal strands and unexpected swirls. As colors are mixed in a marble cake, so functions are mixed in the American federal system."[6] In this view, the Constitution visualized a single mechanism of

[5] Daniel Elazar, *The American Partnership* (Chicago: Univ. of Chicago Press, 1962).
[6] Grodzins, "The Federal Systems," Ch. 12 in *Goals for Americans*, *op. cit.*, p. 265.

government in the United States, with many centers of power, which among them were to perform all the functions required of government by the American people. Even before the Constitution, intergovernmental cooperation was utilized to establish primary and secondary education; and the framers of the Constitution were so conscious of "the essential unity of state and federal financial systems"[7] that they provided for the federal government's assumption of the states' Revolutionary War debts. It is a fundamental principle of American federalism that the national government will use its resources in harmony with state and local programs and policies. During the nineteenth century that principle was manifest in steadily increasing intergovernmental cooperation in all the important functional areas of American government, and the twentieth century confirmed the practice. Shared functions, without regard to neat allocations of responsibility, is thus the core of American governmental operation and of the theory of federalism as well. Intergovernmental collaboration rather than the priority of particular governmental levels is the working principle of the federal system.

Creative Federalism

Creative federalism is that theory of federalism first used and described by Governor Nelson Rockefeller in his Godkin Lectures at Harvard in 1962.[8] The idea was picked up and made central to his program by President Lyndon B. Johnson after his election in 1964. Creative federalism is an extension of cooperative federalism in that it emphasizes cooperation. It differs in its recognition of local and private centers of power as well as national and state

centers, and in its concern for the development of cooperation not only between the national and state governments but between them and local governments and private organizations as well. All are regarded as a working team, dedicated to positive action in solving the problems facing the nation, with perhaps a different combination of forces at work in each different problem area, and with the national government not always the senior partner. In both its stress on the responsibility of the private sector of American life in the problem-solving process and its concern that action and innovation take place before problems become critical, it is unique among the theories of federalism so far espoused in America.

New Federalsm

President Richard Nixon described his concept of "new federalism" in a nationwide television speech on August 8, 1969, and again before the National Governors Conference on September 1. It was later given more explicit form in testimony before Congress by the assistant director of the Bureau of the Budget.[9] Its major theme is to rechannel "power, funds and authority . . . increasingly to those governments closest to the people . . . to help regain control of our national destiny by returning a greater share of control to state and local authorities."[10] It stresses *responsible decentralization*: "Washington will no longer try to go it alone," President Nixon said. Washington will "refrain from telling states and localities how to conduct their affairs and [will] seek to transfer ever-greater responsibilities to

---

[7] *Ibid.*, p. 268.

[8] Nelson A. Rockefeller, *The Future of Federalism* (Cambridge: Harvard Univ. Press, 1962).

[9] See the statement of Richard P. Nathan, September 25, 1969, reprinted in *Congressional Record* 115: S11429 (September 26, 1969). The italicized phrases are from his testimony.

[10] President Nixon before the National Governors Conference, reprinted in *Congressional Record* 115: H7533 (September 4, 1969).

the state level."[11] To make the transfer possible, a system of revenue sharing must be established. It also emphasizes *a strong concern with basic systems.* Instead of piecemeal action on parts of problems, intergovernmental strategies for attacking broad problem areas must be worked out. Welfare and manpower programs were the first two such areas to be singled out for attack. Finally, the "new federalism" places *greater emphasis on the effective implementation of government policies,* particularly at the state and local level, where acceptance of the concept "would impose . . . new obligations and new challenges" on government in terms of improved quality of performance. The thrust of the "new federalism" is to deemphasize the national government's role in the partnership of governments and to strengthen that of state and local governments. "Washington will no longer dictate," President Nixon promised. "We can only toss the ball; the states and localities will have to carry it."[12] The new federalism has not yet developed the specifics as to how to make this possible, particularly in financial terms, and until it does, *The New York Times* remarked editorially, it will likely be little "more than a rhetorical phrase."[13]

A recital in chronological order of the several theories of federalism which have been developed in the United States should not be misinterpreted; the subsequent development of one theory by no means served to crowd its predecessors off the stage. Not only did the first two claimants of attention continue to make themselves heard, but as each new concept was developed, proponents of the earlier theories hardened their positions. Thus the stage became more crowded, more confused, and certainly more noisy.

To a large extent the "debate" over the theories of federalism has not been a debate at all. For the most part, it has been conducted at presidential press conferences and in political addresses, in legislative committee chambers and court rooms, in the pages of the daily press and in scholarly journals and reports, but not in the streets and by the people as a whole. Indeed, it would be difficult to demonstrate that there is now or ever has been a widespread public understanding of federalism. If some southerners seem to have consistently supported one theory as opposed to any of the others, their advocacy is based not so much on participation in the debate and understanding derived therefrom as on habit and stereotype. It has always been difficult to find out what the popular conception of federalism is, and this is because the people are very likely confused as to what federalism means, as much by the several interpretations of the "truth" offered them through the years as by the vacuum left by the framers.

An example of that confusion is found in a survey of federalism as viewed by governmental officials concerned with the administration of federal grant-in-aid programs, recently conducted by the Senate Subcommittee on Intergovernmental Relations.[14] The survey showed that, while none of those interviewed had consciously articulated a theory of federalism or even given much thought to the need to do so, "the respondents [did] have a general idea of what intergovernmental relations are and how they should operate. In short, the survey made it clear . . . [that] they [had] a theory of federalism . . . ,"[15] and that state and local officials involved in federal grant-in-aid programs hold views of federalism quite different from those of federal officials. Moreover, the

---

[11] Quoted in *The New York Times*, September 3, 1969, p. 1.
[12] *Ibid.*
[13] *Ibid.*, p. 46.

[14] *The Federal System as Seen by Federal Aid Officials.* Committee Print. December 15, 1965. 89th Congress, 1st Session.
[15] *Ibid.*, p. 95.

study revealed that neither the state and local officials nor the federal officials were in agreement among themselves as to the several elements of the theories they espoused. As the report itself put it, "These contrasting [theories] . . . are based on contrasting emphases and principles." The federal officials were chiefly concerned with doing a professional job of administering aid programs and generally held an anti-state and anti-local official bias, which understandably made their views "completely unacceptable" to the state and local officials, who generally insisted on a more formal statement of principles and were concerned with such concepts as "balance" and "parity."[16] The views of neither group of officials, however, conformed in every respect to one of the theories described earlier in this chapter. Indeed, the subcommittee concluded, governmental officials probably held atypical views of the federal system.

One is left at the end of even so careful an analysis of concepts of federalism more confused than ever as to just what the theoretical bases of American federalism are—or one's confusion is finally dispelled as he is led to understand once and for all that considerations of theory are irrelevant to an understanding of federalism. For the most important conclusion to be drawn from the Senate study is that most respondents agreed their commitment was to a *process*, to *a way of doing things*, rather than to a set of abstract principles. The most frequently occurring words in the views of both sets of officials are *function, program, activity, administration,* in considering all of which *collaboration* and intergovernmental *relations* are fundamental. Federalism from both points of view—more from the federal than from the state and local, to be sure—is seen as a complex working arrangement to permit the accomplishment of commonly held objectives. It is an arrangement whose virtue lies in what it

permits to be accomplished rather than in the degree to which it adheres to a set of binding tenets. And accomplishment can only be secured by a large amount of interrelation. Above all, the conclusion is inevitable that intergovernmental cooperation is the key to modern federalism. Meeting the problems of modern America with the right programs and policies involves *all* levels of government, working together in a variety of ways. The older competitive theories of federalism took into account only the actions of and relations between the government of the United States and those of the states, and even the more recently developed theories of cooperative and creative federalism are focused chiefly on them. Yet federalism is much more than that. It involves as a matter of inheritance and practical necessity at least three levels of action—national, state, and local—and five sets of relations—national-state, interstate, state-local, interlocal, and national-local. To the extent that theories of federalism overlook this elemental truth, they are inapplicable and invalid from the outset. Only the theory of creative federalism seems to take interaction between all levels of government into account. . . .

Implicit in all the theorizing about federalism is the belief that men plan an act rationally in devising their governmental systems. There is no clear evidence that they do. Even the revered framers of the American Constitution were men affected by many forces, only some of them within the control of their reason, as they worked to create the federal system. It is all well and good to speak, as Paul Ylvisaker does in *Area and Power,*[17] of "the proper areal division of powers." Proper according to what logic? what criteria? what reasoning? Persons working in practical intergovernmentalism are more likely fettered than aided by such notions of "propriety."

---

[16] *Ibid.,* pp. 96, 97, 99.

[17] Arthur Maass, ed., *Area and Power. A Theory of Local Government* (Glencoe, Illinois: Free Press, 1959).

American federalism is based on the theory of limited government. Beyond that, it answers not to theoretical dictates. Nor is it likely that it will be adjusted to meet theoretical demands in the future. Theory, in other words, has not been causative in American federalism. The framers of the Constitution bequeathed us an open-ended system. We can only be the losers if we try to close it off by adopting any set of theoretical principles, any model, any construct. As in so many other areas, the framers in building federalism built better than they knew—and we are the beneficiaries.

14

Revenue Sharing: The Pro and Con Arguments

Michael D. Reagan

Revenue sharing was one of the top policy objectives of the Nixon Administration to achieve the goals of the "New Federalism." Michael Reagan evaluates general revenue sharing as an ongoing program following its enactment and legislative implementation. He finds that the major strengths include political popularity, citizen participation, administrative simplicity, discretionary use of funds, and predictability of funds. Why is revenue sharing so popular? How does it aid capital improvement projects? How is decentralization achieved? What are the administrative advantages as compared with categorical grants? How does the program strengthen elected leaders in relation to department heads? Revenue sharing has been criticized because it allegedly neglects the nation's policy priorities toward the poor, ethnic minorities, and the cities. How has this occurred? What are the fiscal problems of cities compared with suburbs and small towns? How does the program discourage metropolitan area cooperation? What are some of the advantages of federal accountability over the use of program funds? Why are the civil rights provisions considered inadequate? On balance, how can national solutions for domestic policy priorities be accommodated with the appeal of general revenue sharing? Do you agree or disagree with Reagan's suggestions?

There is an interesting change in the character of arguments about the value of a public policy program as it moves from the status of a gleam in the eye of the interest groups and political leaders who propose it to that of an ongoing program having observable, real-world consequences. At the earlier stage, discussion focuses heavily on what the proposal should or should not accomplish; ideological points are prominent. Factual assertions are in part necessarily speculative extrapolations from some analogous precedents. Once a policy proposition has been legislated and implemented for a

couple of years, however, the pros and cons become a good deal more practical. The arguments refer increasingly to specific evidence, and the pattern of who favors and who opposes increasingly reflects the realities of who is gaining and who is losing. Interest becomes more important than ideology, though the latter never disappears.

General revenue sharing—which will almost certainly stand as the most notable domestic policy initiative of the Nixon administration—was enacted as the State and Local Fiscal Assistance Act of 1972. At the time of this writing, it had been operating for two years. Long range effects remain necessarily uncertain (although we are not without some clues), but some of the short run patterns of utilization and immediate impacts, political as well as fiscal, are already becoming apparent. An analysis of the arguments based upon evaluations or experience—which are growing hotter in anticipation of the debate in Congress

I wish to thank John G. Sanzone, a doctoral candidate in political science at the University of California, Riverside, for his excellent bibliographic assistance and for valuable discussions of the relationship of general revenue sharing to metropolitan integration.

regarding extension of the original five-year authorization—will therefore differ in significant respects from the prepassage arguments.[1]

ARGUMENTS IN FAVOR

In this context, the strongest single argument in favor of revenue sharing is no longer Richard Nixon's (or Gerald Ford's) "New Federalism" notion of turning back the tide of history to re-create state-local government autonomy, on the rather naive assumption that doing so would automatically give greater political power (policy determining voice) to the average local citizen; nor is it the liberals' (led by economist Walter Heller) calculation that a once-projected but never reached federal surplus could be channeled into enlargement of the public sector while avoiding the obstacle of conservative objection to enlargement of the specifically national segment. The primary argument now—and it is likely to be a successful one in the renewal debates—is the bread-and-butter political one: governors, mayors, city councils, and the appointed officials who help spend the money all enjoy receiving the quarterly checks.

Some recipients are considerably disillusioned because the inauguration of what they had been led to expect would be an augmentation of discretionary income, supplementing existing grants-in-aid, coincided instead with a decrease of sometimes greater proportion in categorical grant funds. However, the formulae for revenue sharing are working in such a way that a large number of local jurisdictions are being pleasantly surprised to discover that their shares are large, relative to their existing budgets and needs, and can therefore be devoted to one-time special capital projects. That is a delightful situation for any politician, of course; thus the city fathers of hamlets, villages and small towns are now the supporters of revenue sharing as a bulwark of localism— and those small towns are still a most salient factor in the political lives of congressmen.

The significant difference between very large cities and very small towns is exemplified in a break-out of first-year revenue sharing expenditures, which showed that among cities of 500,000 or greater population, only 12 percent went into capital budgets while 88 percent was absorbed by operating budgets; among cities in the 10,000 to 24,999 population range, on the other hand, only 29 percent was used for operating costs and 70 percent was embedded in bricks-and-mortar projects that included city hall buildings, fire houses and golf courses.[2] The contrast could hardly be sharper. The urban fiscal crisis that was widely cited as a major reason for increased federal aid in the late 1960s no longer produces daily headlines. However, the plight of the largest cities, increased by the recent rate of inflation, is such that any additional revenue gets swallowed up immediately in a desperate attempt to remain solvent without cutting back on existing services. Revenue sharing as a stimulus to imagination and innovation has little opportunity to be tested in those jurisdictions. In fact, some alert mayors, very much pressed to keep their basic services going at all in fiscal 1973, anticipated the passage of revenue sharing by a few months and built the projected revenues into their budgets when presenting them in the spring of 1972. This was done in Detroit, Michigan and Rochester, New York, for example.

[1] For examples and summaries of the pre-passage arguments, *see,* U.S., Joint Economic Committee, *Revenue Sharing and Its Alternatives: What Future for Fiscal Federalism?* (a compendium, 3 vols.), 90th Cong., 1st sess., 1967; and Michael D. Reagan, *The New Federalism* (New York: Oxford University Press, 1972), chap. 4.

[2] Advisory Commission on Intergovernmental Relations, *Information Bulletin,* no. 73–9, "General Revenue Sharing After One Year," (November 1973).

Regardless of whether a city had to build its regular operating budget on revenue sharing or was able to treat it as an extra that could be used in a totally discretionary manner for something desired but not necessarily needed by any strict criterion, the tendency has been to look upon revenue sharing checks as "manna from heaven." Any program that cities and states regard as such is obviously going to be popular. And political popularity, whether warranted or not by any rational cost-benefit analysis of the relation between areas of greatest human need and areas of actual expenditure, is the strongest argument a program can have in its favor.

A second major argument that has emerged more prominently in the practice of revenue sharing than in pre-passage discussions is the contribution that its public notification requirements seem to be making for increased citizen participation in at least some cities. One early study reported that about 50 percent of all cities held hearings on revenue sharing to provide an opportunity for citizens to be heard individually and through special interest groups regarding preferred areas of expenditure.[3] In some cities, hearings on the use of revenue sharing funds were, or would have been, almost meaningless. When every available cent has to be used to maintain such basic services as police and fire protection and street maintenance, little room is left for discretionary judgment on the basis of citizen preferences. On the other hand, outside of the largest cities the fiscal situation was perhaps not sufficiently desperate to foreclose completely the making of choices, and the hearings could therefore be of substantive significance. Where special hearings were held on revenue sharing funds—apart from standard general

hearings on a city's entire budget—there seems to have been a great deal of interest elicited.

What remains to be seen is whether increased citizen interest—that is, citizen interest as expressed through leaders of private and public interest groups—which was clearly evident in the early months of revenue sharing, would fade as the early winners in the allocation struggle came to be seen as vested interests no longer amenable to shifting, or whether a true reawakening of a feeling of citizen power was being evidenced. One may speculate that individual and group participation was greater than it might otherwise have been simply because revenue sharing came along at a time when environmental and consumer protection activities had made citizen activism much more common than it had been for some time.

Finally, it should be noted that much of what can be said on this score falls in the realm of speculation, since the experience of revenue sharing is still a new one. It is interesting to note, even on that basis, that a greater percentage of revenue sharing funds—though still a very small percentage—was spent on social services and health services in cities which held public hearings than in those which did not. This is possible evidence of the impact that citizen groups may have, if they stick to their guns. A carryover to general city budgets of the interest generated in direct public input into city budgeting processes would be particularly exciting as a presumably unanticipated spinoff from general revenue sharing. Life would become more hectic for city council members and budget analysts in the offices of city managers, but local democracy would be at least partly revitalized along the rhetorical lines used in the original advocacy of revenue sharing as a part of New Federalism.

Yet another element of revenue sharing that has clearly met with great approbation on the

[3] David A. Caputo and Richard L. Cole, "The Initial Impact of Revenue Sharing in the Spending Patterns of American Cities," in *Public Policy Evaluation*, ed. Kenneth A. Dolbeare (Beverly Hills, Calif.: Sage Publications, 1975), chap. 5.

part of local governments is the administrative simplicity of the program: the absence of federal red tape as compared with the grantsmanship efforts that local governments have to engage in to receive funds under most of the project type grants-in-aid programs. There is a dilemma here, because the intent behind the bureaucratic requirements of the grant in aid programs is, quite properly, to ensure that federal funds are expended in accordance with the specific priorities embedded in the legislation under which Congress has authorized categorical grants; and accountability in the spending of public funds is not easily achieved without some reporting requirements. On the other hand, accountability requirements may largely defeat their own purpose if they ask for an amount or other precise information from the local level that cannot reasonably be attained, or if they involve attempts at control of local minutiae by officials some distance removed. As one close observer of federal aid programs has commented, the "amount of federal administrative regulation has been way out of proportion to the realization of federally prescribed values."[4]

While the absence of most accountability regulations in revenue sharing can also be viewed as a major argument against it (reviewed later in this article), this absence is clearly one of the major plus factors in the eyes of thousands of mayors, city managers and chief county administrative officers. This is probably true even where the absence of federal accountability has not produced any significant change in the use of money from what a particular city might be seeking through categorical grants anyway. That is to say, the absence of paperwork is itself seen as

a major advantage of revenue sharing, even apart from the larger substantive claim that it would reinvigorate state and local government by permitting local definitions of need and local innovations and experimentations based on the knowledge of the people closest to the problem.

Whether revenue sharing constitutes in the long run a decentralization and return of power to state-local levels, or the creation of a much broader (not restricted to specific categories) dependency of those levels on Washington than has ever existed, is an open question.[5] In the short run, however, and at a yearly budget level of decision making within the context of the existing rules of the game, it is true that revenue sharing provides a proportionate shift in decision making power from federal to local hands. Receiving jurisdictions, under general revenue sharing, are required to report to the Office of Revenue Sharing in the Treasury Department their planned pattern of expenditures for the next revenue sharing period and also to show ex post facto expenditures. They do so in a standardized format, but with no directions whatsoever as to where the emphasis in expenditures shall be placed, with the one exception that they are not permitted to spend revenue sharing funds on school operation and maintenance, although they can use these monies for capital outlay of benefit to education. Since this is the only programmatic "string" attached to general revenue sharing, it does indeed give local jurisdictions greater choice in determining what human values will be given priority in the programs of a particular community.

Some other arguments in favor of revenue sharing remain much the same now as they were when the policy was first discussed. Revenue sharing provides aid that can be used

[4] Martha Derthick, Minority Statement in *Revenue Sharing and the Planning Process* (a report of the Subcommittee on the Planning Process and Urban Development of the Advisory Committee to the Department of Housing and Urban Development, Washington, D.C.: National Academy of Sciences, 1974), p. 90.

[5] For a little further elaboration of this argument, *see*, Reagan, *The New Federalism*, pp. 102–105.

for the central functions of local governments —police, fire, health and sanitation, for example—that have been hardest to get categorical aid for, perhaps because they have always been seen as the major local responsibility areas and perhaps because they lack political appeal. The basic housekeeping functions of local governments are, however, at the heart of what makes urbanization possible and hopefully pleasant. Certainly without these core activities, more sophisticated amenities of civilization would be worth little. Yet in many jurisdictions that have not had great need for the special programs funded by Washington through categorical grants, there has nevertheless been a need for improved basic services.

Two additional advantages of revenue sharing may appeal to the elected leaders of local governments particularly. First, the hand of such leaders may be strengthened vis-à-vis their functional department heads. The reasoning here is that under categorical grants the generalist leadership of a city had to rely very heavily upon the specialized skills and specialized contacts of functional department heads, who could bring these skills and contacts to bear in the process of seeking federal grants-in-aid for sewage plants, park and recreation facilities, urban renewal projects, airport construction, or whatever other purpose. Under general revenue sharing, however, it is the generalized elected leadership of mayors and city councils, governors and legislators who hold the purse strings and discretionary authority. Functional department heads must therefore make their cases to local generalist leadership if they are to obtain their share of revenue sharing funds. Thus the direction of dependency is changed about. Another possible consequence of this change is that the department heads may have to become local politicians to a greater degree than previously; that is, they must develop skills in mobilizing electoral and interest group support locally to back up their requests at city hall.

The second advantage of revenue sharing for local leadership is that it provides greater evenness and predictability in the flow of funds than does the project grant system, so far as many localities are concerned. At least during the five-year term of the system, every community can use the official formula to project within reasonably close terms what its revenue sharing income will be each year. Granted that the uncertainty of renewal at the end of five years has been a significant cause for complaint and hesitancy on the part of cities regarding areas that they fear they could not continue to finance if revenue sharing were dropped, it is still a good deal more reliable and predictable than the flow of funds under a project system in which all that is known is that the amount of funds available for each program annually will be considerably less than the amount requested in the form of competitive proposals. Under a project system, some cities do not get anything, and others do not know what they will get until administrative officials of the national government have approved or denied applications. While revenue sharing will almost certainly be continued, though probably not expanded proportionately to other forms of federal grants, the predictability advantage will presumably increase.

ARGUMENTS. AGAINST REVENUE SHARING

Perhaps the most basic group of arguments in favor of specific grants-in-aid as the means the federal government uses to help states and localities financially—and equally the most basic set of arguments against general revenue sharing—revolves around the ideas that there are a number of identifiable national objectives to be obtained through domestic public policies; that the concept of national citizenship establishes an intellectual and ethical base for national criteria of equity in the provision of public services and a national minimum standard of living; that nationally raised funds should not be utilized without some accountability to national criteria; and that proven inefficiency of state and local governments and proven lack of concern of middle class political majorities for the needs of ethnic minorities and the poor require that the national government use financial leverage if equity is to be attained and national social responsibility is to be served. All of these reasons together constitute a very strong argument against simply handing out money with no strings attached.

These arguments continue to be made, but now that revenue sharing has been implemented, certain argumentative aspects stand out more strongly and warrant additional emphasis. That is to say, the particular form of the arguments is now affected by the particular provisions and formulae of the legislation as enacted.

With a total of more than 400 categorical grant-in-aid programs at the peak of the trend, before consolidation into larger block grants got underway at the beginning of the 1970s, it might be said that there were almost as many programs as there were domestic problems. In the shift toward general revenue sharing, it becomes clear that the three broad problem categories which, in de facto political terms, had been most clearly identified as having priority status—namely, problems of the poor, problems of ethnic minorities, and problems of the cities—are the ones which suffer most. This negative rather than positive effect is due to cutbacks in the funding of specific urban-oriented categorical grant programs, such as Model Cities, simultaneously with the start of revenue sharing. In any case, urban minorities who are poor and have for a decade constituted a priority target group for public policies aimed at creating a more equitable society, and the largest cities, with their increasing need for human services simultaneous with a decline in the tax base, are clearly the major losers under general revenue sharing.

Their loss has two primary components: (1)

the loss of national leverage for ensuring that state and local governments direct their efforts toward solving public problems rather than reducing the local tax level or the provision of nonpriority amenities; and (2) a revenue sharing formula that distributes money too much in accordance with population and not enough in accordance with local finances and local needs as related specifically to *national* problem-solving criteria. Closely related to these concerns is the fact that, to the extent that urban problems are partly those of fragmented governmental jurisdictions (which enable the suburbs to have the advantages of the central city without paying an equitable share of the burden), revenue sharing makes things worse: first, by providing funds that enable minor suburban townships to stay afloat (whereas financial pressures might otherwise have induced them to join in metropolitan area governments); and, second, because the totality of funds going to all governments in a metropolitan area cannot under this system be directed toward a single major use, but rather is subject to fragmentation resulting from as many different utilization judgments as there are townships sharing the money.

Granting as a political reality that all distributive legislation has to spread its funds thinner than program objectives require in order to ensure a majority coalition of recipient congressional districts, the general revenue sharing formula seems to have gone much too far in that direction. For example, the Connecticut commuter suburb of Redding received $69,000 as its first revenue sharing check. Questionnaires sent to citizens asking for expenditure suggestions resulted in many requests for a bridle path for horse owners who enjoy a morning ride before commuting to work.[6] Other citizens maintained that the great need was for tennis courts. The Redding Board of Finance apparently represented a different local milieu: it recommended the pur-

[6] *New York Times*, 10 June 1973.

chase of two new highway trucks, a bulldozer, and park improvements. At the time of receiving this $69,000 check, the town of Redding was collecting interest on about $200,000 of surplus funds.

It is argued with considerable justice that there is something wrong with a system of fiscal federalism that does such a tremendously inefficient job of matching revenue availability with pressing social needs. One of the early arguments in favor of revenue sharing was that it would permit localities to define their own needs, on the assumption that they would know those needs best. It is now obvious that, even if this were entirely true rather than partially specious, some jurisdictions' needs constitute another jurisdictions' indefensible frosting on a cake.

Clearly there is something wrong when a central city has absolutely no maneuverability and its revenue sharing funds disappear in the desperate attempt to maintain existing inadequate levels of basic services, while adjoining suburbs solicit ideas for the spending of money that is beyond need or expectation. Ironically, general revenue sharing appears to reward exactly those jurisdictions that were least innovative and least active in attempting to avail themselves of the categorical grant system— whether because of lack of imagination or lack of need. If a city had not been obtaining much or any grant-in-aid money, then it gains from revenue sharing in two ways, in comparison with cities that had become heavily dependent on categorical grants: (1) it suffers no loss from displaced categorical grants, and (2) it obtains new funds that can be used in new ways.

The situation of the central cities is further exacerbated by the extent to which the influx of revenue sharing money was matched by a simultaneous reducton in funds previously obtained on a project grant basis to meet specific central city needs. It is probably not correct, fiscally or politically, to charge that the inaug-

uration of revenue sharing was itself a cause of decline in funding for major urban-oriented grant-in-aid programs. However, it is almost certainly accurate to state that the rise of revenue sharing has been used as an excuse for cutting back on the other kind of aid. As Robert C. Wood, president of the University of Massachusetts and former undersecretary of the Department of Housing and Urban Development, told the Muskie subcommittee in hearings on New Federalism in 1973, general revenue sharing has resembled the old shell game; that is, "Whichever shell you look under, the federal funds you thought were there have vanished." Wood continued:

On the one hand the American people have been told that general revenue sharing is extra money, to be used by the states and cities to relieve the growing tax burden and to fund new programs. But it has not been clear that this "sharing" is coupled with massive cutbacks in educational and social programs upon which the same states and cities depend heavily.

In Boston, Wood pointed out, general revenue sharing was to be $17 million in fiscal 1973, but the city was scheduled to lose $100 million in cuts from such programs as Model Cities, the Public Service Employees Program, and Public Housing. In Wood's view, New Federalism "means the state and local governments of this country will find themselves with responsibility for domestic problems and development without even the present level of resources with which to confront these problems."[7]

Probably even more important than the maldistribution of funds, and certainly at least as important, is the argument that for whatever sums of money it distributes, general revenue sharing lacks the clout that would come from

[7] Wood's testimony is contained in *Hearings, A New Federalism*, U.S., Senate, Committee on Government Operations, Subcommittee on Intergovernmental Relations, 93rd Cong., 1st sess., 1973.

federal priority specifications in the use of the monies. While it is true that the leverage of categorical grants often brought with it "irksome and largely irrelevant supervision over petty details," it is also true, as a National Academy of Sciences advisory committee told its sponsor, the Department of Housing and Urban Development, that:

Neither general nor special revenue-sharing legislation, as presently conceived, can be expected to address nationally recognized problems unless there is a clear local disposition toward their solution. General revenue sharing eliminates virtually all federal direction concerning priorities for local expenditures of funds allocated by the program.

The same subcommittee had stated earlier:

Under revenue sharing, the locus of priority-setting moves from the national to the local level, and the effort to compel conformity to narrowly defined program objectives is abandoned. . . . The question under revenue sharing, is how to ensure that . . . national goals, particularly the effort to reduce racial and economic disadvantage, continue to inform locally based planning and policy development. This question is critical even though racial, social, and economic inequity—and hence effort to address them—are a systemwide problem, and malfunctioning of the system as a whole is virtually impossible to address at the local level.[8]

While the dream of many observers of the urban scene that suburbs and central cities might be fused into single metropolitan-wide governments seems unlikely, some other approaches to the diminution of the consequences of governmental jurisdiction fragmentation seem to have been making some headway, from the "workable plan" requirement of the 1949 urban renewal legislation, through the "701 Comprehensive Planning Assistance" of the Housing Act of 1954 and the Circular A-95

requirement of the Office of Management and Budget for metropolitan area and regional coordination on federally assisted projects. Essentially these were all devices by which a particular local jurisdiction had to pay at least some attention to the relation of its plans to those of neighboring jurisdictions and to some overall conception of the needs and logical development pattern of the metropolitan region as a whole. Under general revenue sharing, all of this stimulus is lost. Worse, a new stimulus is created that necessarily works specifically toward the maintenance of fragmentation, for the jurisdiction that is receiving new monies without having to prove its need through a competitive grant proposal process is confirmed in its autonomy from its own metropolitan area needs.

Another argument against general revenue sharing that relates indirectly to the special needs of very large cities is that, although those needs are still very pressing and can be expected to continue unabated, the more general fiscal crisis of state and local government may well be receding. Melville J. Ulmer has pointed out that education, public welfare, and highway construction now account for more than two-thirds of all state and local expenditures, but that educational expenditures are leveling off because of changes in the birth rate, and huge capital expenditures on school buildings will not be the large drain that they were for the past 20 years. Also, the National Highway Program is nearing completion, and public assistance programs seem to be well on the way toward totally national financing.[9] The state-local fiscal crisis will therefore be ameliorated through these demographic and economic changes.

Critics of unfettered state-local discretion in the use of federal money cite not only the fact

8 The quotations above are from the Subcommittee on the Planning Process and Urban Development, National Academy of Sciences, *Revenue Sharing in the Planning Process*, pp. 60, 61, and 8–9.

9 Melville J. Ulmer, "The Limitations of Revenue Sharing," in *The Annals* 397 (September 1971), pp. 51–52.

that political power may determine which groups are likely to benefit from the expenditures, but they also have great doubts about the administrative capacity of those governments. Except for a few states, the spoils system of personnel appointments, for example, remains amazingly strong. Even where adequate merit systems exist, the salary levels of many cities and counties and some states cannot compete effectively for the best talent among city managers, finance officers, health and welfare officers, housing planners, and the like. For that matter, the rate of increase in federally aided programs over the past 10 years has been so much faster than the rate of production of skilled manpower in many of the needed fields that, regardless of salary level, it would be impossible for all jurisdictions to obtain equally competent persons.

The need for developmental efforts, for technical assistance from the higher jurisdiction with its easier claim to the best talent, and for the use of leverage to ensure that at least minimal professional practices are followed is therefore quite clear. Awareness of this need has produced some of the red tape in federal grant programs in order to ensure effective administration by the receiving government. General revenue sharing would have been a particularly strategic opportunity for enlarging the scope of requirements along these lines, inasmuch as the leverage would run to all governments of general jurisdiction. That opportunity was completely lost, however. Similarly, there was an opportunity for stimulating fiscal reform at the state and local level, and it too was missed.

Revenue sharing funds could be withheld from any state that had not enacted a personal income tax, or they could be withheld from any state or local jurisdiction that did not have a merit personnel system. Since both of these provisions could be enacted without interfering in any way with the shared revenues principle of letting states and localities decide how to spend their funds, it is to be hoped that renewal of the revenue sharing program will not again pass up the opportunity to stimulate improved capacity, fiscal and administrative, of the lower jurisdictions. If this were achieved, a major argument against revenue sharing would be eliminated.

Another problem with revenue sharing, one which was not very much alluded to in advance but is becoming increasingly apparent, is that the institution building function that many federal demonstration grant and pilot program grants had performed is now almost entirely ended. Institution building and demonstration grant programs provide an opportunity for pulling together a critical mass of the best talent available with regard to a specific function, whether it be urban planning, gerontology, the analysis of poverty problems, or defense analyses.

Several major university gerontology centers, for example, have been established through grant programs, and they have produced in a relatively short period of time a significant advance in professionalization of that field and an effective concentration of effort for better understanding of the problems of the aging population. As specific gerontology center grants are phased out, however, such efforts will almost inevitably come to a grinding halt. Whether the equivalent funds are distributed among thousands of jurisdictions through general revenue sharing, or even through special revenue sharing limited to human development problems but still on a formula basis of very wide distribution, the funding pattern will become so scattered that the critical mass will be lost. One could hardly envisage hundreds of local government jurisdictions' getting together on a voluntary basis to contribute pro rata shares for the continuance of a special center located in one jurisdiction.

In other words, revenue sharing is anti-institution building and anti-leadership, though surely not specifically intended to be so. In this regard, it is perhaps ironic that a nation whose general ideology places great faith in competition as a way of ensuring that the best ideas rise to the top should adopt, and hail as an important innovation, a major policy that is extremely uncompetitive in that it does not discriminate between jurisdictions that make bootstrap attempts to solve their own problems, even if with inadequate resources, and those that simply wait for handouts.

One further major argument has developed against revenue sharing as specially legislated in 1972, although this argument is not inherent in the general revenue sharing concept. Under the existing legislation the civil rights, or nondiscrimination, provision has been held by many critics to be totally inadequate and indeed quite regressive as compared with nondiscrimination enforcement provisions in many other pieces of legislation. The Fair Housing Act and the Equal Employment Opportunity Act, for example, have had detailed regulations and specific procedures for acting against alleged violations of the nondiscrimination provision. The general revenue sharing act, however, lacks detailed procedures and even is vague in its definitions of discrimination and "such corrective action as may be appropriate." The enforcement burden is placed largely on the states in the first instance, but obviously it is from some of the states that the greatest unwillingness to honor civil rights has come; and the sanctions for violation of the nondiscrimination provision are minimal in that the ultimate sanction of termination of entitlement payments applies only to the particular program in which noncompliance is found, rather than to the entire unit of government in which it occurs. Although some revisions of a strengthening nature were promulgated in February 1973, an analysis done for the Rand Corporation concluded that discrimination may still be prevalent under revenue sharing.

Apart from the specific civil rights provisions of the revenue sharing act, the problem of discrimination exists in a larger sense. For one thing, revenue sharing puts funds without strings attached in the hands of state and local power structures that in many instances, and not just in the deep South, are very narrowly based in the Anglo middle class. This may result in hard-to-prove discrimination which is in principle subject to the official sanctions of the act but is almost certainly what Nicki King refers to as implicit discrimination, or the use of revenue sharing monies for functions whose beneficiary user groups are the nonpoor, nonminority residents of the area. King cites some examples as follows:

The Capital Improvements Program may be used to refurbish a City Hall. Certainly, this is a legitimate expenditure if the city needs it, but the user group of the modernized City Hall is probably the middle class worker who will then have an air conditioned office. . . . As another example, the recreation program may be used to improve the quality of golf courses in city parks. Certainly, there are lots of golfing devotees who are entitled to an equitable use of their tax dollars, but golfing is largely a middle class diversion, and those devotees are better able to afford costs for private recreational facilities than a poor inner-city resident (who may have never seen a golf course, much less afforded to play the game). By addressing the projects paid for with revenue sharing funds to a non-poor user group, a local official may be implicitly discriminating against a certain racial segment of the population.[10]

While the prohibition against explicit racial discrimination can be strengthened, and stronger enforcement measures devised, implicit discrimination is not so easily dismissed as a problem, inasmuch as it is the logical result of the essence of revenue sharing: to let the locus of responsibility for priority determination in the spending of federal funds be

[10] Nicki King, *Federal Revenue Sharing* (Paper Series P–4994, Santa Monica, Calif.: Rand, 1973), pp. 14–15.

shifted from federal agencies operating under congressionally authorized mandates to local officials operating on a carte blanche basis.

CONCLUSION

Categorical grant-in-aid programs do a much better job than revenue sharing of accommodating expenditures to national social priorities and stimulating innovative programs in states and localities, which must present competitive proposals in order to receive funds. However, revenue sharing is superior to categorical grants in terms of reducing bureaucratic red tape and permitting maximum freedom at the local level to accommodate special needs, even if some of those needs do not fit into the pattern expressed in appropriations priorities by Congress.

Can this dilemma be resolved? The resolution would seem to lie in rational compromise that would focus heavily on block grants, while permitting perhaps 10 percent of the funds in any grant program to be available on a very broad, open-ended competitive proposal basis. Where there was a real desire for innovation and a real sense of healthy local discussion and program formulation in which broad segments of the citizenry participated, providing funds apart from the normal categorical programs would be very worthwhile. The system of fiscal federalism can and should accommodate whatever instances of real local initiatives exist; but the existing general revenue sharing program goes too far in accommodating nonexistent local initiatives and local skills that are no more than the rhetorical dreams of conservative ideology.

15

Sunbelt vs. Frostbelt: A Second Civil War?

Horace Sutton

In recent years the federal system has experienced increasing competition for federal funds between different regions of the country. Such regional rivalries exist alongside the traditional intergovernmental cooperation among states. The so-called Snowbelt states of the Northeast and Midwest contain many distressed cities which have lost population, jobs, and industry to the rapidly growing Sunbelt states of the South and Southwest.

Snowbelt states want targeted federal aid for cities and metropolitan regions to revive local economies. In contrast, the Sunbelt areas want federal aid to deal with regional planning, water and sewer systems, and pollution controls. The Snowbelt-Sunbelt competition has become highly politicized at the national level and is reflected in congressional debates over federal funding formulas.

It was September of 1976, and the party was almost over. The Tall Ships had come and gone. The Freedom Train had puffed across a continent telling how liberty had come to the land. Grown men had played dress-up, donning uniforms of Washington's continentals and marching off to replay campaign tactics that had carried the day against Burgoyne and Cornwallis. The smell of gunpowder, exploded from a thousand pyrotechnic displays, hung over parks and parade grounds like the stale smoke of a giant poker party held the night before.

All this had been done to celebrate the birthday of the Republic born two centuries before, conceived in liberty and welded together in the concept of union. Yet union and celebration were not in the mind of Michael Harrington, congressman from Massachusetts. He was thinking about regionalism. While the deeds of the Adams family, those Massachusetts stalwarts of the Republic, were being dramatized over national television week after week, no place in the nation found itself in more straitened circumstances than Massachusetts

itself. The economic downturn of 1972–73 had devastated the Northeast. Factories had closed or departed for the more felicitous climes of the South. Military bases were, one by one, state by state, slipping into the Sunbelt, that recently designated region knit together of states that lay below a latitudinal line stretching from San Francisco to the point where the northern border of North Carolina falls into the Atlantic.

The inflation set off by the oil embargo was devastating. The price of home heating oil soared from $2 a barrel to anywhere between $11 and $14 a barrel. And in the district represented by Michael Harrington, firm of jaw, florid of face, Harvard '58, there was no way to avoid the crippling expense of heating one's home. Says he, "An awful lot of people saw hope and expectation peeled back for the first time in their lives. Those who had harbored expansive ideas suddenly found that they were among the severely economically disadvantaged." It was very clear to Harrington that those occupying congressional seats had to meet the needs of what some have called The New Poor.

That Bicentennial September, with no recovery in sight, Harrington, having met with representatives of other states in like difficulties, joined with Congressman Henry Reuss of Wisconsin to launch the Northeast-Midwest Economic Advancement Coalition. The toothy name came from Reuss; the philosophy, from Harrington; the membership, from 16 states in New England, the Middle Atlantic, and the Midwest. Ideology and political cant were of no matter. Of disparate strains, the congressmen were welded together by the common problem of regional inequity.

The formation of the Northeast-Midwest coalition was, if anything, a Fort Sumter in reverse. While the coalition's members were certainly not suggesting secession, they served notice that they would act as a body to ensure a fair shake from the federal government, the nation's biggest employer and provider.

With Harrington, Congressman Frank Horton, (a Republican from upstate New York) as cochairman, and Congressman James Oberstar of Minnesota as secretary-treasurer, the coalition assembled a force of 204 representatives backed by its own research bureau. Their concerns varied: Some were interested in the out-migration of industry; some were concerned with welfare; others, with the closing of military bases.

The objectives of the coalition are laid out by John Moriarity, a young Harrington aide who was detached to become the coalition's paid director. "We are not trying to stem the flow of funds to the South. We're trying to balance the flow of funds so they go where the need is greatest," he says.

"When the South was in a position of greatest adversity they had to have a buddy system. We are now creating a buddy system, and we're doing it in a public way. We feel we have a limited amount of time left. After the census of 1980, considering the population shifts, we stand to lose 9 to 10 seats in the Northeast and the Midwest.

"We can't suggest the problems of the East and the Midwest aren't there. We can't suppose there is no poverty in the South. We aren't saying it's our turn to put on the feed bag. We are suggesting that the federal programs must be sensitive to other parts of the country that were once the chief providers that brought forth the New Deal programs that provided the economic opportunity enjoyed by the South today."

It comes hard to the Northeast to realize that its political and economic supremacy is being challenged by sections of the nation that were uncharted Indian country, Polynesian kingdoms, Spanish lands, and even Russian territory when the Founding Fathers put the Republic together. From 1870 to 1940, a span of 70 years, the nation was dominated, as Kirkpatrick Sale points out in *Power Shift*, "in practically every aspect of life . . . by a nexus of industrial, financial, political, academic, and cultural centers based in the Northeast, stretching from Chicago to New York, from Boston to Philadelphia."

This power group influenced the selection of presidents, controlled the Congress, decided foreign policy, and established economic priorities. But the shift came with the start of World War II, which brought with it "new technologies and new priorities." Defense industries, aerospace electronics, oil and gas, and what financial circles call "agribusiness" clustered in the South, Southwest, and West. The population migrated "from the older and colder sections of the Northeast to the younger and sunnier sections of the South and Southwest."

Sale calls this vast bottomland of the U.S. the Southern Rim, but Sunbelt is the name that has caught on. It says in a word—or in an amalgam of two words—what brought it about. If the Sunbelt, or the Southern Rim, were to be an independent nation, as Sale points out, it would have a gross national product larger than that of the United Kingdom, Italy, Sweden, and Norway combined.

It would possess more cars and telephones than any other nation in the world. "It would, in short," Sale writes, "be a world power on the scale of the present superpowers."

While the Sunbelt was growing into a superpower, another phenomenon was under way. The federal government grew into a superspender. The federal budget that stood at about $15 billion before World War II is now over $300 billion. The government's payroll has increased from $613 million to $3 billion. Whereas New York (for all its poverty) is probably the seat of $200 billion in private assets and a source of $30 billion a year for capital backing, Washington's assets are without limits, and as Sale indicates, "the source of something like $300 billion a year for private businesses."

New York the money center has been eclipsed by Washington the superdisburser. With the preeminence went the power. In the years from 1869 to 1945, only two presidents were elected from areas outside the Northeast. But from 1963 until now, all elected presidents —the presidential appointee Gerald Ford excepted—have sprung from the Sunbelt. Control of the presidency and control of major committees give the Sunbelt states a position of advantage in the contest for that mammoth pot of federal dollars. It is the shift in power and poverty that has caused the forces of Frostbelt and Sunbelt to array themselves as if for battle.

When legislators from the Northeast and the Midwest locked arms in a regional coalition, the Sunbelters made no move to match the Yankee offensive. "We don't need a Sunbelt coalition; we've got Jimmy Carter in the White House," Congressman Charlie Rose of North Carolina crowed with some exuberance. Who could consider it a coincidence that in 1977, the first year of Carter's presidency, more money designated for military construction was earmarked for Georgia than for all

the 16 states of the Northeast-Midwest coalition put together?

Sunbelt euphoria faded last spring when the House assembled to vote on HR 6655, a housing and community development bill sparkling with a new formula. The old formula could enable federal aid to be funneled on the basis of poverty, overcrowded housing, and population. Under the new formula, a consideration was added for housing that existed before 1939 as a means of funneling dollars to aging and indigent cities of the East and the Midwest.

Congressman Mark Hannaford, a bouncy, bantam-sized former mayor who represents Long Beach, California, and its adjacent areas, rushed forward with an amendment to HR 6655 that would have neutralized the pre-1939 formula. "This program," Hannaford said from the floor, "looks at old buildings regardless of their state of repair or need as a measure of need, and it mindlessly and arbitrarily passes out money on that basis."

Off the floor the rhetoric was more heated. Hannaford and his cosponsor, Congressman Jerry Patterson, also of California, told the press that the legislation rests on the premise that "we should tax the people of the rest of the country to resolve the problems of neglect faced by the large and old cities of the Midwest and the East." Said Hannaford, "I cannot accept that the suburbs in my district in Los Angeles and Orange counties, some of them with many low-income people, should be taxed to support the revitalization of Detroit or Newark."

Notwithstanding, the so-called Hannaford-Patterson amendment perished by a vote of 149 to 261. The Northeast-Midwest coalition had drawn first blood. The battle was joined.

By November of last year, Hannaford was heading what he has called a task force to monitor Frostbelt-Sunbelt issues and to respond accordingly "when the best interests of the South and the West are at stake."

In his Washington office Hannaford smiles. "I'm a Democrat," he says. "I support cities. I don't want to contribute to sectional cleavage. I'm offering a response to Frostbelt action."

On the hustings, however, he is not likely to stand with sheathed spear. Speaking before the Nucleus Club in Tucson this winter, Hannaford told his audience he was surprised at first by the invitation to come to Arizona. As he began to think about it, however, he realized that Tucson and Long Beach have a common problem. "We are both a part of what is coming to be referred to in Congress as the Sunbelt, and we are being taken to the cleaners together. The Frostbelt in the northeastern and the midwestern states has plans for some of our tax dollars."

Writing for home consumption in *Western City* magazine, Hannaford declared that the Sunbelt is "not prepared to stand with its hands in the air while the rest of the country makes off with its wallet."

Sounding those themes, Hannaford's task force has taken the form of a western coalition, but on the House side it relies on an assigned aide in Hannaford's office and as yet operates without the oiled apparatus functioning on behalf of the Northeast-Midwest coalition.

Western senators, however, rallied to a call sounded by Senator Paul Laxalt, the Nevada conservative Republican who handled the Reagan campaign and who is prominent in the fight against the signing of the new Panama Canal Treaty. Laxalt was able to lasso a bloc of 20 senators representing states stretching from the edge of the Midwest clear to Hawaii and Alaska.

Laxalt has said, "A Northeast senator's effectiveness is measured by how effectively he can raid the federal till," a statement not calculated to endear him to those members of the senate club who hail from the New England and the Middle Atlantic states. At the suggestion of Senator Alan Cranston, a Democrat from California, a Democratic cochairman was

chosen to balance Laxalt on the western coalition. They turned to Dennis DeConcini, an affable forty-year-old freshman senator, the product of an Arizona political family, who had earlier managed Raul Castro's successful campaign for governor of Arizona.

Laxalt offered to run DeConcini's campaign for cochairman, and DeConcini said he would agree to the offer if the senator from Nevada could promise better results than he had obtained on behalf of former governor Ronald Reagan. On that jocular note DeConcini was chosen to head, with Laxalt, the coalition of western senators.

Despite Laxalt's stone flinging at northeastern senators, the western fight is directed more at the federal government than at other parts of the nation. What attracted DeConcini to the cause was the appearance in January 1977 of what he calls "the president's hit list on water projects." It is a circumstance to be noted that "hit list" is also the term used by eastern and midwestern congressmen when they refer to bases that the Pentagon is considering for relocation in Sunbelt areas.

DeConcini worries about such matters as water, Indian claims, and the overbearing presence of federal lands. He is quick to point out that only 13 percent of Arizona is privately held land, the rest belonging to the federal government, the state, and the Indians. Aware of his own local problems, he is more sensitive and more amelioratory on matters that press the East. "I realize more money is spent in New York for welfare, unemployment, and Medicare than is spent in Arizona and a dozen western states, and there is nothing wrong with that," he says.

The argument between Sunbelt and Frostbelt in his view boils down to defense spending. In not all cases, DeConcini claims, does the location of bases and defense facilities derive from political clout. He turns to California as a state without strategic committee representation that nevertheless bristles with defense installations, military bases, and airfields.

"Defense dollars should be spent where they get the most use," DeConcini declares. "Take air training. It makes sense to me to use part of the country where you can have the maximum amount of good weather to fly rather than Michigan or New Hampshire, where the weather is hampering.

"Moving a training center like Luke Air Force Base [Arizona] to Pennsylvania or Massachusetts would not be in the best interests of training and probably would not help the unemployment problem that is there."

That argument is contested with some heat by northern legislators. Harrington's whole fight, the one issue that inspired him to organize the Northeast and the Midwest, was predicated on the Pentagon proposal to move Fort Devens from Massachusetts. Oddly, the new home being considered for Fort Devens is Fort Huachuca, Arizona, near the town of Sierra Vista (population 20,000), a few miles from the Mexican border. There the troops wouldn't have to endure snowed-in winters —only 120-degree summers. No one has measured the cost of northern heating oil in Devens's barracks against the cost of air conditioning in southern Arizona.

On the subject of military displacement, no other senator rings more decibels than Howard Metzenbaum of Ohio. A leader with Senator John Chafee of Rhode Island of the senatorial branch of the Northeast-Midwest coalition, Metzenbaum sits in his expansive office in the Russell Building, chomps on candy from an ever-present bowl, and says, "You can't fight all the wars in the Sunbelt. These are supposed to be military installations. You can't assume every war is going to be fought where the sun is shining.

"One objective of our coalition is to stop the military from literally decimating their installations in the Northeast and the Midwest. I never hear in any conversation with the military that they are going to open a new facility in the Northeast or the Midwest or even expand those they have. But it is a constant battle to keep them from closing the Rickenbacker facility in Columbus or the defense electronics center in Dayton or the defense logistics agency in Columbus.

"It may have to do with the makeup of the committees, but it may have to do with the military, who want to bask in the sunshine and have a swimming pool at their beck and call and who are totally indifferent to the responsibilities to the nation as a whole and indifferent to training in cold zones as well as in hot zones."

To Metzenbaum, who ran for his senatorial seat on the promise that he would bring more jobs to Ohio, the matter of defense spending is basic. And Senator Chafee can give chapter and verse on the effects of diverting defense spending as it affected his home state. As secretary of the navy until he resigned in May 1972, Chafee was completely familiar with the impact of the navy's decision, effected in 1974 to move much of the navy from its traditional home in Rhode Island. The navy extracted from Newport the headquarters of the cruiser-destroyer forces in the Atlantic, as well as a supply depot largely staffed by civilian employees. That wholesale diversion of forces is still being referred to in that city as "the second Pearl Harbor."

Across the bay in Quonset, Rhode Island, a large naval air rework facility that occupied itself with fixed-wing and helicopter aircraft engines and employed nearly 3,000 people was uprooted. Work at Quonset's shipyard, with the ships gone, dried up. At Davisville, a Seabee construction battalion employing 1,000 Rhode Islanders closed down. In all, 17,000 naval personnel were dispatched southward, leaving 6,000 Rhode Islanders jobless.

Why did it happen? Well, the navy, Chafee explains, likes to have its ships overhauled close to their home ports. There the men can work on their ships by day and be at home with their families at night. When the Boston shipyard closed, it followed that Newport be closed. Why did Boston close? Because it was old.

Where are the Seabees today? In Gulfport, Mississippi, the home state of Senator John Stennis, who holds the key position on the Armed Services Committee. Says Chafee, "The southern group is extremely well organized. It is no coincidence that you see Charleston, South Carolina, brimming with defense facilities and Strom Thurmond sitting as ranking Republican on the Armed Services Committee. Or the lovely Naval Air Training facility sitting in Meridian, Mississippi, near where Stennis lives.

"I don't know whether it is cause or effect," Chafee offers disarmingly. "I don't know whether they are there to look after their bases or whether the bases are there because of them."

Harrington, Chafee's neighboring New Englander, wouldn't have to ponder that suggestion very long. The strong, purposeful regionalism that he brought into the House and that was picked up by the Senate is nothing more, he says, than what southern legislators have been practicing all along. "They refined the art," Harrington says. "We have merely adopted it."

Some of the cooperative southern thrust comes from the Southern Growth Policies Board, an interstate agency that is supported by the governments of 13 southern states stretching from the Atlantic to Oklahoma. Delaware and Maryland (which are not Sunbelt states) are eligible to join, and so are Missouri and Texas.

The Southern board operates out of Research Triangle Park, in North Carolina, where it employs a staff of about a dozen, and has offices in Atlanta and a new one in Washington, in view of the Capitol, as well. Each year a governor of a member state serves as chair-

man of the board. This year's chairman is Governor George Busbee of Georgia, who succeeded Jimmy Carter in the statehouse at Atlanta.

Seeking to blunt northern arguments in one blow, the Southern Growth Policies Board has issued a paper entitled "The Snowbelt and the Seven Myths." No fairy tale, it hits hard at these propositions:

1. The South is draining federal funds from the North
2. The South is stealing industry and business from the North
3. The South is actually richer than the North
4. Most poor people live in the North
5. Most distressed cities are in the North
6. Growth lag or lack of percentage increases in income signal the need for federal help
7. Old cities need federal aid

This winter the President convened the White House Conference on Balanced Growth and Economic Development—the name intended no slur at the partisan name of Busbee's group—inviting 500 citizens to participate. Three quarters of the delegates were chosen by the governors and one quarter by the White House. Care had been taken to down-play the hot regional issues. Suggestions along that line, so the story goes, had, been passed to principal speakers by Jack Watson of the White House staff.

Michael Harrington was not invited. The Northeast-Midwest Economic Advancement Coalition opened an office in the Sheraton Park Hotel where the symposium was held, but the coalition was not permitted to include materials in the packets prepared for distribution to delegates.

There were four days of speeches, a number of them by prominent citizens, but. the main event matched two Democrats—George Busbee against Daniel Patrick Moynihan, the junior senator from New York.

Moynihan's address was filled with historical references, quotations plucked from assorted sources, the whole of it dotted, like a fruitcake, with fetching tidbits—an economic lesson here, a fervent plea there. In all, it was an eloquent paper that synthesized, in its lyrical way, the reason for the face-off between Frostbelt and Sunbelt.

The senator observed, first, that the subject of concern was labeled regional growth, but it referred, really, to regional decline. He reminded the assemblage that the federal government had addressed itself to policies of regional growth from the beginning of the nation. Western expansion was nineteenth-century regionalism. In the 1930s, with the coming of the New Deal, Franklin Roosevelt perceived the economic lag in the South and, in 1939, addressed himself to the problem. Said Roosevelt:

It is my conviction that the South presents right now the nation's number one economic problem—the nation's problem, not merely the South's. For we have an economic unbalance in the nation as a whole due to this very condition of the South's. It is an unbalance that can and must be righted for the sake of the South and of the nation.

It has been a tradition of the northeastern states, Moynihan declared, to pursue an ethic of collective provisionism, "which in our time is associated with the activist national liberalism of the New Deal." He reminded the delegates that Roosevelt, a New Yorker of the Hudson Valley, was instrumental in calling for a "considerable transfer of resources from his region . . . to the South and the West." The outpourings were for Roosevelt "the expression of a national purpose which knew little of regional power but concentrated greatly on regional need."

"What happens to this tradition of national liberalism if it turns out, two generations later, that while the South was willing to accept the resources of the North to get it going, it has no intention to reciprocate now that the North-

east is in need?" Moynihan thinks, to answer his own question, there would be a "response in bitterness that would equal what the South expressed and endured after its defeat in the War Between the States." Moreover, it would mean the loss of the national liberalism that the Northeast gave to the nation. Moynihan admitted this to be a fine point but insisted it was at the heart of the issue. "It is not a point easily understood, and it will be fiercely resisted, yet I believe it to be so," he said.

Moynihan presented two propositions. The first was that the federal government cease to make the problems of the Northeast worse by continuing to pour federal money into the South and the West. The heavy concentration of defense facilities in the South, he said, has caused him on prior occasion to remark that "our armed forces are clearly preparing to fight the next war in Nicaragua, or at least someplace where it never freezes."

In his second proposition, the senator called on the federal government to prevent the bankruptcy of New York, an event he considers "somewhere between possible and probable in the next six to thirty months." Such an event, he continued, using a parallel that would not be lost on his audience, "would be to the Northeast what Sherman's march was to the South. It would be a seismic event in the world at large. It will be seen to be a failure of democratic government of an altogether ominous degree. A massive statement that self-government in America is indeed 'all sail and no anchor.' "

If New York City should go bankrupt, he warned, "it will be the only thing the thirty-ninth President is remembered for . . . none of the other things we are talking about at this conference will matter."

When it came his turn, Governor Busbee elected not to defend the matter of military installations in the South. He chose instead to attack the amendment to the Housing and Community Development Act that had slipped through the Congress, when the South had, he said, "its eyes closed and its britches down." On the other hand, he was sympathetic to the plight of New York, but he noted that New York was offering tuition-free college degrees while "I was fighting and bleeding for money to start a statewide kindergarten program."

Both senator and governor warned of the danger of sectionalism and of politicizing regional growth. "Squaring off the governor of Georgia against the senator from New York could mark the formal beginning of such a process," Moynihan said. Busbee, too, decried divisiveness: "The time has come to stop the trend of sectionalism and to address the problems that plague America as Americans. We are as much one nation economically as we are one nation politically." Addressing Moynihan, Busbee assured him that "we are sympathetic to the plight of New York City." Then came the sting. "This is not a divorce proceeding," he said. "You can't expect enough alimony to sustain the manner of life you've been accustomed to."

From the sharp edge of partisan regionalism it is not too long a step to separatism. Regionalists wave off with it-can't-happen-here disdain the specter of Quebec straining at the bonds that tether it to Ottawa. But once in the bloodstream, regionalism is as hard to expunge as dengue fever. One hundred and seventeen years after the outbreak of the War Between the States, we remain a nation where part of the country waves and reveres the flag of the Confederate breakaway states and still sings "Dixie" as if it were "Onward, Christian Soldiers"; a nation where the Lone Star state, which had existed as an independent republic for 9 years and was admitted to the Union on its own petition 133 years ago, still stands to sing "The Eyes of Texas" as if it were its national anthem.

The effects of regionalism are only too vivid in Italy, where sectionalism has broken the threads of the patchwork country sewn to-gether by the *Risorgimento*. The Milanese sniffing at the Neapolitans, the Romans looking askance at the Sicilians, and the Venetians with their own independent mercantile and martial history, a people apart from, say, the Sards. Cracks appear in the unity of France when Bretons strike hard for a revival of their national language and a relief from the second-class citizenship that they feel they have endured because of the remote posture of the land and the singular ways of the people.

And nowhere in western Europe is the lesson clearer than in Spain, where the new constitutional monarchy strives to hold together a nation in which the Catalans and the Basques consider themselves as separate countries and in which the rustlings of independence come from Andalusia and Galicia as well.

In the United States, regionalism in the Congress breeds trade offs in which legislators may vote in favor of measures they basically dislike, or even fear, as a favor to other congressmen who hopefully will be sympathetic when the regionalists' turn comes.

Activists in the regional fray in Washington —senators, congressmen, and heads of sectional groups—have urged caution. It is said that the late Senator Humphrey was against regionalism and was wary of it. Senators Muskie and Kennedy are conspicuous in their absence from the skirmish lines.

Yet, the realities remain. Says the Northeast-Midwest coalition's Moriarity, "If the debate evolves in an acrimonious way, so be it. We are facing the possibility of an eight-year Carter presidency. When Tip O'Neill resigns we stand a chance of seeing the House managed by a southern speaker. And then there are the seats we will lose in the House in '82. Who will stand up for us then?"

In a memorandum written to White House aide Stuart Eizenstat this January, Michael Harrington expressed worry over a backlash against sectionalism that "creates very real political problems." Mark Hannaford has said,

"I don't like this role. I hope the need for it passes. Moreover, if war breaks out over this I'm not going to enlist." No jokes come from Howard Metzenbaum, the senator from Ohio: "I don't look at it as a matter of Balkanization or trying to go into battle with other sections of the country. We are not coming out with our dukes up." But in the backroom trade offs, in the legislative infighting, in the speeches on and off the congressional floor, the tone is less than pacific. If you listen carefully, you can hear the trumpets blow and the trumpets say, "Charge!"

PART
TWO

☆☆☆☆☆☆☆☆☆☆☆☆☆☆☆☆☆☆☆☆☆☆☆☆☆☆☆☆☆☆☆☆☆☆☆☆

POLITICAL PARTICIPATION:
INFLUENCING GOVERNMENT

★★

Interest Groups

5

Interest groups are essential to democracies in providing the people with effective channels to pressure government for the achievement of specific goals. In our modern, post-industrial, technological age, governments have become so large and complex that individuals, acting alone, often find executives, legislators, and administrators inaccessible and unresponsive. By joining interest groups, citizens are able to pool their concerns and are better able to get their views across to government.

Biased policy objectives can threaten the foundations of a democratic political system. James Madison recognized this problem in *Federalist*, No. 10 (Article 16) when he warned against the danger of *factions*. These consist of "a number of citizens, whether amounting to a majority or minority of the whole, who are united and actuated by some common impulse of passion, or of interest, adverse to the rights of other citizens, or to the permanent and aggregate interests of the community." Government needs to modify the conflicting claims of various groups in seeking to promote the public interest.

Interest groups can be understood by a group theory of politics. According to Schattschneider (Article 17), group theory assumes that the struggle between contending groups produces public policy. Individuals with common interests and goals join together to bring their demands to the attention of government. Public policy represents the outcome of bargaining, negotiation, and compromise between different groups, each of which seeks to maximize its power and influence. Coalitions are formed between policy makers and interest groups in order to achieve agreement on the content of public policy. However, Schattschneider argues that any organization is a "mobilization of bias." Special interest groups represent only a narrow range of political bias. In fact, the pressure system has an upper class bias which excludes most citizens. It is unbalanced in favor of a small minority. Consequently, while the people may belong to many different organizations, they rarely participate in developing policy proposals. This is particularly a problem with the representatives of interest group leaders on behalf of the membership and lobbying tactics employed in government.

Interest groups represent nearly every conceivable issue and constituency in our nation. When such groups try to influence public policy, they engage in pressure strategies and lobbying tactics with government. Their strategies may be *positive*—seeking benefits on behalf of their members—or *negative*—trying to prevent government from acting on matters deemed harmful to the group. For example, big business (such as the U.S. Chamber of Commerce or any large corporation) and organized labor (the AFL-CIO or the United Automobile Workers) frequently pressure government on such specific matters as tax benefits, subsidies, investment incentives, collective bargaining, and minimum wages. As government responds to these demands, the special interest groups achieve results for their constituencies that would not be possible otherwise. The effectiveness of interest group demands depends upon their focus on a specific policy area, the information and communication with public officials, and the strength of organizational skills. Additionally, such groups are enhanced by the size of membership, access to monetary and other resources, cohesiveness, leadership skills, and the receptivity of public officials to their demands.

Publicity, lobbying, and pressure are tactics used by interest groups to achieve their objectives. Organized interests seek to mold public opinion to a point of view that creates a favorable image or which assists the groups in attaining particular legislative goals. In this sense, interest groups employ campaigning methods to protect or obtain a public policy objective. For example, the American Medical Association was highly successful for many years in preventing the enactment of medical care for the elderly by organizing a skillful propaganda campaign which attacked medicare as "socialized medicine." The AMA provided literature to physicians for display in their waiting rooms, took out paid advertisements in newspapers and magazines, and engaged in massive letter-writing campaigns to congressmen. Additionally, the AMA took sides in electoral contests by offering campaign funds to legislators who opposed the various medicare bills.

Interest groups also engage in direct lobbying with legislators. Almost every important interest group maintains headquarters in Washington from which lobbyists are sent to congress to discuss legislative proposals. When the lobbyist testifies before a congressional committee, offers advice on a bill, or provides dinners, cocktail parties, and other amenities, he is attempting to influence congressmen to a point of view favored by the group he represents. Lobbying is most effective on issues of a technical or specialized nature. On such matters, the lobbyist can provide expertise, information, and advice to congressmen and the bureaucracy. At the national level, the president, congress, and the voters (or public opinion) are more influential in initiating policy proposals, particularly on those matters of nationwide concern.

There is a very close relationship between interest groups and government policy-makers. These are developed around legal, economic, political and social considerations. Various congressional enactments and executive orders guarantee interest group representation on governmental advisory committees. Politically, the president identifies leading interest group personnel to serve as cabinet level secretaries or assistant secretaries. The interest group can have close economic and social contacts with governmental agencies which deal directly with their needs. The military-industrial complex is a good example, particularly in the areas of defense contracts and weapons systems. The Pentagon is accustomed to dealing with small groups of aerospace and other corporate firms in awarding huge contracts to the private sector.

A crucial problem developing from these relationships is "cooptation," when the governmental agency becomes a captive of the organized private groups. Public policy becomes a product of very narrow interest group demands. The governmental agency may have to yield control over some of its programs to retain support for other policy goals.

According to Theodore Lowi (Article 18), "interest group liberalism" is a result of the excessive influence of pressure groups on public policy. Lowi considers the term "liberal" differently from the designation usually associated with party politics. He considers liberalism comparable to the unrestricted marketplace economics of the early 19th century. The policy "liberal" believes that the public interest is best served by the free competition of private interests. Lowi points out that the consequence of group liberalism is the *status quo*, conservative policy. Public policy thus serves only the corporate or other entrenched elites. Administrative agencies tied to these elites are subject to the pressures of the powerful interests. This creates serious obstacles to policy change.

Unlike private interest groups which seek policy goals to serve their special needs, *public* interest groups attempt to expand public awareness of important and controversial issues. Criticism and publicity are their major instruments of influence. Such groups seek to expose to public criticism those governmental policies unresponsive to the public interest. In particular, the public interest groups frequently focus on irresponsible elites which have gained particular favoritism from governmental bureaucracies such as the military-industrial complex, automobile manufacturers, and the nuclear power industry. A major objective is consumer protection against corporate abuses of power.

In Article 19, Roger Williams analyzes the emergence of public interest lobbies, including Common Cause, the consumer-oriented Ralph Nader task forces, and environmental protection groups. Most of these groups have a middle-class community service orientation. They may represent an outlet to the frustrations toward government but, in the face of powerful private interest groups, they require considerable persistence to achieve their objectives.

As discussed in Article 20, the anti-abortion movement is a good example of a growing trend toward single-issue interest group politics. In recent years, such groups have organized around a controversial policy objective. Their goal is to convince government to act in their favor without regard to traditional political party stands or the so-called liberal or conservative positions on public policy.

Because abortion is such an intensely personal and moral issue affecting the role of women, medical practices, and religious beliefs, it has become a serious controversy for elected officials and judges at all levels of government. Government administrators and many private organizations are involved. When issues of political morality enter the political arena, there are great difficulties in reaching acceptable compromise solutions. Most fundamentally, the abortion debate is a challenge to the role of government in a democratic society. Civil liberty protections under the Bill of Rights and even the basic principles of the Declaration of Independence—"life, liberty and the pursuit of happiness"—are deeply affected.

16

The Federalist, Number Ten

James Madison

Federalist, No. 10 by Madison deals with a central problem of all governmental systems: how to balance majority will with minority rights to prevent tyranny or oppression. Madison warned against the danger of "factions" which might hinder popular control of government. Factions may be "adverse to the rights of other citizens, or to the permanent and aggregate interests of the community." Madison was apprehensive that such factions would influence government out of proportion to their numbers, which would result in a tyranny of the minority; or, conversely, that majority factions would overwhelm the rights and interests of other groups in society causing a tyranny of the majority. Federalist, No. 10 is closely related to Schattschneider's distinction between pressure groups and political parties in Article 17, and the various ideological positions discussed by Deutsch in Article 1. Also, see Federalist, No. 51, Article 5 for an analysis of separation of powers and checks and balances as a structural solution to the problem of factions.

To the People of the State of New York:

Among the numerous advantages promised by a well-constructed Union, none deserves to be more accurately developed than its tendency to break and control the violence of faction. The friend of popular governments never finds himself so much alarmed for their character and fate, as when he contemplates their propensity to this dangerous vice. He will not fail, therefore, to set a due value on any plan which, without violating the principles to which he is attached, provides a proper cure for it. The instability, injustice, and confusion introduced into the public councils, have, in truth, been the mortal diseases under which popular governments have everywhere perished; as they continue to be the favorite and fruitful topics from which the adversaries to liberty derive their most specious declamations. The valuable improvements made by the American constitutions on the popular models, both ancient and modern, cannot certainly be too much admired; but it would be an unwarrantable partiality, to contend that they have as effectually obviated the danger on this side, as was wished and expected. Complaints are everywhere heard from our most considerate and virtuous citizens, equally the friends of public and private faith, and of public and personal liberty, that our governments are too unstable; that the public good is disregarded in the conflicts of rival parties; and that measures are too often decided, not according to the rules of justice and the rights of the minor party, but by the superior force of an interested and overbearing majority. However anxiously we may wish that these complaints had no foundation, the evidence of known facts will not permit us to deny that they are in some degree true. It will be found, indeed, on a candid review of our situation, that some of the distresses under which we labor have been erroneously charged on the operation of our governments; but it will be found, at the same time, that other causes will not alone account for many of our heaviest misfortunes; and particularly, for that

From *The Daily Advertiser*, November 22, 1787. This essay appeared in *The New York Packet* on November 23 and in *The Independent Journal* on November 24.

prevailing and increasing distrust of public engagements, and alarm for private rights, which are echoed from one end of the continent to the other. These must be chiefly, if not wholly, effects of the unsteadiness and injustice with which a factious spirit has tainted our public administrations.

By a faction, I understand a number of citizens, whether amounting to a majority or minority of the whole, who are united and actuated by some common impulse of passion, or of interest, adverse to the rights of other citizens, or to the permanent and aggregate interests of the community.

There are two methods of curing the mischiefs of faction: the one, by removing its causes; the other, by controlling its effects.

There are again two methods of removing the causes of faction: the one, by destroying the liberty which is essential to its existence; the other, by giving to every citizen the same opinions, the same passions, and the same interests.

It could never be more truly said than of the first remedy, that it is worse than the disease. Liberty is to faction what air is to fire, an aliment without which it instantly expires. But it could not be less folly to abolish liberty, which is essential to political life, because it nourishes faction, than it would be to wish the annihilation of air, which is essential to animal life, because it imparts to fire its destructive agency.

The second expedient is as impracticable as the first would be unwise. As long as the reason of man continues fallible, and he is at liberty to exercise it, different opinions will be formed. As long as the connection subsists between his reason and his self-love, his opinions and his passions will have a reciprocal influence on each other; and the former will be objects to which the latter will attach themselves. The diversity in the faculties of men, from which the rights of property originate, is not less an insuperable obstacle to a uniformity of interests. The protection of these faculties is the first object of government. From the protection of different and unequal faculties of acquiring property, the possession of different degrees and kinds of property immediately results; and from the influence of these on the sentiments and views of the respective proprietors, ensues a division of the society into different interests and parties.

The latent causes of faction are thus sown in the nature of man; and we see them everywhere brought into different degrees of activity, according to the different circumstances of civil society. A zeal for different opinions concerning religion, concerning government, and many other points, as well of speculation as of practice; an attachment to different leaders ambitiously contending for pre-eminence and power; or to persons of other descriptions whose fortunes have been interesting to the human passions, have, in turn, divided mankind into parties, inflamed them with mutual animosity, and rendered them much more disposed to vex and oppress each other than to co-operate for their common good. So strong is this propensity of mankind to fall into mutual animosities, that where no substantial occasion presents itself, the most frivolous and fanciful distinctions have been sufficient to kindle their unfriendly passions and excite their most violent conflicts. But the most common and durable source of factions has been the various and unequal distribution of property. Those who hold and those who are without property have ever formed distinct interests in society. Those who are creditors, and those who are debtors, fall under a like discrimination. A landed interest, a manufacturing interest, a mercantile interest, a moneyed interest, with many lesser interests grow up of necessity in civilized nations, and divide them into different classes, actuated by different sentiments and views. The regulation of these various and interfering interests forms the principal task of modern legislation, and involves the spirit of party and faction in the necessary and ordinary operations of the government.

No man is allowed to be a judge in his own cause, because his interest would certainly bias his judgment, and, not improbably, corrupt his integrity. With equal, nay with greater reason, a body of men are unfit to be both judges and parties at the same time; yet what are many of the most important acts of legislation, but so many judicial determinations, not indeed concerning the rights of single persons, but concerning the rights of large bodies of citizens? and what are the different classes of legislators but advocates and parties to the causes which they determine? Is a law proposed concerning private debts? It is a question to which the creditors are parties on one side and the debtors on the other. Justice ought to hold the balance between them. Yet the parties are, and must be, themselves the judges; and the most numerous party, or, in other words, the most powerful faction must be expected to prevail. Shall domestic manufacturers be encouraged, and in what degree, by restrictions on foreign manufactures? are questions which would be differently decided by the landed and the manufacturing classes, and probably by neither with a sole regard to justice and the public good. The apportionment of taxes on the various descriptions of property is an act which seems to require the most exact impartiality; yet there is, perhaps, no legislative act in which greater opportunity and temptation are given to a predominant party to trample on the rules of justice. Every shilling with which they overburden the inferior number is a shilling saved to their own pockets.

It is in vain to say that enlightened statesmen will be able to adjust these clashing interests and render them all subservient to the public good. Enlightened statesmen will not always be at the helm. Nor, in many cases, can such an adjustment be made at all without taking into view indirect and remote considerations, which will rarely prevail over the im-

mediate interest which one party may find in disregarding the rights of another or the good of the whole.

The inference to which we are brought is, that the *causes* of faction cannot be removed, and that relief is only to be sought in the means of controlling its *effects*.

If a faction consists of less than a majority, relief is supplied by the republican principle, which enables the majority to defeat its sinister views by regular vote. It may clog the administration, it may convulse the society; but it will be unable to execute and mask its violence under the forms of the Constitution. When a majority is included in a faction, the form of popular government, on the other hand, enables it to sacrifice to its ruling passion or interest both the public good and the rights of other citizens. To secure the public good and private rights against the danger of such a faction, and at the same time to preserve the spirit and the form of popular government, is then the great object to which our inquiries are directed. Let me add that it is the great desideratum by which this form of government can be rescued from the opprobrium under which it has so long labored, and be recommended to the esteem and adoption of mankind.

By what means is this object attainable? Evidently by one of two only. Either the existence of the same passion or interest in a majority at the same time must be prevented, or the majority, having such coexistent passion or interest, must be rendered by their number and local situation unable to concert and carry into effect schemes of oppression. If the impulse and the opportunity be suffered to coincide, we well know that neither moral nor religious motives can be relied on as an adequate control. They are not found to be such on the injustice and violence of individuals, and lose their efficacy in proportion to the number combined together, that is, in proportion as their efficacy becomes needful.

From this view of the subject it may be concluded that a pure democracy, by which I mean a society consisting of a small number of citizens, who assemble and administer the government in person, can admit of no cure for the mischiefs of faction. A common passion or interest will, in almost every case, be felt by a majority of the whole; a communication and concert result from the form of government itself; and there is nothing to check the inducements to sacrifice the weaker party or an obnoxious individual. Hence it is that such democracies have ever been spectacles of turbulence and contention; have ever been found incompatible with personal security or the rights of property; and have in general been as short in their lives as they have been violent in their deaths. Theoretic politicians, who have patronized this species of government, have erroneously supposed that by reducing mankind to a perfect equality in their political rights, they would, at the same time, be perfectly equalized and assimilated in their possessions, their opinions, and their passions.

A republic, by which I mean a government in which the scheme of representation takes place, opens a different prospect, and promises the cure for which we are seeking. Let us examine the points in which it varies from pure democracy, and we shall comprehend both the nature of the cure and the efficacy which it must derive from the Union.

The two great points of difference between a democracy and a republic are: first, the delegation of the government in the latter to a small number of citizens elected by the rest; secondly, the greater number of citizens and greater sphere of country over which the latter may be extended.

The effect of the first difference is, on the one hand, to refine and enlarge the public views, by passing them through the medium of a chosen body of citizens, whose wisdom may best discern the true interest of their country, and whose patriotism and love of justice will be least likely to sacrifice it to temporary or partial considerations. Under such a regulation, it may well happen that the public voice, pronounced by the representatives of the people, will be more consonant to the public good than if pronounced by the people themselves, convened for the purpose. On the other hand, the effect may be inverted. Men of factious tempers, of local prejudices, or of sinister designs, may by intrigue, by corruption, or by other means, first obtain the suffrages, and then betray the interests of the people. The question resulting is, whether small or extensive republics are more favorable to the election of proper guardians of the public weal; and it is clearly decided in favor of the latter by two obvious considerations.

In the first place, it is to be remarked that, however small the republic may be, the representatives must be raised to a certain number in order to guard against the cabals of a few; and that, however large it may be, they must be limited to a certain number in order to guard against the confusion of a multitude. Hence, the number of representatives in the two cases not being in proportion to that of the two constituents, and being proportionally greater in the small republic, it follows that, if the proportion of fit characters be not less in the large than in the small republic, the former will present a greater option and consequently a greater probability of a fit choice.

In the next place, as each representative will be chosen by a greater number of citizens in the large than in the small republic, it will be more difficult for unworthy candidates to practise with success the vicious arts by which elections are too often carried; and the suffrages of the people being more free, will be more likely to centre in men who possess the most attractive merit and the most diffusive and established characters.

It must be confessed that in this, as in most other cases, there is a mean, on both sides of which inconveniences will be found to lie. By enlarging too much the number of electors, you render the representative too little acquainted with all their local circumstances and lesser interests: as by reducing it too much, you render him unduly attached to these, and too little fit to comprehend and pursue great and national objects. The federal Constitution forms a happy combination in this respect; the great and aggregate interests being referred to the national, the local and particular to the State legislatures.

The other point of difference is, the greater number of citizens and extent of territory which may be brought within the compass of republican than of democratic government; and it is this circumstance principally which renders factious combinations less to be dreaded in the former than in the latter. The smaller the society, the fewer probably will be the distinct parties and interests composing it; the fewer the distinct parties and interests, the more frequently will a majority be found of the same party; and the smaller the number of individuals composing a majority, and the smaller the compass within which they are placed, the more easily will they concert and execute their plans of oppression. Extend the sphere, and you take in a greater variety of parties and interests; you make it less probable that a majority of the whole will have a common motive to invade the rights of other citizens; or if such a common motive exists, it will be more difficult for all who feel it to discover their own strength and to act in unison with each other. Besides other impediments, it may be remarked that, where there is a consciousness of unjust or dishonorable purposes, communication is always checked by distrust in proportion to the number whose concurrence is necessary.

Hence, it clearly appears that the same advantage which a republic has over a democracy in controlling the effects of faction is enjoyed by a large over a small republic,—is enjoyed by the Union over the States composing it.

Does the advantage consist in the substitution of representatives whose enlightened views and virtuous sentiments render them superior to local prejudices and to schemes of injustice? It will not be denied that the representation of the Union will be most likely to possess these requisite endowments. Does it consist in the greater security afforded by a greater variety of parties, against the event of any one party being able to outnumber and oppress the rest? In an equal degree does the increased variety of parties comprised within the Union, increase this security. Does it, in fine, consist in the greater obstacles opposed to the concert and accomplishment of the secret wishes of an unjust and interested majority? Here, again, the extent of the Union gives it the most palpable advantage.

The influence of factious leaders may kindle a flame within their particular States, but will be unable to spread a general conflagration through the other States. A religious sect may degenerate into a political faction in a part of the Confederacy; but the variety of sects dispersed over the entire face of it must secure the national councils against any danger from that source. A rage for paper money, for an abolition of debts, for an equal division of property, or for any other improper or wicked project, will be less apt to pervade the whole body of the Union than a particular member of it; in the same proportion as such a malady is more likely to taint a particular county or district, than an entire State.

In the extent and proper structure of the Union, therefore, we behold a republican remedy for the diseases most incident to republican government. And according to the degree of pleasure and pride we feel in being republicans, ought to be our zeal in cherishing the spirit and supporting the character of Federalists.

PUBLIUS

17

The Scope and Bias of the Pressure System
E. E. Schattschneider

What is the role of interest groups in the American political system? How do such groups develop and what are their goals and objectives? This essay by E. E. Schattschneider provides analysis of the "pressure system," indicating the distinguishing features of group theory, the bias of special interest groups, and the relationships between interest groups and government. He shows that group theory is related to the types of interests involved—special or public—and the differences between organized and unorganized interests. These criteria indicate that organization is a "mobilization of bias," a theme discussed by James Madison in Federalist, No. 10. Also, the pressure system has a strong upper-class bias which excludes most people. Why is this so? What are the major flaws of the pressure system? What does Schattschneider mean by the "socialization of conflict"? What are the relationships between business and the Republican party?

The scope of conflict is an aspect of the scale of political organization and the extent of political competition. The size of the constitutencies being mobilized, the inclusiveness or exclusiveness of the conflicts people expect to develop have a bearing on all theories about how politics is or should be organized. In other words, nearly all theories about politics have something to do with the question of who can get into the fight and who is to be excluded.

Every regime is a testing ground for theories of this sort. More than any other system American politics provides the raw materials for testing the organizational assumptions of two contrasting kinds of politics, *pressure politics* and *party politics*. The concepts that underlie these forms of politics constitute the raw stuff of a general theory of political action. The basic issue between the two patterns of organization is one of size and scope of conflict; pressure groups are small-scale organizations while political parties are very large-scale organizations. One need not be surprised, therefore, that the partisans of large-scale and small-scale organizations differ passionately, because the outcome of the political game depends on the scale on which it is played.

To understand the controversy about the scale of political organization it is necessary first to take a look at some theories about interest-group politics. Pressure groups have played a remarkable role in American politics, but they have played an even more remarkable role in American political theory. Considering the political condition of the country in the first third of the twentieth century, it was probably inevitable that the discussion of special-interest pressure groups should lead to development of "group" theories of politics in which an attempt is made to explain everything in terms of group activity, i.e., an attempt to formulate a universal group theory. Since one of the best ways to test an idea is to ride it into the ground, political theory has unquestionably been improved by the heroic attempt to create a political universe revolving about the group. Now that we have a number of drastic statements of the group theory of politics pushed to a great extreme, we ought to be able to see what the limitations of the idea are.

Political conditions in the first third of the present century were extremely hospitable to the idea. The role of business in the strongly sectional Republican system from 1896 to 1932 made the dictatorship of business seem to be a part of the eternal order of things. Moreover the regime as a whole seemed to be so stable that questions about the survival of the American community did not arise. The general interests of the community were easily overlooked under these circumstances.

Nevertheless, in spite of the excellent and provocative scholarly work done by Beard, Latham, Truman, Leiserson, Dahl, Lindblom, Laski, and others, the group theory of politics is beset with difficulties. The difficulties are theoretical, growing in part out of sheer overstatements of the idea and in part out of some confusion about the nature of modern government.

One difficulty running through the literature of the subject results from the attempt to explain *everything* in terms of the group theory. On general grounds it would be remarkable indeed if a single hypothesis explained everything about so complex a subject as American politics. Other difficulties have grown out of the fact that group concepts have been stated in terms so universal that the subject seems to have no shape or form.

The question is: Are pressure groups the universal basic ingredient of all political situations, and do they explain everything? To answer this question it is necessary to review a bit of rudimentary political theory.

Two modest reservations might be made merely to test the group dogma. We might clarify our ideas if (1) we explore more fully the possibility of making a distinction between public-interest groups and special-interest groups and (2) if we distinguished between organized and unorganized groups. These reservations do not disturb the main body of group theory, but they may be useful when we attempt to define general propositions more precisely. If both of these distinctions can be validated, we may get hold of something that has scope and limits and is capable of being defined. The awkwardness of a discussion of political phenomena in terms of universals is that the subject has no beginning or end; it is impossible to distinguish one subject from another or to detect the bias of the forces involved because scope and bias are aspects of limitations of the subject. It cannot really be said that we have seen a subject until we have seen its outer limits and thus are able to draw a line between one subject and another.

We might begin to break the problem into its component parts by exploring the distinction between public and private interests. If we can validate this distinction, we shall have established one of the boundaries of the subject.

As a matter of fact, the distinction between *public* and *private* interests is a thoroughly respectable one; it is one of the oldest known to political theory. In the literature of the subject, the public interest refers to general or common interests shared by all or by substantially all members of the community. Presumably no community exists unless there is some kind of community of interests, just as there is no nation without some notion of national interests. If it is really impossible to distinguish between private and public interests, the group theorists have produced a revolution in political thought so great that it is impossible to foresee its consequences. For this reason the distinction ought to be explored with great care. . . .

In contrast with the common interests are the special interests. The implication of this term is that these are interests shared by only a few people or a fraction of the community; they *exclude* others and may be *adverse* to them. A special interest is exclusive in about the same way as private property is exclusive.

In a complex society it is not surprising that there are some interests that are shared by all or substantially all members of the community and some interests that are not shared so widely. The distinction is useful precisely because conflicting claims are made by people about the nature of their interests in controversial matters. . . .

The distinction between public and special interests is an indispensable tool for the study of politics. To abolish the distinction is to make a shambles of political science by treating things that are different as if they were alike. The kind of distinction made here is a commonplace of all literature dealing with human society, but *if we accept it, we have established one of the outer limits of the subject;* we have split the world of interests in half and have taken one step toward defining the scope of this kind of political conflict.

We can now examine the second distinction, the distinction between organized and unorganized groups. The question here is not whether the distinction can be made but whether or not it is worth making. Organization has been described as "merely a stage or degree of interaction" in the development of a group.

The proposition is a good one, but what conclusions do we draw from it? We do not dispose of the matter by calling the distinction between organized and unorganized groups a "mere" difference of degree because some of the greatest differences in the world are differences of degree. As far as special-interest politics is concerned the implication to be avoided is that a few workmen who habitually stop at a corner saloon for a glass of beer are essentially the same as the United States Army because the difference between them is merely one of degree. At this point we have a distinction that makes a difference. The distinction between organized and unorganized groups is worth making because it ought to alert us against an analysis which begins as a general group theory of politics but ends with a defense of pressure politics as inherent, universal, permanent, and inevitable. This kind of confusion comes from the loosening of categories involved in the universalization of group concepts.

Since the beginning of intellectual history, scholars have sought to make progress in their work by distinguishing between things that are unlike and by dividing their subject matter into categories to examine them more intelligently. It is something of a novelty, therefore, when group theorists reverse this process by discussing their subject in terms so universal that they wipe out all categories, because this is the dimension in which it is least possible to understand anything.

If we are able, therefore, to distinguish between public and private interests and between organized and unorganized groups we have marked out the major boundaries of the subject; *we have given the subject shape and scope.* We are now in a position to attempt to define the area we want to explore. Having cut the pie into four pieces, we can now appropriate the piece we want and leave the rest to someone else. For a multitude of reasons *the most likely field of study is that of the organized, special-interest groups.* The advantage of concentrating on organized groups is that they are known, identifiable, and recognizable. The advantage of concentrating on special-interest groups is that they have one important characteristic in common; they are all exclusive. This piece of the pie (the organized special-interest groups) we shall call the *pressure system.* The pressure system has boundaries we can define; we can fix its scope and make an attempt to estimate its bias. . . .

By the time a group has developed the kind of interest that leads it to organize, it may be assumed that it has also developed some kind of political bias because *organization is itself a mobilization of bias in preparation for action.*

Since these groups can be identified and since they have memberships (i.e., they include and exclude people), it is possible to think of the *scope* of the system. . . .

The business or upper-class bias of the pressure system shows up everywhere. Businessmen are four or five times as likely to write to their congressmen as manual laborers are. College graduates are far more apt to write to their congressmen than people in the lowest educational category are. . . .

The obverse side of the coin is that large areas of the population appear to be wholly outside the system of private organization. A study made by Ira Reid of a Philadelphia area showed that in a sample of 963 persons, 85 percent belonged to no civic or charitable organization and 74 percent belonged to no occupational, business, or professional associations, while another Philadelphia study of 1,154 women showed that 55 percent belonged to no associations of any kind. . . .

The class bias of associational activity gives meaning to the limited scope of the pressure system, because *scope and bias are aspects of the same tendency.* The data raise a serious question about the validity of the proposition that special-interest groups are a universal form of political organization reflecting *all* interests. As a matter of fact, to suppose that everyone participates in pressure-group activity and that all interests get themselves organized in the pressure system is to destroy the meaning of this form of politics. The pressure system makes sense only as the political instrument of a segment of the community. It gets results by being selective and biased; *if everybody got into the act, the unique advantages of this form of organization would be destroyed, for it is possible that if all interests could be mobilized the result would be a stalemate.*

Special-interest organizations are most easily formed when they deal with small numbers of individuals who are acutely aware of their exclusive interests. To describe the conditions of pressure-group organization in this way is, however, to say that it is primarily a business phenomenon. Aside from a few very large organizations (the churches, organized labor, farm organizations, and veterans' organizations) the residue is a small segment of the population. *Pressure politics is essentially the politics of small groups.*

The vice of the groupist theory is that it conceals the most significant aspects of the system. The flaw in the pluralist heaven is that the heavenly chorus sings with a strong upper-class accent. Probably about 90 percent of the people cannot get into the pressure system.

The notion that the pressure system is automatically representative of the whole community is a myth fostered by the universalizing tendency of modern group theories. *Pressure politics is a selective process* ill designed to serve diffuse interests. The system is skewed, loaded, and unbalanced in favor of a fraction of a minority.

On the other hand, pressure tactics are not remarkably successful in mobilizing general interests. When pressure-group organizations attempt to represent the interests of large numbers of people, they are usually able to reach only a small segment of their constituencies. Only a chemical trace of the fifteen million Negroes in the United States belong to the National Association for the Advancement of Colored People. Only one five hundredths of 1 percent of American women belong to the League of Women Voters, only one sixteenth hundredths of 1 percent of the consumers belong to the National Consumers' League, and only 6 percent of American automobile drivers belong to the American Automobile Association, while about 15 percent of the veterans belong to the American Legion.

The competing claims of pressure groups and political parties for the loyalty of the

American public revolve about the difference between the results likely to be achieved by small-scale and large-scale political organization. Inevitably, the outcome of pressure politics and party politics will be vastly different.

A CRITIQUE OF GROUP THEORIES OF POLITICS

It is extremely unlikely that the vogue of group theories of politics would have attained its present status if its basic assumptions had not been first established by some concept of economic determinism. The economic interpretation of politics has always appealed to those political philosophers who have sought a single prime mover, a sort of philosopher's stone of political science around which to organize their ideas. The search for a single, ultimate cause has something to do with the attempt to explain *everything* about politics in terms of group concepts. The logic of economic determinism is to *identify the origins of conflict and to assume the conclusion.* This kind of thought has some of the earmarks of an illusion. The somnambulatory quality of thinking in this field appears also in the tendency of research to deal only with successful pressure campaigns or the willingness of scholars to be satisfied with having placed pressure groups on the scene of the crime without following through to see if the effect can really be attributed to the cause. What makes this kind of thinking remarkable is the fact that in political contests there are as many failures as there are successes. Where in the literature of pressure politics are the failures?

Students of special-interest politics need a more sophisticated set of intellectual tools than they have developed thus far. The theoretical problem involved in the search for a single cause is that all power relations in a democracy are reciprocal. Trying to find the original cause

is like trying to find the first wave of the ocean. . . .

The very expression "pressure politics" invites us to misconceive the role of special-interest groups in politics. The word "pressure" implies the use of some kind of force, a form of intimidation, something other than reason and information, to induce public authorities to act against their own best judgment. In Latham's famous statement already quoted the legislature is described as a "referee" who "ratifies" and "records" the "balance of power" among the contending groups.

It is hard to imagine a more effective way of saying that Congress has no mind or force of its own or that Congress is unable to invoke new forces that might alter the equation.

Actually the outcome of political conflict is not like the "resultant" of opposing forces in physics. To assume that the forces in a political situation could be diagramed as a physicist might diagram the resultant of opposing physical forces is to wipe the slate clean of all remote, general, and public considerations for the protection of which civil societies have been instituted.

Moreover, the notion of "pressure" distorts the image of the power relations involved. *Private conflicts are taken into the public arena precisely because someone wants to make certain that the power ratio among the private interests most immediately involved shall not prevail.* To treat a conflict as a mere

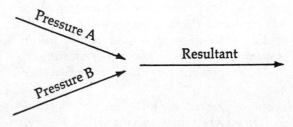

test of the strength of the private interests is to leave out the most significant factors. This is so true that it might indeed be said that the only way to preserve private power ratios is to keep conflicts out of the public arena.

The assumption that it is only the "interested" who count ought to be re-examined in view of the foregoing discussion. The tendency of the literature of pressure politics has been to neglect the low-tension force of large numbers because it *assumes that the equation of forces is fixed at the outset.*

Given the assumptions made by the group theorists, the attack on the idea of the majority is completely logical. The assumption is that conflict is monopolized narrowly by the parties immediately concerned. There is no room for a majority when conflict is defined so narrowly. It is a great deficiency of the group theory that it has found no place in the political system for the majority. The force of the majority is of an entirely different order of magnitude, something not to be measured by pressure-group standards.

Instead of attempting to exterminate all political forms, organizations, and alignments that do not qualify as pressure groups, would it not be better to attempt to make a synthesis, covering the whole political system and finding a place for all kinds of political life?

One possible synthesis of pressure politics and party politics might be produced by *describing politics as the socialization of conflict.* That is to say, the political process is a sequence: conflicts are initiated by highly motivated, high-tension groups so directly and immediately involved that it is difficult for them to see the justice of competing claims. As long as the conflicts of these groups remain *private* (carried on in terms of economic competition, reciprocal denial of goods and services, private negotiations and bargaining, struggles for corporate control or competition for membership), no political process is initiated. Con-

flicts become political only when an attempt is made to involve the wider public. Pressure politics might be described as a stage in the socialization of conflict. This analysis makes pressure politics an integral part of all politics, including party politics.

One of the characteristic points of origin of pressure politics is a breakdown of the discipline of the business community. The flight to government is perpetual. Something like this is likely to happen wherever there is a point of contact between competing power systems. It is the *losers in intrabusiness conflict who seek redress from public authority. The dominant business interests resist appeals to the government.* The role of the government as the patron of the defeated private interest sheds light on its function as the critic of private power relations.

Since the contestants in private conflicts are apt to be unequal in strength, it follows that *the most powerful special interests want private settlements* because they are able to dictate the outcome as long as the conflict remains private. If A is a hundred times as strong as B he does not welcome the intervention of a third party because he expects to impose his own terms on B; he wants to isolate B. He is especially opposed to the intervention of public authority, because public authority represents the most overwhelming form of outside intervention. Thus, if

$$\frac{A}{B} = \frac{100}{1},$$

it is obviously not to A's advantage to involve a third party a million times as strong as A and B combined. Therefore, it is the weak, not the strong, who appeal to public authority for relief. It is the weak who want to socialize conflict, i.e., to involve more and more people in the conflict until the balance of forces is changed. In the schoolyard it is not the bully but the defenseless smaller boys who "tell the teacher." When the teacher intervenes, the balance of power in the schoolyard is apt to change drastically. It is the function of public authority to *modify private power relations by enlarging the scope of conflict*. Nothing could be more mistaken than to suppose that public authority merely registers the dominance of the strong over the weak. The mere existence of public order has already ruled out a great variety of forms of private pressure. Nothing could be more confusing than to suppose that the refugees from the business community who come to Congress for relief and protection *force* Congress to do their bidding.

Evidence of the truth of this analysis may be seen in the fact that the big private interests do not necessarily win if they are involved in public conflicts with petty interests. The image of the lobbyists as primarily the agents of big business is not easy to support on the face of the record of congressional hearings, for example. The biggest corporations in the country tend to avoid the arena in which pressure groups and lobbyists fight it out before congressional committees. To describe this process exclusively in terms of an effort of business to intimidate congressmen is to misconceive what is actually going on.

It is probably a mistake to assume that pressure politics is the typical or even the most important relation between government and business. The pressure group is by no means the perfect instrument of the business community. What does big business want? The *winners* in intrabusiness strife want (1) to be let alone (they want autonomy) and (2) to preserve the solidarity of the business community. For these purposes pressure politics is not a wholly satisfactory device. The most elementary considerations of strategy call for the business community to develop some kind of common policy more broadly based than any special-interest group is likely to be.

The political influence of business depends on the kind of solidarity that, on the one hand, leads all business to rally to the support of *any* businessman in trouble with the government and, on the other hand, keeps internal business disputes out of the public arena. In this system businessmen resist the impulse to attack each other in public and discourage the efforts of individual members of the business community to take intrabusiness conflicts into politics.

The attempt to mobilize a united front of the whole business community does not resemble the classical concept of pressure politics. The logic of business politics is to keep peace within the business community by supporting as far as possible all claims that business groups make for themselves. The tendency is to support all businessmen who have conflicts with the government and support all businessmen in conflict with labor. In this way *special-interest politics can be converted into party policy*. The search is for a broad base of political mobilization grounded on the strategic need for political organization on a wider scale than is possible in the case of the historical pressure group. Once the business community begins to think in terms of a larger scale of political organization the Republican party looms large in business politics.

It is a great achievement of American democracy that business has been forced to form a political organization designed to win elections, i.e., has been forced to compete for power in the widest arena in the political system. On the other hand, *the power of the Republican party to make terms with business rests on the fact that business cannot afford to be isolated*.

The Republican party has played a major role in *the political organization of the business community*, a far greater role than many students of politics seem to have realized. The influence of business in the Republican party is great, but it is never absolute because business is remarkably dependent on the party. The business community is too small, it arouses too much antagonism, and its aims are too narrow to win the support of a popular majority. The political education of business is a function of the Republican party that can never be done so well by anyone else.

In the management of the political relations of the business community, the Republican party is much more important than any combination of pressure groups ever could be. The success of special interests in Congress is due less to the "pressure" exerted by these groups than it is due to the fact that Republican members of Congress are committed in advance to a general probusiness attitude. The notion that business groups coerce Republican congressmen into voting for their bills underestimates the whole Republican posture in American politics.

It is not easy to manage the political interests of the business community because there is a perpetual stream of losers in intrabusiness conflicts who go to the government for relief and protection. It has not been possible therefore to maintain perfect solidarity, and when solidarity is breached the government is involved almost automatically. The fact that business has not become hopelessly divided and that it has retained great influence in American politics has been due chiefly to the over-all mediating role played by the Republican party. There has never been a pressure group or a combination of pressure groups capable of performing this function.

18

Interest Group Liberalism

Theodore J. Lowi

Theodore Lowi introduces the concept of "interest-group liberalism," by which he means that certain dominant elites become highly influential in particular areas of public policy. How widespread is this occurrence in American government? Are Lowi's views consistent with Madison's warnings in Federalist, No. 10? *Do they agree with Schatt-schneider's arguments concerning the upper-class bias of the pressure system? How can interest group liberalism be checked or held accountable? If Lowi's arguments are accurate, what can be done about the excessive influence of private elites in government? This article should be reconsidered in relation to Chapter Eleven, Public Policy.*

The frenzy of governmental activity in the 1960s and 1970s proved that once the constitutional barriers were down the American national government was capable of prompt response to organized political demands. However, that is only the beginning of the story, because the almost total democratization of the Constitution and the contemporary expansion of the public sector has been accompanied by expansion, not contraction, of a sense of distrust toward public objects. Here is a spectacular paradox. It is as though each new program or program expansion had been an admission of prior governmental inadequacy or failure without itself being able to make any significant contribution to order or to well-being. It is as though prosperity had gone up at an arithmetic rate while expectations, and therefore frustrations, had been going up at a geometric rate—in a modern expression of Malthusian Law. Public authority was left to grapple with this alienating gap between expectation and reality.

Why did the expansion of government that helped produce and sustain prosperity also help produce a crisis of public authority? The explanation pursued throughout this volume is that the old justifications for expansion had too little to say beyond the need for the expansion itself. An appropriate public philosophy would have addressed itself to the purposes to which the expanded governmental authority should be dedicated. It would also have addressed itself to the forms and procedures by which that power could be utilized. These questions are so alien to public discourse in the United States that merely to raise them is to be considered reactionary, apolitical, or totally naïve.

Out of the emerging crisis of public authority developed an ersatz political formula that bears no more relation to those questions than the preceding political formula. The guidance the new formula offers to policy formulation is a set of sentiments that elevated a particular view of the political process above everything else. The ends of government and the justification of one policy or procedure over another are not to be discussed. The *process* of formulation is justified in itself. As observed earlier it takes the pluralist notion that government is an epiphenomenon of politics and makes out of that a new ethics of government.

There are several possible names for the new public philosophy. A strong candidate would be *corporatism*, but its history as a concept gives it several unwanted connotations, such as conservative Catholicism or Italian fascism. Another candidate is *syndicalism*, but among many objections is the connotation of anarchy too far removed from American experience. From time to time other possible labels will be experimented with, but, since the new American public philosophy is something of an amalgam of all the candidates, some new terminology seems to be called for.

The most clinically accurate term to capture the American variant of all of these tendencies is *interest-group liberalism*. It is liberalism because it is optimistic about government, expects to use government in a' positive and expansive role, is motivated by the highest sentiments, and possesses a strong faith that what is good for government is good for the society. It is interest-group liberalism because it sees as both necessary and good a policy agenda that is accessible to all organized interests and makes no independent judgment of their claims. It is interest-group liberalism because it defines the public interest as a result of the amalgamation of various claims. A brief sketch of the working model of interest-group liberalism turns out to be a vulgarized version of the pluralist model of modern political science: (1) Organized interests are homogeneous and easy to define. Any duly elected representative of any interest is taken as an accurate representative of each and every member.[1] (2) Organized interests emerge in every sector of our lives and adequately represent most of those sectors, so that one organized group can be found effectively answering and checking some other organized group as it seeks to prosecute its claims against society.[2] And (3) the role of government is one of insuring access to the most effectively organized, and of ratifying the agreements and adjustments worked out among the competing leaders.

This last assumption is supposed to be a statement of how a democracy works and how it ought to work. Taken together, these assumptions amount to little more than the appropriation of the Adam Smith "hidden hand" model for politics, where the group is the entrepreneur and the equilibrium is not lowest price but the public interest.

These assumptions are the basis of the new public philosophy. The policy behavior of old liberals and old conservatives, of Republicans and Democrats, so inconsistent with the old dialogue, is fully consistent with the criteria drawn from interest-group liberalism: *The most important difference between liberals and conservatives, Republicans and Democrats, is to be found in the interest groups they identify with. Congressmen are guided in their votes, presidents in their programs, and administration in their discretion by whatever organized interests they have taken for themselves as the most legitimate; and that is the measure of the legitimacy of demands and the only necessary guidelines for the framing of the laws.*

It is one thing to recognize that these assumptions resemble the working methodology of modern political science. But it is quite another to explain how this model was elevated from a hypothesis about political behavior to an ideology about how our democratic polity ought to work. . . .

[1] For an excellent inquiry into this assumption and into the realities of the internal life of organized interests, see Grant McConnell, *Private Power and American Democracy* (New York: Knopf, 1966); S. M. Lipset et al., *Union Democracy* (New York: Anchor, 1962); and Raymond Bauer et al., *American Business and Public Policy* (New York: Atherton, 1963).

[2] It is assumed that countervailing power usually crops up somehow, but when it does not, government ought help create it. See John Kenneth Galbraith, *American Capitalism* (Boston: Houghton Mifflin, 1952). Among a number of excellent critiques of the so-called pluralist model, see especially William E. Connolly, ed., *The Bias of Pluralism* (New York: Atherton, 1969).

THE COSTS OF INTEREST-GROUP LIBERALISM

The problems of pluralist theory are of more than academic interest. They are directly and indirectly responsible for some of the most costly attributes of modern government: (1) the atrophy of institutions of popular control; (2) the maintenance of old and the creation of new structures of privilege; and (3) conservatism in several senses of the word. These three hypotheses do not exhaust the possibilities but are best suited to introduce the analysis of policies and programs in the next six chapters.

1. In *The Public Philosophy*, Walter Lippmann was rightfully concerned over the "derangement of power" whereby modern democracies tend first toward unchecked elective leadership and then toward drainage of public authority from elective leaders down into the constituencies. However, Lippmann erred if he thought of constituents as only voting constituencies. Drainage has tended toward "support-group constituencies," and with special consequences. Parceling out policy-making power to the most interested parties tends strongly to destroy political responsibility. A program split off with a special imperium to govern itself is not merely an administrative unit. It is a structure of power with impressive capacities to resist central political control.

When conflict of interest is made a principle of government rather than a criminal act, programs based upon such a principle cut out all of that part of the mass of people who are not specifically organized around values salient to the goals of that program. The people are shut out at the most creative phase of policy-making —where the problem is first defined. The public is shut out also at the phase of accountability because in theory there is enough accountability to the immediate surrounding interests. In fact, presidents and congressional committees are most likely to investigate an agency when a complaint is brought to them by one of the most interested organizations. As a further consequence, the accountability we do get is functional rather than substantive; and this involves questions of equity, balance, and equilibrium, to the exclusion of questions of the overall social policy and whether or not the program should be maintained at all. It also means accountability to experts first and amateurs last; and an expert is a person trained and skilled in the mysteries and technologies of that particular program.

Finally, in addition to the natural tendencies, there tends also to be a self-conscious conspiracy to shut out the public. One meaningful illustration, precisely because it is such an absurd extreme, is found in the French system of interest representation in the Fourth Republic. As the Communist-controlled union, the Confédération Générale du Travail (CGT), intensified its participation in postwar French government, it was able to influence representatives of interests other than employees. In a desperate effort to insure that the interests represented on the various boards were separated and competitive, the government issued a decree that "each member of the board must be *independent of the interests he is not representing.*"[3]

2. Programs following the principles of interest-group liberalism tend to create and maintain privilege; and it is a type of privilege particularly hard to bear or combat because it is touched with a symbolism of the state. Interest-group liberalism is not merely pluralism but is *sponsored* pluralism. Pluralists ease our consciences about the privileges of organized groups by characterizing them as representative and by responding to their "iron law of oligarchy" by arguing that oligarchy is simply a negative name for organization. Our consciences were already supposed to be partly reassured by the notion of "overlapping memberships." But however true it may be that overlapping memberships exist and that ol-

[3] Mario Einaudi et al., *Nationalization in France and Italy* (Ithaca: Cornell University Press, 1955), pp. 100–101. (Emphasis added.)

igarchy is simply a way of leading people efficiently toward their interests, the value of these characteristics changes entirely when they are taken from the context of politics and put into the context of pluralistic government. The American Farm Bureau Federation is no "voluntary association" if it is a legitimate functionary within the extension system. Such tightly knit corporate groups as the National Association of Home Builders (NAHB), the National Association of Real Estate Boards (NAREB), the National Association for the Advancement of Colored People (NAACP), or the National Association of Manufacturers (NAM) or American Federation of Labor-Congress of Industrial Organizations (AFL-CIO) are no ordinary lobbies after they became part of the "interior processes" of policy formation. Even in the War on Poverty, one can only appreciate the effort to organize the poor by going back and pondering the story and characters in *The Three Penny Opera*. The "Peachum factor" in public affairs may be best personified in Sargent Shriver and his strenuous efforts to get the poor housed in some kind of group before their representation was to begin. . . .

The more clear and legitimized the representation of a group or its leaders in policy formation, the less voluntary its membership in that group and the more necessary is loyalty to its leadership for people who share the interests in question. And, the more widespread the policies of recognizing and sponsoring organized interest, the more hierarchy is introduced into our society. It is a well-recognized and widely appreciated function of formal groups in modern society to provide much of the necessary everyday social control. However, when the very thought processes behind public policy are geared toward these groups they are bound to take on the involuntary character of *public* control.

3. The conservative tendencies of interest-group liberalism can already be seen in the two foregoing objections: weakening of popular control and support of privilege. A third dimension of conservatism, stressed here separately, is the simple conservatism of resistance to change. David Truman, who has certainly not been a strong critic of self-government by interest groups, has, all the same, provided about the best statement of the general tendency of established agency-group relationships to be "highly resistant to disturbance":

New and expanded functions are easily accommodated, provided they develop and operate through existing channels of influence and do not tend to alter the relative importance of those influences. Disturbing changes are those that modify either the content or the relative strength of the component forces operating through an administrative agency. In the face of such changes, or the threat of them, the "old line" agency is highly inflexible.[4]

If this already is a tendency in a pluralistic system, then agency-group relationships must be all the more inflexible to the extent that the relationship is official and legitimate.

Innumerable illustrations will . . . . be found in new areas of so-called social policy, such as the practice early in the War on Poverty to co-opt neighborhood leaders, thereby creating more privilege than alleviating poverty. . . . Even clearer illustrations will be found in the economic realm, so many, indeed, that the practice is synthesized . . . as "a state of permanent receivership." Old and established groups doing good works naturally look fearfully upon the emergence of competing, perhaps hostile, new groups. That is an acceptable and healthy part of the political game—until the competition between them is a question of "who shall be the government?" At that point conservatism becomes a matter of survival for each group, and a direct threat to the public interest. Ultimately this threat will be recognized.

[4] David B. Truman, *The Governmental Process* (New York: Knopf, 1951), pp. 467–68.

19

The Rise of Middle Class Activism: Fighting "City Hall"

Roger M. Williams

Interest groups are usually considered in terms of such "private" activities as "business" or "labor unions" as discussed previously in the Schattschneider article. Roger Williams describes a more recent form of lobbying activity by "public" interest groups, including Common Cause, the consumer-oriented Ralph Nader task forces, and various environmental protection groups, which have grown in size and membership in the 1970s. He indicates the middle class bias of these groups. Is the middle class view of public policy consistent with the broader interests of the larger community? Williams also discusses the nature of public interest groups, their organizational strengths and weaknesses, and the objectives they seek. Interestingly, he finds that such groups reflect an alternative to the "crisis of confidence" toward government and political leadership. Apparently, there are outlets for individual feelings of powerlessness, alienation, and disillusionment toward government.

In January ABC-TV introduced what the world scarcely needs—another situation comedy. This one, however, is a barometer of something besides our lamentable tastes in television. The program is called "Karen," and its heroine lives near Washington, D.C., and works for a Common Cause-like organization. She is sophisticated, middle-class, and, above all, "involved." Even if "Karen" fails its Nielsen test, ABC should be credited with spotting a significant trend in American life: the growth, in numbers and importance, of public interest groups whose driving forces are the discontent and pent-up energies of the middle class.

From Common Cause to small-city consumer groups, from Nader task forces to local professionals working *pro bono publico*, from housewives angry at children's television in Massachusetts to retired people angry at un-

bridled growth in Colorado, volunteers are banding together to assault the system. They are overwhelmingly middle-class in background and outlook. By the standards of the Sixties, they are unrecognizable as protesters; their dress is neat, their tone moderate, their battlegrounds indoors, not out. Their goals are equally remote from the Sixties. Instead of peace, civil rights, and an end to poverty, the goals are consumer protection, auto and airplane safety, limited growth, pure food, clean air and water, cleaner politics, and especially "accountability"—a term, now almost a cliché, that translates broadly into, "This is bad. Who's gonna fix it?"

One of the most striking "fixit" groups of late has been Citizens for Colorado's Future (C. C. F.), which in the fall of 1972 accomplished the nearly unbelievable feat of keeping the 1976 winter Olympic Games out of Colorado. Faced with the bring-the-games boosterism of business and political leaders, C.C.F. mobilized suburbanites, environmentalists, retired people, and students—almost all of them white, middle-class, and previously uninvolved

Reprinted by permission of the author and publisher from Roger M. Williams, "The Rise of Middle Class Activism: Fighting 'City Hall'." *Saturday Review* (March 8, 1975): 12–16. Copyright © by Saturday Review/World, Inc.

in public controversy. They rounded up 88,000 signatures to get the Olympics issue on the statewide ballot and then passionately argued their case: that the Olympics would bring unwanted growth and environmental blight and that the money to stage such a show could be put to better uses. The proposed $5 million state outlay for the games was voted down by a ratio of almost five to three.

C.C.F. organizer John Parr says that its surprise strength came largely from "a new group of activists—suburban housewives and their professional or executive husbands. A lot of them told us, 'I've been afraid to get involved like this before.' " C.C.F.'s chief spokesman, state representative Michael D. Lamm, rode the Olympics issue (and others of his own making) into the governor's office last fall. His campaign organization was staffed and substantially financed by veterans of the anti-Olympics drive.*

Organized protest is not new to the American middle class—members of the Townsend Movement of the Thirties and the Women's Christian Temperance Union, as well as the early feminists, were certainly middle-class—but it is new on this scale. Except perhaps for the Revolutionary period, organized protest has never reached so deeply into middle-class ranks and involved such a broad range of issues. The protest has made maximum use of the things the middle class does best: organize, propagandize, and work like hell. The press release, the telephone network, and the fold-and-stamp brigade—tools of sales organizations and the Junior League—have been turned loose on government officials and businessmen and anybody else who is "accountable" but not behaving that way. Says Jack Conway, until recently president of Common Cause:

"The Sixties was minority politics. Now we are playing majority politics, because inside the majority is where the decisions are made."

Not everyone is delighted with the new middle-class activism. Labor unions suspect middle-class motives and resent the elevation of environmental and military-spending issues to the detriment of their own traditional concerns, such as job security. Some reformers say the new groups tend to overlook the critical issues. (Says a believer in revenue-sharing as a critical issue: "Those people who fret over children's TV are too much. Why don't they just pull the plug and get to work on something important?") The most serious criticism is that the middle-class groups are not public-interested, but self-interested, elitist in operation and outlook. "Public interest is a middle-class exercise," is the way Anthony Mazzochi of the Oil, Chemical, and Atomic Workers put it not long ago.

The last criticism, at least, is sound, and the most candid of the public interest group spokesmen acknowledge its validity. Environmentalists are especially open to the charge. "They don't simply want to keep the brook clean," a friendly critic observes. "They want to keep other people from fishing in it."

The question is whether middle-class motives, even those of earnest liberals, can serve a broad public interest. It is a tenet of the public interest group faith that they can do. David Brower, the outspoken president of Friends of the Earth, says that those who charge groups like his with acting out of self-interest are "missing the point. There is a paucity of institutions willing to look ahead. This is our job, and it is essential if we give a fig about the next generation."

How large is the public interest movement? It is unmeasured and perhaps unmeasurable, but those close to the field affirm that it is larger than ever before. At present, they say, there are in the United States several thousand activist, public interest organizations—issue-

---

* Also elected last fall, to Congress, was Toby Moffett, a former "Raider" for Ralph Nader and a leader of Connecticut Citizens Action.

oriented rather than service-oriented in the manner of traditional community groups. There are also a few thousand "research" organizations to back them up. The proliferation of the resource organizations is a reliable indicator of how the movement has grown. The membership includes lawyers, scientists, architects, accountants, and advertising executives who donate their time to helping promote causes they deem worthy.

Who is joining the movement? Whites comprise the heavy majority, and they are well above average in education, income, awareness of issues, and disposable time for volunteer activities. That is, they are a large and generally inert portion of the middle-class amalgam. "Part of the middle class is so fearful of change that it turns backward," says David Cohen, chief lobbyist for Common Cause. "Another part accepts change as inevitable, if not welcome, and wants to master it. That second part is the Common Cause group." The same can be said of the other middle-class public interest groups. Many of their activists have been down the protest trail before, in the civil-rights or the anti-war movements. Many are members of more than one public interest group; so their true strength is not so great as a total membership would indicate. Their staying power is limited; the former head of Common Cause in California estimates that only 10 to 15 percent of the organization's membership works actively and that among this group there is a 50 percent annual turnover—a retention rate that he calls "better than most" in the public interest field.

If that is a hell of a way to run a railroad, the train is nonetheless gaining speed. For fuel it has a seemingly inexhaustible supply of middle-class people eager to "get involved" in this or that cause. Their motivations vary. Some of the people have been disillusioned by Watergate and, before that, by Vietnam, by assassinations, and by the 1968 Democratic convention. "People are dismayed that government, set up to serve the public interest, is serving

special interests instead," says Carl C. Clark of the Commission for the Advancement of Public Interest Organizations. "That isn't new, but the perception of it is now getting through." Others are attracted simply because they are joiners, which the American middle class has long been, and because public interest work is currently chic. (One of William Hamilton's "Now Society" cartoons shows his typically "now" female asking her mate, "Don't you think if there'd been no John Gardner and no Common Cause, we'd have found each other anyway?")

But the chief motivations seem to go deeper —to feelings of powerlessness and loss of control over one's life. American society has traditionally been operated by and for the middle class. Ours has been a system based on middle-class values, a system whose riches might be skimmed by economic buccaneers but whose decision-making was in safe, solid, middle-class hands. What has happened, it seems, is that the powerful institutions on which the middle class could always rely—business and government—are no longer reliable, no longer accountable. They serve other interests as well. Business serves itself, in ways that even the middle class finds offensive. Government, more bureaucratized yet more politically sensitive, serves elements of society that formerly were not heard, let alone served: women, blacks, poor people. Not only is the middle class less coddled than before; when it complains, its complaints may go unheeded.

Elevated from specifics to something like a social philosophy, the complaints now have a familiar ring: "We're all nothing but numbers"; "our political institutions are unresponsive"; "other people are getting the benefits that we pay for." Says David Ramage, who heads the Washington-based Center for Community Change: "[The middle class's] perception of control over their lives has been considerably lessened. Not just by the federal government, but by a whole variety of experts who determine what's best. It is a feeling akin to what the lower classes have always felt." In short, there is a growing awareness that major decisions affecting middle-class people are being made without them and often directly against their own interests.

Jack Conway mentions an obvious example, the unemployed aerospace engineer: "He's busted his butt to go to school, become an important man in his community, and—wham!— he's out. Does he feel powerless? You're damned right he does." So does the father who, on $15,000 a year, can no longer be sure of being able to buy a nice house or send his children to college—or even keep a utility from damming or polluting his favorite river. So does the taxpayer, who, try as he may, inevitably resents "subsidizing so many government workers and welfare recipients," as Jack Anderson put it in a recent column on "the submissive majority." John Gardner, the Common Cause chairman, points out that the middle class "has not been victimized. They bought all this themselves: the technology, the bigness, and the centralizing trends that have left them with a feeling of very little power."

It has taken a long while for all this to sink in —because of the middle class's innate go-slow attitudes and because the Fifties was a conservative period. The classes were properly positioned. People who wanted jobs had them, and paychecks covered expenses. The civil-rights movement was still embryonic; the beatniks, who seemed radical at the time, were trying not to change society, but to get away from it. Super-Americanism, which had no patience with protest, was the prevailing ideology, and almost everyone accepted the old maxim, "You can't fight city hall."

For those alert enough to learn, the Sixties provided a valuable lesson. Blacks, Chicanos, and who knew what-all else were raising the devil and getting everyone's attention and some (it looked like a lot) of the things they

wanted. Some nice white middle-class people joined the civil-rights protests; others just watched. But they all learned a little. Then came the anti-war movement, which enlisted nice white middlers by the droves and ruined a President, and they all learned a little more. The war on poverty taught additional lessons, particularly to the middle-class folks who served on the local boards and saw how decisions get made and how money is spent at the grass roots. The nice white middlers began shedding their inhibitions. "By the start of the Seventies," says a veteran of the anti-poverty effort and of Common Cause, "it was okay for *anybody* to organize. You had Suburban Mothers Against the War and Neighbors to Stop High-Rise and God knows how many other groups like them."

The successes of Ralph Nader provided further incentives. Nice white middlers might not have liked Nader's aggressiveness, but they were impressed by the way he challenged unaccountable institutions. In the auto-safety campaign, he not only stood up to some of America's most powerful corporations but even showed them to be dirty pool players. Then he went after phony advertising claims, food additives, government secrecy, and oligarchic corporate boards. He sent his task forces of "Nader's Raiders" in pursuit of water and air polluters, regulatory agencies, the banking industry. Nader's tools have been the exposé and the lawsuit, honed by a righteousness no other public figure can match.

What the middle-class public interest groups lack in righteousness they make up for in skills and in the ability to influence. A high proportion of their members are accustomed to conceptualizing, organizing, and promoting. They are also accustomed to dealing with decision-makers, in and out of government. They are comfortable with the media, and with foundations that have money to give away.

Most of all, members of these groups have a determination to make their presence felt. It was not always thus. "In the old-style service groups, the Boy Scouts and 'friends of the hospital,' " says Carl Clark, "the volunteers weren't really trusted. They were used to carrying out policies that were set by the leadership. It was fine for a Gray Lady to read to a wounded soldier in the hospital, but it wasn't fine for her to ask, 'Why is that soldier lying there all this time without an operation?' In the new public interest groups, people ask questions like that, and they care about the answers." Further, they become impatient with anything short of what they see as direct action to solve a problem. "The people we get don't want study groups or lectures anymore," says Ken Smith of Common Cause. "They say, 'Tell us how to get so-and-so's vote on an issue.' "

A major strength of the public interest groups is the special skills they can call on, usually free of charge. Professional people usually predominate on the boards of directors, and they have little trouble getting colleagues to donate *pro bono* work. Jim Turner, who heads a food and drug consulting group, says he can call on "some of the best-trained people in the world—women with graduate degrees in nutrition, for example, who donate tremendous amounts of time to our projects."

In a potentially far-reaching development, a small band of public activists and foundations recently formed a profit-making corporation whose aim is to challenge shoddy business practices through lawsuits. The corporation, called Public Equity, will take on only cases it considers important and hopes will be lucrative. "The significant thing about Public Equity," says one of its board members, "is that it's getting into economics. It's going to hit business where it lives, in the profit-and-loss statement, and it's going to do that with an All-American institution, the corporation."

Spurred by the national economic situation, consumer action groups have organized in numerous cities. San Francisco Consumer Action is probably the liveliest of the groups.

Since its founding in 1971, the group has published four widely praised handbooks, including guides to banking and pharmaceutical services and a scathing attack on the California Department of Consumer Affairs. It has also threatened "educational picketing" of business firms that do not respond to its demands. Consumer Action has about 2,000 dues-paying members, who are as middle-class as the seven staff members (all college graduates living on "subsistence" pay). The staffers are still a bit embarrassed about their first big case, which involved a woman who had had endless problems with her new Jaguar car. Consumer Action, true to its creed of helping everyone, no matter how well off, picketed the San Francisco office of the British Motor Corporation. British Motors sued for $6 million, but Consumer Action won the case, the right to picket, and good service for the Jaguar for the rest of its natural life.

Suburban Newtonville, Mass., seems an unlikely place for protest, but it is the home of Action for Children's Television, which for several years now has kept unrelenting pressure on the television networks and companies that advertise on their programs for children. ACT wants to improve drastically the dismal quality of children's programs and to banish commercials from them. Although these goals are well nigh unreachable, ACT has made important gains. Under its badgering, the National Association of Broadcasters has agreed to eliminate vitamin advertising and reduce the overall number of commercials on children's shows. ACT is now pressuring both the NAB and Federal Trade Commission to crack down on other commercial practices, such as using program "hosts" to pitch products and bombarding gullible youngsters with come-ons for toys and sugary snacks.

ACT was midwived in Newtonville in the living room of Mrs. Peggy Charren, who called in a few neighbors—two doctors, a lawyer, and their wives—to see what could be done to "change TV." The group decided to forgo boycotts and try instead, in Mrs. Charren's words, "to create a climate that would lead to the broadcaster's giving some real thought to what he was doing." That rather vague battle plan assumes the opposition—also middle-class—to be decent folks who will probably do the right thing when they are shown what that is. If they don't do right, there is always the Naderesque lawsuit.

The networks now anxiously check ACT's ratings of children's programming and brag about ACT's approval if they get it. Not only can the organization make trouble with the FTC; its membership has grown to 5,000 and has spread to almost every state. That's a lot of potential bad-mouthings of a network and its advertisers. These days ACT attracts foundation support, but Mrs. Charren remembers when the embryonic membership had to put up the money from its own pockets. "We can't imagine how people without money could do this kind of thing," she says. "It's difficult to see how the poor can make change."

By the environmentalists' own definition, no other group is more public-interested than they are. Nobody is more middle-class, either —a fact that elicits little concern from environmental leaders. "Yes, our base is too narrow," says David Brower, "but there simply are not enough people around with the time to project their thoughts that far, that often." At Brower's Friends of the Earth and at the Sierra Club, which he formerly headed, the trend is toward involvement in "social issues" with only a tenuous connection to environmentalism: for example, a 1973 strike of Shell Oil refinery workers, to which the Sierra Club gave public support. "Friends of the Earth people are already Socialists," says Sierra Club editor Roger Olmstead, with a chuckle; "so Brower doesn't have to worry. But I think our organization should move cautiously on marginally environmental issues, or we're going to step

on a lot of toes." Some Sierra Club toes already are smarting, because the club still has a healthy complement of conservative members who want to be "involved" only in old-fashioned conservation and the pleasures of the outdoor life.

The flagship of the public interest fleet is Common Cause. It is the biggest, the richest, and —except for the combined Nader enterprises —the most influential of the groups. John Gardner started Common Cause after his original public interest venture, the National Urban Coalition, had failed to develop as anticipated (the Coalition has since undergone substantial staff and budget cutbacks). Common Cause has 320,000 members nationwide and an annual income, from $15 dues and contributions, of more than $6 million. That is a lot of money to be thrown around in anyone's interest, even the public's. Common Cause spends the bulk of it on trying to influence the votes of legislators and the decisions of other government officials, principally in Washington but also in state capitals. It has developed a modern and quite ingenious version of traditional pressure-group politics. The basic instruments are the telephone and the postage meter, which are relentlessly employed by a small staff and legions of volunteers. The system is so efficient that, notified of a critical vote in Congress, Common Cause can put hundreds of letters on the desks of selected congressmen within 24 hours. "They're not form letters, either," says an official of the organization. "They're knowledgeable, articulate, and persuasive."

Virtually alone among public interest groups, Common Cause focuses on procedural, rather than substantive, issues. Instead of attacking poverty, television, or strip-mining, it attacks governmental mechanisms that keep these issues from being effectively addressed. This policy has brought Common Cause itself under attack for allegedly tilting at windmills rather than real fortresses, but there can be little question of the importance of such procedures as the congressional seniority and committee systems. Common Cause won its biggest victory to date last fall, when it led the successful drive for federal campaign-finance reform.

Common Cause affiliates now operate in some 35 states. Last year the California group was instrumental in the passage of Proposition 9, a statewide campaign finance law. It fought for "Prop Nine" with another, very different public interest group, People's Lobby, which specializes in gathering petition signatures (necessary for getting measures like Proposition 9 on the ballot) and which is run from top to bottom by a Los Angeles husband and wife team. The San Francisco office of Common Cause was recently relocated from downtown to Union Street, in part so that it would be more attractive to upper-middle-class lady volunteers from neighboring Pacific Heights. Common Cause officials know that creating an atmosphere is important to the organization's work. To sustain that atmosphere, they have persuaded John Gardner, whenever he visits a city with a Common Cause office, to spend time chatting with its volunteers. But concessions to volunteers' sensitivities stop when the business of politics begins. Common Cause volunteers learn to judge politicians on an issue by issue basis, with no points awarded for good deeds done yesterday. They learn, too, that political protest goes where and how it's needed. In the spring of 1972, one group of Bay Area Common Causists wanted to protest the Vietnam war in the district of Rep. Pete McCloskey, a staunch anti-war man, while another group wanted to march in downtown San Francisco. Instead, both groups were directed to assemble in the district of Rep. William Mailliard, who was pro-war and the senior Republican on the House Foreign Affairs Committee. Even middle-class politics, the lesson was, can be inconvenient.

Leaders of the public interest movement are optimistic about its future. They believe that the movement has established a valuable check and balance on the federal government. They seem confident that middle class feelings of powerlessness will not diminish under a government devoted, as the middle class sees it, to the welfare of other elements of society. But some observers question the tenacity of the middle class in sticking with issues that show little promise of resolution. Others question its willingness to fund a vast array of public interest organizations. (Movement thinkers already are devising ways to tap the federal treasury in behalf of their groups; one idea is for an income tax checkoff, modeled on the present voluntary tax contribution to the two major parties.) A greater danger may well be the failure to build a broader base of support. David Brower favors a new political party that he hopes would attract a wide range of America's disaffected. Although his own Common Cause is far from broadly based John Gardner recognizes the present limitations on the public interest movement. To succeed, he warns, the movement must avoid two pitfalls to which the middle class is peculiarly susceptible: capture by business or foundations or other invaders from the Establishment and infatuation with the idea that it is really *the* voice of the people.

20

The Power of Fetal Politics

Roger M. Williams

The abortion issue has become one of the country's most explosive political and moral controversies. It is also perhaps one of the best examples of single-issue interest group politics. The pro-choice and anti-abortion groups have no room to compromise. Each side attacks the other's motives, tactics, and integrity. An intensely personal issue, abortion has been elevated to the status of the prohibition and women's suffrage battles of the past. What is the political strength of the "right to life" groups? How have they supported and opposed various public officials? Do you agree that they have a right-wing ideological bias? What is the irony of their attacks on Medicaid funding of abortion? What role is played by the Catholic Church in this dispute? What are the prospects of a constitutional amendment prohibiting abortion?

The movement has many faces: from sweet ladies handing out red roses and right-to-life cookbooks, to demonstrators brandishing bottled fetuses and hoodlums attacking medical clinics. It has many voices as well: from righteous ministers preaching the sanctity of unborn souls, to editorials raising the specter of the holocaust, to crowds screaming "murderer" at elected officials who take a different position.

This is the anti-abortion movement, a cause that refuses to yield. Six years ago, the U.S. Supreme Court ruled that the right to have an abortion is beyond the reach of government. Since then, public-opinion polls have consistently shown that a majority of Americans favors making abortion a matter for patient and doctor to decide. Despite these developments, the subject is more politically explosive today than ever before. Opposition to abortion has become the most implacable, and perhaps the nastiest, public-issue campaign in at least a half century.

Anti-abortion forces are eagerly preparing for the elections of 1980 and beyond. U.S. Senators and Representatives, as well as many lesser officials, are being targeted for defeat. Even the forthcoming presidential race is within the movement's sights. "We hope to have at least one of the nominees on our side," says a national anti-abortion leader, "but in any case I assure you we'll have an impact."

Trumpeting their own future influence is part of the basic strategy of most political-pressure groups. But the anti-abortionists have demonstrated that they have muscles as well as mouths. In the 1978 elections they sent severe tremors through the political landscapes of such states as Minnesota and Iowa. In New York, running a gubernatorial candidate whose sole issue was opposition to abortion, they drew 132,000 votes and secured for their Right to Life party an official place on the state ballot.

During the past 18 months, the movement has secured passage of abortion-restricting legislation in a dozen states and municipalities and laid the groundwork in a dozen others.

Fourteen of the necessary 34 state legislatures have passed a call for a constitutional convention aimed at outlawing abortion. In addition, both houses of Congress are being bombarded with prospective constitutional amendments that would accomplish the same purpose. (Some versions make allowances for situations where the mother's life is threatened and for other so-called hard cases.)

Says former Iowa Senator Dick Clark, on whom the anti-abortionists successfully trained their fire last November: "For candidates like me, with a clear-cut voting record on abortion, I see nothing but trouble ahead. The fact is that we're facing a small but very dedicated minority. A while back, I wouldn't have thought their constitutional amendment had a decent prospect. Now, I wouldn't underestimate its chances."

The gloom should not be spread too thick. It can be argued that, in their targeting of 1978 electoral candidates, the anti-abortionists lost as many battles as they won. Michigan Governor William Milliken was reelected despite having angered opponents of abortion by twice vetoing legislation that would have secured one of their principal goals—the elimination of government funding for the operation. In New Jersey, Illinois, and elsewhere, candidates running campaigns based on a right-to-life appeal were heavily outpolled.

Nonetheless, right-to-life successes are sufficiently numerous to demonstrate that the anti-abortion movement has become a significant political force. The question is, How long can it hope to remain one? What chances does it have of sustaining its bright blue flame of moral fury?

The war over abortion has an unusual history. Before the mid-1960s, opponents of abortion were in complete control. Then, within a six-year span, "pro-choice" activists—those who think abortion is a matter for the woman herself to decide—achieved a series of stunning successes: laws that legalized the practice in 18 states; court decisions invalidating prohibitive statutes in a half-dozen other states; and finally, in January 1973, the Supreme Court ruling that gave women an absolute right to have an abortion during the first three months of pregnancy and that severely limited state intervention through the sixth month.

Success, as it turned out, came too easily. The advocates of choice found themselves, like an armored column that has raced deep into enemy territory, outstripping their lines of supply. "The country wasn't with us at that point," concedes Karen Mulhauser, director of NARAL (National Abortion Rights Action League), the leading pro-choice organization. "Had we made more gains through the legislative and referendum processes, and taken a little longer at it, the public would have moved with us."

The Supreme Court decision spurred a number of statewide anti-abortion organizations into forming a National Right to Life Committee (NRLC). Although a welter of other groups is now at work on the issue, NRLC is the acknowledged kingpin. With chapters in all 50 states, it serves as the movement's general lobbying office, clearing house, and strategy center. NLRC maintains especially close ties with the Life Amendment Political Action Committee (LAPAC), which is spearheading the campaign for a constitutional amendment; their offices are located side by side in Washington's National Press Building; until recently, the two organizations were headed by a husband and wife—Judie (NRLC) and Paul (LAPAC) Brown.

Paul Brown (Judi has retired) cheerfully describes himself as a political amateur, a status that always enhances the image of pressure groups. Brown, 40, left a job as manager of a K-Mart store to direct LAPAC. "For the first nine months, the organization consisted of me," he says, "and for three of those months I got no pay." NRLC and LAPAC raise money without the services of professional, conservative-cause fund-raisers; and, if one believes their figures, they spend it with striking cost efficiency. According to the Federal Elections Commission, LAPAC last year reported expenditures of $95,000, with a mere $7,000 of that split among eight candidates whom the committee was especially anxious to see win. NRLC's own political-action committee reported no expenditures at all—a strange foundation for any sort of political action.

At the state level, anti-abortion groups have been working even greater apparent miracles. In Iowa, Senator Clark seems to have been unseated for little more than would buy a new car. In New York, the anti-abortion gubernatorial ticket spent a mere $75,000, most of it for a final-week TV campaign. In state after state, the anti-abortionists' reported expenditures are almost trifling.

Big bangs for small bucks is only one of the surprises that spring from the anti-abortion movement. Most of them involve impressive rationalizations on the part of people who form the mainstay of the movement. It is curious, for example, that Americans who feel most threatened by minorities and the poor are often the most determined to see that their babies are born. The same people are usually hostile to "big government," yet they urge government at all levels to intervene in the personal lives of adult citizens. On a different track, one finds Southern fundamentalist Protestants, who once despised Roman Catholics only a little less than blacks, now making common cause with Catholics on the abortion issue.

The movement transcends these inconsistencies by means of the extraordinary passion of the anti-abortion cause. While right-to-life activity does draw strength from the fears and phobias it holds in common with the New Right, it has a purpose and a life of its own. In our most recent broad-based social movements—civil rights, women's liber-ation, opposition to the Vietnam War—only the extreme fringe has been unwilling to compromise, to make gains piecemeal, to judge candidates for office on some basis other than the movement's own issue. Among anti-abortionists, however, everybody is hardline. For them there is no give and take. A political candidate earns his tireless support or scathing opposition solely by virtue of his position on abortion. (There are *some* limits. When a Missouri Ku Klux Klansman ran for Congress on a pro-life platform, reports a leader of NRLC, "we couldn't support him.")

This singlemindedness—this "devotion," as its practitioners see it—gives rise to the charge that the anti-abortion movement carries one-issue politics to the extreme. Missouri Representative William Clay put the matter forcefully last year when he told his congressional colleagues that, while he personally doesn't believe in abortion, "I am sick and tired of seeing [efforts to prohibit it] pop up on every piece of legislation. . . . It has become an albatross for all legislation, regardless of merit." Clay could have cited District of Columbia statehood as a case in point. Last year *The Wanderer*, a national Catholic newspaper, urged the faithful to oppose D.C.'s statehood on the ground that the new Congressmen would be "virtually certain to be pro-abortion."

The anti-abortion retort amounts to a paraphrase of Barry Goldwater's dictum about extremism and virtue; the defense of life, they insist, transcends all other concerns. Furthermore, they say, many of the complainers were themselves single-issue crusaders. "The black vote, Vietnam—those were strictly one-issue," says LAPAC's Paul Brown. Playing a favorite trump card, he adds, "If you thought a candidate was right on every issue but freedom of the press, would you vote for him?"

Justification based on past movements is only partly convincing. As MIT political scientist Walter Dean Burnham says, "The right-to-lifers *are* doing what others have done, but with a major difference in intensity. The emotional charge coming from opposition to abortion is greater than from civil rights or the right to bear arms or any similar cause. The people who are dedicated right-to-lifers really believe that, in a special religious sense, they are doing the Lord's work."

The effectiveness of the anti-abortion movement stems largely from the wide front along which it attacks. From presidential campaigns to municipal ordinances, the movement slugs away at one or another aspect of the issue.

At the *presidential* level, the movement's influence is indistinct and unpredictable. Theoretically, it could be felt in two ways: through the personal preferences of the major-party candidates or through the influence of convention delegates on party policy. At least for 1980, the latter prospect seems highly unlikely, despite the fact that LAPAC actively encourages right-to-lifers to run for delegate posts; neither party is prone to write a strong platform plank on an issue like abortion.

As for presidential candidates, the movement's prospects appear to be only slightly better. None of the Democrats' 1980 hopefuls is anti-abortion, although President Carter himself is publicly opposed to Medicaid funding of the procedure. Two or three of the probable candidates for the Republican nomination— Ronald Reagan, Philip Crane, perhaps John Connally—are anti-abortion to some degree; but it is at least questionable whether any of them would be willing to thrust the issue to the forefront of a campaign.

At the *congressional* level, the movement has much to show for its efforts. In each of the past three years, Congress has enacted the so-called Hyde Amendment, which prohibits the use of Medicaid money to pay for abortion— and, in the process, discriminates against women who cannot afford private medical care. Congress has also voted to deny government abortions to military personnel and their dependents and to Peace Corps volunteers.

LAPAC has received welcome notoriety from its congressional "hit lists"— rosters of Senators and Representatives who, in its view, must be defeated. "Our [candidate] ratings are 100 percent or zero," says Brown. "There's no middle ground. Take Senator Frank Church [D-Idaho]. He's furious with us because we've targeted him in next year's elections. But Church would accept a 'state's rights' constitutional amendment—to allow individual states to choose whether or not to permit abortion. And he votes for Medicaid funding of abortions. Hell, if he believes in killing 40 percent of those babies, that's no better than killing all of 'em."

LAPAC claims that, as Brown puts it, "We only go after a guy if he can be beaten and if we figure we can generate at least 5 percent of the vote on our own. Some people who should be beaten can't be, or if they can, who you'd get instead makes it not worth the effort." That is sensible pressure politicking, but it doesn't quite explain the right-to-lifers' penchant for consistently right-wing candidates. On LAPAC's 1980 list, for example, there is nobody to the right of center; yet, there appear such stalwarts of the left as Senators George McGovern and Representatives Morris Udall and Robert Drinan.

Texas Senator John Tower, a conservative who has been pro-choice on abortion, allegedly escapes the list under the "unbeatable" or "best available" provisos. According to a former anti-abortion lobbyist, Tower's immunity actually stems from the fact that he's "good on the [other] issues"—a sign that even the single-minded can bow to a higher political cause.

Political analysts are still debating the impact of the movement's 1978 hit list. The consensus seems to be that the abortion issue played a large part in the defeats of Senator Clark and Minnesota Representative Donald

Fraser, who was running for the Senate, and a somewhat smaller part in the defeat of Colorado Senator Floyd Haskell. The Haskell case illustrates how tricky these assessments of influence are; if Haskell was beaten by right-to-life forces, how do we account for the fact that Governor Richard Lamm and two other major pro-choice officeholders in the state won handily?

Congress is also the zone of combat over the proposed constitutional amendment, which has become the top priority for most right-to-life leaders. Brown declares, "Each day we don't have an amendment, 3,000 babies die."

At the *state and local* levels, the movement has pushed legislation that would in effect subvert the court-upheld right to abortion. The first such law, an ordinance passed in early 1978 in Akron, Ohio, has served as a model for most of the others. It provides, among other things, that pregnant women give "informed consent" for the procedure and that parents of any woman under 18 be told of her condition. On their face, these provisions seem reasonable. But many a pregnant teenager would rather risk a surreptitious—and dangerous—abortion than the wrath of Mom and Dad. "Informed consent" usually involves issuing warnings about the emotional and physical dangers of abortion, without corresponding warnings of the emotional dangers of delivering an unwanted baby.

Thus far, at the behest of pro-choice lawyers, every ordinance or law of this nature has been temporarily enjoined by a court, generally on constitutional grounds. But efforts to enact such laws continue unabated. The efforts alone can force pro-choice adherents to retreat: In the New Jersey legislature, for example, they have compromised by introducing an informed-consent bill of their own this year. Although the most militant pro-choicers disparage such concessions, Ms. Fran Avallone, state coordinator of New Jersey's Right to Choose, says it is tactically essential: "Every anti-abor-

tion bill that's been introduced in this assembly has passed. I know the attitudes of the men [legislators] we're dealing with, and our own version of 'informed consent' is the best we can hope to get from them."

New York's Right to Life party has demonstrated the power of this single issue—not so much in terms of total votes as of what politicians call leverage. If the major parties hereafter do not nominate "acceptable" candidates, observes Mrs. Mary Jane Tobin, the right-to-lifer's gubernatorial candidate in New York, "We *do* have the ballot line, and we'll use it. If our candidate can get 3 or more percent in the average district, we can make or break the Republican or Democratic nominee for state assembly."

At any level of political activity, anti-abortion leaders maintain, the strength of the movement lies in the eagerness and energy of its grass-roots adherents. "Our greatest ability is in generating activity," says Brown. "I can make 10 phone calls into a state—spend about $50—and have a hell of an impact." The impact comes in the form of volunteer work and in-kind contributions, that is, donations of supplies or services that normally would have to be paid for. Telephone calls, office space, and pamphlet printing and distribution are standard in-kind donations.

"We never had a campaign headquarters," says Mrs. Tobin. "We worked out of our homes. We're traditional women who have children and don't like to be far away from them." The movement also enjoys large amounts of *pro bono* assistance from lawyers and doctors.

Volunteer support is one major reason for the anti-abortionists' grass-roots success. The other is the cooperation of the Roman Catholic Church and the ready availability of its vast organizational framework. Granted that the right-to-life theme stirs the hearts of many Protestants and some members of other faiths, it finds the bulk of its adherents among Catholics; for them, abortion for any reason amounts to taking the life of an innocent human being and a transgression of the Fifth Commandment, "Thou shalt not kill."

Particularly in the parishes, Catholic Church involvement is continuous and effective. While some of this involvement may be illegal, proving illegalities is very difficult. Under Internal Revenue Service regulations governing tax-exempt organizations, churches are permitted a certain amount of lobbying to influence legislation. The amount is supposed to be "insubstantial." But even if the word were interpreted strictly, which it is not, an insubstantial fraction of a budget the size of the Catholic Church's could be large indeed.

No outsider, including the IRS, knows even vaguely how much the Church and its adherents have put into the anti-abortion movement. At the highest hierarchical level is the support given by individual American bishops—perhaps half the total number in the United States—to the National Committee for a Human Life Amendment; in 1977, the bishops reported contributions of $279,000.

The Church also serves as the focal point of right-of-life activity at the grass-roots. There are abundant examples of parish connections beneficial to the movement. Says an attorney for the pro-choice Center for Constitutional Rights, Rhonda Copelon, who has amassed evidence of the connections: "Money is raised through the parishes in many ways: raffles, dances, and benefits run by church-related groups like the rosary societies and Knights of Columbus." In-kind contributions include using church rooms for right-to-life meetings and church buses to haul demonstrators to right-to-life rallies.

In addition, parishes and their priests do their own versions of candidate targeting. Pennsylvania Congressman Robert Edgar, an opponent of the constitutional amendment, recalls the final Sundays before election day in his victorious 1976 and '78 campaigns: "At every Catholic church in my district there was either a sermon or a handout concerning abortion and, at least by implication, me. I've been named from the pulpit a number of times. We were told these kinds of things are the result of a directive from the archdiocese."

Rosemarie Totaro, a pro-choice member of the New Jersey Assembly, tells of a similar experience last year. According to Totaro, literature favoring her anti-abortion opponent was distributed in the Catholic church she herself attends, and at one Sunday Mass—with Totaro among the worshippers—the priest solicited votes for all the local anti-abortion candidates. "I was really offended," Totaro said recently. "I spoke to the priest about it. All he said was that I was wrong in my position on abortion."

NARAL, which sees the Church's hand in all sorts of anti-abortion funding, believes it has caught a Long Island diocese in a plainly illegal financial contribution. NARAL charges that the diocese, in 1973, made an in-church collection of $36,000 and turned the money over to the New York State Right to Life Committee. At NARAL's behest, the justice department is investigating.

Paul Brown makes a surprisingly strong denial of alleged Catholic control of the anti-abortion movement. In fact, he contends that the Church doesn't do nearly enough in the movement's behalf. He even asserts that "Church for church, we probably get more cooperation from other faiths. Catholic officials are very paranoid about their tax status. I wish they'd *lose* the tax exemption. If they did, we'd have our amendment three days later." In the meantime, Brown says, nervous Church officials should "Go talk to God. Tell Him you weren't able to save any babies this year, but you saved your tax status."

Conservative sectors of the Catholic press have maintained a steady barrage against the advocates and practitioners of abortion. Some of the rhetoric is positively venal, and there are instances of its apparently leading to violence. Two years ago, the St. Paul, Minnesota, diocesan newspaper conducted an editorial campaign against a local planned parenthood/abortion clinic, labeling it "little Dachau." Not long afterward, the clinic was fired upon and burned. Patients and staff have subsequently been harassed, and this past April, windows were broken and epithets ("killers") scribbled on the outside walls. All the attacks took place during the Lenten period. NARAL says a half-dozen other clinics around the country have been physically attacked in the past two years.

Anti-abortionists have no monopoly on gut fighting. Stacked in cartons at NARAL's Washington headquarters are pamphlets whose illustrations slam home the pro-choice contention that banning abortion will only "force" women back into "underground butchery." The contention, is, in fact, buttressed by statistics showing that almost as many women had abortions before they were legalized as have them now. But the pamphlets are excessive, displaying photographs of nude women lying dead on the floors of back-alley abortionists, as well as a grossly deformed fetus and an unwanted newborn burned to death in an incinerator. "We're not proud of those," says Mulhauser, when questioned about the pamphlets. "But sometimes this is necessary to combat the distortions of the other side."

Such a statement points up the frustration the pro-choice leaders feel in trying to match the anti-abortionists' tactical maneuvering. Some pro-choice leaders admit that they have been out-organized and out-generaled. They certainly have been out- "semanticized." The anti-abortionists have succeeded in tagging the pro-choice side "pro-abortion," while appropriating for themselves the seductive phrase "right-to-life." Professional image-makers could hardly have done a better job.

Despite its competitive advantages, the anti-abortion movement faces a very doubtful political future. Passing a constitutional amendment is difficult at best and, as the Equal Rights Amendment forces have learned, especially hard when the campaign resembles a moral crusade. To be politically powerful for more than a couple of years, the movement must push aside a pair of time-tested American propositions. One is that moral certainty and religious precepts seldom sustain political action. The other is that the pluralistic character of our society has a way of fragmenting the most passionate and seemingly unified causes.

A third, more speculative problem for the movement is what Professor Burnham calls "our system-wide political and economic crisis." By that he means a general, long-term reordering of priorities in which issues like abortion will tend to get squeezed out by such overriding concerns as energy and inflation.

All that is little comfort to the pro-choice politician now facing the wrath of a fully mobilized right-to-life constituency. In 1980 and probably beyond, antiabortionists, given the right set of circumstances, will be able to inflict the sting of fetal politics.

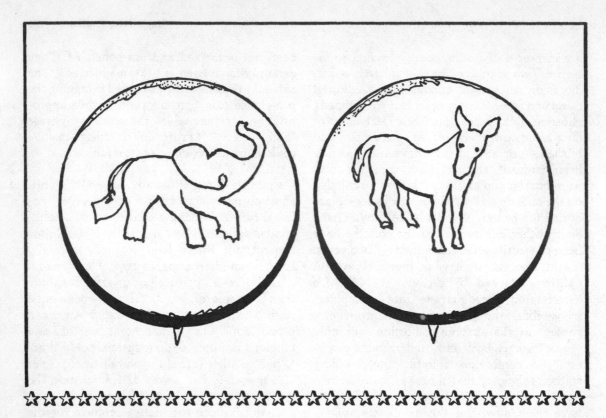

☆☆☆☆☆☆☆☆☆☆☆☆☆☆☆☆☆☆☆☆☆☆☆☆☆☆☆☆☆☆☆☆☆☆☆☆

Political Parties   6

Political parties are instruments for organizing power and providing opportunities for popular participation and control of government in a democratic society. The major objective of a political party is to win elections by mobilizing the voters in order to control the government. As an important link between government and society, political parties offer various groups access to government and a means to participate in the political system.

Political parties are not mentioned in the Constitution. In fact, James Madison warned against the dangers of factions in *Federalist*, No. 10. However, party factions developed as soon as the new government went into effect in 1789. Differences revolved around the extent of national authority in relation to the states. This Federalist–anti-Federalist competition entered the 1800 presidential election when Thomas Jefferson opposed incumbent President John Adams. From that time to the present, political parties have dominated our governmental system.

In contrast to one-party or multiparty systems which exist elsewhere, the United States has a two-party system. Two parties are dominant because minority parties can never hope to capture a majority of votes in the electoral college for president or a majority of seats to control congress. As long as a minority party can never hope to govern, it is clear that two major parties will dominate government. The two-party system provides a majority party with the power to govern and an opposition party that can offer alternatives to the voters with the prospect that someday it can replace the party in power.

The Democratic and Republican parties can be characterized as loosely organized coalitions of *voters, activists,* and *elected officials.* In examining these three groups, what are the major roles of political parties?

First, the chief objective of the Republicans and Democrats is to win public offices at stake in national, state, and local elections. To do so, the parties provide the voters with candidates who articulate their views on relevant issues. The linkage between parties and the electorate is crucial in understanding how and why the voters behave the way they do. In this sense, parties provide channels of expression for public opinion and serve as organizing agents for different groups who wish to participate in elections. This is one of the primary functions of a party: to control and direct the struggle for power.

Second, parties provide opportunities to become actively involved in practical politics. Before the electorate can be organized, the party itself must have an effective scheme of operations. This requires teams of workers who engage in such activities as voter registration, canvassing, and assisting voters to the polls on election day. The party activists may also hold party offices and become involved in fund raising and designating candidates to run in primary elections. They may also seek to attend national or state party conventions which nominate candidates for such high offices as president or governor.

Thirdly, political parties are a means for gaining control over government. After winning elections, the office-holders are in a position to form majority coalitions in government to control the agenda and the outcome of decisions on important issues. Thus, the party in government has the power to make policy decisions based upon the mandate it receives from the voters. Parties often have difficulties in keeping their promises in translating voter expectations into public policies.

Decentralization is another major feature of American political parties. Nominations, campaigns, and electoral contests are predominantly a product of state and local rather than national issues. Loose collections of state and local officials also dominate national party committees; this makeup results in a decentralized structure that is difficult to coordinate except when under the control of a strong national party chairperson. According to William Keefe (Article 21) the federal system, the separation of powers, nominating procedures, and the financing of campaigns all cause a power flow from the decentralized organizations to the top.

Public policy is affected by party decentralization. First, there are many access points in government through which elected officials, interest groups and individuals can take action. Second, there is considerable participation by states and local communities in the development and administration of national programs. The controversies over a national energy policy are a good example of the diversity of regional political conflicts. Third, representatives and senators seek to serve their constituents by reflecting local and state perspectives. Finally, the president attempts to represent the diverse wings of both parties in making cabinet, administrative, and judicial appointments.

In recent years party loyalty has declined drastically. The independent voter, who disavows party labels, regularly splits the ticket in electoral contests. Furthermore, many people are increasingly skeptical about the goals and objectives of the parties. Fewer people are voting today than ten years ago—reflecting a growing dissatisfaction toward party politics.

David S. Broder (Article 22) is quite apprehensive about the continuing fragmentation and disintegration of party politics. His analysis of critical presidential elections and the decline of voter identification with the two major parties questions widely held assumptions about the stability and responsiveness of our two-party system. Unlike the major realignments of the past that were associated with such turbulent events as the Civil War (which established the dominance of the Republican party) and the collapse of the national economy (which forecast the resurgence of the Democrats in 1932), recent social upheavals of the 1960's and 1970's have not transformed either the Democratic or Republican parties.

The parties may become more responsive when they are able to bridge the gap between government and society. Political parties need to develop programs for the "have-nots" and the alienated middle class who are members of a vastly organized and complex technological society. Otherwise, participation in party organizations will become increasingly fragmented.

What are the prospects for party reform? The two key issues are improving public confidence in the performance of political parties and alleviating the tensions between the president and congress over controversial policy problems. Parties could be strengthened by having public financing channeled to the party organizations rather than to individual candidates. Also, the parties need to include groups that have been left out of the political process, for example, youth, women, and minorities.

A major consequence of political party decline is policy conflict between the president and congress. Recent years have witnessed severe confrontations between the executive and legislative branches. These have occurred regardless of whether the president has been a Democrat or a Republican. Jimmy Carter's election in 1976 did not reduce this problem; among other reasons, Carter conducted his presidential campaign largely apart from the regular national Democratic party committee machinery. In fact, Carter campaigned against many of the incumbents of his own party.

The fragmentation of party influence leads to growing public frustration over the levels of governmental performance. The parties face a serious challenge in becoming more responsive to voters and restoring public confidence.

21

The Characteristics of American Parties

William J. Keefe

American political parties are not centralized on a national basis. Instead, as William Keefe indicates, their major characteristic is decentralization, with power flowing from the states and communities to the national party committees. Keefe identifies several causes for party decentralization, *including the federal system, separation of powers, nomination procedures, financing of political campaigns, and a "pervasive spirit of localism." What impact do these limitations have on candidates selected for national office, and what are the effects on public policy?*

There is no lively debate among political scientists concerning the dominant characteristic of American political parties. It is, pure and simple, their decentralization. Viewed at some distance, the party organizations may appear to be neatly ordered and hierarchical—committees are piled, one atop another, from the precinct level to the national committee, conveying the impression that power flows from the top to the bottom. In point of fact, however, the American party is not nearly so hierarchical. The power of national party instrumentalities over state and local organizations is, for the most part, not impressive. The practices that state and local parties follow, the candidates they recruit or help to recruit, the campaign money they raise, the auxiliary groups they form and reform, the innovations they introduce, the organized interests to which they respond, the campaign strategies and issues they create and, most important, the policy orientations of the candidates who run under their label—all bear the distinctive imprints of local and state political cultures, leaders, traditions, and interests.[1]

From *Parties, Politics, and Public Policy* in America, Second Edition, by William J. Keefe. Copyright © 1976 by The Dryden Press. A Division of Holt, Rinehart and Winston. Copyright © 1972 by Holt, Rinehart and Winston. Reprinted by permission of Holt, Rinehart and Winston.

Although there is no mistaking the overall decentralization of American parties, there is evidence that the power of the national party is growing, particularly in terms of control over the presidential nominating process. In 1974 the Democratic party held a mid-term convention for the purpose of drafting a charter—the first in the history of either major party—to provide for the governance of the party. The charter formally establishes the Democratic national convention as the highest authority of the party and requires state parties to observe numerous standards in the selection of convention delegates. As a result of a Supreme Court decision in 1975, moreover, it is now clear that if there is a conflict between national and state party rules concerning the selection of delegates, national party rules must govern. "The convention serves the pervasive national interest in the selection of candidates for national office," the Supreme Court has ruled, "and this national interest is greater than any interest of an individual state."[2]

Weak National Parties

No elaborate argument is needed to establish the point concerning the organizational decentralization of American parties. Evidence is everywhere available that national party agencies cannot dominate state and local party leaders. Should national party leaders seek to influence the nomination of candidates for Congress, for example, the prospects are that they would be met by rebuff and defeat. Although the President obviously has a stake in the policy orientations of candidates his party recruits for Congress—since his legislative program will come before them—there is little he can do to shape the decisions of local party chieftains or electorates. Custom dictates that he follow a "hands-off" policy in the choice of congressional candidates.[3] Moreover, it is exceedingly rare for party leaders in Congress to attempt to discipline fellow party members who stray off the reservation, voting with the other party on key legislative issues or otherwise failing to come to the aid of their party.[4] Congressmen who neglect or demean their party not only escape sanctions but also, by dramatizing their capacity to resist party pressures, may improve their fortunes with the voters back home—such is the case in a relatively loose and decentralized party system.

Finally, the weakness of the national party apparatus is revealed in the character and activities of the national committee. In no important sense can the committee speak for the party as a whole. It has minimum leverage on fellow party members in Congress, on the party's governors, or on officials further down the line. Much of the energy of its leadership is devoted to efforts to keep the party united. And as one would expect in a party composed of divergent interests, the price of unity is usually accommodation. The shaping of party positions on major questions of public policy is therefore well beyond the capacity of the committee.

Factors Contributing to Decentralization

It is no happenstance that the national parties lead a furtive existence, under ordinary circumstances visible only during presidential election campaigns. The situation could hardly be otherwise, given the legal and constitutional characteristics of the American political system. In the first place . . . a decentralized party system appears to be the natural concomitant of a decentralized governmental system. American parties must find their place within a federal system where powers and responsibilities lie with fifty states as well as with the national government. Of particular importance, responsibility for the design of the electoral system in which the parties compete is given to the states, not to the nation. Not surprisingly, party organizations have been molded by the electoral laws under which they contest for power. A vast number of local and state power centers have developed around the thousands of governmental units and elective offices found in the states and localities. With his distinctive constituency (frequently a "safe" district), his own coterie of supporters, and, often, his own channels to campaign money, the typical officeholder has a remarkable amount of freedom in defining his relations to party groups. The organization's well-being and his well-being are not necessarily identical. To press this point, it is not too much to say that officeholders are steadily engaged in the process of evaluating party claims and objectives in the light of their own career aspirations. When the party's claims and the officeholder's aspirations fail to converge, the party ordinarily loses out. To cut short a long story, our decentralized governmental system is the principal sponsor of legal-constitutional arrangements that, on the one hand, often immobilize national party agencies and, on the other hand, open up an extraordinary range of political choices to subnational parties and especially to individual party candidates.

For all of its significance for the party system and the distinctiveness of American politics, however, federalism is but one of several explanations for the decentralization of the major parties. Another constitutional provision, separation of powers, also contributes to the dispersal of governmental and party power. One of the frequent by-products of this system is the emergence of a truncated party majority—that is, a condition under which one party controls one or both houses of the legislature and the other party controls the executive. At worst this leads to a dreary succession of narrow partisan clashes between the branches; at best it may contribute occasionally to the clarification of certain differences between the parties; at no time does it contribute a particle to the development and maintenance of party responsibility for a program of public policy...

A third factor contributing to the decentralization of American parties is the method used to make nominations. It was noted earlier that nominations for national office are sorted out and settled at the local level, ordinarily without interference of any sort by national party functionaries. One of the principal supports of local control over this activity is the direct primary. Its use virtually guarantees that candidates for national office will be tailored to the measure of local specifications. Consider this analysis by Austin Ranney and Willmoore Kendall:

A party's *national* leaders can affect the kind of representatives and senators who come to Washington bearing the party's label only by enlisting the support of the state and local party organizations concerned; and they cannot be sure of doing so even then. Assume, for example, that the local leaders have decided to support the national leaders in an attempt to block the renomination of a maverick congressman, and are doing all they can. There is still nothing to prevent the rank and file, who may admire the incumbent's "independence," from ignoring the leaders' wishes and renominating him. The direct primary, in other words, is *par excellence* a system for maintaining *local* control of nominations; and as long as American localities continue to be so different from one another in economic interests, culture, and political attitudes, the national parties are likely to retain their present ideological heterogeneity and their tendency to show differing degrees of cohesion from issue to issue.[5]

A fourth important explanation for the decentralization of American parties can be found in the financing of political campaigns. Few, if any, campaign resources are more important than money. A large proportion of the political money donated in any year is given directly to the campaign organizations of individual candidates rather than to the party organizations.[6] Candidates with access to campaign money, moreover, are automatically in a strong position *vis-à-vis* the party organization. Not having to rely on the party for campaign funds, the candidate can stake out his independence from it.

Finally, there is a pervasive spirit of localism that dominates American politics and contributes to the deconcentration of political power. There are literally countless ways in which local interests find expression in national politics. Even the presidential nominating convention may become an arena for the settlement of local and state political struggles. Conflicts within state delegations are frequently resolved by the faction that succeeds in identifying and supporting the winning presidential nominee. The cost of backing the "wrong" candidate may be exceedingly high for the losing faction. Very likely some careers will be jeopardized and perhaps cut short; almost certainly members of the losing faction will find both their access to the nominee and their prospects for patronage severely diminished. For a very good reason, national conventions will always have a strong infusion of local politics. The men and women who compose it are, first and foremost, state and local political leaders. They come to the convention not only to select a presidential nominee but also to put new life into their own careers and to advance the interests of their localities.

Congress has always shown a remarkable hospitality to the idea that governmental power should be decentralized. A great deal of the major legislation that has been passed in recent decades, for example, has been designed in such a way as to make state and local gov-

Table 1. Experience of national political leaders in state and local government

Offices Held	Congressional Leaders		Administration Leaders	
	1903	1963	1903	1963
Any state or local office	75%	64%	49%	17%
Elective local office	55	46	22	5
State legislature	47	30	17	3
Appointive state office	12	10	20	7
Governor	16	9	5	4

Source: Samuel P. Huntington, "Congressional Responses to the Twentieth Century," in David B. Truman (ed.), *The Congress and America's Future,* Second Edition, p. 17. Copyright © 1973 by the American Assembly, Columbia University. Reprinted by permission of Prentice-Hall, Inc., Englewood Cliffs, New Jersey, 07632.

ernments participants in the development and implementation of public policies.[7] Locally based political organizations have been strengthened as a result. A basic explanation for Congress's defense of state and local governments lies in the backgrounds of the congressmen themselves. Above all else, congressmen are local products. Unlike most business and political executives, most congressmen reside all their lives in their original hometowns. A substantial majority of them will have been elected to state or local office prior to their election to Congress. (See Table 1, which points up the sharply different career patterns of congressional leaders and administration leaders.) They are steeped in local lore, think in local terms, meet frequently with local representatives, and work for local advantage. Their steady attention to the local dimensions of national policy helps to energize local political organization. . . .

THE INDOMITABLE PARTY?

The party in America is at the center of the political process. Nonetheless, its grip on political power is far from secure. To be sure, the men and women who are recruited for party and public offices, the issues that they

bring before the electorate, the campaigns in which they participate, and the government that they help to organize and direct—all are influenced by party. The basic problem remains, however, that the party is unable to control all the routes to political power. In some jurisdictions, nonpartisan election systems have been developed to try to remove parties from politics, and to a degree they have succeeded. Moreover, so thoroughly are some states and localities dominated by one party that party itself has come to have little relevance for the kinds of men and women recruited for office or for the voters in need of cues for casting their votes. Devices such as the direct primary have also cut into the power of the party organization, serving in particular to discourage national party agencies from attempting to influence nominations, including those for national office, and to open up the nominating process to all kinds of candidates. Perhaps most important, the growing influence of the mass media, public relations experts, and campaign management firms has diminished the role of party organizations in political campaigns.

The wonder of American politics is that the party system functions as well as it does. From the perspective of party leaders, the American Constitution is a vast wasteland, scarcely capable of supporting vigorous parties; federalism, separation of powers, checks and balances, and staggered elections all have proved inimical to the organization of strong parties. The burden of the evidence is that national and state constitutions were drafted by men suspicious of the concentration of power in any hands; their designs have served to fracture or immobilize party power.[8] The party itself is an uneasy coalition of individuals and groups brought together for limited purposes. Within government, power is about as likely to be lodged in nooks and crannies as it is in central party agencies. Conflict within the parties is sometimes as intense as it is between the parties. As for the individual party member, he has a great many rights but virtually no responsibilities for the well-being of the party.

Public disillusionment over the parties places a further strain on their capacities. Many voters believe that the parties have not posed imaginative solutions for such nagging issues as racial injustice, urban decay, and poverty. Similarly, citizens are concerned over the "old" politics that seems to dominate the parties, manifested in a preoccupation with patronage, perquisites, and the welfare of the organization rather than with public policy. The parties also come in for harsh criticism for their apparent willingness to yield to the blandishments of pressure groups and local interests, while too frequently ignoring broad national interests and problems. For many citizens, it is all too clear, the parties appear as starkly conservative institutions, fearful of innovation and unable to shape intelligent responses to contemporary dilemmas. At no time in the last century have the American major parties occupied such troubled ground as they do today.

Despite their present difficulties, it is by no means clear that the major parties are in the process of withering away, to be replaced by government without parties or government by multiple-party coalitions. But stock-taking is

surely in order. Viewed broadly, what seems to be required for party revitalization is the development of a new responsiveness within the parties, one that extends to all the interests that comprise the American polity. The importance of restoring the parties ought to be obvious. It is inconceivable that democracy could exist in the absence of a viable party system.

NOTES

[1] American political parties not only are more decentralized than their counterparts in European nations, they are clearly among the most decentralized parties in the world. For evidence on this point, see Kenneth Janda, "American and European Parties Compared on Organization, Centralization, Coherence, and Involvement," a paper delivered at the Annual Meeting of the American Political Science Association, Chicago, Illinois, August 29-September 2, 1974, especially pp. 23-24.

[2] *Cousins v. Wigoda*, 95 S. Ct. 549 (1975). This case involved the seating of the Illinois delegation to the 1972 Democratic national convention. The Court upheld the right of the Democratic convention to refuse to seat the Illinois delegation which, according to the findings of the credentials committee, had violated national party rules concerning the selection process for delegates and whose make-up inadequately represented youth, women, and minorities.

[3] History dictates the same course. Disturbed by congressional opposition to certain New Deal legislation, President Franklin D. Roosevelt attempted in 1938 to "purge" several southern Democrats by openly endorsing their primary opponents. His action ended in embarrassment for him and disaster for his plan, for the voters' response was to elect the very men he had marked for defeat. The lesson is evident that national party leaders must tread warily on local party grounds.

[4] Exceptions can be noted. During the 89th Congress (1965-1966), the House Democratic caucus, in an unusual exercise of disciplinary powers, took away the seniority rights of two southern Democrats who had publicly endorsed the Republican presidential candidate, Barry Goldwater, in the 1964 election. An even more extraordinary action occurred in 1975 when the House Democratic caucus removed three committee chairmen.

[5] Austin Ranney and Willmoore Kendall, *Democracy and the American Party System* (New York: Harcourt Brace Jovanovich, 1956), p. 497. Another comprehensive analysis of the decentralization of

American parties may be found in David B. Truman's essay on "Federalism and the Party System" in Arthur W. MacMahon (ed.), *Federalism: Mature and Emergent* (New York: Doubleday, 1955), pp. 115-136.

[6] This will continue to be the case under the public financing provisions of the Federal Election Campaign Act of 1974. Public financing applies only to presidential primaries and elections.

[7] See James M. Burns, *The Deadlock of Democracy* (Englewood Cliffs, N.J.: Prentice-Hall, 1963), especially Chapters 1 and 2.

[8] Ibid., especially Chapters 1 and 2.

22
Of Presidents and Parties
David S. Broder

Is American party politics disintegrating to the point where new alternatives must be developed? David S. Broder places American parties in the context of "critical elections" or various presidential contests which resulted in fundamental realignments of American voters in their party allegiances. Such realignments were preceded by considerable dissatisfaction and discontent over basic policy problems and the role of government in solving them. The most recent critical election was in 1932. What accounted for the massive voter shift to Franklin Roosevelt and the Democratic party? Broder's view is that since 1952, the New

Deal coalition has disintegrated. American voters are less attracted to party labels than to the personalities of the candidates. Four factors—television, education, affluence, and participation—have affected this change. The Watergate debacle severely weakened the Republicans without resulting in any major strengthening of the Democrats. In fact, the campaign finance reforms of 1974 hindered both party organizations. What accounts for the voter alienation toward party labels? Do you agree with Broder's pessimistic conclusions regarding the disintegration of party politics? What are the consequences of independent voting?

Four months after Inauguration Day, President Carter invited his party's congressional leadership to the White House for a breakfast-table briefing on the economic policies of the new administration. Charles L. Schultze, chairman of the Council of Economic Advisers, displayed charts showing that, with full cooperation from business, labor, and consumers, it might just be possible to generate enough economic growth to balance the federal budget by 1980, as the President had promised.

Bert Lance, as director of the Office of Management and Budget, followed with a sermon on the stiff discipline that would be required to meet that goal, pointing out that many past Democratic programs would have to be pared in the process. As the climax to the briefing, the President introduced Arthur Burns, chairman of the Federal Reserve Board and living

symbol of a cautious, conservative economic policy, and Burns gave his heartfelt blessing to the whole Carter approach.

That was just a little too much for House Speaker Thomas P. (Tip) O'Neill (D-Mass.) to swallow with his coffee and Danish. "Something has changed around here," O'Neill growled, "and I don't think it's me."

Indeed it had. The Democrats' jubilation over their first presidential victory since 1964 was quickly tempered by the realization that, as *New York Times* columnist Tom Wicker noted, they had nominated and elected the most conservative Democratic President since Grover Cleveland.

Part of their shock, of course, reflected little more than the belated recognition that the American public had grown weary of the liberal federal programs that were the meat and potatoes of the Democratic Party and had nurtured Tip O'Neill in the Irish wards of Cambridge and Boston. The ideas that had sus-

From *The Wilson Quarterly*, Winter 1978. Copyright © 1978 by the Woodrow Wilson International Center for Scholars.

tained most Democrats from the New Deal through the days of the Great Society had lost their allure, if not their relevance. And no new ideas had replaced them.

The new President had grown up in an environment largely untouched by traditional Democratic ideals, even when they possessed vitality. An Annapolis graduate, a south Georgia farmer-businessman, he was as far removed from the Northern urban Democratic coalition of labor, ethnic, and racial blocs as could be imagined. He ran for President as a critic of Big Government-bureaucratic Washington, but he was more of an outsider than even his own rhetoric suggested.

Such a man could have emerged to lead the Democratic Party only after its presidential-selection process had undergone a thoroughgoing transformation. The new procedures allowed Mr. Carter to reap great advantage from the early support of a plurality of Democratic activists in primary elections in such relatively conservative states as Iowa, New Hampshire, and Florida. Traditional Democratic power-brokers—leaders of organized labor, big city mayors, governors, and congressional leaders—were late and, in some cases, reluctant boarders of the Carter bandwagon.

Tax funds, available for the first time in significant amounts for a presidential campaign, provided sustenance for Carter's homebred campaign organization (of the $13.2 million he spent to win the nomination, $3.5 million was in matching federal funds); and the legislated limits on individual financial contributions prevented his chief rivals (Henry Jackson, Birch Bayh, Morris Udall, Jerry Brown, and Frank Church) from fully exploiting their potential advantage in soliciting large-scale individual or interest-group contributions.

The whole meaning and role of national political parties had changed in the quarter century since O'Neill was elected to Congress in 1952. Being a Democrat or a Republican means less today than it did then to almost everyone from the candidate down to the average voter.

The current decline of national political parties got under way just about the time Jimmy Carter left the Navy in 1953 and began the career that was to take him to the White House. After 1955, the symptoms could be found in the sorry record of unimplemented and underfunded government programs, of uncompleted reforms, of political careers ended abruptly in violence or frustration.

There has been general agreement on what a responsible two-party system means and what has caused it to erode over the past generation. As early as 1950, the American Political Science Association had catalogued a lengthy list of reforms to achieve "a more responsible two-party system." "An effective party-system," the Association's report stated, "requires first, that the parties are able to bring forth programs to which they commit themselves, and, second, that the parties possess sufficient internal cohesion to carry out these programs." The test of an effective party, in other words, would be its capacity to give the voters a credible pledge to pursue a plausible agenda and to achieve the consensus and discipline required to act on it, once the party was in office.

THE AMERICAN SUPERSTATE

The last time such a two-party system existed on any kind of a durable basis was the period of Democratic dominance from 1932 to 1952. Franklin D. Roosevelt had his difficulties with Democrats in Congress and suffered political setbacks along the way, but for a full generation, under Roosevelt's New Deal and Truman's Fair Deal, the Democrats mounted major attacks on America's social and economic ills and led the nation through World War II and the Korean crisis. In helping to establish the Atlantic Alliance and the United Nations, they also created the American superstate, with its enduring military and welfare bureaucracies that even today, a generation later, consume 90 percent of the federal budget. Moreover, they did this as Democrats, provoking from the Republican Party a challenge to almost every major policy decision, foreign and domestic. During that long period, despite each party's regional differences and factional splits, American voters were rarely in the dark about what was at stake in national elections.

To political scientists, the New Deal realignment, or Roosevelt Coalition, was the dominant force in the fifth major-party system since the birth of the Republic. Before 1932,

---

Carter's 1976 vote as a percentage of votes cast for top Democratic candidates for statewide office

Alabama 101%	Montana 76%
Alaska 129%	Nebraska 74%
Arizona 65%	Nevada 72%
Arkansas 82%	New Hampshire 102%
California 105%	New Jersey 86%
Colorado 101%	New Mexico 114%
Connecticut 115%	New York 99%
Delaware 125%	North Carolina 85%
Florida 90%	North Dakota 88%
Georgia 105%	Ohio 103%
Hawaii 90%	Oklahoma 78%
Idaho 77%	Oregon 81%
Illinois 141%	Pennsylvania 107%
Indiana 109%	Rhode Island 104%
Iowa 87%	South Carolina 89%
Kansas 137%	South Dakota 201%
Kentucky 131%	Tennessee 109%
Louisiana 153%	Texas 94%
Maine 79%	Utah 65%
Maryland 98%	Vermont 105%
Massachusetts 82%	Virginia 136%
Michigan 93%	Washington 82%
Minnesota 82%	West Virginia 88%
Mississippi 103%	Wisconsin 74%
Missouri 102%	Wyoming 89%

Source: *Guide to 1976 Elections*, Washington, D.C.: Congressional Quarterly, July 1977.

An analysis of voting data from the November 1976 election shows that in 27 of the 50 states President Carter drew fewer votes than the most popular Democratic candidate for statewide office.

---

four other critical elections inaugurated a new party system.

The first was the victory of Thomas Jefferson in 1800, which ended Federalist Party dominance of the young Republic. The second was the election of Andrew Jackson in 1828, a triumph for frontier democracy. The third was the election of Abraham Lincoln in 1860, bringing the new Republican Party to power and precipitating the Civil War. The fourth was the election of Republican William McKinley in 1896, in which industrialism won a victory over the agrarian-populist forces that had captured the Democratic Party with the nomination of William Jennings Bryan. The fifth was the Depression-induced victory of Roosevelt and the New Deal Democrats.

Each of these realignments saw millions of voters shifting allegiance in response to what they perceived as new and vital issues and making the kind of emotional commitment to their new party that could be eroded only over a long period of time.

Because that process of erosion—and realignment—has occurred at fairly regular intervals, many scholars have formulated a cyclical or generational theory of party realignment. According to that theory, America should have had another critical presidential election in 1964 or 1968. Nothing like that happened. Instead, we have seen a series of random movements during the last two decades, in which near landslides for one party or the other (1956, 1964, 1972) alternated with near dead heats (1960, 1968, 1976), all the while granting the Democrats a comfortable congressional majority.

The old pattern began breaking up in 1952. The immediate catalyst was the personality of Dwight D. Eisenhower. As a war hero and a national figure, "above party," Eisenhower played a major role in breaking the habit of party-voting. He, more than any other individual, introduced ticket-splitting into American politics. An analysis of the 1952 election made by the University of Michigan Center for Political Studies found that "three out of five of those Democrats and Independents who voted for Mr. Eisenhower in 1952 were not willing to support the rest of the Republican slate."

THE BROKEN LINK

That lack of support was underlined two years later when the Republicans lost control of Congress despite Eisenhower's vigorous campaign efforts, thus inaugurating a long era of divided government. During 14 of the 22 years between 1954 and 1976, Republicans controlled the executive branch while Democrats reigned on Capitol Hill. No such lengthy period of divided party control can be found in America's previous history.

The 1952 election was notable for another reason. It marked the rise of Lyndon B. Johnson to leadership of the Senate Democrats. Johnson shared Eisenhower's belief that partisanship is the enemy, not the servant of responsible and effective government. For eight critical years the two men managed to divorce party labels from pertinent issues and to practice what Johnson liked to call "consensus" government. It was during this period of Eisenhower-Johnson hegemony that the vital links that joined the public to government through the political party mechanism were broken. Once broken, the links were not repaired. John F. Kennedy, invoking the memory of Franklin Roosevelt, made a start at restoring party government but died before much had been achieved. None of the later Presidents cared much, or tried.

At the same time, other factors were influencing U.S. voting patterns. Four of these are important enough to be identified:

Television.   In the last 20 years, television has established itself as the prime medium of political communication. The most significant point to be made about television, as compared to printed media, is that it is personality dominated. It deals with political figures, not political institutions. It is first and foremost the President's instrument, but it is available to any politician with wit and flair, as George Wallace and Ronald Reagan have demonstrated.

Political parties as such have almost no role in television's portrayal of the political drama. Efforts by the opposition party to gain access to television to respond to presidential statements have been frustrated more often than not by the networks, the Federal Communications Commission, and the courts.

Television cameras focus on the parties only at convention time; then, they move in so massively that they almost overwhelm the convention, making it impossible for professional politicians to conduct the kind of negotiations that formerly characterized convention week. Under the gaze of the television cameras, party conventions have been largely transformed into carefully scripted theatrical productions for the ratification of decisions already made elsewhere. It is no accident that no convention has gone beyond one ballot in the selection of a President during the television era.

Education.   As mass education has grown and spread, the behavior of voters has changed. In my own interviewing, I have found a significant difference between the political perceptions of those with at least a high school education and those who left school before eighth grade.

Educated voters are not content merely to vote the party ticket. They consider themselves capable of making sophisticated judgments on the individual worth of the candidates they have seen on their living-room screens. They tell you proudly, "I don't vote for the party; I vote for the man" (or, if their consciousness has been raised, "for the person"). And they do. The percentage of ticket-splitting voters has risen significantly in the last quarter century.

Affluence. Prosperity has blurred the economic issues that once served to differentiate the two parties. The New Deal was essentially a class realignment, with important racial, religious, and ethnic elements. For the most part, Republicans represented the affluent classes and the Democrats the less well-off—except in the South, where it was many years before better-off whites were willing to ally themselves with the party of Lincoln.

Post-World War II prosperity and the industrialization of the South have taken many

Percentage of ticket splitters

	1952	1964	1968	1972	1976
Pres./Gov.	26.1	18.1	25.9	28.0	24.8
Pres./Sen.	10.8	20.6	28.6	29.0	25.4
Pres./Gov./Sen.	22.0	28.3	37.0	42.9	43.1
All of the above	19.6	22.3	30.5	33.3	31.1

Source: Howard L. Reiter, assistant professor of Political Science, University of Connecticut, based on data from the Survey Research Center, University of Michigan.

The chart shows the growing trend of voters to support the Presidential candidate of one party and the Governor and/or Senate candidate of another. The highly partisan 1976 election slightly reversed the trend.

Americans far from their economic origins and thereby blurred old party allegiances. Overall, the country has become more inflation-conscious and conservative in the past decade—but not more Republican.

Participation. With education and affluence came an ideological demand—not confined to any single sector of the populace but led by the college-educated—for a greater direct voice in decisions that affect people's lives.

The activism of the civil-rights movement (not to mention the peace movement, the environmental movement, the consumer movement, the equal-rights movement, the right-to-life movement, and all the opposition movements they have spawned) has carried over into the political parties, where it is expressed largely as a demand for participation, for "opening up the system." One result has been a great rush of rule-writing, designed to bring the informal processes of political brokering under prescribed and publicized codes, so that everybody, not just the insiders, can understand how the game is played.

Another result has been the sudden proliferation of state primary elections—from 16 in 1952 to 31 today—as a device for increasing public participation in the party's most important decision, the choice of its presidential nominee. Since 1952, the key to nomination has been performance in the primaries, and as a result, the role and influence of party cadre, the professionals, has steadily declined.

Most of these trends were evident at the time I wrote *The Party's Over* in 1971. The tone of that book was gloomy, for in the Washington of that day a policy stalemate between a President and a Congress of opposing parties was frustrating effective action on crises ranging from Vietnam to Detroit and Newark. That stalemate was duplicated in almost half the states, where divided governments were also struggling to cope.

I quoted—but did not sufficiently heed—the words of Stephen K. Bailey, the Syracuse University political scientist, who had written that "as long as we lack strong national parties operating as catalysts in the Congress, the executive branch, and the national government as a whole, and between the national government and state and local governments, power will continue to be dangerously diffused, or, perhaps what is worse, will whipsaw between diffusion and presidential dictatorship."

I commented, "We have been through that

dreadful cycle once...from diffusion of power under Eisenhower to the excessive concentration under Johnson . . . and with Nixon, we may be starting on a second run through that frustrating course." Obviously, I did not anticipate that shortly after *The Party's Over* was published, the Watergate scandals would reveal the covert, illegal steps Richard Nixon had taken, partly to relieve his frustration and gain the power he and his party had failed to win legitimately in the election of 1968.

EBBING PARTY STRENGTH

Unfortunately, there is little sign of a revival of the two-party system. Watergate decimated the Republicans on both national and state levels. When Nixon was forced to resign in August 1974, they lost the only card-carrying, life-long Republican President in two generations. They also lost most of their carefully cultivated reputation as the party of law and order and the party of America's "respectable people." In the 1974 Watergate-year election, they approached their all-time Depression low,

losing 43 House seats, 4 Senate seats, and 5 governorships.

While the Republican party has been badly weakened, the Democrats have barely held their own. In Maine, public disillusionment with both parties was so great in 1974 that James Longley was able to become the first Independent governor in 38 years. Fundamentally, the Democrats have been losing strength as markedly as Republicans. In 1976, both parties were 8 points below their peak strength of the previous decade, measured by voters' self-identification. The Democrats had dropped from 53 to 45 percent; the Republicans, from 30 to 22 percent. It was the Independents who gained strength.

Institutional changes are also weakening the grip of the political parties. It is a remarkable irony that the single most important "reform" legislation stemming from Watergate, the Federal Election Campaign Act of 1974, may severely damage both political parties. Its framers rejected the opportunity to strengthen the parties by making them the conduits for public subsidy of presidential candidates. Instead, it gave money directly to candidates

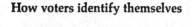

How voters identify themselves

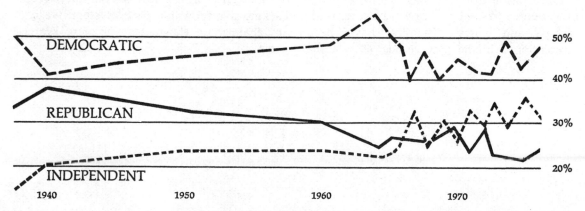

Source: Gallup Opinion Index, March 1973; June 1976.

($67 million in 1976), while allocating only a few million to the parties for convention expenses ($2 million to the Democrats, $1.6 million to the Republicans), thus further widening the breach between presidential candidates and their parties.

At the same time that the share of the parties in financing candidates is being minimized, their role in the choice of nominees is being significantly reduced. The result of changes in the Democratic delegate-selection rules has been a proliferation of primaries. The Republicans, who have dabbled with minor rules reforms of their own, have been carried along in the Democrats' wake to a primary-dominated presidential-selection system. In 1976, more than 70 percent of the delegates to both conventions were chosen in the primaries, not in state caucuses and conventions, where party cadres normally dominate the proceedings and often produce a sharper definition of what the party stands for.

Instead, we have what amounts to a national primary conducted state by state from late February to early June, with television amplifying the (generally inconclusive) results of early tests into giant waves of personal publicity that drown out almost any other consideration of qualifications for the office.

Only inside Congress has there been a bit of a counter-trend. Party caucuses, party leadership, and party discipline have been strengthened in the past decade, as first the Republicans and then the Democrats sought leverage with which to protect their legislative jurisdiction against the inroads of an unchecked President.

Advocates of responsible party government must welcome the reassertion of these party functions in the Congress, but they do so with bittersweet recognition that so long as the President remains largely outside the party system, this development is almost certain to result in greater conflict between the White House and the legislature. To many people, the greatest surprise of the early months of the Carter administration was the spectacle of frequent battles between the White House and the Democratic majorities in Congress. But those who understood that Carter truly was an outsider, the product of a selection process in which the party cadre, including many senior congressmen, had little voice, were not surprised.

Such analysts understand that the party system has now deteriorated to the point where it is possible for a President to face an "opposition" Congress organized and run by members of his own party.

In 1971, in *The Party's Over*, I argued that the result of the decline of our parties was stalemate in government. With the advantage of hindsight, I would now amend that to read: Lacking a responsible party system, we can anticipate more stalemates—or more Watergates.

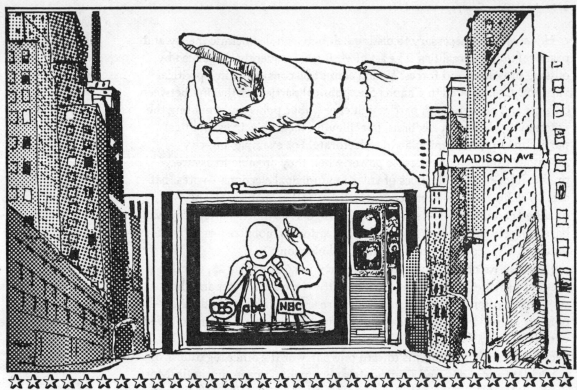

Voting, Campaigns, and Elections 7

Voting is one of the basic means for active citizen participation in a democratic society. Accordingly, democratic theory holds that voting should be a rational choice made by informed citizens. Thomas Jefferson believed that grassroots democracy was ensured when citizens participated equally in governing community affairs. Voting in town meetings was meaningful because all citizens shared power, control, and responsibility over local policies—a model of participation rooted in the ancient Greek city-state. More recently, the Supreme Court decisions in the legislative reapportionment cases established the "one man, one vote" principle, which, coupled with the Voting Rights Act, affirms that all votes should count the same, that no discrimination may be used to prevent voting, and that voting is an individually determined choice made between competing candidates.

However, it is necessary to distinguish between democratic theory and practical political realities. The act of voting is frequently influenced by outside pressures and forces. Voting cannot be considered in a political vacuum. As indicated in Chapter Six, political parties are the link between citizens and government; parties influence public policy by providing the voters with choices in elections. In achieving their objectives, political parties may try to manipulate the electorate. For example, big-city machines exercise considerable power when they are able to assure predictable and reliable blocs of votes in municipal elections—votes that are, by definition, for party-endorsed slates rather than for the best qualified candidates. The strength of Chicago's Mayor Richard Daley was based largely on the ability of his organization to mobilize Democratic voters in city, county, state, and national elections.

How can we characterize the American voter? In Article 23, Gerald Pomper provides two contrasting views: the *dependent* voter and the *responsive* voter. Political science survey research of the 1950s developed a portrait of the voting public as poorly informed and relatively uninvolved with public affairs. Voting was a response to such factors as family background, predispositions toward one party or the other regardless of particular candidates, and a candidate's personality, image, and style. Most voters did not make careful evaluations of substantive policy differences. The voter was basically non-rational and voting choices could be controlled by the media, persuasion, symbolism, and slogans.

In contrast, the responsive voter of the 1960s and 1970s, according to Pomper, reflects increasing participation, the rejection of traditional authority symbols, the national integration of major policy issues, and the growth of ideology or group consciousness by blacks, women, ethnic groups, and students. Consequently, people vote as they do because they are making a selective choice between alternatives presented to them. If the voters do not have a meaningful choice, they will not be able to make a meaningful decision. Voters behave as rationally as they can depending on the clarity of alternatives and available information. This means that the perceptions of parties and public leaders are crucial in determining voter responses. If political leaders appeal to fear, hate, and divisiveness, voters will respond emotionally. In contrast, if public office-seekers present clear choices on serious issues, the voters will have a basis to make a reasoned decision at the polls. This further explains why many people do not vote. If political leaders systematically exclude issues relevant to the voters or make it difficult to vote, it should not be surprising that participation will be low. According to Michael Parenti in Article 24, nonparticipation does not reflect voter apathy but the alienation of excluded groups toward the political process.

In recent years, voter participation has declined among the middle class. The 1976 presidential election had a very low turnout and less than forty percent of the eligible voters participated in the 1978 midterm elections. This was surprising because many potential voters were seriously concerned about inflation and energy shortages. Refusing to vote may have reflected several concerns, including issue complexity, confused solutions offered by candidates or general disbelief that government could do anything about solving the problems.

With the advent of mass communications media, particularly television, traditional campaign techniques have merged with both psychological and advertising methods of *mass persuasion*. Modern advertising attempts to condition large audiences to purchase goods and services. When political candidates buy television time, they are more concerned with creating a favorable image that reinforces voter beliefs than they are in discussing the merits of substantive issues. Campaign strategists therefore seek to reassure the voters that a candidate's views are safe, comforting, and reliable. This means that a candidate's television appeal is to communicate a brief message rather than to stimulate serious thought or discussion.

What should television newscasts and candidate's purchase of TV advertising emphasize in appealing to the voters? Unfortunately, much of TV news and spot advertising is aimed at the lowest common denominator in the electorate. Patterson and McClure point out in Article 25 that such an approach seriously underestimates the basic intelligence of the voters. Many years ago, political scientist V. O. Key argued that the "voice of the people is an echo"—the perceptions of the TV networks and the candidates are crucial in determining voter responses.

Presidential candidates spend large sums for TV advertising, although the impact and outcome are not always predictable. In 1976, Jimmy Carter became the first challenger since 1932 to defeat an incumbent president. Malcolm MacDougall (Article 26) indicates why President Ford's media efforts could not overcome Carter's early lead in the campaign. Another key factor was Carter's performance during the televised debates with Ford. Unlike 1960 when John F. Kennedy was perceived as the clear "winner" in the first TV debate with Richard Nixon, Carter did not achieve that kind of advantage. He certainly was not considered as the loser, however. The early momentum of Carter's efforts proved to be just enough in winning a very close victory over Ford.

23

The Obscure American Voter

Gerald M. Pomper

Voting is one of the basic instruments for citizen participation in government. Elections determine who controls executive and legislative offices and the shaping of public policy. The nature of voting behavior is important to understanding how American government will respond to societal problems. Are voters easily manipulated or do they exercise independent choices? This is a key problem considering the vast number of officials that voters elect. Gerald Pomper offers two contrasting views of voter behavior: The dependent voter responds to his or her socioeconomic class and to party labels with relative lack of concern for issues. The responsive voter is issue-oriented, carefully considering his or her vote in relation to the major problems of the times. Why was dependent voting so characteristic of the 1950's and responsive voting more a feature of the 1960's and 1970's? What are the problems with political leadership and how does this relate to decline of party influence discussed in Chapter 6? How do Pomper's views compare and contrast with Parenti's "nonparticipation" arguments in article 24?

Who is the American voter?

Although founded on the premise that legitimate government requires "the consent of the governed," the United States has long puzzled over its own electorate. The power of the voters has been proclaimed and restrained, as the wisdom of their choices has been praised and condemned. The self-portrait of the American voter is of both a hero and a villain.

The conflict in American attitudes has been evident throughout the nation's existence. Alexander Hamilton contemptuously concluded, "your people, sir, are a great beast," but still argued for direct popular election of the Congress.[1] George Mason, on the other hand, was one of the most democratic members of the Constitutional Convention of 1787, but found popular election of the president as irrational as "to refer a trial of colors to a blind man."[2] Even as James Madison insisted that "a de-

pendence on the people is the primary safeguard of good government," he supported institutional barriers against "the superior force of an interested and overbearing majority."[3] As Hamilton wryly observed, the persons "most tenacious of republicanism were as loud as any in declaring against the vices of democracy."[4]

Our uncertain stance toward the voters has been evidenced in ambiguous institutions. Popular sovereignty is recognized in electoral choice of a half-million officials from precinct committeemen to president. The wisdom of the voters is assumed in asking them to decide on state constitutional amendments and legislation by referenda and to determine the details of school budgets in local votes. Yet popular decisions are severely limited by restrictions on terms of office, judicial review, fixed tenure of officials, and the reservation of important functions to nonelected commissions and public authorities. The world's first mass democracy also imposes the most elaborate legal restrictions on the right to vote. The world's most powerful person, the president, is still formally elected by an unknown Electoral College of 538 members. . .

The Dependent Voter. Two portraits of the American voter have been drawn. There are some similarities in these two portraits, but their foci are substantially different. The first is that of the dependent voter, based on a series of surveys of presidential elections beginning in 1940. The focus of this portrait is on the long-term factors affecting the electorate and the voters' consequently limited attention to contemporary issues and individuals. Although the findings are sometimes distorted when retold, the central thrust of these studies is denigrating to the electorate. It is described as choosing candidates because of influences established considerably before a given campaign, such as social characteristics, or traditional party loyalty. Dependent voters pay little attention to political events generally, and even less to specific issues of public policy.

The dependent voter does not rely primarily on his own resources and opinions in making political choices. Rather, he relies on the cues of his social groups—his economic class or race or accustomed party. Following these cues often may serve an individual's objective interests, but the association is highly contingent. The dependent voter does not make an autonomous choice on the basis of the issues and candidates. He relies instead on indirect and uncertain relationships.

"It is abundantly clear," as one author summarized this description, "that the voter of today does lack both high political interest and an urge to participate in the political discourse. The voting studies indicate that political discourse is limited, sparse and desultory. Indeed, most voters make up their minds, and act ultimately on that decision, even before the campaigns begin. Family background, cultural milieu, all of the inchoate pressure of 'socioeconomic status' seem subtly to work on the voter in a process which is neither rational nor accompanied by high interest."[5]

Substantial research supports these conclusions. In particular, the voting studies provide data on two related subjects: the political capacity of individual voters and the causal influences on balloting. Dependent voters are deficient on both grounds. Few give serious consideration to public matters. Even the majority who do vote are not greatly concerned over the outcome. Beyond voting, most refrain from further participation in organized political life, such as financial contributions, attending political rallies, or membership in community organizations.[6]

The capacity of dependent voters for informed judgment is limited. On the two most vital issues of the 1948 campaign, for example, only a sixth of the voters could report accurately the position of both Harry Truman and Thomas Dewey.[7] On a longer series of issues in 1956, no more than a third was able to offer an informed opinion on any particular policy relevant to the election choice.[8] A broader perspective on politics is still rarer. In 1956, only 2.5 percent of the population were "ideologues," who "clearly perceived a fundamental liberal-conservative continuum on which various of the political objects might be located." If less elaborate conceptual schemes of politics are included, this group still constituted only an eighth of the population.[9] Similarly, when asked to explain such terms as "liberal" and "conservative," only 15 percent could provide an extended explanation.[10]

In place of individual judgment, group influences determine the dependent voter's choice. "A person thinks, politically, as he is, socially,"[11] for "his vote is formed in the midst of a group decision—if, indeed, it may be called a decision at all."[12] Therefore, "the Catholic vote or the hereditary vote is explainable less as principle than as a traditional social allegiance. The ordinary voter, bewildered by the complexity of modern political problems, unable to determine clearly what the consequences are of alternative lines of action, remote from the arena, and incapable of bringing information to bear on principle, votes the way trusted people around him are voting."[13]

Of the various influencing groups, the most important for this voter is his party. Affinity to the Republicans and Democrats is not unique, but provides a social reference point, much like membership in a union or religious community. Party "is a type of social group, a group that happens to be political. Attachment to this group is therefore psychological in character, and is not essentially a political phenomenon."[14] The theme of electoral studies, thus, has been "primarily the role of enduring partisan commitments in shaping attitudes toward politics."[15] The voter's evaluations of candidates and issues are distorted by his partisanship. His choices are "guided by essentially nonrational political partisanship that is culturally transmitted from generation to generation in the course of normal socialization processes—the same as is 'character,' 'breeding,' or any other of the abstruse terms used to describe a cultural heritage."[16]

While partisanship strongly affects voting choices, this connection is not based on policy preferences. Party loyalty has not been founded on a general liberal or conservative posture, nor on opinions about international issues, and has been related to only five of twenty-four specific policy questions. Both Democrats and Republicans have favored such proposals as federal aid to education, while large proportions in both parties have been unenthusiastic about suggestions such as public ownership of natural resources.[17]

Unable to focus upon issues, dependent voters cannot substantially affect public policy. Only a small proportion of the electorate meets democratic ideals: "Once below the higher deciles of the population, there are major barriers to understanding that disrupt the processing of even that information about

public policy to which the person attends." As a result, the citizenry "is almost completely unable to judge the rationality of government actions; knowing little of particular policies and what has led to them, the mass electorate is not able to appraise either its goals or the appropriateness of the means chosen to serve these goals."[18] Policy decisions are necessarily left to unmandated government officials, for "individual voting decisions have no direct consequences for public policy; and conversely, the actions of government from election to election have no discernible resonance in the minds of voters."[19]

The portrait of the dependent voter has been widely accepted as a faithful likeness, but varying ideological judgments have followed. The conservative conclusion has been to employ the findings to develop a new normative theory of democracy, aptly termed the "theory of democratic elitism."[20] The electorate, pictured as unresponsive and unknowing, is potentially dangerous according to this theory.[21] The inability of the undemocratic mass to affect policy is therefore seen as desirable, since decisions will be left to those more informed and more supportive of American institutions. Furthermore, voter apathy, ignorance, and lack of principle are actually beneficial, for such attitudes promote stability and moderation.[22] The prevalent absence of commitment softens the clashes of the few intense partisans and ideologists. Individual vices become public virtues, for "the very low affect of most voters, their lack of ideological commitment, and the low faith in the efficacy of politics makes political concord relatively easy to achieve."[23]

The same portrait, however, has been employed for very different purposes. Radical writers have seen the voting studies as demonstrating the disappearance of democracy in America. In their view the public citizen has been reduced to the mass man: "He cannot detach himself in order to observe, much less to evaluate, what he is experiencing, much less what he is not experiencing. Rather than that internal discussion we call reflection, he is accompanied through his life-experience with a sort of unconscious, echoing monologue. He has no projects of his own: he fulfills the routines that exist."[24] Under these conditions, the choices of voters are easily manipulated. "The prevailing level of opinion has become a level of falsehood," where officials are "elected under conditions of effective and freely accepted indoctrination."[25]

These conclusions, whether conservative or radical, are alike in their basic contempt of the electorate. If voters are essentially nonrational, their choices can be deliberately controlled. Issue appeals can be abandoned, while the uninformed, conceptually limited, and indoctrinated electorate is approached through attention-getting but irrelevant campaigns. A winning smile or religious enmity or an empty slogan wll promote political careers better than a concern with relevant problems. An academic portrait of the dependent voter is the unintended intellectual foundation of the merchandized candidate.[26]

The Responsive Voter. National events have spurred revisionary research on electoral behavior. In recent years, political involvement has clearly increased, although the locus of participation has been not only in polling places but still more in marches, gathering of petitions, and demonstrations. Accepted political truths are called into question when the Republicans nominate a pure ideological conservative for president and the Democrats choose a pure ideological liberal, when the South becomes heavily Republican and Congress consistently Democratic, and when benevolent presidential power turns toward autocracy. New issues of race, war, and life-style have reached and divided the citizenry. The substance of politics is no longer Tocqueville's "lesser controversies," but the ultimate questions of who should live and who should die.

In this context, an alternative portrait of the electorate has been drawn, that of the responsive voter. The character of this voter, and the influences upon his choices, are not permanent, but change with the circumstances of the times and with political events. Issues are often important to the responsive voter. In the proper environment, public questions and the candidates' issue positions become critical to the electoral decision. Variety in electoral behavior is most evident, not determinism.

The variation in the stimuli provided by political leadership, parties, and candidates is particularly important in this view of the voter, for the popular response will be strongly conditioned by these stimuli. "The voice of the people is but an echo," wrote V. O. Key. "Even the most discriminating popular judgment can reflect only ambiguity, uncertainty or even foolishness if those are the qualities of the input into the echo chamber. If the people can choose only from among rascals, they are certain to choose a rascal."[27] When issues are raised effectively, however, the popular reaction changes. "In the moment of truth in the polling booth, how the parties and candidates look on the issues seems the most relevant cue for much of the American electorate if conditions permit issues to be used."[28] This argument is the basic undercoating of the responsive-voter portrait.

Responsive voters are affected by their social characteristics such as race and economic position. However, these characteristics are essentially permanent in nature. If they alone affected ballot choices, every election would have the same result, and there would be neither short-term nor long-term shifts in the vote. In fact, other influences also are important, and elections cannot be understood by emphasizing single features. Rather than determinism, analysis reveals that "social characteristics move into and out of the zone of political relevance, that they 'explain' the actions of some people and not those of others, and that insofar as social characteristics determine political preference they encounter considerable friction."[29]

There is a further problem in the deterministic approach, for it does not explain the particular partisan direction of a social group. While businessmen or blacks each have distinct group interests, there is no inherent, nonpolitical reason why these interests always must be expressed as black support of the Democrats or business backing for the Republicans. Historically, in fact, each group has changed its partisanship. Sociological influence "indeed explains a certain uniformity of choice but not the political direction of the choice. An explanation will always have to be sought in outside factors, and it is probable that, in the last resort, these factors will be the activities of the parties and the government in the present and past."[30]

While the responsive voter evidences party loyalty, this attachment does not determine his vote. In the aggregate, in fact, the combination of steadfast independence and temporary defections from party loyalty means that "electoral dynamism of some sort seems almost as normal as electoral stability."[31] On the individual level, partisanship does not necessarily mean loyalty devoid of issue content, but may indeed be a rational course for the voter. To vote along party lines can be an efficient means for the individual to reduce the personal costs of participation, while still expressing his general judgment on the government and opposition.[32] Adhering to a party can also be an effective expression of the voter's particular interests.[33] "There is a rational component to party identifications rooted in group norms,"[34] for the interests of a group may be best expressed by support of a particular party. Blacks' support of the Democrats, or businessmen's support of the Republicans may not be thoughtless conformity to a social group, but an expression of a policy reference. Moreover, over time, there is an increasing parallelism between the electorate's issue positions and its partisan choices.[35]

The fact of group or party loyalty therefore can be viewed in two different ways. In the portrait of the dependent voter these facts are interpreted as demonstrating the inattention and incapacity of the electorate. In the portrait of the responsive voter, the same facts may be interpreted as consistent with the issue and candidate preferences of the voters. The accuracy of the second interpretation will be tested by the consistency between these preferences and actual ballot choices. A businessman voting Republican simply to follow his social group is dependent on that group for political guidance, while a businessman voting Republican to promote his policy objectives is responsive to contemporary issues.

Contrary to the deterministic portrait, the responsive voter evidences considerable awareness of ideology and issues. However, voting choice may be reasonable but inarticulate, for "the reasoning that lies behind the choice is often made in private language which the chooser never learns to translate into words intelligible to others because there is ordinarily no need for him to do so."[36] Direct questions may underestimate voter awareness. When other techniques are employed, popular attitudes become more comprehensible.[37] For example, lengthy interviews, even among persons of limited education and articulateness, evoke an underlying ideological viewpoint.[38] Another method is to rely on multiple questions, rather than a single indicator, as an index of consciousness. Through these broader techniques, over a fifth of the electorate was found to be ideologically aware in 1956, using concepts such as liberalism and conservatism explicitly, or by implication in references to "the individual and the state, the role and power of government, welfare, free enterprise, and posture toward change."[39] These proportions increase substantially in later elections.

The public judgments of the responsive voter can have a substantial impact on his vote, depending on the salience of issues and the campaign strategies of a particular election. Many persons change their partisan choice from one election to the next, and these changes are closely related to their positions on the issues and their assessment of the abilities of the candidates. The resulting portrait "is not one of an electorate strait-jacketed by social determinants or moved by subconscious urges triggered by devilishly skillful propagandists. It is rather one of an electorate moved by concern about central and relevant questions of public policy, of governmental performance, and of executive personality."[40]

But the electorate can choose only from the options presented to it, and these alternatives are not always distinct on any single issue, and are never distinct on all dimensions of judgment. Even when the choices are clear, the individual voter is unlikely to agree fully with one candidate on all questions. In a contest between a rabid segregationist and an advocate of compulsory statewide busing, for whom does the gradual integrationist vote? He is likely to ignore the issue or to select the candidate closer to his own intermediate position, even though dissatisfied partially with both. Fuller explanations of elections must consider not only the voters, but also the alternative candidates and parties, and the voters' closeness or proximity to them on various attitudes. "It is not theoretically sound, nor even particularly logical, to attempt to explain a voter's behavior solely on the basis of his own positions on issues, disregarding his perception of the locations of the candidates and/or parties on those same dimensions."[41] The behavior of the voters varies with the character of the available choices.

Electoral sensitivity to issues has been particularly evident in recent presidential contests. A concern for specific issues is evident in 1964 and is as closely correlated to the vote as

party identification itself.[42] Evaluations of policy on Vietnam and civil rights, and of the performance of the Johnson administration were the vital influences in the 1968 contest;[43] while "overall relative proximity to the candidates and parties on the issues is the best predictor of the vote,"[44] surpassing party identification in its effect. Again in 1972, "ideology and issue voting in that election provide a means for better explaining the unique elements of the contest than do social characteristics, the candidates, the events of the campaign, political alienation, cultural orientations or partisan identification."[45]

The portrait of the responsive voter that appears in these recent elections has been drawn by different methodological instruments than were used to draw the dependent voter. The different results may have been obtained, then, from variations in technique. Yet it seems more likely that the differences reflect variation in behavior in different periods. Time itself must be considered as a crucial contextual variable. Rather than being an unchanging behavior, voting varies with circumstances, for "elections differ enormously in their nature, their meaning and their consequences."[46]

Any conclusions drawn from a given election may therefore reflect, not permanent voter characteristics, but rather that contest's particular influences—composition of the parties, specific issues or their absence, and the given candidates. The basic findings of electoral stability in the pioneering voting studies are not necessarily enduring truths, but may be a product of "investigator's misfortune" in analyzing campaigns in which the tides of change were weak.[47] The particular conclusion of low ideological awareness among the voters during the Eisenhower period may have resulted from the generally low level of ideological stimulation during this period.

The different circumstances of the 1960s and 1970s parallel change in the electorate. In explaining the greater impact of policy issues in the latter period, the simple fact that research is conducted in a different environment is more important than changed techniques. Whatever the measure employed, ideology was more evident after 1960 than in earlier years.[48] Even if they deliberately replicated previous research, analysts would find an immense increase in the internal consistency of the views of the American public, which can only be explained by its reactions to the times.[49]

There is no single answer, then, to the question, "who is the American voter?" The question must be further specified by "when" and "where." . . . Certainly American voters are not persistently interested and active, and surely the Jeffersonian dream of independent yeomen discussing politics learnedly is unachievable. Coherent and well-argued political philosophies are no more to be expected at shopping centers than in college classrooms. Yet, if voters are unlikely to be philosopher-kings, neither must they be regarded as insignificant helots. Americans are concerned about their futures and their country's future. Recent research argues that they can understand issues and can express their concerns. Although those concerns may be expressed in the streets, they can also be expressed at the polling place. Not fixed in their allegiances by party tradition or group memberships, the electorate can respond differently when the times and the alternatives favor change. For the future, the behavior of the voters will depend on what the future brings into their view. . .

NOTES

[1] Max Ferrand, ed., *The Records of the Federal Convention of 1787* (New Haven: Yale University Press, 1911), I, 364.

[2] *Ibid.*, II, 31.

[3] James Madison, *The Federalist*, Nos. 51, 10.

[4] Farrand, I, 288.

[5] Eugene Burdick, "Political Theory and the Voting Studies," in Burdick and Arthur Brodbeck, *Ameri-can Voting Behavior* (New York: The Free Press, 1959), p. 139 f.

[6] Angus Campbell, Philip Converse, Warren Miller, and Donald Stokes, *The American Voter* (New York: Wiley, 1960), p. 91, and Sidney Verba and Norman Nie, *Participation in America* (New York: Harper and Row, 1972), Chap. 4.

[7] Bernard Berelson, Paul Lazarsfeld, and William McPhee, *Voting* (Chicago: Chicago University Press, 1954), p. 227.

[8] *The American Voter*, p. 182, and see Chap. 8 below.

[9] *Ibid.*, pp. 227–234.

[10] Philip Converse, "The Nature of Belief Systems in Mass Publics," in David Apter, ed., *Ideology and Discontent* (New York: The Free Press, 1964), pp. 219–223.

[11] Paul Lazarsfeld, Bernard Berelson, and Helen Gaudet, *The People's Choice*, 2nd ed. (New York: Columbia University Press, 1948), p. 27.

[12] *Voting*, p. 321.

[13] *Ibid.*, p. 309.

[14] Peter B. Natchez, "Images of Voting: The Social Psychologists," *Public Policy*, XVIII (Summer, 1970), 564. While Natchez attacks this view, it is supported by Lee Benson, *The Concept of Jacksonian Democracy* (Princeton: Princeton University Press, 1961), p. 281.

[15] *The American Voter*, p. 135.

[16] David Wallace, *First Tuesday* (Garden City: Doubleday, 1964), p. 272.

[17] See Herbert McClosky, "Conservatism and Personality," *American Political Science Review*, LII (March, 1958), 45; V. O. Key, *Public Opinion and American Democracy* (New York: Knopf, 1961), Chaps. 2, 3; McClosky, "Issue Conflict and Consensus among Party Leaders and Followers," *American Political Science Review*, LIV (June, 1960), 406–427.

[18] *The American Voter*, pp. 253, 543.

[19] Natchez, p. 577; cf. *The American Voter*, pp. 543–548.

[20] See Peter Bachrach, *The Theory of Democratic Elitism* (Boston: Little Brown, 1967), and Jack Walker, "A Critique of the Elitist Theory of Democracy," *American Political Science Review*, LX (June, 1966), 285–295.

[21] Supportive data have been drawn from Samuel Stouffer, *Communism, Conformity and Civil Liberties* (Garden City: Doubleday, 1955), and Herbert McClosky, "Consensus and Ideology in American Politics," *American Political Science Review*, LVIII (June, 1964), 361–382.

[22] Talcott Parsons, " 'Voting' and the Equilibrium of the American Political System," in Burdick and Brodbeck (above, n.5), Chap. 4.

[23] Burdick, "Political Theory and the Voting Studies," p. 145.

[24] C. Wright Mills, *The Power Elite* (New York: Oxford University Press, 1956), p. 322.

[25] Herbert Marcuse, *One-Dimensional Man* (Boston: Beacon Press, 1964), pp. 117, 40.

[26] The connection can be seen in Murray Levin, *The Compleat Politician* (Indianapolis: Bobbs-Merrill, 1962), and in Joe McGinniss, *The Selling of the President* (New York: Trident Press, 1968).

[27] V. O. Key, Jr., with the assistance of Milton C. Cummings, Jr., *The Responsible Electorate* (Cambridge: Harvard University Press, 1966), p. 2 f.

[28] David Kovenock, Philip Beardsley, and James Protho, "Status, Party, Ideology, Issues, and Candidate Choice: A Preliminary Theory—Relevant Analysis of the 1968 American Presidential Election," a paper prepared for the Congress of the International Political Science Association (Munich, 1970), p. 24.

[29] V. O. Key and Frank Munger, "Social Determinism and Electoral Decision: The Case of Indiana," in Burdick and Brodbeck (above, n. 5), p. 297f.; cf. Morris Janowitz and Warren Miller, "The Index of Political Predisposition in the 1948 Election," *Journal of Politics*, XIV (November, 1952), 710–727.

[30] H. Daudt, *Floating Voters and the Floating Vote* (Leiden: Stenfert Kroese, 1961), p. 94.

[31] Richard M. Merelman, "Electoral Instability and the American Party System," *Journal of Politics*, XXXII (February, 1970), 116.

[32] Anthony Downs, *An Economic Theory of Democracy* (New York: Harper, 1957), Chaps. 12 and 13.

[33] Arthur Goldberg, "Social Determinism and Rationality as Bases of Party Identification," *American Political Science Review*, LXIII (March, 1969), 5–25.

[34] *Ibid.*, p. 21.

[35] Everett Ladd, Jr., and Charles Hadley, *Political Parties and Political Issues: Patterns in Differentiation Since the New Deal* (Beverly Hills: Sage Professional Papers in American Politics, 1973), Part III. See also Chap. 8 below.

[36] John Plamenatz, "Electoral Studies and Democratic Theory: A British View," *Political Studies*, VI (February, 1958), 9.

[37] See Robert Axelrod, "The Structure of Public Opinion on Policy Issues," *Public Opinion Quarterly*, XXXI (Spring, 1967), 51–60, and Norman Luttbeg, "The Structure of Beliefs Among Leaders and the Public," *Public Opinion Quarterly*, XXXII (Fall, 1968), 398–409.

[38] Robert Lane, *Political Ideology* (New York: The Free Press of Glencoe, 1962), and "The Fear of Equality," *American Political Science Review*, LIII (March, 1959), 35–51.

[39] J. O. Field and R. E. Anderson, "Ideology in the Public's Conceptualization of the 1964 Election," *Public Opinion Quarterly*, XXXIII (Fall, 1969), 386.

[40] *The Responsible Electorate*, p. 7 f.

[41] Kovenock, p. 9 f; cf. Gerald Finch, "Policy and Candidate Choice in the 1968 American Presidential Election," Ph.D. dissertation (University of Minnesota, 1973).

[42] David RePass, "Issue Salience and Party Choice," *American Political Science Review*, LXV (June, 1971), 389–400.

[43] Richard Boyd, "Popular Control of Public Policy: A Normal Vote Analysis of the 1968 Election," *American Political Science Review*, LXVI (June, 1972), 429–449; Finch, pp. 70–79.

[44] Kovenock, p. 21.

[45] Arthur Miller, Warren Miller, Alden Raine, and Thad Brown, "A Majority Party in Disarray: Policy Polarization in the 1972 Election," a paper presented to the annual meetings of the American Political Science Association (1973), p. 5, and forthcoming, in part, in the *American Political Science Review* (1975).

[46] V. O. Key, "A Theory of Critical Elections," as cited in this context by John K. Wildgen, "The Detection of Critical Elections in the Absence of Two-Party Competition," *Journal of Politics*, XXXVI (May, 1974), 467.

[47] Donald Stokes, "Some Dynamic Elements of Contests for the Presidency," *American Political Science Review*, LX (March, 1966), 19.

[48] John Pierce, "Party Identification and the Changing Role of Ideology in American Politics," *Midwest Journal of Political Science*, XIV (February, 1970), 25–42.

[49] Norman Nie, with Kristi Andersen, "Mass Belief Systems Revisited: Political Change and Attitude Structure," *Journal of Politics*, XXXVI (August, 1974), 547–554. Also see Chap. 8 below.

24

The Politics of Discouragement: Nonvoters and Voters

Michael Parenti

Michael Parenti challenges the notion that non-voting reflects either "apathy" or "the politics of happiness." Instead, he argues that American politics frequently excludes the very groups— blacks, minorities, the poor, youth—that usually have the lowest voting participation. Parenti claims that elite and middle-class values dominate the electoral system, thereby making it difficult for the lower-class to participate. Consider, for example, voter registration and residency requirements or absentee voting for students attending college away from home. Nonvoters are not apa-thetic but alienated. Nonvoting may be more rational than voting. Do you agree? How do Parenti's arguments compare with Pomper's view (Article 23) that recent years have witnessed great increases in electoral participation and more concern for issues in voting behavior? For example, what have been the effects of the 1965 Voting Rights Act and the 26th Amendment (see the Constitution in the Appendix)? And, if alienation results in nonparticipation, how are the limitations of exclusionary politics overcome?

Much has been written about the deficiencies of ordinary voters, their prejudices, lack of information and low civic involvement. More should be said about the deficiencies of the electoral-representative system that serves them. It has long been presumed that since the present political system represents the best of all worlds, those who show an unwillingness to vote must be manifesting some failing in themselves. Seldom is nonparticipation treated as a justifiable reaction to a politics that has become somewhat meaningless in its electoral content and disappointing in its policy results.

In the United States during the nineteenth century, the small-town democratic system "was quite adequate, both in partisan organization and dissemination of political information, to the task of mobilizing voters," according to Walter Dean Burnham.[1] But by the turn of the century most of the political means for making important decisions had been captured by powerful industrial elites. Business interests perfected the arts of pressure politics, wielding a heavy influence over state legislatures, party organizations, governors and Congressmen. At the same time, the judiciary extended its property-serving controls over the national and state legislatures, imposing limitations on taxation powers and on regulatory efforts in the fields of commerce, industry and labor. "Confronted with a narrowed scope of effective democratic options an increasingly large proportion of the eligible adult population either left, failed to enter or—as was the case with the Southern Negro . . . was systematically excluded from the American voting universe."[2] Much of the blame for the diminishing popular participation, Burnham concludes, must rest with "the political system itself."

NONVOTING AS A RATIONAL RESPONSE

The percentage of nonvoters has climbed to impressive levels, running as high as 55 to

[1] Walter Dean Burnham, "The Changing Shape of the American Political Universe," *American Political Science Review*, 59, March 1965, p. 22.

[2] *Ibid.*, p. 26.

60 percent in congressional contests and 40 to 45 percent in recent presidential elections. In many local elections, voter participation is so low as to make it difficult to speak of "popular" representation in any real sense. Observing that in a municipality of 13,000 residents an average of 810 voters elected the city council, Prewitt comments:

Such figures sharply question the validity of thinking that "mass electorates" hold elected officials accountable. For these councilmen, even if serving in relatively sizable cities, there are no "mass electorates"; rather there are the councilman's business associates, his friends at church, his acquaintances in the Rotary Club, and so forth which provide him the electoral support he needs to gain office.[3]

The political significance of low participation becomes apparent when we consider that nonvoters are disproportionately concentrated among the rural poor, the urban slum dwellers, the welfare recipients, the underemployed, the young, the elderly, the low-income and non-union workers and the racial minorities. The entire voting process is dominated by middle-class styles and conditions which tend to discourage lower-class participation.[4] Among the reasons poor whites in one city gave for not voting were the humiliating treatment they had been subjected to by poll attendants in previous elections, the intimidating nature of voting machines, the belief that they were not entitled to vote because they had failed to pay their poll tax (a misapprehension encouraged by tax collectors and town clerks), the feeling that they lacked whatever measure of education, specialized information and ability gives one the right to participate in the electoral process, and the conviction that elections are a farce and all politicians are ultimately out to "line their own pockets."[5] Residency requirements and the registration of voters at obscure locations during the political off-season discriminate against the less informed and less established community elements, specifically the poor, the unemployed and transient laborers.[6]

Working long hours for low pay, deprived of the kind of services and material security that the well-to-do take for granted, made to feel personally incapable of acting effectively and living in fear of officialdom, those of lower-class background frequently are reluctant to vote or make political commitments of any kind. The entire social milieu of the poor militates against participation. As Kimball describes it:

Tenements, rooming houses, and housing projects —the dormitories of the ghetto electorate—provide . . . a shifting, changing human environment instead of the social reinforcements that encourage political involvement in more stable neighborhoods. And the immediate struggle for subsistence drains the reservoirs of emotional energy available for the distant and complex realms of politics. . . . Elections come and go, and the life of poverty goes on pretty much as before, neither dramatically better nor dramatically worse. The posturing of candidates and the promises of parties are simply irrelevant to the daily grind of marginal existence.[7]

Nor is it unreasonable that lower-strata groups are skeptical that any one candidate can change things. Their suspicions might be summarized as follows: (1) the reform-minded candidate is still a politician and therefore is as deceptive as any other; (2) even if he is sincere, the reformer is eventually "bought

[3] Kenneth Prewitt, "Political Ambitions, Volunteerism, and Electoral Accountability," *American Political Science Review*, 64, March 1970, p. 9.

[4] Penn Kimball, *The Disconnected* (New York: Columbia University Press, 1972); Giuseppe Di Palma, *Apathy and Participation: Mass Politics in Western Societies* (New York: Free Press, 1970).

[5] Opinions reported by Democratic campaign workers in Burlington, Vt., in 1972. I am indebted to Cheryl Smalley for gathering the information.

[6] See Charles E. Merriam and Harold F. Gosnell, *Non-voting, Causes and Methods of Control* (Chicago: University of Chicago Press, 1924), pp. 78 ff.; and Kimball, *The Disconnected*, p. 15.

[7] Kimball, *The Disconnected*, p. 17.

off" by the powers that be; (3) even if he is not bought off, the reformer can do little against those who run things. The conviction that politics cannot deliver anything significant leaves many citizens unresponsive, even if not unsympathetic, toward those who promise meaningful changes through the ballot box.[8]

It has been argued that if nonvoters tend to be among the less informed, less educated and more apathetic, then it is just as well they do not exercise their franchise. Since they are not all that capable of making rational choices and are likely to be swayed by prejudice and demagogy, their activation would constitute a potential threat to our democratic system.[9] Behind this reasoning lurks the dubious presumption that the better-educated, upper-income people who vote are more rational, less compelled by narrowly defined self-interests, and less bound by racial, political and class prejudices, an impression which itself is one of those comfortable prejudices that upper- and middle-class people (including social scientists) have of themselves. As Kimball reminds us: "The level of information of the most informed voters is not very high by objective standards. The influence of ethnic background, family upbringing, and party inheritance is enormous in comparison to the flow of political debate. The choices in a given situation are rarely clear-cut, and the decision to vote for particular candidates can be highly irrational, *even at the highest levels of education and experience*."[10]

Some writers argue that the low voter turn-out in the United States is symptomatic of a "politics of happiness": people do not bother to participate because they are fairly content with the way things are going.[11] But the 40 to 50 million adult Americans outside the voting universe are not among the more contented but among the less affluent and more alienated, displaying an unusual concentration of socially deprived characteristics.[12] The "politics of happiness" may be nothing more than a cover for the politics of discouragement or what Lane describes as the "alienation syndrome": "I am the object not the subject of political life. . . . The government is not run in my interest; they do not care about me; in this sense it is not my government. . . ."[13] The nonparticipation of many people often represents a feeling of powerlessness, a conviction that it is useless to vote, petition or demonstrate, useless to invest precious time, energy and hope and risk insult, eviction, arrest, loss of job and police assault, useless to do anything because nothing changes and one is left only with an aggravated sense of affliction and impotence. For many ordinary citizens, nonparticipation is not the result of brutish contentment, apathy or lack of civic virtue but an understandable negative response to the political realities they experience.[14]

---

[8] Michael Parenti, "Power and Pluralism: A View from the Bottom," *Journal of Politics*, August 1970, p. 515; and Kimball, *The Disconnected*, pp. 61–62.

[9] A typical example of this kind of thinking is found in Seymour M. Lipset, *Political Man* (Garden City, N.Y.: Doubleday, 1960), pp. 215–219.

[10] Kimball, *The Disconnected*, p. 63. Italics added. Occasionally there is an admission by the well-to-do that voting should be limited not to protect democracy but to protect themselves. A letter to the *New York Times* (December 6, 1971) offered these revealing words: "If

. . . everybody voted, I'm afraid we'd be in for a gigantic upheaval of American society—and we comfortable readers of the Times would certainly stand to lose much at the hands of the poor, faceless, previously quiet throngs. Wouldn't it be best to let sleeping dog lie?"

[11] Heinz Eulau, "The Politics of Happiness," *Antioch Review*, 16, 1956, pp. 259–264; Lipset, *Political Man*, pp. 179–219.

[12] Burnham, "The Changing Shape of the American Political Universe," p. 27; and Kimball, *The Disconnected*.

[13] Robert Lane, *Political Ideology* (New York: Free Press, 1962), p. 162.

[14] A similar conclusion can be drawn from Studs Terkel, *Division Street: America* (New York: Pantheon,

With that in mind, we might question those public-opinion surveys which report that underprivileged persons are more apathetic and less informed than better-educated, upper-income citizens. If by *apathy* we mean the absence of affect and awareness, then the poor, the elderly, the young, the racial minorities and the industrial workers who have repeatedly voiced their outrage and opposition to various social conditions can hardly be described as "apathetic." Apathy should not be confused with antipathy and alienation. Nor is it clear that these dissident groups are "less informed." What impresses the investigators who actually take the trouble to talk to low-income people is the extent to which they have a rather precise notion of what afflicts them. Certainly they have a better sense of the difficulties that beset their lives than the many middle-class officials who frequently do not even recognize the reality or legitimacy of their complaints.[15]

VOTING AS AN IRRATIONAL RESPONSE

Civic leaders, educators and opinion-makers usually characterize nonvoters as "slackers" and seldom as people who might be justifiably cynical about the electoral system. Conversely, they portray voters as conscientious citizens performing their civic responsibilities. Certainly many voters seem to agree, especially those who report that they vote primarily because of a "sense of citizenship duty"; often they believe their vote makes no difference and have little regard for the outcome of the election. Thus in the 1956 presidential campaign, 58 percent of those who described themselves as "not much interested" in the campaign voted anyway. Fifty-two percent of those who "didn't care at all" about who won the election voted. Only 13 percent of those with a "low-sense of citizenship duty" voted, while 85 percent who had a "high" sense voted. The crucial variable in predicting turnout was "sense of citizenship duty" and not interest in substantive issues.[16] For many citizens, then, the vote seems to be more an exercise of civic virtue than civic power. This raises the interesting question of who really is the "deadwood" of democracy: the "apathetic" or the "civic minded," those who see no reason to vote or those who vote with no reason?

There are, of course, other inducements to voting besides a sense of civic obligation. The tendency to vote for the lesser, or lesser known, of two evils has already been noted. Once it is presumed that there are significant differences between the parties, the location of undesirable traits in one party suggests the relative absence of these traits in the other and sometimes becomes enough reason for partisan choice. Thus, the suspicion that Democrats might favor blacks and hippies leads some middle-class whites to assume that the Republican party is devoted to their interests, a conclusion that may have no basis in the actual performance of Republican officeholders. Similarly, the identification of Republicans as "the party of big business" suggests to some working-class voters that, in contrast, the Democrats are *not* for business but for the "little man," a conclusion that may be equally unfounded. Not unlike the masks worn by players in Greek drama, the party label gives distinct identities to otherwise indistinguish-

1967); Kimball, *The Disconnected*; Levin; *The Alienated Voter*; Harold V. Savitch, "Powerlessness in an Urban Ghetto: The Case of Political Biases and Differential Access in New York City," *Polity*, 5, Fall 1972, pp. 17–56; Parenti, "Power and Pluralism"; Lewis Lipsitz, "On Political Belief: The Grievances of the Poor," in Philip Green and Sanford Levinson (eds.), *Power and Community* (New York: Pantheon, 1969), pp. 142–172.

[15] See the citations in the previous footnote.

[16] Angus Campbell et al., *The American Voter* (New York: Wiley and Sons, 1960), pp. 103–106.

able and often undistinguished political actors, identifying some as villains and others as heroes. By acting as instigators of partisan spirit and partisan anxiety, the parties encourage participation, stabilize electoral loyalties and build reservoirs of trust and mistrust that survive the performances of particular candidates.

Some people vote because it is "the only thing the ordinary person can do."[17] Not to exercise one's franchise is to consign oneself to *total* political impotence, an uncomfortable condition for those who have been taught that they are self-governing. An awareness that there are men in exalted positions who exercise fateful power over ordinary people makes it all the more imperative for some citizens to feel that they exercise a control over their leaders. The need to *feel* effective can lead to the mistaken notion that one *is* effective. A faith in the efficacy of voting also allows one to avoid the risks of more unconventional actions and attitudes.

Voting not only induces a feeling of efficacy, it often results from such a feeling. Studies show that persons with a high sense of political efficacy are more likely to vote than those with a low sense. High efficacy is related to a citizen's educational and class level: better-educated people of comfortable income who feel more efficacious in general also tend to feel more politically efficacious than lower-income persons.[18] But while many studies relate sense of political efficacy to voting, there is almost nothing relating sense of political efficacy to actual efficacy. In fact there may be little relationship between the two.[19]

The argument is sometimes made that if certain deprived groups have been unable to win their demands from the political system, it is because they are numerically weak compared to white middle-class America. In a system that responds to the democratic power of numbers, a minority poor, for instance, cannot hope to have its way. The representative principle works well enough, but the poor are not strong enough nor numerous enough. Therefore, the deficiency is in the limited numbers of persons advocating change and not in the representative system, which in fact operates according to majoritarian principles. What is curious about this argument is that it is never applied to more select minority interests—for instance, oilmen. Now oilmen are far less numerous than the poor, yet the deficiency of their numbers, or of the other tiny minorities like bankers, industrialists and millionaire investors, does not result in any lack of government responsiveness to their wants. On many—probably most—important matters the government's policy is determined less by the majoritarian principle and more by the economic strength of policy advocates and the strategic positions they occupy in the wider social structure. The fact that government does little for the minority poor, and even shares in the middle-class hostility toward the poor, does not mean that government is devoted to the interests of the great bulk of belabored "middle Americans" nor that it operates according to majoritarian principles.

[17] See Lane, *Political Ideology*, p. 166: Gabriel Almond and Sidney Verba, *The Civic Culture* (Boston: Little, Brown, 1963), p. 131.

[18] See Robert R. Alford and Harry M. Scoble, "Sources of Local Political Involvement," *American Political Science Review*, 62, December 1968, pp. 1192–1206.

[19] See Alan Wertheimer, "In Defense of Compulsory Voting" (unpublished monograph, University of Vermont, 1972).

25

Responsible Journalism and Rational Candidates

Thomas E. Patterson and Robert D. McClure

Television today is an influential aspect of presidential campaigns. While more expensive than any other communications media, television reaches more potential voters and brings the candidates directly into the voters' homes. Yet despite the massive sums of campaign funding spent on TV, voter turnout on election day has been declining. McClure and Patterson argue that the major TV networks and presidential candidates seriously underestimate the basic good sense and intelligence of the voters. TV news programs dramatize motorcades and mass audiences following the candidates in an endless stream of newsreels. In-depth news coverage of the issues is generally avoided; the electorate is not educated on the issues, merely entertained. Candidates need to do more than develop effective images. Patterson and McClure contend that "information persuasion" is a better candidate strategy than simplistic, irrational, and emotional appeals. Do you agree? Should TV "spot" advertisements be reduced in favor of more detailed analyses of the issues?

The problem with television's entry into national politics is that network news departments and presidential candidates consistently misuse the medium and underrate their audiences.

Primarily because network campaign news contains so little meaningful information, it fails to have any meaningful effect on the viewers' feelings about the candidates and knowledge of the issues. Television's only effect on the American voter is to cheapen his conception of the campaign process and to stuff his head full of nonsense and trivia.

The networks could not maintain this charade without the active cooperation of presidential candidates who tailor their campaigns to every dictate of the television camera.

The networks broadcast the pap and the candidates agree to provide it because both

believe the myths about the power of television and because both have a false conception of the capacities and expectations of the American voter. The networks' appeals to viewers, and the candidates' appeals to voters, are premised on a low regard for the basic good sense and intelligence of the public. The result is that the electorate is deprived of vital information; the networks fail to live up to the standards of responsible journalism; and the candidates, in addition to cheating the voters of a meaningful choice, cheat themselves by acting in a manner unlikely to persuade even the most uninformed and uninterested voter.

THE NETWORK DEFENSE: A FRAIL ARGUMENT

The networks contend that they are acting responsibly. Television news says repeatedly "that it does operate in the public interest because it gives the public 'what it wants'." According to the standard network argument, the viewing audience demands good pictures and a snappy format, even at the cost of informative news coverage. And by responding to this demand, the networks feel they meet their public obligation. (A corollary is the networks' fear that, if they fail to furnish such news coverage, much of their audience and the advertising revenue that accompanies it will be lost.)

The network argument has two flaws. First, it fails to acknowledge the news media's traditional role in informing the electorate. No amount of evidence that the public is satisfied with network election coverage can hide the media's obligation for serving as a public educator. If television news is obsessed with campaign hijinks; if it does not consider careful reporting of the candidates and issues as its primary task; if it is not concerned with searching for significance, then television network news is not living up to its Fourth Estate responsibilities. The news must be more than a source of revenue. It must also serve the serious needs of a democratic society.

A second flaw in the network argument is that no solid evidence exists for the contention that the viewing public must be treated to an unending reel of dramatic film or it will stop watching the news. Although many observers other than network news personnel believe this, it is not an established fact that the size of the *national* news audience actually depends directly on the proportion of exciting pictures contained in a given broadcast. First, no reliable studies have been conducted to determine exactly what the viewing audience will tolerate in network news presentations. Second, the networks have never really experimented with their format in the market place to discover the limits of public toleration. From inception, the networks have had a policy of action pictures at the expense of informative reporting. From inception, and harking back to the breathless shouting days of radio news, the networks have given the viewers

just the headlines in order to make the news breeze along. So when they claim that the public insists on this shoddy journalism, the networks are merely endorsing the only television news product the American people have been offered.

Some observers point to the obvious success of certain local affiliates, which have abandoned any pretense of serious journalism, as proof that entertainment, not information, attracts news viewers. These "happy time" local newscasts are glutted with easy bantering, sheer sensationalism, and outright clowning, and they attract large audiences. But do people have the same expectations for network *national* news as they do for *local* news, weather, and sports? Probably not. At least none of the networks have been willing to risk their present audience, or their journalistic reputations, to find out whether a total entertainment orientation would lead to an even greater national audience.

In defending their news practices, the networks themselves have pointed more to the lack of audience interest in prime-time documentaries. News documentaries do not draw large audiences, and the networks have often claimed that this "proves" that most viewers are not interested in *any* serious television journalism.

This facile conclusion is also troublesome. It is problematic because people do not see all "news" in the same way. There is "daily" news that tells them what is happening in the world. And there is "other" news that provides in-depth looks at special topics. Their interest in "other" news is not a suitable basis for judging their likely reactions to "daily" news. Consider the newspaper reader as an example. The reader is not deterred by the serious journalism that he finds on the front page. In fact, many more Americans read the front page of a newspaper than watch the nightly news. But it is also clear that only a small portion of newspaper readers trouble themselves with the serious journalism of in-depth newspaper stories. Should the newspaper editor take this fact as a mandate to eliminate serious journalism from the front page? Of course not. Reasons quite beyond the seriousness of the journalism account for people's lack of interest in either special, in-depth newspaper stories or special television news documentaries. This news material, by definition, is likely to appeal only to those few people who are particularly interested in the topic. "Daily" news has a wider market. Further, television viewers have different expectations during the dinner hour than during prime-time hours. To watch television in prime time is to expect and seek entertainment, not information from news documentaries. To watch during the dinner hour is to expect the "daily" news.

When it comes to this daily news, people will accept it in the form of serious journalism, or in the form of not-so-serious journalism. More than to be entertained, they want to satisfy their simple desire "to find out what's happening." They will take what they get.

Now certainly, the television news audience expects a visual presentation of the news, and networks face audience problems that newspapers do not. Some people without any interest in the news leave on their television sets. Although good pictures may be about the only thing that occasionally attracts the attention of such viewers, they are a distinct minority. Most viewers watch to "get the news," and it is doubtful they notice which nights provide better pictures. It is much more likely they notice when the news events themselves are dull.

Moreover, most Americans do not even care which network provides their daily news. The best predictor of audience size for any network nightly newscast is the audience size for the program that precedes it. In those locations where ABC's pre-news programs have the most viewers, ABC Evening News draws the biggest audience. The same holds true for

CBS and NBC. This tendency is the well documented influence of "audience flow"—the tendency for most television programs to inherit many of their viewers from the preceding show. *All in the Family* may inspire many viewers to switch a given channel, but network news does not. Some people, out of habit or because they like a particular anchorman, may prefer one network's newscast over the others, but the bulk of the viewing audience does not shop between the networks to determine which newscast is likely to provide the most exciting pictures and snappiest format.

It seems clear: The networks have more freedom to practice responsible journalism than they have granted themselves. There is room for change. Perhaps not for fundamental change, since viewers do expect to see the news in film and expect all of the day's major stories to be reported. But these audience expectations may be rather flexible. Would viewers notice the difference if, most evenings, only 8 or 10 stories rather than 15 or 20 were carried? Would they perceive a change if slightly less news film were used and if that film contained a greater portion of "talking heads" and less action? It seems unlikely.

At the least, networks could alter the portion of their newscasts that every fourth year is granted to coverage of the presidential campaign. These national elections are special opportunities for network television news. As a news medium that reaches the entire nation, network television cannot cover election contests at the state and local level with enough frequency or depth to inform those constituencies. For those races, the local newspaper carries the democratic responsibility to keep the public informed. But at the presidential level, network news can and should meet its obligations to the electorate. The networks even have the advantage that during presidential campaigns the voters are more attentive to political information than at any other time.

In making this contribution, the networks might simply substitute more news stories on the candidates' qualifications and issue positions for news reports based on campaign hoopla. It can be said, however, that these stories would be too brief and fleeting to be very informative. Candidates' records, their abilities, and their policies are not easily absorbed by the eye and ear when they fly past in a news mix involving nearly a score of stories.

So during presidential elections, the networks would provide a more valuable service if they set aside up to 10 minutes each night for in-depth comparisons of the candidates on important issues or leadership dimensions. These stories might involve several types of news presentation: a simple statement of what is to be examined; and exposition of the background, using available film and visual material; and an analysis through informed commentary, using guest commentators if the networks' personnel lacked the necessary expertise. Such reports would be a significant step toward changing network election coverage for the better.

One network tried a similar approach during the last week of the 1972 campaign. Using imaginative graphics and existing film footage, CBS Evening News presented a few lengthy reports on the election issues. These reports were a clear departure from what the networks usually do as, point-by-point, Walter Cronkite explained the different positions of Nixon and McGovern on several major issues. If the nightly newscasts of ABC, CBS, and NBC are to contribute substantially to the electorate's information about the candidates and issues, however, reports like the one on CBS would have to be a regular feature of their election coverage.

How would television viewers react to more serious election journalism? The odds at least favor their *passive* acceptance of it. For one thing, viewers have no real enthusiasm for the manner in which presidential campaigns are covered now. Each night seems like a rerun of the night before. About sixty percent of all network reports that contain film of a presidential candidate picture him at an election rally, surrounded by a huge crowd. The city changes—one evening it is Minneapolis, the next it is St. Louis, then Portland, and around the continental merry-go-round. On camera, however, each rally looks very much the same, and viewers come to find it all very boring:

It's the same thing every night. The candidate out shaking hands. I'm tired of it.
                              —31-year-old sales clerk

Saw the same thing last night that I see every night. George McGovern at one of those rallies.
                              —53-year-old factory worker

It's so repetitious. I don't pay any attention any more.
                              —42-year-old housewife

Once you see one of those things [election rallies], you've seen them all.
                              —44-year-old craftsman

And when questioned more systematically, most people indicate a desire for election reports that, in effect, would make campaign coverage more informative. Although the networks assume that viewers want campaign action, not substance, because the first is entertaining and the second is boring, people's preferences reveal no such demand. By six to one, people said they want to see *fewer* network reports showing the "candidates moving through crowds of people." By two to one, people indicated a desire for *fewer* reports picturing the "candidates speaking at political rallies." In contrast, people claimed, by three to one, that they want *more* stories showing the "candidates being interviewed by reporters." And by two to one, people expressed a preference for *more* reports in which experts and voters were pictured "talking about the candidates."

Evidence such as this must be interpreted with care. In the past, what people have said they want from television and what they have actually watched have sometimes been quite different. In truth, people's preferences in election reporting may say more about how the voters feel a campaign should be reported than what they would actually prefer to watch. The public understands fully what presidential elections are supposed to be. The American voter knows that the ideal election is one where the issues are made clear and the candidates are subject to scrutiny. It is this sentiment, as much as people's viewing "tastes," that is represented in their news preferences.

Television networks could try to appeal to this higher instinct in the American voter. Exciting campaign pictures may or may not be the lowest common denominator for the television election audience, but at least the audience knows it should want more. To date, however, journalistic responsibility and the democratic ideal have lost out to the networks' low opinion of the typical news viewer.

THE CANDIDATE AND TELEVISION: PURSUING AN UNWISE STRATEGY

It is a fitting irony that patently meaningless television imagery fails to convince the American electorate. Presidential candidates' self-interest, as well as the nation's best interest, would be better served by television campaigns based on political substance.

Believability is the first requirement for effective media propaganda. Voters must accept what is being said; the message must become part of their thinking about the candidate. It is quite true that to accept a candidate's message is not always to be persuaded by it. A voter may change his thinking about a candidate and still vote against him. But message acceptance is a necessary first step on the road to winning votes.

Television image-making fails to make it past the believability barrier. Television style

and superficial mannerisms leave no impression with viewers about a candidate's fitness for the presidency. Voters simply fail to get the message that empty imagery is contrived to convey.

A candidate's issue positions, however, do get past this obstacle. They can be communicated effectively. Even people who intend to vote for his opponent get the message when a candidate makes clear his stand on important policy questions. Equally well communicated through the mass media are a candidate's group commitments, his personal record, his past accomplishments, and his personal background. The reason why these messages register with the electorate is that they are, for the most part, factual. And several decades of media research have demonstrated that "facts" get communicated.[1]

What does it gain a candidate, however, to build his media campaign around issues, his group commitments, and his personal and political history? George McGovern and Barry Goldwater tried that, and they lost nearly every state in the Union. So conventional political wisdom suggests that speaking too loudly and too clearly on the issues is a strategy for defeat.

But observers have misinterpreted these ruinous candidacies and have ignored other evidence—well-documented in careful research conducted by political scientists—that the electorate is becoming increasingly responsive to issues.[2] This same research would say that the candidacies of Goldwater and McGovern fell apart, not because issues were prominent, but because many of their issue proposals were poorly conceived and totally unwanted by overwhelming majorities of voters. The proper lesson from the Goldwater and McGovern defeats is not that issues make poor propaganda but that, because voters are increasingly concerned about issues, a candidate who advocates what most voters oppose is in serious trouble. If issues did not matter, neither Goldwater nor McGovern would have been so decisively whipped.

By comparison, if the thinking behind television image-making was correct, Goldwater and McGovern would have fared well. Each candidate was more photogenic and had a "cooler" personality, in the McLuhan sense, than his opponent. At their engineered-for-television rallies, each candidate drew more enthusiasm from his followers than did his opponent. Operating on assumptions about television imagery, it was Johnson and Nixon who should have been in trouble.

Voters simply are not fools. Some individuals do choose their candidate for strange reasons. But most of the electorate is "moved by concern about central and relevant questions of public policy, of governmental performance, and of executive personality." Issues and candidates' qualifications also are the focus of people's attention to the campaign.

Because the bulk of the electorate can separate wheat from chaff, few citizens are interested in campaign rallies and candidate motorcades. Consider this list of reasons why people say they pay attention to a political campaign. "Excitement" is last on the list.

Percent Agreeing

To judge what presidential candidates are really like.	60%
To help me make up my mind who to vote for.	59%
To see what each presidential candidate would do if elected.	53%
To keep up with the main issues of the day.	53%
To see what presidential candidates would do for people like me.	51%
To remind me of the strong points of the presidential candidate I support.	38%
To get information to talk politics with others.	27%
To judge which presidential candidate is likely to win the election.	18%
To enjoy the excitement of a presidential election.	16%

Candidates have assumed that people are bored by issues and hard facts about their qualifications and that they find imagery and hoopla both more interesting and more persuasive. Candidates simply have been wrong in this judgment.

A media campaign where issues and candidate character are the themes can work. However, it must be the right kind of media campaign.

Both Goldwater and McGovern faltered by selecting the unsuccessful strategy of *opinion persuasion*. They adopted issue positions favored by a minority of the public and then tried to convince the bulk of the people that the minority position was preferable. Efforts such as those are certain to fail. A presidential campaign is no place to change people's opinions and values. Much evidence documents that, when people are in the midst of overt attempts to persuade and propagandize, they protect themselves. Their psychological barriers against manipulation are mobilized. They are wary, and their more cherished opinions cannot be altered. Opinion persuasion simply will not work in the charged atmosphere of a presidential campaign.

Substantive campaigns can win votes, however, through *information persuasion*. Information persuasion is the process of altering people's views of a candidate by providing them information ("facts") that change their perceptions of the candidate rather than trying to change their own stands on the issues. Consider a candidate who has been a firm advocate of busing. He cannot persuade people who oppose busing to believe that busing is good. Nor can he say that he has had a change of heart and is now against this means of school integration. Voters would be suspicious of such an appeal occurring during the heat of the campaign. But the candidate's media propaganda, provided his past record makes it plausible, can state and state again his commitment to a strong military defense. Most voters will accept his commitment as valid, and this information will expand their store of knowledge about him. The candidate will still be seen in the voters' eyes as probusing, but now they will also consider him a firm advocate of defense preparedness. If the candidate can further persuade voters that a strong defense is a more compelling national concern than forced busing, and something a President can do more about, he has made an inroad toward picking up votes.

A second illustration may further clarify information persuasion. Take a candidate whose political activity has always been strongly probusiness. Media appeals that declare his support for the working man will fail. Contrary information overwhelms any such obvious propaganda. Nor will he be able to convert people with antibusiness attitudes to his probusiness position. But campaign messages that document the candidate's ability to get important legislation through Congress will be believed by most voters, if the evidence is clear. The candidate will still be seen as probusiness, but voters will also regard him as a politician who can get things accomplished. By getting them to regard this capacity as a very important element in the execution of the presidency, the candidate will have begun the process of winning votes.

Although oversimplified, the examples suggest why information persuasion is the only reasonable objective of media appeals in a presidential campaign. First, it involves the communication of material that people will accept. The candidate cannot be served by media messages that do not register in voters' minds. Second, it operates within the framework established by existing public opinion and merely attempts to link the candidate with political positions and abilities that voters think are desirable. After establishing that linkage, it works to convince voters that this new information should play an important part in their final candidate evaluations. No attempt is ever made to change resistant attitudes.

Today, in the past, and for the foreseeable future, the real persuasive message is what the candidate stands for. One of the more mischievous beliefs to gain hold on the minds of presidential candidates has been Marshall McLuhan's dictum that the medium is the message. Maybe over long periods of time and in subtle ways, the television medium has altered the public mind. But in the short run of a presidential campaign, people still react to candidates in very traditional ways. To get people to change their minds, the candidate must make his positions clear on the right issues, select the appropriate groups and publicize well his support for their goals, and pick the more favorable aspects of his public record and make them broadly known.

In the backroom, on the stump, in the newspaper, this is the political candidate's best strategy for persuasion. It is also his best strategy for political persuasion in the mystical medium of television.

Pursuit of this strategy would also benefit the electorate. Without question, information about the candidates' policies, commitments, and executive abilities provides voters a far more meaningful basis for choosing between the candidates than trivial televised pictures. Although some critics would argue that this strategy eliminates elections as a time for truly major political change, an election can only serve that function when the public wants it, as happened in 1932. The candidate cannot remold public opinion during the campaign, but he can inform the people how he meets their political needs and wants. And that, by any reckoning, is no small improvement over a campaign of meaningless television imagery.

NOTES

[1] See the communication research findings discussed in Joseph T. Klapper, *The Effects of Mass Communication* (New York: The Free Press, 1960).

[2] See, e.g., Richard W. Boyd, "Popular Control of

Public Policy: A Normal Vote Analysis of the 1968 Election," *American Political Science Review* 66 (1972), pp. 429–449; Richard A. Brody and Benjamin I. Page, "Comment: The Assessment of Policy Voting," *American Political Science Review* 66 (1972), pp. 450–458; Philip E. Converse, et al., "Continuity and Change in American Politics: Parties and Issues in the 1968 Election," *American Political Science Review* 63 (1969), pp. 1083–1105; Martin Fishbein and Fred Coombs, "Basis for Decision: An Attitudinal Approach Toward an Understanding of Voting Behavior," paper presented at the 67th Annual Meeting of the American Political Science Association, Chicago, September 7–11, 1971; John H. Kessel, "Comment: The Issues in Issue Voting," *American Political Science Review* 66 (1972), pp. 459–465; V. O. Key, Jr., op. cit.; Norman H. Nie, "Mass Belief Systems Revisited: Political Change and Attitude Structure," unpublished paper, University of Chicago, 1972; Gerald M. Pomper, "From Confusion to Clarity: Issues and American Voters, 1956–1968," *American Political Science Review* 66 (1972), pp. 415–428; David E. Repass, "Issue Salience and Party Choice," *American Political Science Review* 65 (1971), pp. 389–400; Michael J. Shapiro, "Rational Political Man: A Synthesis of Economic and Socio-Psychological Perspectives," *American Political Science Review* 60 (1966), pp. 19–28.

26

How Madison Avenue Didn't Put a Ford in Your Future

Malcolm D. MacDougall

The 1976 presidential campaign between President Ford and Jimmy Carter was an excellent example of how television advertising was used to promote candidates. Interestingly, Carter gained more widespread recognition and attention by the voters before Ford. Although Carter, an unknown, had a tremendous uphill battle, his anti-Washington, anti-Watergate themes were attractive to many voters. Even more attractive were his moral-istic stands, which superseded discussion of the issues. MacDougall indicates that this posed a number of problems for Ford's campaign which could not be overcome even with intensive use of TV spot advertisements. How does Mac-Dougall's analysis of Ford's campaign compare and contrast with the rational candidate arguments made by Patterson and McClure in Article 25?

When I got the phone call, a week before the Republican convention, I knew for certain that Jimmy Carter would be the next president of the United States. I had just been hit four times by what I thought was the slickest political campaign ever engineered.

I was listening to *Sports Huddle*, Boston's most popular radio talk show, when Lillian Carter called in from Plains, Georgia. She wanted to talk about wrestling. I was spellbound. So, I was sure, were 100,000 avid Boston sports fans. I pictured her hanging up to dial city after city, talk show after talk show. It was a brilliant ploy.

Later I went out for cigarettes and noticed three different paperback biographies of Jimmy Carter piled right next to the checkout counter. When I got home, I turned on the evening news. Jimmy Carter was playing softball in faded dungarees. He was the pitcher. I switched channels and there he was again, pitching from a slightly different camera angle. A few days earlier, Barbara Howar had appeared as a guest on *The Tonight Show*. She didn't want to talk about her new book. She wanted to talk about her chat with Jimmy Carter, on his back porch in Plains, Georgia. Jimmy Carter was going to save our country, she said. And then she reminded us that President Ford eats tamales with the wrappers on.

As I headed for bed, I was in awe of the marketing genius that had created this Jimmy Carter. I understood the strategy, and as an advertising guy I couldn't help but be deeply impressed. Before the networks and the talk shows and the paper stores woke up, the Carter family would be better known and better loved than the Waltons.

I got the phone call the next morning. "How would you like to do a presidential campaign?"

He didn't even say "hello." It was John Deardourff calling from Washington. I hadn't heard from him in six years. I knew that he and his best friend, Doug Bailey, ran a successful political consulting firm. I didn't have to ask which presidential campaign he had in mind. He handled only Republicans.

I told him that I was grateful that he'd thought of me but that it was absolutely impossible for me to get involved in Ford's campaign. Besides, the time for creative work on the Ford campaign was over. The advertising would have to start running in a few more weeks. It wouldn't be right to bring in a new creative director at this late date.

"They have no advertising plans at all," John said. "They just called Doug and me this week."

"They have nothing?" I asked.

"Nothing," John said.

"Then I have another reason why I can't do it," I said. "It can't be done."

"That's what makes it so interesting," John said.

Two days later I found myself having lunch with John and Doug at the Federal City Club in Washington. I learned that not a single thought had been applied as yet to the Ford advertising campaign. I learned that we would have over $10 million to spend in advertising —and we would have direct access to the President. I also learned that John and Doug had contracted to do eight other major election campaigns. They were having a busy season too.

That afternoon I went to the White House to meet Dick Cheney, the President's chief of staff.

Indeed, there was no advertising plan. They were dead broke, and there would be no more money until after the convention.

"I'll tell you how bad it is," Cheney said. "I'm going to have to pay my own way to Kansas City. *That* bad!" Then he ticked off what he called the "real" problems.

The Democrats had twice as many voters to begin with . . . they had a six-month head start . . . they were ahead by 33 points in the polls . . . they had a united party . . . the unions were pouring in the money and the energy . . . for the first time in history the Republicans didn't have a financial advantage . . . the convention was so late there hadn't been time to gear up for the real campaign . . . we had Watergate around our neck . . . and their candidate was better known.

"But our candidate is the President!" I pointed out, startled.

"People know Ford's the president—the *ap-* *pointed* President—but they don't know Ford the *man*," Cheney said. "They know that Jimmy Carter is a peanut farmer—which, by the way, he isn't. They know all about Plains, Georgia. And Miss Lillian. But nobody knows Jerry Ford. *That's* the job you've got to do."

"The right advertising can do that," John said confidently.

"You have one problem though," Cheney said. "President Ford freezes on camera."

THE PLANET FORD

Bob Teeter, a cheerful guy in his early thirties, was the first research expert I'd ever met who made me feel comfortable.

Teeter's men had been polling the voters for months and there didn't seem to be a single blip in the voters' psyches that they hadn't measured. And I would have guessed most of their findings dead wrong.

People were antibusing, antiabortion, antipornography, antimarijuana, anti-gun control, and anti-big government. Although they were more or less in favor of national health insurance, most people thought poverty was simply the result of laziness. By far their biggest concern was the issue of honesty in government. It was twice as important as unemployment, five times as important as education, and ten times as important as protecting the environment. Over 74 percent of the people seemed convinced that the government was run by a few special interests, was wasting their money, and that people in high places were basically immoral. I was beginning to wish that Jerry Ford was just a little ol' peanut farmer from Plains, Georgia. Someone who could appear to be as antigovernment as the voters themselves were.

Teeter then took us through the numbers on an issue I had thought might hurt Carter— religion. Most of the people I knew thought Carter was something of a freak on religion. I quickly learned *we* were the freaks.

"Here are the facts," Teeter said, flipping to a well-worn section in one of the books of statistics.

Thirty-nine percent of the people had had an actual experience with Jesus Christ that they could identify—time and place. Fourteen percent had actually seen or touched Jesus Christ. Seventy-two percent read the Bible regularly and said it was the main source of comfort in their lives.

"Billy Graham," Doug muttered, as Bob reeled off statistics about people in prayer groups. "We've got to have Billy Graham on the ticket."

"Or Oral Roberts," John suggested.

Teeter went to the back of the room and picked up what I had thought was a large cardboard chart. He turned it around and placed it on the table. It wasn't a chart at all. It looked to me like a precisely drawn map of the solar system. There were neat circles that resembled planets in a sky that had been divided by a grid.

"This is something that's never been done before," Bob said. "I call it a perceptual map."

A computer, with Teeter at the controls, had projected the candidates into two-dimensional space. Hence the planets in the sky. It had then placed the voters' perceptions of the candidates in space. These voter perceptions were represented by little dots drawn on acetate sheets. There were about fifteen acetate sheets representing key issues and important feelings that people had toward the various candidates.

Teeter laid the acetate sheets against the solar candidate map one by one. A pattern quickly began to emerge.

The planet just above and to the left of the center of the map represented Jimmy Carter. As the voters' perceptions were laid on the top of the map, thousands of little dots began to cluster around Jimmy Carter. Blue-collar workers started clinging to the Carter circle. Intellectuals gathered around him. Catholics and Jews, a little more hesitantly, circled in orbit around him. Blacks and Chicanos smothered him with their dots. People who cared about busing dropped at his feet. People who were for gun control hung around him. People who were against gun control sided with him as well. Conservative women kissed his feet Liberal women hugged his head. Environmentalists swarmed around him. The rich people touched him. The poor people clung to him.

About four squares below him and six squares to the right of him another pattern was emerging. This was the planet Ford. As the acetate sheets were laid on the grid we saw a small cluster of Republicans falling on Ford . . . a few farmers hanging around . . . some suburban third-generation Catholics looking in . . . and a nice bevy of women 18 to 34 standing directly at his side. The Ford planet looked lonely.

Directly above Ford, about eight squares away, a bigger and louder group circled the planet Reagan—the "anti" satellites: anti-gun control, anti-abortion, anti-poor people, anti-black people. There were a lot of them. Over half of that group stuck right by Reagan. The rest of them landed on a planet many squares above him. It was the planet Wallace.

"What a team that would have been," Teeter said, pointing to the Reagan and Wallace clusters. "A Reagan-Wallace ticket would have siphoned off a ton of voters from here"—he swept his hand from the Carter planet to a space between Reagan and Wallace— "and put them here."

"They wouldn't win," said Doug, "but they sure would scare the hell out of a lot of people."

When all the acetate sheets had been placed over the sky of candidates, one thing was very apparent: Carter was the king of the perceptual map.

THE KANSAS CITY PLAN

I spent the Republican convention in Kansas City cooped up in Ford headquarters, writing the advertising plan with John and Doug.

I tried to approach the plan the way I'd approach any marketing problem. We had to increase our market share by 33 points and we had to do it in a little more than two months. We had to get those points from undecided voters and from weak supporters of Jimmy Carter. There were plenty of both, and we had good information about those voters to work with. We wrote a 40-page plan, based on four major objectives:

1. Strengthen Ford's human dimension.
2. Strengthen Ford's leadership dimension.
3. Portray his accomplishments in office in a believable way.
4. Cut Jimmy Carter down to size.

We outlined a series of five-minute, 60-second, and 30-second commercials aimed at accomplishing those objectives. Our five-minute commercials were to be documentary films on the President's life, on his leadership qualities, on his family, and on his accomplishments during the two and a half years that he'd been president. Our one-minute commercials were designed to dramatize Ford's accomplishments. Our 30-second commercials were to be anti-Carter spots, regional spots, and issue spots. We wound up with over 50 spots.

I had written a line on the plane to Kansas City. It was corny, and I hesitated to show it to John and Doug. But I found that Doug had included something close to the same line in a speech he had just written: "President Ford is helping to make us proud again." I had written: "President Ford—the man who made us proud again."

We had our theme: "He's making us proud again."

Our plan was a good one—I was certain of that. Jimmy Carter's apparent lead in the polls seemed nonsense. What's more, our campaign hadn't even begun. When President Ford made his acceptance speech in Kansas City—by far

the greatest speech of his life—I started thinking about my wardrobe for the inaugural ball.

Just a few hours later I reconsidered briefly. Bob Dole had been picked over Bill Ruckelshaus for vice-president.

INSTANT MADISON AVENUE

We had just three weeks from the time the President approved the plan we had drawn up in Kansas City to the night the first commercial was scheduled. We eliminated all the normal precampaign steps. We had no meetings, no storyboards, no preproduction sessions, no production bids, no creative reviews. We hired a minimum of creative people. Three writers, one art director, and three television producers turned out the entire Ford campaign —which during its course came to over 300 separate print and TV assignments.

To save money and time, we set up our own TV production facilities. We hired our own cameramen, sound men, and film editors. As soon as a film had been shot, it would be rushed to New York and we would start editing it immediately. Scripts were written after the films had been edited. To eliminate film-laboratory delays, all the commercials were finished on tape. Winkler Video handled the incredible postproduction logistics problems—getting the right spot to the right TV station at the right time.

Somehow our jerry-built advertising agency worked. We never missed a deadline. No one lost his temper.

The chief reason for the smoothness was probably that we had just one client. Things are much easier when you deal directly with the top.

Unfortunately, President Ford was not another Frank Perdue—a good client who is also a good actor.

I spent nine and ten hours a day, for days on end, in a tiny room with Jerry Ford. I watched and listened and replayed the film over and over again as he talked about his childhood, about his family, about his years in Congress, about the kind of president he thought he was, about the kind of leadership he could give America, about the concerns he had for the future, about his accomplishments as president. I was absolutely convinced of his sincerity. He was so uncertain, so awkward. I began to wish that there were some way that we could put him on television just as he was, with all the "umms" and the "errs." I wished that I could show him dropping his pipe in mid-sentence. I wished that I could show him fumbling for words, and fumbling for matches. It was so damn real. There was not a trace of glibness, not a possibility of deception.

But I knew that it was impossible to run an unedited Ford commercial. Americans want their presidents to be terrific actors.

MISSING THE TARGETS

By far the biggest chunk of our advertising budget, over $5 million, went into spot TV. We wanted to concentrate our dollars in the states where we had the best chance of collaring the electoral votes. "Priority one" states were California (45 electoral votes), Illinois (26), Michigan (21), New Jersey (17), Ohio (25), Pennsylvania (27), and New York (41). "Priority two" states were Texas (26), Missouri (12), Maryland (10), Washington (9), Wisconsin (11), Connecticut (8), Virginia (12), Iowa (8), Florida (17), Kentucky (9), and Tennessee (10).

Those eighteen states represented 334 electoral votes. We needed 270 to win.

It's easy to point out that we lost half of those priority states. But the fact remains, the election was closest in the states where we concentrated the dollars. Those were the key states, all right. We just didn't find the right key. Texas and New York are two excellent examples. We had good issues in Texas, and we didn't use them properly. We had serious

problems in New York, and we didn't address them.

In Texas, Carter had made some serious mistakes. In his *Playboy* interview, he had spoken of Lyndon Johnson as "cheating," and his strange religious remarks had infuriated a lot of Texas Baptists. His vague position on the energy issue had Texans scared. His statements on registering handguns had Texas cowboys up in arms. His willingness to sign a bill doing away with state right-to-work laws could have hurt Texas working people. He was vulnerable as hell.

We felt that the ideal person to attack Carter on those specific issues was Ronald Reagan, who had a tremendous approval rating in Texas. Unfortunately, Reagan was willing only to do a vague and general commercial, prepared by his own scriptwriters, about the Republican platform. In desperation, I flew down to Texas and filmed John Connally. He was terrific. Fire glinted in his eyes when he laid into Carter for "betraying the workers of Texas," for trying to take guns away "from our ranchers," for his "dangerous waffling" on the energy issue. He put on a great show— but he just wasn't the man for Texas voters.

I was bitterly amused recently to see Ronald Reagan on *60 Minutes* bragging about carrying California for Ford and pointing out that Connally failed to carry Texas. The fact is, Ford carried California by himself. Reagan wouldn't even appear on the crucial half-hour television show just before the election. And it is my strong opinion that if he had really worked for Ford in Texas and Mississippi we could have won those states.

It seems to me, in fact, that the only effective campaign work done by Ronald Reagan was for Jimmy Carter. Reagan's attacks on Ford during the primary were heavily featured in a series of spots that Jimmy Carter ran throughout the South in the closing weeks of the campaign.

Our biggest problem in New York was that famous headline in the *Daily News:* FORD TO

CITY: DROP DEAD. Ford, of course, had never told New York to drop dead. He had forced the city to clean up its act before he approved a $2.3-billion loan that saved the city from bankruptcy. But that didn't stop Jimmy Carter from plastering the subways with large posters saying, "I guarantee I will never tell the greatest city on Earth to drop dead." The issue could have been defused. At first we wanted Nelson Rockefeller to do it, but after he appeared on the front page of the New York *Post*, giving the finger to a heckler, he might just as well have been giving the finger to us. Then Telly Savalas agreed to do the commercial for us. He would have been perfect, but just as we were ready to film him, he disappeared. The word we got was that a Greek organization had persuaded him not to do anything for Ford. Finally, on the next to the last night of the campaign, Senator Jacob Javits, on a live half-hour show, gave a brilliant explanation of the "drop dead" affair, giving one of the strongest statements on Ford's behalf that I heard during the whole campaign. It was too late.

When some of the southern states began to show promise, I again wanted to use Ronald Reagan talking about specific issues. I had to settle for Strom Thurmond. If Joe DiMaggio had batted for Joe Morgan in the last World Series, I doubt that Cincinnati would have won.

And that brings me to what I think was the biggest single mistake of our Ford campaign: We utterly failed to communicate with the Black voters of America. Blacks voted ten to one for Jimmy Carter. The Black vote elected Jimmy Carter.

Republican presidential candidates normally expect about 30 percent of the Black vote. Based on polling data and on the constant talk about voter apathy in the press, it seemed safe to assume that the Black turnout would be relatively low. Ford had a good civil-rights record, he had put a Black in his Cabinet, and hell, Carter was a Southerner. We put Lionel Hampton's song "Call Ford Mr. Sunshine" on Black radio. The listeners, apparently, did not sing along.

I sometimes think that Jimmy Carter won the election the day he walked into Harlem. With cameras.

CUTTING CARTER DOWN TO SIZE

I think that the advertising battle might have been a lot rougher if both sides hadn't been so afraid of being accused of Nixonian "dirty tricks."

We knew that Carter had prepared a brutal spot on Ford's pardon of Nixon. As described to us, the commercial opened on a shot of Nixon saying he was not a crook. Cut to Ford saying that Nixon was not a crook. Cut to Nixon leaving the White House in disgrace. Cut to Ford announcing his pardon of Nixon. I'm sure they tested the spot and concluded that it could hurt them more than us.

Late in the campaign, the Carter people brought in Tony Schwartz—the "hit man" who had created the most controversial television ad in political history, the "daisy girl" spot that was used, very briefly, against Barry Goldwater in 1964. The commercial opened with a pretty little girl picking petals off a daisy, and the scene suddenly burst into an atomic mushroom cloud.

I hoped he'd try something like that again, but no such luck. The Schwartz commercials had Carter reeling off a laundry list of things that the Nixon-Ford administration had done wrong. The mind boggles at all that malfeasance in 30 seconds.

We checked all of Carter's commercials, of course, and the closing of one of his spots gave us a great opening for one of ours. His ad ended with a picture of Carter, and an announcer dramatically stating that "what he did as governor of Georgia he will do as president."

Our spot opened with that tag. Then we cut to a map of Georgia and graphically showed that Carter had increased government spending by 57 percent, government employees by 27 percent, and bonded indebtedness by 20 percent. Our announcer—equally dramatic—said, "Don't let him do as president what he did as governor of Georgia."

I think that the most effective advertising that we did were the man-in-the-street commercials. We weren't just trying to find people who would say nasty things about Carter. We wanted to reflect an existing national attitude. My favorite, and the most famous, was the one made up entirely of Georgians. Six different people allowed as how Jimmy Carter hadn't been much of a governor. Then an attractive woman said, "I'd like to have someone from Georgia become president—but not Carter."

And then there was the "wishy-washy" commercial. During interviews in five cities, the same phrase kept coming up. Doug strung them all together: "He seems a little wishy-washy to me" . . . "I guess I'd describe him as wishy-washy" . . . "It seems that he's, well, I'd say he was wishy-washy."

Those commercials worked. They worked because they reflected the existing feelings of many people. Other interviews had much nastier things to say, but we didn't use them because they wouldn't have worked.

IF ONLY . . .

What's the difference between selling a president and selling soap? Frankly, the disciplines are basically the same. But you don't get quite so emotionally invoked with a box of soap. When I first started working on the campaign. I thought I'd stick to my part of the show. I

soon learned, however, that we were all on that damned roller coaster together.

The night Bob Dole was falsely accused of taking illegal campaign contributions from Gulf Oil, I threw my shoe at the evening news.

When Carter's *Playboy* interview broke, I bet $200 on Ford.

When I heard about the infamous Earl Butz remark, before it became public, I lost three nights' sleep.

When I watched the second debate, I ate half a box of Gelusil.

The night it was announced that the Watergate prosecutor was investigating Ford's personal finances, I kicked a chair so hard that I limped for days.

The day the Watergate prosecutor cleared Ford, I took six people to dinner at the Palm.

When John Dean went on *Today* to hype his book by falsely accusing Ford of trying to stop the Watergate investigation, I felt murder in my heart.

When, in spite of everything, our final ten-day blitz began to take hold, when we started to move up in the polls, day after day, I was in euphoria.

When CBS gave Texas to Carter, I had to leave our "victory party."

All in all, it was quite an emotional experience—especially for a guy who just two months earlier wasn't even sure whom he'd be voting for.

And now that it's over and I know that a swing of a few votes here or there would have changed the outcome, I have to live with the *if only's* . . .

If only we'd started sooner . . .

If only the economy hadn't soured . . .

If only Butz . . .

If only Reagan . . .

If only the blacks . . .

If only John Dean . . .

If only we had something more satisfying to look back on than a long list of *if only's*. . . .

PART THREE

✮✮

POLITICAL ACTION: THE MACHINERY OF GOVERNMENT

The President and the Bureaucracy

The presidency occupies a central role in American government. The chief executive is the focus of leadership, authority, and policy direction. Presidential power expands in response to demands for decisive action that neither Congress nor the courts can fulfill. The dispersal and decentralization of Congress delays and limits swift, unified decisions in critical situations. Congress is more likely to follow presidential initiatives, particularly in defense policy and international relations. The president has access to secret and complex information from his advisers and the executive bureaucracy which Congress cannot effectively challenge. The Supreme Court cannot initiate new policy in redefining constitutional powers or interpreting legislation, but must wait for appeals and cases and controversies brought by contending parties, which can often be a very slow and time-consuming process. Furthermore, the courts must depend on Congress for appropriations and the president to enforce its decisions.

Only the president, with his control of the executive branch and his overview of public policy priorities, can respond to the extraordinarily chaotic events of the twentieth century—two world wars, the cold war with the Soviet Union, the threat of nuclear holocaust, the Korean and Vietnam wars, conflict in the Middle East between Israel and the Arab states, economic depression and recovery, and various energy, poverty, and urban crises. These and many other problems have required presidential leadership to protect, defend, and define the national interest.

The president's leadership skills are much more than the product of formal constitutional powers. When the Founding Fathers wrote the Constitution, they were reacting, in part, to the excesses and abuses of executive power imposed by the British Crown during the colonial and Revolutionary War experiences. Consequently, the framers focused major attention on the details of legislative representation and authority as a check on executive power. They designed a tripartite system of separation of powers and checks and balances to achieve an equilibrium between the executive and legislative branches (see *Federalist*, No. 51). In Article II of the Constitution, the framers were vague in specifying the substance of the president's executive, administrative, military, and diplomatic powers. It was left to future occupants of the office to determine the precise nature of executive leadership.

In the *Federalist*, No. 70, Alexander Hamilton struck a particularly modern note by arguing for "energy" in the executive as "a leading character in the definition of good government." A strong president would protect the nation against foreign attacks, administer the laws, and secure liberty against the dangers of ambition, faction, and anarchy. Today, presidential power is defined in such active and positive terms rather than in negative or passive ways. Most modern presidents have positive leadership approaches which include promoting executive policy initiatives in Congress, extolling the president's ceremonial role as the leader of the entire nation, rising above party politics, having heroic qualities, and establishing charismatic leadership in direct communication with the masses. Most presidents no longer accept the Madisonian view of limited presidential authority. An example of such an approach was William Howard Taft who considered the roles of Congress and the courts as considerably more important than the president, and who, as *chief magistrate*, would not undertake any new initiatives unless specifically authorized by the Constitution, acts of Congress, or judicial rulings.

Abraham Lincoln was the most important nineteenth century president to provide precedents for extraordinary presidential authority in confronting wartime crisis. At the outbreak of the Civil War, Lincoln found it necessary and expedient to suspend various constitutional provisions. In attempting to restore national unity, he assumed legislative and judicial powers and suspended the civil liberties of certain Southern agitators. Such constitutional usurpation was temporary. When the crisis subsided, the president restored the full provisions of the "peacetime" constitution.

Theodore Roosevelt was the first modern president to define the activist role of the chief executive in shaping public policy. He argued that the president is the "steward" of the national interest, a leader who may undertake new authority unless he is specifically restricted by the Constitution, Congress, or Supreme Court decisions. Thus, the president has a general constitutional prerogative to expand his powers in response to particular situations that require his involvement.

World war required Woodrow Wilson and Franklin D. Roosevelt to assume new powers in controlling the national economy and in conducting diplomatic negotiations with foreign nations. The 1917 Lever Act represented a significant legislative delegation of power to the president in preparing the national economy for entry into World War I. In 1936, the Supreme Court decided that the president has exclusive authority to represent the nation in foreign affairs. The president's preeminent role gives him discretion and freedom from statutory restrictions "which would not be admissible were domestic affairs alone involved." Subsequently, President Roosevelt entered into secret arrangements with Prime Minister Winston Churchill to trade American warships for British bases in the West Indies before the United States formally entered World War II. Roosevelt then presented his *fait accompli* policies to Congress which were approved in the Lend Lease Act of 1941.

William Lammers (Article 27) indicates three competing perspectives on modern presidential leadership. The first includes the strong presidency views associated with Lincoln, Theodore and Franklin Roosevelt, and Wilson. In his book, *Presidential Power* (1960), Richard E. Neustadt, a leading proponent of this outlook, argues that effective presidential leadership requires persuasion and influence rather than commands or coercion. Neustadt views the president's role within the context of a Washington establishment, consisting of influential members of the bureaucracy, Congress, pressure groups, advisers, and the press. All of these actors have their own sources of power. Effective presidential leadership requires skillful management of this influence structure. Presidential commands diminish power and reputation because the president uses his leadership resources which he might employ in other policy areas.

In contrast, the separationists take a "balance of power" stance by arguing for strong executive and legislative participation in shaping public policy. Congressional authority is crucial in representing diverse regional viewpoints and in checking abuses of presidential power. Article 31 is a case study which shows that such separationism can lead to executive-legislative deadlock over important issues of domestic policy.

The separationist position gained widespread public support during the congressional investigations of the Watergate scandals in 1973–74. During the summer months of 1973, the Senate Select Committee on Presidential Campaign Activities heard more than thirty witnesses testify about the break-in of the Democratic National Party Head-quarters in June of 1972. The national TV audience, the seven senators, and their legal staff expressed disbelief that President Nixon's most trusted advisers never informed him about either the Watergate burglary or the subsequent cover-up. John Dean, the counsel to the president, revealed many sensational details about Watergate and directly impli-cated the president after revealing Nixon's efforts to keep the de-fendants silent. Presidential advisers Ehrlichman and Haldeman strongly defended Nixon. More than a year after Dean's disclosures, President Nixon, under the pressure of Judge John Sirica, Special Prosecutor Leon Jaworski, and the House Judiciary Committee, disclosed that he indeed had obstructed the administration of justice by directing the Central Intelligence Agency to stop an investigation of Watergate by the FBI just a few days after the break-in had occurred.

Presidential cover-ups in Watergate and the disastrous foreign policy consequences of the Vietnam War have resulted in a third view of the modern presidency, expressed through the skeptics. Their concern is with executive accountability. For example, George Reedy's *Twilight of the Presidency* (1970) argues that presidents tend to be treated as "kings" because they are frequently isolated from criticism by approving staff members. Presidents begin to consider themselves omnipotent, without the necessity of checks by Congress or public opinion.

Presidential leadership can also be viewed from the perspective of cross-pressures on White House occupants. In Article 28, Thomas Cronin argues that public demands and expectations of presidents are so complex that chief executives frequently face contradictory situations.

Paradoxical behavior results in a "no-win" or "Catch-22" condition for the president. Can any one person, let alone the president, be "gentle and decent" but "forceful and decisive" at the same time? Can the chief executive be "apolitical" in representing all the people and "political" with Congress in promoting and defending his legislative programs?

Personal character analysis may also offer insights into presidential leadership. This is the highly individualized approach suggested by James David Barber in Article 29. Barber argues that presidents can be assessed by their character traits, world views, and political styles. In Barber's opinion, "active-positive" presidents are the most desirable and beneficial for the country while "active-negatives" are potentially the most dangerous.

The active-positives include Franklin Roosevelt, Harry Truman, and John F. Kennedy. These men had confidence, flexibility, and enjoyed working to achieve their policy objectives. They had well-defined goals and sought to implement them even though they were not always successful. Active-positives are strong chief executives.

The active-negatives are also power-seekers. They, however, exhibit tendencies of ambitious striving, aggressiveness, and struggling for power against a hostile environment. They can become compulsive, withdrawn, and increasingly isolated if their policy views do not succeed and as they are not willing to admit mistakes. Lyndon B. Johnson and Richard M. Nixon are two recent examples of active-negative presidents.

From Barber's perspective, presidential candidates should be carefully evaluated prior to elections. The active-negatives should be sifted out. Otherwise the nation faces the possibility of damaging confrontations over domestic and foreign policy issues.

The president is the manager of the vast federal bureaucracy. In recent years, much criticism has been directed toward federal administrative agencies. Entrenchment, resistance to change, and unresponsiveness are among the problems most frequently cited. People feel that government bureaucracy is too large, costly, and impersonal.

These concerns are explored by John Herbers in Article 30. Ironically, as more people and organizations look to Washington for assistance and financial aid, criticism of the bureaucracy has increased. The key issue is that many special interest groups, including public and private organizations and state and local governments, want to maintain or increase funding and support for their pet projects and programs. Yet, these very same groups are severely critical of the "bureaucracy" serving others. For example, conservative Republicans support huge defense budgets for the Pentagon but consider welfare benefits to the poor as a waste of the taxpayers' money.

Herbers explores interest group alliances with the bureaucracy. Presidents have considerable difficulties dealing with the so-called "triple alliance" or "iron triangle." This consists of the lobby which supports a program, the congressional subcommittee which provides appropriations for it, and the federal agency which administers it. For example, President Carter encountered massive opposition to new energy legislation when the oil companies joined with legislators from the oil-producing states, a partnership the Energy Department was unable to counteract (see Article 31). To overcome this pressure the chief executive must mobilize strong lobbying campaigns from the White House to develop congressional majorities.

The president is generally considered as the major *initiator* and *formulator* of important policy proposals. As chief executive, he can draw upon the advice and resources of the White House staff, the cabinet secretaries, and the vast bureaucracy of the executive branch. This gives the president a comprehensive overview of the nation's priorities. After considering various policy proposals, the president then formally sends his suggestions to Congress in the State of the Union address, special messages for particular legislation, and the annual budget and economic report. Congress usually responds to presidential initiatives by refining policy requests. Responsibility is delegated to the standing committees which deal with specialized aspects of legislative proposals. For example, Congress does not consider all domestic policy together but as aspects of agricultural, urban, social services, or environmental matters which are the separate responsibilities of the standing committees. Also, Congress conducts hearings and investigations to clarify and revise executive proposals. The two houses must then agree on the substance of a bill which incorporates the policy. Following legislative adoption and presidential signing, the policy goes into effect. This requires an administering agency which may have authority to design specific rules and regulations to attain legislative policy goals. Frequently, the effect of a new policy may not be fully determined until the bureaucracy and other participants—clientele and special interest groups—become involved.

These formal procedures of executive-legislative relations do not indicate what can occur when the president and Congress disagree over major public policy disputes. In recent years, frequent executive-legislative deadlocks have resulted from such disagreements. Energy policy, as described in Article 31, is an excellent case study example of such a problem. In 1977, President Carter anticipated future fuel shortages when he declared that congressional approval of his energy program was absolutely essential as a "moral equivalent of war" against the energy crisis. Most public opinion polls, however, indicated general disbelief of fuel (gasoline and natural gas) shortages. The public felt that such difficulties were directly attributable to the greed of the giant oil producers. Through a variety of tax and regulatory measures, Carter tried to convince Congress to take action before it was too late. But the president did not sell his program effectively and his lobbying efforts were weak. Consequently, there was a hostile and fragmented legislative response. Special interest groups helped to defeat nearly all of Carter's key proposals.

27

Three Views of the President's Role
William W. Lammers

As the American presidency has become immensely prestigious and powerful, different varieties of presidential leadership indicate how the office was shaped and developed. The constitutional provisions of Article 2 dealing with the executive branch are rather brief (see Appendix), although Alexander Hamilton argued for a vigorous and energetic presidency in Federalist, No. 70. William Lammers shows that three perspectives have developed on the contemporary presidency: strong-presidency views, separatism, and skepti- *cism. Associated with each outlook are different views of institutional operations, key problems of the chief executive, and prospects for reform. Strong president proponents encountered considerable criticism by the skeptics following the policies of the Johnson and Nixon administrations during the 1960's and early 1970's. Why did this happen? What are the arguments made by the separationists? How is Jimmy Carter's presidency affected by post-Vietnam and post-Watergate developments?*

The proper role for the Presidency in American politics has long been in dispute. Even at the outset, the able group of men gathered at Philadelphia in the summer of 1787 were troubled by the manner in which the executive office was to be developed. They spelled out the activities and powers of Congress with some precision, but used only vague references in the stipulations for the executive—a telltale sign of uncertainty.[1] The debates themselves were marked by considerable vacillation, with basic issues often resolved fairly late in the proceedings. Even the decision providing for election by an electoral college rather than selection by Congress (which had been proposed as the Virginia Plan) came only in the final deliberations. The widespread view that George Washington would be the first executive in the new system served to reduce some

of the apprehension, but not to reduce uncertainties.

In retrospect, the initial uncertainty is not surprising. The men at Philadelphia were, after all, seeking to chart unfamiliar ground in avoiding a monarchy and yet having an executive who could help to overcome problems of inadequacy in policy development which had plagued the fledgling government created by the Articles of Confederation. There were few obvious models to follow in outlining a non-monarchical executive as of 1787.

Initial uncertainty about presidential roles was followed by considerable fluctuation in both presidential behavior and major thinking about the nature of the institution. Presidential roles tended to evolve more from individual actions and specific situations than from a consistent view of the office. Andrew Jackson served to expand popular support for the Presidency through the party system, yet there was limited formal assessment of the change which was taking place. The actions of two Republicans, Abraham Lincoln and

Theodore Roosevelt, were instrumental in creating precedents for active leadership roles. The Republican Party at the same time remained the frequent repository of concepts emphasizing limited presidential roles. Roosevelt's successor, portly William Howard Taft, was a frequent spokesman for a restrained interpretation of the Presidency.[2]

In recent decades, the Democratic Party has included a large number of the spokesmen for the importance of encouraging major presidential leadership roles. Woodrow Wilson contributed to this development, with his emphasis on the opinion-leading role and the importance of party leadership. The tendency for Democrats to advocate a strong set of presidential roles increased substantially as the Democratic Party developed a major coalition for controlling that office. The debate over the nature of the Presidency has intensified in recent years, along with the expansion in key roles being performed.

The major views of proper presidential roles today have their dominant moorings in the conflicts which emerged out of the changes in the Presidency spawned by Franklin Roosevelt. Although there are numerous statements by earlier participants and some students of government, the most extensive ideas emerge in the controversy over the changes and growth since the 1930s. It is thus appropriate to focus our review of conflicting perspectives on that debate.

Those taking a specific presidential perspective can be categorized into three broad groups: strong-presidency advocates, separationists, and contemporary skeptics.[3] The table below, entitled "Perspectives on the Contemporary Presidency," provides an overview of key positions. In part, the three positions involve differing views of actual institutional operations. Also, one finds major differences in how key problems with the Presidency are viewed. In turn, the nature of the reform agenda differs dramatically in the respective views.

Each of these positions has often been incorporated in a set of policy preferences, partisan orientations, and rather definite views of power relationships in American politics. The consideration of differing perspectives is thus appropriately followed by an overview of the differing interpretations of power relationships.

Perspectives on the contemporary presidency		
General View	*Major Problems Seen for the Political System*	*Reform Possibilities*
Strong presidency	Fragmentation: lack of leadership; slow policy response	Stronger parties Selection of skilled politicians Expanded staff
Separationist	President has too much power; can easily abuse it	Strengthen Congress Decentralize
Contemporary skepticism	Presidential isolation Electoral manipulation by incumbents Selection process which produces inadequate individuals	Open communication systems Greater sharing of functions

STRONG-PRESIDENCY VIEWS

Those emphasizing the necessity of strong presidential leadership, in the modern context, have to a striking degree been talking of the way in which Franklin Roosevelt is seen to have operated the Presidency. In particular, one finds a fondness for the manner in which Roosevelt mobilized electoral support and gained legislative victories in Congress. The strong-presidency writers have envisioned particular ways in which the president will gain his strength, and not all situations in which a president will have a major impact on the course of public policy. Now, however, given some dimensions of Nixon's Presidency, it is especially important to be specific about the manner in which the president is to be influential.

The overall picture of presidential politics which emerges from strong-presidency writers emphasizes the extent to which presidential leadership is needed if there is to be effective policy change. Congress is seen as typically too slow moving to provide major initiatives in getting new legislation promoted and accepted by the public and in Congress itself. The fear, for strong-presidency writers, has been that without a strong president, there will simply be a stalemate in American politics. Not insignificantly, this emphasis was especially pronounced during the days of domestic lethargy in the Eisenhower Presidency and the period under Kennedy, during which Congress would be characterized by some as almost literally engaging in a sit-down strike, and legislative proposals involving civil rights, aid to education, and a tax cut all languished.

The need for strong presidential leadership is thus a major theme in Richard Neustadt's classic, *Presidential Power*.[4] Writing at the end of the Eisenhower Presidency, Neustadt displayed a strong dislike for the handling of the Presidency by Eisenhower, and looked back at the Roosevelt Presidency as one in which effective use of presidential power did produce policy results. Similarly, in the early 1960s, the works of James Burns and Louis Koenig stressed the need for presidential leadership to overcome tendencies toward stalemate and lack of policy response. Koenig was most emphatic, claiming, "Our system of government tends toward paralysis except when a strong President is on hand."[5]

A strong Presidency was in turn seen as the best means of achieving policies which recognized the needs of those who were not specifically organized to plead their cases in Congress. The Presidency was seen as the place where policies for aiding middle and lower-class segments of American society gained initiation and often passage during Roosevelt's Presidency, and the institution offering the greatest chance for the "other Americans" of the 1960s to gain political recognition of their needs. Blacks, the elderly, and the rural poor were thus encouraged to seek helpful action in the orbit of presidential politics. Congress was viewed as particularly responsive to special interests, and the Presidency as more apt to speak for the entire nation. Such former key Nixon aides as H. R. Haldeman and John Ehrlichman, in arguing that only the President was speaking for all of the people, took a position which jarred many in Congress, but they were certainly expressing an idea which strong-presidency advocates had given wide circulation.

The strong president was additionally seen as providing the best opportunities for coordination and use of expertise in developing policy. This argument was more often expressed in foreign than in domestic policy areas, but could also be found in the writings which pointed to the importance of economic advice for the president. Congress again was found wanting. Its fragmented committee structure and a reluctance to develop expertise of its own constituted, for the strong-presidency advocate, a clear indication that only the Presidency could provide needed coordination and expertise. The "whiz kids" of McNamara's analytic staff in the Pentagon and the thrust toward systematic budgeting procedures under Johnson in 1965 constituted the type of development which was viewed as necessary in national politics and also more apt to occur within the Presidency rather than in Congress.

Strong-presidency writers, finally, looked to the president for the provision of necessary policy leadership in relating to the electorate. Here in particular the Roosevelt example is strong. Roosevelt's shrewd use of "fireside chats" for radio audiences and his sustained efforts at building support for such policy moves as the adoption of social security were highly praised. In *Presidential Power*, Neustadt emphasizes the opinion-leadership role with a major chapter devoted to opportunities, restraints, and techniques involved in building policy interest and support.[6] Both Eisenhower and Kennedy often received critical reviews for tending to enjoy high personal popularity but not pushing for specific policy support, especially on domestic issues. Rather than simply enjoying high popularity, the president was expected to engage in efforts at public education to gain support for policy changes.

Policy leadership with Congress, mobilization of public support, and the development of policy based upon coordination and the use of expertise have thus been key roles in the strong-presidency view. These roles have been deemed necessary because of the tendency for the political system to have too many veto points, and too often to be sluggish in its policy responses. Inertia, rather than abuses of power, has constituted the major concern.

In the wake of the Watergate scandals, one must emphasize the aspects of presidential politics which strong-presidency writers have tended *not* to fear. Possible abuse of presidential power, of great concern to the separationists, was of limited concern to the advocates of the strong presidency. In sharp contrast with the separationists and many current skeptics, before Watergate the strong-presidency advocates saw adequate alternative restraints. Interpretations of both power relationships in American politics and personal power orientations reinforced a lack of concern for possible abuses of presidential power.

Emphasis on the importance and desirability of a strong presidency was high at a time when power relationships were characterized as highly competitive. The label *pluralism* was often attached to views stressing large amounts of group competition. Such widely read works as David Truman's *The Governmental Process* described a political process with differing groups in such areas as agriculture, labor, and business competing with each other for the favor of the president.[7] Group competition in elections was seen as especially extensive, thus making elections an important check on presidential power. The pluralist view, as subsequent analysis shows, has fallen into substantial question in the face of both additional analysis and the movement toward greater concentration of economic power in American society. The belief in a pluralistic political system was nonetheless essential for the strong-presidency advocate. One could rely upon group competition rather than such formal structural arrangements as separation of power to prevent abuses by the president.

Along with group competition, the strong-presidency advocate emphasized the importance of political socialization in developing restrained and uncorrupt presidential behavior. Such leading political scientists as Robert Dahl went to great lengths to argue that the formal checks and balances of the constitutional system were overrated, and that leaders behaved with restraint in considerable part because of their learning of norms for presidential behavior.[8] A similar emphasis on the tendency for the possession of a position of power to be infrequently associated with a willingness to abuse power was developed by Lasswell and Rogow.[9] In their view, many individual factors tended to reduce the likelihood that the old maxim "Power corrupts and absolute power corrupts absolutely" would be valid. Several examples were cited of instances in which individuals behaved with greater rectitude *after* assuming the Presidency as an indication that whatever a politician's earlier involvement with petty political patronage and corruption might be, his presidential behavior would be less corrupt. A learning of norms for proper presidential behavior, coupled with a competitive political system, constituted in these writings an adequate basis for minimizing the fears some were expressing regarding dangers inherent in a strong Presidency.

Strong-presidency advocates saw various routes for the better achievement of the preferred presidential roles. Generally, a reduction in the key veto points in Congress was stressed. This typically included the seniority system, as it gave considerable power to individual committee chairmen; the use of filibusters in the Senate; and the opportunities for delay in the House stemming from the power of the House Rules Committee in deciding which measures would be debated on the floor of the House. Discussions in the early 1960s stressed problems with Congress in particular, as Kennedy faced continual frustrations with his legislative programs.

Possible strengthening of political parties emerged as an additional reform thrust. Some political scientists, looking favorably at the British party system, hoped for more cohesive political parties to provide a vehicle for presidents to gain greater support in Congress. This view did not fit well with a selection process emphasizing different constituencies for members of Congress. As analysis of the recent selection process shows, furthermore, the degree of party control seems actually to be declining. This is particularly true of the presidential selection itself. For such writers

as James Burns, however, the best means of strengthening the Presidency was through modification in the party system. The attractiveness of that idea found its way, more recently, into journalist David Broder's *The Party's Over*.[10]

A different approach was voiced by Richard Neustadt, as he discounted formal changes as a feasible means for strengthening the Presidency. For Neustadt, it was crucial to elect presidents who possessed a good political sense. In his analysis, the best operation of presidential politics was to be achieved as skilled politicians guarded their choices to make sure that they maintained support in the electorate and developed high ratings among key Washington constituents. With this emphasis, such politically active presidents as Franklin Roosevelt, with their obvious enjoyment of political calculations and operations, received the high marks. Erwin Hargrove asserted a similar view in giving the personally ambitious presidents higher evaluations than their more apolitical counterparts in the major roles of leading public opinion, persuading Congress, and controlling the bureaucracy. In this view, the best means of achieving needed presidential leadership was to place skilled and ambitious politicians in the Oval Office.[11]

Supporters of the strong-presidency view, as subsequent chapters show in several contexts, came generally from the academic community, from some Democrats in Congress, and from segments of the electorate most interested in policy change. Public perceptions of the strong-presidency view have been illusive—subject to the influence of policy preferences, the popularity of particular Presidents, and even the manner in which opinion poll questions have been worded[12] It is a fair judgment of the literature, however, to say that the popularity of the strong-presidency ideas was greater among those who thought extensively about the Presidency than within the electorate generally. In the period following World War

II, a substantial segment of the electorate was more committed to the value of separation of power and a strong role for Congress than were major writers on presidential politics.

The reader may well have concluded by now that the strong-presidency ideas seem, at least at some points, to be rather dated. Credibility gaps, indictments of key presidential aides, and impeachment proceedings are surely not a part of the standard litany of the strong-presidency writers. While the views on several grounds may seem rather simplistic, it is important to stress several summary points. First, these views had a significant impact on the manner in which the Presidency was operating by the time Richard Nixon arrived at the White House. Coalition politics, with the Democratic Party often in strong support, helped carry some of these ideas into fruition. Second, however one now views these ideas, they stand as a frequent theme in many discussions of ways in which public policy can be made more effectively. Although the set of ideas involved in the strong-presidency view are most easily seen in the context of American politics in the 1950s and 1960s, the recent traumas in presidential politics have not altered the important issues in that advocacy. Thus Richard Neustadt's more recent writings, for example, caution against an over-response to Watergate abuses that could make it too difficult for other presidential personalities to function effectively.

Finally, it must be reemphasized that there are various ways in which a president can exercise a strong role in policy development. With the Roosevelt model in mind, and particularly the early years involving domestic policy, strong-presidency writers tended to talk in terms of building public support and working to gain legislative victories. That was, after all, a dominant thrust of FDR's Presidency. His constitutional fight, in contrast to the dominant early thrust of the Nixon Presidency, was with the Courts and not with

Congress. President Nixon, as we will see, somewhat confounded ideas of the strong Presidency. Like Roosevelt, he sought to build a new coalition and to have an overarching impact on American politics for a substantial period. Yet because he lacked support in Congress, and distrusted the media, he was often at war with Congress, and was in the position of telling the electorate what he had done recently which was good for it, rather than building sustained support for policy decisions. To question Richard Nixon's Presidency is not necessarily to question the strong-presidency ideas altogether.

THE OPPOSITE VIEW: SEPARATIONISM

A second group of writers and political figures has long argued that the proper answer to questions of presidential power comes with a definite effort at restraining opportunity for the abuse of power. Traditionally, the most common basis for this position has been emphasis on the importance of both strengthening Congress and reducing presidential power. The label *separationist* characterizes this position. In policy terms, the separationists have not felt the same urgency expressed by most strong-presidency advocates for moving toward new or expanded policy commitments.

The separationist view has been, in the period since the 1930s, substantially a critique of the strong-presidency ideas, rather than a developed interpretation of the manner in which the American system actually operates. This is partly due to the limited interest in the separationist position within the academic community. Willmoore Kendall and Alfred deGrazia are strong exceptions to the lack of interest and academic support for the separationist position. Supporters of the Nixon Presidency during his years in office, interestingly enough, produced some discussion of decentralization but no flowering of the separationist view. Given some of Nixon's actions, this is not surprising. Nonetheless, that lack of interest constituted an important shift in traditional divisions between parties since the 1930s.

Separationists sharply disagree with the strong-presidency enthusiasts over the nature of the majorities reflected in the presidency and in Congress. For strong-presidency advocates, congressional procedures and committee structures has created, historically, a tendency for vetoes by such varying minorities as Southern whites, local elites, and business interests. The separationists argue differently. In their eyes, the Presidency emerges as the institution with a strong minority slant. The tendency for electoral college majorities in large, urban states to play a key role in presidential elections produces, for the separationist, a tendency for periodic swings toward new programs which are of primary interest to a minority within the electorate. Presidents, rather than speaking uniquely for a national interest, thus simply emerge as spokesmen for different segments of the nation. As a result, the separationist tends to view the dominant voices in Congress as having at least as much claim to full expression in the development of policy as those which tend to be most frequently heard in the orbit of presidential politics.

The amount of coordination and expertise which is applied to public policy within the executive branch is also called into question by the separationists. Alfred deGrazia considers these claims to be a gigantic myth.[13] In his view, the Presidency is like Congress—but with a tent over it. Beneath the often seeming unanimity of executive pronouncements, he sees a hidden process which, if more generally known, would make the Presidency seem more like Congress in its wrenching and groping toward policy positions.

Constitutional checks, for the separationists, are essential for avoiding abuses of power. In their eyes, formal concentration of power has long been an open invitation to abuse. It is simply not adequate to argue, for separationists, in terms of electoral checks or a prevailing competitiveness among interest groups and elites. One must maintain a formal, constitutional check in the form of separation of branches, to avoid having an executive abuse the rights of at least segments of American society. The characteristically Southern emphasis on the importance of constitutional checks which emerged in the commentary of Chairman Sam Ervin during the Senate Watergate Committee investigations in late spring of 1973 vividly reflected the separationist position.

Possible means of attainment have not been spelled out very specifically in the separationist view. Generally, there is an interest in adhering to a concept of separation of power and a tendency to equate separation with effective policy development. Proposals for making Congress more efficient occur periodically, but proposals are less often directed toward such key power questions as committee chairmanships. At the same time, the president is to be held more accountable through less general delegation of power and a reduced legislative willingness to support his proposals as a normal course of events.

Since the New Deal, the basis of support for the separationist position has come predominantly from the Republican Party and some segments of the Southern Democrats in Congress. Not a single Republican in either house of Congress, for example, voted against the Twenty-second Amendment with its limitation of presidents to two terms. The interest of white Southerners in using Congress as a base for defense against integration proposals coming from the White House was most apparent, particularly in the period prior to their fundamental defeats on civil rights matters in 1964 and 1965.

Traditional separationists can rightly note

with a measure of relief—and perhaps be-musement—that several aspects of their posi-tion are now being widely expressed by aca-demic writers and liberals in Congress. Senator McCarthy became an early skeptic as he voiced concern over abuse of presidential power (largely on foreign policy matters, and particularly Vietnam) in the 1968 presidential primaries. His shift marked a clear departure from the traditional strong-presidency ideas often expressed by Northern Democrats. One has witnessed a growing chorus of concern with presidential power coming from those who once advocated the strong-presidency po-sition, or at least share some of the policy desires of many strong-presidency advocates. The contemporary skeptics show both several similarities and important differences as they are compared with the traditional sep-arationists.

CONTEMPORARY SKEPTICISM

Increasingly skeptical interpretations of the Presidency have grown dramatically since the mid-1960s. The impact of the Vietnam War and the operation of the Presidency under Richard Nixon have been instrumental in this shift. Contemporary skeptics often share with the separationists a concern for the impact of office on an individual and the likelihood that he will become arrogant in his use of power. Skeptics have also questioned the ex-tent to which a president, often viewed as isolated from public moods and sound advice, will in fact promote policies which are in a majority interest. Fundamentally, the con-temporary skeptics have come to question whether the totality of restraints on presiden-tial operations (both constitutional and in com-peting power relationships among elites and interest groups) are sufficient to prevent abuse of power. Contemporary skeptics are apt to question the supposed pluralism of American

politics, in sharp contrast to their strong-presi-dency compatriots of an earlier day. The con-temporary skeptics are highly divided on the question of what should be done, however, and they tend to differ sharply with the separation-ists in terms of the degree of confidence ex-pressed in separation as the necessary and suf-ficient step for overcoming contemporary problems.

George Reedy's *Twilight of the Presidency* stands as a major contribution to the con-temporary skepticism position.[14] For Reedy, writing after serving as press secretary for Lyndon Johnson, the contemporary Presidency dangerously isolates its occupant in an atmo-sphere where he is treated virtually as a mon-arch, and has a staff which is anxious to ad-vance personally rather than to bring needed information and viewpoints to presidential at-tention. Writing before the Watergate scan-dals, Reedy saw service in the Presidency as not necessarily producing direct corruption, but rather a situation in which the president becomes increasingly unable to make accurate political judgments. The president, in Reedy's eyes, becomes while in office an increasingly isolated bungler.

The major review of presidential personali-ties undertaken by James Barber has also em-phasized sobering aspects of the presidential character.[15] Barber is less convinced than Reedy that the experience itself is adverse in the evolution of presidential behavior. Rather, Barber emphasizes that the type of personality we have been elevating has often been what he characterizes as an active-negative. Both John-son and Nixon are described in this category. For the active-negative, there is a rush of ac-tivity, but a nagging sense of personal uncer-tainty and a perception of the political en-vironment as essentially hostile. He must succeed by constantly striving and never let-ting himself be done in by opposing forces. Rather than being confident, as was Neu-stadt, that an experienced politician was apt to develop skills as an effective president, Barber worries that we are now increasingly apt to get individuals in office who will make serious miscalculations because of their basic personality weaknesses. Contemporary skeptics, in short, have taken a far less optimistic view of presidential personalities than have the strong-presidency advocates.

Contemporary skepticism has seriously questioned the likelihood that presidential politics constitutes the best avenue for the achievement of policy outcomes aiding the less well organized and the less privileged in American society. For some, a dependency on presidential initiative is unrealistic simply because the president is apt to be too busy with foreign policy matters and, increasingly, questions of economic management. The president's ability to build policy support has been seriously questioned, with the suggestion that domestic policy steps are apt to reduce the popularity of a president, rather than helping in expanding support. Rather than building new support, a domestically active president is seen as often finding that he makes more enemies than new friends. The question of likely policy thrusts has been heightened mightily, as well, by the revelation of the access patterns enjoyed by business interests within the White House under Richard Nixon. The revelation of the close ties between business interests and not only the cabinet departments and regulatory commissions, but also the White House Staff under Richard Nixon simply made the concern acute.

The staunch critic of the Presidency as it has existed, especially at the hands of Richard Nixon, has added up recent tendencies as a fundamental threat to democratic politics. The picture of the Presidency which emerges in this critique is one in which an isolated White House threatens each of the checks traditionally placed on presidential action. Elections can be manipulated, at least at the hands of an incumbent. Congress can be bypassed, rather than persuaded. Interest groups held in disfavor can simply be ignored, and restraining voices in the bureaucracy dampened by a downgrading and ridiculing of the federal bureaucracy. Press criticism, in turn, can be reduced by a heavy-handed handling of access —and even threats to the freedom of reporters to operate without personal sanctions being imposed. Rather than a competitive political system, with the president bargaining and working to build public support, skeptics see little competition—and considerable manipulation and abuse of power.

Questions raised by the contemporary skeptics, and the crucial issue of what can be done, are central to the issues considered here. They become, indeed, vital questions for all Americans. For now, key summary points deserve emphasis. First, ideas about the operation of presidential politics have been closely tied to coalition positions and favored policy outcomes. This has been true historically, and is certain to be at least partially the case in the evolution away from the traumas of the Nixon Presidency. Second, it is the strong-presidency ideas which have come into particular question. They have been the most extensively developed, and are the ones which have been most directly tied to concern for the expansion of the capacity of the federal government in dealing with needed policy change. Third, positions on reform have often masked far too little knowledge of actual operations of presidential politics. The differences on factual questions found among the respective presidential perspectives underscore the importance of an expanded knowledge of actual practices and patterns. Fortunately, the emerging body of presidential scholarship is beginning to fill that void. Finally, one finds views of presidential politics closely tied to views of power relationships in American politics.

NOTES

[1] A useful general account of these struggles is contained in Charles C. Thach, *The Creation of the*

Presidency, 1775–1789, Baltimore, Johns Hopkins Press, 1922.

[2] Presidential statements and early scholarly views are presented in Robert S. Hirschfield, ed., *The Power of the Presidency*, Chicago, Aldine, 1968.

[3] For another classification scheme, see David Paletz, "Perspectives on the Presidency," *Law and Contemporary Problems*, Summer 1970, chap. 1.

[4] Richard E. Neustadt, *Presidential Power: The Politics of Leadership*, New York, Wiley, 1960. For his more recent view, see "The Constraining of the President: The Presidency after Watergate," *British Journal of Politics* 4 (October 1974), 383–397.

[5] Louis Koenig, *The Chief Executive*, New York, Harcourt, Brace, and World, 1968, pp. 186.

[6] Neustadt, op. cit., chap. 5.

[7] David B. Truman, *The Governmental Process*, New York, Knopf, 1951.

[8] Robert A. Dahl, *A Preface to Democratic Theory*, Chicago, University of Chicago Press, 1956.

[9] See Arnold Rogow and Harold Lasswell, *Power, Corruption, and Rectitude*, Englewood Cliffs, N.J., Prentice-Hall, 1963.

[10] David Broder, *The Party's Over*, New York, Harper & Row, 1972.

[11] Hargrove, op. cit. For his more recent views, see Erwin C. Hargrove, *The Power of the Modern Presidency*, New York, Knopf, 1974.

[12] Changing public perceptions are traced in Donald Devine, *The Political Cultures of the United States*, Boston, Little, Brown, 1972, pp. 151–161.

[13] See Alfred deGrazia, "The Myth of the President," in *The Presidency*, ed. by Aaron Wildavsky, Boston, Little, Brown, 1969, pp. 49–73.

[14] George Reedy, *The Twilight of the Presidency*, New York, Mentor, 1970.

[15] James David Barber, *The Presidential Character: Predicting Performance in the White House*, Englewood Cliffs, N.J., Prentice-Hall, 1972.

28

The Presidency and Its Paradoxes

Thomas E. Cronin

Presidents are confronted with a variety of public expectations, many of which may conflict with each other. As the most visible national leader, the president has heavy demands on his time, energy, and resources. As Clinton Rossiter once argued, the president's list of required leadership talents includes everything from a to z, such as head of the political party, of congress, of the bureaucracy, of foreign policy, etc. In Article 28,

Thomas Cronin focuses on a crucial set of problems: What happens to presidents when contradictory demands are made in particular political, personal, or policy-making situations? Can we continue to have a "paradoxed" presidency? Cronin's article deserves close attention, particularly its discussion of effective leadership and the assessment of candidate types who seek the presidency.

Why is the presidency such a bewildering office? Why do presidents so often look like losers? Why is the general public so disapproving of recent presidential performances, and so predictably less supportive the longer a president stays in office?

The search for explanations leads in several directions. Vietnam and the Watergate scandals must be considered. Then too, the personalities of Lyndon Johnson and Richard Nixon doubtless are factors that soured many people on the office. Observers also claim that the institution is structurally defective; that it encourages isolation, palace guards, "groupthink" and arrogance.

Yet something else seems at work. Our expectations and demands on the office are frequently so paradoxical as to invite two-faced behavior by our presidents. We seem to want so much so fast that a president, whose powers are often simply not as great as many of us believe, gets condemned as ineffectual. Or a president often will overreach or resort to unfair play while trying to live up to our demands. Either way, presidents seem to become locked into a rather high number of no-win situations.

The Constitution is of little help in explaining any of this. Our founding fathers purposely were vague and left the presidency defined imprecisely. They knew well that the presidency would have to provide the capability for swift and competent executive action, yet they went to considerable lengths to avoid enumerating specific powers and duties so as to calm the then persuasive popular fear of monarchy.

In any event, the informal and symbolic powers of the presidency today account for as much as the formal ones. Further, presidential powers expand and contract in response to varying situational and technological changes. Thus, the powers of the presidency are interpreted in ways so markedly different as to seem to describe different offices. In some ways the modern presidency has virtually unlimited authority for nearly anything its occupant chooses to do with it. In other ways, however, our beliefs and hopes about the presidency very much shape the character and quality of the presidential performances we get.

The modern (post-Roosevelt II) presidency

Presented at the American Political Science Association Meetings, Chicago, Illinois, September 1–6, 1976. An earlier version of this essay appears in *Skeptic Magazine* (Sept./Oct. 1976).

is bounded and constrained by various expectations that are decidedly paradoxical. Presidents and presidential candidates must constantly balance themselves between conflicting demands. It has been suggested by more than one observer that it is a characteristic of the American mind to hold contradictory ideas simultaneously without bothering to resolve the potential conflicts between them. Perhaps some paradoxes are best left unresolved. But we should at least better appreciate what it is we expect of our presidents and would-be presidents. For it could well be that our paradoxical expectations and the imperatives of the job make for schizophrenic presidential performances.

We may not be able to resolve the inherent contradictions and dilemmas these paradoxes point up. Still, a more rigorous understanding of these conflicts and no-win or near no-win situations should encourage a more refined sensitivity to the limits of what a president can achieve. Exaggerated or hopelessly contradictory public expectations tend to encourage presidents to attempt more than they can accomplish and to overpromise and overextend themselves.

Perhaps, too, an assessment of *the paradoxed presidency* may impel us anew to revise some of our unrealistic expectations concerning presidential performance and the institution of the presidency and encourage in turn the nurturing of alternative sources or centers for national leadership.

A more realistic appreciation of presidential paradoxes might help presidents concentrate on the practicable among their priorities. A more sophisticated and tolerant consideration of the modern presidency and its paradoxes might relieve the load so that a president can better lead and administer in those critical realms in which the nation has little choice but to turn to him. Like it or not, the vitality of our democracy still depends in large measure on the sensitive interaction of presidential

leadership with an understanding public willing to listen and willing to provide support when a president can persuade. Carefully planned innovation is nearly impossible without the kind of leadership a competent and fair-minded president can provide.

Each of the paradoxes is based on apparent logical contradictions. Each has important implications for presidential performance and public evaluation of presidential behavior. A better understanding may lead to the removal, reconciliation, or more enlightened tolerance of the initial contradictions to which they give rise.

1. The paradox of the gentle and decent but forceful and decisive president. Opinion polls time and again indicate that people want a just, decent, humane "man of good faith" in the White House. Honesty and trustworthiness repeatedly top the list of qualities the public values most highly in a president these days. However, the public just as strongly demands the qualities of toughness, decisiveness, even a touch of ruthlessness.

Adlai Stevenson, George McGovern and Gerald Ford were all criticized for being "too nice," "too decent." (Ford's decisive action in the Mayaguez affair was an exception—and perhaps predictably his most significant gain in the Gallop Poll—11 points—came during and immediately after this episode.) Being a "Mr. Nice Guy" is too easily equated with being too soft. The public dislikes the idea of a weak, spineless or sentimental person in the White House.

Morris Udall, who was widely viewed as a decidedly decent candidate in the 1976 race for the Democratic nomination, had to advertise himself as a man of strength. He used a quote from House Majority Leader Thomas P. O'Neill in full-page newspaper ads which read: "We need a Democratic president who's tough enough to take on big business." "Mo Udall is tough." The image sought was unquestionably that of toughness of character.

Perhaps, too, this paradox may explain the unusual extraordinary public fondness for President Eisenhower. For he was at one and the same time blessed with a benign smile and reserved, calming disposition and yet he also was the disciplined, strong, no-nonsense five-star general with all the medals and victories to go along with it. His ultimate resource as president was this reconciliation of decency and decisiveness, likeability alongside demonstrated valor.

During the 1976 presidential campaign, Jimmy Carter appeared to appreciate one of the significant byproducts of this paradox. He noted that the American male is handicapped in his expressions of religious faith by those requisite "macho" qualities—overt strength, toughness and firmness.

Carter's personal reconciliation of this paradox is noteworthy: "But a truer demonstration of strength would be concern, compassion, love, devotion, sensitivity, humility—exactly the things Christ talked about—and I believe that if we can demonstrate this kind of personal awareness of our own faith we can provide that core of strength and commitment and underlying character that our nation searches for."

Thus this paradox highlights one of the distinctive frustrations for presidents and would-be presidents. Plainly, we demand a double-edged personality. We in effect demand the *sinister* as well as the *sincere*, President *Mean* and President *Nice;* tough and hard enough to stand up to a Khrushchev or to press the nuclear button, compassionate enough to care for the ill-fed, ill-clad, ill-housed. The public in this case seems to want a soft-hearted son of a bitch. It's a hard role to cast; a harder role to perform for eight years.

2. *The paradox of the programmatic but pragmatic leader.* We want both a *programmatic* (i.e., committed on the issues and with a detailed program) and a *pragmatic* (i.e., flexible and open, even changeable) person in the White House. We want a *moral* leader yet the job forces the president to become a *constant compromiser.*

On the one hand, Franklin Roosevelt proclaimed that the presidency is preeminently a place for moral leadership. On the other hand, Governor Jerry Brown aptly notes that "a little vagueness goes a long way in this business."

A president who becomes too committed risks being called rigid; a president who becomes too pragmatic risks becoming called wishy-washy. The secret, of course, is to stay the course by stressing character, competence, rectitude and experience, and by avoiding strong stands that offend important segments in the population.

Jimmy Carter was especially criticized by the press and others for avoiding commitments and stressing his "flexibility" on the issues. This prompted a major discussion of what became called the "fuzziness issue." Jokes spread the complaint. One went as follows: "When you eat peanut butter all your life, your tongue sticks to the roof of your mouth, and you have to talk out of both sides." Still, his "maybe I will and maybe I won't" strategy proved very effective in overcoming critics and opponents who early on claimed he didn't have a chance. Carter talked quietly about the issues and carried a big smile. In fact, of course, he took stands on almost all the issues, but being a centrist or a pragmatic moderate his stands were either not liked or dismissed as non-stands by liberals and conservatives.

What strikes one person as fuzziness or even duplicity appeals to another person as remarkable political skill, the very capacity for compromise and negotiation that is required if a president is to maneuver through the political minefields that come with the job.

Most candidates view a campaign as a

fight to win office, not an opportunity for adult education. Barry Goldwater in 1964 may have run with the slogan "We offer a *choice* not an echo" referring to his unusually thematic strategy, but Republican party regulars, who, more pragmatically, aspired to win the election preferred "a *chance* not a *choice*." Once in office, presidents often operate the same way; the electoral connection looms large as an issue-avoiding, controversy-ducking political incentive. Most presidents also strive to *maximize their options*, and hence leave matters up in the air or delay choices. J.F.K. mastered this strategy, while on Vietnam L.B.J. permitted himself to be trapped into his tragically irreparable corner because his options had so swiftly dissolved. Indeed this yearning to maximize their options may well be the core element of the pragmatism we so often see when we prefer moral leadership.

3. The paradox of an innovative and inventive yet majoritarian and responsive presidency.

One of the most compelling paradoxes at the very heart of our democratic system arises from the fact that we expect our presidents to provide bold, innovative leadership and yet respond faithfully to public opinion majorities.

Walter Lippmann warned against letting public opinion become the chief guide to leadership in America, but he just as forcefully warned democratic leaders: Don't be right too soon, for public opinion will lacerate you! Hence, most presidents fear being in advance of their times. They must *lead us*, but also *listen to us*.

Put simply, we want our presidents to offer leadership, to be architects of the future, providers of visions, plans and goals, and at the same time we want them to stay in close touch with the sentiments of the people. To *talk* about high ideals, New Deals, Big Deals and the like is one thing. But the public resists being *led* too far in any one direction.

Most of our presidents have been conserva-

tives or at best "pragmatic liberals." They have seldom ventured much beyond the crowd. John Kennedy, the author of the much acclaimed *Profiles in Courage*, was often criticized for presenting more profile than courage; if political risks could be avoided, he shrewdly avoided them. Kennedy was fond of pointing out that he had barely won election in 1960 and that great innovations should not be forced upon a leader with such a slender mandate. Ironically, Kennedy is credited with encouraging widespread public participation in politics. But he repeatedly reminded Americans that caution was needed, that the important issues are complicated and technical, and best left to the administrative and political experts. As Bruce Miroff writes in his *Pragmatic Illusions*, Kennedy seldom attempted to change the political context in which he operated:

More significantly, he resisted the new form of politics emerging with the civil rights movement: mass action, argument on social fundamentals, appeals to considerations of justice and morality. Moving the American political system in such a direction would necessarily have been long range, requiring arduous educational work and promising substantial political risk. The pragmatic Kennedy wanted no part of such an unpragmatic undertaking.

Presidents can get caught whether they are coming or going. The public wants them to be both *leaders* of the country and *representatives* of the people. We want them to be decisive and rely mainly on their own judgment, yet we want them to be very responsive to public opinion, especially to the "common sense" of our own opinions. It was perhaps with this in mind that an English essayist once defined the ideal democratic leader as "an uncommon man of common opinions."

4. The paradox of the inspirational but don't-promise-more-than-you-can-deliver leader.

We ask our presidents to raise hopes, to educate us, to inspire. But too much inspiration will invariably lead to dashed hopes, disillusion and cynicism. The best of leaders often suffers from one of their chief virtues—an instinctive tendency to raise aspirations, to summon us to transcend personal needs and subordinate ourselves to dreaming dreams of a bolder, more majestic America.

We enjoy the upbeat rhetoric and promises of a brighter tomorrow. We genuinely want to hear about New Nationalism, New Deals, New Frontiers, Great Societies, and New American Revolutions; we want our fears to be assuaged during "fireside chats" or "a conversation with the president," to be told that "the torch has been passed to a new generation of Americans . . . and the glow from that fire can truly light the world."

We want our fearless leaders to tell us that "peace is at hand," that the "only fear we have to fear is fear itself," that "we are Number One," that a recession has "bottomed out" and that "we are a great people." So much do we want the "drive of a lifting dream," to use Mr. Nixon's trite phrase, that the American people are easily duped by presidential promises.

Do presidents overpromise because they are congenital optimists or because they are pushed into it by the demanding public? Surely it is an admixture of both. But whatever the source, few presidents in recent times were able to keep their promises and fulfill their intentions. Poverty was not ended, a Great Society was not realized. Vietnam dragged on and on. Watergate outraged a public that had been promised an open presidency. Energy independence remains an illusion just as crime in the streets continues to rise.

A president who does not raise hopes is criticized as letting events shape his presidency, rather than making things happen. A president who eschewed inspiration of any kind would be rejected as un-American. For as a poet once wrote, "America is promises." For people everywhere cherishing the dream of individual liberty and self-fulfillment, America has been the land of promises, of possibilities, of dreams. No president can stand in the way of this truth, no matter how much the current dissatisfaction about the size of big government in Washington, and its incapacity to deliver the services it promises.

William Allen White, the conservative columnist, went to the heart of this paradox when he wrote of Herbert Hoover. President Hoover, he noted, is a great executive, a splendid desk man. "But he cannot dramatize his leadership. A democracy cannot follow a leader unless he is dramatized."

5. The paradox of the open and sharing but courageous and independent presidency. We unquestionably cherish our three-branched system with its checks and balances and its theories of dispersed and separated powers. We want our presidents not only to be sincere but to share their powers with their cabinet, the Congress and other "responsible" national leaders. In theory, we oppose the concentration of power, we dislike secrecy and we resent depending on any one person to provide for all our leadership. In more recent years (the 1970's in particular) there have been repeated calls for a more open, accountable and deroyalized presidency.

The other side of the coin, however, rejects a too secularized presidency. It rejects as well the idea that complete openness is a solution; indeed it suggests instead that the great presidents have been the strong presidents, who stretched their legal authority, who occasionally relied on the convenience of secrecy and who dominated the other branches of government. This point of view argues that the country in fact often yearns for a hero in the White House, that the human heart ceaselessly reinvents royalty, and that Roosevelts and Camelots, participatory democracy notwithstanding, are vital to the success of America.

If some people feel we are getting to the point where all of us would like to see a de-mythologized presidency, others claim we need myth, we need symbol. As a friend of mine put it: "I don't think we could live without the myth of a glorified presidency, even if we wanted to. We just aren't that rational. Happily, we're too human for that. We will either live by the myth that has served us fairly well for almost two hundred years, or we will probably find a much worse one."

The clamor for a truly open or collegial presidency was opposed on other grounds by the late Harold Laski when he concluded that Americans in practice want to rally round a president who can demonstrate his independence and vigor:

A president who is believed not to make up his own mind rapidly loses the power to maintain the hold. The need to dramatize his position by insistence upon his undoubted supremacy is inherent in the office as history has shaped it. A masterful man in the White House will, under all circumstances be more to the liking of the multitude than one who is thought to be swayed by his colleagues.

Thus it is that we want our president not only to be both a lion and a fox, but more than a lion, more than a fox. We want simultaneously a secular leader and a civil religious mentor; we praise our three branched system but we place capacious hopes upon and thus elevate the presidential branch. Only the president can give us heroic leadership, or so most people feel. Only a president can dramatize and symbolize our highest expectations of ourselves as an almost chosen people with a unique mission. Note too that only the president is regularly honored with a musical anthem of his own: "Hail to the Chief." If it seems a little hypocritical for a semi-sovereign people to delegate so much hierarchical defer-

ence and semi-autocratic power to their president, this is nonetheless precisely what we continually do.

We want an open presidency and we oppose the concentration of vast power in any one position. Still, we want forceful, courageous displays of leadership from our presidents. Anything less than that is condemned as aimlessness or loss of nerve. Further, we praise those who leave the presidency stronger than it was when they entered.

6. The taking-the-presidency-out-of-politics paradox. The public yearns for a statesman in the White House, for a George Washington or a second "era of good feelings": anything that might prevent partisanship of politics-as-usual in the White House. In fact, however, the job of a president demands a president to be a gifted political broker, ever-attentive to changing political moods and coalitions.

Franklin Roosevelt illustrates well this paradox. Appearing so remarkably nonpartisan while addressing the nation, he was in practice one of the craftiest political coalition builders to occupy the White House. He mastered the art of politics—the art of making the difficult and desirable possible.

A president is expected to be above politics in some respects and highly political in others. A president is never supposed to act with his eye on the next election; he's not supposed to favor any particular group or party. Nor is he supposed to wheel and to deal or twist too many arms. That's politics and that's bad! No, a president, or so most people are inclined to believe, is supposed to be "president of all the people." On the other hand, he is asked to be the head of his party, to help friendly members of Congress get elected or reelected, to deal firmly with party barons and congressional political brokers. Too, he must build political coalitions around what he feels needs to be done.

To take the president out of politics is to

assume, incorrectly, that a president will be so generally right and the general public so generally wrong that a president must be protected from the push and shove of political pressures. But what president has always been right? Over the years, public opinion has been usually as sober a guide as anyone else on the political waterfront. Anyway, having a president constrained and informed by public opinion is what a democracy is all about.

In his reelection campaign of 1972, Richard Nixon in vain sought to reveal himself outwardly as too busy to be a politician: he wanted the American people to believe he was too preoccupied with the Vietnam War to have any personal concern about his election. In one sense, Mr. Nixon may have destroyed this paradox for at least a while. Have not the American people learned that we *cannot* have a president *above* politics?

If past is prologue, presidents in the future will go to considerable lengths to portray themselves as unconcerned with their own political future. They will do so in large part because the public applauds the divorce between presidency and politics. People naively think that we can somehow turn the job of president into that of a managerial or strictly executive post. (The six-year single term proposal reflects this paradox.) Not so. The presidency is a highly political office, and it cannot be otherwise. Moreover, its political character is for the most part desirable. A president separated from or somehow above politics might easily become a president who doesn't listen to the people, doesn't respond to majority sentiment or pay attention to views that may be diverse, intense and at variance with his own. A president immunized from politics would be a president who would too easily become isolated from the processes of government and too removed from the thoughts and aspirations of his people.

In all probability, this paradox will be an enduring one. The standard diagnosis of what's gone wrong in an administration will be that the presidency has become too politicized. But it will be futile to try to take the president out of politics. A more helpful approach is to realize that certain presidents try too hard to hold themselves above politics—or at least to give that appearance—rather than engaging in it deeply, openly and creatively enough. A president in a democracy has to act politically in regard to controversial issues if we are to have any semblance of government by the consent of the governed.

7. *The paradox of the common man who gives an uncommon performance.*   We like to think that America is the land where the common sense of the common man reigns. We prize the common touch, the "man of the people." Yet few of us settles for anything but an uncommon performance from our presidents.

This paradox is splendidly summed up by some findings of a survey conducted by Field Research Corp., the California public opinion organization. Field asked a cross section of Californians in 1975 to describe in their own words the qualities a presidential candidate should or should not have. Honesty and trustworthiness topped the list. But one of his more intriguing findings was that "while most (72%) prefer someone with plain and simple tastes, there is also a strong preference (66%) for someone who can give exciting speeches and inspire the public."

It has been said that the American people crave to be governed by men who are both Everyman and yet better than Everyman. The Lincoln and Kennedy presidencies are illustrative. We might cherish the myth that anyone can grow up to be president, that there are no barriers, no elite qualifications. But the nation doesn't want a person who is too ordinary. Would-be presidents have to prove their special qualifications—their excellence, their stamina, their capacity for uncommon leadership.

The Harry Truman reputation, at least as it flourished in the mid 1970's, demonstrates the apparent reconciliation of this paradox. Fellow-commoner Truman rose to the demands of the job and became an apparent gifted decision-maker, or so his admirers would have us believe.

Candidate Carter in 1976 nicely fit this paradox as well. Local, down-home, farm boy next door, makes good! The image of the peanut farmer turned gifted governor and talented campaigner contributed greatly to Carter's success as a national candidate, and he used it with consummate skill. Early on in his presidential bid Carter enjoyed introducing himself as a peanut farmer *and* a nuclear physicist—yet another way of suggesting he was down-to-earth and yet cerebral as well.

A president or would-be president must be bright, but not too bright; warm and accessible, but not too folksy; down to earth, but not pedestrian. Adlai Stevenson was witty and clever, but these are talents that seldom pay in politics. Voters prefer plainness and solemn platitudes, but these too can be overdone. Thus, Ford's talks, no matter what the occasion, dulled our senses with the banal. Both suffered because of this paradox. The "Catch 22" here, of course, is that the very fact of an uncommon performance puts distance between a president and the truly common man. We persist, however, in wanting both at the same time.

8. *The national unifier/national divider paradox.* One of the paradoxes most difficult to alleviate arises from our longing simultaneously for a president who will pull us together again and yet be a forceful priority setter, budget manager and executive leader. The two tasks are near opposites.

We remain one of the few nations in the world that calls upon our chief executive also to serve as our symbolic, ceremonial head of state. Elsewhere these tasks are spread around.

In some nations there is a monarch *and* a prime minister; in other nations there are three visible national leaders—the head of state, a premier, and a powerful party head.

In the absence of an alternative, we demand that our presidents and our presidency act as a unifying force in our lives. Perhaps it all began with George Washington who so artfully performed this function. At least for a while he truly was above politics and a near unique symbol of our new nation. He was a healer, a unifier and an extraordinary man for all seasons. Today we ask no less of our presidents than that they should do as Washington did.

However, we have designed a presidential job description that impels our contemporary presidents to act as national dividers. They necessarily divide when they act as the leader of their political party; when they set priorities that advantage certain goals and groups at the expense of others; when they forge and lead political coalitions; when they move out ahead of public opinion and assume the role of national educator; when choosing one set of advisors over another. A president, as creative leader, cannot help but offend certain interests. When Franklin Roosevelt was running for a second term some garment workers unfolded a great sign that said, "We love him for the enemies he has made." Such is the fate of a president on an everyday basis; if he chooses to use power he usually will lose the good will of those who preferred inaction over action. The opposite is of course true if he chooses not to act.

Look at it from another angle. The nation is torn between the view that a president should primarily preside over the nation and merely serve as a referee among the various powerful interests that actually control who gets what, when and how and a second position which holds that a president should gain control of governmental processes and powers so as to use them for the purpose of furthering public, as opposed to private interests. Obviously the position that one takes on this question is relevant to how you value the presidency and the kind of person you'd like to see in the job.

Harry Truman said it very simply. He noted there are fourteen or fifteen million Americans who have the resources to have representatives in Washington to protect their interests, and that the interests of the great mass of other people, the hundred and sixty million or so others, is the responsibility of the President of the United States.

Put another way, the presidency is sometimes seen as the great defender of the people, the ombudsman or advocate-general of "public interests." Yet it is sometimes also (and sometimes at the same time) viewed as hostile to the people, isolated from them, wary of them, antagonistic, as inherently the enemy.

This debate notwithstanding, however, Americans prize the presidency as a grand American invention. As a nation we do not want to change it. Proposals to weaken it are dismissed. Proposals to reform or restructure it are paid little respect. If we sour on a president the conventional solution has been to find and elect someone else whom we hope will be better.

9. *The longer he is there the less we like him paradox.* Every four years we pick a president and for the next four years we pick on him, at him, and sometimes pick him entirely apart. There is no adequate pre-presidential job experience, so much of the first term is an on-the-job learning experience. But we resent this. It is too important a job for on-the-job learning, or at least that's how most of us feel.

Too, we expect presidents to grow in office and to become better acclimated to the office. But the longer they are in office, the more they find themselves with more crises and less public support. There is an aprocryphal presidential lament which goes as follows: "Every

time I seem to grow into the job, it gets bigger."

Simply stated, the more we know of a president, or the more we observe his presidency, the less we approve of him. Familiarity breeds discontent. Research on public support of presidents indicates that presidential approval peaks soon after a president takes office, and then slides downward at a declining rate over time until it reaches a point in the latter half of the four-year term, when it bottoms out. Thereafter it rises a bit, but never attains its original levels. Why this pattern of declining support afflicts presidents is a subject of debate among social scientists. Unrealistic early expectations are of course a major factor. These unrealistic expectations ensure a period of disenchantment.

Peace and prosperity, of course, can help stem the unpleasant tide of ingratitude, and the Eisenhower popularity remained reasonably high in large part because of his (or the nation's) achievements in these areas. For other presidents, however, their eventual downsliding popularity is due nearly as much to the public's inflated expectations as to a president's actions. It is often as if their downslide in popularity would occur no matter what the president did. If this seems unfair, even cruel, this is nonetheless what happens to those skilled and lucky enough to win election to the highest office in the land.

And all this occurs despite our conventional wisdom that the *office makes the man:* "that the presidency with its built-in educational processes, its spacious view of the world, its command of talent, and above all its self-conscious historic role, does work its way on the man in the Oval Office," as James MacGregor Burns put it. If we concede that the office in part does make the man, we must admit also that time in office often unmakes the man.

10. *The what it takes to become president may not be what is needed to govern the na-*

tion paradox. To win a presidential election it takes ambition, ambiguity, luck, and masterful public relations strategies. To govern the nation plainly requires all of these, but far more as well. It may well be that too much ambition, too much ambiguity and too heavy a reliance on phony public relations tricks actually undermine the integrity and legitimacy of the presidency.

Columnist David Broder offers an apt example: "People who win primaries may become good Presidents—but 'it ain't necessarily so.' Organizing well is important in governing just as it is in winning primaries. But the Nixon years should teach us that good advance men do not necessarily make trustworthy White House aides. Establishing a government is a little more complicated than having the motorcade run on time."

Likewise, ambition (in very heavy doses) is essential for a presidential candidate, but too much hunger of the office or for "success-at-any-price" is a danger to be avoided. He must be bold and energetic, but carried too far this can make him cold and frenetic. To win the presidency obviously requires a single-mindedness of purpose, and yet we want our presidents to be well rounded, to have a sense of humor, to be able to take a joke, to have hobbies and interests outside the realm of politics—in short to have a sense of proportion.

Another aspect of this paradox can be seen in the way candidates take ambiguous positions on issues in order to increase their appeal to the large bulk of centrist and independent voters. Not only does such equivocation discourage rational choices by the voters, but it also may alienate people who later learn, after the candidate has won, that his views and policies are otherwise. LBJ's "We will not send American boys to fight the war that Asian boys should be fighting," and Richard Nixon's "open presidency" pledges come readily to mind. Their pre-presidential stands were later violated or ignored.

Political scientist Samuel Huntington calls attention to yet another way this paradox works. To be a winning candidate, he notes, the would-be president must put together an *electoral coalition* involving a majority of voters appropriately distributed across the country. To do this he must appeal to all regions and interest groups and cultivate the appearance of honesty, sincerity and experience. But once elected, the electoral coalition has served its purpose and a *governing coalition* is the order of the day. This all may sound rather elitist, but Harvard Professor Huntington insists that this is what has to be:

The day after his election the size of his majority is almost—if not entirely—irrelevant to his ability to govern the country. What counts then is his ability to mobilize support from the leaders of the key institutions in society and government. He has to constitute a broad governing coalition of strategically located supporters who can furnish him with the information, talent, expertise, manpower, publicity, arguments, and political support which he needs to develop a program, to embody it in legislation, and to see it effectively implemented. This coalition must include key people in Congress, the executive branch, and the private-sector "Establishment." The governing coalition need have little relation to the electoral coalition. The fact that the President as a candidate put together a successful electoral coalition does not insure that he will have a viable governing coalition.

Presidential candidate Adlai Stevenson had another way of saying it in 1956. He said he had "learned that the hardest thing about any political campaign is how to win without proving that you are unworthy of winning." The process of becoming president is an extraordinarily taxing one that defies description. It involves, among other things, an unending salesmanship job on television.

Candidates plainly depend upon television to transform candidacy into incumbency. Research findings point out that candidates spend well over half their funds on broadcasting.

Moreover, this is how the people "learn" about the candidates. Approximately two-thirds of the public report that television is the best way for them to follow candidates and about half of the American public acknowledge they got their best understanding of the candidates and issues from television coverage.

Thus, television is obviously the key. But the candidate has to travel to every state and hundreds of cities for at least a four-year period to capture the exposure and the local headlines before earning the visibility and stature of a "serious candidate." For the most part, it becomes a grueling and gasping ordeal, as well as a major learning experience. In quest of the Democratic nomination for president Walter F. Mondale of Minnesota spent most of 1974 traveling some 200,000 miles, delivering hundreds of speeches, appearing on countless radio and television talk shows, and sleeping in Holiday Inn after Holiday Inn all across the country. He admits that he enjoyed much of it, but says, too, that he seldom had time to read or to reflect, not to mention having time for a sane family life. Eventually he withdrew on the grounds that he simply had neither the overwhelming desire nor the time to do what was necessary in order to win the nomination.

Mondale's was not a sufficiently power-hungry ambition, witness his remarks:

I love to ponder ideas, to reflect on them and discuss them with experts and friends over a period of time, but this was no longer possible. It struck me as being unfortunate and even tragic that the process of seeking the Presidency too often prevents one from focusing on the issues and insights and one's ability to express them, which are crucially important. I believe this fact explains many of the second-rate statements and much of the irrational posturing that are frequently associated with Presidential campaigns. In any case, after eighteen months I decided this wasn't for me. It wasn't my style and I wasn't going to pretend that it was. Instead of controlling events in my life, I was more and more controlled

by them. Others have had an easier time adapting to this process than I did, and I admire them for it. But one former candidate told me, three years after his campaign had ended, that he *still* hadn't fully recovered emotionally or physically from the ordeal.

What it takes *to become* president may differ from what it takes *to be* president. It takes a near-megalomaniac who is also glib, dynamic, charming on television and hazy on the issues. Yet we want our presidents to be well-rounded, not overly ambitious, careful in their reasoning and clear and specific in their communications. It may well be that our existing primary and convention system adds up to an effective testing or obstacle course for would-be presidents. Certainly they have to travel to all sections of the country, meet the people, deal with interest group elites and learn about the bracing issues of the day. But with the Johnson and Nixon experiences in our not-too-distant past, we have reason for asking whether our system of producing presidents is adequately reconciled with what is required to produce a president who is competent, fair-minded, and emotionally healthy.

CONCLUSIONS

Perhaps the ultimate paradox of the modern presidency is that it is always too powerful and yet it is always too inadequate. Always too powerful because it is contrary to our ideals of a government by the people and always too powerful as well because it must now possess the capacity to wage nuclear war (a capacity that unfortunately doesn't permit much in the way of checks and balances and deliberative, participatory government). Yet, always too inadequate because it seldom achieves our highest hopes for it, not to mention its own stated intentions.

The presidency is always too strong when we dislike the incumbent. On the other hand the limitations are bemoaned when we believe the incumbent is striving valiantly to serve the public interest as we define it. For many people the Johnson presidency captured this paradox vividly: many of the people who felt that he was too strong in Vietnam felt too that he was too weakly equipped to wage his war on poverty (and vice versa).

The dilemma for the attentive public is that curbing the powers of a president who abuses the public trust will usually undermine the capacity of a fair-minded president to serve the public interest. In the 187 years since Washington took office, we have multiplied the requirements for presidential leadership and we have made it increasingly more difficult to lead. Certainly this is not the time for a mindless retribution against the already fragile, precarious institution of the presidency.

Neither presidents nor the public should be relieved of their respective responsibilities of trying to fashion a more effective and fair-minded leadership system simply because these paradoxes are pointed out and even widely agreed upon. It is also not enough to throw up our hands and say: "Well, no one makes a person run for that crazy job in the first place."

The situation I have analyzed in this essay doubtless also characterizes governors, city managers, university presidents and even many corporate executives. Is it a new phenomenon or are we just becoming increasingly aware of it? Is it a permanent or a transitory condition? My own view is that it is neither new nor transitory, but more comparative and longitudinal analysis is needed before we can generalize more systematically. Meanwhile, we shall have to select as our presidents persons who understand these contrary demands and who have a gift for the improvisation that these paradoxes demand. It is important for us to ask our chief public servants to be willing occasionally to forego enhancing their own short term political fortunes for a greater good of simplifying, rather than exacerbating, the paradoxes of the presidency.

While the presidency will doubtless remain one of our nation's best vehicles for creative policy change it will also continue to be an embattled office, fraught with the cumulative weight of these paradoxes. We need urgently to probe the origins and to assess the consequences of these paradoxes and to learn how presidents and the public can better coexist with them. For it is apparent that these paradoxes serve to isolate and disconnect a president from the public. Like it or not, the growing importance of the presidency and our growing dependence on presidents seem to ensure that presidents will be less popular and increasingly the handy scapegoat when anything goes wrong.

Let us ask our presidents to give us their best, but let us not ask them to deliver more than the presidency—or any single institution —has to give.

Bibliographical Note:

Because of the essay nature of this article I have not provided footnotes, nor have I cited the considerable number of articles and books that have assisted me in its writing. Let me acknowledge here my debt to many of the more important items cited and not. Especially helpful were Arthur Schlesinger's *The Imperial Presidency* and James MacGregor Burns' *Presidential Government.* I have profited too from numerous essays written by Fred Greenstein, Michael J. Robinson, James Stimson, Rexford G. Tugwell and Aaron Wildavsky. See also, Bruce Miroff, *Pragmatic Illusions* (McKay, 1976), Henry Fairlie, *The Kennedy Promise* (Doubleday, 1973), Walter F. Mondale, *The Accountability of Power* (McKay, 1975), Harold Laski, *The American Presidency* (Harper, 1940) and Michael Novak, *Choosing Our King* (Macmillan, 1974). The writings of David Broder, James David Barber and Alexander George always inform essays such as this. See finally, Harlan Cleveland's *The Future Executive* (Harper & Row, 1972) and *The American Commonwealth, 1976* (Basic Books, 1976), especially the essays by Samuel Huntington and Aaron Wildavsky.

29

Presidential Character and How To Foresee It

James David Barber

James David Barber argues that a president's personality, as shaped by his character, world view, and political style, will affect his performance as chief executive. Presidential personalities fall into a typology of four variables: activism or passivity and postive or negative effects. Barber establishes four categories: active-positive; active-negative; passive-positive; and passive-negative. Consider-ing these types, the reader may find it interesting to play a classification game by rating presidential personalities and giving reasons for the type selected. Another key point is Barber's belief that presidential performance can be predicted. Do you agree or disagree? Also, are there differences in domestic and foreign policy that affect presidential performance?

. . . [C]rucial differences can be anticipated by an understanding of a potential President's character, his world view, and his style. This kind of prediction is not easy; well-informed observers often have guessed wrong as they watched a man step toward the White House. One thinks of Woodrow Wilson, the scholar who would bring reason to politics; of Herbert Hoover, the Great Engineer who would organize chaos into progress; of Franklin D. Roosevelt, that champion of the balanced budget; of Harry Truman, whom the office would surely overwhelm; of Dwight D. Eisenhower, militant crusader; of John F. Kennedy, who would lead beyond moralisms to achievements; of Lyndon B. Johnson, the Southern conservative; and of Richard M. Nixon, conciliator. Spotting the errors is easy. Predicting with even approximate accuracy is going to require some sharp tools and close attention in their use. But the experiment is worth it because the question is critical and because it lends itself to correction by evidence.

My argument comes in layers.

First, a President's personality is an impor-tant shaper of his Presidential behavior on nontrivial matters.

Second, Presidential personality is patterned. His character, world view, and style fit together in a dynamic package understandable in psychological terms.

Third, a President's personality interacts with the power situation he faces and the national "climate of expectations" dominant at the time he serves. The tuning, the resonance—or lack of it—between these external factors and his personality sets in motion the dynamic of his Presidency.

Fourth, the best way to predict a President's character, world view, and style is to see how they were put together in the first place. That happened in his early life, culminating in his first independent political success.

But the core of the argument . . . is that Presidential character—the basic stance a man takes toward his Presidential experience—comes in four varieties. The most important thing to know about a President or candidate is where he fits among these types, defined according to (a) how active he is and (b) whether or not he gives the impression he enjoys his political life.

Let me spell out these concepts briefly before getting down to cases.

PERSONALITY SHAPES PERFORMANCE

I am not about to argue that once you know a President's personality you know everything. But as the cases will demonstrate, the degree and quality of a President's emotional involvement in an issue are powerful influences on how he defines the issue itself, how much attention he pays to it, which facts and persons he sees as relevant to its resolution, and, finally, what principles and purposes he associates with the issue. Every story of Presidential decision-making is really two stories: an outer one in which a rational man calculates and an inner one in which an emotional man feels. The two are forever connected. Any real President is one whole man and his deeds reflect his wholeness.

As for personality, it is a matter of tendencies. It is not that one President "has" some basic characteristic that another President does not "have." That old way of treating a trait as a possession, like a rock in a basket, ignores the universality of aggressiveness, compliancy, detachment, and other human drives. We all have all of them, but in different amounts and in different combinations.

THE PATTERN OF CHARACTER, WORLD VIEW, AND STYLE

The most visible part of the pattern is style. *Style is the President's habitual way of performing his three political roles: rhetoric, personal relations, and homework.* Not to be confused with "stylishness," charisma, or appearance, style is how the President goes about doing what the office requires him to do—to speak, directly or through media, to large audiences; to deal face to face with other politicians, individually and in small, relatively private groups; and to read, write, and calculate by himself in order to manage the endless flow of details that stream onto his desk. No President can escape doing at least some of each. But there are marked differences in stylistic emphasis from President to President. The *balance* among the three style elements varies; one President may put most of himself into rhetoric, another may stress close, informal dealing, while still another may devote his energies mainly to study and cogitation. Beyond the balance, we want to see each President's peculiar habits of style, his mode of coping with and adapting to these Presidential demands. For example, I think both Calvin Coolidge and John F. Kennedy were primarily rhetoricians, but they went about it in contrasting ways.

A President's world view consists of his primary, politically relevant beliefs, particularly his conceptions of social causality, human nature, and the central moral conflicts of the time. This is how he sees the world and his lasting opinions about what he sees. Style is his way of acting; world view is his way of seeing. Like the rest of us, a President develops over a lifetime certain conceptions of reality—how things work in politics, what people are like, what the main purposes are. These assumptions or conceptions help him make sense of his world, give some semblance of order to chaos of existence. Perhaps most important: a man's world view affects what he pays attention to, and a great deal of politics is about paying attention. The name of the game for many politicians is not so much "Do this, do that" as it is "Look here!"

"Character" comes from the Greek word for engraving; in one sense it is what life has marked into a man's being. As used here, *character is the way the President orients himself toward life*—not for the moment, but enduringly. Character is the person's stance as he confronts experience. And at the core of character, a man confronts himself. The President's fundamental self-esteem is his prime personal resource; to defend and advance that, he will sacrifice much else he values. Down there in the privacy of his heart, does he find himself superb, or ordinary, or debased, or in some intermediate range? No President has been utterly paralyzed by self-doubt and none has been utterly free of midnight self-mockery. In between, the real Presidents move out on life from positions of relative strength or weakness. Equally important are the criteria by which they judge themselves. A President who rates himself by the standard of achievement, for instance, may be little affected by losses of affection.

Character, world view, and style are abstractions from the reality of the whole individual. In every case they form an integrated pattern: the man develops a combination which makes psychological sense for him, a dynamic arrangement of motives, beliefs, and habits in the service of his need for self-esteem.

THE POWER SITUATION AND "CLIMATE OF EXPECTATIONS"

Presidential character resonates with the political situation the President faces. It adapts him as he tries to adapt it. The support he has from the public and interest groups, the party balance in Congress, the thrust of Supreme Court opinion together set the basic power situation he must deal with. An activist President may run smack into a brick wall of resistance, then pull back and wait for a better moment. On the other hand, a President who sees himself as a quiet caretaker may not try to exploit even the most favorable power situation. So it is the relationship between President and the political configuration that makes the system tick.

Even before public opinion polls, the President's real or supposed popularity was a large factor in his performance. Besides the power mix in Washington, the President has to deal with a national climate of expectations, the predominant needs thrust up to him by the people. There are at least three recurrent themes around which these needs are focused.

People look to the President for *reassurance*, a feeling that things will be all right, that the President will take care of his people. The psychological request is for a surcease of anxiety. Obviously, modern life in America involves considerable doses of fear, tension, anxiety, worry; from time to time, the public mood calls for a rest, a time of peace, a breathing space, a "return to normalcy."

Another theme is the demand for a *sense of progress and action*. The President ought to do something to direct the nation's course—or at least be in there pitching for the people. The President is looked to as a take-charge man, a doer, a turner of the wheels, a producer of progress—even if that means some sacrifice of serenity.

A third type of climate of expectations is the public need for a sense of *legitimacy* from, and in, the Presidency. The President should be a master politician who is above politics. He should have a right to his place and a rightful way of acting in it. The respectability—even religiosity—of the office has to be protected by a man who presents himself as defender of the faith. There is more to this than dignity, more than propriety. The President is expected to personify our betterness in an inspiring way, to express in what he does and is (not just in what he says) a moral idealism which, in much of the public mind, is the very opposite of "politics."

Over time the climate of expectations shifts and changes. Wars, depressions, and other national events contribute to that change, but there also is a rough cycle, from an emphasis on action (which begins to look too "political") to an emphasis on legitimacy (the moral uplift of which creates its own strains) to an emphasis on reassurance and rest (which comes to seem like drift) and back to action again. One need not be astrological about it. The point is that the climate of expectations at any given time is the political air the President has to breathe. Relating to this climate is a large part of his task.

PREDICTING PRESIDENTS

The best way to predict a President's character, world view, and style is to see how he constructed them in the first place. Especially in the early stages, life is experimental; consciously or not, a person tries out various ways of defining and maintaining and raising self-esteem. He looks to his environment for clues as to who he is and how well he is doing. These lessons of life slowly sink in: certain self-images and evaluations, certain ways of looking at the world, certain styles of action get confirmed by his experience and he gradually adopts them as his own. If we can see that process of development, we can understand the product. The features to note are those bearing on Presidential performance.

Experimental development continues all the way to death; we will not blind ourselves to midlife changes, particularly in the full-scale prediction case, that of Richard Nixon. But it is often much easier to see the basic patterns in early life histories. Later on a whole host of distractions—especially the image-making all politicians learn to practice—clouds the picture.

In general, character has its *main* development in childhood, world view in adolescence, style in early adulthood. The stance toward life I call character grows out of the child's experiments in relating to parents, brothers and sisters, and peers at play and in school, as well as to his own body and the objects

around it. Slowly the child defines an orientation toward experience; once established, that tends to last despite much subsequent contradiction. By adolescence, the child has been hearing and seeing how people make their worlds meaningful, and now he is moved to relate himself—his own meanings—to those around him. His focus of attention shifts toward the future; he senses that decisions about his fate are coming and he looks into the premises for those decisions. Thoughts about the way the world works and how one might work in it, about what people are like and how one might be like them or not, and about the values people share and how one might share in them too—these are typical concerns for the post-child, pre-adult mind of the adolescent.

These themes come together strongly in early adulthood, when the person moves from contemplation to responsible action and adopts a style. In most biographical accounts this period stands out in stark clarity—the time of emergence, the time the young man found himself. I call it his first independent political success. It was then he moved beyond the detailed guidance of his family; then his self-esteem was dramatically boosted; then he came forth as a person to be reckoned with by other people. The *way* he did that is profoundly important to him. Typically he grasps that style and hangs onto it. Much later, coming into the Presidency, something in him remembers this earlier victory and re-emphasizes the style that made it happen.

Character provides the main thrust and broad direction—but it does not *determine*, in any fixed sense, world view and style. The story of development does not end with the end of childhood. Thereafter, the culture one grows in and the ways that culture is translated by parents and peers shapes the meaning one makes of his character. The going world view gets learned and that learning helps channel character forces. Thus it will not necessarily be true that compulsive characters have reactionary beliefs, or that compliant characters believe in compromise. Similarly for style: historical accidents play a large part in furnishing special opportunities for action —and in blocking off alternatives. For example, however much anger a young man may feel, that anger will not be expressed in rhetoric unless and until his life situation provides a platform and an audience. Style thus has a stature and independence of its own. Those who would reduce all explanation to character neglect these highly significant later channelings. For beyond the root is the branch, above the foundation the superstructure, and starts do not prescribe finishes.

FOUR TYPES OF PRESIDENTIAL CHARACTER

The five concepts—character, world view, style, power situation, and climate of expectations—run through the accounts of Presidents in the chapters to follow, which cluster the Presidents since Theodore Roosevelt into four types. This is the fundamental scheme of the study. It offers a way to move past the complexities to the main contrasts and comparisons.

The first baseline in defining Presidential types is *activity-passivity*. How much energy does the man invest in his Presidency? Lyndon Johnson went at his day like a human cyclone, coming to rest long after the sun went down. Calvin Coolidge often slept eleven hours a night and still needed a nap in the middle of the day. In between the Presidents array themselves on the high or low side of the activity line.

The second baseline is *positive-negative affect* toward one's activity—that is, how he feels about what he does. Relatively speaking, does he seem to experience his political life as happy or sad, enjoyable or discouraging, positive or negative in its main effect. The feeling I am after here is not grim satisfaction in a job well done, not some philosophical conclusion. The idea is this: is he someone who, on the surfaces we can see, gives forth the feeling that he has *fun* in political life? Franklin Roosevelt's Secretary of War, Henry L. Stimson wrote that the Roosevelts "not only understood the *use* of power, they knew the *enjoyment* of power, too. . . . Whether a man is burdened by power or enjoys power; whether he is trapped by responsibility or made free by it; whether he is moved by other people and outer forces or moves them—that is the essence of leadership."

The positive-negative baseline, then, is a general symptom of the fit between the man and his experience, a kind of register of *felt* satisfaction.

Why might we expect these two simple dimensions to outline the main character types? Because they stand for two central features of anyone's orientation toward life. In nearly every study of personality, some form of the active-passive contrast is critical; the general tendency to act or be acted upon is evident in such concepts as dominance-submission, extraversion-introversion, aggression-timidity, attack-defense, fight-flight, engagement-withdrawal, approach-avoidance. In everyday life we sense quickly the general energy output of the people we deal with. Similarly we catch on fairly quickly to the affect dimension— whether the person seems to be optimistic or pessimistic, hopeful or skeptical, happy or sad. The two baselines are clear and they are also independent of one another: all of us know people who are very active but seem discouraged, others who are quite passive but seem happy, and so forth. The activity baseline refers to what one does, the affect baseline to how one feels about what he does.

Both are crude clues to character. They are leads into four basic character patterns long familiar in psychological research. In summary form, these are the main configurations:

Active-positive. There is a congruence, a consistency, between much activity and the enjoyment of it, indicating relatively high self-esteem and relative success in relating to the environment. The man shows an orientation toward productiveness as a value and an ability to use his styles flexibly, adaptively, suiting the dance to the music. He sees himself as developing over time toward relatively well defined personal goals—growing toward his image of himself as he might yet be. There is an emphasis on rational mastery, on using the brain to move the feet. This may get him into trouble; he may fail to take account of the irrational in politics. Not everyone he deals with sees things his way and he may find it hard to understand why.

Active-negative. The contradiction here is between relatively intense effort and relatively low emotional reward for that effort. The activity has a compulsive quality, as if the man were trying to make up for something or to escape from anxiety into hard work. He seems ambitious, striving upward, power-seeking. His stance toward the environment is aggressive and he has a persistent problem in managing his aggressive feelings. His self-image is vague and discontinuous. Life is a hard struggle to achieve and hold power, hampered by the condemnations of a perfectionistic conscience. Active-negative types pour energy into the political system, but it is an energy distorted from within.

Passive-positive. This is the receptive, compliant, other-directed character whose life is a search for affection as a reward for being agreeable and cooperative rather than personally assertive. The contradiction is between low self-esteem (on grounds of being unlovable, unattractive) and a superficial optimism. A hopeful attitude helps dispel doubt and elicits encouragement from others. Passive-positive types help soften the harsh edges of politics. But their dependence and the fragility of their hopes and enjoyments make disappointment in politics likely.

Passive-negative. The factors are consistent—but how are we to account for the man's *political* role-taking? Why is someone who does little in politics and enjoys it less there at all? The answer lies in the passive-negative's character-rooted orientation toward doing dutiful service; this compensates for low self-esteem based on a sense of usefulness. Passive-negative types are in politics because they think they ought to be. They may be well adapted to certain nonpolitical roles, but they lack the experience and flexibility to perform effectively as political leaders. Their tendency is to withdraw, to escape from the conflict and uncertainty of politics by emphasizing vague principles (especially prohibitions) and procedural arrangements. They become guardians of the right and proper way, above the sordid politicking of lesser men.

Active-positive Presidents want most to achieve results. Active-negatives aim to get and keep power. Passive-positives are after love. Passive-negatives emphasize their civic virtue. The relation of activity to enjoyment in a President thus tends to outline a cluster of characteristics, to set apart the adapted from the compulsive, compliant, and withdrawn types.

30

Washington: An Insider's Game

John Herbers

*The federal government has a permanent bureauc-
racy of more than two million civil servants working in various departments and agencies. Although
the federal government has offices scattered
throughout the country, Washington has become
the focus of public discontent over many issues.
John Herbers indicates that many believe the federal government "tolerates inefficiencies and stifles reform." How does the Washington lifestyle
contribute to these problems? Why has the federal
government become so difficult to manage? What
is the "iron triangle"? How does this affect the
policies of the regulatory agencies? What are the
prospects for overcoming bureaucratic fragmentation?*

More than any other period of American history, the decade of the 70's is the time when
the seat of the Federal Government has become the national center for the petition of
grievances. Millions have marched here, lob-
bied here, fought pitched battles with troops
and police here, bought and extracted influence here for causes just and unjust, for private and public privilege, for a share of the
half-billion dollars a year handed out by the
Federal treasury.

And in recent years, the national Government itself has become a major source of griev-
ance. Across the country, politicians are saying
that the current tax revolt is really aimed at
Washington, which is perceived as wasteful,
indifferent and impenetrable. And they see
the move to call a constitutional convention
to require the Federal Government to keep a
balanced budget as an extension of the tax
revolt.

Albert H. Quie, the mild-mannered studious

Republican from Minnesota, served two
decades in the House of Representatives
before deciding that Washington had gotten
so out of touch with the country that he had
to get out. He returned home last year and ran
successfully for governor. The other day he
returned for a meeting of the National Governors Association and said quietly, "The
people are feeling as strongly about the Federal Government now as they did about the
King of England at the time of the Revolution."

In Washington, there are those who attribute the uprising to a middle class that has
become self-centered and cynical about government at all levels, whether good or bad.
Others say that after a quarter century of
expanding prosperity many Americans now
find the good life slipping from them and
are striking out at the largest extractor of
their taxes.

Yet a close look at Washington today makes
it hard to dismiss the argument that the national Government serves itself first, that it
tolerates inefficiencies and stifles reform.
Through prosperity, recession, war and peace,
one thing has been consistent: The Federal

apparatus centered in Washington has grown and prospered.

Washington has been unique since it was superimposed on a swamp on the Potomac a century and a half ago, a geographical compromise that assured it would be almost exclusively a Government town. A generation ago, Washington was a relaxed and plain company town with a strong Southern flavor that those on the Upper Eastern Seaboard considered a trifle boorish. Not anymore. It is now a megapolis of the well-to-do, a magnet for some of the best Ivy League graduates, a haven for tens of thousands of middle-level civil servants who enjoy the equivalent of faculty tenure and who would never do so well in the private sector.

Washington, with a metropolitan-area population of three million, consisting chiefly of the government complex and the business people who serve it, has become the per capita wealthiest of the big cities. In 1977, it had a spendable income per household of almost $23,000, or 33 percent above the national average. In this recession-proof town, the average house sells for $100,000. Here, mile after mile of fine homes stretching out to the farmlands of Virginia and Maryland are occupied by professional couples earning $60,000 to $100,000 or more a year. It is a city of the four-day weekend, or the seven-day weekend if any two days of a week are holidays.

Here, even the urban poor are made almost invisible by the influx of professionals. And while there is street crime, it is down more than in most cities, partly because the District has 20 different law-enforcement agencies on the streets, a security apparatus that would make a police state jealous.

In the last five years Washington has attracted some of the nation's most expensive shopping centers. It is the nation's leading market for new cars, especially classy imports. All of this, some say, has bred insensitivity to the needs of the rest of the nation that supplies all the wealth.

By now, many Americans believe that the Washington apparatus has a life of its own, that it does not matter who is President or who gets elected to Congress or which party is in or out of power. Washington has its own way of absorbing invaders and malcontents.

The new chairman of the Federal Communications Commission ordered his employees to change their work hours—9:30 to 5:30 instead of 8:30 to 4:30—so that people on the West Coast would not find the office closed at 1:30 P.M. their time. The order raised such a howl that it was redrawn to include only new employees.

A few years ago, John McLaughlin, then a Jesuit priest, came to Washington as an anti-Washington-establishment speechwriter for Richard Nixon (he became known as one of Mr. Nixon's ardent defenders during the Watergate scandal). Today, he is a prosperous consultant to business corporations, advising them on what is likely to happen on such questions as the limitation of strategic arms, environmental enforcement and bottle disposal.

A Republican administration, it was once believed, is good for reforming, trimming and reorganizing innovations put in place by impractical Democrats. During the eight years of the Nixon and Ford Administrations, high officials brought in to *do something* about government traveled the country, as did the two Presidents, decrying Washington bigness and interference and preaching decentralization. Yet during that period Federal regulation took a quantum jump, and layer after layer of bureaucracy and confusion was added.

In his first term, Mr. Nixon yielded to political pressures in order to get elected to a second, and thus he went along with new programs and regulations enacted by the Democratic Congress. In his second term, Mr. Nixon sought to gain control of the Government through a centralization that included the placing of political appointees in permanent positions in the civil service.

Jimmy Carter himself ran for President on an anti-Washington platform. Now, he too has been impaled. His reorganization team wanted to combine many of the programs that overlap and cause confusion—in the urban and economic-development areas, for example. But interest groups from mayors to business leaders registered so much opposition that the plan never got out of the White House.

Mr. Carter's zero-based budgeting, which will make every agency justify its existence from the beginning—is virtually forgotten. His budget restraints are aimed at controllable domestic items, not at throwing out programs that do not work. He learned his lesson when his attempt to stop construction of dubious water projects angered much of the West.

And Mr. Carter's attempts at reforming the civil service have fared no better. After years of shoring up one kind of protection or another for Government workers, the civil-service bureaucracy has made it virtually impossible to fire incompetents. When he first took office, Mr. Carter waded into this quagmire like a marine fresh out of boot camp, but he soon found himself up against employee unions, the sizable constituency of the Washington area, and court decisions which have held that Government jobs cannot be denied without due process. The result of Mr. Carter's efforts at reform has been a series of compromises that still leave a formidable array of procedures that will have to be exhausted before an incompetent can be fired. Time is on the side of the Government worker; the civil service has a way of waiting out and wearing down every reform effort.

Some have referred to the Washington of today as Versailles-on-the-Potomac. But this does not quite fit, not when members of the court—those closest to the President—work 15 hours a day. Others see only the corrupting influence of power. An axiom in the newspaper business has it that any good reporter on any day in any city can go out and get a story on corruption and misuse of funds in the General Services Administration or the Comprehensive Employment and Training Act programs, to name two Federal functions that have become notorious for their corruption in the lower ranks.

The corruption, some say, is an inevitable offshoot of modern politics—with its single-issues interest groups all operating independently of one another; fragmentation of authority in the Congress; the runaway financing of Congressional campaigns by special interests; the decline in public confidence in government.

The Washington of today might more aptly be described as a medieval fair, with all manner of people doing their juggling acts, bartering, agitating, cajoling, preaching, stealing. By now everyone has gotten the word: If you are going to accomplish anything in this country, you must go to Washington and set up a booth. It is everyone for himself. It can be great fun for the participants, but don't expect those left in Peoria to understand what is going on.

In effect, there are now—as there have been since the late 1960's—two governments. The government of the Eisenhower era remains, with its center in the White House. There, in concert with Congress, the President can control to some degree foreign policy, the Pentagon and the Federal budget. He can do things like decree more aid to the South Bronx. He can wheel and deal with Congress on public works, water projects, highway construction. He can make his policies felt through appointments. Americans understand this government and know that certain excesses in politics and the bureaucracy are to be expected. This government can be controlled, after a fashion, by the democratic processes.

It is the other, more complex government which is not only out of control but which has been superimposed over the older government. This second government is one owned not by the public but piece by piece by interest groups—mayors, veterans, homebuilders, poor people, rich people, the handicapped, police chiefs, farmers, the auto industry, the elderly, truckers, or by people purporting to represent them. It is not a new phenomenon, but what was once a mouse is now an elephant.

This government has no center. Instead— in a democracy gone rampant—a multitude of groups clamor for a positive response from the Federal Government. Neither the President nor the leadership of Congress in recent years has found a way to get control of the second government, to strengthen what is good, weed out what is bad and make priorities that are in the national interest. This government is too large and diverse to be publicly understood. Even in Washington, no one knows and understands all of it, only pieces of it.

The second government is made up in part by a plethora of regulatory agencies. Eighteen of these, mostly the oldline ones, such as the Interstate Commerce Commission, are independent by law. Congress created them and the President appoints their members. Each was established to protect the people, but the tendency has been for the interest under regulation to gain control of the agency so that the special interest, rather than the public, is protected. At present, there are about 72 other regulatory agencies in the executive branch. New ones include the National Highway Traffic Safety Administration (in the Department of Transportation), and the Occupational Safety and Health Administration, or OSHA (in the Labor Department).

President Carter, besides offering overall regulatory-reform legislation, is trying to gain control of those 60 agencies nominally under his command. After all, somebody has to decide between competing goals—between jobs and clean water, for example, or inflation and more energy. Whether the President can stand outside the fray to be an effective arbiter of what is best for the country is another matter. The A.F.L.-C.I.O. has taken the Administration to court in a case involving, among other factors, White House efforts to delay an order by OSHA to establish a lower level of lint in textile plants. OSHA is interested in workers' health; the White House, in worker safety as well as the inflationary impact of such an order. And the issue of control is not likely to be settled soon. Lloyd N. Cutler, a lawyer and member of the American Bar Association's Commission on Law and the Economy, said in regard to regulatory government: "Where Harry Truman was fond of saying, 'The buck stops here,' they [the interest groups] prefer a system in which the buck stops nowhere."

A larger part of the second government is composed of about 500 separate grants-in-aid programs, most of them enacted by the Congress in the years since 1965. Each was designed and funded to serve a particular purpose, usually at the urging of some group, but these programs frequently overlap and clash against each other. The town of Junior, W. Va., has spent five years trying to satisfy the conflicting demands of six Federal agencies involved in its effort to build a sewage treatment plant.

The programs are easy to start but almost impossible to eliminate because each develops a strong constituency. When Attorney General Griffin Bell first came to Washington, he took one look at the Law Enforcement Assistance Administration—which has handed out billions to police departments without making much impact on crime—and decided the agency had served its purpose and had to go. But the L.E.A.A. is still alive and well; the Carter Administration decided it did not need to have all the police chiefs, sheriffs and mayors in the country on its neck.

Furthermore, the programs—for oversight and enabling legislation—are spread among an almost equal number of committees and subcommittees. Any interest strong enough to form a substantial lobby, says Representative David R. Obey, Democrat of Wisconsin and head of a committee that tried to correct some of the fragmentation in the House, can find a port of entry into the Government by attaching itself to a subcommittee.

Congress is a land of many entrances but few exits. If a group is blocked at the entrance, such as that supporting a consumer-protection agency, it is because the lobby against it—in this case, the business lobby—is stronger than the lobby for it.

By and large, Government officials are sincere about the programs they oversee and view them as providing needed services. When there is evidence that the programs do not work—such as the seeming inability of a succession of job programs to make a dent on the unemployment rates for young people, particularly minorities—they are brought in for fine tuning. What this usually means, observed Richard W. Boone, acting director of the Field Foundation, a public-interest group in New York, is the "adding of more technical assistance personnel so that we have an enormous army of middle-management people who are supposed to be the bridges between the Federal system and the needs of poor people."

This is true of a number of other programs as well, and the personnel added are not always Federal employees. Many programs are run and maintained by "the iron triangle," a term given currency a couple of years ago by Daniel Evans, then Governor of Washing-

ton, who complained that no elected official outside the District of Columbia could penetrate it. An oversimplified definition is that the three sides are made up of (1) the staffs of the Congressional committees involved, (2) that section of the Federal bureaucracy charged with administering the program and (3) the lobby supporting the program. Revolving doors may connect the three sides with professionals moving freely back and forth.

Triangles gain control because they write the laws and the regulations, and they run the programs. Members of Congress, the argument goes, cannot give much time to the details because they are too busy acting as ombudsmen for their constituents—that is, defending them from the alleged abuses of other triangles, or seeking services or grants for them. Neither can the White House staff intervene to any degree. There is too much going on for the political appointees, who come in born yesterday with each administration, to follow. Even the Office of Management and Budget, whose 600 or so professionals serve as the President's watchdogs over the entire Government, has only limited effect on what the triangles achieve.

Triangles come in all shapes and sizes. The veterans triangle is an old one made of the finest of carbon steel. Nobody messes around for long with this triangle. Over the years, it has been able to maintain a steadily growing separate structure of welfare, social and medical services for veterans, and it displayed its strength again last year by defeating President Carter's plan to end veterans' preference for Government jobs except for those discharged in the past few years.

Triangles require more staff. There never seem to be enough Government buildings for the executive branch and appendages—consultants, lawyers, journalists, newsletter writers, think tanks, lobbyists, copying machines by the carloads. And the Senate is erecting its third office building—at a cost of $135 million, according to the latest estimate.

What is happening in Washington is a fragmentation that feeds defensiveness. Almost every elected official in Washington from the President on down is an independent, the end result of the steady decline in the party system. The White House has to put together a different coalition for every issue, and frequently it is as dependent on Republicans as Democrats to win a vote. The city is abloom with hundreds of new interest groups, each seeking its own narrow purpose. In the District of Columbia Telephone book there are more than 200 listings under "National Association": the National Association of Distributive Education Teachers; the National Association of Independent Insurers; the National Association of Mature People; the National Association of Margarine Manufacturers. . . .

Many industries, cities and states send agents to Washington purely for defensive purposes—to see that they are not short-changed in the great push for money and favorable regulation. Substantial political organizations have grown up around single, narrow issues: anti gun control vs. pro gun control; anti abortion vs. pro choice.

The 357,000 or so civil servants who labor in the labyrinths of Government buildings have been pulled and tugged, too, and have become defensive in the process. Government service is a land of extremes. Political appointees and the highest grades of the civil service work much harder and for longer hours than their counterparts in the private sector. The 7-to-11 day is nothing unusual, with week-end work as well. However, a number of officials estimate that about 10 percent of workers at various levels of government spend much of their time in passive or active revolt against their superiors.

Occasionally, reports of blatant inefficiency will appear in public. In a man-bites-dog story, an agricultural official who had been depicted in a news item as having nothing to do but prop his feet on his desk was awarded a medal by fellow employees, who wanted to show their disapproval of any public criticism of a colleague.

A number of Government officials have become discouraged by the bureaucracy and by trying to make programs work against seemingly insurmountable odds. Frequently the difficulty with a program comes from another agency having different goals and priorities. As a result, all involved spend an inordinate amount of time in meetings to resolve the disagreements. Many of the malcontents would have left except that they could not do as well in either salary or pensions outside government.

The existing problems in the civil service explain in part the muddle over consultants. When President Carter took office he asked for the simple facts: How many consultants are there on the Government payroll and how much are they paid? He still does not know. The agencies kept submitting different figures under different definitions of what constituted "consulting arrangements." The Department of Agriculture, for one, hired a consultant to find out how to cut the cost of meat and poultry inspection. When the findings in the study were challenged by consumers and packers, the department hired another consultant to study the study. Total cost: $330,000.

The number of consultants probably ranges in the thousands, and some place the cost at about $2 billion a year. Consultants can be useful for performing a limited task in an agency that does not have the expertise to do it itself. But frequently it is easier for an agency to get the job done by a consultant than to move its own employees to do so. And the use of consultants can be a way of getting around the limit on the number of employees.

Last year, an audit of the Nuclear Regulatory Commission showed it had tried to conceal the existence of a large force of consultants, including two former Congressmen, who were paid up to $465 a day, more than twice the amount ($182) that the law allows.

There does not seem to be much awareness in Washington of its being out of sync with the rest of the country, possibly because the standards are different here. Secretary of the Treasury W. Michael Blumenthal, former chairman of Bendix Corporation, said the other day that in business it was the reality of a situation that in the end determined success. "In government there is no bottom line and that is why you can be successful if you appear to be successful."

With one of the largest public-relations apparatuses anywhere, the executive branch, the Congress and the appendages of government strive each day for the appearance of success. In recent years, probably the most spectacular failure was President Ford's anti-inflation program called Whip Inflation NOW (WIN). The White House consistently defended it as effective, until everyone, including Mr. Ford, forgot about it and it died quietly. This practice of living by appearances is in the spirit of the advice given in 1966 by Senator George Aiken, Republican of Vermont, to Lyndon Johnson for ending the Vietnam War: Declare it won and get out.

A lot of people are offering prescriptions for cutting Washington down to size, including a number of Presidential candidates—Jerry Brown, Ronald Reagan, Philip Crane, among others—who seem more determined than Richard Nixon or Jimmy Carter. Some scholars and political leaders believe that certain initiatives now under way will help sort out priorities and result in reforms. One is public financing of Congressional campaigns, which would mean that members of Congress would be less beholden to special interests and thus

better able to undo the excesses of the past decade. An Administration bill to achieve that was defeated last year, but it is now before the new Congress. Senator Edmund G. Muskie, Democrat of Maine, and others believe that "sunset" legislation also before Congress would help; it would allow a number of programs to expire unless their continued existence can be justified.

To achieve deeper change, however, the prescriptions fall into two categories. One would be the revival of strong political parties capable of disciplining their members in order to achieve broad national goals. The Committee for Party Renewal, formed by a group of political scientists, is proposing that if public financing of Congressional campaigns is ever achieved, the money should be funneled through the parties to give them more authority.

The second prescription calls for the President to find a way to get control of the jungle of programs and regulatory agencies in order to answer to the people who elected him. Whether any President can inspire enough people to permit this, with all the checks and balances intact, is questionable. Reforms of this kind are easier achieved in a second term, but we may now be in an era of one-term Presidents.

At the same time, there are those who say that a scaled-down role for the Federal Government may be in order, that Washington may have taken on too much for a country of such diversity. There are a number of things the Federal Government does well: the collection of taxes, the redistribution of income through Social Security and other cash payments to individuals and local governments, and acting as referee and protector of the underdog in a number of areas when the rules are properly prescribed—in civil-rights and antitrust matters, for example.

What it does not do well, according to an abundance of evidence, is in running big, complex, highly structured programs over a number of diverse regions. The money goes too much into enriching the armies of managers and technicians, and although the effects of those 500 Federal programs can be seen everywhere—in colleges, cities, the rural countryside—the loss and slippage between Washington and the local level is enormous. Many of the programs were started with the intention of concentrating the money where it is most needed, in urban and rural slums, in education for the most severely handicapped, in regions having the most economic distress. But Washington almost always finds a way to spread the money around, among the needy and nonneedy, and the conflicts among the regions over Federal-fund formulas in the past two years have raised the prospect that it will never be any other way.

Efforts to decentralize the Federal Government have not worked. People simply bypass the regional offices and go to Washington, where the power is. Trusting state and local governments and other institutions with the programs is fraught with danger, but those who propose doing so say that at least this way the inefficiencies and outrages would be dispersed throughout the country where people could better attack them. And, taking a lesson from China, it might be good for those long established in Washington to get a taste of the provinces.

31

The 1977 Energy Bill
Congressional Quarterly

The end of the 1970's brought nationwide gasoline shortages. Long waiting lines, station closings, and high prices resulted in a crisis of confidence over the nation's reliance on automobiles. Meanwhile, the OPEC countries continued to raise the price of imported oil with no limits in sight. The prospects for providing sufficient supplies of home heating fuel were ominous; there was no national energy policy. President Carter, preoccupied with this issue during his first year in office, put forth highly complex proposals which included a variety of taxation and regulatory measures. Yet Congress rejected or severely modified all but the least controversial of these. What were the reasons for the executive-legislative deadlock? What was the role played by special interest groups? What was the nature of the President's lobbying effort? What are the future prospects for developing a comprehensive national energy policy?

Jimmy Carter's crusade for a comprehensive national energy policy dominated Congress and public affairs more than any other domestic issue during his first year as President.

Both the new Democratic President and the Democratic congressional leaders made passage of a national energy policy their top legislative priority for 1977.

And yet, when the year ended, there was no comprehensive energy policy signed into law. Congress did not finish the job. Both the House and Senate passed versions of the program, but the Senate went far afield from the President's approach in two key areas—natural gas regulation and energy tax policy. Conference committees settled other issues but bogged down over gas and taxes. Conferees quit Dec. 22; they did not meet again until February 1978.

At his last 1977 press conference Dec. 15, Carter asserted that the inability to erect an energy policy was "the only major failure this year. . . ." The story behind that failure tells a

lot about Congress, President Carter and the formation of American public policy in 1977.

The need. It had been painfully evident to policymakers since the Arab oil embargo of 1973–74 that America was in need of a national energy plan. That need was underscored as Jimmy Carter prepared to take the oath of office. An unprecedented cold wave caused such rapid depletion of the nation's declining natural gas supplies that many schools and factories were closed and workers went jobless. Special legislation was needed to divert supplies to gas-short areas.

Both the oil embargo and the gas crisis four years later provided vivid evidence that America no longer was producing enough fuel to power its growing economy. The difference was increasingly made up by expensive imports of foreign fuels.

With worldwide energy consumption growing faster than supply availability, the clear trend was that a devastating energy crisis loomed in the future. The Central Intelligence Agency (CIA) warned in an April 1977 study that such a crisis probably would occur by

1985 unless energy conservation measures were "greatly increased."

A month later a prestigious panel of international experts assembled by the Massachusetts Institute of Technology (MIT) warned that a worldwide shortage of oil would occur before the year 2000 and possibly as soon as 1981 unless extraordinary efforts were made to conserve energy.

Carter's Plan. Upon taking office, President Carter ordered a small team of energy planners to construct a comprehensive national energy program in 90 days; the deadline was met.

The primary goal of Carter's vaunted "National Energy Plan" was to cut America's appetite for oil and natural gas and to use energy more efficiently.

His answer was an exceedingly complex package of regulatory and tax measures. The Carter plan would have empowered the federal government: to require industries to make products meeting mandated standards of energy efficiency; to tell businesses to burn certain fuels but not others; to sponsor massive programs encouraging property owners to insulate their buildings; to levy stiff taxes against cars that guzzled too much gasoline, against businesses that burned oil or natural gas and against purchasers of domestically produced oil. The taxes were aimed at spurring energy conservation; their effect would be to drive energy prices higher.

By his own admission, Carter did not expect his program to be popular. But, he said, it was necessary.

Pushing it. Carter and the Democratic congressional leaders pushed hard to complete action on the program in 1977, before the next election year.

Carter spoke to the nation via evening television addresses only three times during his first year in Washington; each time the subject was energy. The first was a fireside chat about the natural gas crisis. The next two were to rally support for his energy program. The only speech Carter made to a joint session of Congress during his first year was also on the subject of his energy program.

When the going got tough on Capitol Hill against his plan, the President dispersed his Cabinet across the country to plug for the energy plan. Though his critics at times faulted Carter's tactics, it was clear that no other single domestic issue received so much presidential attention in 1977.

The same could be said of Congress. The first session of the 95th Congress could be said to have had two agendas: energy, and everything else. In the House, Speaker Thomas P. O'Neill Jr., D-Mass., used all the powers he could muster to strongarm the Carter program to passage in record time, passing it as one bill (HR 8444) Aug. 5, 244-177.

Next, Senate Majority Leader Robert C. Byrd, D-W. Va., cleared all other bills from the Senate agenda to give the energy program undivided attention. It was passed as five major bills between Sept. 28 and Oct. 31.

And yet, the Carter energy program did not make it through.

ANALYSIS

There was no single, simple answer why President Carter's energy program encountered so many difficulties in Congress. But there were a number of clearly identifiable contributing factors.

Five basic problems plagued the program from the beginning:

• It was a plan tackling inherently difficult political problems that was drafted virtually in secret by nonpolitical technicians without outside consultation. That alienated not only Capitol Hill, but also interest groups and even members of the Carter administration who held relevant expertise but were not consulted.

• Its drafting was rushed and consequently the plan suffered from technical flaws, which undermined confidence in it.

• It was the object of intense and negative lobbying by a broad range of powerful special interest groups.

• It was poorly sold to Congress by Carter's lobbyists.

• It lacked a constituency.

Despite those factors, the Carter energy program managed to pass the House virtually intact Aug. 5. Then it ran into the Senate, where it was butchered. In addition to the five basic problems listed above, which continued to plague the Carter plan in the Senate, at least four other problems were thrown on the scales, tilting the balance against the President:

• There was a complete loss of momentum between House passage and Senate consideration, caused principally by two things: the August recess and the troubles of Bert Lance, then Carter's budget director.

• The two Senate committees handling the Carter energy plan were dominated by a different predisposition toward energy policy than were their two counterpart committees in the House.

• The Senate was guided by a different style of leadership than was the House, due in part to the nature of the Senate and in part to the nature of Majority Leader Byrd.

• The administration misread the Senate almost to the end, hoping it would come through somehow for the President as had the House.

THE BASIC PROBLEMS

Drafting

From the outset of his term, President Carter vowed to present a comprehensive national energy program to the nation by April 20, 1977, exactly 90 days after he took office.

Later Carter abandoned his early habit of forcing arbitrary deadlines for completion of complicated policy proposals. But on energy, the deadline was met.

The challenge was handed to his energy adviser, James R. Schlesinger. The Harvard-trained economist and former Nixon-Ford cabinet member gathered around him a small, close-knit team of fewer than two dozen economists, lawyers and Washington-wise administrators.

To beat the clock, they were forced to work almost in isolation. Though the plan came to rest largely on energy tax proposals, Treasury Department tax experts later complained they had not been consulted. Though the plan would need congressional approval to become law, key members of Congress were not invited to help shape the policy and they were miffed. Likewise, experts from private industry were left out, though the plan as conceived would touch every phase of American life.

The political consequence of such a policy formation process was that many who were left out felt little or no obligation to support the final product.

Tacitly recognizing that danger, the White House attempted to present an image of openness via an innovative public relations campaign featuring "mini-conferences" with industry leaders, citizen town meetings and 450,000 letters to citizens requesting energy policy suggestions.

White House protestations to the contrary, most observers were convinced these efforts were all show. They believed the real decisions on the new energy policy were being made in isolation by Schlesinger's small band in the second floor offices of the Old Executive Office Building next door to the White House.

But the deadline was met. And with it came one of the most complex legislative packages ever devised. The Schlesinger team had strung together 113 separate interlocking provisions that together would affect virtually every facet of American society.

Technical Flaws

"The legislation itself was written at white heat, and as a result there are serious technical problems."

That observation came in early May, 1977, from Frank M. Potter, staff director of the House Commerce Subcommittee on Energy and Power. That panel held jurisdiction over most non-tax aspects of the Carter energy plan.

The "technical problems" Porter mentioned began to show up soon after administration officials began defending the plan before congressional committees. The whole program was held together by numbers—estimates of how much energy this proposal would save, how much money that proposal would cost—and with embarrassing frequency, the administration's numbers conflicted with each other.

There were repeated examples of this in May testimony before the House Ways and Means Committee. Administration witnesses from Schlesinger's team provided different answers than Treasury Department tax experts to the same queries.

Doubts about the soundness of the Carter program were magnified during the summer as four comprehensive analyses of the plan performed by non-partisan Capitol Hill research units were unveiled. In each case, the four congressional agencies—the Congressional Budget Office, the General Accounting Office, the Library of Congress and the Office of Technology Assessment—concluded that Carter's program would fall far short of attaining its energy goals.

Lobbying

When things got tough for the White House during Congress' eight-month 1977 examination of the energy plan, the President's men would scream "lobbyists."

On June 9, a House Commerce subcommittee voted to decontrol new natural gas prices, contrary to Carter's plan. The House Ways and Means Committee the same day overwhelmingly rejected the President's proposed gasoline tax, tossed out a proposed rebate for buyers of fuel-efficient cars and weakened Carter's proposed tax on "gas guzzling" autos.

The next day Jody Powell, Carter's press secretary, howled "lobbyists." Gas decontrol, he said, was a "ripoff of the American consumer. . . . [Y]esterday, the oil companies, the auto companies and their lobbies won significant preliminary victories," Powell said.

At a news conference June 13, the President added his voice to that theme, decrying the "inordinate influence" of the oil and auto industries on Capitol Hill.

Later, the full Commerce Committee overturned its subcommittee vote on gas deregulation and Carter's position was muscled through the House. And though his gasoline tax never resurfaced, the President got most of what he wanted from Ways and Means as well. There was no more talk from the White House about lobbies until the energy bill reached the Senate.

On Oct. 13, the White House screamed louder than ever. The Senate Finance Committee recently had rejected all of the President's key energy tax proposals. At a televised news conference, Carter suggested the nation's oil companies were preparing for "war profiteering in the impending energy crisis. . . . [T]he oil companies apparently want it all," Carter said.

There is no doubt that the formidable oil and gas industry lobby was working overtime against Carter's program during most of 1977. Their efforts were concentrated on natural gas regulation, but many company representatives were also working to either defeat Carter's taxes or to ensure that the proceeds from the taxes went to the oil industry instead of to consumers, as Carter preferred.

The automobile industry was well represented, especially at sessions on Carter's proposed tax on gas guzzling cars. Union lobbyists, consumer groups and environmentalists all were heavily involved. The nation's major utilities were scrambling all over, opposing Carter's proposed utility rate reforms, his tax on utility use of oil and gas and his proposal to force utilities to burn coal instead of oil and gas.

And those were just the major actors. There were scores of narrowly focused lobbies. Small oil refiners worked their own angles. One lobbyist represented shopping center associations concerned about a possible ban against master utility meters.

In short, the Capitol was crawling with lobbyists of every shape, stripe and persuasion from the day Carter sent his energy package to Congress. But blaming lobbyists alone for Congress' failure to clear the bill is too simplistic. The House, which essentially adopted Carter's program, was no less besieged by pleaders for special interests than was the Senate, which rejected much of the President's program. Lobbyists were an ever-present factor, but hardly the only one.

Selling It

From April 29, the day the White House delivered the energy program to Congress in formal legislative language, complaints were raised on both sides of the Capitol about White House salesmanship.

Key energy legislators did not receive adequate individual attention from White House liaison, they said. They felt disregarded, left out, and most importantly, in the dark.

When they did receive personal attention and briefings, it came late; too often the administration pitchmen did not know the issues sufficiently well to be of much help, members said.

And, both Senate and House members added, there were too many administration aides trying to explain the various portions of the complex package. No one White House salesman save Energy Secretary Schlesinger could make sense of the whole program, some said.

"I don't think they had anyone who could fully explain the package," said Sen. Spark M. Matsunaga, D-Hawaii. "It was a truly awful mess." Matsunaga cast votes on both the Senate Energy and Finance Committees, which together ruled on every facet of Carter's energy program.

A partial exception to the criticism of the White House sales effort was President Carter himself, whose personal efforts were considered diligent and effective. He made telephone calls to round up wavering votes throughout. He held repeated White House meetings with select groups of energy legislators. His major personal slip-up was to not keep the public pressure on the Senate when it was gearing up to tackle the energy program.

No Constituency

In his speech to the nation April 18,1977, explaining the need for his energy program, President Carter observed:

"I am sure each of you will find something you don't like about the specifics of our proposal. . . . We can be sure that all the special interest groups in the country will attack the part of this plan that affects them directly."

Six months later, Carter again tried to sell the public his energy program via television Nov. 8, and he noted: "I said six months ago that no one would be completely satisfied with this national energy plan. Unfortunately, that prediction has turned out to be right."

Gallup Polls throughout the year demonstrated one of the biggest obstacles Carter faced: About half the nation refused to take the energy crisis very seriously.

In mid-December, Gallup reported that 40 per cent of the nation's people believed that the U.S. energy situation was "very serious"; another 42 percent viewed it as "fairly serious." Fifteen per cent, Gallup said, saw the problem as "not at all" serious.

Those figures had remained virtually unchanged since early April, before the President's plan was presented, Gallup said. ". . . [A]pproximately half of the public can be said to be relatively unconcerned about our energy problems," Gallup wrote in late June. Despite all the political fury in Washington, despite repeated presidential addresses and unceasing media attention, the American public's views on energy changed barely at all in 1977.

The absence of a strong body of public opinion behind Carter's program made it difficult to repel sophisticated lobbying campaigns against the plan waged by committed special interests. As Energy Secretary Schlesinger summed up Oct. 16 on CBS television's "Face the Nation:"

". . . [T]he basic problem is that there is no constituency for an energy program. There are many constituencies opposed. But the basic constituency for the program is the future. . . ."

COMPLICATING FACTORS

As noted earlier, all those problems were present from the start, yet the House accepted the heart of the Carter plan, and the Senate did not. After House passage Aug. 5, new and critical factors came into play.

Momentum

The House, to the surprise of many—including a good number of its own members—managed to meet Speaker O'Neill's ambitious schedule and passed the Carter energy plan almost unchanged before the August recess.

Passage marked the high point of Carter's legislative year; afterwards Congress closed

down for a month until Sept. 7. Carter never regained the momentum in 1977.

Having momentum, as every football coach knows, is like having an extra player on the team. The same is true in politics. Jimmy Carter still had some of the luster of political wizardry and a shiny new presidency about him going into the August recess. All that changed over the next few weeks.

Part of the explanation for the loss of momentum lies simply in the nature of the August recess. Washington tends to slow down and catch its breath. The heat is oppressive; people take their vacations while Congress is gone. Members of Congress go home, talk to people, do a little politicking. There is a collective taking of stock, looking back and looking forward. And then after Labor Day, Washington comes back and starts a new cycle.

It is hard to sustain a sense of momentum through such a break. But for Carter in August 1977 it was impossible. During that period the Carter administration had a few holes blown in its bow and was gasping for air by the time Congress returned in September.

The reason for the abrupt turn of events was the Bert Lance fiasco. The President's budget director, close friend and adviser got caught in a scandal stemming from his pre-Washington banking days. With Washington lacking in competing news during August, the Lance affair dominated the news media for weeks. In the end Lance resigned, on Sept. 21, 1977.

Lance's loss was a major blow to the young administration. Apart from the substance of the charges against him, the Lance case was also a very real power fight between the new Carter team and its established institutional opponents in Congress, the bureaucracy and the news media.

The President made it clear he did not want to yield, but in the end he was forced to. Carter looked very vulnerable once he announced

Lance's resignation Sept. 21. While difficult to measure, there was no doubt that the Lance debacle contributed to a loss of influence by the Carter team that continued to weaken the President throughout 1977.

Committee Contrasts

The President's energy plan went to the House first, then to the Senate. In the House, though five committees reviewed portions of the bill, the large majority of the work fell to only two panels. Most non-tax proposals were handled by the Interstate and Foreign Commerce Committee, while all energy tax proposals went to Ways and Means.

In the Senate there were only two committees with jurisdiction. Non-tax concerns came under the new Energy and Natural Resources Committee; tax proposals went to the Finance Committee.

It was predictable that Carter's energy plan would receive a more favorable hearing before the two House panels than it did from their Senate counterparts. The House committees had compiled strong records of support for precisely the kinds of energy policies that Carter proposed. The Senate panels either had records of support for opposite kinds of policies, or no records at all.

Utility rate reform provided a good example. In 1976, House Commerce's Subcommittee on Energy and Power held eight days of thorough hearings on that complex subject. A massive record of expert testimony was compiled. The subcommittee chairman, John D. Dingell, D-Mich., sponsored a bill that year growing out of those hearings. Dingell's bill was distinctly pro-consumer.

One of the major sections of President Carter's energy plan dealt with utility rate reform, and his proposals bore a marked resemblance to Dingell's of the previous year. This was more than coincidence; one of Dingell's chief aides in drawing up his 1976

bill was committee counsel Robert Riggs Nordhaus. In early 1977, Nordhaus joined Carter's team of energy planners.

Consequently, Carter's utility rate reform proposals sailed through the Commerce Committee, and later, the House.

It was a different story in the Senate. The Energy Committee was new in 1977. Built on the old Interior Committee, its members had never examined electric rate reform before.

In 1977, the panel's Subcommittee on Energy Conservation and Regulation held two days of hearings in late July and three more in September on Carter's rate reform proposals. By the subcommittee's own admission, its members did not know enough about that exceedingly complex field to legislate responsibly.

Also working against Carter on that topic was simply the dominant value position on the subcommittee. Unlike Dingell's panel, its Senate counterpart had not built a similar record of pro-consumer positions on energy issues. It seemed simply to be a more conservative forum.

Natural gas deregulation was another exemplary issue. In the House, Dingell failed narrowly to carry his subcommittee behind the Carter proposal. Carter wanted to continue federal regulation over natural gas prices.

But when the issue reached the full House Commerce Committee, its pro-consumer majority backed Carter and reversed the subcommittee.

The Senate Energy Committee was different. There was no pro-consumer majority. The issue went straight to the full committee and it deadlocked, 9-9. Later, in a major defeat for Carter, the full Senate voted 50–46 to end federal regulation over new gas sales.

The House and Senate committees handling energy taxes were distinctly different as well. The House Ways and Means Committee was large, with 37 members. Since its authoritarian chairman, Wilbur D. Mills, D-Ark. 1939–77, was deposed in 1975, it had been much more democratic in its deliberations and much more responsive to the House leadership. Its approval of an ill-fated, tough energy tax bill in 1975 demonstrated that under Chairman Al Ullman, D-Ore., it had built a record of support for the kind of energy initiatives Carter proposed. And like the Energy Committee in the Senate the Finance Committee had not.

The Senate Finance Committee was a relatively small group with only 18 members. Unlike Ullman, who worked closely with his party's leadership, Senate Finance was headed by Russell B. Long, D-La., who tended to function as a kind of supreme leader apart from either party's official leadership on tax matters. Long, far more than Ullman, was a master of both the tax code and his committee.

And on matters of energy taxes, unlike Ullman, Long's philosophical bent was very different than President Carter's.

Long represented Louisiana, heartland of the nation's oil and gas industry. He looked out for that industry's interests. From the day Carter announced his energy plan in April, Long said he thought the plan did not provide adequate incentives to the industry for production.

Long's committee was no more sympathetic to Carter's energy taxes than its chairman; arguably less so. After rejecting virtually all of Carter's energy tax proposals, the Finance Committee in October wrote its own vastly different energy tax bill. Rather than trying to induce conservation through penalty taxes, the Finance Committee bill tried to induce additional energy production primarily through tax incentives to industry.

Different Leadership

It had become a commonplace in Washington by the end of 1977 that Jimmy Carter's best ally in the capital during his first year was House Speaker O'Neill. Certainly that was true on the energy bill.

O'Neill saw to it that the Carter energy program got through the House, fast. He made it clear that he saw the energy program as a test of Congress and a test of whether the Democratic Party could govern when it controlled both the executive and legislative branches.

The House Speaker saw the Carter energy plan as the Democrats' plan, and he made it the O'Neill plan as well. He went all out to pass it.

His first move was to create a special blue-ribbon select committee to coordinate House review of the program. To it he appointed 40 hand-picked members, with a majority top-heavy with senior Democrats favorably inclined toward the Carter plan.

Next he set strict short deadlines for the regular standing committees to meet in conducting hearings and mark-ups on the complex bill. He insisted that the deadline be honored and it was; the committees finished work in six weeks and sent the bill to the select committee.

His select committee rushed the bill through in three days, proposing a handful of strengthening amendments. Then the measure was sent to the House Rules Committee, stacked with O'Neill lieutenants who obeyed his directions to protect the bill by issuing a modified closed rule, limiting floor debate and amendments.

O'Neill kept abreast of the measure's progress at every point, and when the legislation appeared in trouble on the floor, he stepped in directly to help.

Delivering a thundering oration, the Speaker appealed to party unity and congressional responsibility and helped block a move to overturn Carter's policy on natural gas.

As with so many other things, leadership on the bill was quite different in the Senate.

On April 20, after Carter outlined his energy plan to Congress, the reaction of Senate Majority Leader Byrd was noticeably cooler than was O'Neill's: ". . . The President cannot expect every jot and tittle to be enacted as he proposed it," Byrd warned.

Byrd's commitment to the Carter energy plan was of quite a different kind than O'Neill's. The West Virginian's deepest commitment is not to party or President, or to legislative policy, but to the Senate. Though pledged to back the plan and evidently dedicated to working with Carter as smoothly as possible, Byrd stopped short of O'Neill-like efforts.

Byrd's strongest exertions were aimed at getting the energy bill through Congress in 1977, one way or the other. His commitment was, in a phrase he repeated time and again, to "let the Senate work its will" on the program, not necessarily to force the Senate to adopt it.

But even if Byrd had wanted, he would not have been able to manipulate the Senate as O'Neill did the House. Senate rules simply do not allow a leader such power.

"I don't know that anybody today could run this Senate" as strong majority leaders have in the past, observed Sen. Lloyd Bentsen, D-Texas, in an October interview.

Administration Misreading

If the Carter administration saw trouble coming in the Senate, it was slow to react.

There was little evidence that the White House was alarmed at all by initial votes against the plan in the Senate. President Carter himself conceded Oct. 13 that he was perhaps remiss in not leaning more heavily on the Senate during August and September to pass his program.

But as late as Oct. 16 there was strong evidence that the administration still was expecting the Senate to somehow come through for the President, even though by that time

the Senate had finished action on four of the five basic portions of the Carter plan and the fifth had been gutted in the Finance Committee.

On Oct. 16, in an appearance on CBS television's "Face the Nation" program, Energy Secretary Schlesinger downplayed the Senate's actions to date.

"When the original package went to the House," he recalled, "there were all these comments to the effect that the program was being gutted or riddled and so on. Then in August, when the House voted out virtually the entire package, everyone said it was a remarkable triumph. I would not be surprised if we went through the same cycle with regard to the Congress as a whole."

Conference Action

The White House and congressional leaders held out hope following completion of Senate action Oct. 31 that conference agreements on the Carter package could be reached and final action attained before the year's end.

But that was not to be. The reason, basically, was that there were such wide gulfs to be bridged between Senate and House that time simply ran out. A secondary reason was that conferees set a fairly relaxed pace in pursuing their negotiations.

Conferees took up the first of the five basic portions of the Carter energy package—general energy conservation—Oct. 18. They reached agreement on it Oct. 31, just under two weeks later. On Oct. 31, they started the second bill—coal conversion—and completed it Nov. 11, again in less than two weeks. On the third bill—utility rates—they reached their key agreement in four days, took a 10-day Thanksgiving recess and returned to finish the bill after five days more.

On each of those bills, the conferees seldom worked more than five hours a day and often took three-day weekends. Nevertheless, for

Energy boxscore

A chart detailing House and Senate action on key parts of President Carter's energy program follows. The dates given for approval of the various pieces reflect final floor votes. The dates for rejection of programs are the days on which floor votes on the questions were taken or when committee reports were issued that did not contain those Carter proposals.

Carter Energy Proposal	House Action	Senate Action	Conference	Final Action
Tax credits for home insulation (HR 5263)	Approved Aug. 5, 1977	Approved Oct. 31, 1977	Maximum $300 credit approved and conference report filed Oct. 12, 1978	Senate and House passed conference report Oct. 15, 1978
Boost in gasoline tax	Rejected Aug. 4, 1977	Rejected by Finance Committee Oct. 21, 1977		
Tax on "gas guzzling" cars (HR 5263)	Approved Aug. 5, 1977	Rejected; ban on their production approved instead Sept. 13, 1977, as part of HR 5037	Approved and conference report filed Oct. 12, 1978	Senate and House passed conference report Oct. 15, 1978
Rebate of "gas guzzler" tax to buyers of gas saving cars	Rejected by Ways and Means Committee June 9, 1977	Not considered		
Mandatory energy efficiency standards for home appliances (HR 5037)	Approved Aug. 5, 1977	Approved Sept. 13, 1977	Approved Oct. 31,1977; conference report filed Oct. 10, 1978	Senate passed conference report Oct. 9, 1978; House passed conference report Oct. 15, 1978
Extention of natural gas price controls, with higher price ceiling (HR 5289)	Approved Aug. 5, 1977	Rejected; approved ending federal price controls for new gas Oct. 4, 1977	Agreement to end federal price controls on new natural gas by 1985, reached May 24, 1978; conference report filed Aug. 18	Senate passed conference report Sept. 27, 1978; House passed conference report Oct. 15, 1978
Tax on crude oil (HR 5263)	Approved Aug. 5, 1977	Rejected by Finance Committee Oct. 21, 1977	Killed by conference	
Tax on utility and industrial use of oil and natural gas (HR 5263)	Approved, weaker than Carter plan Aug. 5, 1977	Approved, but weaker than House or Carter plan Oct. 31, 1977	Killed by conference	
Authority to force utility, industrial conversion from oil, gas to coal (HR 5146)	Approved Aug. 5, 1977	Approved, but weaker than House version Sept. 8, 1977	Compromise reached Nov. 11, 1977; conference report filed July 14, 1978	Senate passed conference report July 18, 1978; House passed conference report Oct. 15, 1978
Reform of electric utility rates (HR 4018)	Approved Aug. 5, 1977	Rejected by Finance Committee Sept. 19, 1977	Compromise reached Dec. 1, 1977; conference report filed Oct. 6, 1978	Senate passed conference report Oct. 9, 1978; House passed conference report Oct. 15, 1978

such far-reaching and complex legislation, working out conference agreements between radically different bills in less than two weeks each cannot be considered unusually slow by normal standards.

It was when they reached natural gas regulation that the conference completely bogged down. That conference started Dec. 2. Battle lines on that question were rigid and there was little middle ground for compromise. Complicating negotiations immensely was the fact that Senate conferees were evenly split, 9–9, and could not agree among themselves on anything.

Completing the conference breakdown was the fact that negotiators on the complex energy tax proposals refused to do much of anything until the natural gas bill was worked out.

Because House Speaker O'Neill was insistent that the House would not vote on any conference agreement until all could be combined for a single up or down vote, none of the Carter energy plan could be sent to the floor for final congressional action until the conferees finished natural gas pricing and taxes.

Consequently, Congress adjourned Dec. 15 with three conference agreements on Carter's energy package on the shelf while two more were still caught in intense negotiations.

Congress

9

In examining the three branches of the national government, we find that Congress occupies a central role in making public policy. The Founding Fathers considered Congress as a major participant in formulating, developing, and approving public policy through the legislative process. In addition to the lawmaking function, which is found in Article I, Section 8 of the Constitution, Congress has several other responsibilities:

1. the housekeeping function—control over its own internal procedures;
2. the fiscal function—authority over taxation, revenue raising, borrowing, and spending;
3. the Senate's confirmation role—approval of presidential appointments and treaties;
4. the judicial function—impeachment of civil officers accused of high crimes;
5. the electoral function—counting of electoral votes cast for president and vice president, and the House of Representatives selecting the president if no candidate receives a majority of the electoral votes; and
6. the constitutional role—proposing amendments to the Constitution.

How do members of Congress and senators perceive their duties and responsibilities?

First, the elected representative is an *agent* of the constituency. Such a role seeks to promote and support the interests, needs, and desires of the people back home. Several important questions arise here: How does the legislator get to know the needs of the constituents? Who does he or she listen to? Does he or she represent all of the constituency, the political party, or special interest groups? How is the legislator's record made known to the voters so they are assured he is acting in their best interests?

A second possible role is that of *trustee*—a relatively free actor who is not always bound to constituency demands. This role was suggested by Edmund Burke who, upon his election to Parliament, claimed that he would not sacrifice his judgment, conscience, or unbiased opinion to his constituents. The problem is that the legislative trustee who is not responsive to his district may suffer electoral defeat if he cannot show any tangible results to the voters.

A third legislative response combines the agent and trustee roles. Most legislators do not automatically respond to all constituency demands (which is clearly impossible); neither do they ignore their districts, which is a serious political risk. Rather, they determine their own priorities by responding to issues, selecting those persons upon whom they can build a reliable following, and recognizing those pressures which are most persuasive and important.

According to Morris Fiorina (Article 32), congressmen and-women engage in three types of activities: lawmaking, pork-barreling, and casework. The *agent* role is most relevant to serving constituency needs through "pork barrel" legislation, or the targeting of federal grants and programs to the home district. Visible public works projects are tangible evidence of providing jobs and direct local benefits to constituents, thereby building a strong case for the legislator's re-election prospects.

Although Fiorina argues that incumbency—the regular re-election of legislators over long periods of time—is a powerful foundation of legislative influence, Tom Bethell (Article 33) contends that many legislators are leaving Washington voluntarily. This can be attributed to more generous pension benefits, but early retirements also result from a variety of other problems, including financial disclosure laws, criticism by journalists, and the tedious treadmill of the job. Consequently, the legislative task is becoming so burdensome that the prospects for exercising power are no longer as alluring as they once were.

Casework is also important to a legislator's success. This is the daily response to the huge volume of requests and favors by the people back home for information, services, and inquiries to intervene in the federal bureaucracy for favorable actions or decisions. Most legislators try to build good reputations in acting as go-betweens for constituents in cutting bureaucratic red tape.

The *lawmaking* function involves the congressional representative or senator in policy-making. Here, Congress responds to the proposals suggested by the president, various executive agencies, special interest groups, constituency pressures, and public opinion. Additionally, the House and Senate develop policy by investigating administration, increasing or withholding appropriations for existing programs, and confirming or disapproving of presidential appointments. The House and the Senate may be distinguished by their separate contributions. The House considers technical details of pending bills. Because of its large size (435 members), the House must have a highly structured committee and subcommittee system through which members can gain expertise on specialized legislative matters. Thus, decentralization of power in the House is essentially in accord with the technical and specialized substance of policy proposals. On the other hand, the Senate is a forum for cultivating national constituencies; that is, individual senators seek to develop questions for debate that affect the national interest. In contrast to the considerable formalized structure of the House, the Senate is more loosely organized to permit the introduction and cultivation of new policy proposals. Thus, the Senate serves as a forum of policy innovation.

For many years, Congress was considered a weak "second cousin" to the president. When it followed presidential advice, Congress was accused of being a rubber-stamp of the executive branch. On the other hand, when Congress consistently opposed the president, it was ridiculed for obstructing the public will. During the strong presidency years of Franklin D. Roosevelt and following World War II, Congress faced an institutional crisis. It lost power and influence at the very time that the president and interest groups enhanced their roles in shaping public policy. This could be attributed to three major problems: the *insulation* of legislators from the centers of influence resulting from their narrowly based affiliations; the *dispersal of legislative power* among many committees rather than effective party leadership to deal with the president's considerable authority and leadership; and the shift away from developing legislation to *supervising administrative performance*.

The aftermath of the "imperial presidency" years under Lyndon Johnson and Richard Nixon resulted in a changed environment for executive-legislative relations. Congress has become less insulated and more assertive. Important presidential policy initiatives are now subjected to careful congressional scrutiny. For example, President Carter gained approval of the Panama Canal treaty only after an intense struggle in the Senate. Similarly, the SALT II treaty on arms control between the United States and the Soviet Union underwent protracted debate in the Senate. On the domestic side, President Carter encountered severe resistance to nearly every one of his major policy proposals. The 1977 energy bill was perhaps one of the most extreme examples of congressional limitation of a crucial domestic policy initiative (see also Article 31).

As indicated in Article 34, Congress has developed independent sources of power and influence which can limit the success of presidential programs. For example, the triple alliance of key legislators and bureaucratic and interest group actors can counterbalance the strength of the chief executive. This may result in an institutional deadlock that makes it very difficult to develop agreement on controversial new policies and programs.

Tad Szulc (Article 35) offers a contrasting view of congressional policy independence from the executive. The presidential-congressional tensions over controversial policy measures have resulted in a tremendous drain on legislative efficiency. The breakdown of party loyalty to the president is another complicating factor along with the growing influence of single-issue lobbyists. Is Congress obsolete? Is reform possible? Procedural and mechanical changes for Congress are difficult to achieve, and structural changes do not always guarantee better public policies. Congress needs to improve its effectiveness in developing alternatives to presidential proposals. Also, new bases of legislative-executive cooperation need to be established. Otherwise, both executive and legislative actors will continue to have serious difficulties in achieving their policy goals.

32

Big Government: A Congressman's Best Friend

Morris P. Fiorina

Individual legislators face a variety of pressures from their home constituencies, interest groups, the president, and the bureaucracy. What is the relationship between legislators' roles and the various decisions they make? Morris Fiorina argues that congressmen and senators are part of the Washington establishment. Their major objective is re-election. This is facilitated by three major activities: lawmaking, pork-barreling, and casework. How do legislators respond to the pressures placed upon them? What are the differences between constituency casework and committee responsibilities? What are the most important constituency influences affecting a legislator's record, especially when he or she seeks re-election?

In this article I will set out a theory of the Washington establishment(s). The theory is quite plausible from a common sense standpoint, and it is consistent with the specialized literature of academic political science. Nevertheless, it is still a theory, not proven fact. Before plunging in let me bring out in the open the basic axiom on which the theory rests: the self-interest axiom.

I assume that most people most of the time act in their own self-interest. This is not to say that human beings seek only to amass tangible wealth, but rather to say that human beings seek to achieve their own ends—tangible and intangible—rather than the ends of their fellow men. I do not condemn such behavior nor do I condone it (although I rather sympathize with Thoreau's comment that "if I knew for a certainty that a man was coming to my house with the conscious design of doing me good, I should run for my life"). I only claim that political and economic theories that presume self-interest behavior will prove to be more widely applicable than those that build on more altruistic assumptions.

What does the axiom imply when used in the specific context of this article, a context peopled by congressmen, bureaucrats, and voters? I assume that the primary goal of the typical congressman is reelection. Over and above the $57,000 salary plus "perks" and outside money, the office of congressman carries with it prestige, excitement, and power. It is a seat in the cockpit of government. But in order to retain the status, excitement, and power (not to mention more tangible things) of office, the congressman must win reelection every two years. Even those congressmen genuinely concerned with good public policy must achieve reelection in order to continue their work. Whether narrowly self-serving or more publicly oriented, the individual congressman finds reelection to be at least a necessary condition for the achievement of his goals.

Moreover, there is a kind of natural selection process at work in the electoral arena. On average, those congressmen who are not primarily interested in reelection will not achieve reelection as often as those who are interested.

We, the people, help to weed out congressmen whose primary motivation is not reelection. We admire politicians who courageously adopt the aloof role of the disinterested statesman, but we vote for those politicians who follow our wishes and do us favors.

What about the bureaucrats? A specification of their goals is somewhat more controversial. The literature provides ample justification for asserting that most bureaucrats wish to protect and nurture their agencies. The typical bureaucrat can be expected to seek to expand his agency in terms of personnel, budget, and mission. One's status in Washington is roughly proportional to the importance of the operation one oversees. And the sheer size of the operation is taken to be a measure of importance. As with congressmen, the specified goals apply even to those bureaucrats who genuinely believe in their agencies' missions. If they believe in the efficacy of their programs, they naturally wish to expand them and add new ones. All of this requires more money and more people.

And what of the third element in the equation, us? What do we, the voters who support the Washington system, strive for? Each of us wishes to receive a maximum of benefits from government for the minimum cost. This goal suggests maximum government efficiency, on the one hand, but it also suggests mutual exploitation on the other. Each of us favors an arrangement in which our fellow citizens pay for our benefits.

With these brief descriptions of the cast of characters in hand, let us proceed.

THE FIRST PRIORITY

What should we expect from a legislative body composed of people whose first priority is their continued tenure in office? We should expect, first, that the normal activities of its members are those calculated to enhance their chances of reelection. And we should expect, second, that the members would devise and maintain institutional arrangements that facilitate their electoral activities.

For most of the twentieth century, congressmen have engaged in a mix of three kinds of activities: lawmaking, pork-barreling, and casework. Congress is first and foremost a lawmaking body, at least according to constitutional theory. In every postwar session Congress "considers" thousands of bills and resolutions, many hundreds of which are brought to a record vote (over 500 in each chamber in the 93rd Congress). Naturally the critical consideration in taking a position for the record is the maximization of approval in the home district. If the district is unaffected by and unconcerned with the matter at hand, the congressman may then take into account the general welfare of the country. (This sounds cynical, but remember that "profiles in courage" are sufficiently rare that their occurrence inspires books and articles.) Politicians have propounded an ideology that maintains that the good of the country on any given issue is simply what is best for a majority of congressional districts. This ideology provides a philosophical justification for what congressmen do while acting in their own self-interest.

A second activity favored by congressmen consists of efforts to bring home the bacon to their districts. Many popular articles have been written about the pork barrel, a term originally applied to rivers and harbors legislation but now generalized to cover all manner of federal buildings, sewage treatment plants, urban renewal projects, etc. as sweet plums to be plucked. The average constituent may have trouble translating his congressman's vote on some civil rights issue into a change in his own personal welfare. But the workers hired and supplies purchased in connection with a big federal project provide benefits that are widely appreciated.

The importance congressmen attach to the pork barrel is reflected in the rules of the House. That body accords certain classes of legislation "privileged" status: they may come directly to the floor without passing through the Rules Committee, a traditional graveyard for legislation. What kinds of legislation are privileged? Taxing and spending bills, for one: the government's power to raise and spend money must be kept relatively unfettered. But in addition, the omnibus rivers and harbors bills of the Public Works Committee and public lands bills from the Interior Committee share privileged status. The House will allow a civil rights or defense procurement or environmental bill to languish in the Rules Committee, but it takes special precautions to insure that nothing slows down the approval of dams and irrigation projects.

SPEEDING UP THE PROCESS

A third major activity takes up perhaps as much time as the other two combined. Traditionally, constituents appeal to their congressmen for myriad favors and services. Sometimes only information is needed, but often constituents request that their congressmen intervene in the internal workings of federal agencies to affect a decision in a favorable way, to reverse an adverse decision, or simply to speed up the glacial bureaucratic process. On the basis of extensive personal interviews with congressmen, Charles Clapp writes:

"Denied a favorable ruling by the bureaucracy on a matter of direct concern to him, puzzled or irked by delays in obtaining a decision, confused by the administrative maze through which he is directed to proceed, or ignorant of whom to write, a constituent may turn to his congressman for help. These letters offer great potential for political benefit to the congressman since they affect the constituent personally. If the legislator can be of assist-

ance, he may gain a firm ally; if he is indifferent, he may even lose votes."

Actually congressmen are in an almost unique position in our system, a position shared only with high-level members of the executive branch. Congressmen possess the power to expedite and influence bureaucratic decision. This capability flows directly from congressional control over what bureaucrats value most: higher budgets and new program authorizations. In a very real sense each congressman is a monopoly supplier of bureaucratic unsticking services for his district.

BLEEDING ALL OVER THE CAPITAL

Every year the federal budget passes through the appropriations committees and subcommittees of Congress. Generally these committees make perfunctory cuts. But on occasion they vent displeasure on an agency and leave it bleeding all over the capital. The most extreme case of which I am aware came when the House committee took away the entire budget of the Division of Labor Standards in 1947 (some of the budget was restored elsewhere in the appropriations process). Professors Richard Fenno and Aaron Wildavsky have provided extensive documentary and interview evidence of the great respect (and even terror) federal bureaucrats show for the House Appropriations Committee. Moreover, the bureaucracy must keep coming back to Congress to have its old programs reauthorized and new ones added. Again, most such decisions are perfunctory, but exceptions are sufficiently frequent that bureaucrats do not forget the hand that feeds them. For example, the Law Enforcement Assistance Administration and the Food Stamps Program had no easy time of it this last Congress. The bureaucracy needs congressional approval in order to survive, let alone expand. Thus, when a congressman calls about some minor bureaucratic decision or regulation, the bureaucracy considers his accommodation a small price to pay for the goodwill its cooperation will produce, particularly if he has any connection to the substantive committee or the appropriations subcommittee to which it reports.

From the standpoint of capturing voters, the congressman's lawmaking activities differ in two important respects from his pork barrel and casework activities. First, legislative programs are inherently controversial. Unless his district is homogeneous, a congressman will find his district divided on many major issues. Thus when he casts a vote, introduces a piece of non-trivial legislation, or makes a speech with policy content, he will displease some elements of his district. Some constituents may applaud the congressman's civil rights record, but others believe integration is going too fast. Some support foreign aid, while others believe it's money poured down a rat hole. Some advocate economic equality, others stew over welfare cheaters. On such policy matters the congressman can expect to make friends as well as enemies.

In contrast, the pork barrel and casework are relatively less controversial. New federal projects bring jobs, shiny new facilities, and general economic prosperity, or so people believe. Snipping ribbons at the dedication of a new post office or dam is a much more pleasant pursuit than disposing of a constitutional amendment on abortion. Republicans and Democrats, conservatives and liberals, all generally prefer a richer district to a poorer one. Of course, in recent years the river-damming and streambed-straightening activities of the Army Corps of Engineers have aroused some opposition among environmentalists. Congressmen happily reacted by absorbing the opposition and adding environmentalism to the pork barrel: water treatment plants are currently a hot congressional item.

Casework is even less controversial. Some poor, aggrieved constituent becomes enmeshed in the tentacles of an evil bureaucracy and calls upon Congressman St. George to do battle with the dragon. Again, Clapp writes:

"A person who has a reasonable complaint or query is regarded as providing an opportunity rather than as adding an extra burden to an already busy office. The party affiliation of the individual, even when known to be different from that of the congressman, does not normally act as a deterrent to action. Some legislators have built their reputations and their majorities on a program of service to all constituents irrespective of party. Regularly, voters affiliated with the opposition in other contests lend strong support to the lawmaker whose intervention has helped them in their struggle with the bureaucracy."

Even following the revelation of his sexual improprieties, Wayne Hays won his Ohio Democratic primary by a two-to-one margin. According to a *Los Angeles Times* feature story, Hays' constituency base was built on a foundation of personal service to constituents:

"They receive help in speeding up bureaucratic action on various kinds of federal assistance—black lung benefits to disabled miners and their families, Social Security payments, veterans' benefits, and passports.

"Some constituents still tell with pleasure of how Hays stormed clear to the seventh floor of the State Department and into Secretary of State Dean Rusk's office to demand, successfully, the quick issuance of a passport to an Ohioan." Practicing politicians will tell you that word of mouth is still the most effective mode of communication. News of favors to constituents gets around and is no doubt embellished in the process.

In sum, when considering the benefits of his programmatic activities, the congressman must tote up gains and losses to arrive at a net profit. Pork-barreling and casework, however, are basically pure profit.

A second way in which lawmaking differs from casework and the pork barrel is the difficulty of claiming credit for the former as compared with the latter. No congressman can seriously claim that he was responsible for the 1964 Civil Rights Act, the ABM, or the 1972 Revenue Sharing Act. Most constituents do have some vague notion that their congressman is only one of hundreds and their senator one of an even hundred. Even committee chairmen, let alone a rank-and-file congressman, may have a difficult time claiming credit for a piece of major legislation.

THE SNAP TO ATTENTION

Ah, but casework, and the pork barrel. In dealing with the bureaucracy, the congressman is not merely one vote of 435. Rather, he is a nonpartisan power, someone whose phone calls snap an office to attention. The constituent who receives aid believes that his congressman and his congressman alone got results. Similarly, congressmen find it easy to claim credit for federal projects awarded their districts. The congressman may have instigated the proposal for the project in the first place, issued regular progress reports, and ultimately announced the award through his office. Maybe he can't claim credit for the 1965 Voting Rights Act, but he can take credit for Littletown's spanking new sewage treatment plant.

Overall then, programmatic activities are dangerous, and programmatic accomplishments are difficult to claim credit for. While less exciting, casework and pork-barreling are both safe and profitable. For a reelection-oriented congressman the choice is obvious.

The key to the rise of a semi-permanent Washington establishment (and the fall of the non-safe congressional seat) is the following observation: *the growth of an activist federal government has stimulated a change in the mix of congressional activities.* Specifically, a lesser proportion of congressional effort is now go-

ing into programmatic activities and a greater proportion into pork-barrel and casework activities. As a result, today's congressmen make relatively fewer enemies and relatively more friends among the people of their districts. Hence, more safe seats.

To elaborate, a basic fact of life in twentieth-century America is the growth of the federal role and its attendant bureaucracy. Bureaucracy is the characteristic mode of delivering public goods and services. *Ceteris paribus*, the more the government attempts to do for people, the more extensive a bureaucracy it creates. As the scope of government expands, more and more citizens find themselves in direct contact with the federal government. Consider the rise in such contacts upon passage of the Social Security Act, work relief projects, and other New Deal programs. Consider the millions of additional citizens touched by the veterans' programs of the postwar period. Consider the untold numbers whom the Great Society and its aftermath brought face to face with the federal government. In 1930 the federal bureaucracy was small and rather distant from the everyday concerns of Americans. Nowadays it is neither small nor distant.

As the years have passed, more and more citizens and groups have found themselves dealing with the federal bureaucracy. They may be seeking positive actions—eligibility for various benefits and awards of government grants. Or they may be seeking relief from the costs imposed by bureaucratic regulations—on working conditions, racial and sexual quotas, market restrictions, and numerous other subjects. While not malevolent, bureaucracies make mistakes in their dealings with the citizenry, both of commission and omission, and normal attempts at redress often meet with unresponsiveness and inflexibility and sometimes seeming incorrigibility. Whatever the problems, the citizen's congressman is a source of succor. The greater the scope of government activity, the greater the demand for his services.

CREATIVE PORK-BARRELING

In addition to greatly increasing casework, let us not forget that the growth of the federal role has also greatly expanded the federal pork barrel. The creative pork-barreler need not limit himself to dams and post offices— rather old-fashioned interests. Today, creative congressmen can cadge LEAA money for the local police, urban renewal and housing money for local politicians, and educational program grants for the local education bureaucracy. There are also sewage treatment plants, worker training and retraining programs, health services, and programs for the elderly. The pork barrel is full to overflowing. The conscientious congressman can stimulate applications for federal assistance (the sheer number of programs makes it difficult for local officials to stay current with the possibilities), put in a good word during consideration, and announce favorable decisions amid great fanfare.

In sum, everyday decisions by a large and growing federal bureaucracy bestow significant tangible benefits and impose significant tangible costs. Congressmen can affect these decisions. Ergo, the more decisions the bureaucracy has the opportunity to make, the more opportunities there are for the congressman to build up credits.

The nature of the Washington system is thus quite clear. Congressmen (typically the majority Democrats) earn electoral credits by establishing various federal programs (the minority Republicans typically earn credits by fighting the good fight). The legislation is drafted in very general terms, so some agency, existing or newly established, must translate a vague policy mandate into a functioning program, a process that necessitates the promulgation of numerous rules and regulations and, incidentally, the trampling of numerous toes. At the next stage, aggrieved and/or hopeful constituents petition their congressmen to intervene in the complex (or at least obscure) decision processes of the bureaucracy. The cycle closes when the congressman lends a sympathetic ear, piously denounces the evils of bureaucracy, intervenes in the latter's decisions, and rides a grateful electorate to ever more impressive electoral showings. Congressmen take credit coming and going. They are the alpha and the omega.

The popular frustration with the permanent government in Washington is partly justified, but to a considerable degree it is misplaced resentment. *Congress is the linchpin of the Washington establishment.* The bureaucracy serves as a convenient lightning rod for public frustration and a convenient whipping boy for congressmen. But as long as the bureaucracy accommodates congressmen, they will oblige with ever larger budgets and grants of authority. Congress does not just react to big government—it creates it. All of Washington prospers. More and more bureaucrats promulgate more and more regulations and dispense more and more money. Fewer and fewer congressmen suffer electoral defeat. Elements of the electorate benefit from government programs, and all of the electorate is eligible for congressional ombudsman services. But the general, long-term welfare of the United States is no more than an incidental by-product of the system.

33

The Disadvantaged Congress

Tom Bethell

What determines legislative success? Historically, the power of incumbents has been very influential in shaping public policy. However, the 96th Congress contained 97 newcomers, or 18 percent of the House and Senate membership. Tom Bethell explores the reasons for congressional turnovers.

The Ninety-Sixth Congress, which convened in January, includes seventy-seven new Representatives and twenty new Senators, the latter constituting the largest freshman class in the U.S. Senate since 1947. Overall, "new faces" make up 18 percent of the Congress. Looked at historically, this is a low figure. Throughout most of the nineteenth century, for example, when the new Congress assembled on Capitol Hill about half would be newcomers. Sometimes the figure would be higher (73 percent in 1843, 61 percent in 1853). But these percentages began to drop off quickly in the twentieth century. Parliamentary changes made power proportional to seniority, for one thing, so rewarding tenure. Washington itself became a more tolerable city to live in after the swamps were drained and the streets paved. Later on, air conditioning encouraged lawmakers to stay on in the summer months, when they would pass more laws (further proof, if any is needed, that technology doesn't necessarily bring progress in its wake). Finally, the Congressman's job itself became relatively more important in the scheme of American government. "By 1890," Morris Fiorina writes

Early retirements can be explained by higher pension benefits. There are, however, also several negative factors which discourage legislators from remaining in Washington. Which are the most important? How does legislative turnover affect public policy considerations by Congress?

in *Congress: Keystone of the Washington Establishment*, "it was no longer true that the Virginia state legislature was more important than the U.S. Congress."

So more and more Congressmen arrived in Washington, saw that it was good, and resolved to stay on as long as possible. Congress gradually became a career, its incumbents burdened by the weight of "public service"—a burden that was lightened every year as the comforts, perquisites, and importance of the job grew. To this tradition, to cite a more than normally candid case, comes Geraldine A. Ferraro, newly elected to New York's Ninth District (Queens), her aspirations duly recorded by the *New York Times* a month after her election: "Her aim, she said, is to do a good job for the neighbors and get reelected in 1980."

But—who knows?—she may change her mind after she has been in Washington a few months. The new political wisdom on everyone's lips is that Congress is becoming a less enjoyable place to work. Here are some figures to back this up. Table 1 shows the percentage of first-term members in the House of Representatives since World War II. No great trend is discernible. Table 2 shows the number of incumbent Congressmen defeated in reelection

Table 1

House of Representatives:
Percent of First-Term Members

1945	15.8	1963	15.2
1947	24.1	1965	20.9
1949	22.3	1967	16.8
1951	14.9	1969	8.9
1953	19.5	1971	12.9
1955	11.7	1973	15.9
1957	9.9	1975	21.1
1959	18.2	1977	15.0
1961	12.6	1979	17.7

Source: Foundation for the Study of Presidential and Congressional Terms.

Table 2

House of Representatives: Number of Incumbents Defeated in Reelection Bid

1954	29	1968	8
1956	22	1970	21
1958	40	1972	19
1960	33	1974	48
1962	27	1976	16
1964	52	1978	24
1966	52		

Source: National Journal

Table 3

Retirements from House and Senate

Year	House	Senate	Total
1946	33	7	40
1948	27	7	34
1950	25	4	29
1952	41	3	44
1954	24	2	26
1956	20	5	25
1958	33	6	39
1960	26	4	30
1962	24	4	28
1964	33	2	35
1966	21	3	24
1968	22	6	28
1970	28	4	32
1972	39	6	45
1974	44	7	51
1976	49	9	58
1978	49	10	59

Source: Congressional Quarterly

Table 4

Senate Freshman Class

1941	12	1961	9
1943	13	1963	12
1945	14	1965	8
1947	23	1967	7
1949	18	1969	15
1951	14	1971	11
1953	16	1973	13
1955	14	1975	11
1957	10	1977	18
1959	10	1979	20

Source: Congressional Quarterly

bids since 1954. There has been a drop-off in the numbers, although 1974 (the year of retribution for Watergate) was an exception. In other words, the security of incumbents has increased. Table 3 shows the number of retirements from the House and Senate—a number that has steadily increased in the past decade. (Table 4 shows the size of the Senate freshman class since 1941.) Thus, the statistics confirm the political wisdom, which is a relief —and also a mild surprise.

But why are legislators more inclined to retire these days? Probably the most important reason is the one that is least mentioned: retirement benefits have improved considerably in the past decade. "A man lies if he says the pension is not a factor," says Teno Roncalio of Wyoming, who recently retired after ten years in the House. In fact, so alluring are retirement benefits that the Foundation for the Study of Presidential and Congressional Terms, which supports a constitutional amendment limiting Congressional service to twelve years, might well consider that if it wants legislators to come and go more frequently, the simplest method might be to prod Congress to increase its pensions once again—get them to make themselves an offer they can't refuse. (This was tried last year by

House Speaker Thomas P. [Tip] O'Neill, Jr., but his maneuver failed at the last minute.)

In 1967 Congress took the first step toward making retirement more attractive by adding a "cost-of-living escalator" to pensions. This protected members against inflation, which they themselves, in their generosity to constituents, were causing. No longer, then, would retired legislators have to worry about the hazards of living on a fixed income. Until 1972 the Congressional pension was calculated by averaging the salary the Congressman received in his or her last five years and multiplying it by 2.5 percent times the number of years in federal service. This was changed in 1972 to the average of the last three years, and Tip O'Neill's proposal would have reduced this to the salary in the final year: convenient, because the Congressional salary was increased from $42,500 to $57,500 in 1977, and thus members could have taken full advantage of this by retiring in 1978. As the formula stands, those contemplating retirement will have to hang on for one more term. Put another way, we can expect a lot more retirements in 1980.

It is, incidentally, quite difficult to find out the precise pensions of individual members. Capitol Hill, a mine of information on most matters, is guarded on the subject of pensions, which somehow come under the purview of the Privacy Act. *Congressional Quarterly* has been reduced to calculating "approximate pensions" of departing legislators. (The maximum allowable pension is $46,000 a year. Some *CQ* estimates: Sen. Bill Scott of Virginia, $44,000; Rep. John J. Flynt, Jr., of Georgia, $38,000; and Rep. John E. Moss of California, $36,000.)

This explains the popularity of departure. But why has incumbency itself become unpopular? One reason is the "financial disclosure" requirement embodied in the new Code of Ethics. Senators, for example, have to fill out an eight-page form giving details of property transactions, personal property ("examples of reportable items are savings accounts, loans, . . . farm equipment and livestock, stocks, bonds . . ."), liabilities, patent rights, and so on. Those who announced their retirement before April 30 last year, however, were exempted from this scrutiny. Even so, Sen. George McGovern's disclosure report shows that it is possible to fill out these forms in a nonrevealing manner. Under "personal property" he simply wrote "None."

Another thing incumbents don't like these days is the limitation on outside income, which takes effect this year. Members of Congress, who previously have been allowed to earn up to $25,000 in extra cash, are now limited to $8,625. This will come as a blow to Sen. Daniel Patrick Moynihan, for example, who earned $165,393 in 1976 (i.e., before he was elected), primarily by making speeches. Others will suffer, including Sens. Herman Talmadge, Robert Packwood, and George McGovern, the top three Senatorial moneymakers in 1976, all earning more than $20,000 that year in honoraria. Now they will have to speak for less, or speak less.

Actually, this may not be necessary, because there is a good chance that the ethics bill will quietly be revised to strike the limitation on outside income, which was imposed in order to mollify public opinion after the recent Congressional pay raise. Now that that is forgotten, someone is bound to point out that there is something illogical about the income limitation. Why, for example, limit earned income, but not income from stocks and bonds? It doesn't make sense. Reformist zealotry sometimes goes too far. "We seem to be operating under one giant guilt complex resulting from Watergate and the overreaction of politicians who already have the highest ethical standards of any parliamentary body," said James Mann of South Carolina, who recently retired from Congress.

This brings to mind another reason why

Congressmen don't like Washington so much these days: the journalists. One could call this the Fishbowl Factor. As is by now well known, journalists have discovered that by staking out a high moral ground for themselves, they are in a good position to look down upon their fellow men. Sometimes they will come down from Mount Olympus to sniff cocaine or smoke a marijuana cigarette, and will gladly do so in the company of an elected or appointed official. But that is "not a story," and everyone is safe. At other times a Congressman, unbuttoned of an evening, drink in hand after a wearying session on the floor, must fervently hope that he is not spotted by an earnest Pulitzer-seeker.

The most interesting Congressional lament heard today is that the job has become, as one study group found, an "exhausting treadmill" with eleven-hour days (an average of four-and-a-half hours on the House floor), in the course of which the Congressman has to absorb a barrage of complaints, requests, and advice from constituents—admittedly mostly by mail. Not just his public behavior, but his legislative performance is now being monitored by the voters as never before.

A brief digression here, to a favorite topic of conversation in Washington and an essential element in our story: the well-established advantage of incumbency. An incumbent Congressman can, among other things, send out six mass mailings a year—addressed simply to "Postal Patron"—covering his entire district. There is no need, even, to go to the trouble of getting the names of constituents. Myriad pieces of mail go out (containing such messages as "My number one goal is to eliminate inflation and to see this nation achieve a balanced budget"), and although the recipient may not be flattered to receive mail that doesn't even have his name on it he cannot help noticing the *Congressman's* name, always prominently displayed.

In sending out this mail, for which the federal government reimburses the Post Office, members are aware of the following survey data: On average, only 34 percent of the electorate know who represents them in Congress. But 79 percent can pick their representative's name from a list of five. This means that on election day a small but important percentage of the electorate can reliably be expected to vote on the basis of name recognition alone. The free mailings to a large extent create this name recognition, and, as a result, incumbents are hard to beat.* The rate of "incumbent return" to the House since 1966 has been 95 percent; to the Senate, 84 percent.

What happens next has a certain poetic justice. Constituents, having heard so often from this friendly fellow in Washington, who claims to be able to do so much on their behalf, begin to write back *asking* him to do things—and not just that, *telling* him to do things, such as which way to vote on various issues. In fact, incumbents often literally ask for this, by including questionnaires in their mass mailings: What do you think about abortion? Defense spending? The unspoken question is: How should I vote?

An increasing number of Congressmen commission professional polls in their districts. Further—in a significant development that no one seems to have noticed—many will publish the results of these polls in the *Congressional Record*. Not only does a Congressman want to know that 55 percent of his constituents favor an increased defense budget; he wants the world to know that he knows it. You would think he might want to keep quiet about the personal aimlessness implied by such polling; but no, the poll in effect legitimizes his vote.

* According to one estimate, the financial advantage enjoyed by incumbents is as much as $1.2 million per Congressional term. This takes into account mailing privileges, office use, and salaries, with the estimate that 80 percent of staff work is aimed at reelection, not legislation. Congressmen have a staff-salaries allowance of $288,156 per annum.

Many Congressmen are now openly saying, "I will abide by the wishes of the majority of my constituents." Leadership is thus transformed into followership. Notice the volte-face of California's Governor Brown after Proposition 13. The striking thing about this was its utter shamelessness. And Brown was quite right, pragmatically. As his November victory margin showed, the voters didn't mind a bit.

If it is true that the philosophy of government now tacitly accepted by many American politicians is that they are there to obey rather than command (President Carter, certainly, manages to convey this impression), then two important effects follow. The first is that such a philosophy explains with ease the great political conundrum that everyone has again been mulling over for the past few months: Why has voter turnout been dropping? Immensely complicated studies of this question have been undertaken recently. But the answer is surely obvious. If elected officials now consider it their duty to do what the majority wants, then it doesn't make any difference which of the rival candidates you vote for. Either will do, because both will be inclined to do what they are told. Therefore, why vote? Better to be polled than to go to the polls.

The other effect is the complaint now being heard in Congress: The job is no fun anymore. Of course it's no fun if all you are expected to do is follow orders from constituents. "Follow orders" is, of course, putting the case a little too strongly, but once a Congressman volunteers to become his constituents' ombudsman, he is well on the way to becoming their lackey. A retiring Congressman, James Hastings of New York, once put it this way: "All a member of Congress needs to do to win reelection is run a good public-relations operation and answer his constituent mail promptly. What kind of a whore am I?"

Let us take a look at the dynamics of this in a little more detail. The enormously increased legislative budget has allowed Congressional staffs to grow rapidly. (The overall legislative budget, more than $1 billion, has quadrupled since 1968; the number of staff employees has tripled.) More and more Congressmen are opening offices in their districts. Then they put out the shingle and invite business. "Need help with a federal problem?" the card in the constituent's mailbox will ask. "Please feel free to communicate with your Congressman, in person, by phone, or by mail."

In response to such soliciting, the mail begins to arrive—and continues arriving; so much of it that computers have perforce been installed on Capitol Hill to deal with the problem of replying to the flood of letters. An increase in the Congressional operating budgets took care of the expense of such computers. Some (not yet all) Congressmen now have the appropriate computer terminals in their offices. The necessary data from incoming letters are fed into the computer (name and address of constituent, subject of inquiry), and when the Congressman and his staff have gone home for the night, the obedient machine clatters out 700 or so "personalized" replies. The staff returns the next morning to fold the letters into envelopes and send them on their way.

Then more letters come back. The Congressman increasingly becomes the slave of this communications technology. He initiates the flurry of mail, but ends up being snowed under by it. He is hoist with his own petard. Mounting numbers of his constituents are on the alert, watching every move, trying to prod him this way or that.

There is much to be said for this, of course. It is, in effect, democracy carried to its logical conclusion. But it does render the Congressman slightly superfluous. It almost reaches the point where he could be replaced by a . . . computer. Come to think of it, the "ayes" and "noes" are now totaled on the House floor by a computer (called an "electronic voting device"). Only a few relatively simple changes would be needed for the constituents' "pro" and "con" letters on given issues to be fed into the letter-writing computer, which, instead of writing letters, would relay the opinions to the machine tallying the votes on the House floor . . . and there you would have it: the Congressman neatly short-circuited, entirely superfluous. Computers would mediate between the voters in the districts and the final tally on the floor. The beauty of this arrangement is that no one would have to worry about paying these computerized lawmakers pensions, or limiting their outside income, or getting them to submit financial-disclosure statements, or straightening out their ethics, or providing sensational copy for journalists. No wonder the flesh-and-blood Congressmen are getting restless.

34

The Great Congressional Power Grab
Business Week

Executive-legislative relations have changed significantly as a result of presidential abuses in Vietnam and Watergate (see also discussion in Chapter 7). The so-called "imperial presidency," as developed under Lyndon B. Johnson and Richard Nixon, has been modified by an increasingly assertive Congress. While the chief executive remains the initiator of major policies, the House and the Senate demand greater participation in amending, revising or opposing presidential requests. President Carter has encountered serious problems with Congress. What are some of the policy areas where problems have occurred? What is meant by the breakdown of congressional discipline? How is "interest-group government" related to the "iron triangle" discussion by Herbers in Article 25? What has been the impact of reform?

Throughout the 200-year history of the American republic there has been a constant ebb and flow of power between the country's two wellsprings of national policy: Congress and the White House. For much of the 20th century, mainly because of world wars, the Depression, and the cold war, the Presidency had grown nearly supreme. But over the past decade there has been a remarkable and historic shift of power back to Congress. It began under Democratic President Lyndon B. Johnson over Vietnam and intensified during the "imperial Presidency" of Republican Richard M. Nixon, whom Congress drove from office over Watergate. And it is now bedeviling the Administration of President Carter.

Many assumed that the election of Democrat Carter to the White House would end the growing tug-of-war between a Democratic-controlled Congress and the executive branch. But if anything, the power shift has accelerated. The overwhelmingly Democratic 95th

Congress has wrested policy control from the executive over energy and taxes, interferes more than ever in foreign policy, and is openly contemptuous of executive leadership.

At the same time, Congress itself has been undergoing profound institutional changes that have sapped its ability to exercise its new-found power. Party discipline has broken down, allowing regional and narrow special interests increasingly to dominate deliberations. Seniority no longer determines committee chairmanships, often resulting in a debilitating diffusion of power. A massive turnover in both parties and both houses has brought an influx of younger, more independent members who reject the old rule: "To get along, go along." The probity of Congress itself has been thrown into doubt by the Korea bribery scandal.

The cost of all this is increasingly apparent. After 16 months, Congress is only now at a stage where it is ready for a final vote on Carter's energy program. That, in turn, has played no small role in the slide of the dollar. And the unpredictability of what Congress may do about a tax cut both reflects confusion

Table 1: Milestones in the march of congressional power

War Powers Act of 1973: Congress significantly expanded its involvement in foreign policy by requiring the President to obtain congressional assent within 60 days of any armed action or undeclared state of war

The Watergate hearings of 1973: They launched the most serious arraignment of a sitting President in a century, decisively altering the relationship of the President and Congress for decades

Vietnam supplemental appropriation: Denial by Congress of supplemental money to wind down the Vietnam war in 1974 was perhaps the most direct intervention into foreign policy since the refusal of the Senate to ratify the Treaty of Versailles in 1919

Turkish arms embargo: Congressional refusal in 1975 to permit the Ford Administration to sell arms to Turkey in the Greek-Turkish imbroglio over Cyprus was a major new incursion into foreign policy

Budget & Impoundment Control Act of 1974: Congressional limitation of executive discretion was extended, preventing the President from holding up spending of funds authorized and appropriated by Congress

Legislative veto: Although the right of one or both houses of Congress to disapprove executive actions by simple majority vote dates back to 1932, it grew increasingly popular in the 1970s. It appears in both the War Powers and Budget acts, in the National Highway Traffic Safety Act, in petroleum allocation, and in a variety of laws covering federal regulation

Simultaneous transmittal: Increasingly, Congress is trying to circumvent Office of Management & Budget control of federal agency budgets by requiring that agencies transmit their budget requests to the relevant congressional committee when they send them to OMB. The most prominent such requirement is in the act that set up the Consumer Product Safety Commission in 1972

Congressional staff expansion: Staff for congressmen and for committees experienced a huge expansion between 1969 and 1975, giving Congress the resources and expertise that permit it for the first time to exercise judgments independent of the executive branch over the economic outlook and adds to it, making control of inflation much more difficult. "It's hard to get Congress to focus on the fact that government is the dominant force in the U. S. economy, and that what they do has more than localized effects," says a White House aide.

More broadly, while Congress has succeeded in grasping power, it has so far used that power more to block White House initiatives than to exercise constructive leadership. "There is a clear picture of disarray" in Washington, says Senate Budget Committee Chairman Edmund S. Muskie (D-Me.). No one, including the feisty members of Congress, believes that Congress is capable of setting national policy, or even providing national leadership. "No matter how assertive [Congress] is, or how creative and qualified for leadership individual members are," says Muskie, "maybe the institution is not really equipped to act as a strong leader." Adds James L. Sundquist, senior fellow at the Brookings Institution: "If Congress doesn't follow the President, it doesn't go anywhere. And today, the President doesn't seem to have any more influence than a citizen with one vote."

Carter's Show of Firmness

Already a small but growing band of congressmen is beginning to wonder whether things have gone too far. "I'm starting to hear talk in the cloakrooms now that wouldn't it be nice if we had a stronger President who could provide solid leadership and Congress could focus a little better on what needed to be done," says House Interior Committee Chairman Morris K. Udall (D-Ariz.).

That judgment is echoed at the White House. "Congress has overasserted its power, and to a large degree it is our fault," confides one White House aide. "There's a compelling institutional responsibility for us to be firmer

[with Congress] than we have been." Such a belief prompted Carter's veto of the defense authorization bill, and other vetoes appear in the offing.

But toughness in the White House seems unlikely to alter the new power relationship. For one thing, this fall's elections will bring yet another wave of new members—at least 50 in the House and 10 in the Senate—who are unlikely to be any more accommodating to the White House than those they will replace.

Moreover, there is a widespread belief on Capitol Hill that despite some excesses, the shift in power is both beneficial and long overdue. "We went through a period of developing Presidential power for many years, beginning with the Depression, and that made it inevitable that power was going to be abused," says Senate Majority Whip Alan Cranston (D-Calif.). "I think it's an overstatement to say we're entering a period of parliamentary government," says Senate Minority Leader Howard H. Baker Jr. (R-Tenn.). "We had one brush with that after the Civil War, and it was a failure."

Most members are also convinced that the public favors their growing influence. Indeed, talk by some top Carter aides of running against Congress in 1980 draws a skeptical review on Capitol Hill. "It would be foolish," says Senate Majority Leader Robert C. Byrd (D-W. Va.). "The American people expect a Democratic Congress and a Democratic President to work together, or they will seek an alternative."

Even a dramatic upturn in Carter's popularity would have only a limited impact on Congress, for the current mood of independence has been building since the late 1960s. The bitter dissent against Johnson's prosecution of the war in Vietnam marked the beginning of a major and expanding congressional role in foreign policy. "Older veterans around here," says Udall, "remember when foreign policy was very largely and exclusively the domain of Presidents, and Congress' role was only to appropriate money and occasionally give a little advice." Those days are gone. Passage of the War Powers Act in 1973 firmly established congressional review of any armed action overseas. That power was further enhanced when Congress in 1974 reserved the right to approve arms sales abroad. And legislators of both parties are consistently skeptical of Administration proposals in general. The debate on a SALT II treaty next year, for instance, could easily prove to be as difficult and contentious as was this year's over the Panama Canal treaties.

Congressional insistence on a greater role in policy is hardly limited to foreign relations. Capitol Hill has increasingly sought to limit the executive branch's discretion in administering legislation. Such attempts—the inclusion of one-house vetoes in laws ranging from pesticide regulation to energy pricing—recently drew complaints from Carter that their "proliferation threatens to upset the constitutional balance of responsibilities between the branches of government." Yet 48 of these provisions, which enable Congress to block a proposed regulation, have been enacted in the last four years.

Even more worrisome, in the eyes of many executive branch officials, is Congress' growing tendency to write ever more detailed laws. Health, Education & Welfare Secretary Joseph A. Califano Jr. complains that appropriations bills now have "literally hundreds of directives they want to set us about doing. We just can't move." Adds Senate Minority Leader Baker: "We've taken to passing 1,000-page bills instead of 10-page bills. What we are doing, if you examine that critically, is trying to act like executive department officials. . . . I think that's a distortion of the function of Congress."

Beginning roughly with the Clean Air Act amendments of 1970, Congress has drafted regulatory legislation in a way that gives agencies, such as the Environmental Protection Agency, as little "wiggle room" as possible. Congress "is becoming a 'super executive' branch as well as a 'super regulator,'" says Ralph Nader. "It wasn't designed to cross all the Ts and dot all the Is—it was designed as a compass simply to point the government in the proper direction. Now it's trying to dominate."

The Breakdown of Discipline

In response to the Nixon Administration's penchant for simply refusing to spend money on programs it did not want, Congress also moved to take greater control over federal spending and fiscal policy in general. Under the Congressional Budget & Impoundment Control Act of 1974, Congress required the executive to give it review power over any administrative decision not to spend money authorized and appropriated by Congress. In practice that has meant growing White House acquiescence to congressional spending plans. "We were saying, 'We're not going to let you discipline us, we're going to discipline ourselves,'" says Muskie. "But disciplining yourself always leaves open the option of not disciplining yourself."

That, critics claim, is precisely the problem. For, as Congress sought to impose greater discipline on the executive branch, its own internal structures were breaking down. A tremendous influx of new and independent members—fully 37% of the House and 33% of the Senate have served four years or less—was in part responsible. But serious efforts to break down the power of often autocratic committee chairmen had been under way for years.

The 94th Congress, which took office in 1974, marked the high point of that drive. That year the House Democratic Caucus removed three longtime committee chairmen—

F. Edward Hebert (D-La.) from Armed Services, W. R. Poage (D-Tex.) from Agriculture, and Wright Patman (D-Tex.) from Banking. The Senate, which also established procedures for removing chairmen, has yet to fire one. "But the mere fact that it happened in the House and that we've established a way of doing it in the Senate has caused those who might be inclined to be tyrannical not to be," says Cranston. "Members are in a better position to punish a chairman than a chairman is to punish them," says one Administration lobbyist.

In theory, a weakening of committee chairmen should have strengthened the hand of the leadership in both houses. Both House Speaker Thomas P. O'Neill Jr. (D-Mass.) and Senator Byrd generally win high marks for trying, but it is clear that their powers are limited. As Speaker, says Udall, "you're supposed to be a head-counter and a persuader, and you're supposed to produce the votes for the committee chairmen and the President any time a major bill hits the floor. There's a limit to what any human being can do." The Senate leadership "is trying to manage in a very difficult situation," says one senior State Dept. official. "You would have to be a cross between Solomon and Genghis Khan to run that place."

'INTEREST-GROUP GOVERNMENT'

The leadership's problems, and those of the White House, have been immensely complicated by the massive decline in party loyalty and party discipline. That is a reflection in part of Carter's close win over former President Gerald Ford in 1976. "Remember, most of us ran ahead of Carter in our districts," says Representative Leon E. Panetta (D-Calif.), president of the 1976 freshman class, "so we feel pretty independent of the old straight-loyalty-to-leadership appeal." The

nature of the two major parties has changed as well. "You can define a Democratic Party by states, but that's all," says Anne Wexler, a newly appointed White House political aide. "You don't have the party cohesion you had 20 years ago."

The nature of the issues Congress faces has also had a major impact in diminishing the importance of the parties. "There's not the cleavage [on issues] there used to be," says Senate Appropriations Committee Chairman Warren G. Magnuson (D-Wash.), a 32-year veteran of the Senate. "I remember in the Roosevelt days, if you had a piece of legislation you equated it to how it fit into the so-called 'New Deal.' Now they all come up with their own, and they don't equate it to any particular philosophy."

Moreover, the increasingly technical detail of congressional debates over such issues as energy and the environment makes it harder to discern normal partisan lines. "How can you get in a political fight over storing nuclear waste?" asks Magnuson. "Everybody wants to store it in the safest place, and the fight becomes somebody taking sides with this expert and somebody taking sides with that expert."

That development, when combined with the lack of discipline, has worked to the advantage of narrow interest groups. "The fragmentation of society into interest groups, together with the fragmentation of congressional authority into subgroups," says Stuart E. Eizenstat, top White House domestic policy adviser, "gives you a situation where every penny is defended by some group or another."

The enormous expansion of highly specialized subcommittees has also made it difficult for Congress to consider any major policy in its entirety. "The fact that the energy appropriations bill has to go through three subcommittees in each House, and the energy authorization bill through two committees in the House," says one White House aide, "makes it virtually impossible for Congress to exercise a judgment about overall energy policy." Notes Fred Wertheimer, senior vice-president of Common Cause: "We're coming really close to interest-group government, and it makes it almost impossible for Congress to take holistic approaches—everything gets sliced up."

Compounding these problems is the obvious ineptitude of the Carter Administration in working with Congress. Though most members, both Republican and Democrat, profess to see improvements, it has been a painfully slow process. Most of the problem has been laid to the inexperience of Carter and his staff with the institution. "It's like trying to play the piano by reading a book, or having somebody tell you how," says Muskie. "You have to actually play the instrument to make sweet music."

A Monumental Problem

Carter's "outsider" role has had another telling effect. A President's success on Capitol Hill, argues one top official of the Office of Management & Budget, "is fundamentally based on personal relationships with members. Even a guy like Jerry Ford won some fights he had no right to win on political grounds because he had champions on the Hill, old friends who carried the load for him." Indeed, just such a relationship is responsible as much as anything else for the survival of Carter's natural gas bill—although the relationship is not Carter's. Senate Energy Committee Chairman Henry M. Jackson (D-Wash.) was never enamored of the bill's thrust towards higher price. But out of personal pride as the Senate's energy expert and his long-standing friendship with Energy Secretary James R. Schlesinger, he went the extra mile, Administration officials believe.

But even had Carter been the consummate Washington insider, his relations with Congress would have been rocky. "Anybody who took that oath on that January day in 1977 was going to face a diminished Presidency and a resurgent Congress," says Udall. "You could have resurrected Lincoln, Washington, and Franklin Roosevelt, had a synthesis of them all, and I'm sure that President would have had a lot more trouble than any of his recent precedessors."

Whatever the reasons, Carter's problems with the two-thirds Democratic Congress have been monumental. After an early spate of victories last year—creation of the Energy Dept. and quick passage of an economic stimulus package among them—he has seen more and more proposals either rejected or totally overruled. The energy package, even if natural gas deregulation finally passes, has been diminished substantially by the death of the key wellhead tax on crude oil. The tax bill that emerged from the House is 180 degrees different in its thrust from Carter's reform-minded plan. Carter's ambitious reorganization plans for the government have slowed in the face of congressional hostility.

Even Carter's major victories this year—approval of the Panama Canal treaties, lifting the arms embargo on Turkey, and approval of Middle East arms sales—came with a twist that bodes ill for Carter. All three hinged on substantial Republican support, and that may not be forthcoming in the future. "In each case the initiative has begun in Ford's Administration or Nixon's . . . which makes it easier for us," says Baker. "But you're running out of old issues. You've got to get out of Ford issues and into Carter issues."

In fact, the deep divisions among congressional Democrats, and between them and the White House, have afforded Republicans more power than their numbers would suggest. House Ways & Means Committee Chairman

Al Ullman (D-Ore.), when faced with split Democratic ranks, was finally forced to turn to the panel's united Republicans to get any tax bill out of the committee. "We [Republicans] wrote the tax bill," says House Minority Leader John J. Rhodes (R-Ariz.), with only some exaggeration.

The Republicans' unusual influence shows signs of rekindling the flames of partisanship among congressional Democrats. But more important are the doubts on both sides over the direction in which the newly assertive Congress is headed. "Congress has become a little confused" about its role, says Representative Barber B. Conable Jr. (R-N. Y.), ranking Republican on the Ways & Means Committee. "They think if they can block, they can lead. But Congress leads in every which way."

Reform Reconsidered

In the House, such doubts have prompted some of those prominent in the reform battles of the early 1970s to reconsider the impact of their sweeping changes. Udall, who led the first attack on the committee seniority system in 1967 when Representative Adam Clayton Powell (D-N. Y.) was stripped of his Education & Labor Committee chairmanship, reflects that concern. "The question now," says Udall, "is can we reexamine what we did, and adjust it so we get the benefits of reform without paying quite as heavy a price in terms of confusion, the flood of ill-considered legislation, and the inability to do the oversight [of the executive] we ought to be doing?"

The worries extend beyond those members, such as Udall, who rank somewhere in the middle in seniority and are just now moving into positions of power in the House. Even the rebellious junior members elected in the wake of Watergate are showing concern. "I think the general tone is not bad—independent and a sense of questioning," says first-termer Panetta. "But the product is something else."

Much of the problem stems from the tremendous increase in workload that followed in part from the reform goal of giving individuals, no matter how junior, more say in legislation, and with it more committee slots and more staff. "We'd like to limit committee assignments," says Representative Norman Y. Mineta (D-Calif.), a leader of the 1974 freshman caucus in the House. "The current system is bad. Guys meet themselves coming and going. It doesn't allow for a coherent train of thought."

The new Congress that convenes in January could well see some changes to that end. Representative Thomas S. Foley (D-Wash.), chairman of the House Democratic Caucus, which sets House rules, is appointing a committee to look into procedures. "Their mandate is going to be to bring in to the December caucus meeting a set of proposals to deal with a whole gamut of things," says Udall, including the number of committee assignments and number of subcommittees as well as size of staff.

Limiting Filibusters

In the Senate, where reforms never had the impact they had on the House, there is a growing sense that the institution has failed to change to meet the demands now put upon it. "The founding fathers wanted Congress to move slowly and carefully," says Magnuson, "but that was in the days when the world was moving a little more slowly."

Of particular concern is the devastating impact that filibusters can have upon the Senate, preventing decisions on matters it simply cannot ignore. "There was a time when we could [afford] to spend a certain percentage of each session on filibusters and delays," says Muskie. But this Congress, which saw lengthy filibusters on natural gas and labor law reform, has prompted the leadership on both sides to search for ways to limit their effect. "There have got to be some rule changes in the Senate to limit filibusters," says Cranston. "There will be."

But such changes, if they increase the day-to-day efficiency of Congress, could make it a more effective competitor with the executive branch. And there are signs that Congress is more than eager to compete. "Congress is not meant to be a rubber stamp of any President," says Byrd. "What we have seen is a balancing act, which is in conformity with the constitutional system as it was intended to operate." Besides, after years under the executive's thumb, the newly assertive Congress is clearly enjoying its role. "The power of Congress is a new sort of idea," says Udall. "Members haven't tired of it yet."

35

Is Congress Obsolete?

Tad Szulc

Congress has a huge volume of legislative bills to consider, a burden which causes tremendous difficulties in making sense out of complex public policy proposals. Additionally, legislative staffs have grown to serve individual congressmen, committees, and subcommittees. Coupled with the in- *fluence of lobbyists, the congressional bureaucracy has become burdensome and unwieldy. Tad Szulc argues that legislative inefficiency is a serious problem. How does this affect voter responses in congressional elections? What are the prospects for legislative reform?*

Emerging from the Capitol shortly before eight o'clock on a Sunday morning last October, a red-eyed and exhausted senator stopped to talk to a friend before getting into his car for the drive home. In a hoarse whisper, he said: "You know, I've been in the Senate for 14 years, but I have never seen anything like the last 24 hours. This just can't be allowed to happen again." What the lawmaker didn't wish to see repeated was the paroxysm of wild, last-minute legislating that had held congressmen captive on the floor of both houses since early Saturday morning, with the midterm elections only three weeks away. In the course of an around-the-clock closing session, the Senate had passed 22 bills, and the House of Representatives 14, spending hours on countless amendments to such crucial legislation as those governing taxation and energy.

But this Congress, the 96th (in session since January 15), may very well conclude with the same eleventh-hour frenzy. The staggering volume and complexity of legislation, which was primarily responsible for its predecessor's last-minute snarl, is a problem that will not go away. The legislative burden, however, is

From Tad Szulc, "Is Congress Obsolete?" *Saturday Review* (March 3, 1979): 20, 22–23. Reprinted by permission of the author.

only one cause of the disease with which Congress is now afflicted. The recent establishment of a vast system of subcommittees, intended to reduce the power of committee chairmen, has so diffused authority that crucial legislation is continuously being bottled up for months in subcommittees before emerging in barely recognizable form. Meanwhile, this same fragmentation is repeated in the members' ties to party and to ideology. On several occasions President Carter has found himself in the embarrassing position of depending on Republican votes to avert defeat, despite heavy Democratic majorities in both houses. And the one-issue candidate, with his nonchalance toward the broad ideals that have defined the two parties, has become a commonplace of political analysis. Finally, and perhaps most insidious of all, congressmen have become ever more dependent on lobbyists and special-interest groups for advice—even including instructions on how to vote—and for underwriting the skyrocketing costs of campaigns.

These problems, by and large, are not matters of happenstance; they are embedded in the structure of Congress and American politics. Looking toward the future with this in mind, one cannot avoid asking a fundamental question: Is Congress an obsolete institution? Without a radical change in the way that it governs, can Congress act as an efficient lawmaking body in the Eighties and beyond?

A midwestern senator sums up the situation in dismal tones: "We are losing control of what we are doing here . . . there isn't enough time in a day to keep abreast of everything we should know to legislate responsibly, dealing with so many bills, having to attend so many committee and subcommittee meetings, listening to the lobbyists, having to worry about problems of constituents, and, of course, keeping a close eye on politics back home. You know, one *has* to get reelected. . . ."

Any analysis of Congress's basic problems must begin with the incredible legislative burden that it now tries to shoulder. The numbers alone are overwhelming. In the 1977–78 session, congressmen introduced 22,313 public and private bills and resolutions. The House took 1,810 seriously enough to file reports on them, the Senate, 1,413. In the end, they passed 3,211 bills and resolutions, with 804 bills finally enacted into law. These figures included fundamental lawmaking, as well as such matters as providing for the display of the U.S.S. *Wyoming's* nameplate, bell, and silver service at the Wyoming State Museum. And as if that weren't enough, the Congress had to act in the last two years to confirm 124,730 military and civilian nominations submitted by the President.

The problem of overwork is aggravated by the complexity of legislation, which has come more and more to embrace highly detailed, technically difficult issues. The 1978 tax bill, for example, was 184 pages long, though it was an amendment to the 1954 Internal Revenue Code rather than a new piece of legislation. Few congressmen could honestly claim to understand every ramification of the bill that they ultimately passed. Since every member of the Congress cannot be an expert in every field—most will carve out a specialty or

two—the majority come to depend on the judgment of the recognized experts, their staffs, lobbyists, and representatives of special interests.

"I don't know what the answer to this problem can be," a young southern representative commented. "I try to do my homework, but, say, on taxes, I will be guided by the views of Al Ullman (chairman of the Joint Internal Revenue Taxation Committee) or Russell Long (chairman of the Senate Finance Committee). I have a legislative assistant boning up on taxation, and, like everybody else, I get my ear bent by lobbyists. In the end, I'm not sure if I vote intelligently every time, especially on the more complex issues."

Congressmen have taken to appointing more and more staff members in order to stem this vast tide of information. A full 5,000 staffers are now attached to congressmen, committees, and subcommittees. Their influence may be pernicious or benign; but in any case it is expanding rapidly, so that staffers have become the unacknowledged legislators of the Congress. Some are counted among the most powerful figures in Washington on particular topics. For example, Richard Perle, Senator Henry Jackson's (D-Wash.) principal adviser on defense issues, is credited with substantially influencing key arms-control thinking in the Senate, and has been called "the quintessential Washington operator." Many Capitol Hill experts give the credit for the 1978 energy compromise not to Speaker Thomas P. O'Neill, Jr., but to his 25-year-old legislative assistant, Ariel Weiss. But whether staffers even fulfill their original purpose of saving their boss's time is open to doubt, since staff members are themselves responsible for more and longer bills, more hearings, more reports, more unfathomable issues.

Other efforts to deal with the flood of legislation have proved no more successful. The subcommittee system, greatly augmented by the post-Watergate "freshman class" of 1974, has smothered or splintered legislation more often than it has expedited it. The 96th Congress has inherited 29 standing committees and 151 subcommittees in the House, 21 committees and 112 subcommittees in the Senate (outnumbering the 100 senators), four joint committees, and seven joint subcommittees. The House also has six Democratic and Republican partisan committees, while the Senate has seven. The average representative sits on three subcommittees, the average senator, five. Not only do these groups-within-groups keep legislation holed up for as long as a year, but the tendency of their interests to overlap further adds to the confusion.

Most congressmen find themselves unable to devote adequate time and thought to their various assignments; instead, they flit in and out of hearings, spending an hour in a committee, and minutes in some of the subcommittees. "I can't be everywhere at the same time," a New York congressman said. "And I also have to race to the floor for quorum votes or votes on bills whenever that damned bell rings. It's insane."

A further attempt to deal with the huge volume of work is the so-called "suspension calendar." Under this procedure, originally intended to dispose rapidly of lesser legislation, the House sets aside part of Monday and Tuesday for floor votes without allowing amendments. But this aim is often subverted by the inclusion of important money bills that sneak past unwary congressmen on the suspension docket.

One of the most alarming aspects of the functioning of Congress is the new primacy of lobbyists. An estimated 15,000 of them currently spend $1 billion a year pursuing congressmen around Capitol Hill, and probably another $1 billion a year for related activities in the home districts. The growing reach of Congress into highly specific, detailed legislation touching on the interests of particular groups has made this new muscle necessary for them; and this same complexity, forcing

congressmen into the hands of technical experts, has made it possible. Whether he represents a defense contractor, a labor union, the association of restaurant-owners (who campaigned successfully against President Carter's attempt to remove tax deductions from "three-martini lunches"), or a public interest group, the lobbyist is the master of his subject. He may know even more about it than a Hill staffer. In this sense, he becomes a "technical adviser" to the congressmen, many of whom gladly accept his assistance.

"There is obviously no bribing," a senator said, "because the lobbyists and congressmen are, by and large, too sophisticated for such crude business. But lobbyists can be enormously convincing politically, outlining for their targeted congressmen the pluses and minuses, in terms of political impact in their districts, of how a vote is cast. And, believe me, it works."

It is a common sight in the lobbies of the House and Senate—literally—for groups of lobbyists to congregate before a vote and indicate with thumb-up or thumb-down signals what a member should do on the floor. Others do it from public galleries. William S. Cohen, the Maine Republican who was elevated last November from the House to the Senate, says that he developed the habit of hunching his shoulders and lowering his head as he made his way through clusters of lobbyists from the front door to the elevator. "I just didn't want to see their signals," he says.

A more recent innovation is the political action committee (PAC). Under the 1974 election law, corporations and unions can contribute $5,000 to as many PACs as they wish. Formed by corporate employees, trade groups, or stockholders, as well as by unions, close to 1,900 PACs contributed over $64 million to congressional candidates in the 1978 elections.

Though business PACs have been accused of giving to front-runners no matter what their affiliation, most of the giving is anything but indiscriminate. A study of federal election returns shows that committee chairmen received especially lavish gifts, and that the industries or professions for which the chairman legislated led the list of donors. The average House chairman received $45,000 from political committees, double the 1976 total. Thomas Foley (D-Wash.), chairman of the House Agriculture Committee, took in $145,000 from special interests, 57 percent of his campaign treasury. Rep. John M. Murphy (D-N.Y.), chairman of the Merchant Marine Committee, received nine contributions of $2,500 or over from maritime and transportation groups. Few of these congressmen even needed the money, since they were already outspending their opponents, and almost all won handily.

There is no question that lobbyists and special interests affect legislation. The most spectacular display of their power was mustered around the tough energy-conservation package that President Carter submitted to the Congress on April 20, 1977. It sought to curb the use of oil by taxing it at the wellhead and other measures. The bill was approved by the House in autumn of 1977, but it came unraveled in the Senate a year later, when special interests—oil and natural-gas companies and oil and gas-producing states among them—arrayed a formidable army against the Carter proposals.

The lobbyists advocated the deregulation of the price of natural gas, which the White House (at least at the outset) and consumer groups opposed, and the removal of the tax features of the bill. The legislation remained stalled for a year in Senate committees, then in House-Senate conferences, and finally in a House Ad Hoc Committee on Energy. The committee reached a compromise on the deregulation issue in early October, but the House didn't complete voting on the energy package until 7:30 a.m. on the last day of the session. (The Senate acted a few days earlier.) Though oil and gas interests professed dissatisfaction, they got what they wanted.

The session's other major piece of legisla-tion, the tax reform bill, was just as badly mauled. The legislation that finally emerged after a year's struggle in Senate and House committees and on the floor of both houses provided precious little relief for the average American family—and the rise in Social Security levies, particularly in a time of inflation, meant that most Americans would be even worse off than before. Only the powerful fared well: Rich taxpayers got a break on capital gains, while business received a cut in the maximum corporate tax rate.

While members of Congress lose sight of central concerns amid the vast welter of legislation and the badgering of lobbyists, consensus becomes an ever more evanescent ideal. Appeals to loyalty, either to basic principles or to the party that is supposed to embody those principles, simply do not carry the strength that they used to. President Carter's difficulty in gaining support for such issues as the energy and tax reforms, or the two Panama Canal treaties, was due not only to his lack of personal magnetism or shrewdness, but also to the growing resistance of congressmen to being mustered along party lines. The Canal treaties, for example, were ratified by exactly the required two-thirds majority only because Senate Minority Leader Howard Baker of Tennessee and a number of moderate Republican leaders concluded that the United States—and not the Carter administration—should be spared the foreign policy embarrassment of a rejection. Meanwhile, nine Democrats voted against the treaties.

On such issues as budget-cutting, tax reform, and defense spending, the distinction between the two parties has been blurred beyond recognition. This has led, paradoxically, to less cohesion rather than more, since loose ideological coalitions can form and dissolve around specific issues when parties fail to dictate clear and opposing points of view. "I'm no longer sure whom the Congress represents," says a veteran California representative. "It's getting to be more and more atomized. On lots of issues, we go for the lowest common denominator so that we can legislate at all."

Is it any wonder, then, that congressional elections rouse so little enthusiasm in the public? Only 37.9 percent of eligible voters went to the polls to elect the 96th Congress, the lowest midterm turnout since 1942. As recently as 1970, 43.5 percent of eligible Americans queued up at polling stations. A further depressing discovery is the massive number of young voters who declined to vote, a scant six years after the much-heralded lowering of the voting age to 18.

Nor is enthusiasm within the Congress itself running at a very high pitch. Fifty-eight members of the House, a record number, chose not to seek reelection in 1978. Three senators did likewise. The reasons ranged from frustration over a member's inability to influence legislation constructively, to just plain overwork, the sacrifice of family life, and—often—the realization that a congressman, particularly if he is a lawyer, can earn more money in private life.

In the end, there is no reason to expect that the 96th Congress will behave or perform any better than its predecessor. Aware as members are of all the shortcomings in the functioning of the Congress, there is no outlook for any serious changes or reforms. The truth is that few congressmen are prepared to upset the applecart: Their personal interests are, by and large, well served by the status quo.

One reform mentioned periodically is the extension of the House term from two to four years, so that congressmen can spend a smaller percentage of their terms worrying about reelection or mollifying the special-interest pressures emanating from the home district. But the extension of congressional terms can be accomplished only through a constitutional amendment, an idea received very coolly in Washington.

The sorry spectacle of a Congress unable to legislate has led some thinkers to advance truly radical proposals for reform. Retired Massachusetts congressman Michael Harrington has proposed "a distinctly American parliamentary setup," in which the President and the Cabinet would be selected by the Congress and serve concurrently with it. The Cabinet would take on many of the lesser responsibilities of Congress, which would then be free to engage in the kind of serious policy debate so rarely heard in its chambers. The executive and legislative branches would cooperate, of course, far more closely than they do today. Whatever the merits of this system, however, it is certain to be ignored by a body incapable even of minor reform.

Calls for change have been lukewarm at best. Meeting early in December, the Democratic Caucus agreed to limit service on House subcommittees to five panels per member, a minute improvement, and to reduce the time-wasting number of roll-calls (a suggestion since accepted by Congress). There are no other proposals to win action.

With the next presidential and congressional elections less than two years away, the harsh realities of politics combined with the inertia already paralyzing Capitol Hill should prevent Americans from expecting too much from their beleaguered lawmakers. It would be a near-miracle if a sensible compromise emerges on national health legislation, one of the priorities in the 96th Congress. Action may be required to cope with the worsening energy crisis, but it could be just a rerun of the 1978 stalemate. The same may apply to possible anti-inflation legislation. The Senate ratification of the new arms agreement with the Soviets is a toss-up. The legislative logjam shows no sign of unclogging. Leaders will go on with uphill battles to corral majorities.

It looks like bad business as usual for the 96th Congress.

The Supreme Court

10

The Supreme Court, the "court of last resort" in the nation's judicial
system, has played a unique role in shaping and influencing important
policy decisions through critical stages of American political development. No other Western democratic government has a high court
where powers are comparable to the Supreme Court's substantial powers
in the political process. The Supreme Court is more than the highest
appellate court for settling legal disputes. With its special role as
constitutional interpreter, the Supreme Court has co-equal authority
and status with the legislative and executive branches of the national
government.

How has this non-elective judicial branch of government achieved
such important powers? As shown in Article 36, much of the Supreme
Court's influence can be traced to the leadership of Chief Justice John
Marshall who established the basis of judicial review in the case of

Marbury v. *Madison* (1803). Although the constitutional framers had not provided for judicial review in Article III of the Constitution—even though Alexander Hamilton argued in *Federalist*, No. 78 that the court had such authority—Marshall asserted that the Supreme Court has the right to nullify acts of Congress when such legislation conflicts with the Constitution. Why? The Chief Justice argued that "It is emphatically the province and duty of the judicial department to say what the law is." Moreover, it is "the very essence of judicial duty" for the Supreme Court to uphold the Constitution when an act of Congress violates the basic charter, because "the Constitution is superior to any ordinary Act of the Legislature," and "the Constitution, and not such ordinary Act, must govern the case to which they both apply."

Judicial review of federal legislation was used rarely during the early course of the nation's development. In fact, the Marshall Court was more involved with state challenges to national authority than with congressional enactments. With the exception of the *Marbury* case, the Supreme Court was more concerned with state laws that conflicted with national constitutional supremacy. The second occasion for judicial review placed the Supreme Court in the political crisis over the slavery issue. In deciding the *Dred Scott* case (1857), Chief Justice Roger Taney struck down the Missouri Compromise, a ruling which contributed to the nation's internal disunity and the Civil War.

The most serious clash between judicial and legislative power took place during the 1930s when the Supreme Court used judicial review and statutory interpretation to nullify much of President Roosevelt's New Deal legislation. Roosevelt had attacked the nation's economic crisis with a wide range of reforms, particularly in labor-management relations and controls over industrial production. The Supreme Court viewed these sweeping and comprehensive measures as unconstitutional delegations of power from Congress to the president. This led Roosevelt to propose a court packing plan, which would have permitted him to appoint additional Justices to the court to sit alongside the men who had reached age 70. Even though Roosevelt had just won a landslide victory in 1936, his court packing plan was politically unacceptable. The Court ended the crisis by adjusting its internal alignments, and by 1937 a majority of the Justices were approving the same economic reforms that only a few months before they had opposed.

The Court's role as constitutional interpreter is buttressed by its authority to determine the meaning of legislation, by the prestige which judges have in the political system, and by the legitimacy and acceptability of judicial decisions by other agencies of government. At the same time, the judiciary is limited by the forces of public opinion, by various legal and technical checks which delay court decisions, and by the self-restraint which judges impose upon themselves to limit their interference into politically sensitive areas of public policy.

Perhaps the most significant check on judicial authority is the filling of court vacancies. Since all federal judges are appointed rather than elected, both the president and the Senate can influence the composition of the judiciary by the persons they select. According to Henry Abraham (Article 37), this is most clearly evident in presidential appointments to the Supreme Court. In using such criteria as professional achievement, ideological appropriateness, political affiliation, personal attractiveness, and religious, racial, and geographic considerations, the president can have a significant influence over the membership and future directions of Supreme Court decisions.

The U.S. Supreme Court has a complex decision-making process. In Article 38, Nina Totenberg identifies the various stages of the Court's deliberations. In *selecting* cases, the Court was assisted by the 1925 Judge's bill, designed by Chief Justice William Howard Taft to reduce the obligatory right of appealing cases to the Supreme Court. This was considerably narrowed through the process of *certiorari*, which gave the Court discretionary authority to select the most important cases for review. This considerably reduced the volume of cases brought before the Court. A writ of certiorari is granted only when four of the Justices vote affirmatively. The Supreme Court is also unique in having *oral argument* before the nine justices in important cases. A former Justice, John Harlan, suggested four major purposes of the oral argument, including *selectivity* of issues presented, *simplicity* of form and expression, *candor* or frankness in responding to Justices' inquiries, and *resiliency* or flexibility toward the Court, particularly since the Justices may interject questions or comments during any stage of the oral argument. Other interesting aspects of the Court's decision making include internal debate over the case, assigning and writing of opinions, and announcing opinions publicly.

The Court's policy-making role is examined by Levine and Becker in Article 39. The Warren Court (1954–1968) was highly instrumental in strengthening the Bill of Rights and protecting the individual against the power of the state. For example, the school desegregation decision in *Brown* v. *Board of Education* (1954) (see also Article 8) provided the constitutional basis for eliminating the system of separate school facilities for black and white students. President Nixon appointed justices with "law and order" and "strict constructionist" views. The four Nixon appointees—Chief Justice Burger and Associate Justices Blackmun, Powell, and Rehnquist—eroded many of the liberal decisions of the Warren Court. Rather than nullifying judgments in school desegregation, civil rights, and civil liberties, the Burger Court changed the scope of such decisions and limited the impact of previous rulings. Most controversial have been recent rulings in such areas as school busing, abortion, and the death penalty in state criminal cases. In any event, the Supreme Court remains at the center of political controversy since it must deal with issues that other branches of government cannot resolve and with legal disputes that are not settled by the lower federal and state courts. For this reason, the Court is as much a part of the political process as the executive and legislative branches.

36

Marbury v. Madison
U.S. Supreme Court

The power of judicial review—the authority of the Supreme Court to declare acts of Congress unconstitutional—is not specifically found in Article III of the Constitution, although Alexander Hamilton argued, in Federalist, No. 78, that such power was implicit. Judicial review over the constitutionality of state laws was part of the "supremacy clause" of Article VI and included in section 25 of the 1789 Judiciary Act. Chief Justice Marshall's opinion in Marbury v. Madison *(1803) established this doctrine in the context of a bitter political controversy between the Federalist party (which had just lost the presidential election of 1800) and the Jeffersonian Republicans. Just before John Adams left the presidency he attempted to pack the courts with Federalist appointees, acting under authority of the 1801 Judiciary Act, which was adopted after Jefferson's presidential victory. Marbury, one of these last-ditch appointees, had been selected for a justice of the peace in the District of Columbia. His commission to take office was signed and sealed by John Marshall, then serving as Secretary of State as well as Chief Justice. But Jefferson ordered his new Secretary of State, James Madison, to withhold the commission to Marbury. Conse-quently, Marbury filed suit with the Supreme Court to issue a writ of mandamus under the 1789 Judiciary Act to force Madison to deliver his commission. The case thus involved a dispute between the presidency and the Supreme Court. Marshall knew that the Court could not force the issue since the Jefferson Administration would refuse to obey the court order if it was issued. Marshall also knew that he would be severely criticized by the Federalists if he refused to issue the order for Marbury's commission. How did Marshall resolve the dispute? As indicated in the text of the opinion, the solution was to agree that Marbury's commission should be granted but that the Supreme Court could not intervene in the matter because the section of the 1789 Judiciary Act granting such authority to the Court was unconstitutional. Marshall's opinion has been called a masterwork of indirection, that is, a brilliant example of side-stepping danger while seeming to court it, to advance in one direction while his opponents were looking in another. It also should be noted that the Supreme Court is much more inclined to use statutory interpretation rather than judicial review to avoid confrontations with either Congress or the presidency.*

Mr. Chief Justice Marshall delivered the opinion of the Court, saying in part:

In the order in which the court has viewed this subject, the following questions have been considered and decided.

1st. Has the applicant a right to the commission he demands? . . . [The Court finds that he has.]

2d. If he has a right, and that right has been violated, do the laws of his country afford him a remedy? . . . [The Court finds that they do.]

3d. If they do afford him a remedy, is it a mandamus issuing from this court? . . .

This, then, is a plain case for a mandamus, either to deliver the commission, or a copy of it from the record; and it only remains to be inquired,

Whether it can issue from this court.

The act to establish the judicial courts of the

1 Cranch 137; 2 L. Ed. 60 (1803)

United States authorizes the Supreme Court "to issue writs of mandamus in cases warranted by the principles and usages of law, to any courts appointed, or persons holding office, under the authority of the United States."

The Secretary of State, being a person holding an office under the authority of the United States, is precisely within the letter of the description, and if this court is not authorized to issue a writ of mandamus to such an officer, it must be because the law is unconstitutional, and therefore absolutely incapable of conferring the authority, and assigning the duties which its words purport to confer and assign.

The Constitution vests the whole judicial power of the United States in one Supreme Court, and such inferior courts as Congress shall, from time to time, ordain and establish. . . .

In the distribution of this power it is declared that "the Supreme Court shall have original jurisdiction in all cases affecting ambassadors, other public ministers and consuls, and those in which a state shall be a party. In all other cases, the Supreme Court shall have appellate jurisdiction." . . .

If it had been intended to leave it in the discretion of the legislature to apportion the judicial power between the supreme and inferior courts according to the will of that body, it would certainly have been useless to have proceeded further than to have defined the judicial power, and the tribunals in which it should be vested. The subsequent part of the section is mere surplusage, is entirely without meanings, . . . the distribution of jurisdiction, made in the Constitution, is form without substance. . . .

It cannot be presumed that any clause in the Constitution is intended to be without effect; and, therefore, such a construction is inadmissible, unless the words require it. . . .

To enable this court, then, to issue a man-

damus, it must be shown to be an exercise of appellate jurisdiction, or to be necessary to enable them to exercise appellate jurisdiction. . . .

It is the essential criterion of appellate jurisdiction, that it revises and corrects the proceedings in a cause already instituted, and does not create that cause. Although, therefore, a mandamus may be directed to courts, yet to issue such a writ to an officer for the delivery of a paper, is in effect the same as to sustain an original action for that paper, and, therefore, seems not to belong to appellate but to original jurisdiction. Neither is it necessary in such a case as this to enable the court to exercise its appellate jurisdiction.

The authority, therefore, given to the Supreme Court, by the Act establishing the judicial courts of the United States, to issue writs of mandamus to public officers, appears not to be warranted by the Constitution; and it becomes necessary to inquire whether a jurisdiction so conferred can be exercised.

The question, whether an Act, repugnant to the Constitution can become the law of the land, is a question deeply interesting to the United States; but, happily, not of an intricacy proportioned to its interest. It seems only necessary to recognize certain principles, supposed to have been long and well established, to decide it.

That the people have an original right to establish, for their future government, such principles as, in their opinion, shall most conduce to their own happiness, is the basis on which the whole American fabric has been erected. The exercise of this original right is a very great exertion; nor can it nor ought it to be frequently repeated. The principles, therefore, so established, are deemed fundamental. And as the authority from which they proceed is supreme, and can seldom act, they are designed to be permanent.

This original and supreme will organizes the

government, and assigns to different departments their respective powers. It may either stop here, or establish certain limits not to be transcended by those departments.

The government of the United States is of the latter description. The powers of the legislature are defined and limited; and that those limits may not be mistaken, or forgotten, the Constitution is written. To what purpose are powers limited, and to what purpose is that limitation committed to writing, if these limits may, at any time, be passed by those intended to be restrained? The distinction between a government with limited and unlimited powers is abolished, if those limits do not confine the persons on whom they are imposed, and if acts prohibited and acts allowed are of equal obligation. It is a proposition too plain to be contested, that the Constitution controls any legislative Act repugnant to it; or, that the legislature may alter the Constitution by an ordinary Act.

Between these alternatives there is no middle ground. The Constitution is either a superior paramount law, unchangeable by ordinary means, or it is on a level with ordinary legislative Acts, and, like other Acts, is alterable when the legislature shall please to alter it.

If the former part of the alternative be true, then a legislative Act contrary to the Constitution is not law; if the latter part be true, then written constitutions are absurd attempts, on the part of the people, to limit a power in its own nature illimitable.

Certainly all those who have framed written constitutions contemplate them as forming the fundamental and paramount law of the nation, and, consequently, the theory of every such government must be, that an Act of the Legislature, repugnant to the Constitution, is void.

This theory is essentially attached to a written Constitution, and, is consequently, to be considered, by this court, as one of the fundamental principles of our society. It is not therefore to be lost sight of in the further consideration of this subject.

If an Act of the Legislature, repugnant to the Constitution, is void, does it, notwithstanding its invalidity, bind the courts, and oblige them to give it effect? Or, in other words, though it be not law, does it constitute a rule as operative as if it was a law? This would be to overthrow in fact what was established in theory; and would seem, at first view, an absurdity too gross to be insisted on. It shall, however, receive a more attentive consideration.

It is emphatically the province and duty of the judicial department to say what the law is. Those who apply the rule to particular cases, must of necessity expound and interpret that rule. If two laws conflict with each other, the courts must decide on the operation of each.

So if a law be in opposition to the Constitution; if both the law and the Constitution apply to a particular case, so that the court must either decide that case conformably to the law, disregarding the Constitution; or conformably to the Constitution, disregarding the law, the court must determine which of these conflicting rules governs the case. This is of the very essence of judicial duty.

If, then, the courts are to regard the Constitution, and the Constitution is superior to any Act of the Legislature, the Constitution, and not such ordinary Act, must govern the case to which they both apply.

Those, then, who controvert the principle that the Constitution is to be considered, in court, as a paramount law, are reduced to the necessity of maintaining that courts must close their eyes on the Constitution, and see only the law.

This doctrine would subvert the very foundation of all written constitutions. It would declare that an Act which, according to the principles and theory of our government, is entirely void, is yet, in practice, completely obligatory. It would declare that if the legislature shall do what is expressly forbidden, such Act, notwithstanding the express prohibition, is in reality effectual. It would be giving to the legislature a practical and real omnipotence, with the same breath which professes to restrict their powers within narrow limits. It is prescribing limits, and declaring that those limits may be passed at pleasure.

That it thus reduces to nothing what we have deemed the greatest improvement on political institutions, a written constitution, would of itself be sufficient, in America, where written constitutions have been viewed with so much reverence, for rejecting the construction. But the peculiar expressions of the Constitution of the United States furnish additional arguments in favor of its rejection.

The judicial power of the United States is extended to all cases arising under the Constitution.

Could it be the intention of those who gave this power, to say that in using it the Constitution should not be looked into? That a case arising under the Constitution should be decided without examining the instrument under which it arises?

This is too extravagant to be maintained.

In some cases, then, the Constitution must be looked into by the judges. And if they can open it at all, what part of it are they forbidden to read or to obey?

There are many other parts of the Constitution which serve to illustrate this subject.

It is declared that "no tax or duty shall be laid on articles exported from any State." Suppose a duty on the export of cotton, of tobacco, or of flour; and a suit instituted to recover it. Ought judgment to be rendered in such a case? ought the judges to close their eyes on the Constitution, and see only the law?

The Constitution declares "that no bill of attainder or ex post facto law shall be passed."

If, however, such a bill should be passed, and a person should be prosecuted under it, must the court condemn to death those victims whom the Constitution endeavors to preserve?

"No person," says the Constitution, "shall be convicted of treason unless on the testimony of two witnesses to the same overt act, or on confession in open court."

Here the language of the Constitution is addressed especially to the courts. It prescribes, directly for them, a rule of evidence not to be departed from. If the legislature should change that rule, and declare one witness, or a confession out of court, sufficient for conviction, must the constitutional principle yield to the legislative Act?

From these, and many other selections which might be made, it is apparent, that the framers of the Constitution contemplated that instrument as a rule for the government of courts, as well as of the legislature.

Why otherwise does it direct the judges to take an oath to support it? This oath certainly applies in an especial manner to their conduct in their official character. How immoral to impose it on them, if they were to be used as the instruments, and the knowing instruments, for violating what they swear to support!

The oath of office, too, imposed by the legislature, is completely demonstrative of the legislative opinion on this subject. It is in these words: "I do solemnly swear that I will administer justice without respect to persons, and do equal right to the poor and to the rich; and that I will faithfully and impartially discharge all the duties incumbent on me as ———, according to the best of my abilities and understanding, agreeably to the Constitution and laws of the United States."

Why does a judge swear to discharge his duties agreeably to the Constitution of the United States, if that Constitution forms no rule for his government—if it is closed upon him, and cannot be inspected by him?

If such be the real state of things, this is worse than solemn mockery. To prescribe, or to take this oath, becomes equally a crime.

It is also not entirely unworthy of observation, that in declaring what shall be the supreme law of the land, the Constitution itself is first mentioned; and not the laws of the United States generally, but those only which shall be made in pursuance of the Constitution, have that rank.

Thus, the particular phraseology of the Constitution of the United States confirms and strengthens the principle, supposed to be essential to all written constitutions, that a law repugnant to the Constitution is void; and that courts, as well as other departments, are bound by that instrument.

The rule must be discharged.

37

Judges and Justices: Qualifications and Nominations
Henry J. Abraham

Unlike the president or Congress, all federal judges are appointed rather than elected to office. (See Constitution, Article 3, Section 1 in the Appendix.) Considering the life tenure of federal judges and the impact they have on the law and public policy, the criteria and standards used to select judges are important. While most states have formal requirements of legal training for judges, this is only an unwritten, although very important, requirement at the federal level. Senatorial courtesy is a political factor in confirming presidential appointments to the lower federal courts. Prior judicial experience, while always said to be important, has not been an obstacle for some of the most outstanding members of the Supreme Court, including such luminaries as Chief Justice Marshall and Chief Justice Earl Warren. Every time the presi-

dent has the opportunity to nominate a Supreme Court Justice, a national guessing game takes place. Abraham indicates five of the most important factors considered by the president. What is objective merit? How are political availability and ideological appropriateness related? How important is personal friendship with the president? Since Abraham wrote this selection, what have been the trends in presidential appointments to the Supreme Court? Why did President Nixon encounter such difficulty with the Senate with two of his nominees who were rejected? Should there be a woman nominated to the Supreme Court? How are presidential nominating standards related to actual performance on the Supreme Court?

QUALIFICATIONS AND NOMINATIONS

On the whole, the only *statutory* requirement for judicial nomination present in the states for most courts is a law degree, for others not even an LLB. is required (e.g., certain magistrates). No statutory requirement, *whatsoever*, exists on the federal level, but the need for a law degree is unquestionably an unwritten law: no nonlawyer stands even the slightest chance of nomination, no matter how learned he may be otherwise.

The matter of *judicial experience* is in a different category: considerable lip-service is paid to it, and some Chief Executives have

insisted upon it for certain levels (e.g., President Eisenhower for his nominees to the Supreme Court after Earl Warren); but its absence has by no means been a block to nomination even to the United States Supreme Court. Of the 96 men who had served on that tribunal between 1789 and late 1968, only twenty had had ten years or more on any lower court levels at the time of their appointment; the last one with that much experience was Mr. Justice Cardozo, who had served for eighteen years on New York benches when President Hoover nominated him to succeed Mr. Justice Holmes in 1932. Forty-one had had none at all—yet among these are some of the most revered and illustrious names in America's judicial annals: six of the 14 Chief Justices—Marshall, Taney, S. P. Chase, Waite, Fuller, and Warren; and such Associate Justices as Story, Miller, Bradley, Brandeis,

Reprinted by permission of the publisher from Henry J. Abraham, *The Judiciary: The Supreme Court in the Governmental Process*, 2nd Edition (Boston: Allyn and Bacon, 1969). Copyright © 1969 by Allyn and Bacon, Inc.

Sutherland, Roberts, Frankfurter, and Robert Jackson. In the oft-quoted words of one of these, Mr. Justice Frankfurter, neither judicial experience nor geographic considerations nor political affiliation should play the slightest role in considerations leading to appointment to even the highest bench in the land—such selection should be "wholly on the basis of functional fitness." To him, the essential qualities of a Supreme Court Justice were but three: those of the philosopher, historian, and prophet (to which, as we have already noted, Mr. Justice Brennan added a fourth: "inordinate patience"). To seal his basic contention, Frankfurter told an attentive audience of lawyers and law students:

One is entitled to say without qualification that the correlation between prior judicial experience and fitness for the Supreme Court is zero. The significance of the greatest among the Justices who had such experience, Holmes and Cardozo, derived not from that judicial experience but from the fact that they were Holmes and Cardozo. They were thinkers, and more particularly, legal philosophers.

Nonetheless, the issue of judicial experience is never quite dormant, and there is no doubt that at least some consideration is given to it, depending upon the stance of the nominating authority. Individual members of Congress call sporadically for some statutory requirement—usually providing for upwards of five years of service on lower court benches—but no such legislation has ever been passed. And it is not likely to be, given continued opposition by the Bar, the Executive, and the Judiciary itself.

Presidential nominating motivations. A favorite indoor sport of the practitioners of the law and politics as well as of the public at large is to speculate upon the reasons why an individual is nominated by the Chief Executive—federal or state—to serve on a tribunal. This becomes a particularly intriguing guessing game at the level of the Supreme Court of the United States, whose appointees obviously receive more public prominence than those at lower levels. For the sake of both brevity and comprehensive illustration, the following observations will thus concentrate upon that body.

There is no doubt that presidential motivations in selecting a future justice of the Supreme Court are both complex and multiple and vary with each President. It is possible, however, to ascertain a fairly reliable quintet of factors that seem to be more or less present in most presidential choices to the august tribunal. In no particular order they are the nominee's:

1. objective merit;
2. political "availability";
3. ideological "appropriateness";
4. personal "attractiveness" to the President;
5. geographical, religious, and other socio-political background.

Not all of these five considerations necessarily plays a role in each selection, but a majority of them unquestionably does; one of them is usually uppermost in significance; and probably all are given at least some thought by the President and his advisers. A few specific cases will serve to illustrate this important fact of the political process.

Thus, the *merit* factor proved to be decisive in President Hoover's reluctant designation of Mr. Justice Cardozo, but the other four also played key roles, affirmatively or negatively. Hoover did not really wish to nominate Cardozo, although he recognized clearly the judicial greatness and personal integrity of this dedicated, experienced, principled, and brilliant New York jurist—a bachelor, a Democrat, and a Sephardic Jew. Public and private demands for Cardozo's nomination to succeed to the Holmes seat on the Court were both clear and persistent, and were spearheaded by such important figures as Idaho's influential and powerful Republican Senator William E. Borah—not commonly known for his love of Easterners—and by Mr. Justice Stone who offered to relinquish his seat in favor of Cardozo when Hoover raised the argument that the Court already had two New Yorkers on the bench (Stone and Mr. Chief Justice Hughes). When Hoover suggested possible "religious and sectarian" repercussions—Mr. Justice Brandeis also being Jewish—Borah told the President that "anyone who raises the question of race [sic] is unfit to advise you concerning so important a matter." Amidst universal public applause, Hoover then surrendered, and the Senate unanimously confirmed Cardozo within moments after his nomination reached the floor.

Political "availability" includes both the official party allegiance of the designee and his acceptability—or at least his "nonobnoxiousness"—to his home state Senators, provided these are of the President's own political party. By and large, an old political maxim governs here, namely, that "there are just as many good *Republican* (or *Democratic*, as the case may be) lawyers—so why appoint someone from the enemy camp?" There have been deviations from this concept, and there are always a few "sops" thrown to the opposition, but there is no mistaking the pattern. To illustrate: President Wilson appointed 73 Democrats and one Republican as federal jurists; Harding, Coolidge, and Hoover a total of 198 Republicans and 20 Democrats; F.D.R. 194 Democrats and eight Republicans; Truman 128 Democrats and 13 Republicans; Eisenhower 178 Republicans and 11 Democrats; Kennedy 105 Democrats, ten Republicans, one Independent, and one member of the New York Liberal Party; and by the start of 1968, Johnson 130 Democrats and 10 Republicans. Thus the pattern is clear. It is true that twelve Supreme Court justices of opposite party allegiance were appointed, yet ready explanations governed each instance.

Ideological "appropriateness" played a role in most of the above twelve cases. This concept is also known as a nominee's "real politics"—i.e., what is surmised to be, on the basis of an educated guess, the candidate's actual personal philosophy, regardless of formal party adherence—a philosophy that the appointing authority presumes, with fingers crossed, to express itself on the bench. As President Theodore Roosevelt put it succinctly in a well-known statement to Senator Henry Cabot Lodge (R.-Mass.) concerning the "appropriateness" of Horace H. Lurton, ". . . the *nominal* politics of the man has nothing to do with his actions on the bench. His *real* politics are all important. . . ." And he then proceeded to outline how "right" he was on sundry public questions. But more than once have a Chief Executive's hopes and advance analysis proved to be erroneous. The case of Madison's appointment of Joseph Story, Theodore Roosevelt's of Holmes, and Wilson's of James C. McReynolds are obvious illustrations of the point. Consequently, it is not easy to "pack" the Court—although many have tried, perhaps most famously President Franklin D. Roosevelt in 1937, but initially President Washington, who insisted on a set of five criteria for his nominees. In characteristic language and with candor President Truman observed that "packing the Supreme Court can't be done, because I've tried it and it won't work. . . . Whenever you put a man on the Supreme Court he ceases to be your friend. I am sure of that."

A nominee's *personal "attractiveness"* to the President may play a decisive role in a President's decision to select an individual, regardless of the other factors at issue. Close personal friendship thus unquestionably accounted in large measure for the Supreme Court nomination of Messrs. Vinson, Clark, and Minton by President Truman, that of Byron R. White by President Kennedy, and that of Abe Fortas by President Johnson.

The last of the quintet of outstanding factors that generally seem to motivate chief executives embraces the American meltingpot considerations of *religion, geography*, and now race. They are usually present—either negatively or positively. The case of Mr. Justice Cardozo illustrates the first: neither the presence of two other New Yorkers nor that of his co-religionist Brandeis was permitted to stand in the way, although President Hoover saw them as genuine and overriding barriers. In the "positive" sense, President Eisenhower's designations of Charles Evan Whittaker of Illinois and Potter Stewart of Ohio reflected his concern with the absence of the Midwest on the Court. And the fact that thirty states had sent justices to the Supreme Court as of its 1968–69 term would appear to bear out the regional factor consideration. The same is true for religion: the fact that William J. Brennan was from New Jersey (key state) and a Roman Catholic (a religion then not "represented" on the Court) was surely not lost on President Eisenhower and his advisers when Brennan was nominated to the Supreme Court during the presidential election year of 1956. Although President Truman ignored the "religious" factor when he appointed Tom C. Clark to succeed Mr. Justice Murphy in 1949, it has become an accepted axiom of American politics that there should be a Jew and a Roman Catholic on the highest bench at all times. As of the 1968–69 term, six Roman Catholics and five Jews had served on the Court, the other 85 being Protestants. The pressure to establish a niche for another minority group, the Negro, culminated in President Johnson's appointment of Thurgood Marshall in June 1967.

The typical justice of the Supreme Court of the United States. A composite of the typical jurist on the highest bench of the land, reflecting the various aspects and factors of the selection process as well as statistical facts of the past would look as follows at the time of his accession to the Court:

A 50–55 year-old male; white (the first Negro came to the Court in 1967); generally Protestant; of Anglo-Saxon stock (all except six to date); high social status; reared in an urban environment; well-educated; member of an economically comfortable, civic-minded, politically active family; with B.A. and LL.B. degrees; experienced in some public or civic office.

38

Behind the Marble, Beneath the Robes
Nina Totenberg

While the U.S. Supreme Court may be an unrepresentative elite appointed for life and even a "secret society" in conducting its work, the nine Justices are required to agree (or disagree) on all cases and to write formal opinions indicating their decisions. Unlike the president or Congress, the written opinions of the Court form a permanent record of every major action taken. In this sense, the Supreme Court is accountable for what it does. The bargaining, negotiation, and compromise needed to reach agreement are an entirely closed process, however. Nina Totenberg attempts to lift the veil of secrecy. The three key steps in the closed decision-making process are: (1) decision to accept or reject cases for review; (2) assigning of opinions; and (3) drafting of written opinions. The "open" parts of the process are: (1) oral argument and (2) formal announcement of the Court's opinion. Totenberg's research uncovered some important questions about the internal processes of the Court. How can dissent on petitions to grant review sometimes change the way a case is ultimately handled? Why did the Court change its earlier position on jury verdicts for capital punishment cases? What are some of the major criticisms against Chief Justice Burger, especially in the busing and abortion cases? Why is Burger criticized for the way he assigns opinions? How did the decision of the Nixon tapes case develop? Is the Court's workload too heavy?

Washington. It was Saturday, and the United States Supreme Court, like the rest of Washington's public buildings, looked lonely and deserted. But inside, five of the Justices were hard at work. A sixth had interrupted his routine to visit with a friend from out of town. The fire in the Justice's chambers crackled warmly as the two men talked. The visitor ventured the opinion that the Court's biggest case of that year would be a capital-punishment decision and asked if the Justice had made up his mind yet. The Justice didn't answer. The visitor, suddenly aware that he had asked an improper question, started to apologize. But his voice caught in his throat at the sight of his old friend. The Justice was slumped ashen-faced in his chair, eyes closed; his words seemed almost a whisper. "My God, all those lives."

The visitor was dismayed. He quickly changed the subject. But the moment of good cheer was gone. The Justice was preoccupied.

There is probably no more secret society in America than the Supreme Court. Its nine Justices are among the most powerful, yet least visible, men in the United States. It is unheard-of for a Justice to reveal anything specific about the Court's case work; law clerks, too, are sworn to secrecy. The Court's written decisions are supposed to speak for themselves. It is the least accountable branch of Government, and in the common understanding, its Justices are robed symbols of seriousness, wisdom and the majesty of the law.

And yet to those who are familiar with the Court's daily functioning, the Justices are also people—nine men who work terribly hard and are sometimes very smart, men who constantly fight to overcome their own prejudices and backgrounds, men who sometimes win that battle and sometimes lose it, men who agonize, strain and manipulate to reach joint conclusions, and sometimes change their minds. "Judicial decision-making," wrote a former Supreme Court law clerk in a recent Harvard Law Review, "involves, at bottom, a choice between competing values by fallible, pragmatic and at times nonrational men engaged in a highly complex process in a very human setting."

What follows is an attempt to lift the Court's curtain of secrecy a bit so that the Justices and their work may be better understood. It does not pretend to be a definitive picture; rather, it is one reporter's attempt to put together in one place information gleaned from scores of interviews with Supreme Court law clerks, friends of the Justices, law professors, attorneys who practice regularly before the Court, and the Justices themselves. All of the facts reported here have been obtained from or verified by at least two of these sources.

The basic event in the Court's decision-making process is a weekly conference, usually scheduled for Wednesday afternoon and all day Friday, at which cases are discussed. On Friday, the Justices arrive punctually at 9:30 a.m. Some, like William H. Rehnquist and Potter Stewart, are "night people" who look solemn-faced as they fight the morning doldrums. Others, like Justice William J. Brennan Jr., who rises each morning at 5:30, are cheerful and wide awake.

In the center of the oak-paneled room is a massive mahogany table, surrounded by nine high-backed chairs and about 25 carts. The carts, wheeled in from each Justice's office before the conference, are loaded with briefs, transcripts, memos from clerks, notebooks—everything the Justice thinks he will need for every case that may come up during the exhausting all-day session. The Justices pour themselves coffee from a silver urn. Then they shake hands, as has been the custom since 1888, and sit down to do battle.

The first function of the conference might be called deciding to decide. Each year roughly 5,000 cases come before the Court. The Justices sift through these cases and decide which ones are worthy of their full consideration. Last year, for example, the Justices agreed to hear only 170 cases.

Copies of each case go to every Justice. Justice Brennan is the only one of the nine men who reads virtually all the petitions asking for review. Three other Justices share this chore to varying extents with their three law clerks and have their clerks write summarizing memos. Still others—the four Nixon appointees plus Justice Byron R. White—have in recent years created a rotating pool of their law clerks to write summary memos. Each Justice then makes an independent, tentative judgment as to whether the case provides a substantial Federal question that is ready to be resolved by the nation's highest court. If a Justice thinks a case presents a substantial Federal question, he asks that it be put on the conference list for discussion. With the exception of a small fraction of cases that fall into a technical legal category, no case is put on the conference list unless at least one Justice requests that it be considered. The vast majority of cases, having aroused no Justice's interest, automatically go on what is known as "the dead list" and are denied further consideration.

Once on the conference list, a case faces an even bigger hurdle, for it takes the votes of four Justices to grant it review. The votes to grant review are not always routine or trivial, and the arguing over them may turn out to be highly significant, as it was when the Court was asked to rule on whether President Nixon could refuse to release his tapes to those investigating his subordinates. When the case came to the Court, the legal question was whether the Justices should leapfrog the appeals process to expedite a crucial question. Justice Stewart is reported to have argued forcefully that it was up to the judiciary to settle quickly an issue that was so terribly paralyzing the other institutions of Government and so deeply affecting the national well-being. Stewart was joined by Justices Lewis F. Powell Jr. and William O. Douglas, and soon they had won over two more of their colleagues, leaving Chief Justice Warren E. Burger, Justice Harry A. Blackmun and Justice White to dissent, in a vote that until now had been kept secret. (Justice Rehnquist had disqualified himself from the case.) This procedural vote, coming when it did, was pivotal in forcing the rapid resolution of Watergate and the impeachment process.

Occasionally, when there are not enough votes to grant review, one Justice will write a dissent from the refusal to hear the case. And here the game gets really interesting, for it is not unusual for the dissent to be so persuasive that the other Justices change their minds. The briefs in a case are often so poor that the Justice's dissent provides the only available serious presentation of the case.

For example, in 1968 the Justices voted not to hear the case of Representative Adam Clayton Powell, who claimed he had been unconstitutionally barred from his seat in Congress. Powell had lost his case in the lower courts, and there were strong feelings on the Supreme Court that to grant review of the case might involve the Court in a potentially serious clash with Congress. But Justice Douglas disagreed and wrote a dissent that persuaded the Court to take the case. The Douglas dissent, of course, has never been made public (as it would have been had the Court held to its original position) for seven months later, the Justices overruled the lower court by a vote of 7 to 1.

This kind of persuasive dissent is not seen much these days at the Court. According to Court sources, the liberal Justices have an "un-written agreement" to try to keep many cases out of the hands of the Court so long as the conservatives have the five-vote majority needed to carry a decision. Thus, for example, if an important First Amendment case comes up on appeal, the liberals will vote not to hear it—even if it involves what they consider a horrendous lower-court decision—for fear a conservative majority would result in a Supreme Court decision restricting First Amendment rights. It is better to save final resolution of the issue for another day and a more liberal Court, they reason.

In any event, once the Court agrees to hear a case, it is scheduled for oral arguments some months later. In the interim, lawyers for both sides file lengthy written briefs—usually 60 to 80 pages long—arguing the case. Sometimes as many as 10 or 20 other "friend of the court" briefs are filed by other parties who claim an interest in the case.

Finally, the day for oral argument comes. Each side generally has a half-hour to make its points. The Justices pepper the attorneys with questions. Oral argument is like verbal fencing; at its best, it can be a lawyer's virtuoso performance.

At the end of the week, the following Friday, the case is back in conference, this time to be decided tentatively. Beginning with the Chief Justice and then in order of seniority, each Justice voices his views. They argue, cajole, persuade and finally they vote, this time with the junior Justice going first. Depending on the personalities and mood of the Justices, the conversation can get quite heated. It is said that in the days when Felix Frankfurter and Hugo Black were on the Court, the guards stationed outside the conference room could hear the Justices yelling at each other. The Burger Court, at least on the surface, is more civilized.

Nobody except the Justices is permitted in the conference room. All the notes are taken by the Justices themselves. The Chief Justice, if he is on the majority side, assigns a Justice to write the opinion. The dissenters usually agree among themselves who will write their opinion. Then the negotiating begins. The Court has a tradition that up to the moment when an opinion is announced in public, any Justice can change his mind, and occasionally it takes less than an hour for a majority arranged in the conference to fall apart. "You can leave that conference room thinking you are to write the majority opinion, and one hour and one telephone call later you can be converting it into the minority opinion," explains one Justice.

Some capital-punishment cases illustrate how the Court wrestles over a single subject in the face of shifting issues and events. In 1969, the Court had agreed to hear *Maxwell* v. *Bishop*, which presented a test of two key capital-punishment issues. The first question involved "split-verdict," as opposed to "single-verdict," trials. In a single-verdict trial, the jury hears the evidence, then retires to determine both guilt and punishment. The defendant in the Maxwell case contended that this one-step system forced him to choose between his right not to incriminate himself and his chance to explain his actions before he was sentenced. He asserted that in capital cases the Constitution required a split-verdict system under which the jury would first determine guilt and then return to hear the defendant's evidence in mitigation—insanity or intoxication, for example—before passing sentence. Defendant Maxwell's second argument was that he had been denied due process of law when the jurors condemned him to die without having been given detailed standards to guide them in their decision.

The Supreme Court heard the case and, according to Court sources, voted 6 to 3 to require a split-verdict system. Standardless discretion for juries was upheld. But the split-verdict requirement would have knocked out

death sentences in all but six states and required massive resentencings. The six-man majority included Chief Justice Earl Warren, the conservative Justice John Harlan, and liberal Justices Abe Fortas, Thurgood Marshall, Brennan and Douglas. Justices Stewart, White and Black dissented. Justice Douglas was assigned to write the opinion. But he couldn't hold onto the majority. Later in the year, Fortas was forced to resign from the Court, leaving the case at a 5-to-3 vote. Then Justice Harlan said he wanted to write a concurring opinion, that he was not in complete agreement with the reasoning of the majority. In the process of writing his concurring opinion, Harlan changed his mind, deciding that the Constitution did not require split trials.

The Court then found itself locked in a 4–4 tie and ordered the case reargued the following year, when it would have a full nine-man court. The next year, however, Chief Justice Burger replaced Warren, and Blackmun replaced Fortas. Since Blackmun had served previously on a lower court that ruled on the Maxwell case, he was disqualified from ruling on it again. So the Justices washed out the Maxwell case and took another set of cases that presented the same issues. The new cases, known as *McGautha* v. *California*, were finally decided in the spring of 1971. The High Court, by the same numerical vote of 6 to 3, this time rejected both the split-verdict and the standards arguments. And Justice John Harlan wrote the opinion.

Once the Court had disposed of these two issues, the problem the Justices faced was whether to grant a case testing the ultimate constitutionality of capital punishment in light of the Eighth Amendment prohibition against cruel and unusual punishment.

In 1969, when they had voted to require split verdicts, the Justices had tentatively decided not to accept any more death cases for review. Warren, Black and Harlan firmly believed that the death penalty was constitutional. The majority who wanted split verdicts reasoned that they would make imposition of the death penalty as fair as possible and then leave the ultimate question of cruel and unusual punishment to be decided by another Court far, far in the future. By 1971, there were 600 people on death row, and the split-verdict ruling, as finally decided, would not require massive resentencings. The Justices were divided on the issue of whether to grant review of the ultimate capital punishment question.

Justice Thurgood Marshall, at the time, voiced the private opinion that he was the only vote on the Court for total abolition of the death penalty. And Justice Douglas proposed that the Court hear a rape case in which the death penalty was imposed. He reasoned that the Court could forbid capital punishment in cases where nobody was killed and the Court opinion at the same time could make clear that the death penalty was permissible in murder cases. But the Justices finally decided to grant review of a series of murder cases in which the death penalty was imposed. The Court was finally going to try to decide the ultimate question.

On June 29, 1972, the High Court ruled 5 to 4 that capital punishment as then administered in the United States was unconstitutionally cruel and unusual punishment. Surprisingly, Justices White and Stewart, who had consistently voted to oppose a split-verdict requirement, this time voted against the death penalty. And their reasoning was that it was imposed so arbitrarily as to be capricious. Of course, split verdicts and standards for imposition of the death penalty might have mitigated the arbitrary nature of the death penalty as it came to be administered. But, as a former Supreme Court law clerk observes, "the Court doesn't sit as a legislature—with a clean slate to write on. A legislature can do pretty much what it wants, but the Court has to take cases as they come up, and this sometimes forces the

Justices to do things they wouldn't do if they had been able to choose the order in which issues arose."

The Court has reversed itself midstream on other issues as well. For example, in the 1967–68 term, the Court heard *Shapiro* v. *Thompson*, which tested the constitutionality of state residence requirements for welfare recipients. The Justices originally voted to uphold residence requirements, but the dissenting opinion changed a number of minds. The Court eventually struck down state residence requirements as unconstitutional.

Another big switch occurred in *Time Inc.* v. *Hill*, in which Hill claimed that magazine photos of the Broadway play "Desperate Hours," used to depict his family's ordeal at the hands of criminals, violated his constitutional rights. Hill was represented by attorney Richard Nixon, and the case pitted the right to privacy against freedom of the press. Initially, the Justices sided with Nixon, for the right to privacy. Justice Fortas, the man Nixon would later help push off the Court, was assigned to write the opinion. Justice Hugo Black, when he saw Fortas's opinion, said it was the worst First Amendment opinion he had seen in a dozen years. Indeed, Black was so outraged that he said it would take him all summer to write his dissent, that it would be the greatest dissent of his life. Black knew full well that no opinion is ever issued without its dissent and that any case not completed in a term is reargued the following year. Indeed, the Court did order the case reargued the following year. By then, Black had changed enough minds, and the case came out the opposite way, with Fortas writing the dissent.

The shifts in votes are usually what most people assume them to be—changes of mind that result from the ongoing efforts of the Justices to apply their best judgment and knowledge of the law to their best understanding of subtle or ambiguous facts. But Court insiders say that judicial minds are sometimes changed for less elevated reasons. Most recently such criticism has focused on Chief Justice Burger.

Critics of Burger cite his voting behavior in the Court's first big busing case—the 1971 Charlotte, N.C., case—in which he wrote the Court's unanimous decision ordering extensive busing to desegregate Southern schools. The first vote in conference was said to have been 6 to 3 against busing. In an unusual move, each Justice went back to his chambers and drafted an opinion. Justice Harlan's was said to have been the toughest pro-busing opinion. Then several Justices had second thoughts and switched their votes. Soon the vote was 6 to 3 for busing, with Burger, Blackmun and Black dissenting. Eventually, the three capitulated—Black being the last holdout. And Burger, who had envisioned himself writing the opinion against busing, ended up writing the opinion for it and incorporating much of the language from the drafts of the more liberal Justices.

Some who know the Chief Justice well contend that he changed his vote for personal and political reasons rather than reasons of legal judgment. At the time, they speculate, Burger did not wish to be a part of a small minority if that stance would cause people to think of him as an automatic supporter of positions favored by then-President Nixon. Critics point to other examples of Burger's fighting hard in conference to get a conservative position upheld, only to switch to the other side when he saw he had lost. This occurred, they say, in the Court's unanimous ruling in 1972 that the Government could not wiretap domestic radicals without first obtaining a court-approved warrant—a stunning rebuff to the Nixon Administration. In that case, Burger and Blackmun are said to have originally supported the view that no warrant was necessary, though they eventually switched their votes. And in the abortion case, Burger is said to have fought doggedly for the position that states have the right to prohibit abortions.

But when it became clear that a majority would vote the other way, he voted with it.

Burger has attracted further criticism in legal circles and, according to sources close to the Court, generated hostility among the other Justices because of the ways he has chosen to assign opinions. The power to assign the writing of opinions is tremendously important, since the choice of an author often determines whether the opinion will be written on narrow or broad grounds, whether it will be cautious or sweeping. The assignments may also be made with an eye to enhancing the eventual impact of the decision—such as the national security wiretapping case, when Justice Douglas assigned the opinion to Lewis Powell. Powell, as a lawyer, had spoken out publicly for the Government's right to conduct warrantless wiretapping of domestic radicals. Thus, his judicial opinion to the contrary was perhaps doubly respected. Similarly, it was generally thought inside the Court that Chief Justice Burger would assign the Detroit busing opinion to Justice Stewart, who provided the swing vote giving the conservatives their first majority on busing. But Burger assigned the case to himself.

The cases assigned to each Justice frequently determine whether that Justice feels happy and satisfied in his job. It is said that one of the ways Chief Justice Warren exerted such tremendous leadership over the Court was that he assigned the most tedious and difficult opinions to himself and tried to assign to other Justices the opinions he knew would interest them.

Burger's assignments, however, have been criticized for the way they reflect personal or political conflict with other Justices. Law clerks and law professors say that his assignments have resulted in "the complete emasculation of Brennan and Stewart." And it does appear that remarkably few "juicy" opinions—those that arise from big, controversial cases—are being assigned to them.

There is perhaps some explanation for Brennan's getting fewer important opinions than he used to. He tends to be more in the liberal minority these days and agreed with Burger in only 45 percent of the cases decided in the last term. But Stewart agreed with Burger 77 percent of the time and he was assigned virtually nothing of major public importance. Indeed, a quick scanning of the record indicates that last term Burger assigned the most important cases to himself or to the two most junior Justices, Powell and Rehnquist, and to a lesser extent, to White.

Burger's critics also charge that he has used his traditional power to assign opinions in ways that could be interpreted as tactical. The abortion case, for example, was first decided in the 1971–72 Court term. The vote was 5 to 2, with Burger and White dissenting. (The vacancies resulting from the health-related resignations of Justices Black and Harlan had not been filled). Burger, in disregard of tradition, assigned the opinion instead of letting the senior Justice in the majority—in this case, Douglas—do it. And he assigned the opinion to his old friend Blackmun, the most conservative Justice in the majority. Burger did this, his critics speculate, in the hope that Blackmun would write a very narrow opinion or perhaps even change his mind. Then, they assert, Burger persuaded Blackmun that the case should not be decided at all, that it should be reargued before a full, nine-man Court the following year, when the vacancies were filled, a practice the court had followed on similar occasions.

Blackmun agreed, and since the feelings of the man who is writing the opinion carry great weight, the full Court went along with the suggestion that the case should be reargued. But when Burger saw that the majority would hold and that Powell was joining it to make the majority 6 to 3, the Chief Justice changed his vote. The public saw only the final decision: 7 to 2, with Burger in favor of more liberal abortion laws and White and Rehnquist the only dissenters.

The abortion case was the most flagrant example—so flagrant that it provoked Justice Douglas to write an internal protest memo—but according to those familiar with the Court's operations, it was not the first time Burger assigned a majority opinion when he was in the minority. Some Justices thought the assignments, which are posted a few days after the Friday conferences, were "just mistakes—inefficiency," and since voting in these early deliberations may be tentative, and since the only records are those kept by the Justices themselves, the votes may in fact be subject to different interpretations. But others saw the apparently mistaken assignments as a part of a deliberate attempt by Burger to usurp traditional powers. Some Justices even believe that the Chief Justice has on occasion cast "phony votes" in conference—voting with the majority so that he can assign the opinion and then dissenting from it when it is finally written.

Certainly other Courts and Chief Justices have had their personality difficulties. The late constitutional scholar Alexander Bickel, who was a law clerk when Fred Vinson was Chief Justice, once described that Court as "nine scorpions in a bottle." But Vinson, whatever his shortcomings, was never accused of so serious a break with tradition as assigning opinions when he was in the minority.

Burger, for his part, vehemently denies the critical allegations, calling them "utter absurdity." He has told friends that anyone who says he ever made a mistaken assignment is "either stupid or lying." However, these serious allegations about Burger began with the Justices themselves, not their clerks.

Writing any sort of Supreme Court opinion —important or routine—is a long and arduous process. Each Justice runs his chambers differently. One Justice likens the Court to "nine separate law firms." But each Justice has only three law clerks to assist him. Daniel J. Meador, who clerked for Justice Hugo Black in 1954, described in The Alabama Law Review the process of writing an opinion:

"When 'the Judge,' as his clerks called him, is assigned a case for an opinion, he dives into reading the record and all the briefs. He absolutely masters the facts and the arguments. Then he moves into the relevant literature— cases, statutes, treatises and law reviews. The clerks often read along with him or dig out additional material and feed it to him. The issues will be discussed intermittently. After a while, Black will feel that he is ready to do a first draft. . . . The draft is then turned over to the clerks, and with all the confidence of youth, they work it over. Then the fun begins. The . . . clerks and Black gather around his large desk and start through the draft, word by word, line by line. This may go on for hours. When the Judge has an opinion in the mill, he does not drop it for anything else. The discussion often . . . last[s] until midnight. Often revisions result; sometimes a clerk can get a word or comma accepted, but the substance and decision are never anything but Black's alone."

The Justices take their obligation to research opinions so seriously that in one area of law —obscenity—the result has led to a lot of snickering both on and off the bench. Since 1957, the Court has tried repeatedly to define obscenity. The subject has become so familiar at the Supreme Court building that a screening room has been set up in the basement for the Justices and their clerks to watch the dirty movies submitted as exhibits in obscenity cases. Justice Douglas never goes to the dirty movies because he thinks all expression— obscene or not—is protected by the First Amendment. And Chief Justice Burger rarely, if ever, goes because he is offended by the stuff. But everyone else shows up from time to time.

Justice Blackmun watches in what clerks describe as "a near-catatonic state." Justice Marshall usually laughs his way through it all, occasionally nudging a colleague and wisecracking. Justice White rocks back and forth in a straight-backed chair; on leaving, he has been heard to mutter about "filth." Justice Powell, the aristocratic Virginian, was appalled by the first film he saw, "Without a Stitch," which is quite mild by today's popular standards. Justice Brennan has gotten used to porn, though it is said that it took him more than a decade to overcome his upbringing on the subject. The late Justice Harlan used dutifully to attend the Court's porno flicks even though he was virtually blind; Justice Stewart would sit next to Harlan and narrate for him, explaining what was going on in each scene. Once every few minutes, Harlan would exclaim in his proper way, "By George, extraordinary!"

The dirty movies have provided some of the Court's most funny, and most private, moments. For example, there was the time that the movie began with a psychiatrist telling the audience about the sad life of a nymphomaniac named Laura. The psychiatrist's voice continued to narrate while the film showed Laura engaged in various sexual feats. At the end, the psychiatrist came back on the screen. By this time Justice Marshall was already out of his seat and walking toward the door. The psychiatrist lamented that Laura "is still not cured." Marshall, hand on the door knob, declared, "And neither are you." Then he opened the door, adding, "But I am," and walked out.

Most Justices begin their work on cases during the three-month summer vacation that Congressmen annually complain about. Justice Powell, for example, reads through all the briefs in cases that have already been scheduled for argument in the coming term. He then dictates a lengthy memo on each case. In addition, he picks out 15 to 18 cases he thinks will be particularly important and has his clerks do extra research on them. Each case is assigned to a clerk. Then, during the Court term, shortly before the case is to be argued, Powell sits down with the clerk in charge of the case, and they discuss the issues presented.

Once Powell is assigned an opinion, either he or his clerk roughs out a draft opinion. Who does the first draft depends on what the workload is in the office at the time. The opinion then goes back and forth between the Justice and his clerk like a shuttle-cock, being worked and reworked, drafted and redrafted, until both are satisfied. Then the opinion is given to a second clerk, who goes over it like an editor, looking for mistakes, poor reasoning, unclear writing. Then the opinion is sent to the print shop the Court maintains inside the building. Then the third Powell clerk reads the opinion, acting as an editor-proofreader.

Once the opinion is written so that a Justice is satisfied with it, it is circulated to the other Justices. "You wait for the join memos from the people who voted with you and pray," one Justice says. And then the memos begin to fly.

"It can be very difficult to get one Court opinion, even if people agree with the judgment," explains one Justice. "To write a Court opinion you have to sew a big enough umbrella for five guys to get under, and that can require some pretty fancy sewing." It's even harder to write a unanimous opinion, as evidenced in the Nixon tapes case.

By the time the tapes case was argued before the Court last July 9, the Justices had all done vast research on the issues at hand. Many had written lengthy memorandums on every conceivable position. Moreover, the Justices had completed all their work for the term and could devote full time to this single case.

When the historic case went to conference, there was only one vote. According to Court sources, the Justices were in immediate agreement on all the basic issues. The Chief Justice assigned himself the opinion and received memorandums from each of his colleagues.

However, when Burger circulated his first opinion draft, it met with a wholly negative response. For unknown reasons—some relating to its technical execution and some to its substance—the other Justices were completely dissatisfied with the opinion. The job then became one of getting Burger to accept language drafted by other Justices—principally Powell and Stewart. But the other Justices—sometimes alone and sometimes in groups of two or three—produced new opinions almost every day.

By a process of erosion, they finally got Burger to incorporate their language. The section that Burger is reported to have held to most strenuously, and successfully, acknowledges for the first time that there is a presumption of executive privilege in the Constitution.

Negotiations in less important cases can be as tortured and involved. "You know, you work your brains out and you finally circulate something," remarks one Justice. "Then one guy sends you a note saying, 'I'll be happy to join with you in *Smith* v. *Jones* if you'll take out that paragraph on the top of page 5.' And then you get a note from someone else saying he'll be happy to join you if you strengthen that paragraph at the top of page 5." Or more frequently, one Justice requests a change, and another Justice objects to it when he sees the new draft of the opinion.

In either event, negotiations then begin in earnest. Justice White is said to be a master at working the telephone. But some Justices feel it is improper to lobby their colleagues. And it is not unusual for a Justice to dispatch his clerks to "feel out the territory" among the clerks from another Justice's chambers.

What happens when minor differences cannot be reconciled? As one former law clerk put it: "That's when you fudge it, and then the law professors complain that the Court doesn't write clear opinions. Or else you leave out the point altogether. And then the law professors complain that there is a step missing in the Court's logic."

Sometimes, notes one Justice, an opinion is circulated and someone has "a whole new concept he wants in, and if you've got only a five-man majority, you have to listen to all suggestions very seriously or you might lose the whole thing." (That problem was illustrated in Justice Blackmun's maiden opinion, *Wyman v. James*. He was severely criticized by many legal scholars because his opinion equated welfare with charity. In fact, this whole notion wasn't Blackmun's at all and was put in at the insistence of another Justice.)

Each time a new draft of an opinion is circulated, all changes are marked in the margin with a black line. By the time a decision is announced, it has sometimes undergone as many as 10 drafts in a Justice's chambers and 17 or 18 more to satisfy other Justices. Each Justice writes between 13 and 18 opinions each year, plus nearly as many dissenting and concurring opinions. In addition, each Justice must review those thousands of cases that are appealed to the High Court each year in hopes of a hearing. So it is no wonder that most Justices work six or seven days a week, that Justice Brennan begins his work day with a walk at dawn, or that Justice Rehnquist closes his briefcase each night at about midnight.

Is the Court's workload too great for nine human beings to handle properly? Some believe that it is, and in fact the four Nixon appointees to the Court, led by Chief Justice Burger, have protested lustily that the Court is overworked. A number of committees, one appointed by Burger, have recommended changes in the Court's structure to limit the number of cases the Court must review.

But it is noteworthy that four of the more senior Justices—Douglas, Marshall, Brennan and Stewart—have spoken out against these proposals for change. Indeed, some Justices even object to Burger's hiring of additional administrative staff for the Court. They fear that enlarging the staff may make the Court into another Government bureaucracy. And if the alternative is for the Justices to cope with a superhuman workload, they declare, that is what the Justices will have to do. "Sure, it's hard and exhausting," remarks one Justice, "but we weren't put here because we're lightweights." Indeed, the Justices are deceptively ordinary looking people. As the late Justice Oliver Wendell Holmes once observed, "We are very quiet here, but it is the quiet of a storm center."

39

The Unmasking of the Supreme Court

James P. Levine and Theodore L. Becker

Among Western democracies the U.S. Supreme Court differs from nearly every other court because of its political function in shaping public policy. Through its great powers of constitutional and statutory interpretation, the Court can affect government in many important ways. Levine and Becker discuss the myths of political impartiality, moral leadership, and omnipotence frequently associated with the Court. How and why did these myths develop? President Roosevelt's court-packing plan represented a political assault in response to a series of negative decisions. What was the result of this presidential effort? The Warren Court (1954–69) expanded the Bill of Rights to protect the individual against the state. What were some of the key decisions of the Warren Court? What was the liberal orientation of these decisions? The Burger Court, according to the authors, has returned to its more traditional role. Discuss some of the important rulings which illustrate this. Do you agree that "The time is ripe for a reexamination of the . . . Court as a national policy-maker?"

The Supreme Court of the United States, the most ethereal and mysterious of our Federal institutions, has a dreamlike quality about it for many American citizens.

The dream of political impartiality Although it is a governmental body, the Supreme Court is made to appear apolitical, above the level of mundane, daily politics. Nine strangely clad individuals sit on-high, perched above contending attorneys, listening intently to an arcane and esoteric language. All this is prelude to their main role—making pronouncements *ex cathedra*, many months hence.

These ultimate utterances are "the supreme law of the land" and, after all, American government (we are told) is a "government of law, not men." Somehow, the justices are not human, but an unearthly medium through which the law is revealed. The "real" meanings of the Constitution, statutes, past precedents, and the English language can be divined by a conscientious and thorough search of the law. The law, according to this tale, is what Oliver Wendell Holmes once called "the brooding omnipresence in the sky" (*Southern Pacific Co.* v. *Jensen*).

There is a distant and misty aura about all this—like a dream. It is the American Dream of Political Impartiality, said to be inherent and incarnate in this one branch of government. This scenario has it that some people, some government officials, actually transcend the bloody struggles of politics by donning the robes of Supreme Court Justices. Almost miraculously, the clash of interests and the conflicts of values which influence other government decisions stop at the courthouse door.

The dream of moral leadership However, there is another scene to the American Dream about the Supreme Court. Because of its non-partisan nature, one of its major functions is to provide moral leadership for the American people on how to conduct their public affairs. According to this script, the Court is assigned as prime keeper of the American Political Conscience. It is supposed to be best-suited for elaborating those sacred ideals that embody, and are embodied in, the U.S. Constitution, and that document has provisions that comprise the essence of the American Dream of Governance—a limited, accountable, responsive government of, by, and for the people, with firm guarantees of individual liberty against the tyrannical tendencies inherent in all governments.

Moreover, the Court is to save America from its worst impulses—intolerance, injustice, and majoritarian despotism. Only celestial figures, like U.S. Supreme Court Justices, should be trusted to expound upon these values, to protect us from the excesses of the *political* branches of government, at all levels, in all locales, at all times.

The dream of omnipotence   There is yet another dream about the Court and The Law. It is a vision that the law, particularly in a democracy, matters to the people and affects their daily lives. What is important about laws is what they mean to people and how people respond to them. There is a vast difference between the "law on the books" and the "law in action"—regulations that actually control human behavior.

We all know that there are many laws that are honored more in the breach than in the observance. For example, few people come to full stops at stop signs; no one worries much about ignoring the many laws prohibiting a wide variety of sex acts in private; and tens of millions of Americans blithely and even brazenly violate criminal laws against smoking marijuana. However, these are statutes—laws passed by politicians regarded by many as cynical, corrupt, or out-of-date. One expects different results from judicial declarations, particularly when proclaimed from the highest tribunal in the country.

Thus, part of the American Political Dream is that what the Supreme Court states to be The Law will matter to the American people and that they will obey and cherish it. Article VI is supposed to say it all: the Constitution shall be the "supreme law of the land." Since the judiciary interprets and applies the Constitution, what the Court sayeth, goeth.

PRESERVING THE DREAMS

Ever since the 1803 decision of *Marbury* v. *Madison*, in which the Supreme Court seized the power of judicial review, the Court has been steeped in politics. Whether it was upholding the U.S. National Bank in *McCulloch* v. *Maryland*, overturning the Missouri Compromise and protecting slavery in the *Dred Scott* case, or declaring the income tax unconstitutional in *Pollock* v. *Farmers' Loan and Trust Company*, the Court has created major controversies through its decision-making. Moreover, the history of the Supreme Court is replete with attempts to rebuff the Court and undermine its decisions.

However, through tactical concessions and strategic retreats, the Court was able to weather the political storms and maintain its independence for nearly 150 years. Thus, when the Southern-dominated Taney Court was apparently about to strike down important provisions of the post-Civil War Reconstruction Act and the Congress abruptly took away its authority to hear the cases involved, the Court, in the *McCardle* case, capitulated by acquiescing in the cutting down of its jurisdiction. Also, the Fuller Court occasionally deviated from its ideologically rigid conservatism at the beginning of this century to permit a few pieces of social welfare legislation to survive the Constitutional onslaught against laws protecting workers.

Because these maneuvers have been cloaked in "legalese," however, the political adaptivity of the Court has been disguised. Always, the Court has issued disclaimers about actively making policy—we only *interpret* the laws; we simply *apply* the Constitution; ours is a modest task. In the (disingenuous) words of Justice Roberts in *U.S.* v. *Butler:*

When an act of Congress is . . . challenged in the courts as not conforming to the Constitutional mandate the judicial branch of the Government has only one duty—to lay the article of the Constitution which is invoked beside the statute which is challenged and to decide whether the latter squares with the former. . . . This Court neither approves nor condemns any legislative policy.

Moreover, the craft of legal argumentation includes many technical devices that enable the Court to exercise enormous discretion without appearing to do so—distinguishing cases, qualifying precedents, defining words, assessing facts. Up through, roughly, the first third of the 20th century, the Court was able to disguise its true nature, and the several dreams about the Court remained very much alive. All of the legal sorcery engaged in by the Justices succeeded in keeping the Court enshrouded in mystery, protecting its godlike reputation.

THE RUDE AWAKENINGS

Sometime during the early gestation of the New Deal, however, an abrasive reality began to shatter these images. The Supreme Court went too far and the nation was in no mood to tolerate the Court's autonomy—no matter what semantics they employed. The Court's well-preserved bubble began to burst.

Specifically, much of Pres. Roosevelt's attempt to reconstruct American capitalism during the debacle of the Great Depression ran afoul of a Republican-dominated Supreme Court. Using the power of judicial review, the Court sabotaged one key social program after another designed to help farmers, laborers, and the unemployed since a majority of the Justices entertained a decidedly different philosophy of government and economics than did the strong Democratic president and his new coalition of labor leaders, city bosses, southern politicians, and ethnic elites. The wheels of fate kept Roosevelt from having even one new appointment in his first term of office, so judges from a previous day ruled supreme.

One way of looking at this is that the "separation of powers" doctrine was working as intended. Independent, principled judges were adamantly defying an aggressive, power-hungry chief executive. Judges from a crustier era were resisting a president who wanted to promote a radical reweaving of the political-social-economic fabric in violation of Constitutional limitations. The majority of the Justices wanted to "conserve" some older values, some traditional ways of doing things.

Another way of looking at it was that a few survivors of a conservative era were holding back the forces of progress and the will of the people. In the 1936 election, "the people" returned FDR to the White House by a record margin. Roosevelt took this to be an endorsement, if not a mandate, to continue his work in pursuit of social reform, but there was that Court, an obnoxious obstruction. It had to be checked. The institution *itself* had to be modified.

FDR's response was to devise a "court-packing" bill. According to this plan, the size of the Court was to be altered. Instead of nine, there were to be as many as 15 Justices, with the President permitted to select a new Justice for every one over the age of 70. The ostensible rationale of this change was that a Court dominated by elderly judges could not operate effectively. This would have enabled Roosevelt to appoint six new Justices and to immediately transform the Court into one dominated by judges more sympathetic to his social welfare policies.

This frontal attack on the Court shocked both FDR's friends and foes. More significantly, it jolted the Court itself, for the sitting Justices, like their predecessors, were not nearly so blind to political realities as they were supposed to be about The Law. They saw the political handwriting on the wall and two previously antagonistic Justices suddenly embraced the New Deal—the famous "switch in time that saved nine." On issue after issue, these "above-politics" Justices altered their views on major legislative matters. They defected to the liberal minority and made it, presto chango, a liberal majority.

Thereafter, the Court regularly imprinted its Constitutional rubber stamp on crucial planks in FDR's program. The dream of apoliticality and independence was deflated, but the liberals tried to make it appear otherwise. After all, the "court-packing" plan had been defeated, had it not? True, but the results were the same. It was clear that the judicial fortress could be penetrated when the stakes were high, but now the liberals were inside, so they lost interest in changing the basic *structure* of the Court. The erstwhile critics of the Court relented to the tune of an old refrain —all's well that ends well.

Enter the Roosevelt Court Life teaches a hard lesson—what is morality to one person is sin to another. The Supreme Court ultimately administered a sound beating to the Republican morality of "free enterprise." A new set of values became dominant. Some call it the "welfare state" and others defined it as "corporate socialism," but, whatever its name, central government regulation of the economy represented a new political ideology. Thus, a large group of Americans, once believing the Court to be an untouchable wellspring of morality, now began to perceive the Court as a source of immorality—a willing collaborator in the national drift toward socialism or "Big Government." Some moral leader! Another part of the American Political Dream faded as a new era dawned.

Now, we had the Roosevelt Court. Until then, when Supreme Courts had been given names of people, it was the Chief Justice who was honored because of his presumed influence on the sum and substance of The Law —*e.g.*, the Marshall Court, the Taney Court, etc. Reflecting the new reality, modern courts have come to be baptized after certain Chief Executives who shaped them. This accurately mirrored the growing recognition of the Court's subservience to the "powers that be" —the dominant national political alliance.

Slowly, the Supreme Court became something else on the American political scene. With a large number of fresh appointments, the legacy of FDR, the new philosophy of the Supreme Court was being labelled "liberal" or "progressive," but it took a surprise appointment of a California politician by an ex-General to coalesce an even more liberal Court, one with a deep sense of moral purpose. Just as many were ready to dismiss the Court as a bunch of grovelling political hacks who meekly followed public opinion, the Supreme Court blew its trumpet, flexed its muscle, and emphatically attempted to lead the nation into new paths of idealism.

Enter the Warren Court For a decade-and-a-half (1954–69), under the shrewd and firm leadership of Chief Justice Earl Warren, the Supreme Court won the plaudits of many Americans previously unenthusiastic about the Court as an American political institution. Most of these new supporters were from the "liberal" end of the American political spectrum, for, unlike its predecessors, the Warren Court decided a large number of cases in favor of purer democracy, individual liberty, and equal opportunity at the expense of arbitrary, discriminatory, or repressive governmental power.

For example, it ruled that public schools which separated black children from white ones were "inherently" unconstitutional, giving new hope to a race that had been oppressed in America for 300 years (*Brown* v. *Board of Education*); decided that police had the duty to advise suspects of their constitutional rights in no uncertain terms and that their failure to do so would void convictions based on confessions (*Miranda* v. *Arizona*); and, in another momentous holding, decided that every American citizen would have his or her vote equal to every other American (*Reynold* v. *Sims*) and that the then-prevalent malapportionment of voters in districts with greatly varying populations violated this principle (*Wesberry* v. *Sanders*).

All these decisions, and many more, were hailed by the "liberal" wings of the political and legal establishment as being what the Supreme Court had a right, even an obligation, to do. Previous courts were known for relatively pro-*status quo* postures. After all, according to common law, courts were supposed to decide cases on the basis of past precedent, not make new policies. Since these innovative decisions were now adhering to the "right" (read: liberal) ideology, employing "correct" (read: liberal) statistics, and using "sound" (read: liberal) legal argumentation, it was all right, acceptable, and admirable—to some.

Somewhat coincidentally, just as the Warren Court reached its peak of activism in the early and mid-1960's, a vast body of empirical research was produced that demonstrated how totally politicized the Court had become. Many studies of the Justices' voting patterns unequivocally showed that the Court fell into rather neat liberal, conservative, and "swing" blocs that were aligned on all kinds of seemingly disparate Constitutional issues.* The team of Warren, Hugo Black, William O. Douglas, William J. Brennan, Jr., and Arthur Goldberg seemed to stand together no matter what—acting more predictably than members of Congress, who frequently steer an independent course. It became crystal clear that it was the Justices' *political* attitudes and values that were decisive factors in decision-making, with the legal arguments merely furnishing the necessary rationalizations. "Liberal" academics also went along, because the "good guys" were in the driver's seat (or on the bench).

There were vast multitudes, however, who were wildly hysterical about these judicial dictates and angry about this aggressive Federal interference with their lives. These persons loved the Warren Court the way the Hatfields loved the McCoys. They saw some formerly friendly judges now assaulting states' rights, tampering with their preferences in education, and mucking up the effectiveness of their local police forces. Nothing was beyond the Supreme Court's mischief. These opponents of the Court tried to drum up impeachment proceedings—to no avail. They tried to reverse the more egregious decisions through constitutional amendments, but these efforts also failed.

So, many Americans who knew what the Court was saying and doing began to ignore, defy, and non-comply with what they knew was "the law of the land." In other words, they disregarded the supposed legitimacy of the Court and marched to a different drummer. Some of these people were public officials at the state and local level. They were governors, legislators, schoolteachers, principals, and superintendents. They were judges. They were policemen. They were voting registrars. They

* Glendon Schubert, *The Judicial Mind: Attitudes and Ideologies of Supreme Court Justices, 1946–1963* (Evanston, Ill.: Northwestern University Press, 1965).

acted silently and alone. They acted in concert. They delayed. They distinguished their actions from those prohibited directly by the Court. They pleaded special circumstances. There was a war against the Court being waged from coast to coast by an uncoordinated, but mutually sympathetic, army of average Americans.

Some were more direct in their political rebellion against the Court, and developed political plans against Earl Warren and his brand of judicial policy. Some were violent, like the mobs that tried to keep Central High School in Little Rock, Ark., from integrating. What all these activities had in common—whether legalistic, political, or disruptive—was an intention to sabotage The Law. For all these people, there was a "higher law" than Earl Warren's Constitution—their own interests, values, laws, and ways of life.

Finally, after tireless, but largely futile, efforts to foil the Court, these detractors found a handsome knight, a former champion on the comeback trail, who came to their rescue. His name was Richard Milhouse Nixon and, along with another "conservative" stalwart, Sen. Strom Thurmond of South Carolina, they worked out an electoral strategy to win the coveted Presidency. Nixon promised, while running for election in 1968, that, if he won, he would select forthwith a number of "strict constructionist" Justices for the Court, men who would return the Court to a less-activist, less-liberal, sounder position. Simply put, he vowed to change the personnel of the Court, and thus its *political position*, and thus its *decisions*. Unlike so many politicians, he made good on his promises (notwithstanding a couple of initial blunders—the infamous Clement Haynsworth and G. Harrold Carswell Supreme Court appointments that were rejected by the Senate). Nixon proved dramatically that, as far as the Supreme Court was concerned, this was surely a government of men, not laws.

Enter the Burger Court   Within a short period of time, Nixon appointed Warren Earl Burger as the new Chief Justice, along with Harry A. Blackmun, Lewis F. Powell, Jr., and ultra-conservative William Rehnquist, who had served as Nixon's Assistant Attorney General. This quartet rapidly emerged as a new majority bloc in collaboration with one or two older members of the Court. Nixon's appointee to the Presidency, Gerald Ford, added a fifth Justice, John P. Stevens, who solidified the new hegemony on the Court.

What did the new Court do? In general (and with some exceptions), it reverted back to its rather traditional role of protecting the affluent and supporting the *status quo*. Thus, it essentially stymied attempts to integrate public schools in large cities with overwhelming black student populations by ruling that courts could not order metropolitan-wide busing of students between inner cities and surrounding suburbs that are predominantly white (*Milliken* v. *Bradley*). Environmentalists were given a series of blows by various decisions limiting the right of plaintiffs to bring suits in Federal courts (*Sierra Club* v. *Morton*). The one-person, one-vote doctrine of the Warren Court was qualified to permit (under some circumstances) ownership of property to be legitimate grounds for giving some individuals extra voting power at the ballot box (*Salver Land Co.* v. *Tulare Water Storage Dist.*).

Indeed, in a whole series of cases, the Court has disallowed claims that government discrimination based on wealth (or the lack of it) is an unconstitutional violation of the Equal Protection clause of the Fourteenth Amendment. Exclusionary zoning ordinances passed by many small towns and suburbs requiring houses or lots to be of minimal size were upheld, thereby limiting construction of low-cost housing and relegating the poor to live in the deteriorating sections of the central city (*Arlington Heights* v. *Metropolitan Housing Development Corp.*). The use of the property tax to finance public education was sustained, although this enables wealthy suburbs to receive far more state aid per student than their neighboring cities, which have lower and declining tax bases (*San Antonio Independent School Dist.* v. *Rodriguez*). For all practical purposes, poor women had their Constitutional right to an abortion drastically curtailed when the Court ruled that states could cut off Medicaid funds to subsidize abortions (*Maher* v. *Roe*). Thus, the Burger Court has given short shrift to the plight of the poor.

The most pronounced reversal of previous trends made by the Burger Court concerns criminal procedure and due process. Simply put, the Court has adopted a "law and order" perspective on these cases. It has upheld the use of the death penalty against convicted murderers (*Gregg* v. *Georgia*). Convictions have been fostered by permitting the use of small juries of fewer than 12 people (*Williams* v. *Florida*) and jury decision rules that permit guilty verdicts to be reached without unanimity (*Apodaca* v. *Oregon*). The so-called "Miranda rule," which requires police to tell suspects their rights after they are arrested, has been watered down by permitting the introduction of illegally seized confessions to undermine the credibility of a defendant's testimony on the stand (*Harris* v. *New York*).

The Court's turnabout in criminal procedure cases becomes even more apparent if we examine statistics on outcomes. In 1967, during the heyday of the Warren Court, when six of the Justices could clearly be identified as "liberals," 80% of all criminal cases were decided in favor of the defendant. However, in 1975, when the number of liberals had dwindled to three, only 23% of the decisions were won by defendants. What this "score card" reveals is a clearcut change in the dominant ideology on the Court. In 1968, a majority of the electorate had supported Nixon's "get tough" approach to crime and, within a few short years, the Supreme Court's decisions reflected this popular sentiment. In short, the Supreme Court followed the election returns!

The impact of all these policy shifts has been to support plutocracy, inequality, and national polarization—to favor the haves at the expense of the have-nots Whether we deal with equal protection, due process, interstate commerce, or other Constitutional concepts, the Burger Court has by and large manipulated the law for the sake of the privileged. Once again, the Court has played politics—*obvious* politics.

THE FUTURE OF THE SUPREME COURT

The combined effect of the furor during the Warren era and the quick backtracking of the Burger Court which followed has been to destroy the several dreams about the Court— the dreams of independence, super-morality, and supremacy. It is now realized that the Court is invariably controlled by particular political factions—sometimes liberal, but more often conservative, and when the Court is out of kilter with prevailing national politics, it must engage in an uphill struggle (often unsuccessful) to force its policies on a resisting body politic. The Supreme Court is a non-supreme, non-court—it *is* a political institution *par excellence*.

For years, the mythology about legal objectivity and the Court's own cleverness warded off a close scrutiny of the proper role of the High Court in American society. Now that the emperor's clothes (*i.e.*, robes) have been stripped, the time is ripe for a reexamination of the Court as a national policy-maker.

Among the questions that should be asked are the following: How can we take the appointment of Justices out of routine politics, while maintaining some degree of accountability? Is it possible and desirable to make the composition of the Court more representative of the various strains of the population? Can we devise better ways for those offended by Supreme Court decisions to fight back than the largely futile path of Constitutional amendment and the lawless course of outright defiance? How can the Court improve its legitimacy in the eyes of the public, its efficacy in making its voice heard, and its success in gaining compliance? Then there is the age-old question: How can we reconcile judicial review with democratic government?

Since the founding of the Republic in 1787, we have witnessed several Constitutional revolutions, resulting in profound changes in the fundamental law of the nation. However, the institution which has wrought many of these changes has escaped significant alterations—let alone a major overhaul. At this time, we present no concrete plans for restructuring and revitalizing the Supreme Court, but we do urge that the future of the Court be given the national attention which this issue deserves.

Dilemmas about the Supreme Court will not be resolved by merely choosing the "right" kind of Justice when the next vacancy occurs. The Court will not be saved by the likes of a Barbara Jordan or an Archibald Cox, no matter how worthy their credentials may be, for a sudden flip-flop back to liberal policies will only breed more cynicism among an already contemptuous public.

It is the Supreme Court itself which needs change—in one way or another. The upheavals of the last quarter-century have undermined its credibility. It is no exaggeration to state that the Supreme Court is at the crossroads.

PART FOUR

★★★

THE OUTPUTS OF GOVERNMENT

Public Policy

11

Public policy is the productive output of government in response to external and internal political pressures. Governmental policy-making includes a variety of actors who may initiate, formulate, approve, or administer different kinds of program objectives. The actors may represent either broad or narrow interests. Their involvement and intensity of participation in the policy process will depend upon the range of issues, the demands for action, different priorities, timing of decisions, available resources, and the necessity to reach satisfactory compromises over conflicting goals.

National government policies can be classified into three general categories: domestic, defense, and foreign affairs. The scope of public policy requires the government to make decisions, to implement and maintain programs, and to resolve controversies. As the responsibilities of the federal government have increased in the twentieth century, the

president, Congress, the bureaucracy, and the courts have assumed
important roles in the policy-making process.

Although the policy-making process is generally well understood by
most students of American government, less attention has focused on
the *substance* of particular policies except as illustrations of various
components of the governmental structure. In Article 40, Shank and
George argue that more emphasis is needed on policy substance which
may assist in explaining how government functions. For example, the
various aspects of revenue sharing or welfare reform policy may
provide insight on how the national government works. After reviewing
a variety of policy process and substance approaches, the authors
recommend a policy sequence framework which asks key questions
relating to the development and evolution of policy proposals. The
major aspects of the framework deal with policy history and problem
identification, policy sequences, and policy content.

The remaining three articles illustrate controversial public policy issues
and how they relate to the major *processes* and *structures* of American
government. Their purpose is to show how several of these components
come together in the public policy arena. The policy articles can be
used separately or as further illustration of key points discussed in
the previous chapters.

The tax revolt, as demonstrated so effectively in the California vote
on Proposition 13, is a challenge to the federal system. In Article 41,
Arthur Blaustein indicates the devastating impact of tax cuts on
government services. Since many programs depend on intergovernmental aid, the California cutbacks reduced the federal share of assisting
people in that state. The most severely affected groups are the poor,
the needy, minorities, the handicapped, and school-age children.

Second, Proposition 13 shows that voter participation goes beyond
electing candidates. In many states, with California being the leading
example, the public can also pass judgment on ballot measures—
by the initiative and referendum procedures—that directly affect
critical public policy issues. The impact of such voter participation
raises serious questions about the proper agency of government—
citizens or the legislature—as the source of enacting policy measures.

Third, the California voters were effectively organized by strong
interest group campaigning. The leader, Howard Jarvis, became a
gadfly, constantly attacking government waste, inefficiency, and bureaucracy. The Jarvis campaign overcame the opposition of many powerful
groups that argued against Proposition 13. In fact, Jarvis' efforts

resulted in Governor Jerry Brown becoming an advocate of Proposition 13 even though he had vigorously opposed it before the voters acted.

Finally, Proposition 13 has led to other policy goals and objectives. After the successful vote in California, several other states began referendum drives to limit taxes and government spending. Proposition 13 gained tremendous media attention in the press and television. A movement began to limit federal spending by means of a constitutional amendment. In this time of runaway inflation, the taxpayers' revolt is certain to continue.

Racial segregation is a continuing problem of American public policy. Previous articles in Chapter 3 focused on court decisions dealing with segregated public schools and job discrimination. Another perplexing issue is housing discrimination. Segregated housing is directly linked to other maladies of distressed central cities, including unemployment, public welfare, and high crime rates. Over the years, the federal government has taken the lead in providing housing aid to the urban poor and minorities as well as developing various civil rights statutes and executive orders to combat housing discrimination. Most observers agree, however, that the severity of this problem has not been alleviated. Instead, blacks and other minorities are largely confined to the worst neighborhoods and slums of the central cities. Article 42 offers a public policy strategy for the federal government to combat segregated housing by a stronger coordinated interagency effort that would promote fair housing.

On March 28, 1979, the nation's worst nuclear power plant accident occurred at the Three Mile Island facility near Harrisburg, Pennsylvania. The accident caused a severe dilemma for national energy policy. Seeking to reduce U.S. dependence on foreign oil, President Carter encouraged expansion of power plants relying on coal or nuclear energy. By 1979, the nation had seventy-two reactors producing 12.5 percent of all electricity. Then the Three Mile Island accident occurred, raising issues of plant safety, the role of the Nuclear Regulatory Commission, possible "cover-ups" by the utility company, the potential explosive capacity of reactors, and the serious radioactive hazards to urban populations. President Carter appointed a 12-member panel to recommend policy changes that would help to alleviate future accidents. Excerpts from their October 1979 report are included in Article 43.

40

Analyzing Public Policy
Alan Shank and Neil J. George

Public policy consists of the wide variety of decisions, actions, and programs of government. In Article 40, Shank and George analyze various approaches to understanding how American government produces public policy. The authors consider the advantages and shortcomings of different "process" and "content" models. The goal is to develop a framework which asks the most relevant and specific questions about policy-making in general. The authors argue that the process approaches—elitism, group theory, and the systems model—identify the components of policy-making without focusing on the content of specific policies. Why is this so? What are the problems with relying on the elite approach? What is the major strength of the group model? Why is the systems approach too general? Why is the rational actor model more applicable to foreign policy than to domestic policy? How is bureaucratic politics related to the group model? What is incrementalism? What is Lowi's classification system? How does the sequential framework link process and content studies of policy? What are the various stages of the sequential framework?

APPROACHES TO ANALYZING PUBLIC POLICY

Public policy analysis includes a variety of approaches which generally fall into two categories: process or content. *Policy process* models examine variables or components of governmental policy-making activity. Such processes identify policy actors, the sources of their power and influence, their institutional roles, bargaining activity, and interaction which lead to various kinds of policy decisions and program actions. *Policy content* models show that policy occurs within specific decisional or institutional arrangements. Also, such approaches classify and categorize different types of policies. Depending upon the type of policy considered, certain kinds of processes may or may not occur.

This essay was especially prepared for this book. Earlier versions were presented in papers delivered at the 1976 Annual Meeting of the National Conference on Public Administration in Washington, D.C. and the 1976 Annual Meeting of the Midwest Political Science Association in Chicago, Illinois.

Neither process nor content models are employed exclusively in policy analysis. In fact, the linkage of process and content considerations provides the most effective analysis of public policy. The integration of process and content promotes policy research of a far richer quality than traditional case studies in producing new generalizations and hypotheses about public policy.

Most past policy research has focused on process rather than content. In process approaches, public policy is considered as the *dependent* variable. The goal is to explain what political actors do, for example in the political party process, the interest group process, or the legislative process. Attention focuses on the behavior of actors and policy is considered the outcome of their activities. According to Lewis A. Froman, Jr.,[1] public policy can also be considered as the *independent* variable, that is, policy can be used to identify and explain how government functions. The *content* approaches begin by identifying the kind of policy being considered and then explaining what political actors do to achieve the particular kind of policy. The actual parameters and functions of the governmental process are related to the content of the policy.

Our subsequent discussion provides a brief review and critique of policy process and policy content theories and models. The purpose is to provide a summary exposition and analysis of relevant political science literature, indicating that scholars have established various types of systematic approaches.

POLICY PROCESS

Elite Theories and Models

The elite model assumes that public policy reflects the actions of a small group of powerful decision-makers who occupy strategic positions in the policy process. Decision-making is considered as a relatively closed activity in a hierarchical or pyramidal power arrangement. Such elites may either be monolithic in dominating all major policy decisions or they may be part of a competitive system in which participation is related to issue-areas of particular interest (democratic elitism).

One of the best process model examples of monolithic elite dominance is found in *The Power Elite*. C. Wright Mills argued that a military-industrial complex constituted an all-powerful elite which controls American society.[2] He contended that our entire political system is diminated by the military, giant corporations (defense contractors) and a "political directorate" with all three of these power blocs acting in harmony with each other. The three groups form an integrated power pyramid with the military-industrial leaders at the top, key White House executives and Pentagon administrators at a secondary level of power, and the powerless (and nearly helpless) masses on the bottom.

Similarly, the community power literature includes elitist interpretations of power and influence. In *Community Power Structure* (1953),[3] Floyd Hunter examined "Regional City" (Atlanta, Georgia). Hunter used a "reputational" research method to identify the most influential local leadership. He submitted lists of prominent persons in business, government, civic associations, and social activities to a panel of fourteen "judges" or local citizens presumed knowledgeable about community affairs. The judges responded by designating forty top leaders, who comprised primarily the business elite of Atlanta.

Hunter's process model indicated that the forty top leaders controlled Atlanta. This ruling elite differed from the general population in socioeconomic characteristics. The elite usually acted benevolently and assumed civic responsibilities. The leadership group had a relatively stable membership, maintained its influence over long periods of time, and controlled the agenda for most important community actions. The power structure formed into decision-initiating cliques or power pyramids to activate policy proposals. Their decisions were forwarded for implementation to subordinate managers, executives, and elected officials.

Thomas R. Dye and Harmon Zeigler argue the case for responsiveness of elites in a democratic political system.[4] In their view, democratic elitism does not imply rule by conspiracy or purely self-motivated power objectives. Instead, the governing elites must reflect the wishes of the people. The public is usually poorly informed about policy and has difficulty in translating general demands into specific policy proposals. With more power and resources at their disposal, the elites can shape public opinion and also develop policy initiatives. This maintains governmental stability. Elites must act when the masses are ill-informed, passive, and apathetic. Also, elites generally agree on the "rules of the game" by which they conduct their affairs.

The elite model has the advantage of focusing attention on the role of leadership groups in policy-making. The policy process includes the identification of key leaders who initiate, formulate, adopt and implement public policy. The policy-making arena occurs in a hierarchical organizational structure comprised of relatively few actors. In substantive policy matters at the national governmental level, the elite model is useful in identifying the formal elective and appointive positions of actors in the executive, legislative, and administrative agencies who interact in public policy issues. However, the elite model does not explain the content of public policies unless it is assumed that elite interaction is the only variable significantly affecting substantive issues under consideration. Also, it is difficult to demonstrate the responsiveness claims of democratic elitism without examining the purposes, goals, and objectives of specific public policies. Finally, the elite model assumes that all policy matters are activated by elites. While this may be the case, it may also be possible that the content of public policy strengthens or benefits other groups in society which are not a part of the elite decision-making process.[5]

Group Theories and Models

Group theory considers that the struggle between contending groups produces public policy. It assumes that individuals with common interests and goals join together to bring their demands to the attention of government. According to Earl Latham, "What may be called public policy is the equilibrium reached in this group struggle at any given moment, and it represents a balance which the contending factions or groups constantly strive to weigh in their favor."[6]

A group struggle in policy-making was recognized by James Madison in *Federalist*, No. 10. In commenting upon the federal constitution in 1787, Madison warned against the danger of "factions" which might hinder popular control of the national government. According to Madison, factions are "a number of citizens, whether amounting to a majority or a minority of the whole, who are united and actuated by some common impulse of passion, or of interest, adverse to the rights of other citizens, or to the permanent and aggregate interests of the community." Madison was apprehensive that such factions would influence government out of proportion to their numbers, resulting in a tyranny of the minority, or, conversely, that majority factions would overwhelm the rights and interests of other groups in society.

According to this model, public policy represents the outcome of bargaining, negotiation, and compromises between different groups, each of which seeks to maximize its power and influence. Coalitions are formed between policy makers and interest or clientele groups in order to achieve agreement on the content of public policy. Earl Latham, a group theorist, describes the role of government in the battle of contending forces:

The legislature referees the group struggle, ratifies the victories of the successful coalitions, and records the terms of the surrenders, compromises, and conquests in the form of statutes. Every statute tends to represent compromises because the process of accommodating conflicts of group interests is one of deliberation and consent. . . . Administrative agencies of the regulatory kind are established to carry out the terms of the treaties that the legislators have negotiated and ratified. . . .[7]

The group model can also be employed to develop a pluralistic interpretation of public policy. Robert A. Dahl in a study of New Haven, Connecticut (*Who Governs?*, 1961)[8] argued that actual participation in selected community issues can reveal the most active and influential actors. He focused upon the resolution of community problems by competing actors in three key issue-areas: political party nominations, urban redevelopment, and public education.

Dahl discovered that power in New Haven was dispersed among many groups rather than concentrated in a small elite. There was relatively little overlapping of key actors in the three public policy issues. With the exception of Mayor Richard Lee, community affairs were decided by "rival sovereignties fighting it out."[9] These multiple power centers included many competing participants seeking different objectives. Community participation depended upon levels of citizen interest, time, and resources in key issues.

The group model is useful in identifying the roles of interest groups which bring supports and demands to the attention of governmental policy-makers. Public officials may also use pressure and lobbying tactics to promote or oppose particular policies. Group theory also helps to explain the formation of coalitions and the nature of bargaining, negotiation, and compromise in the policy process. In contrast to the elite model, group theory distinguishes between different issues and shows that power and influence are relatively dispersed rather than centralized in the political system. But exclusive reliance on the group model suggests a limitation for policy analysis. This approach is ineffective in understanding policy content because interest group influence is only one part of the policy process. While groups may generate policy proposals, elected officials usually develop, initiate, and formulate the content of policy. The group struggle seems most applicable in the legislative arena where voting coalitions are developed around controversial issues. Similarly, clientele groups can influence administrative agencies which carry out policies that directly affect the interests of such groups.

Systems Theory

While the elite and group models are distinguished by their emphasis on the roles of formal institutional leaders or the pressure exerted by interest groups in the policy arena, systems theory considers public policy as part of a reciprocal input-output systems relationship occurring within a political environment. As developed by David Easton,[10] the systems model includes the *environment*, which consists of any conditions, constraints, or events outside of the political system. The environment establishes the parameters for policy activity within the political system. From this environment arise *inputs* or *demands* and *supports* for government. The *inputs* or external pressures affect the governmental processes, structures, and decisions which have authority and legitimacy in allocating values to society. Governmental institutions or machinery convert the *inputs* into *outputs*, which are the actions, results, consequences, or policies which directly affect the political environment. There is a reciprocal relationship between outputs and inputs identified as *feedback*, which ties the systems model together and makes it an ongoing, viable process.

The systems model has the problem of considerable generality as it is applied to public policy. One difficulty is that the different parts of the model need to be more precisely specified. Additionally, systems theory does not explain the processes by which inputs are converted into outputs. More specificity in model construction is needed to analyze how policies are produced. Also, the outputs are aggregated into decisions, actions, and results. Public policy is the product of more than a single decision. Finally, the linkage between outputs and inputs (feedback) needs clearer definition in terms of policy impacts and results. We need to know the content of public policy in order to compare it with demands and supports on the input side.

Even with these drawbacks, the systems model does draw attention to the constraints and boundaries of policy activity imposed by an external environment. As the most inclusive of the policy process models, the systems approach does, as indicated by James E. Anderson, raise such important questions as: How do environmental inputs affect the content of public policy and the nature of the political system? How does public policy affect the environment and subsequent demands for action? What forces or factors in the environment act to generate demands upon the political system? How is the political system able to convert demands into public policy able to preserve itself over time?[11]

POLICY CONTENT

Rational Actor Theories

In contrast to the policy process approaches which are limited by their focus on the actions of elites or groups, policy content models provide guidelines for both decision-making and/or the classification of public policy. Discussion begins with a substantive policy matter and analysis seeks to explain how and why the policy is shaped, developed, and put into effect. Public policies are explained in terms of rational action, bureaucratic politics, or incrementalism. Policy-making decisions and actions are then classified by such types as distributive, regulative, or redistributive.

According to rational actor theories, public policy is the product of specific goals sought by participants. Various alternatives are considered, a calculation is made of the consequences of each alternative, and the policy selected most efficiently attains the specific goal, purpose, or objective being sought. According to Graham Allison, the government is considered as a single actor. This actor has "one set of specified goals, one set of perceived options, and a single estimate of the consequences that follow from each alternative."[12] Action is chosen in response to the problem under consideration. Such action is viewed as the "sum of activity of representatives of the government relevant to a problem."[13] The selection of a policy represents the most reasonable choice or "one best way." Analysis focuses on the choice of strategy that best maximizes goals and objectives.

The rational actor model seems less applicable to domestic policy than to foreign policy decisions involving crisis situations. First, it is difficult to characterize domestic policy activities as the product of a single actor when coalition support is necessary to achieve policy goals. In contrast, crisis decisions in foreign policy frequently involve national responses where the policy actors are considered as representing the entire nation. According to Spanier and Uslander, "crisis decisions . . . cannot wait for an internal consensus among the various governmental actors to 'emerge.' Indeed, they require immediate action, the type of action best taken by a President plus a small number of top-level advisors."[14] With policy made at the top level of the governmental hierarchy, the President has a key role in interpreting events and the national stakes in the crisis. Bureaucratic interests are subordinated to make a rational decision to safeguard the national interest. Finally, congress is usually not involved in the decision-making process, but simply receives presidential briefing after the policy decision has been made.

Bureaucratic Politics

Bureaucratic politics and decision-making are closely related to the group model. The difference is that the policy actors' roles are affected by policy-relevant questions. Bureaucratic theories assume that many actors are involved in policy-making, each seeking different goals and objectives. Policy actors include an inner circle of the President and his key advisors, a secondary ring of lower-level bureaucrats, a third circle of congressional, political party and interest group participants, and an outer ring comprising public opinion and the mass media.[15] Unlike the centralized power arrangement of the rational actor model, bureaucratic politics is more dispersed and decentralized.

Policy is the result of considerable bargaining, negotiation, and compromise in a pluralistic environment. As the policy process unfolds, efforts are made to reconcile different preferences of the various actors. Since compromise is the key to resolving conflict, policy outcomes are those most acceptable to all actors involved. It is important to know the stakes and interests of the actors to determine how policy disputes are resolved.[16]

The advantage of the bureaucratic politics model is that it focuses upon the resolution of conflict by achieving minimally acceptable policy decisions. Most domestic policy conflicts are considerably complex, extending over relatively long periods of time. Complexity may be comprehended by disaggregating policy-making and focusing upon specific actions which required compromises to resolve conflict situations. Also, this approach identifies bargaining styles, interests, and positions of the various actors involved.

A general problem with this approach is that it does not clearly distinguish the various stages of policy-making, including formulation, adoption, and implementation. Bargaining games occur most frequently at the legislative or adoption stage of policy-making. Presidential dominance over formulating major policy initiatives generally precedes the coalition-building required in the legislative process. Another difficulty is the relationship between bargaining games and minimally acceptable policy decisions. Bureaucratic politics seems to be most closely related to incremental rather than innovative policies. As discussed below, incrementalism is considered as a building block process to policies already in effect.

Incrementalism

Unlike the rational actor model which assumes agreement on policy goals, the incremental approach deals with limited adjustments to policies already in effect. Charles E. Lindblom summarizes the differences between rational-ism and incrementalism in terms of a "root" and a "branch" method, with the former "starting from fundamentals anew each time," and the latter "continually building out step-by-step and by small degrees."[17] The solution of policy problems depends upon the relationship of goals and objectives to alternatives selected. Only some of the alternatives are considered and these differ only slightly from ongoing policies. Policies are not considered anew, but adjustments are made to existing policies. There is no single or "one best way" solution for a policy problem; rather the policy option selected is the one most acceptable or applicable in a given situation. Thus, the incremental approach is a remedy to current problems rather than an effort to promote long-range solution of problems.

The advantages of incremental policy-making include political expediency, reducing the risks and costs of uncertainty, recognizing that decision makers lack the time and resources to analyze comprehensively all solutions to a problem, and the desirability of pragmatic and minimally acceptable solutions rather than the "best" solutions.[18]

Incremental policy making suffers from entrenched attitudes of actors who may become captives of interest or clientele groups that gain the most benefits from small adjustments to existing policies. If incremantalism occurs within a closed bargaining environment, participation will be limited to those actors with the most expertise seeking to maintain a policy without interference by outside groups. Bureaucratic politics may tend toward this direction to reduce the scope of policy conflict. The manageability and pragmatic aspects of incrementalism may lead to the closed elite problems discussed in an earlier section of this paper.

Lowi's Classification System

Theodore Lowi provides a classification system for categorizing public policies that tend to result from the utilization of rational actor, bureaucratic politics, or incremental policy studies. He suggests that policy-making can best be understood by focusing on three substantive types: *distributive, regulative,* and *redistributive.* Distributive policies provide broad benefits to members of a political coalition. Government distributes resources in such a way that all members of the political coalition are relatively satisfied, thereby reducing the scope of conflict and controversy. Further, government is requested to enter such activity because neither the private sector nor individuals acting alone can obtain the desired benefits. Distributive policies include political patronage, subsidies, or pork barrel legislation.

Regulative policies involve forms of government control over the private sector of the economy. Political actors are part of a conflict situation where some are restrained while others are benefited. According to Lowi, "the impact of regulatory decisions is clearly one of directly raising costs and/or reducing or expanding the alternatives of private individuals. . . . Regulatory policies are distinguishable from distributive in that in the short run the regulatory decision involves a direct choice as to who will be indulged and who deprived."[19] Therefore, the scope of conflict in regulative policies is over limited resources and a group struggle occurs in which the outcome represents either the formation of a coalition, pluralistic competition, or bargaining, negotiation, and compromise. Regulative policies usually occur in the context of the group struggle or bureaucratic politics.

Redistributive policies involve the most controversy among contending political actors because the distribution of resources involves a shift from one social class to another. Benefits and burdens are reallocated among broad socioeconomic groups. Unlike distributive policies which include large classes of winners, redistributive policies shift resources in such a way that some groups consider themselves as winners while others are losers. Organized pressure groups are involved in redistributive policies involving "haves and have-nots, bigness, and smallness, bourgeoisie and proletariat."[20] Such policies promote long-term conflict, particularly when their purposes and objectives are irreconcilable for contending groups. In such situations, policy deliberations are initially perceived by the principal actors as a zero-sum game. After redistributive policies become politically acceptable, the contenders may consider them as distributive and the policy context shifts to incremental decision making. For example, many of the social welfare programs of President Johnson's Great Society were perceived primarily as redistributive on behalf of the poor and blacks. This caused controversy in such areas as the implementation of the 1964 antipoverty program. In contrast, the Social Security program, while having redistributive objectives of providing pensions to the elderly, has become a distributive policy with incremental adjustments made over the years of its existence.

Lowi's classification of public policy content is useful in shifting the focus from process to substance. Clearly, it is necessary to understand the linkage between process and resultant policies. According to Randall Ripley, "if an individual knows how the political actors view what they are doing in making specific policy decisions, then he can predict such things as what kinds of coalitions can form, where the final decision will be made in the political system, and where the decision will be implemented."[21]

Lowi's classification system has one serious limitation. It is difficult to apply his scheme to domestic policies unless one knows how the policy was produced. In other words, Lowi's classification is more applicable to policy outcomes or results rather than to how policy is formulated, adopted, and implemented. If several policy outcomes are compared, the relationship between distribution, regulation, and redistribution becomes clearer.[22] Also, within a single policy, there may be conflicting objectives which involve aspects of distribution, regulation, or redistribution. In fact, the success or failure of a policy may be related to the adjustment or lack of accommodation in resolving the distributional or non-redistribution aspects of the policy. Policy analysis must connect policy-making processes with substantive policy outcomes or results. We turn next to a framework which attempts to provide such process-substantive linkages.

POLICY ANALYSIS

Linking Process and Content

Our previous discussion and critique argues that public policy analysis requires consideration of both process and content approaches to account for the interrelationship of actor involvement, decision-making contexts, and policy substance. These considerations cannot be divorced from each other. Clearly, policy is a combination of these variables. Also, policy analysis requires the creative interweaving of many models since any kind of political science model is only an artificial abstraction from the real world. Erwin Hargrove effectively summarizes this position:

Political science is just beginning to develop crude models of policymaking processes in government organizations. These models are simplified versions of what is thought to go on in a given kind of organizational process. The key is to identify the important variables and then suggest possible relationships between them and likely consequences for policymaking. . . . Every case is a different combination of factors and thus no model will automatically explain a case. Nor is any one model adequate to explain all elements of any single complex case. Several models may be required. Models have to be used selectively, as sources of hypotheses, about what actually happened and why.[23]

It must be emphasized that all analytical constructs distort reality. Each one selects certain factors and dismisses others as insignificant. The test is which model or models provide the least distortion and the fullest explanation. As seen in the previous discussion, the two dominant orientations—process and content—have unacceptable liabilities. Neither promotes sufficient explanation of public policy. The integration or linkage of process and content is intellectually warranted as a giant step in the right direction. Otherwise, one is forced to recognize that the previous analytical summary generates a null hypothesis, namely, that reliance on either of the two dominant model orientations leaves out essential features of the other. Clearly, this is counterproductive in understanding public policy as a totality.

What is required, then, is a framework for identifying the key variables of actor involvement, decisional contexts, and policy outcomes. Such a framework should provide guidelines for analyzing public policy case studies by determining if there are specific kinds of answers to questions dealing with a sequence of regularized policy process stages. If there are no answers to some of the questions, then we can assume gaps exist in the policy research. Finally, if the answers are provided, we have a basis for comparing and contrasting the findings of different policy studies.

The framework, as presented below, represents an adaptation from the one originally developed by Charles O. Jones.[24] He provides a sequential framework of (1) problem identification, (2) policy formulation, (3) policy adoption, (4) policy application, and (5) policy evaluation. This provides a wide range of opportunities to examine both policy processes and policy outcomes. Jones' contributions are at best suggestive and embryonic. They are consistent with our view that policy analysis requires the integration of process and content. We consider that the sequential framework should be expanded to overcome the shortcomings of the process and content approaches. We seek to integrate the best aspects, components, and features of existing models dealing with process and content considerations. We also add elements that do not appear in the process or content orientations. The goal is to promote a framework that integrates prior research and also has the potential for greater explanation without being overly complex so as to be unworkable.

We begin with the basic sequential design that examines the regularized or step-by-step stages of policy making. To this, we add a substantive historical background to indicate the political environment within which the policy issue is considered. Next, we examine the decision-making contexts (rational actor, bureaucratic politics or incrementalism) of the formulation-legitimation-application stages. Finally, in evaluating the policy case, we apply Lowi's classification scheme of distributive, regulative, redistributive to the policy outcome.

OUTLINE OF A POLICY SEQUENCE FRAMEWORK

I. Prelude: Case Study Summary or Overview
    What was the background chronological development of the policy under consideration?
    What was the nature of the political environment in providing flexibility for or imposing restraints on policy makers?
II. Problem Identification
    How did the issue or problem come to the attention of government?
    What groups or individuals identified with the issue and brought it to the attention of others?
    Was the problem a matter of mass concern, interest group activity, electoral pledges, or elite concern?
III. Policy Initiation and Formulation
    Who initiated, who formulated (developed a plan for solving the problem), and who responded to the policy?
    Did policy initiation and formulation occur at one time or did it evolve over time?

What was the decisional context of initiation and formulation?
IV. Policy Adoption
    How was the policy approved, modified, or rejected after it was sent by the executive to congress?
    What strategies were involved, *i.e.*, what was the decisional context in the legislature?
    What were the interests of the major actors and how did they respond to the pressures placed upon them?
    Who won and who lost in the policy enactment?
V. Policy Application
    How was the policy implemented in the administration?
    Were any new agencies established by the policy?
    How was the policy financed?
    Who were the beneficiaries of the policy?
    What was the decisional context?
VI. Policy Evaluation
    How is this policy classified: Distributive, Regulative, or Redistributive?
    Did the policy effectively solve the problem brought to the attention of government?

NOTES

[1] Lewis A. Froman, Jr., "The Categorization of Policy Contents," 44–48 in Austin Ranney, ed., *Political Science and Public Policy* (Chicago: Markham, 1968).

[2] C. Wright Mills, *The Power Elite* (New York: Oxford University Press, 1956).

[3] Floyd Hunter, *Community Power Structure* (Garden City, New York: Doubleday, Anchor, 1964).

[4] Thomas R. Dye and L. Harmon Zeigler, *The Irony of Democracy* (Belmont, California: Wadsworth, 1970).

[5] The dangers of self-fulfilling prophesies seem particularly acute in the literature employing the elite model.

[6] Earl Latham, *The Group Basis of Politics* (New York: Octagon Books, 1965), p. 36.

[7] *Ibid.*, pp. 35–36, 38–39.

[8] Robert A. Dahl, *Who Governs?* (New Haven: Yale, 1961).

[9] *Ibid.*, pp. 199–201.

[10] David Easton, *A Framework For Political Analysis* (Englewood Cliffs, N.J.: Prentice-Hall, 1965), pp. 108–17.

[11] James E. Anderson, *Public Policy-Making* (New York: Praeger, 1975), p. 19.

[12] Graham T. Allison, *Essence of Decision* (Boston: Little, Brown, 1971), pp. 32–33.

[13] *Ibid.*, p. 33.

[14] John Spanier and Eric M. Uslaner, *How American Foreign Policy Is Made* (New York: Praeger, 1974), p. 107.

[15] *Ibid.*, pp. 55.

[16] Allison, *Essence of Decision*, pp. 162–80.

[17] Charles E. Lindblom, "The Science of 'Muddling Through'," *Public Administration Review*, 19 (Spring 1959), pp. 79–88. Also, reprinted in Fred A. Kramer, *Perspectives On Urban Bureaucracy* (Cambridge, Mass.: Winthrop, 1973), pp. 123–41.

[18] Anderson, *Public Policy-Making*, p. 13.

[19] Theodore J. Lowi, "Distribution, Regulation, Redistribution: The Functions of Government," in Randall B Ripley, ed., *Public Policies and Their Politics* (New York: Norton, 1966), p. 28.

[20] *Ibid.*

[21] Randall B. Ripley, *American National Government and Public Policy* (New York: The Free Press, 1974), p. 226.

[22] See, for example, the seventeen case studies compared in Theodore J. Lowi, "Four Systems of Policy, Politics, and Choice," *Public Administration Review*, 32, (July/August 1972), pp. 298–310.

[23] Erwin C. Hargrove, *The Power of the Modern Presidency* (New York: Knopf, 1974), pp. 123–24.

[24] Charles O. Jones, *An Introduction to the Study of Public Policy* (Belmont, California: Wadsworth, 1970).

☆ TAXATION AND THE STATES ☆

41

Proposition 13—Catch 22

Arthur I. Blaustein

When California voters approved Proposition 13 in 1978, the so-called "taxpayers revolt" gained tremendous momentum. Many other states began campaigns to limit government spending. During a time of runaway inflation, voter concern with big government, inefficient bureaucracy, and waste was expressed in the most direct way: California statewide property taxes were drastically reduced by 57 percent and the state legislature could not increase other taxes except by a two-thirds vote in both houses. What was the impact of Proposition 13 on California public services? Who were the major winners and losers in this battle? How did Howard Jarvis and Paul Gann develop the campaign? What interest groups were involved? How did Governor Jerry Brown respond? What is the effect of the tax revolt on the federal system? How does it affect future congressional and presidential politics and elections?

The reactionary dream of George Wallace and Ronald Reagan, repudiated by the nation at large in 1968 and again in 1976, has come to pass in California under the rubric of "a people's tax revolt." Four months after the passage of Proposition 13 by an enthusiastic majority in that benighted state, politicians elsewhere in the country have declared themselves in possession of a new revelation. In primary and election campaigns this fall they have been saying that big government needs to be reduced, and they advertise themselves as courageous representatives of an electorate righteously aroused. Before the rest of the nation joins the headlong rush to the sea, the fine print in Proposition 13 deserves a slightly more careful examination than has been provided by the wise men of the doting media.

A number of states have adopted the initiative and referendum process, but none has used it so often as California. Since its inception sixty-seven years ago, the initiative has not proved to be a very sound means of enacting legislation. Initiatives are typically reflexive, emotional reactions to an issue, poor substitutes for the hearings, debates, compromises, and deliberations that distinguish the legislative process. And so with Proposition 13.

A disarmingly simple initiative of 389 words, it limits the taxes levied on any piece of real property—houses, apartments, factories, and businesses—and makes the limitation binding on the state legislature as an amendment to the constitution. Proposition 13 promised to cut California's high property taxes by some $7 billion per year, from $12 billion to $5 billion. It immediately reduces property-tax bills approximately 57 percent by rolling back the maximum rate of tax to 1 percent of the property's 1975-76 assessed valuation, and restricts future levies to 2 percent per year. The initiative further requires a two-thirds majority in both houses of the state legislature to approve increases in any other state tax.

Under Proposition 13, the tax savings for a typical $60,000 house will amount to about $765 per year, a seductive figure indeed for California homeowners like myself whose taxes have risen 40 percent in the past two years.

Howard Jarvis, the chief architect of the initiative in concert with Paul Gann, a retired real estate salesman, spent $28,000 to secure 1,264,000 signatures, more than twice the 500,000 needed to place his petition on the ballot. And amid the hoopla of his lavish public relations campaign, a number of insidious provisions in the initiative were obscured. For example, Proposition 13 states that property will be assessed at *current market value* "when purchased, newly constructed, or change in ownership has occurred." Unfortunately, California homeowners are the most mobile in the nation: on average, houses are sold once every seven years. Thus the conditions by which assessments will be unfrozen ensure that tax relief for most homeowners will be at best temporary. As houses are built and change hands, they will receive far higher assessments than voters were led to believe. And because families move more often than such corporate leviathans as Standard Oil, Lockheed, Kaiser, and Ford, the heaviest property tax burden must shift from the corporations best able to bear it to individuals. (A recently completed study of the impact of Proposition 13 in San Mateo County found that, by 1983, homeowners will pay 60 percent of the county's property tax; prior to the passage of Proposition 13, the homeowners' share of the total was only 50 percent.)

Fewer houses will be built as a result of Proposition 13's requirement of a two-thirds majority of the electorate to pass the bonds that subdividers depend upon to finance such public facilities as schools, fire stations, and water works. Because available housing stock will diminish, market prices are bound to soar and with them the taxes new homeowners will have to pay.

Landlords will realize a considerable tax cut under Proposition 13 that may or may not be passed on in equitable amounts to tenants. Although rent reductions and controls are being debated in city councils throughout the state, appended to local ballots as referenda, and likely to be introduced as bills before the legislature, tenants at present can depend only upon the good will of their landlords—a group not noted for its charity. With profits increasing dramatically, the market value of rental property will inevitably rise. In effect, then, landlords enjoy both an "increase value" windfall and a "tax free" windfall. Thus, here again relief is greatest where it is needed least. The only way these windfalls might have been avoided was through a transfer tax or capital gains tax on property sales, as Jarvis understood only too well and thus prohibited in his initiative. (Voters would have been wise to question Jarvis's selflessness given his position as head of the Apartment Association of Los Angeles County and the fortune he has made in various business enterprises.)

A less stringent alternative was available to Californians, if they had only been willing to consider it. Governor Jerry Brown and the state legislature, stung by Jarvis's achievement, drafted a compromise measure that appeared on the ballot as Proposition 8. Sponsored by Republican State Senator Peter Behr, Proposition 8 would have given homeowners a 30 percent cut in property taxes, paid for lost revenue through state budget surplus, and placed a cost-of-living ceiling on state and local expenditures. Proposition 8 offered no relief to landlords and businesses. (Thus the San Mateo study found that if Proposition 8 had passed, homeowners in that county would be paying only 41.5 percent of the total property tax in 1983, against a much higher and more equitable business share of 58.5 percent.)

Proposition 8 was further distinguished from the Jarvis-Gann amendment by offering special tax breaks to tenants—who are ignored by Proposition 13—and to the elderly. Proposition 8 was designed to limit the growth of the state treasury rather than to diminish its existing size, as Proposition 13 will do. Further, Proposition 8 could have been amended by the legislature. Proposition 13 can be altered only by a two-thirds majority of California voters in another popular referendum, and thus binds the state to a condition of fiscal extremity.

With all its contradictions and at best dubious advantages, the amendment's passage nearly defies reason. One understands the success of Proposition 13 only by noting the influence of mass media, and the cultivated susceptibility of their audiences to buzz-words like "the new revolution," "momentum," "avalanche," and "steam-roller." By simple repetition, these words established their own credibility and the amendment's virtue. Thus the three networks, *Time*, *Newsweek*, the *New York Times*, and the *Washington Post* anticipated the passage of Proposition 13 as a re-enactment of the Boston Tea Party and the Battle of Bunker Hill. Howard Jarvis was afforded the celebrity status more appropriately reserved for Charlemagne or Douglas MacArthur. Dazzled by hyperbole and captivated by their own greed, California voters rallied like yokels at a county fair to win something for nothing. Unwilling to evaluate the contents of the amendment, they were singularly unprepared to confront the realities of its passage—which were swiftly made manifest.

At present, the leadership of California is best described as a government by provisional catastrophe. The state legislature is being muscled for funds from all directions and county boards of supervisors are still meeting far into the night trying to figure out priorities. Do they shut down schools or hospitals, museums or transportation systems, firehouses or police stations, senior citizens' centers, parks, playgrounds, community colleges, or sanitation dumps? Howard Jarvis told the voters that his initiative would trim the rolls of politicians and bureaucrats. But

as voters might have guessed, the best estimates are that not one bureaucrat or politician is going to lose *his* job. Instead, more than a quarter of a million public-service employees and 10,000 CETA (Comprehensive Employment and Training Act) workers will be threatened in the next eight months by the pink slip.

With one pie to cut, some will eat their fill, more will go hungry. Banks, savings and loan associations, and corporate California were written into the initiative as beneficiaries by Mr. Jarvis. It is no small wonder that the United Bank of California chose the day after the election to release its survey of the state's major corporations. The survey showed that these corporations raised their profits at a rate nearly double that of comparable companies outside California in the first quarter of 1978.

Jarvis made a point of reminding homeowners about their $7 billion windfall. He failed to mention that $2.5 billion will be transferred to the federal government in the form of higher income taxes because Californians will have less property tax to deduct. He neglected to mention that $3 billion would go to out-of-state corporations and individuals who own land in California. After corporations in California take their share, the bottom line in this "middle-class tax revolt" is less than $1 billion in the pockets of homeowners.

If corporations and property owners are the winners, the losers are the disadvantaged and the poor. Senior citizens will lose their centers and the public transportation on which they depend; fewer young Chicanos and blacks will be educated at community colleges; women who seek jobs will face a market glutted with the sudden addition of numerous unemployed. All this to save the typical homeowner in Orange County $900 in taxes. But he will have ample time to contemplate the consequences of his choice when the local fire department takes fifteen minutes to respond instead of five; at least he will be able to view the fire from the comfort of his kidney-shaped pool.

It is a curious paradox that the so-called revolt of the middle class should begin in suburban California, where the middle class enjoys more material luxury than it does anywhere else in the country. Suburban Californians are a nervous breed of the "newly arrived." They suffer the neurosis of having too much and not knowing how well they have it. Fear of displacement makes the newly arrived rather unpleasant people to live with, and Jarvis and company played to that fear.

The nervous suburbanites ask themselves every morning what will save them from labor unions, taxes, blacks, Cesar Chavez, the women's movement, busing, illegal aliens, fluoridation, and, worst of all, from government. They waited for a message that would preserve them from these evils, and Howard Jarvis gave them the message. He said that Proposition 13 was their constitutional guarantee "to life, liberty, and the pursuit of *property*." Apparently happiness *is* property, according to Jarvis. And a majority of California voters agreed. No matter that libraries would close, that schoolrooms would overflow with sixty-five children to a class, that thousands of people would lose their jobs. The crowds danced on election night. We have not come very far from Conrad's *Heart of Darkness*: Kurtz sitting on his little piece of private property with his neighbor's head on a pole.

Mr. Jarvis made no bones about it: he likes money, knows how to amass property, and these activities pose no philosophical dilemma, since his morality and his self-interest are conveniently identical. Ironically, Jerry Brown, his chief opponent, had been working the same side of the street for four years, as had Reagan before him.

Taking a page from *Don Quixote*, if Howard Jarvis played the Knight of the Rueful

Figure, then Jerry Brown played the Knight of the Mirror. But we must bear in mind that Cervantes' characters possessed an ethical consistency not shared by the heroes of California's contemporary romance. Chanting "limitation" mantras and raising karma, Jerry Brown helped to create the hostile antigovernment atmosphere in the state that yielded Proposition 13. In his four years as governor, Brown failed to secure decent tax reform. He accumulated the largest state budget surplus in the nation's history, and this proved the most effective weapon in the arsenal of the initiative's advocates.

The surplus, estimated during the campaign at $3–$5 billion, was intended to be Jerry Brown's ticket to the White House. The governor could only enhance his candidacy in 1980 by pointing to the huge surplus as evidence of his frugality. But Howard Jarvis discovered Jerry Brown's pot of gold, and he beat Brown at his own game. When critics of Proposition 13 objected that its passage would cripple the government's ability to provide essential human services, Jarvis had only to cite the surplus in rebuttal. It was left to the voter to imagine what would become of those services once the surplus was depleted—as it is expected to be within a year.

The conservatives who supported Proposition 13 were betting that the state would step in and bail out the local communities. But they must have known that with the power of the purse comes control. It has seemed to me that the two cardinal tenets of conservatism are home rule and antibureaucracy. Yet the ink was scarcely dry on the amendment before a special bipartisan Proposition 13 committee of the state legislature was organized to work out the necessary legislation that would keep schools, cities, counties, and special districts operating when the amendment became effective on July 1. The committee secured immediate agreement that the state should provide $4 billion in direct assistance and another $1 billion in emergency loans for the coming fiscal year. Oddly, it was the Democrats in the legislature, led by State Senator Leo McCarthy, who urged that the money be distributed by straight formula, with no strings attached. To the contrary, Assembly GOP leader Paul Priolo asserted the conservatives' preference for "earmarking" to special interests. Although it was argued that local officials were already hard-pressed and needed no additional restrictions on their limited funds, the conservatives fought to sell out the principle of home rule. Now some communities are refusing any state money to avoid becoming enmeshed in the strings attached. Local governments, over which individuals have traditionally been able to assert most direct influence, are now becoming more aware and fearful of the threat of state authority.

Now that the amendment has passed, Brown speaks as if it had been his own idea from the first. His chidings at the National Governors' Conference late this summer might have been uttered by Howard Jarvis himself. Whatever ideological differences may exist between the two are invisible to the naked eye.

Side by side, the new Left and the old Right spin their fantasies. In the 1960s the Left argued the hothouse notion that one could bring down the system by going after Pacific Gas & Electric, Bank of America, Safeway, and Pacific Telephone. It advocated such direct action as stealing from coin boxes, forging credit cards and checks, and tossing home-made bombs at power lines. It never occurred to these ideologues that the companies so harassed would simply pass the costs on to the consumer, and that the people hurt most would be the poor.

In like manner, Howard Jarvis found eager recruits in his battle against "the politicians." But politicians from Sacramento to Capitol Hill reserve a special maneuver for such assaults: one step to the right and one step backward. They raise a finger to the wind and "get tough." Getting tough means slashing budgets for social programs. Just as the corporations pass business costs on to those who can least afford them, politicians pass social costs on to the poor, the minorities, women, and young people.

Jarvis's sales pitch had a deceptively libertarian sheen calculated to inspire backlash. His ballyhoo about cutting government and taxes down to size was so much snake oil to soothe the consciences of landlords and moneyed taxpayers. It expiated their guilt by suggesting that self-interest is consistent with principle: a neat trick.

Proposition 13 indeed proclaims a message, but it is not the one sung in popular chorus. The issue of big government versus small government is moot; big government is here to stay. The real issue is whether government will be dominated by privileged interests and their hucksters or whether ordinary people will have some say through the conventional political process. The paradox of the California referendum is that so many ordinary people voted their power away.

42

To Ensure Equal Opportunity in Housing

Alan Shank

Housing discrimination against blacks and other minorities is a serious public policy problem. Restricted residential opportunities in urban and suburban areas limit access to better jobs, schools, and public services, perpetuating a segregated, and thus inherently unequal, society. Although the federal government has statutory powers to pre-

vent housing discrimination, such civil rights protections are not adequately enforced. What kinds of discriminatory actions in housing were prohibited under Title VIII of the 1968 Civil Rights Act? What are the proposed goals of interagency coordination in fair housing?

More effective and vigorous civil rights enforcement must be part of a new national urban policy. The Fair Housing Law (Title VIII of the 1968 Civil Rights Act) mandates equal opportunity in housing and urban development and affirmative action on the part of all relevant departmental and agency programs that affect cities and metropolitan areas. Such mandates are clearly necessary because, as this paper will show, various federal programs have contributed to racial segregation in housing. Without positive guarantees that equal opportunity will be part of and undergird a national urban policy, racial segregation will continue. Such residential racial segregation is invidious since it limits housing choice, which perpetuates the ghettoization of minority groups.

Central cities are troubled today precisely because they have become the haven of the poor, the underprivileged, and the unskilled. The older central cities of the Northeast and

This is a revised version of a report prepared by the author in October 1977, while on assignment as a NASPAA Faculty Fellow at the Office of Fair Housing and Equal Opportunity of the U.S. Department of Housing and Urban Development. The report was submitted to the HUD Task Force working on President Carter's national urban policy proposals.

Midwest regions have experienced long-term economic decline, manifested by such problems as the loss of jobs and industry, increases in welfare dependency, housing abandonment, high crime rates, eroding tax bases, increasing costs of public services, and housing discrimination. Housing discrimination can be defined as the denial of housing opportunities to minorities, women, and low-income groups on the basis of race, sex, national origin, or ethnic heritage. Refusal to sell or to lease housing units are blatant examples of racial discrimination. More subtle forms of discrimination are racial steering, whereby only a portion of the housing market is shown to minorities, and minority brokers are excluded from listing services.

Residential segregation separates blacks and other minorities from whites by neighborhood within the city and between the central city and the surrounding suburbs. The private real estate industry has contributed to residential segregation by convincing whites that there are only three types of residential areas within cities: *black areas*, where no white persons would want to live; *white areas*, where no "ethical" real estate person would sell to a black; and *changing or turning areas*, where neighborhoods are "declining," "aging," or "deteriorating," which translates into perceived neighborhood transition from white to black. In these "changing" areas, real estate firms tend to hasten the change by engaging in such practices as blockbusting and other persuasive measures to hasten the neighborhood transition from white to black.

This paper addresses the role of the federal government in attacking housing discrimination through the wide range of departmental and agency programs that affect urban development. Five major areas are included: (1) a brief perspective of housing discrimination, with examples of the effects of discrimination upon particular groups, locational patterns in metropolitan areas, and the residual effects of past federal policies which either ignored housing discrimination or contributed to exacerbating it; (2) linkages between housing discrimination and other urban problems, such as employment, schools, public welfare, and central city tax burdens; (3) linkage of federal housing programs to the activities of other federal departments and agencies; (4) the nature and content of major federal Fair Housing policies; and (5) proposed solutions and recommendations.

The federal government has a special responsibility to eliminate past injustices as they affect minority groups. The United States Constitution, various Supreme Court decisions, and the Civil Rights enactments of the 1960's all emphasize the leadership role of the national government to ensure equal opportunity in housing. Otherwise, persistent discrimination against minority groups will continue.

PERSPECTIVES ON HOUSING DISCRIMINATION

Housing discrimination is the denial of housing opportunities to minorities, women and low-income groups on the basis of race, sex, national origin, or ethnic heritage. Racist, exclusionary, sexist, and discriminatory attitudes, actions and institutional structures are clearly evident in housing. For example, locational patterns in metropolitan areas exhibit residential discrimination in the separation of blacks from whites in housing. Women have experienced discrimination on the dubious grounds that they are inherently unstable and incapable of conducting their own affairs in meeting rent payments, maintaining apartments, or controlling the behavior of their children. Economic discrimination deliberately excludes low- and moderate-income housing from middle- and upper-income residential areas. Suburban governments restrict housing choice by imposing minimum lot size limits on multifamily units, and other restrictive zoning, building, and subdivision policies.

Housing discrimination is linked to the residual effects of past public policies which either ignored the problem or contributed to it. Until recently, federal policies contributed to racial concentration in the cities, the decline of older neighborhoods, and the elimination of vast numbers of low and moderate-income housing units. For example, the urban renewal program destroyed more dwellings occupied by blacks and other minorities than it provided. Public housing contained a disproportionate percentage of minority occupants. And the Federal Housing Administration provided far more insured mortgage loans to whites seeking suburban housing than to blacks wanting to reside in the central cities. Until 1968, the federal government did not have a comprehensive antidiscrimination policy in housing and related urban development programs.

Linkage of Housing Discrimination to Other Urban Problems

Housing discrimination is an identifiable public policy problem directly linked to other social and economic maladies in metropolitan areas. When any particular group—blacks, Hispanics, women or the poor—are denied equal housing opportunities, the urban area manifests other debilitating conditions which deeply affect the quality and character of urban life, including:

Inequality in job opportunities: Segregated housing generally produces residential patterns of inner-city slums surrounded by nearly all-white suburbs. Job opportunities are severely restricted in slum neighborhoods thereby forcing persons to seek work long distances away from their homes, usually in factories or low-paying public service jobs. High unemployment rates are particularly severe among young people living in inner-city areas.

Racially impacted schools: Restricted educational opportunities in low-income housing areas affect the equality of public education available to students living in such areas. Despite various court rulings against *de jure* school segregation, the restricted patterns of housing choice produce conditions of *de facto* segregation in the public schools.

Disproportionately high concentration of public welfare recipients: Unusually high unemployment rates are directly related to the concentration of welfare recipients in the inner-city segregated neighborhoods. The welfare burden falls particularly upon unmarried black women with dependent children who are forced to rely upon public assistance to survive.

Higher central city tax burden: Since the inner-city neighborhoods have a higher concentration of the poor, unemployed, and welfare recipients. more municipal services and subsidies are required to aid them. Higher city taxes to provide such services discourage the middle class and contribute to white flight to the suburbs. Consequently, the central city tax base is eroded, requiring municipalities to seek aid from other levels of government, particularly the federal government.

Linkage of Federal Housing Programs to Other Federal Agencies

In addition to the various housing programs sponsored and funded by the Department of Housing and Urban Development, many other federal departments and agencies perform a variety of activities that directly impact on housing in cities, suburbs, and metropolitan areas. The following is a description of selected departmental activities that directly or indirectly affect housing patterns in urban areas:

Department of Commerce: The Economic Development Administration of the Commerce Department promotes long-range economic development of areas with severe unemployment and low family income problems. It aids in the development of public facilities and assists private enterprise in trying to create new, permanent jobs. EDA's authorizing legislation mandates that the agency's programs be directed to target populations which include significant numbers of minorities. Programmatically, a large portion of EDA funds are directed to water and sewer projects. As a condition for the approval of every project, a community survey is conducted to ascertain the civil rights posture of the recipient community. Consequently, it is evident that EDA activities and funding affect housing patterns in cities and metropolitan areas. Program emphases on *distressed areas* by EDA directly affect the location and condition of housing.

Department of Defense: Programs of the Defense Department affect housing patterns in two direct ways. First, the location of Defense Department installations and the awarding of Defense Department contracts impact on housing facilities available to either Defense Department military and civilian personnel at such installations or to the required housing facilities for workers in industries having Defense Department contracts. Secondly, the termination of Defense Department installations or Defense contracts can have a very direct effect on the economic conditions in an urban region, thereby impacting on housing conditions.

Environmental Protection Agency: EPA administers the Wastewater Treatment Works Construction Grant Program, which provides substantial grants to municipalities to construct sewer treatment plants. Sewer treatment is directly related to housing, since household waste products must usually be tied to a sewer line. Consequently, the location and condition of housing in cities and metropolitan areas is directly affected by the construction of new sewer treatment plants.

Transportation Department: The Transportation Department provides funding for the construction of Interstate Highways and for urban mass transit. The location of highways directly affects the location and condition of housing. New housing construction may be predicated upon the location of new highways. Urban mass transit affects the access of commuters to jobs in the city and metropolitan areas. Residential patterns are directly affected by the availability and cost of urban mass transit.

The above discussion is intended to illustrate a few of the federal agency programs that have direct or indirect effects on housing patterns in cities, suburbs, and metropolitan areas. A fuller discussion would include activities of at least the following additional federal agencies: the various lending and mortgage insurance activities of the Federal Home Loan Bank Board and the Veterans Administration; the Department of Health, Education and Welfare; the Labor Department, which administers the Comprehensive Employment and Training Act (CETA) programs that affect the availability of jobs; and the Treasury Department, which administers General Revenue Sharing, a program that distributes considerable funds to states and localities which may subsequently undertake activities with General Revenue Sharing Funds that directly or indirectly affect housing.

Federal Fair Housing Policies

As a consequence of the recognition of racism in the housing field, the federal government, beginning in 1962, became involved in the issue of civil rights in housing. The four major developments were: (1) Executive Order 11063 of 1962; (2) the United States Supreme Court decision in *Jones* v. *Mayer* in 1968; (3) enactment of the Federal Fair Housing Law, as contained in Title VIII of the 1968 Civil Rights Act, and (4) Section 109 of Title I of the Housing and Community Development Act of 1974.

Executive Order 11063 of 1962 This Executive Order was intended to prevent discrimination due to race, color, or creed in all federally-furnished housing. President Kennedy's Executive Order affected only FHA mortgage insurance, Veterans's Administration loans, guarantees, and federally-assisted public housing. All conventionally financed housing was *not covered* and the Executive Order affected only those federally-assisted housing programs developed after November 20, 1962.

The principal problems of Executive Order 11063 were *limited coverage* and *lack of enforcement* by federal administrators. FHA exempted all one- and two-family owner-occupied units. Federal agencies did not adopt an affirmative action program to prevent discrimination, but relied only upon a complaint process. Builders and owners were required to certify no discrimination against tenants and owners. There were no follow-up procedures to ensure that certifications were met unless complaints were filed.

U.S. Supreme Court decision in Jones v. *Mayer* On June 17, 1968, the U.S. Supreme Court in a 7–2 decision ruled that the 1866 Civil Rights Law prohibited *all* housing discrimination practices by private citizens as well as by government agencies. The 1866 law provided that citizens "of every race and color, without regard to any previous conditions of slavery . . . shall have the same right, in every state and territory in the United States, to make and enforce contracts, to sue, be parties, and give evidence, to inherit, purchase, lease, sell, hold, and convey real and personal property . . . as is enjoyed by white citizens."

The impact of the *Jones* v. *Mayer* decision was more symbolic than real in prohibiting racial discrimination in housing. The mandate of the Supreme Court decision left a number of unanswered questions in implementing the goal of fair housing: Were successful plaintiffs under the 1866 law entitled to monetary damages as well as injunctive relief in the courts? Would "class actions" be permitted to enforce the 1866 law as opposed to actions by one plaintiff at a time?

Title VIII of the 1968 Civil Rights Act The Civil Rights Act of 1968 prohibits discrimination on the basis of race, color, religion, national origin or sex in the sale and rental of both federally-assisted and private sector housing. Title VIII does not apply, however, to owner-occupied dwellings with four or less units or to sales by private owners without using brokers or advertising.

More specifically, Title VIII prohibits housing discrimination on the basis of race, color, religion, sex, or national origin, regarding:

1. *Refusal to Deal:* Refusal to sell or rent after making of a bona fide offer, or to refuse to negotiate for the sale or rental of a dwelling. Section 804(a).
2. *Discrimination In Terms, Conditions and Privileges:* Discrimination in terms, conditions and privileges in the sale or rental of a dwelling or in the provisions of services or facilities connected therewith. Section 804(b).
3. *Discriminatory Advertising:* With respect to sale or rental of a dwelling. Section 804(c).
4. *False Representation:* To represent to any person that any dwelling is not available for inspection, sale or rental when such dwelling is in fact so available. Section 804(d).
5. *Blockbusting:* For profit, to induce or attempt to induce any person to sell or rent any dwelling by representations regarding the entry or prospective entry into the neighborhood of a person or persons of a particular race, color, religion, sex or national origin. Section 804(e).
6. *Discrimination In Financing:* Discrimination in financing by any bank, building and loan association, insurance company or any other such corporation making commercial real estate loans to a person for the purpose of purchasing, constructing, improving, repairing or maintaining a dwelling. Section 805.
7. *Discrimination in Membership in Multi-Listing Services and Real Estate Brokers' Organizations:* Denial of any person to membership in such organizations. Section 805.

Section 109 of Title I of the Housing and Community Development Act of 1974 This law provides for nondiscrimination in any program or activity funded under the Community Development Block Grant Program. HUD implementing regulations for Section 109 require that (1) local government must refrain from discrimination in all activities or programs funded under the Title; and (2) must take reasonable action to overcome the effects of prior discriminatory practices or conditions which have otherwise limited participation by persons of a particular race, color, national origin, or sex.

Despite the existence of the Fair Housing Law, various HUD regulations, and Section 109 of Title I of the Housing and Community Development Act of 1974, federal efforts to reduce involuntary residential discrimination have not resulted in changing segregated housing patterns in cities and metropolitan areas. The reason for this is clear: until there is a national urban policy which supports Fair Housing as an identifiable and attainable goal, the implementation of Fair Housing will remain a hope rather than an integral part of public policy.

A new national urban policy must address the practical implementation of Fair Housing, because all other aspects of such a policy—jobs, more federal aid, revitalized neighborhoods, and improved city-metropolitan area relationships—are directly tied to the housing discrimination problem. Central cities will remain distressed areas until minority groups have equal opportunity in our society.

We do not need more civil rights laws to attack the housing discrimination problem. Title VIII of the 1968 Civil Rights Act provides a sufficient basis for assuring equal opportunity in housing to minority groups.

This is not to suggest that the Act could not be strengthened; it most certainly could use stronger enforcement power, but this is a matter of amending or adjusting the basic Act, not creating an additional Act. What is needed is a new approach to *implementing* Title VIII. Such an approach requires no new program or additional funding from Congress. No additional federal departments are required.

PROPOSED SOLUTIONS AND RECOMMENDATIONS

Our basic recommendation for substantially reducing housing discrimination is the substantive implementation of Title VIII of the 1968 Civil Rights Act. Instead of waiting for individual complaints to be filed, the federal government should *coordinate* its civil rights efforts under Title VIII to reduce existing patterns of residential segregation.

Title VIII of the 1968 Civil Rights Act has two such affirmative action requirements which can provide the basis for a new initiative in federal interagency coordination: Section 808(d) requires all executive departments to administer their programs and activities relating to housing and urban development in a manner affirmatively to further the purposes of Fair Housing and to cooperate with the Secretary of Housing and Urban Development to further such purposes. Section 808(e) of the same law indicates that the Secretary of HUD "shall administer the programs and activities relating to housing and urban development affirmatively to further the *policies* (emphasis added) of this title."

To implement Sections 808(d) and 803(e) (5), we propose that a Fair Housing Interagency Committee be established to determine how the resources of the federal government can be used to expand housing opportunities for citizens of all income and racial groups. This Committee would implement Section 808(d) by developing coordinated policy implementation agreements among the participating agencies that will be *directly* incorporated into ongoing and future departmental programs. The goal is to ensure a specific Federal agency commitment to equal opportunity and affirmative action for Fair Housing as an integral part of all federally-sponsored programs to the nation's cities and metropolitan areas.

The Fair Housing Interagency Committee should be chaired by the Secretary of Housing and Urban Development, as specified in Section 808(d) of Title VIII of the 1968 Civil Rights Act. At a minimum, the following departments and agencies should be members of the Committee; Housing and Urban Development, Commerce, Treasury, Justice, Health, Education and Welfare, Labor, Transportation, Environmental Protection Agency, and Community Services Administration. The Interagency Committee would have the following initial tasks:

1. Develop a brief historical perspective of housing discrimination, and its effects on other urban problems, for example, unemployment and education, and the federal role in such discrimination, both negative and positive.
2. Catalogue and analyze current regulatory and/ or other requirements in each department or agency designed to further Fair Housing pursuant to Section 808(d).
3. Develop an overall policy initiative for all participating federal agencies.
4. Develop implementation techniques, by program, for each participating federal agency in conjunction with overall policy objectives.

Assuming that the participating federal agencies will develop agreements to coordinate Fair Housing standards into their respective policies and programs, a major problem will remain with *enforcing* Title VIII Fair Housing requirements between granting federal agencies and recipient cities, towns, and other local governments in metropolitan areas. Therefore, we propose that after the federal agencies have established cooperative and mutually supporting Fair Housing program standards, they should develop a National Fair Housing Impact Plan. Such a plan would contain specific indicators regarding the existence and reduction of housing discrimination and involuntarily segregated residential areas in cities, suburbs, and metropolitan areas. Federal aid programs to recipient communities should be directly tied in with National Fair Housing Impact Plan. The national plan would have targeted dates and goals for recipient cities and other local governments to reduce discrimination and involuntary segregation. If such recipients did not meet the targeted alleviation goals, the requested federal aid would be withheld from them until the disputed issues were resolved.

The National Fair Housing Impact Plan would be modeled, in part, after the 1973 guidelines of the Council on Environmental Quality to implement federal agency policy for Environmental Impact Statements under Section 102(2)(c) of the National Environmental Policy Act. The guidelines would contain, but not be limited, to the following objectives:

1. Antidiscrimination in housing and related urban development projects should be considered at the earliest stage of agency decisions.
2. Any adverse housing discrimination affecting minority groups should be avoided in agency programs which provide federal aid to urban areas, including direct housing programs and related urban development programs.
3. Antidiscrimination in housing should also be related to other urban development programs, including, for example, job training, water and sewer grants, highway construction, etc.
4. Public comment and participation should be included in drafting the Fair Housing Impact Plan. The Plan should be made available to the public after it has been prepared. All participating federal agencies should have the opportunity to comment on the Impact Plan.

The three major goals of the National Impact Plan would be: (1) to bring all housing and related urban development policy into line with Title VIII requirements; (2) to provide a systematic approach to coordinating policy of participating federal agencies; and (3) to ensure that Fair Housing policy is open to public scrutiny and participation.

In addition to the National Fair Housing Plan, local governments seeking federal aid programs would be required to develop Fair Housing Impact Statements. Such statements would develop local targeted dates and goals for reducing residential housing discrimination and involuntary segregation. Such targeted goals would follow the guidelines developed in the National Impact Plan. The local impact statements would also incorporate the same objectives as the national impact plan, that is, incorporation of Fair Housing at the earliest stage of agency decision; avoid undesirable consequences of housing discrimination on minority groups; integrate Fair Housing with other urban development projects; and ensure public participation in the drafting of the impact statement.

To assure adequacy in implementing these recommendations, it will be necessary to (1) establish procedures that are mutually agreeable and practical at the interagency level; (2) clearly inform localities of the Fair Housing indicators in the National Impact Plan; (3) provide the interagency committee with adequate resources, staff personnel, and budget to develop the National Impact Plan; and (4) assure the maximum opportunity for interagency review, information, and communication to develop the impact plan. Finally, it is recommended that the impact plan be periodically updated and revised to meet changing national housing needs and conditions.

43

The Accident at Three Mile Island

President's Commission

The nuclear power plant accident at Three Mile Island near Harrisburg, Pennsylvania focused public attention on the dangers of such facilities located in or near metropolitan populations. This accident was the worst in the nation's history since atomic power had been adapted for producing electricity to consumers. Advocates of nuclear power point to it as a "clean" source of energy, its relative cost compared to oil or natural gas, and as a source of U.S. energy independence from the OPEC oil cartel. Opponents are worried about safety, radioactive dangers, plant accidents, and the disposal of nuclear waste. President Carter's special commission offered several recommendations in dealing with the future of nuclear power policy. Do you agree with the commission that the risks of nuclear power can be "kept within tolerable limits?"

OVERALL CONCLUSION

After a six-month investigation of all factors surrounding the accident and contributing to it, the commission has concluded that:

To prevent nuclear accidents as serious as Three Mile Island, fundamental changes will be necessary in the organization, procedures, and practices—and above all—in the attitudes of the Nuclear Regulatory Commission and, to the extent that the institutions we investigated are typical, of the nuclear industry.

This conclusion speaks of necessary fundamental changes. We do not claim that our proposed recommendations are sufficient to assure the safety of nuclear power.

Given the nature of its President's mandate, its time limitations, and the complexity of both energy and comparative "risk-assessment" issues, this commission has not undertaken to examine how safe is "safe enough" or the broader question of nuclear versus other forms of energy. The commission's findings with respect to the accident and the regulation of the

Excerpted from the *Overview* of the Commission's Report to President Carter. Washington, D.C.: U.S. Government Printing Office, 1979.

nuclear industry—particularly the current and potential state of public safety in the presence of nuclear power—have, we believe, implications that bear on the broad question of energy. But the ultimate resolution of the question involves the kind of economic, environmental, and foreign policy considerations that can only be evaluated through the political process.

Our findings do not, standing alone, require the conclusion that nuclear power is inherently too dangerous to permit it to continue and expand as a form of power generation. Neither do they suggest that the nation should move forward aggressively to develop additional commercial nuclear power. They simply state that if the country wishes, for larger reasons, to confront the risks that are inherently associated with nuclear power, fundamental changes are necessary if those risks are to be kept within tolerable limits.

ATTITUDES AND PRACTICES

Equipment can and should be improved to add further safety to nuclear power plants, and some of our recommendations deal with this subject. But as the evidence accumulated, it became clear that the fundamental problems are people-related problems and not equipment problems.

Our investigation has revealed problems with the "system" that manufactures, operates, and regulates nuclear power plants. There are structural problems in the various organizations, there are deficiencies in various processes, and there is a lack of communication among key individuals and groups.

In the testimony we received, one word occurred over and over again. That word is "mindset."

After many years of operation of nuclear power plants, with no evidence that any member of the general public has been hurt, the belief that nuclear power plants are sufficiently safe grew into a conviction. One must recognize this to understand why many key steps that could have prevented the accident at Three Mile Island were not taken. The commission is convinced that this attitude must be changed to one that says nuclear power is by its very nature potentially dangerous, and, therefore, one must continually question whether the safeguards already in place are sufficient to prevent major accidents. A comprehensive system is required in which equipment and human beings are treated with equal importance.

This commission believes that it is an absorbing concern with safety that will bring about safety—not just the meeting of narrowly prescribed and complex regulations.

We find a fundamental fault even with the existing body of regulations. A preoccupation developed with largebreak accidents as did the attitude that if they could be controlled, we need not worry about the analysis of "less important" accidents.

This was the tragedy of Three Mile Island, where the equipment failures in the accident were significantly less dramatic than those that had been thoroughly analyzed, but where the results confused those who managed the accident. A potentially insignificant incident grew into the T.M.I. accident, with severe damage to the reactor. Since such combinations of minor equipment failures are likely to occur much more often that the huge accidents, they deserve extensive and thorough study. In addition, they require operators and supervisors who have a thorough understanding of the functioning of the plant and who can respond to combinations of small equipment failures.

The most serious "mindset" is the preoccupation of everyone with the safety of equipment, resulting in the down-playing of the importance of the human element in nuclear power generation. The N.R.C. and the industry have failed to recognize sufficiently that the human beings who manage and operate the plants constitute an important safety system.

CAUSES OF THE ACCIDENT

Other investigations have concluded that, while equipment failures initiated the event, the fundamental cause of the accident was "operator error." It is pointed out that if the operators (or those who supervised them) had kept the emergency cooling systems on through the early stages of the accident, Three Mile Island would have been limited to a relatively insignificant incident. While we agree that this statement is true, we also feel that it does not speak to the fundamental causes of the accident.

Let us consider some of the factors that significantly contributed to operator confusion.

First of all, it is our conclusion that the training of T.M.I. operators was greatly deficient.

Second, we found that the specific operating

procedures, which were applicable to this accident, are at least very confusing and could be read in such a way as to lead the operators to take the incorrect actions they did.

Third, the lessons from previous accidents did not result in new, clear instructions being passed on to the operators.

We find that there is a lack of "closure" in the system—that is, important safety issues are frequently raised and may be studied to some degree of depth, but are not carried through to resolution; and the lessons learned from these studies do not reach those individuals and agencies that most need to know about them.

These shortcomings are attributable to the utility, to suppliers of equipment, and to the Federal commission that regulates nuclear power. Therefore—whether or not operator error "explains" this particular case—given all the above deficiencies, we are convinced that an accident like Three Mile Island was eventually inevitable.

SEVERITY OF THE ACCIDENT

Just how serious was the accident? Based on our investigation of the health effects of the accident, we conclude that in spite of serious damage to the plant, most of the radiation was contained and the actual release will have a negligible effect on the physical health of individuals. The major health effect of the accident was found to be mental stress.

The amount of radiation received by any one individual outside the plant was very low. However, even low levels of radiation may result in the later development of cancer, genetic defects, or birth defects among children who are exposed in the womb. Since there is no direct way of measuring the danger of low-level radiation to health, the degree of danger must be estimated indirectly. Different scientists make different assumptions about

how this estimate should be made and, therefore, estimates vary. Fortunately, in this case the radiation doses were so low that we conclude that the overall health effects will be minimal. There will either be no case of cancer or the number of cases will be so small that it will never be possible to detect them. The same conclusion applies to the other possible health effects.

We found that the mental stress to which those living within the vicinity of Three Mile Island were subjected was quite severe. There were several factors that contributed to this stress. Throughout the first week of the accident, there was extensive speculation on just how serious the accident might turn out to be. At various times, senior officials of the N.R.C. and the state government were considering the possibility of a major evacuation. There were a number of advisories recommending steps short of a full evacuation. Some significant fraction of the population in the immediate vicinity voluntarily left the region. N.R.C. officials contributed to the raising of anxiety in the period from Friday to Sunday (March 30–April 1). On Friday, a mistaken interpretation of the release of a burst of radiation led some N.R.C. officials to recommend immediate evacuation. And on Friday Governor Thornburgh advised pregnant women and preschool-aged children within five miles of T.M.I. to leave the area. On Saturday and Sunday, other N.R.C. officials mistakenly believed that there was an imminent danger of an explosion of a hydrogen bubble within the reactor vessel, and evacuation was again a major subject of discussion.

There was very extensive damage to the plant. While the reactor itself has been brought to a "cold shutdown," there are vast amounts of radioactive material trapped within the containment and auxiliary buildings. The utility is therefore faced with a massive cleanup process that carries its own potential dangers to public health. The ongoing cleanup operation at T.M.I. demonstrates that the plant was inadequately designed to cope with the cleanup of a damaged plant. The direct financial cost of the accident is enormous. Our best estimate puts it in a range of $1 to $2 billion, even if T.M.I.-2 can be put back into operation. (The largest portion of this is for replacement power estimated for the next few years.) And since it may not be possible to put it back into operation, the cost could even be much larger.

Worldwide Concerns Raised

The accident raised concerns all over the world and led to a lowering of public confidence in the nuclear industry and in the N.R.C.

Since the accident was due to a complex combination of minor equipment failures and major inappropriate human actions, we have asked the question: "What if one more thing had gone wrong?"

Some of these scenarios lead to a more favorable outcome than what actually happened. Several other scenarios lead to increases in the amount of radioactive iodine released, but still at levels that would not have presented a danger to public health. But we have also explored two or three scenarios whose precise consequences are much more difficult to calculate. They lead to more severe damage to the core, with additional melting of fuel in the hottest regions.

At this stage we approach the limits of our engineering knowledge of the interactions of molten fuel, concrete, steel, and water, and even the best available calculations have a degree of uncertainty associated with them. Our calculations show that even if a meltdown occurred, there is a high probability that the containment building and the hard rock on which the T.M.I.-2 containment building is built would have been able to prevent the escape of a large amount of radioactivity.

These results derive from very careful calculations, which hold only insofar as our assumptions are valid. We cannot be absolutely certain of these results.

We strongly urge that research be carried out promptly to identify and analyze the possible consequences of accidents leading to severe core damage.

These uncertainties have not prevented us from reaching an overwhelming consensus on corrective measures. Our reasoning is as follows: Whether in this particular case we came close to a catastrophic accident or not, this accident was too serious. Accidents as serious as T.M.I. should not be allowed to occur in the future.

HANDLING OF THE EMERGENCY

Another area of our investigation dealt with the questions of whether various agencies made adequate preparations for an emergency and whether their responses to the emergency were satisfactory. Our finding is negative on both questions.

We are disturbed both by the highly uneven quality of emergency plans and by the problems created by multiple jurisdictions in the case of a radiation emergency. We found an almost total lack of detailed plans in the local communities around Three Mile Island.

We favor the centralization of emergency planning and response in a single agency at the Federal level with close coordination between it and state and local agencies.

PUBLIC AND WORKER HEALTH AND SAFETY

We have identified a number of inadequacies with respect to procedures and programs to prevent or minimize hazards to health from radiation exposure from the operations of nuclear power plants.

We make recommendations with respect to improving the coordination and collaboration among Federal and state agencies with radiation-related responsibilities in the health area. We believe more emphasis is required on research on the health effects of radiation to provide a sounder basis for guidelines and regulations related to worker and public health and safety. We believe that both the state and the utility have an opportunity and an obligation to establish more rigorous programs for informing workers and the public on radiation health-related issues and procedures to prevent adverse health effects of radiation.

RIGHT TO INFORMATION

The President asked us to investigate whether the public's right to information during the emergency was well served. Our conclusion is again in the negative. However, there were many different causes, and it is both harder to assign proper responsibility and more difficult to come up with appropriate recommendations. There were serious problems with the sources of information, with how this information was conveyed to the press, and also with the way the press reported what it heard.

We do not find that there was a systematic attempt at a "cover-up" by the sources of information.

The media generally attempted to give a balanced presentation which would not contribute to an escalation of panic. There were, however, a few notable examples of irresponsible reporting and some of the visual images used in the reporting tended to be sensational.

Another severe problem was that even personnel representing the major national news

media often did not have sufficient scientific and engineering background to understand thoroughly what they heard, and did not have available to them people to explain the information.

We therefore conclude that, while the extent of the coverage was justified, a combination of confusion and weakness in the sources of information and lack of understanding on the part of the media resulted in the public being poorly served.

THE NUCLEAR REGULATORY COMMISSION

We had a broad mandate from the President to investigate the Nuclear Regulatory Commission. When N.R.C. was split off from the old Atomic Energy Commission, the purpose of the split was to separate the regulators from those who were promoting the peaceful uses of atomic energy. We recognize that the N.R.C. has an assignment that would be difficult under any circumstances. But, we have seen evidence that some of the old promotional philosophy still influences the regulatory practices of the N.R.C. While some compromises between the needs of safety and the needs of an industry are inevitable, the evidence suggests that the N.R.C. has sometimes erred on the side of the industry's convenience rather than carrying out its primary mission of assuring safety.

Two of the most important activities of N.R.C. are its licensing function and its inspection and enforcement (I.&E.) activities. We found serious inadequacies in both.

The existence of a vast body of regulations by N.R.C. tends to focus industry attention narrowly on the meeting of regulations rather than on a systematic concern for safety. Furthermore, the nature of some of the regulations in combination with the way rate bases are established for utilities, may in some instances have served as a deterrent for utilities or their suppliers to take the initiative in proposing measures for improved safety.

N.R.C. is vulnerable to the charge that it is heavily equipment-oriented, rather than people-oriented. Evidence for this exists in the weak and understaffed branch of N.R.C. that monitors operator training, in the fact that inspectors who investigate accidents concentrate on what went wrong with the equipment and not on what operators may have done incorrectly, in the lack of attention to the quality of procedures provided for operators, and in an almost total lack of attention to the interaction between human beings and machines.

In addition to all the other problems with the N.R.C., we are extremely critical of the role the organization played in the response to the accident. There was a serious lack of communication among the commissioners, those who were attempting to make the decisions about the accident in Bethesda, the field offices, and those actually on site. This lack of communication contributed to the confusion of the accident. We are also skeptical whether the collegial mode of the five commissioners makes them a suitable body for the management of an emergency, and of the agency itself.

Managerial Problems

We found serious managerial problems within the organization. These problems start at the very top. It is not clear to us what the precise role of the five N.R.C. commissioners is, and we have evidence that they themselves are not clear on what their role should be. The huge bureaucracy under the commissioners is highly compartmentalized with insufficient communication among the major offices. We do not see evidence of effective managerial guidance from the top, and we do see evidence of some of the old A.E.C. promotional philosophy in key officers below the top.

We therefore conclude that there is no well-thought-out, integrated system for the assurance of nuclear safety within the current N.R.C.

For all these reasons we recommend a total restructuring of the N.R.C. We recommend that it be an independent agency within the executive branch, headed by a single administrator, who is in every sense chief executive officer, to be chosen from outside the N.R.C.

We have also recommended a number of other organizational and procedural changes designed to make the new agency truly effective in assuring the safety of nuclear power plants. Included in these are an oversight committee to monitor the performance of the restructured N.R.C. and mandatory review by H.E.W. of radiation-related health issues.

Nuclear power requires management qualifications and attitudes of a very special character as well as an extensive support system of scientists and engineers. We feel that insufficient attention was paid to this by the General Public Utilities Corporation (G.P.U.).

While the utility has legal responsibility for a wide range of fundamental decisions, from plant design to operator training, some utilities have to rely heavily on the expertise of their suppliers and on the Nuclear Regulatory Commission. Our report contains a number of examples where this divided responsibility, in the case of T.M.I., may have led to less than optimal design and operating practices.

The legal responsibility for training operators and supervisors for safe operation of nuclear power plants rests with the utility. However, Met Ed, the G.P.U. subsidiary which operates T.M.I., did not have sufficient expertise to carry out this training program without outside help. They, therefore, contracted with Babcock & Wilcox, supplier of the nuclear steam system, for various portions of this training program. While B.&W. has substantial expertise, they had no responsibility for the quality of the total training program, only for carrying out the contracted portion. And coordination between the training programs of the two companies was extremely loose.

It is our conclusion that the role that the N.R.C. plays in monitoring operator training contributes little and may actually aggravate the problem. Since the utility has the tendency of equating the passing of an N.R.C. examination with the satisfactory training of operators, N.R.C. may be perpetuating a level of mediocrity.

There were significant deficiencies in the management of the T.M.I.-2 plant. Shift foremen were burdened with paper work not relevant to supervision and could not adequately fulfill their supervisory roles. There was no systematic check on the status of the plant and the lineup of valves when shifts changed. Surveillance procedures were not adequately supervised. And there were weaknesses in the program of quality assurance and control.

We agree that the utility that operates a nuclear power plant must be held legally responsible for the fundamental design and procedures that assure nuclear safety. However, the analysis of this particular accident raises the serious question of whether all electric utilities automatically have the necessary technical expertise and managerial capabilities for administering such a dangerous high-technology plant. We, therefore, recommend the development of higher standards of organization and management that a company must meet before it is granted a license to operate a nuclear power plant.

THE TRANSITION

We recognize that even with the most expeditious process for implementation, recommendations as sweeping as ours will take a significant amount of time to implement. Therefore, the commission had to face the issue of what should be done in the interim with plants that are currently operating and those that are going through the licensing process.

The commission unanimously voted:

Because safety measures to afford better protection for the affected population can be drawn from the high standards for plant safety recommended in this report, the N.R.C. or its successor should, on a case-by-case basis, before issuing a new construction permit or operating license: (a) assess the need to introduce new safety improvements recommended in this report, and in N.R.C. and industry studies; (b) review, considering the recommendations set forth in this report, the competency of the prospective operating licensee to manage the plant and the adequacy of its training program for operating personnel; and (c) condition licensing upon review and approval of the state and local emergency plans.

A WARNING

We have not found a magic formula that would guarantee that there will be no serious future nuclear accidents. Nor have we come up with a detailed blueprint for nuclear safety. And our recommendations will require great efforts by others to translate them into effective plans.

Nevertheless, we feel that our findings and recommendations are of vital importance for the future of nuclear power. We are convinced that, unless portions of the industry and its regulatory agency undergo fundamental changes, they will over time totally destroy public confidence and, hence, they will be responsible for the elimination of nuclear power as a viable source of energy.

☆☆☆☆☆☆☆☆☆☆☆☆☆☆☆☆☆☆☆☆☆☆☆☆☆☆☆☆☆☆☆☆☆☆☆☆

APPENDIX

The Declaration of Independence

The 1976 bicentennial of the Declaration of Independence drew nation-wide attention to one of the fundamental documents of American government. John Adams, one of the founders of the nation, had prescribed the Fourth of July celebration as a "great anniversary Festival . . . with pomp and parade, with shows, games, sports, guns, bells, bonfires, and illuminations, from one end of the continent to the other, from this time foreward, forevermore." The major events in the chronology of the Declaration included: (1) Richard Henry Lee's resolution in the Continental Congress on June 7, 1776 which was referred to a committee of five to draft a declaration; (2) the drafting of the declaration by Thomas Jefferson; (3) revision of Jefferson's draft by the committee and presentation to Congress on June 28th; (4) adoption of the Lee-Adams resolution of independence on July 2nd by a vote of twelve colonies in favor, none against, and New York abstaining; (5) discussion of the Declaration with revisions and editing, with approval of the final document on July 4th by a vote of 12-0, New York again abstaining; and (6) printing of the Declaration and signing by 55 delegates, presided over by President John Hancock on July 19th, with the signing completed by August 2nd. The Declaration consisted of three parts: the preamble and philosophical statement, the list of grievances or causes, and the actual declaration itself, which incorporated the Lee-Adams resolution of independence passed on July 2.

IN CONGRESS, JULY 4, 1776.

The Unanimous Declaration of the Thirteen United States of America

When in the Course of human events, it becomes necessary for one people to dissolve the political bands which have connected them with another, and to assume among the Powers of the earth, the separate and equal station to which the Laws of Nature and of Nature's God entitle them, a decent respect to the opinions of mankind requires that they should declare the causes which impel them to the separation.

We hold these truths to be self-evident, that all men are created equal, that they are endowed by their Creator with certain unalienable Rights, that among these are Life, Liberty and the pursuit of Happiness. That to secure these rights, Governments are instituted among Men, deriving their just powers from the consent of the governed, That whenever any Form of Government becomes destructive of these ends, it is the Right of the People to alter or to abolish it, and to institute new Government, laying its foundation on such principles and organizing its powers in such form, as to them shall seem most likely to effect their Safety and Happiness. Prudence, indeed, will dictate that Governments long established should not be changed for light and transient causes; and accordingly all experience hath shown, that mankind are more disposed to suffer, while evils are sufferable, than to right themselves by abolishing the forms to which they are accustomed. But when a long train of abuses and usurpations, pursuing invariably the same Object evinces a design to reduce them under absolute Despotism, it is their right, it is their duty, to throw off such Government, and to provide new Guards for their future security.—Such has been the patient sufferance of these Colonies; and such is now the necessity which constrains them to alter their former Systems of Government. The history of the present King of Great Britain is a history of repeated injuries and usurpations, all having in direct object the establishment of an absolute Tyranny over these States. To prove this, let Facts be submitted to a candid world.

He has refused his Assent to Laws, the most wholesome and necessary for the public good.

He has forbidden his Governors to pass Laws of immediate and pressing importance, unless suspended in their operation till his Assent should be obtained; and when so suspended, he has utterly neglected to attend to them.

He has refused to pass other Laws for the accommodation of large districts of people, unless those people would relinquish the right of Representation in the Legislature, a right inestimable to them and formidable to tyrants only.

He has called together legislative bodies at places unusual, uncomfortable, and distant from the depository of their public Records, for the sole purpose of fatiguing them into compliance with his measures.

He has dissolved Representative Houses repeatedly, for opposing with manly firmness his invasions on the rights of the people.

He has refused for a long time, after such dissolutions, to cause others to be elected; whereby the Legislative Powers, incapable of Annihilation, have returned to the People at large for their exercise; the State remaining in the mean time exposed to all the dangers of invasion from without, and convulsions within.

He has endeavoured to prevent the population of these States; for that purpose obstructing the Laws for Naturalization of Foreigners; refusing to pass others to encourage their migrations hither, and raising the conditions of new Appropriations of Lands.

He has obstructed the Administration of Justice, by refusing his Assent to Laws for establishing Judiciary Powers.

He has made Judges dependent on his Will alone,

for the tenure of their offices, and the amount and payment of their salaries.

He has erected a multitude of New Offices, and sent hither swarms of Officers to harass our people, and eat out their substance.

He has kept among us, in times of peace, Standing Armies without the Consent of our legislatures.

He has affected to render the Military independent of and superior to the Civil Power.

He has combined with others to subject us to a jurisdiction foreign to our constitution, and unacknowledged by our laws; giving his Assent to their acts of pretended Legislation:

For quartering large bodies of armed troops among us:

For protecting them, by a mock Trial, from Punishment for any Murders which they should commit on the Inhabitants of these States:

For cutting off our Trade with all parts of the world:

For imposing taxes on us without our Consent:

For depriving us in many cases, of the benefits of Trial by Jury:

For transporting us beyond Seas to be tried for pretended offences:

For abolishing the free System of English Laws in a neighbouring Province, establishing therein an Arbitrary government, and enlarging its Boundaries so as to render it at once an example and fit instrument for introducing the same absolute rule into these Colonies:

For taking away our Charters, abolishing our most valuable Laws, and altering fundamentally the Forms of our Governments:

For suspending our own Legislatures, and declaring themselves invested with Power to legislate for us in all cases whatsoever.

He has abdicated Government here, by declaring us out of his Protection and waging War against us.

He has plundered our seas, ravaged our Coasts, burnt our towns, and destroyed the lives of our people.

He is at this time transporting large armies of foreign mercenaries to compleat the works of death, desolation and tyranny, already begun with circumstances of Cruelty & perfidy scarcely paralleled in the most barbarous ages, and totally unworthy the Head of a civilized nation.

He has constrained our fellow Citizens taken Captive on the high Seas to bear Arms against their Country, to become the executioners of their friends and Brethren, or to fall themselves by their Hands.

He has excited domestic insurrections amongst us, and has endeavoured to bring on the inhabitants of our frontiers, the merciless Indian Savages, whose known rule of warfare, is an undistinguished destruction of all ages, sexes and conditions.

In every stage of these Oppressions We have Petitioned for Redress in the most humble terms: Our repeated Petitions have been answered only by repeated injury. A Prince, whose character is thus marked by every act which may define a Tyrant, is unfit to be the ruler of a free people.

Nor have We been wanting in attentions to our British brethren. We have warned them from time to time of attempts by their legislature to extend an unwarrantable jurisdiction over us. We have reminded them of the circumstances of our emigration and settlement here. We have appealed to their native justice and magnanimity, and we have conjured them by the ties of our common kindred to disavow these usurpations which, would inevitably interrupt our connections and correspondence. They too have been deaf to the voice of justice and of consanguinity. We must, therefore, acquiesce in the necessity, which denounces our Separation, and hold them, as we hold the rest of mankind, Enemies in War, in Peace Friends.

We, therefore, the Representatives of the united States of America, in General Congress, Assembled, appealing to the Supreme Judge of the world for the rectitude of our intentions, do, in the Name, and by authority of the good People of these Colonies, solemnly publish and declare, That these United Colonies are, and of Right ought to be Free and Independent States; that they are Absolved from all allegiance to the British Crown, and that all political connection between them and the State of Great Britain, is and ought to be totally dissolved; and that as Free and Independent States, they have full power to levy War, conclude Peace, contract Alliances, establish Commerce, and to do all other Acts and Things which Independent States may of right do. And for the support of this Declaration, with a firm reliance on the Protection of Divine Providence, we mutually pledge to each other our Lives, our Fortunes and our sacred Honor.

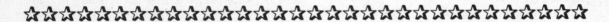

The Constitution of
the United States

The Constitution, framed to replace the Articles of Confederation, is
the fundamental legal charter of American government. The relatively
plain language of Article I, Sections 2 and 3 conceals the intensive
struggles in the convention to reach agreement over the structure of
legislative representation. Article I, Section 8 discusses the delegated
powers of Congress (see Chapter 9) which were considerably
strengthened by Chief Justice Marshall's interpretation of the
"necessary and proper" clause in *McCulloch* v. *Maryland*. Article II
specifies the powers of the president. The framers were most concerned
with the manner of electing the president and designed the rather
curious system of the electoral college in Section 1. Section 2 is the
source of the president's foreign policy and national defense authority.

Note: Parts of the Constitution no longer in effect are printed in italics.

Section 3 provides the chief executive's legislative powers. (See Chapters 8 and 9). Article III deals with the Supreme Court and the federal judiciary. Notice the omission of "judicial review" as a power of the Supreme Court, although Hamilton, in *Federalist*, No. 78, implied such power from Article VI and Marshall incorporated it in *Marbury* v. *Madison*. The Constitution also includes the Bill of Rights—the first ten amendments which were considerably strengthened by the Warren Court (see Chapter 3). Additional amendments reflect various changes made since the Constitution went into effect on March 4, 1789. Particularly important for the cause of civil rights were amendments 13, 14, and 15, which were adopted after the Civil War.

PREAMBLE

We, the People of the United States, in Order to form a more perfect Union, establish Justice, insure domestic Tranquility, provide for the common defence, promote the general Welfare, and secure the Blessings of Liberty to ourselves and our Posterity, do ordain and establish this Constitution for the United States of America.

ARTICLE I
Legislative Branch
SECTION 1.

Legislative power; in whom vested. All legislative powers herein granted shall be vested in a Congress of the United States, which shall consist of a Senate and House of Representatives.

SECTION 2.

House of Representatives, how chosen, qualifications. Impeachment power. The House of Representatives shall be composed of members chosen every second year by the people of the several states, and the electors in each state shall have the qualifications requisite for electors of the most numerous branch of the state legislature.

No person shall be a representative who shall not have attained to the age of twenty-five years, and been seven years a citizen of the United States, and who shall not, when elected, be an inhabitant of that state in which he shall be chosen.

Representatives and direct taxes shall be apportioned among the several states which may be included within this union, according to their respective numbers, *which shall be determined by adding to the whole number of free persons, including those bound to service for a term of years, and excluding Indians not taxed, three-fifths of all other persons.*[1] The actual enumeration shall be made within three years after the first meeting of the Congress of the United States, and within every subsequent term of ten years, in such manner as they shall by law direct. The number of representatives shall not exceed one for every 30,000, but each state shall have at least one representative; *and until such enumeration shall be made, the state of New Hampshire shall be entitled to choose three, Massachusetts eight, Rhode Island and Providence Plantations one, Connecticut five, New York six, New Jersey four, Pennsylvania eight, Delaware one, Maryland six, Virginia ten, North Carolina five, South Carolina five, and Georgia three.*[2]

When vacancies happen in the representation from any state, the executive authority thereof shall issue writs of election to fill such vacancies.

The House of Representatives shall choose their speaker and other officers; and shall have the sole power of impeachment.

SECTION 3.

Senators; how chosen, classified; qualifications. Power to try impeachments. The Senate of the United States shall be composed of two senators from each state, *chosen by the legislature thereof,*[3] for six years; and each senator shall have one vote.

Immediately after they shall be assembled in conse-

[1] Changed by Amendment XIV, Section 2, "counting the whole number of persons in each State." The "other persons" were slaves, and all Indians are now subject to federal taxation.

[2] A temporary provision, superseded by Congressional reapportionments based on each decennial Census.

[3] Changed by Amendment XVII, paragraph 1, "elected by the people thereof."

quence of the first election, they shall be divided as equally as may be into three classes. The seats of the senators of the first class shall be vacated at the expiration of the second year, of the second class at the expiration of the fourth year, and of the third class at the expiration of the sixth year, so that one-third may be chosen every second year; and if vacancies happen by resignation, or otherwise, during the recess of the legislature of any state, the executive thereof may make temporary appointments until the next meeting of the legislature, which shall then fill such vacancies.[4]

No person shall be a senator who shall not have attained to the age of thirty years, and been nine years a citizen of the United States, and who shall not, when elected, be an inhabitant of that state for which he shall be chosen.

The Vice President of the United States shall be president of the Senate, but shall have no vote, unless they be equally divided.

The Senate shall choose their other officers, and also a president pro tempore, in the absence of the Vice President, or when he shall exercise the office of President of the United States.

The Senate shall have the sole power to try all impeachments. When sitting for that purpose, they shall be on oath or affirmation. When the President of the United States is tried, the chief justice shall preside: And no person shall be convicted without the concurrence of two-thirds of the members present.

Judgment in cases of impeachment shall not extend further than to removal from office, and disqualification to hold and enjoy any office of honor, trust or profit under the United States; but the party convicted shall nevertheless be liable and subject to indictment, trial, judgment and punishment, according to law.

SECTION 4.

Times and manner of holding elections. The Times, Places and Manner of holding Elections for Senators and Representatives, shall be prescribed in each State by the Legislature thereof; but the Congress may at any time by Law make or alter such Regulations, except as to the Places of chusing Senators.

The Congress shall assemble at least once in every year, and such meeting *shall be on the first Monday in December,*[5] unless they shall by law appoint a different day.

[4] Filling of vacancies modified by Amendment XVII, paragraph 2.

[5] Changed by Amendment XX, Section 2; "shall begin at noon on the 3rd day of January."

SECTION 5.

Membership, quorum, rules, power to punish or expel. Each house shall be the judge of the elections, returns and qualifications of its own members, and a majority of each shall constitute a quorum to do business; but a smaller number may adjourn from day to day, and may be authorized to compel the attendance of absent members, in such manner, and under such penalties as each house may provide.

Each house may determine the rules of its proceedings, punish its members for disorderly behavior, and, with the concurrence of two-thirds, expel a member.

Each house shall keep a journal of its proceedings, and from time to time publish the same, excepting such parts as may, in their judgment, require secrecy; and the yeas and nays of the members of either house on any question, shall, at the desire of one-fifth of those present, be entered on the journal.

Neither house, during the session of Congress, shall, without the consent of the other, adjourn for more than three days, nor to any other place than that in which the two houses shall be sitting.

SECTION 6.

Compensation, privileges, disqualifications. The Senators and Representatives shall receive a Compensation for their Services, to be ascertained by Law, and paid out of the Treasury of the United States. They shall in all Cases, except Treason, Felony and Breach of the Peace, be privileged from Arrest during their Attendance at the Session of their respective Houses, and in going to and returning from the same; and for any Speech or Debate in either House, they shall not be questioned in any other Place.

No Senator or Representative shall, during the Time for which he was elected, be appointed to any civil Office under the Authority of the United States, which shall have been created, or the Emoluments whereof shall have been increased during such time; and no Person holding any Office under the United States, shall be a Member of either House during his Continuance in Office.

SECTION 7.

Revenue bills. Vetoes. Orders, resolutions. All Bills for raising Revenue shall originate in the House of Representatives; but the Senate may propose or concur with Amendments as on other Bills.

Every Bill which shall have passed the House of Representatives and the Senate, shall, before it become a Law, be presented to the President of the United States; if he approve he shall sign it, but if not he shall return it, with his Objections to that House in which it shall have originated, who shall enter the Objections at large on their Journal, and proceed to reconsider it. If after such Reconsideration two thirds of that House shall agree to pass the Bill, it shall be sent, together with the Objections, to the other House, by which it shall likewise be reconsidered, and if approved by two thirds of that House, it shall become a Law. But in all such Cases the Votes of both Houses shall be determined by Yeas and Nays, and the Names of the Persons voting for and against the Bill shall be entered on the Journal of each House respectively. If any Bill shall not be returned by the President within ten Days (Sundays excepted) after it shall have been presented to him, the Same shall be a Law, in like Manner as if he had signed it, unless the Congress by their Adjournment prevent its Return, in which Case it shall not be a Law.

Every Order, Resolution, or Vote to which the Concurrence of the Senate and House of Representatives may be necessary (except on a question of Adjournment) shall be presented to the President of the United States; and before the Same shall take Effect, shall be approved by him, or being disapproved by him, shall be repassed by two thirds of the Senate and House of Representatives, according to the Rules and Limitations prescribed in the Case of a Bill.

SECTION 8.

Powers of Congress. The Congress shall have Power to lay and collect Taxes, Duties, Imposts and Excises, to pay the Debts and provide for the common Defence and general Welfare of the United States; but all Duties, Imposts and Excises shall be uniform throughout the United States;

To borrow money on the credit of the United States;

To regulate Commerce with foreign Nations, and among the several States, and with the Indian Tribes;

To establish an uniform Rule of Naturalization, and uniform Laws on the subject of Bankruptcies throughout the United States;

To coin Money, regulate the Value thereof, and of foreign Coin, and fix the Standard of Weights and Measures;

To provide for the Punishment of counterfeiting the Securities and current Coin of the United States;

To Establish Post Offices and post Roads;

To promote the Progress of Science and useful Arts, by securing for limited Times to Authors and Inventors the exclusive Right to their respective Writings and Discoveries;

To constitute Tribunals inferior to the supreme Court;

To define and punish Piracies and Felonies committed on the high Seas, and Offenses against the Law of Nations;

To declare War, grant Letters of Marque and Reprisal, and make Rules concerning Captures on Land and Water;

To raise and support Armies, but no Appropriation of Money to that Use shall be for a longer Term than two Years;

To provide and maintain a Navy;

To make Rules for the Government and Regulation of the land and naval Forces;

To provide for calling forth the Militia to execute the Laws of the Union, suppress Insurrections and repel Invasions;

To provide for organizing, arming, and disciplining the Militia, and for governing such Part of them as may be employed in the Service of the United States, reserving to the States respectively, the Appointment of the Officers, and the Authority of training the Militia according to the discipline prescribed by Congress;

To exercise exclusive Legislation in all Cases whatsoever, over such District (not exceeding ten Miles square) as may, by Cession of particular States, and the acceptance of Congress, become the Seat of the Government of the United States, and to exercise like Authority over all Places purchased by the Consent of the Legislature of the State in which the Same shall be, for the Erection of Forts, Magazines, Arsenals, dock-Yards, and other needful Buildings;—And

To make all Laws which shall be necessary and proper for carrying into Execution the foregoing Powers, and all other Powers vested by this Constitution in the Government of the United States, or in any Department or Officer thereof.

SECTION 9.

Immigration, habeas corpus, bills of attainder. Taxes, apportionment. How money to be drawn from Treasury. Ban on titled nobility. The migration or importation of such persons as any of the states now existing shall think proper to admit, shall not be prohibited by the Congress prior to the year 1808, but a tax or duty may be imposed on such importations, not exceeding ten dollars for each person.[6]

The privilege of the Writ of Habeas Corpus shall not be suspended, unless when in Cases of Rebellion or Invasion the public Safety may require it.

No Bill of Attainder or ex post facto Law shall be passed.

[6] Made obsolete January 1, 1808, when Congress prohibited all further importation of slaves.

No capitation, or other direct, Tax shall be laid, unless in Proportion to the Census or Enumeration herein before directed to be taken.[7]

No Tax or Duty shall be laid on Articles exported from any State.

No preference shall be given by any Regulation of Commerce or Revenue to the Ports of one State over those of another: nor shall Vessels bound to, or from, one State be obliged to enter, clear, or pay Duties in another.

No money shall be drawn from the Treasury, but in Consequence of Appropriations made by Law; and a regular Statement and Account of the Receipts and Expenditures of all public Money shall be published from time to time.

No Title of Nobility shall be granted by the United States: And no Person holding any Office of Profit or Trust under them, shall, without the Consent of the Congress, accept of any present, Emolument, Office, or Title, of any kind whatever, from any King, Prince, or foreign State.

SECTION 10.

Powers prohibited the States.   No State shall enter into any Treaty, Alliance, or Confederation; grant Letters of Marque and Reprisal; coin Money; emit Bills of Credit; make any Thing but gold and silver Coin a Tender in Payment of Debts; pass any Bill of Attainder, ex post facto Law, or Law impairing the Obligation of Contracts, or grant any Title of Nobility.

No State shall, without the Consent of the Congress, lay any Imposts or Duties on Imports or Exports, except what may be absolutely necessary for executing its inspection Laws; and the net Produce of all Duties and Imposts, laid by any State on Imports or Exports, shall be for the Use of the Treasury of the United States; and all such Laws shall be subject to the Revision and Control of the Congress.

No State shall, without the Consent of Congress, lay any duty of Tonnage, keep Troops, or Ships of War in time of Peace, enter into any Agreement or Compact with another State, or with a foreign Power, or engage in War, unless actually invaded, or in such imminent Danger as will not admit of delay.

ARTICLE II

The Executive

SECTION 1.

The President, term, electors, qualification, death or removal, compensation, oath.   The executive Power

shall be vested in a President of the United States of America. He shall hold his Office during the Term of four Years,[8] and, together with the Vice-President, chosen for the same Term, be elected as follows:

Each State[9] shall appoint, in such Manner as the Legislature thereof may direct, a Number of Electors, equal to the whole Number of Senators and Representatives to which the State may be entitled in the Congress: but no Senator or Representative, or Person holding an Office of Trust or Profit under the United States, shall be appointed an Elector.

The electors shall meet in their respective states, and vote by ballot for two persons, of whom one at least shall not be an inhabitant of the same state with themselves. And they shall make a list of all the persons voted for, and of the number of votes for each; which list they shall sign and certify, and transmit sealed to the seat of the government of the United States, directed to the president of the Senate. The president of the Senate shall, in the presence of the Senate and House of Representatives, open all the certificates and the votes shall then be counted. The person having the greatest number of votes shall be the President, if such number be a majority of the whole number of electors appointed; and if there be more than one who have such majority, and have an equal number of votes, then the House of Representatives shall immediately choose by ballot one of them for President; and if no person have a majority, then from the five highest on the list, the said House shall, in like manner, chose the President. But in choosing the President, the votes shall be taken by states, the representation from each state having one vote; a quorum for this purpose shall consist of a member or members from two-thirds of the states, and a majority of all the states shall be necessary to a choice. In every case, after the choice of the President, the person having the greatest number of votes of the electors shall be the Vice President. But if there should remain two or more who have equal votes, the Senate shall choose from them by ballot the Vice President.[10]

The Congress may determine the time of choosing the electors, and the day on which they shall give their votes; which day shall be the same throughout the United States.

No person except a natural born citizen, *or a citizen of the United States, at the time of the adoption of this Constitution,* shall be eligible to the office of President; neither shall any person be eligible to that

---

[7] Amendment XVI exempts the federal income tax from this provision.

[8] Amendment XXII limits a President to two terms.

[9] Extended by Amendment XXIII.

[10] This whole paragraph is superseded by Amendment XII.

office, who shall not have attained to the age of thirty-five years, and been fourteen years a resident within the United States.[11]

In case of the removal of the President from office, or of his death, resignation, or inability to discharge the powers and duties of the said office, the same shall devolve on the Vice President, and the Congress may by law provide for the case of removal, death, resignation, or inability, both of the President and Vice President, declaring what officer shall then act as President, and such officer shall act accordingly, until the disability be removed, or a President shall be elected.[12]

The President shall, at stated times, receive for his services, a compensation, which shall neither be increased nor diminished during the Period for which he shall have been elected, and he shall not receive within that Period any other Emolument from the United States, or any of them.

Before he enter on the Execution of his Office, he shall take the following Oath or Affirmation: "I do solemnly swear (or affirm) that I will faithfully execute the Office of President of the United States, and will to the best of my Ability, preserve, protect and defend the Constitution of the United States."

SECTION 2.

President as Commander-in-Chief; role of cabinet; power to pardon and make treaties. The President shall be Commander in Chief of the Army and Navy of the United States, and of the Militia of the several States, when called into the actual Service of the United States; he may require the Opinion, in writing, of the principal Officer in each of the executive Departments, upon any subject relating to the Duties of their respective Offices, and he shall have Power to grant Reprieves and Pardons for Offenses against the United States, except in Cases of Impeachment.

He shall have Power, by and with the Advice and Consent of the Senate, to make Treaties, provided two thirds of the Senators present concur; and he shall nominate, and by and with the Advice and Consent of the Senate, shall appoint Ambassadors, other public Ministers and Consuls, Judges of the supreme Court, and all other Officers of the United States, whose Appointments are not herein otherwise provided for, and which shall be established by Law; but the Congress may by Law vest the Appointment of such inferior Officers, as they think proper, in the President alone, in the Courts of Law, or in the Heads of Departments.

[11] See Amendment XII: "But no person constitutionally ineligible to the office of President shall be eligible to that of Vice President of the United States."
[12] Extended by Amendment XX, Sections 3 and 4.

The President shall have Power to fill up all Vacancies that may happen during the Recess of the Senate, by granting Commissions which shall expire at the End of their next Session.

SECTION 3.

Presidential powers re Congress; to receive ambassadors, execute laws, commission officers. He shall from time to time give to the Congress Information of the State of the Union, and recommend to their Consideration such Measures as he shall judge necessary and expedient; he may, on extraordinary Occasions, convene both Houses, or either of them, and in Case of Disagreement between them, with Respect to the Time of Adjournment, he may adjourn them to such Time as he shall think proper; he shall receive Ambassadors and other public Ministers; he shall take Care that the Laws be faithfully executed, and shall Commission all the Officers of the United States.

SECTION 4.

Forfeiture of office. The President, Vice President, and all civil Officers of the United States, shall be removed from Office on Impeachment for, and Conviction of, Treason, Bribery, or other high Crimes and Misdemeanors.

ARTICLE III
The Judiciary
SECTION 1.

Judicial powers, tenure, compensation. The judicial Power of the United States, shall be vested in one supreme Court, and in such inferior Courts as the Congress may from time to time ordain and establish. The Judges, both of the supreme and inferior Courts, shall hold their Offices during good Behaviour, and shall, at stated Times, receive for their Services a Compensation which shall not be diminished during their Continuance in Office.

SECTION 2.

Scope of judicial power. The judicial Power shall extend to all Cases, in Law and Equity, arising under this Constitution, the Laws of the United States, and Treaties made, or which shall be made, under their Authority;—to all Cases affecting Ambassadors, other public Ministers and Consuls;—to all Cases of admirality and maritime Jurisdiction;—to Controversies to which the United States shall be a Party;—to Controversies between two or more States;—*between a State and Citizen of another State;*—between Citizens of different States;—between Citizens of the same

State claiming Lands under Grants of different States, and between a State, or the Citizens thereof, and foreign States, *Citizens or Subjects.*[13]

In all Cases affecting Ambassadors, other public Ministers and Consuls, and those in which a State shall be Party, the supreme Court shall have original Jurisdiction. In all the other Cases before mentioned, the supreme Court shall have appellate Jurisdiction, both as to Law and Fact, with such Exceptions, and under such Regulations as the Congress shall make.

The trial of all Crimes, except in Cases of Impeachment, shall be by Jury; and such Trial shall be held in the State where the said Crimes shall have been committed; but when not committed within any State, the Trial shall be at such Place or Places as the Congress may by Law have directed.

SECTION 3.

Treason. Treason against the United States, shall consist only in levying War against them, or, in adhering to their Enemies, giving them Aid and Comfort. No Person shall be convicted of Treason unless on the Testimony of two Witnesses to the same overt Act, or on Confession in open Court.

The Congress shall have power to declare the Punishment of Treason, but no Attainder of Treason shall work Corruption of Blood, or Forfeiture except during the Life of the Person attained.

ARTICLE IV

The States

SECTION 1.

Full faith and credit. Full faith and Credit shall be given in each State to the public Acts, Records, and judicial Proceedings of every other State. And the Congress may by general Laws prescribe the Manner in which such Acts, Records and Proceedings shall be proved, and the Effect thereof.

SECTION 2.

Privileges of citizens of each State. The Citizens of each State shall be entitled to all Privileges and Immunities of Citizens in the several States.

A Person charged in any State with Treason, Felony, or other Crime, who shall flee from Justice, and be found in another State, shall on demand of the executive Authority of the State from which he fled, be delivered up, to be removed to the State having Jurisdiction of the Crime.

[13] These two italicized passages are limited by Amendment XI.

No person held to service or labor in one state, under the laws thereof, escaping into another, shall, in consequence of any law or regulation therein, be discharged from such service or labor, but shall be delivered up on claim of the party to whom such service or labor may be due.[14]

SECTION 3.

Admission of new States. New States may be admitted by the Congress into this Union; but no new State shall be formed or erected within the Jurisdiction of any other State; nor any State be formed by the Junction of two or more States, or parts of States, without the Consent of the Legislatures of the States concerned as well as of the Congress.

The Congress shall have Power to dispose of and make all needful Rules and Regulations respecting the Territory or other Property belonging to the United States; and nothing in this Constitution shall be so construed as to Prejudice any Claims of the United States, or of any particular State.[15]

SECTION 4.

Republican form of government guaranteed. The United States shall guarantee to every State in this Union a Republican Form of Government, and shall protect each of them against Invasion; and on Application of the Legislature, or of the Executive (when the Legislature cannot be convened) against domestic Violence.

ARTICLE V

Amendment of Constitution

The Congress, whenever two-thirds of both Houses shall deem it necessary, shall propose Amendments to this Constitution, or, on the Application of the Legislatures of two-thirds of the several States, shall call a Convention for proposing Amendments, which, in either Case, shall be valid to all Intents and Purposes, as part of this Constitution, when ratified by the Legislatures of three-fourths of the several States, or by Conventions in three-fourths thereof, as the one or the other Mode of Ratification may be proposed by the Congress; Provided that *no Amendment which may be made prior to the Year One thousand eight hundred and eight shall in any Manner affect the first and fourth Clauses in the Ninth Section of the first*

[14] Made obsolete as to slaves by Amendment XIII.
[15] Relating to unsettled boundaries at the time of adoption of the Constitution.

Article; and that[16] no State, without its Consent, shall be deprived of its equal Suffrage in the Senate.

ARTICLE VI

Supremacy of Constitution

All Debts contracted and Engagements entered into, before the Adoption of this Constitution shall be as valid against the United States under this Constitution, as under the Confederation.

This Constitution, and the Laws of the United States which shall be made in Pursuance thereof; and all Treaties made, or which shall be made, under the Authority of the United States, shall be the supreme Law of the Land; and the Judges in every State shall be bound thereby, any Thing in the Constitution or Laws of any State to the Contrary notwithstanding.

The Senators and Representatives before mentioned, and the Members of the several State Legislatures, and all executive and judicial Officers, both of the United States and of the several States, shall be bound by Oath or Affirmation, to support this Constitution; but no religious Test shall ever be required as a Qualification to any Office or public Trust under the United States.

ARTICLE VII

Ratification

The Ratification of the Conventions of nine States shall be sufficient for the Establishment of this Constitution between the States so ratifying the Same.

DONE in convention by the unanimous consent of the states present, the 17th day of September, in the year of our Lord 1787, and of the Independence of the United States of America the 12th. In witness whereof we have hereunto subscribed our names.

GEORGE WASHINGTON, *President, and Deputy from Virginia*

Attest:

William Jackson, *Secretary*

New Hampshire
  John Langdon
  Nicholas Gilman
Massachusetts
  Nathaniel Gorham
  Rufus King

Connecticut
  William Samuel
    Johnson
  Roger Sherman
New York
  Alexander Hamilton

New Jersey
  William Livingston
  David Brearley
  William Paterson
  Jonathan Dayton
Pennsylvania
  Benjamin Franklin
  Thomas Mifflin
  Robert Morris
  George Clymer
  Thomas FitzSimons
  Jared Ingersoll
  James Wilson
  Gouverneur Morris
Delaware
  George Read
  Gunning Bedford, Jr.
  John Dickinson
  Richard Bassett
  Jacob Broom
Maryland
  James McHenry
  Daniel of
    St. Thomas Jenifer
  Daniel Carroll

Virginia
  John Blair
  James Madison, Jr.
North Carolina
  William Blount
  Richard Dobbs
    Spaight
  Hugh Williamson
South Carolina
  John Rutledge
  Charles Cotesworth
    Pinckney
  Charles Pinckney
  Pierce Butler
Georgia
  William Few
  Abraham Baldwin

Dates of Ratification by States

The Constitution was ratified by the thirteen original states in the following order:

Delaware, *December 7, 1787*
Pennsylvania, *December 12, 1787*
New Jersey, *December 18, 1787*
Georgia, *January 2, 1788*
Connecticut, *January 9, 1788*
Massachusetts, *February 6, 1788*
Maryland, *April 28, 1788*
South Carolina, *May 23, 1788*
New Hampshire, *June 21, 1788*
Virginia, *June 25, 1788*
New York, *July 26, 1788*
North Carolina, *November 21, 1789*
Rhode Island, *May 29, 1790*

Vermont, by convention, ratified January 10, 1791; and Congress, February 18, 1791, admitted that State into the Union.

[The Continental Congress on September 13, 1788, proclaimed the ratification by nine states, and ordered the convening of the new government on March 4, 1789.]

[16] A temporary provision protecting the slave trade until 1808.

THE FIRST TEN AMENDMENTS— THE BILL OF RIGHTS

Note: The first ten amendments, usually called the Bill of Rights, went into effect December 15, 1791.

ARTICLE I.

Freedom of Speech, Press, Religion, Petition

Congress shall make no law respecting an establishment of religion, or prohibiting the free exercise thereof; or abridging the freedom of speech, or of the press; or the right of the people peaceably to assemble, and to petition the Government for a redress of grievances.

ARTICLE II.

Right to Keep and Bear Arms

A well-regulated militia, being necessary to the security of a free State, the right of the people to keep and bear arms, shall not be infringed.

ARTICLE III.

Quartering of Soldiers

No soldier shall, in time of peace be quartered in any house, without the consent of the owner, nor in time of war, but in a manner to be prescribed by law.

ARTICLE IV.

Search and Seizure, Warrants

The right of the people to be secure in their persons, houses, papers, and effects, against unreasonable searches and seizures, shall not be violated, and no warrants shall issue, but upon probable cause, supported by oath or affirmation, and particularly describing the place to be searched, and the persons or things to be seized.

ARTICLE V.

Provisions Concerning Prosecution, Trial and Punishment, Double Jeopardy, Due Process, Self-Incrimination

No person shall be held to answer for a capital, or otherwise infamous crime, unless on a presentment or indictment of a Grand Jury, except in cases arising in the land or naval forces, or in the militia, when in actual service in time of war or public danger; nor shall any person be subject for the same offense to be twice put in jeopardy of life or limb; nor shall be compelled in any criminal case to be a witness against himself, nor be deprived of life, liberty, or property, without due process of law; nor shall private property be taken for public use without just compensation.

ARTICLE VI.

Right to Speedy Trial, Witnesses, Counsel

In all criminal prosecutions, the accused shall enjoy the right to a speedy and public trial, by an impartial jury of the State and district wherein the crime shall have been committed, which district shall have been previously ascertained by law, and to be informed of the nature and cause of the accusation; to be confronted with the witnesses against him; to have compulsory process for obtaining witnesses in his favor, and to have the assistance of counsel for his defense.

ARTICLE VII.

Right of Trial by Jury

In suits at common law, where the value in controversy shall exceed twenty dollars, the right of trial by jury shall be preserved, and no fact tried by a jury shall be otherwise re-examined in any court of the United States, than according to the rules of the common law.

ARTICLE VIII.

Excessive Bail or Fines, Cruel Punishment

Excessive bail shall not be required, nor excessive fines imposed, nor cruel and unusual punishments inflicted.

ARTICLE IX.

Rule of Constitutional Construction

The enumeration in the Constitution, of certain rights, shall not be construed to deny or disparage others retained by the people.

ARTICLE X.

Rights of States under Constitution

The powers not delegated to the United States by the Constitution, nor prohibited by it to the States, are reserved to the States respectively, or to the people.

AMENDMENTS SINCE THE BILL OF RIGHTS

ARTICLE XI.

Judicial Powers Construed

The judicial power of the United States shall not be construed to extend to any suit in law or equity, commenced or prosecuted against one of the United States by citizens of another State, or by citizens or subjects of any foreign state.

(Proposed by Congress in March 1794; declared to have been ratified January 8, 1798.)

ARTICLE XII.

Manner of Choosing President and Vice President

The Electors shall meet in their respective States[1] and vote by ballot for President and Vice-President, one of whom, at least, shall not be an inhabitant of the same State with themselves; they shall name in their ballots the person voted for as President, and in distinct ballots the person voted for as Vice-President, and they shall make distinct lists of all persons voted for as President, and of all persons voted for as Vice-President, and of the number of votes for each, which lists they shall sign and certify, and transmit sealed to the seat of Government of the United States, directed to the President of the Senate; the President of the Senate shall, in the presence of the Senate and House of Representatives, open all the certificates and the votes shall then be counted;— The person having the greatest number of votes for President, shall be the President, if such number be a majority of the whole number of Electors appointed; and if no person have such majority, then from the persons having the highest numbers not exceeding three on the list of those voted for as President, the House of Representatives shall choose immediately, by ballot, the President. But in choosing the President, the votes shall be taken by States, the representation from each State having one vote; a quorum for this purpose shall consist of a member or members from two-thirds of the States, and a majority of all the States shall be necessary to a choice. And if the House of Representatives shall not choose a President whenever the right of choice shall devolve upon them, before the fourth day of March[2] next following, then the Vice-President shall act as Presi-

dent, as in case of the death or other constitutional disability of the President. The person having the greatest number of votes as Vice-President shall be the Vice-President, if such number be a majority of the whole number of Electors appointed, and if no person have a majority, then from the two highest numbers on the list, the Senate shall choose the Vice-President; a quorum for the purpose shall consist of two-thirds of the whole number of Senators, and a majority of the whole number shall be necessary to a choice. But no person constitutionally ineligible to the office of President shall be eligible to that of Vice-President of the United States.

(Proposed December 1803; ratification completed June 15, 1804.)

ARTICLE XIII.

Abolition of Slavery

1. Neither slavery nor involuntary servitude, except as punishment for crime whereof the party shall have been duly convicted, shall exist within the United States, or any place subject to their jurisdiction.
2. Congress shall have power to enforce this article by appropriate legislation.

(Proposed January 1865; ratification completed December 6, 1865.)

ARTICLE XIV.

Citizenship Rights; Apportionment of Representatives; Validity of Public Debt

1. All persons born or naturalized in the United States, and subject to the jurisdiction thereof, are citizens of the United States and of the State wherein they reside. No State shall make or enforce any law which shall abridge the privileges or immunities of citizens of the United States; nor shall any State deprive any person of life, liberty, or property, without due process of law; nor deny to any person within its jurisdiction the equal protection of the laws.
2. Representatives shall be apportioned among the several States according to their respective numbers, counting the whole number of persons in each State, *excluding Indians not taxed*.[3] But when the right to vote at any election for the choice of Electors for President and Vice-President of the United States, Representatives in Congress, the executive and judicial officers of a State, or the members of the Legislature thereof, is denied to any of the male inhabitants

---

[1] Extended by Amendment XXIII.

[2] Changed by Amendment XX, Section 1, "at noon on the 20th day of January."

[3] All Indians are now subject to federal taxation.

of such State, being twenty-one years of age, and citizens of the United States, or any way abridged, except for participation in rebellion, or other crime, the basis of representation therein shall be reduced in the proportion which the number of such male citizens shall bear to the whole number of male citizens twenty-one years of age in such State.[4]

3. No person shall be a Senator or Representative in Congress, or Elector of President and Vice-President, or hold any office, civil or military, under the United States, or under any State, who, having previously taken an oath, as a member of Congress, or as an officer of the United States, or as a member of any State Legislature, or as an executive or judicial officer of any State, to support the Constitution of the United States, shall have engaged in insurrection or rebellion against the same, or given aid or comfort to the enemies thereof. But Congress may by a vote of two-thirds of each House, remove such disability.

4. The validity of the public debt of the United States, authorized by law, including debts incurred for payment of pensions and bounties for services in suppressing insurrection or rebellion, shall not be questioned. But neither the United States nor any State shall assume or pay any debt or obligation incurred in aid of insurrection or rebellion against the United States, or any claim for the loss or emancipation of any slave; but all such debts, obligations and claims shall be held illegal and void.

5. The Congress shall have power to enforce, by appropriate legislation, the provisions of this article.

(Proposed June 1866; declared to have been ratified in July 1868.)

ARTICLE XV.

Equal Voting Rights for White and Colored Citizens

1. The right of citizens of the United States to vote shall not be denied or abridged by the United States or by any State on account of race, color, or previous condition of servitude.

2. The Congress shall have power to enforce this article by appropriate legislation.

(Proposed February 1869; declared to have been ratified on March 30, 1870.)

ARTICLE XVI.

Income Taxes Authorized

The Congress shall have power to lay and collect taxes on incomes, from whatever sources derived,

without apportionment among the several States, and without regard to any census or enumeration.

(Proposed July 1909; ratification completed February 3, 1913.)

ARTICLE XVII.

Direct Election of U.S. Senators

1. The Senate of the United States shall be composed of two Senators from each State, elected by the people thereof, for six years; and each Senator shall have one vote. The electors in each State shall have the qualifications requisite for electors of the most numerous branch of the State Legislatures.

2. When vacancies happen in the representation of any State in the Senate, the executive authority of such State shall issue writs of election to fill such vacancies: Provided, That the Legislature of any State may empower the Executive thereof to make temporary appointments until the people fill the vacancies by election as the Legislature may direct.

3. This amendment shall not be so construed as to affect the election or term of any Senator chosen before it becomes valid as part of the Constitution.

(Proposed May 1912; ratification completed April 8, 1913.)

ARTICLE XVIII.

Liquor Prohibition

1. After one year from the ratification of this article the manufacture, sale, or transportation of intoxicating liquors within, the importation thereof into, or exportation thereof from the United States and all territory subject to the jurisdiction thereof, for beverage purposes is hereby prohibited.

2. The Congress and the several states shall have concurrent power to enforce this article by appropriate legislation.

3. This article shall be inoperative unless it shall have been ratified as an amendment to the Constitution by the legislatures of the several states, as provided in the Constitution, within seven years from the date of submission hereof to the states by the Congress.

(Proposed December 1917; ratification completed January 16, 1919. Amendment repealed by Article XXI, effective December 5, 1933.)

ARTICLE XIX.

Nationwide Suffrage for Women

1. The right of citizens of the United States to vote shall not be denied or abridged by the United States or by any State on account of sex.

---

[4] This provision has never been enforced.

2. Congress shall have power to enforce this Article by appropriate legislation.

(Proposed June 1919; ratification certified August 26, 1920.)

ARTICLE XX.

Beginning Date of Terms of President, Vice President, Members of Congress

1. The terms of the President and Vice-President shall end at noon on the 20th day of January and the terms of Senators and Representatives at noon on the 3rd day of January, of the years in which such terms would have ended if this article had not been ratified, and the terms of their successors shall then begin.

2. The Congress shall assemble at least once in every year, and such meeting shall begin at noon on the 3rd day of January, unless they shall by law appoint a different day.

3. If, at the time fixed for the beginning of the term of the President, the President elect shall have died, the Vice-President elect shall become President. If a President shall not have been chosen before the time fixed for the beginning of his term, or if the President elect shall have failed to qualify, then the Vice-President elect shall act as President until a President shall have qualified, and the Congress may by law provide for the case wherein neither a President elect nor a Vice-President shall have qualified, declaring who shall then act as President, or the manner in which one who is to act shall be selected, and such person shall act accordingly until a President or Vice-President shall have qualified.[5]

4. The Congress may by law provide for the case of the death of any of the persons from whom the House of Representatives may choose a President whenever the right of choice shall have devolved upon them, and for the case of the death of any of the persons from whom the Senate may choose a Vice-President whenever the right of choice shall have devolved upon them.

5. Sections 1 and 2 shall take effect on the 15th day of October following the ratification of this article [Oct., 1933].

6. This article shall be inoperative unless it shall have been ratified as an amendment to the Constitution by the Legislatures of three-fourths of the

[5] The Presidential Succession Act of 1886, as amended in 1947, fixes the order of succession as follows: Speaker of the House, President of the Senate, Secretary of State, of Treasury, of Defense, Attorney-General, Postmaster-General, Secretary of Interior, of Agriculture, of Commerce, of Labor, and of Health, Education and Welfare.

several States within seven years from the date of its submission.

(Proposed March 1932; ratification completed January 23, 1933.)

ARTICLE XXI.

Repeal of Eighteenth Amendment

1. The eighteenth article of amendment to the Constitution of the United States is hereby repealed.

2. The transportation or importation into any State, Territory, or Possession of the United States for delivery or use therein of intoxicating liquors, in violation of the laws thereof, is hereby prohibited.

3. This article shall be inoperative unless it shall have been ratified as an amendment to the Constitution by conventions in the several States, as provided in the Constitution, within seven years from the date of the submission hereof to the States by the Congress.

(Proposed February 1933; ratification completed December 5, 1933, by State conventions rather than legislative bodies.)

ARTICLE XXII.

Limit on Number of Presidential Terms

1. No person shall be elected to the office of the President more than twice, and no person who has held the office of President, or acted as President, for more than two years of a term to which some other person was elected President shall be elected to the office of the President more than once. But this Article shall not apply to any person holding the office of President when this Article was proposed by the Congress, and shall not prevent any person who may be holding the office of President, or acting as President, during the term within which this Article becomes operative from holding the office of President or acting as President during the remainder of such term.

2. This article shall be inoperative unless it shall have been ratified as an amendment to the Constitution by the Legislatures of three-fourths of the several States within seven years from the date of its submission to the States by the Congress.

(Proposed March 1947; ratification completed February 27, 1951.)

ARTICLE XXIII.

Presidential Vote for Residents of the District of Columbia

1. The District constituting the seat of Government of the United States shall appoint in such manner as the Congress may direct:

A number of electors of President and Vice President equal to the whole number of Senators and Representatives in Congress to which the District would be entitled if it were a State, but in no event more than the least populous State; they shall be in addition to those appointed by the States, but they shall be considered, for the purposes of the election of President and Vice President, to be electors appointed by a State; and they shall meet in the District and perform such duties as provided by the twelfth article of amendment.

2. The Congress shall have power to enforce this article by appropriate legislation.

(Proposed June 1960; ratification completed March 29, 1961.)

ARTICLE XXIV.

Prohibition of Poll Tax in Federal Elections

1. The right of citizens of the United States to vote in any primary or other election for President or Vice President, for electors for President or Vice President, or for Senator or Representative in Congress, shall not be denied or abridged by the United States or any State by reason of failure to pay any poll tax or other tax.

2. The Congress shall have power to enforce this article by appropriate legislation.

(Proposed August 1962; ratification completed January 23, 1964.)

ARTICLE XXV.

Presidential Inability and Succession

1. In case of the removal of the President from office or of his death or resignation, the Vice President shall become President.

2. Whenever there is a vacancy in the office of the Vice President, the President shall nominate a Vice President who shall take office upon confirmation by a majority vote of both houses of Congress.

3. Whenever the President transmits to the President pro tempore of the Senate and the Speaker of the House of Representatives his written declaration that he is unable to discharge the powers and duties of his office, and until he transmits to them a written declaration to the contrary, such powers and duties shall be discharged by the Vice President as Acting President.

4. Whenever the Vice President and a majority of either the principal officers of the executive departments or of such other body as Congress may by law provide, transmit to the President pro tempore of the Senate and the Speaker of the House of Representatives their written declaration that the President is unable to discharge the powers and duties of his office, the Vice President shall immediately assume the powers and duties of the office as Acting President.

Thereafter, when the President transmits to the President pro tempore of the Senate and the Speaker of the House of Representatives his written declaration that no inability exists, he shall resume the powers and duties of his office unless the Vice President and a majority of either the principal officers of the executive department or of such other body as Congress may by law provide, transmit within four days to the President pro tempore of the Senate and the Speaker of the House of Representatives their written declaration that the President is unable to discharge the powers and duties of his office. Thereupon Congress shall decide the issue, assembling within forty-eight hours for that purpose if not in session. If the Congress, within twenty-one days after receipt of the latter written declaration, or, if Congress is not in session, within twenty-one days after Congress is required to assemble, determines by two-thirds vote of both houses that the President is unable to discharge the powers and duties of his office, the Vice President shall continue to discharge the same as Acting President; otherwise, the President shall resume the powers and duties of his office.

(Proposed July 1965; ratification completed February 10, 1967.)

ARTICLE XXVI.

Lowering Voting Age to 18 Years

1. The right of citizens of the United States, who are 18 years of age or older, to vote shall not be denied or abridged by the United States or any state on account of age.

2. The Congress shall have the power to enforce this article by appropriate legislation.

(Proposed March 1971; ratification completed June 30, 1971.)